Digital Logic Circuit Analysis and Design

Victor P. Nelson
Auburn University

H. Troy Nagle
North Carolina State University

Bill D. Carroll
University of Texas–Arlington

J. David Irwin
Auburn University

Prentice Hall, Upper Saddle River, New Jersey 07458

Library of Congress Cataloging-in-Publication Data

Digital logic circuit analysis and design / Victor P. Nelson ... [et.
al.]
      p.   cm.
    Developed from: Introduction to computer logic. 1974.
    Includes bibliographical references and index.
    ISBN 0-13-463894-8
    1. Logic circuits--Design and construction. 2. Electronic digital
computers--Circuits--Design and construction. I. Nelson, Victor P.
(Victor Peter)   II. Nagle, H. Troy   Introduction
to computer logic.
TK7888.4.D54 1995
621.39'5--dc20   94-35122
                                              CIP

Acquisitions Editor: Don Fowley
Production Editor: Joe Scordato
Copy Editor: Bill Thomas
Designer: Amy Rosen
Cover Designer: Warren Fischbach
Buyer: Bill Scazzero

Printed in the United States of America

10   9   8   7

ISBN 0-13-463894-8

PRENTICE-HALL INTERNATIONAL (UK) LIMITED, LONDON
PRENTICE-HALL OF AUSTRALIA PTY. LIMITED, SYDNEY
PRENTICE-HALL CANADA INC., TORONTO
PRENTICE-HALL HISPANOAMERICANA, S.A., MEXICO
PRENTICE-HALL OF INDIA PRIVATE LIMITED, NEW DELHI
PRENTICE-HALL OF JAPAN, INC., TOKYO
PEARSON EDUCATION ASIA PTE. LTD., SINGAPORE
EDITORA PRENTICE-HALL DO BRASIL, LTDA., RIO DE JANEIRO

Contents

Preface

The Need for This Book

This text has been developed from a previous work, *An Introduction to Computer Logic* (1974) by Nagle, Carroll, and Irwin, which was a widely adopted text on the fundamentals of combinational and sequential logic circuit analysis and synthesis. The original book was praised for its clarity and teaching effectiveness, and despite rapid changes in the field in the late 70's and early 80's, the book continued to enjoy wide use many years after its original publication date, underscoring the interesting fact that during most of the period since the publication of that book, the mainstream educational approach to introductory-level courses in digital design evolved quite slowly, even while major technological changes were rapidly being adopted in industry.

How things have changed! Recently, the astronomical proliferation of digital circuit applications and phenomenal increases in digital circuit complexity have prompted significant changes in the methods and tools used in digital design. Very Large Scale Integrated (VLSI) circuit chips now routinely contain millions of transistors; computer-aided design (CAD) methods, standard cells, programmable logic devices, and gate arrays have made possible rapid turnaround from concept to finished circuit, supported by increased emphasis on hierarchical, modular designs utilizing libraries of standard cells and other predesigned circuit modules. We have developed a text which supports those changes, but we have also worked carefully to preserve the strong coverage of theory and fundamentals.

An effective digital design engineer requires a solid background in fundamental theory coupled with knowledge of practical real-world design principles. This text contains both. It retains its predecessor's strong coverage of fundamental theory. To address practical design issues, over half of the text is new material that reflects the many changes that have occurred in recent years, including modular design, CAD methods, and the use of programmable logic, as well as such practical issues as device timing characteristics and standard logic symbols.

◗ Intended Audience

This book is intended for sophomore, junior, and senior-level courses in digital logic circuits and digital systems for engineers and scientists who may be involved with the design of VLSI circuits, printed circuit boards, multi-chip modules, and computer circuits.

No particular background in electronic circuits or computer systems is assumed or required, and thus the text is suitable for a first course in digital systems. However, the book contains sufficient advanced material and depth to support the needs of more advanced students. This text has been designed to allow each instructor the flexibility to select topics according to the needs of his or her specific course.

This text is also suitable for the reader who wishes to use the self-study approach to learn digital design, and is useful as a reference for practicing engineers.

◗ Significant Features

This book is a unique work representing the combined efforts of the four authors at three universities. In addition to extensive publisher-sponsored reviewing, the manuscript was used in courses at all three schools during its development, with feedback from students and instructors incorporated into the book.

Noteworthy features include:

- Solid coverage of fundamental concepts and theory coupled with practical real-world design methods
- A strong emphasis on developing and using systematic problem solving and design methodologies, abundantly supported by over 250 numbered, worked examples
- Heavy emphasis on visualization, supported by over 600 two-color illustrations
- Numerous problems with a wide range of difficulty levels at the ends of the chapters
- CAD issues integrated in-depth throughout the text without relying heavily on CAD products from specific vendors
- Coverage of hierarchical modular design and standard digital circuit modules
- A chapter containing comprehensive design projects
- Two chapters describing programmable logic devices and their applications in implementing digital circuits
- An in-depth introduction to testing and design for testability
- Support of both breadboarding labs and CAD-based modeling and simulation labs
- An Instructors' Manual with fully worked solutions to each problem

▶ Coverage of Computer-Aided Design

Most modern digital circuit design projects require the use of computer-aided design methods and tools. For this reason, CAD is covered throughout the text at the end of each chapter, allowing CAD methods to be applied to the basic fundamental concepts and design principles presented in that chapter.

The coverage of CAD methods and tools was designed to be generic in nature, rather than specific to any particular vendor's tools. This will allow students to apply these concepts to whichever CAD tools may be available, including comprehensive packages running on engineering workstations from such vendors as Mentor Graphics, Cadence, and Viewlogic, and lower-end tools designed for use on personal computers. A number of the latter are available at nominal pricing for students and educators.

The CAD coverage in the chapters is as follows:

Chapter 2 introduces the computer-aided design process as used in the design and analysis of digital logic circuits and systems. Topics covered include design representation with schematic diagrams and hardware description languages, schematic capture, and logic simulation for design verification and timing analysis.

Chapter 3 discusses CAD methods for simplification and optimization of combinational logic circuits. Chapter 4 extends the CAD coverage to support of hierarchical, modular combinational logic circuit designs. Chapter 5 describes CAD tools for designing and modeling circuits to be implemented in programmable logic devices, including hardware description languages.

In the sequential circuit section of the book, Chapter 8 discusses CAD methods used in the design and analysis of sequential logic circuits, including timing analysis and detection of timing constraint violations. Chapter 11 extends this discussion to methods used for modeling sequential logic circuits to be implemented in programmable logic devices.

▶ Laboratory Support

Courses in digital design often utilize laboratory experiments to reinforce concepts presented in class. In some cases, schematic capture or other CAD tools are used to model circuits of varying degrees of complexity, and simulation tools are used to study the operation of these circuits. This text supports both CAD-based and traditional breadboarding laboratories.

The traditional breadboarding lab usually involves the construction of digital circuits with standard TTL small scale integrated (SSI) and medium scale integrated (MSI) circuit modules. Many examples of such modules are covered throughout the book, discussing the design and operation of each module and the design of higher-level circuits using these modules.

In addition to short laboratory exercises, it is often desirable to use comprehensive design projects to have students assimilate the different concepts learned in a course. To illustrate the planning and design steps in such projects, the final chapter of this text presents four case studies based on projects done by students at North Carolina State University and Auburn University.

▶ Chapter Descriptions

The material in this text has been organized into several sections. In each section, fundamental concepts and theory are first developed to provide a solid foundation. Then the theory is applied to the design and analysis of simple circuits, and extended to the design of optimal circuits. Finally, practical design issues and methods are discussed, including the use of modular design methods, computer-aided design techniques, and programmable logic devices. Extensive examples are presented throughout each section to illustrate and reinforce the concepts presented in that section.

Background

Since no particular prerequisites are assumed, the first two chapters present background material that will aid in the understanding of digital circuit design.

Chapter 0 introduces digital circuits and digital computers, including the primary software and hardware components of a computer.

Chapter 1 presents number systems and representation of information, with emphasis on binary codes used to represent numbers and other information in digital computers and other circuits. Arithmetic with binary numbers is also discussed, as a prelude to the design of digital computer circuits that perform such operations.

Combinational Logic Circuits

The analysis and design of combinational logic circuits is the topic of the next section of the book, beginning with fundamentals in chapter 2, and progressing through optimization in Chapter 3, modular design in Chapter 4, and design with programmable logic in Chapter 5.

Chapter 2 begins with a presentation of Boolean and switching algebras, which form the basis of logic circuit design. Digital logic gates are introduced next, followed by coverage of analysis techniques for circuits constructed with basic gates. The synthesis and design of logic circuits from various types of specifications are presented next. The chapter concludes with an introduction to computer-aided design of digital logic circuits.

Chapter 3 presents algorithms and methods for simplifying combinational logic circuits. The use of Karnaugh maps and the tabular Quine-

McCluskey method are presented in detail, and then computer-aided methods for simplification of combinational logic circuits are discussed.

Chapter 4 discusses hierarchical, modular design of digital circuits. The design and use of various modules in such designs are described, including decoders, multiplexers, and arithmetic circuits. CAD tool support of hierarchical, modular design activities is presented to conclude the discussion.

Chapter 5 describes the basic operation of programmable logic devices, and the implementation of combinational logic circuits with programmable arrays. The three basic device architectures, PLA, PROM, and PAL, are described, along with examples of commercially-available modules. CAD tools to support the modeling of combinational logic circuits to be implemented with programmable devices are presented.

Sequential Logic Circuits

Sequential logic circuits, which involve memory, are discussed in the next section of the book. Chapter 6 describes the memory elements used in sequential circuits and Chapter 7 examines the design and operation of a number of standard circuit modules based on these memory elements. Chapter 8 presents the fundamentals of synchronous circuit analysis and design, with Chapter 9 discussing methods for optimizing these circuits. Chapter 10 discusses the unique problems associated with the analysis and design of asynchronous sequential circuits. Finally, Chapter 11 describes the use of programmable logic devices in sequential circuit design.

Chapter 6 begins by introducing sequential logic circuits, including the role played by memory elements in these circuits. The design and operation of the two basic types of memory devices, latches and flip-flops, are then discussed, and the features of a number of commercially-available modules containing such devices are described.

Chapter 7 describes the design and operation of a number of standard sequential logic circuit modules, including registers, shift registers, and counters. For each module type, the basic design and theory of operation are presented, and then the features and use of a number of representative standard TTL modules are described.

Chapter 8 presents fundamentals and techniques for analysis and synthesis of synchronous sequential logic circuits, including timing diagrams, state tables, and flip-flop excitation tables. The chapter concludes with an overview of CAD methods for modeling and simulating the operation of synchronous sequential circuits and for analyzing the unique timing characteristics of such circuits.

Chapter 9 discusses optimization of synchronous sequential logic circuits. Methods are presented for eliminating redundant states to reduce the number of memory elements needed to implement a design, and methods for optimal assignment of state variables to minimize the number of required combinational logic gates.

Chapter 10 discusses pulse mode and fundamental mode asynchronous sequential circuits. Methods for analysis and synthesis of each type of circuit are presented, including the identification of races in fundamental mode circuits and methods for preventing critical races.

Chapter 11 concludes the sequential circuit section by describing programmable logic devices used to implement synchronous and asynchronous sequential circuits, including registered PALs and PLAs, and flexible macro-cell-based devices. Also covered are field programmable gate arrays. The chapter includes an overview of CAD methods for modeling sequential circuits to be synthesized with programmable logic devices.

Testing and Design for Testability

Chapter 12 provides an introduction to faults in digital logic circuits and testing methods, including the process of deriving test sets for logic circuits. Testing of a digital circuit represents a significant cost, especially as circuits grow in size. To facilitate testing and minimize testing cost, design for testability is critical. Therefore, this chapter discusses a number of digital circuit design techniques that can improve testability at the gate and circuit board levels, including the use of built-in testing circuits.

Digital Design Case Studies

Chapter 13 concludes the text by presenting four case studies based on actual comprehensive digital design projects done by students at North Carolina State University and Auburn University: a slot machine game, an automobile keyless entry system, a traffic controller to coordinate two-way traffic on a single-lane road, and a cash register controller.

Suggested Course Outlines

The material in this course may be used in a quarter or semester course, or may be extended to two quarters. A 10-week quarter course might use the following outline.

Chapter 0:   General introduction

Chapter 1:   Binary number codes and binary arithmetic

Chapter 2:   Boolean algebra and switching functions, logic gates, combinational circuit analysis and design

Chapter 3:   Minimization—one method (typically K-maps)

Chapter 4:   Modular, hierarchical design and standard circuit modules

Chapter 6:   Basic operation and design of flip-flops and latches

Chapter 7:　Simple sequential shift register and counter modules

Chapter 8:　Analysis and synthesis of synchronous sequential circuits

A second 10-week quarter course can spend more time on computer-aided design, programmable logic, asynchronous circuits, and testing.

A 16-week semester course can simply follow the book outline, adding the optimization topics in chapters 3 and 9, coverage of programmable logic devices in chapters 5 and 11, and testing from chapter 12.

Acknowledgments

The authors are appreciative of the students at Auburn University, North Carolina State University, and the University of Texas at Arlington, who used the manuscript in class in lieu of a finished text. Also, colleagues and graduate assistants who participated in teaching courses from the manuscript offered many valuable suggestions, including Mr. Bruce Tucker, Mr. Bill Dillard, Prof. Adit Singh, Prof. Dharma Agrawal, Prof. Alexandra Duel-Hallen, Mr. Kam Yee, Prof. Hee Yong Youn, and Prof. Vijay K. Raj.

The authors also thank our editor Don Fowley for his many helpful suggestions and contributions in both the preparation of the manuscript and the design of the textbook. Additional thanks go to Miss Meredith Nelson for her assistance in typing the initial draft and Mr. Gregory Nelson for his work on the Solutions Manual.

The comments of several reviewers were valuable in the development of the manuscript, in particular those of Michael A. Driscoll of Portland State University, David Bray of Clarkson University, Karan Watson of Texas A & M, Dong Ha of Virginia Polytechnic Institute, and Kewal Saluja of the University of Wisconsin-Madison.

Finally, we would like to express our appreciation to our wives, Margaret, Susan, Marsha, and Edie, for their support and patience during the seemingly endless process of developing this manuscript.

Victor P. Nelson
H. Troy Nagle
Bill D. Carroll
J. David Irwin

We are living in an age that sociologists have called the computer revolution. Like any true revolution, it is widespread and all-pervasive and will have a lasting impact on society. It is as fundamental to our present economic and social order as was the industrial revolution in the nineteenth century. It will affect the thinking patterns and life-styles of every individual. Whereas the major effect of the industrial revolution was to augment our physical powers, the computer revolution is extending our mental powers.

Computers are composed of electronic, mechanical, and/or optical elements known as the hardware and of programs and data known as the software. This book introduces the subject of computer hardware. In particular, we will study the analysis and design of logic circuits that form the basis for most computer electronic hardware. But first, let's take a closer look at the history and the organization of the digital computer.

Introduction

0.1 History of Computing

A *computer* is a device capable of solving problems or manipulating information, according to a prescribed sequence of instructions (or *program*), using some mechanical or electrical process. Since people first began solving problems thousands of years ago, ways have been sought to simplify various problem-solving tasks. Of primary interest over the millenia has been the automation of arithmetic operations. The advent of computer technology provided an inexpensive way to perform simple arithmetic, and, as the technology matured, computer techniques were rapidly extended to solving complex numeric problems, storing, retrieving, and communicating information, and controlling robots, appliances, automobiles, games, manufacturing plants, and a variety of other processes and machines. What is most amazing is that this computer revolution has occurred all within the past 50 years! The following is a brief synopsis of these developments.

0.1.1 Beginnings: Mechanical Computers

The first computer was probably the abacus, which has been used in the Orient for over 3000 years. This device, still in use today, had little competition until the 1600s when John Napier used logarithms as the basis for a device that multiplied numbers. His work led to the invention of the slide rule. Then, in 1642, Blaise Pascal built an adding machine that had geared wheels much like the modern odometer.

In 1820, Charles Babbage built the first device that used the principles of modern computers. His machine, the *difference engine*, evaluated polynomials by the method of finite differences (see [1]). He also conceived a mechanical machine that resembled modern-day computers with a store and arithmetic unit. However, the precision required for constructing the mechanical gears was beyond the capabilities of the craftsmen of his time.

0.1.2 Early Electronic Computers

The first real progress toward electronic digital computers came in the late 1930s when Howard Aiken of Harvard University and George Slibitz of Bell Telephone Laboratories developed an automatic calculator using relay networks; the *relay* is an electromagnetically controlled switch. Other relay machines were developed during World War II for artillery ballistic calculations. Although these machines were relatively slow and comparatively large, they demonstrated the versatility of the electronic computer. Then, in the early 1940s, John Mauchly and J. Presper Eckert, Jr., of the University of Pennsylvania designed and built a vacuum tube computer, which they called the electronic numerical integrator and calculator (ENIAC); it was completed in 1945 and installed at Aberdeen Proving Ground, Maryland. ENIAC used 18,000 electron tubes, which required tremendous amounts of power; its failure rate was high and it was difficult to program because a plugboard was required.

Three very important discoveries were then made, which began the rapid evolution toward today's digital computer. First, John von Neumann proposed that the program reside in the computer's memory where it could be changed at will, solving the programming difficulties of ENIAC; second, in 1947 the transistor was invented by John Bardeen, Walter H. Brattain, and William Shockley, which drastically reduced the size and power requirements by replacing the electron vacuum tube; and, third, J. W. Forrester and his associates at the Massachusetts Institute of Technology developed the magnetic core memory, which made large amounts of storage feasible.

0.1.3 The First Four Generations of Computers

ENIAC and other vacuum tube computers appearing in the late 1940s and through the 1950s have been labeled *first-generation* digital computers. The advent of transistors in the late 1950s brought about the *second generation* of machines, which were smaller in size and faster and featured increased capabilities over their ancestors. In the late 1960s and throughout the 1970s, the *third generation* of machines appeared. These machines are characterized by their use of *integrated circuits* consisting of subminiature packages of multiple transistor circuits, which provided still another drastic reduction in size. Improvements in packaging and memory technology also contributed to the improved third-generation machines.

The late 1960s also brought the emergence of the minicomputer. In addition to large complex machines, often called mainframes, many manufacturers offered these smaller, limited-capability, general-purpose computers. Minicomputers, which derived their name from their size and cost, have been used in many diverse applications and have played a major role in popularizing the use of computers. The minicomputer widely increased computer usage in the scientific and engineering communities. Machines found their way into industrial and university research laboratories. Computerized process control in industry became commonplace.

The *fourth generation* of computers was ushered in during the late 1970s and early 1980s with the appearance of machines based on large scale integrated (LSI) and very large scale integrated (VLSI) circuit hardware components. VLSI made it feasible to build small but powerful computers known as personal computers or workstations. The central component of these machines is the *microprocessor*, which is an entire central processing unit of a computer implemented in a single VLSI component. Intel Corporation and Motorola have led the way in microprocessor technology development. This development is illustrated in Fig. 0.1, which shows the evolution over a 20-year period of the Intel VLSI microprocessor chips used in the IBM and IBM-compatible personal computers.

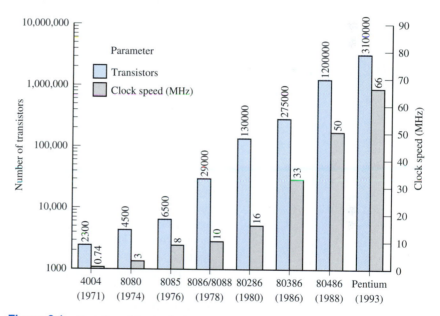

Figure 0.1   Evolution of the Intel microprocessors.

Perhaps the appearance of personal computers such as the IBM Personal Computer, based on Intel microprocessors, and the Apple Macintosh, based on Motorola microprocessors, has had the most dramatic impact on expanding the range of computer applications than has any other occurrence. Before the personal computer became widespread, one could safely say that most computers were used by computer experts. Now computers are commonly used by experts and nonexperts alike. Computer networks have become commonplace during the fourth generation as well. Networks have increased access to computers and have spawned new applications, such as electronic mail.

0.1.4 The Fifth Generation and Beyond

When will the fifth generation of computers begin? Or has it already begun? Using the classical measure, the switch to a new hardware technology base, the answer is no. But should hardware technology be the only indicator of computer generations? Probably not. It is clear that advances in software have had profound effects on the way computers are used. New user interfaces, such as voice activation, or new computational paradigms, such as parallel processing and neural networks, may also characterize the next-generation machine. Whatever the case may be, it is likely that parallel processing, artificial intelligence, optical processing, visual programming, and gigabit networks will play key roles in computer systems of the future. We will likely be in the fifth generation of computers for some time before it becomes apparent.

Armed with these perspectives, let us now review some important computer terminology that we will need to analyze and design circuits for computers and other digital systems.

0.2 Digital Systems

0.2.1 Digital versus Analog Systems

A *digital* system or device is a system in which information is represented and processed in discrete rather than continuous forms. Systems based on continuous forms of information are called *analog* systems or devices. A watch that displays time with hour, minute, and second hands is an example of an analog device, whereas a watch that displays the time in decimal digits is a digital device. Information on traditional audio cassette tapes is recorded in analog form, whereas compact laser disks hold information in digital form. A more modern form of audio tape, the digital audio tape (DAT), stores information in digital form.

For example, Fig. 0.2a shows an analog signal as might be found on a strip of magnetic audio tape. Figure 0.2b shows the same signal sampled at uniform time intervals and converted to a discrete number of values. Figure 0.2c shows this information in digital form, with each sample represented by a binary number written vertically on the tape.

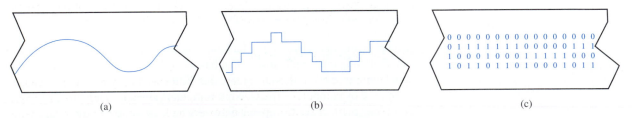

Figure 0.2 Magnetic tape containing analog and digital forms of a signal.
(a) Analog form. **(b)** Sampled analog form. **(c)** Digital form.

Although the modern computer is the most visible example of a digital system, there are many other examples, including digital watches, traffic light controllers, and pocket calculators. All these examples (other than the computer) are systems with fixed functionalities that cannot be modified by the user. On the other hand, the computer is a *programmable* system; that is, it can be modified to change the tasks or applications that it performs. In other words, computers are general-purpose systems, while the other examples are application specific.

In a rapidly growing trend, computers are being used in place of application-specific circuits in such products as automobile engines, home appliances, and electronic games by developing programs to perform the tasks required of the application and then embedding the programmed computer within the product. The ability to program a computer to perform any arbitrary task allows embedded computers to be used in place of a wide variety of fixed circuits, usually at a much lower cost.

Analog computers and other analog systems were in use long before digital devices were perfected. Why then have digital systems supplanted analog systems in most application areas? There are several reasons.

- In general, digital techniques offer more flexibility than do analog techniques in that they can be more easily programmed to perform any desired algorithm.
- Digital circuits provide for more powerful processing capabilities in terms of speed.
- Numeric information can be represented digitally with greater precision and range than it can with analog signals.
- Information storage and retrieval functions are much easier to implement in digital form than in analog.
- Digital techniques allow the use of built-in error detection and correction mechanisms.
- Digital systems lend themselves to miniaturization more than do analog systems.

0.2.2 Digital System Design Hierarchy

Digital systems may be designed and studied at many different levels of abstraction, ranging from a purely behavioral model, in which no hardware details are specified, down to the physical level, in which only structures of physical materials are specified. Several levels of design abstraction are listed in Table 0.1.

The System and Register Levels

At its highest level, a digital system can be viewed as one or more interacting functional modules. The behavior of each module is described without specifying implementation details. For example, a desktop computer viewed at the system level comprises a microprocessor, memory modules, and control circuits for the monitor, keyboard, printer, and other peripheral devices.

TABLE 0.1 HIERARCHY OF DIGITAL SYSTEM DESIGN ABSTRACTION

Design Level	Level of Abstraction	Amount of Detail	Type of Model
System	Highest	Lowest	Behavioral
Register	.	.	Behavioral/structural
Gate	.	.	Structural
Transistor	.	.	Structural
Physical	Lowest	Highest	Structural

At the register level, a digital system is viewed as a collection of elements called *registers* that store information, interconnected in some fashion by signal lines. Information is processed by the system by transferring it between registers along these signal lines. In some cases the information is transformed during these register transfers by routing it through one or more functional modules. Figures 0.3a and b illustrate the system- and register-level models of a digital

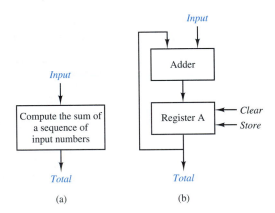

Figure 0.3 Models of a digital system that adds lists of numbers. **(a)** system level. **(b)** register level.

system that computes the sum of a sequence of binary numbers, supplied one at a time as inputs to the system. At the system level, all that is known is the basic function of the system, which is to compute:

$$\text{Total} = \sum_{i=1}^{N} \text{Input}_i$$

At the register level, as in Fig. 0.3b, it is seen that the system comprises a storage register, A, and an adder circuit. The *Total* is computed by first clearing register A, using control signal *Clear*, and then adding each input number, $Input_i$, to the contents of register A, replacing the contents of register A with the new sum, using control signal *Store*. Hence, the sum of a list of numbers is computed by performing the following register transfers in the proper sequence.

$$Clear: \quad A \leftarrow 0$$

$$Store: \quad A \leftarrow A + \text{input}$$

The Gate Level

At its lowest level, the behavior of a digital system is specified as a set of logic equations from switching algebra that can be realized in hardware by logic circuits. The smallest logical unit of digital hardware is called a *gate*. Gates are switching elements that implement the fundamental operators of switching algebra. Logic equations are realized in hardware by interconnecting gates to form *combinational logic circuits*, as illustrated in Fig. 0.4. Note that the circuit has six gates. The inputs in this example are labeled $x_1, \ldots, x_5$, and the output $f(x_1, \ldots, x_5)$ is a function only of the present value of the input signals. Hence, a distinguishing feature of the combinational logic circuit is that it possesses no memory of previous input signals. The analysis and design of combinational logic circuits consume a major portion of this text.

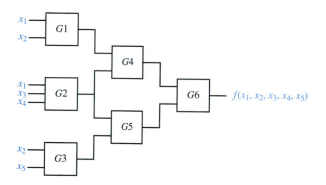

Figure 0.4 A combinational logic circuit with six gates.

All digital computers contain memory devices called *registers* that serve as temporary stores for information. These registers and certain parts of the control unit are called sequential logic circuits. A *sequential* logic circuit is, in general, a combinational logic circuit with memory, as modeled in Fig. 0.5. Unlike combinational logic circuits, the outputs of a sequential logic circuit are functions of not only the present value of the input signals, but also depend on the past history of inputs, as reflected by the information stored in the registers. Sequential logic circuit analysis and design comprise the second focal point of this text. Only after readers have mastered the fundamentals of combinational and sequential circuits can they proceed with the design and construction of digital systems hardware.

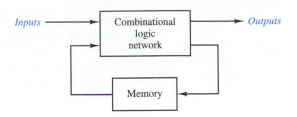

Figure 0.5 Sequential logic circuit.

Transistor and Physical Design Levels

Combinational and sequential logic circuits completely define the logical behavior of a digital system. Ultimately, each logic gate must be realized by a lower-level transistor circuit, which in turn is realized by combining various semiconductor and other materials. The technologies used to construct gates and other logic elements have evolved from mechanical devices to relays to electron tubes to discrete transistors to integrated circuits. Figure 0.6 illustrates several of these devices. Modern computers and application-specific digital systems are usually built of integrated circuits that are arranged to realize the registers and control circuits necessary to implement the computer's instruction set or the system's functions.

An *integrated circuit* (IC) contains multiple logic elements. The number of gates or gate equivalents per IC determines the scale of integration. Small scale integration (SSI) refers to ICs with 1 to 10 gates, medium scale integration (MSI) corresponds to 10- to 100-gate ICs, large scale integration (LSI) to 100 to 10,000 gates, and very large scale integration (VLSI) to ICs with more than 100,000 gates.

It is beyond the scope of this text to consider transistor and physical-level design of logic gates. However, it is important to have a basic understanding of various electrical and physical properties of different gate circuits so that the logical operation, performance, cost, and other parameters of a digital system design may be evaluated.

Electronic Technologies

Numerous *families* of electronic technologies have been developed to provide characteristics such as speed, power consumption, packaging density, functionality, and cost that hardware designers prefer. Usually, it is impossible to provide all the desired characteristics in one family. Hence, there is an ongoing quest for improvements in proven technologies or the development of new technologies. Tables 0.2 and 0.3 list the most significant technologies and corresponding characteristics that have been used since the beginning of the transistor era.

The packaging of logic gates and other logic elements has changed significantly over the years. Early electronic logic elements were typically constructed from large electron tubes, discrete resistors, and capacitors, were mounted on

TABLE 0.2 IMPORTANT ELECTRONIC TECHNOLOGIES

Technology	Device Type
Resistor–transistor logic (RTL)	Bipolar junction
Diode–transistor logic (DTL)	Bipolar junction
Transistor–transistor logic (TTL)	Bipolar junction
Emitter-coupled logic (ECL)	Bipolar junction
Positive metal oxide semiconductor (pMOS)	MOSFET
Negative metal oxide semiconductor (nMOS)	MOSFET
Complementary metal oxide semiconductor (CMOS)	MOSFET
Gallium Arsenide (GaAs)	MESFET

TABLE 0.3 CHARACTERISTICS OF ELECTRONIC TECHNOLOGY FAMILIES

Technology	Power Consumption	Speed	Packaging
RTL	High	Low	Discrete
DTL	High	Low	Discrete, SSI
TTL	Medium	Medium	SSI, MSI
ECL	High	High	SSI, MSI, LSI
pMOS	Medium	Low	MSI, LSI
nMOS	Medium	Medium	MSI, LSI, VLSI
CMOS	Low	Medium	SSI, MSI, LSI, VLSI
GaAs	High	High	SSI, MSI, LSI

an aluminum chassis, and were interconnected with copper wire. Tube technology advances resulted in reduced sizes, and printed circuit boards replaced the wires. Later, discrete transistors replaced the tubes, but the resistors, capacitors, and printed circuit boards remained in use, although their sizes were smaller. The advent of the integrated circuit in the early 1960s produced further reduction in the size of printed circuit boards and other passive elements.

Integrated circuits can be manufactured in standard, semicustom, and custom forms. Standard ICs provide the parts necessary to build systems for most applications. However, some applications may require semicustom or custom circuits to meet special functions, lower cost, or smaller size requirements. Custom circuits are manufactured to the exact requirements of a specific customer. On the other hand, semicustom circuits are programmed to satisfy a customer's need. The term *application-specific integrated circuits* (ASICS) is often used to describe semicustom devices.

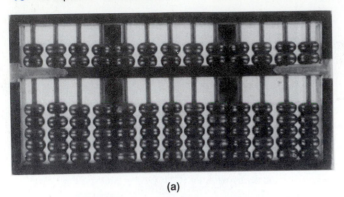

(a)

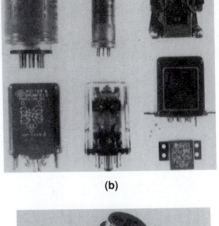

(b)

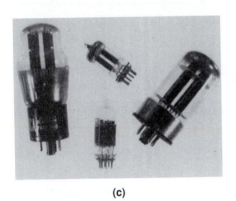

(c)

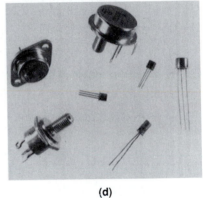

(d)

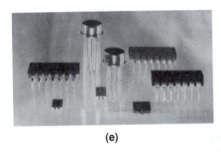

(e)

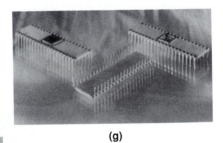

(g)

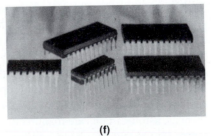

(f)

Figure 0.6 Photographs of computer hardware. **(a)** abacus; **(b)** relays; **(c)** electron tubes; **(d)** transistors; **(e)** small-scale integrated circuits; **(f)** medium-scale integrated circuits; **(g)** large-scale integrated circuit.

Figure 0.6 (Continued). **(h)** internal view of an integrated circuit chip (MC74450) (courtesy of Motorola Semiconductor Products, Inc.); **(i)** internal view of an electronically programmable logic device (courtesy of Xilinx); **(j)** internal view of an electronically programmable logic device (courtesy of Xilinx); **(k)** a very large-scale integrated circuit in a flat pack with pin-grid input/output leads (courtesy of Xilinx); **(l)** multichip module containing three chips—a microprocessor, an electronically programmable read-only memory, and an application-specific integrated circuit (courtesy of Texas Instruments).

◗ 0.3 Organization of a Stored Program Digital Computer

Now that we have been introduced to the basic elements used to construct digital logic circuits, let us take a look at the organization of a digital computer. A digital computer is a system whose functional elements consist of arithmetic/logic units (ALUs), control units, memory or storage units, and input/output (I/O) equipment. The interaction of these elements is shown in Fig. 0.7. Every computer system has a native set of instructions, called *machine instructions*, that specify operations to be performed on data by the ALU and other interactions between the ALU, memory, and I/O devices. The memory elements contain the data plus a stored list of machine instructions called a *program*.

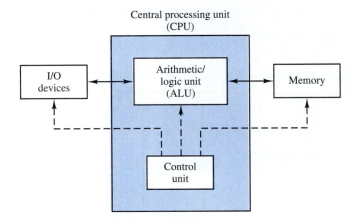

Figure 0.7   High-level organization of a digital computer.

The control unit coordinates all operations of the ALU, memory, and I/O devices by continuously cycling through a set of operations that cause instructions to be fetched from memory and executed. The *instruction cycle* of a simple digital computer, illustrated in Fig. 0.8, includes the following basic steps:

1. Fetch the next instruction of the current program from memory into the control unit.
2. Decode the instruction; that is, determine which machine instruction is to be executed.
3. Fetch any operands needed for the instruction from memory or from input devices.
4. Perform the operation indicated by the instruction.
5. Store in memory any results generated by the operation, or send the results to an output device.

Instructions are taken from memory in sequential order unless a special kind of instruction is encountered called, synonymously, a *branch*, *jump*, *skip*, or *transfer*. The branch instructions allow looping and decision-making programs to be written.

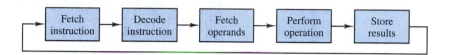

Figure 0.8   Instruction cycle of a stored program computer.

0.3.1 Computer Instructions

As the control unit of a digital computer fetches an instruction from memory for execution, several types of operations may result.

1. *Arithmetic instructions* cause the binary data to be added, subtracted, multiplied, or divided as specified by the computer programmer in the program.

2. *Test and compare operations* are available and determine the relation (greater than, less than, equal to, or other) of two pieces of binary data.

3. *Branch or skip instructions* may be employed that alter the sequential nature of program execution, based on the results of a test or compare. This type of function adds considerable flexibility to programs.

4. *Input and output commands* are included for reading messages into the computer, writing messages from the computer, and controlling peripheral devices.

5. *Logical and shifting operations* provide the computer with the ability to translate and interpret all the different codes it uses. These instructions allow bit manipulation to be accomplished under program control.

All instructions for any digital computer may be grouped into one of these five categories.

0.3.2 Information Representation in Computers

We have briefly discussed the instructions and data stored in the digital computer's memory unit, but no mention was made of the form of these items. Information in a computer system can generally be divided into three categories: numeric data, nonnumeric data, and instruction codes.

Numeric Data Representation

Numbers are stored in the computer's memory in the binary (base 2) number system. Binary numbers are written using the two binary digits (bits), 1 and 0. By contrast, we use 10 decimal digits in writing decimal numbers.

For example, 129 in decimal means $1 \times 10^2 + 2 \times 10^1 + 9 \times 10^0$, or each digit's position represents a weighted power of 10. Note that the 10 digits are 0 through $10 - 1 = 9$. Each digit in a binary number, say 1101, is represented by a weighted power of 2, or $1 \times 2^3 + 1 \times 2^2 + 0 \times 2^1 + 1 \times 2^0$. To convert the binary number to decimal, this weighted sum is determined as $(1101)_2 = 1 \times 8 + 1 \times 4 + 0 \times 2 + 1 \times 1 = (13)_{10}$ or one-one-zero-one in binary equals 13 in decimal. The rules for converting numbers between decimal and binary are covered in detail in Chapter 1.

Data in the form of binary numbers are stored in registers in the computer and are represented as follows:

$$1011000111$$

This is a 10-bit register, which might reside in the arithmetic or memory unit. In memory, the data in a single register are called a *word* (the word length is 10 bits in this example). Patterns of ones and zeros are the only information that can be stored in a computer's registers or memory. The assignment of a meaning to the bit patterns is called *coding*, and the codes used in most computers for data are simply variations of the binary weighting scheme just presented.

Nonnumeric (Input/Output) Codes

Although the computer employs binary data, users prefer alphabetic and numeric data representations, for example, records of sales, lists of names, or test grades. The set of alphanumeric symbols allowed for many computers is called the character set and has a special binary-like code called the *American Standard Code for Information Interchange* (ASCII). In this code the alphanumeric and other special characters (punctuation, algebraic operators, and the like) are coded with 8 bits each; a partial listing of this code is given in Chapter 1. Suppose we wanted to give the digital computer a message "ADD 1". This message has five characters, the fourth one being a space or blank. In the ASCII code, our message becomes

Symbol	ASCII Code
A	01000001
D	01000100
D	01000100
	00100000
1	00110001

After our message is sent to the computer, a program in the computer's memory accepts it and acts accordingly.

Instruction Codes

The computer's instructions reside in main memory and therefore, by definition, are also represented by patterns of ones and zeros. The instructions are generally broken down into subfields that are coded separately. These subfields are the operation code (op code) and the memory address. The operation code specifies the specific function to be performed.

0.3.3 Computer Hardware

Now, let us further examine the interaction of the computer's components shown in Fig. 0.7. Programs are stored in the computer's memory as discussed previously. However, the programs are inserted into memory by the control unit in conjunction with the input/output (I/O) equipment, sometimes called *peripheral devices*. Programs are usually given to the computer from magnetic or optical peripheral storage devices. The computer then fetches the instructions of the program from memory and executes them. Data to be used by a program are likewise transferred into memory from keyboards, scanners, magnetic disks, and other peripheral devices.

Control Unit

The control unit follows the stored list of instructions, directing the activities of the arithmetic unit and I/O devices until the program has run to completion. Each unit performs its task under the synchronizing influence of the control unit.

Arithmetic/Logic Unit

Arithmetic/logic units (ALUs) are combinational or sequential logic circuits that perform various operations on data, as instructed by the control unit. Each ALU is characterized by the type of data that it can manipulate and the set of operations that it can perform on those data. Most ALUs support operations on integers of various sizes and may also include operations to manipulate fixed-point and floating-point numbers and various nonnumeric data. Typical ALU operations include the following:

- Arithmetic: add, subtract, multiply, divide.
- Logical: AND, OR, exclusive-OR, complement (these will be defined when we examine combinational logic circuits in Chapter 2).
- Shift and rotate data.
- Convert data from one type to another.

Control unit and ALU circuits are usually constructed from semiconductor devices packaged in a wide variety of schemes. Models of the second generation have transistors, resistors, diodes, and so on, mounted on printed circuit boards, while models of the third generation use small scale integrated circuits on circuit boards. Fourth-generation machines use large scale and very large scale integrated circuits.

Memory Units

Computer memory units are classified as *primary memory* if they can be accessed directly by the control unit; otherwise they are classified as *secondary memory*.

Primary memory units in today's digital computers are usually constructed using high-speed semiconductor elements called *RAMs* (random-access memory) and *ROMs* (read-only memory). Most systems built prior to 1980, some of which are still in operation today, utilized arrays of magnetic cores as their primary memory elements. A few specialized systems, particularly in space vehicles, utilized plated wire as a replacement for magnetic core in some applications where radiation hardness was required.

Memory units are divided into cells called *words*, and each cell is known by its physical location, or memory address. The concept of a memory address for a memory cell is equivalent to a mailing address for a mailbox. For example, every post office has rows of mailboxes, each identified by a unique numbered position. Similarly, each memory cell resides in a unique numbered position, the number being the memory address.

Memory units may be characterized by their access and cycle times; *memory access time* may be defined as the length of time required to extract (read) a word from the memory, and *memory cycle time* may be defined as the minimum interval of time required between successive memory operations. The access time of a memory determines how quickly information can be obtained by the CPU, whereas the cycle time determines the rate at which successive memory accesses may be made.

Secondary memory devices are used for bulk or mass storage of programs and data and include rotating magnetic devices, such as floppy and hard disks, magnetic tapes, magnetic bubble memories, optical devices such as CDROMs (compact disk read-only memory), and a variety of other devices. In contrast to primary memory, information in secondary memory devices is not accessed directly. Instead, a special controller searches the device to locate the block of information containing the desired item. When found, the entire block is usually transferred into primary memory, where the desired items can be accessed in a more convenient fashion.

Input/Output Equipment

The computer may output data to several types of peripherals; a magnetic disk or laser printer is typical. Cathode-ray tubes (CRTs) and liquid crystal display (LCD) panels are also available to display the results of a program's calculations. Analog-to-digital converters, digital-to-analog converters, plotters, magnetic reading and recording devices, and laser and ink-jet printers are the most commonly used input/output equipment.

0.3.4 Computer Software

Software consists of the programs and data stored in the computer's memory. The software determines how the computer hardware is utilized and can be broadly classified as either application programs or system programs.

Application Programs

Programming the digital computer is the process of designing a list of instructions for the computer so that it can efficiently perform a specified task. The digital computer's instructions must be coded in patterns of ones and zeros before the computer can interpret them. If all programs had to be written in this form, digital computers would enjoy very limited use. The patterns of ones and zeros are called machine language instructions, and very few programmers ever attempt to write programs in this manner.

A symbolic representation of the machine language of a computer, called *assembly language*, is often used to develop programs. This is especially true for small microcomputers embedded into kitchen appliances, electronic games, and automotive equipment. Assembly language allows a programmer to specify the operations to be performed on data stored in the internal registers and memory of a processor without becoming bogged down in patterns of ones and zeros.

However, most programmers prefer to use higher-level, more reasonable, symbolic languages in which to program their problems. By using high-level languages such as C, Pascal, Ada, or FORTRAN, the programmer has a wide range of instructions in a form that he or she can easily understand and efficiently use, with the instructions of each language tailored to specific types of problems. The full flexibility of machine language is difficult to incorporate into high-level languages, but a magnificent amount has been retained, especially in C.

System Programs

System programs comprise all the software provided on a computer system to aid programmers in the process or developing and executing application programs. For example, whenever a symbolic language, either assembly language or a high-level language, is used to write a program, the program must be translated into machine language before it can be executed by the computer. The question now arises as to who shall perform this laborious translation chore. The most efficient translator is not the programmer, but the digital computer itself. Any job done by a computer is done under program control; therefore, the program that translates higher-level languages into machine language has been given a special name, the *compiler*. This translation process is illustrated in Fig. 0.9. Likewise, the program that translates assembly language into machine language is called an *assembler*. Compilers and assemblers are typical examples of system programs, as are the text editors used to type and alter program statements.

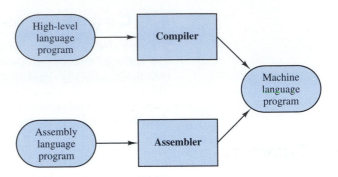

Figure 0.9 Translation of computer programs into machine language.

Now, let us contemplate the manner in which a given digital computer might be operated. A special program called the *operating system* handles the routine tasks needed to change from one user's program to the next. This special program falls into a category of programs called system software. In particular three different operating systems will be discussed: single user, batch processing, and time sharing.

If a machine is operated by each user who executes a program, it is dedicated to this program and no one else may use the computer until the current user is finished. The computer is then dependent on human intervention during the time between programs, and hence much time can be spent idling. This operating system is convenient for the user if the computer is available when the user needs it, for once an individual is "on the machine," that user may modify and reexecute programs or execute several successive programs before turning the machine over to the next user. The MS-DOS and Macintosh operating systems are examples of single-user operating systems.

The batch operating system eliminates most of the computer idle time by establishing one operator who collects all the user programs and feeds them to the computer continuously. The operating system program resides in the memory unit, and the memory locations it uses are protected from each user. Thus, although idle time is reduced, the available memory storage for the user is also reduced. In addition, the user must wait for the operator to return her or his program, which is always a source of irritation and confrontation.

A more advanced operating system called *time sharing* allows multiple users to execute their programs almost simultaneously. Common examples are the UNIX operating system, used on a wide variety of personal computers, workstations, and larger machines, and the VMS operating system used on computers from Digital Equipment Corporation. Remote terminals consisting of limited input/output devices are connected to the digital computer, and each terminal is assigned to a single user. The users are relatively slow while the computer is extremely fast. This speed differential allows the computer to skip around between users, or time-share, in such a manner as to convince each user that he has the machine all to himself. Although this operating system seems very attractive, it has disadvantages, the first of which is cost. Also the time-sharing system program is complicated and long, which means it uses a lot of memory space and computer time. In addition, since all users' programs are stored in memory simultaneously, each individual's available portion of memory is limited. Therefore, time sharing usually requires the maximum number of memory elements that a particular computer can accommodate.

0.4 Summary

In this introductory chapter we have provided motivation for the material that follows. We have briefly explained what a computer is, how it is organized, the codes it employs, the manner in which it is programmed, and the hardware of which it is composed. The material contained in the remaining chapters is prerequisite to any hardware design or implementation for digital computers or other complex digital systems. The reader is referred to [1, 2, 3, 4] for further reading.

REFERENCES

1. J. P. HAYES, *Computer Architecture and Organization,* 2nd ed. New York: McGraw-Hill Book Co., 1988.

2. D. A. PATTERSON AND J. L. HENNESSY, *Computer Organization & Design: The Hardware/Software Interface.* San Mateo, CA: Morgan Kaufmann Publishers, 1993.

3. D. A. HODGES AND H. G. JACKSON, *Analysis and Design of Digital Integrated Circuits,* 2nd ed. New York: McGraw-Hill Book Co., 1988.

4. J. F. WAKERLY, *Digital Design Principles and Practices,* 2nd ed. Englewood Cliffs, NJ: Prentice Hall, 1994.

Computers and other digital systems process information as their primary function. Therefore, it is necessary to have methods and systems for representing information in forms that can be manipulated and stored using electronic or other types of hardware.

In this chapter we cover number systems and codes that are often employed in computers and digital systems. Topics covered include binary, octal, and hexadecimal number systems and arithmetic; base conversion techniques; negative number representation methods such as sign-magnitude, two's complement, and one's complement; numeric codes for fixed- and floating-point numbers; character codes, including binary coded decimal and ASCII; Gray and excess codes; and error detection and correction codes. Later chapters of the book cover the analysis and design of hardware to process information represented in the forms described here.

Number System and Codes

1.1 Number Systems

A number system consists of an ordered set of symbols, called *digits*, with relations defined for addition (+), subtraction (-), multiplication (x), and division (÷). The *radix* (*r*), or *base*, of the number system is the total number of digits allowed in the number system. Number systems commonly used in digital system design and computer programming include *decimal* ($r = 10$), *binary* ($r = 2$), *octal* ($r = 8$), and *hexadecimal* ($r = 16$). Any number in a given system may have both an integer part and a fractional part, which are separated by a radix point (.). The integer part or the fraction part may be absent in some cases. Now let's examine the *positional* and *polynomial* notations for a number.

1.1.1 Positional Notation

Suppose you borrow one hundred twenty-three dollars and thirty-five cents from your local bank. The check you are given indicates the amount as $123.35. In writing this number, positional notation has been used. The check may be cashed for 1 one hundred dollar bill, 2 ten dollar bills, 3 one dollar bills, 3 dimes, and 5 pennies. Therefore, the position of each digit indicates its relative weight or significance.

In general, a positive number N can be written in positional notation as

$$N = (a_{n-1}a_{n-2}\ldots a_1 a_0 \; . \; a_{-1}a_{-2}\ldots a_{-m})_r \qquad (1.1)$$

where

$. =$ radix point separating the integer and fractional digits

$r =$ radix or base of the number system being used

$n =$ number of integer digits to the left of the radix point

$m =$ number of fractional digits to the right of the radix point

$a_i =$ integer digit i when $n - 1 \geq i \geq 0$

$a_i =$ fractional digit i when $-1 \geq i \geq -m$

$a_{n-1} =$ most significant digit

$a_{-m} =$ least significant digit

Note that the range of values for all digits a_i is $r - 1 \geq a_i \geq 0$. Using this notation, the bank loan amount would be written $\$(123.35)_{10}$. The parentheses and the subscript denoting the radix may be eliminated without loss of information if the radix is either known by the context or otherwise specified.

Polynomial Notation

The $(123.35)_{10}$ dollar loan amount can be written in polynomial form as
$$N = 1 \times 100 + 2 \times 10 + 3 \times 1 + 3 \times 0.1 + 5 \times 0.01$$
$$= 1 \times 10^2 + 2 \times 10^1 + 3 \times 10^0 + 3 \times 10^{-1} + 5 \times 10^{-2}$$
Note that each digit resides in a weighted position and that the weight of each position is a power of the radix 10. In general, any number N of radix r may be written as a polynomial in the form

$$N = \sum_{i=-m}^{n-1} a_i r^i \qquad (1.2)$$

where each symbol is defined the same as in Eq. 1.1. For the bank loan, $r = 10$, $a_2 = 1, a_1 = 2, a_0 = 3, a_{-1} = 3, a_{-2} = 5,$ and $a_i = 0$ for $i \geq 3$ and for $i \leq -3$.

1.1.2 Commonly Used Number Systems

The decimal, binary, octal, and hexadecimal number systems are all important for the study of digital systems. Table 1.1 summarizes the fundamental features of each system and illustrates a limited range of positive integers in each. All the numbers in Table 1.1 are written in positional notation.

Digital systems are usually constructed using two-state devices that are either in an off state or an on state. Hence, the binary number system is ideally suited for representing numbers in digital systems, since only two digits, 0 and 1, commonly called *bits*, are needed. A bit can be stored in a two-state storage device often called a *latch*. Binary numbers of length n can be stored in an n-bit long device known as a *register*, which is built with n latches. An 8-bit register loaded with the binary number 10011010 is shown in Fig. 1.1.

Figure 1.1   An 8-bit register.

◗ 1.2 Arithmetic

Every child learns the rudiments of arithmetic by memorizing the base-10 addition and multiplication tables as shown in Tables 1.2a and b, respectively. Subtraction can be accomplished by using the addition table in reverse. Similarly, long division uses trial and error multiplication and subtraction to obtain the quotient. The foundation for arithmetic in any base is a knowledge of the addition and multiplication tables for the given base. Given these tables, arithmetic operations proceed in a similar manner for all bases. Arithmetic in the binary, octal, and hexadecimal number systems will be introduced in the remainder of this section.

TABLE 1.1   IMPORTANT NUMBER SYSTEMS

Name	Decimal	Binary	Octal	Hexadecimal
Radix	10	2	8	16
Digits	0, 1, 2, 3, 4,	0, 1	0, 1, 2, 3,	0, 1, 2, 3, 4, 5,
	5, 6, 7, 8, 9		4, 5, 6, 7	6, 7, 8, 9, *A, B,*
				C, D, E, F
First	0	0	0	0
seventeen	1	1	1	1
positive	2	10	2	2
integers	3	11	3	3
	4	100	4	4
	5	101	5	5
	6	110	6	6
	7	111	7	7
	8	1000	10	8
	9	1001	11	9
	10	1010	12	*A*
	11	1011	13	*B*
	12	1100	14	*C*
	13	1101	15	*D*
	14	1110	16	*E*
	15	1111	17	*F*
	16	10000	20	10

1.2.1 Binary Arithmetic

Addition

Tables 1.3a and b show the addition and multiplication tables, respectively, for the binary number system. The tables are very small since there are only two digits, or *bits*, in the system. Binary arithmetic is very simple as a result. Note that the addition $1 + 1$ produces a sum bit of 0 and a carry bit of 1. The carry must be added to the next column of bits as addition proceeds in the normal pattern from right to left. Two examples of binary addition are given next.

EXAMPLE 1.1

Add the two binary numbers $(111101)_2$ and $(10111)_2$.

	1	*1*	*1*	*1*	*1*	*1*		Carries
		1	1	1	1	0	1	Augend
+			1	0	1	1	1	Addend
	1	0	1	0	1	0	0	Sum

TABLE 1.2 (a) DECIMAL ADDITION TABLE; (b) DECIMAL MULTIPLICATION TABLE.

+	0	1	2	3	4	5	6	7	8	9
0	0	1	2	3	4	5	6	7	8	9
1	1	2	3	4	5	6	7	8	9	10
2	2	3	4	5	6	7	8	9	10	11
3	3	4	5	6	7	8	9	10	11	12
4	4	5	6	7	8	9	10	11	12	13
5	5	6	7	8	9	10	11	12	13	14
6	6	7	8	9	10	11	12	13	14	15
7	7	8	9	10	11	12	13	14	15	16
8	8	9	10	11	12	13	14	15	16	17
9	9	10	11	12	13	14	15	16	17	18

(a)

×	0	1	2	3	4	5	6	7	8	9
0	0	0	0	0	0	0	0	0	0	0
1	0	1	2	3	4	5	6	7	8	9
2	0	2	4	6	8	10	12	14	16	18
3	0	3	6	9	12	15	18	21	24	27
4	0	4	8	12	16	20	24	28	32	36
5	0	5	10	15	20	25	30	35	40	45
6	0	6	12	18	24	30	36	42	48	54
7	0	7	14	21	28	35	42	49	56	63
8	0	8	16	24	32	40	48	56	64	72
9	9	9	18	27	36	45	54	63	72	81

(b)

TABLE 1.3 (a) BINARY ADDITION TABLE. (b) BINARY MULTIPLICATION TABLE.

+	0	1
0	0	1
1	1	10

(a)

×	0	1
0	0	0
1	0	1

(b)

In Example 1.1, two columns were encountered that had two 1 bits and a carry bit of 1, which had to be totaled. This addition of three 1's can be more easily viewed as

$$1 + 1 + 1 = (1 + 1) + 1$$
$$= (10)_2 + (01)_2$$
$$= 11$$

Thus both the sum bit and the carry bit are 1's.

When a long list of binary numbers must be added, the computation is easily performed by adding the numbers in pairs, as demonstrated in the following example.

EXAMPLE 1.2

Add the four numbers $(101101)_2$, $(110101)_2$, $(001101)_2$, and $(010001)_2$.

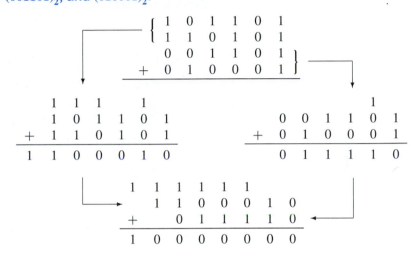

However, we may choose to perform the addition directly to avoid the intermediate steps required by the preceding approach. The direct method is illustrated in the following example.

EXAMPLE 1.3

Repeat the previous example by adding one entire column at a time.

10	10	10	10	1	10		Carries
		1	0	1	1	0	1
		1	1	0	1	0	1
		0	0	1	1	0	1
+		0	1	0	0	0	1
1	0	0	0	0	0	0	0	Sum

Note that the sum of the digits in the first column is $1 + 1 + 1 + 1 = (100)_2$. This results in a sum digit of 0 in that column and a carry of 10 to the next column to the left.

Subtraction

Subtraction may be thought of as the inverse of addition. The rules for binary subtraction follow directly from the binary addition table in Table 1.3a and are

$$1 - 0 = 1$$
$$1 - 1 = 0$$

$$0 - 0 = 0$$

$$0 - 1 = 1 \quad \text{with a borrow of 1, or } 10 - 1 = 1$$

The last rule shows that if a 1 bit is subtracted from a 0 bit then a 1 must be borrowed from the next most significant column. Borrows propagate to the left from column to column, as illustrated next.

EXAMPLE 1.4

Subtract $(10111)_2$ from $(1001101)_2$.

6	5	4	3	2	1	0	Column
	1			*10*			*Borrows*
0	*1̸*	*0̸*	*10*	0	*0̸*	*10*	*Borrows*
1̸	0̸	0̸	1̸	1̸	0̸	1	Minuend
−			1	0	1	1	1	Subtrahend
1	1	0	1	1	0	Difference

In this example, a borrow is first encountered in column 1. The borrow is taken from column 2, resulting in a 10 in column 1 and a 0 in column 2. The 0 now present in column 2 necessitates a borrow from column 3. No other borrows are necessary until column 4. In this case, there is no 1 in column 5 to borrow. Hence, we must first borrow the 1 from column 6, which results in 0 in column 6 and 10 in column 5. Now column 4 borrows a 1 from column 5, leaving 1 in column 5 $(10 - 1 = 1)$ and 10 in column 4. This sequence of borrows is shown above the minuend terms.

Multiplication and Division

Binary multiplication is performed in a similar fashion as decimal multiplication except that binary multiplication operations are much simpler, as can be seen in Table 1.3b. Care must be taken, however, when adding the partial products, as illustrated in the following example.

EXAMPLE 1.5

Multiply $(10111)_2$ by $(1010)_2$.

			1	0	1	1	1	Multiplicand
×				1	0	1	0	Multiplier
		0	0	0	0	0		
	1	0	1	1	1			
0	0	0	0	0				
1	0	1	1	1				
1	1	1	0	0	1	1	0	Product

Note that there is one partial product for every multiplier bit. This procedure can be performed more efficiently by merely shifting one column to the left, rather than listing an all-zero partial product for a multiplier bit of 0. We can see from this example how easily this procedure can be accomplished.

Binary division is performed using the same trial and error procedure as decimal division. However, binary division is easier since there are only two values to try. Copies of the divisor terms are subtracted from the dividend, yielding positive intermediate remainder terms. The following example illustrates binary division.

EXAMPLE 1.6

Divide $(1110111)_2$ by $(1001)_2$.

```
                              1  1  0  1   Quotient
   Divisor   1  0  0  1 | 1  1  1  0  1  1  1   Dividend
                          1  0  0  1
                          _____
                             1  0  1  1
                             1  0  0  1
                             _____
                                1  0  1  1
                                1  0  0  1
                                _____
                                   1  0   Remainder
```

1.2.2 Octal Arithmetic

The addition and multiplication tables for the octal number system are given in Table 1.4. Given these tables, octal arithmetic can be done using the same procedures as for the decimal and binary systems, as is illustrated in the following four examples.

EXAMPLE 1.7

Compute $(4163)_8 + (7520)_8$.

```
      1     1           Carries
      4  1  6  3        Augend
  +   7  5  2  0        Addend
  _____
  1   3  7  0  3        Sum
```

EXAMPLE 1.8

Compute $(6204)_8 - (5173)_8$.

```
         1  10          Borrows
      6  2̸  0̸  4        Minuend
  -   5  1  7  3        Subtrahend
  _____
      1  0  1  1        Difference
```

EXAMPLE 1.9

Compute $(4167)_8 \times (2503)_8$.

```
                  4  1  6  7   Multiplicand
           ×      2  5  0  3   Multiplier
           _____
                1  4  5  4  5   Partial products
          2  5  1  2  3  0
    1  0  3  5  6
    _____
    1  3  1  0  5  0  4  5   Product
```

TABLE 1.4   (a) OCTAL ADDITION TABLE (b) OCTAL MULTIPLICATION TABLE

+	0	1	2	3	4	5	6	7
0	0	1	2	3	4	5	6	7
1	1	2	3	4	5	6	7	10
2	2	3	4	5	6	7	10	11
3	3	4	5	6	7	10	11	12
4	4	5	6	7	10	11	12	13
5	5	6	7	10	11	12	13	14
6	6	7	10	11	12	13	14	15
7	7	10	11	12	13	14	15	16

(a)

X	0	1	2	3	4	5	6	7
0	0	0	0	0	0	0	0	0
1	0	1	2	3	4	5	6	7
2	0	2	4	6	10	12	14	16
3	0	3	6	11	14	17	22	25
4	0	4	10	14	20	24	30	34
5	0	5	12	17	24	31	36	43
6	0	6	14	22	30	36	44	52
7	0	7	16	25	34	43	52	61

(b)

EXAMPLE 1.10

Compute $(4163)_8 \div (25)_8$.

```
                    1  4  7   Quotient
    Divisor   2  5 | 4  1  6  3   Dividend
                     2  5
                    ─────
                     1  4  6
                     1  2  4
                    ──────
                        2  2  3
                        2  2  3
                       ───────
                           0   Remainder
```

1.2.3 Hexadecimal Arithmetic

The hexadecimal addition and multiplication tables are more complex than those for the number systems studied previously and are given in Table 1.5. However, as with other number systems, a knowledge of these tables permits

TABLE 1.5   HEXADECIMAL ADDITION AND MULTIPLICATION TABLES (a) HEXADECIMAL ADDITION TABLE (b) HEXADECIMAL MULTIPLICATION TABLE

+	0	1	2	3	4	5	6	7	8	9	A	B	C	D	E	F
0	0	1	2	3	4	5	6	7	8	9	A	B	C	D	E	F
1	1	2	3	4	5	6	7	8	9	A	B	C	D	E	F	10
2	2	3	4	5	6	7	8	9	A	B	C	D	E	F	10	11
3	3	4	5	6	7	8	9	A	B	C	D	E	F	10	11	12
4	4	5	6	7	8	9	A	B	C	D	E	F	10	11	12	13
5	5	6	7	8	9	A	B	C	D	E	F	10	11	12	13	14
6	6	7	8	9	A	B	C	D	E	F	10	11	12	13	14	15
7	7	8	9	A	B	C	D	E	F	10	11	12	13	14	15	16
8	8	9	A	B	C	D	E	F	10	11	12	13	14	15	16	17
9	9	A	B	C	D	E	F	10	11	12	13	14	15	16	17	18
A	A	B	C	D	E	F	10	11	12	13	14	15	16	17	18	19
B	B	C	D	E	F	10	11	12	13	14	15	16	17	18	19	1A
C	C	D	E	F	10	11	12	13	14	15	16	17	18	19	1A	1B
D	D	E	F	10	11	12	13	14	15	16	17	18	19	1A	1B	1C
E	E	F	10	11	12	13	14	15	16	17	18	19	1A	1B	1C	1D
F	F	10	11	12	13	14	15	16	17	18	19	1A	1B	1C	1D	1E

(a)

×	0	1	2	3	4	5	6	7	8	9	A	B	C	D	E	F
0	0	0	0	0	0	0	0	0	0	0	0	0	0	0	0	0
1	0	1	2	3	4	5	6	7	8	9	A	B	C	D	E	F
2	0	2	4	6	8	A	C	E	10	12	14	16	18	1A	1C	1E
3	0	3	6	9	C	F	12	15	18	1B	1E	21	24	27	2A	2D
4	0	4	8	C	10	14	18	1C	20	24	28	2C	30	34	38	3C
5	0	5	A	F	14	19	1E	23	28	2D	32	37	3C	41	46	4B
6	0	6	C	12	18	1E	24	2A	30	36	3C	42	48	4E	54	5A
7	0	7	E	15	1C	23	2A	31	38	3F	46	4D	54	5B	62	69
8	0	8	10	18	20	28	30	38	40	48	50	58	60	68	70	78
9	0	9	12	1B	24	2D	36	3F	48	51	5A	63	6C	75	7E	87
A	0	A	14	1E	28	32	3C	46	50	5A	64	6E	78	82	8C	96
B	0	B	16	21	2C	37	42	4D	58	63	6E	79	84	8F	9A	A5
C	0	C	18	24	30	3C	48	54	60	6C	78	84	90	9C	A8	B4
D	0	D	1A	27	34	41	4E	5B	68	75	82	8F	9C	A9	B6	C3
E	0	E	1C	2A	38	46	54	62	70	7E	8C	9A	A8	B6	C4	D2
F	0	F	1E	2D	3C	4B	5A	69	78	87	96	A5	B4	C3	D2	E1

(b)

hexadecimal arithmetic to be performed using well-known procedures. The following four examples illustrate hexadecimal arithmetic.

EXAMPLE 1.11

Compute $(2A58)_{16} + (71D0)_{16}$.

```
              1            Carries
      2   A   5   8        Augend
  +   7   1   D   0        Addend
  ─────────────────
      9   C   2   8        Sum
```

EXAMPLE 1.12

Compute $(9F1B)_{16} - (4A36)_{16}$.

```
              E   11       Borrows
      9   F   1̸   B        Minuend
  −   4   A   3   6        Subtrahend
  ─────────────────
      5   4   E   5        Difference
```

EXAMPLE 1.13

Compute $(5C2A)_{16} \times (71D0)_{16}$.

```
              5   C   2   A        Multiplicand
      ×       7   1   D   0        Multiplier
  ───────────────────────
          4   A   E   2   2   0    Partial products
          5   C   2   A
  2   8   5   2   6
  ───────────────────────────
  2   8   F   9   6   C   2   0    Product
```

EXAMPLE 1.14

Compute $(27FCA)_{16} \div (3E)_{16}$.

```
                          A   5   1    Quotient
  Divisor   3   E │ 2   7   F   C   A    Dividend
                    2   6   C
                  ─────────
                        1   3   C
                        1   3   6
                      ─────────
                            6   A
                            3   E
                          ─────────
                            2   C    Remainder
```

1.3 Base Conversions

Users and designers of computers and other digital systems often encounter a need to convert a given number in base A to the equivalent number in base B. Algorithms for performing base conversions will be presented and illustrated in this section.

1.3.1 Conversion Methods

Series Substitution

The polynomial representation of a number previously given by Eq. 1.2 forms the basis of the *series substitution* conversion method. The equation can be written in an expanded form as follows:

$$N = a_{n-1}r^{n-1} + \ldots + a_0 r^0 + a_{-1} r^{-1} + \ldots + a_{-m} r^{-m} \qquad (1.3)$$

A number in base A can be converted to a number in base B in two steps.

1. Form the series representation of the number in base A in the format of Eq. 1.3.

2. Evaluate the series using base B arithmetic.

The following four examples illustrate this procedure.

EXAMPLE 1.15

Convert $(10100)_2$ to base 10.

We make this conversion by substituting for each digit, according to its weight. Counting from right to left in $(10100)_2$, we find that the rightmost digit, 0, has a weight of 2^0, the next digit, 0, has weight 2^1, and so on. Substituting these values into Eq. 1.3 and evaluating the series with base 10 arithmetic gives:

$$N = 1 \times 2^4 + 0 \times 2^3 + 1 \times 2^2 + 0 \times 2^1 + 0 \times 2^0$$
$$= (16)_{10} + 0 + (4)_{10} + 0 + 0$$
$$= (20)_{10}$$

EXAMPLE 1.16

Convert $(274)_8$ to base 10.

$$N = 2 \times 8^2 + 7 \times 8^1 + 4 \times 8^0$$
$$= (128)_{10} + (56)_{10} + (4)_{10}$$
$$= (188)_{10}$$

EXAMPLE 1.17

Convert $(1101.011)_2$ to base 8.

The integer part of the number is converted as in the previous examples. With digits that are to the right of a binary point, we count from left to right. The first digit to the right of the binary point, 0, has weight 2^{-1}, the next digit, 1, has weight 2^{-2}, and the third digit, 1, has weight 2^{-2}. Substituting into Eq. 1.3 gives

$$N = 1 \times 2^3 + 1 \times 2^2 + 0 \times 2^1 + 1 \times 2^0 + 0 \times 2^{-1} + 1 \times 2^{-2} + 1 \times 2^{-3}$$
$$= (10)_8 + (4)_8 + 0 + (1)_8 + 0 + (.2)_8 + (.1)_8$$
$$= (15.3)_8$$

EXAMPLE 1.18

Convert $(AF3.15)_{16}$ to base 10.

$$N = A \times 16^2 + F \times 16^1 + 3 \times 16^0 + 1 \times 16^{-1} + 5 \times 16^{-2}$$
$$= 10_{10} \times 256_{10} + 15_{10} \times 16_{10} + 3_{10} \times 1_{10}$$
$$+ 1_{10} \times 0.0625_{10} + 5_{10} \times 0.00390625_{10}$$
$$= 2560_{10} + 240_{10} + 3_{10} + 0.0625_{10} + 0.01953125_{10}$$
$$= (2803.08203125)_{10}$$

Note in the preceding examples that the computations were easier for conversions from base A to base B when $A < B$. Conversion methods will now be described where the converse is true.

Radix Divide Method

The *radix divide* conversion method can be used for converting an integer in base A to the equivalent base B integer. To understand the method, consider the following representation of integer N_I.

$$(N_I)_A = b_{n-1} B^{n-1} + \ldots + b_0 B^0 \qquad (1.4)$$

In Eq. 1.4, the b_i's represent the digits of $(N_I)_B$ in base A. The least significant digit, $(b_0)_A$, can be found by dividing $(N_I)_A$ by $(B)_A$ as follows:

$$N_I / B = (b_{n-1} B^{n-1} + \ldots + b_1 B^1 + b_0 B^0)/B$$
$$= \underbrace{b_{n-1} B^{n-2} + \ldots + b_1 B^0}_{Quotient, Q_1} + \underbrace{b_0}_{Remainder, R_0}$$

In other words, $(b_0)_A$ is the remainder produced when $(N_I)_A$ is divided by $(B)_A$. In general, $(b_i)_A$ is the remainder, R_i, produced when quotient, Q_i, is divided by $(B)_A$. The conversion is completed by converting each $(b_i)_A$ to base B. However, this last step is trivial if $B < A$. The radix divide conversion procedure is summarized as follows.

1. Divide $(N_I)_A$ by the desired base $(B)_A$, producing quotient Q_1 and remainder R_0. R_0 is the least significant digit, d_0, of the result.

2. Compute each remaining digit, d_i, for $i = 1 \ldots n - 1$, by dividing quotient Q_i by $(B)_A$, producing quotient Q_{i+1} and remainder R_i, which represents d_i.

3. Stop when quotient $Q_{i+1} = 0$.

The radix divide method is illustrated in the next two examples.

EXAMPLE 1.19

Convert $(234)_{10}$ to base 8.

We solve this problem by repeatedly dividing integer $(234)_{10}$, that is $(N)_A$, by 8, that is $(B)_A$, until the quotient is 0.

$$
\begin{array}{r}
2\ \ 9 \\
8\ \overline{\big|\ 2\ \ 3\ \ 4} \\
1\ \ 6 \\
\overline{\ 7\ \ 4} \\
7\ \ 2 \\
\overline{\ \ \ 2}\quad = b_0
\end{array}
\qquad
\begin{array}{r}
3 \\
8\ \overline{\big|\ 2\ \ 9} \\
2\ \ 4 \\
\overline{\ \ \ 5}\quad = b_1
\end{array}
\qquad
\begin{array}{r}
0 \\
8\ \overline{\big|\ 3} \\
0 \\
\overline{\ \ 3}\quad = b_2
\end{array}
$$

Hence, $(234)_{10} = (352)_8$. These calculations may be summarized in the following shorthand format:

$$
\begin{array}{rrrll}
8 & \big|\ 2\ \ 3\ \ 4 & 2 & \uparrow & \text{LSB} \\
& 8\ \big|\ 2\ \ 9 & 5 & & \\
& & 8\ \big|\ 3 & 3 & \quad \text{MSB} \\
& & & 0 &
\end{array}
$$

EXAMPLE 1.20

Convert $(234)_{10}$ to base 16.

$$
\begin{array}{r}
1\ \ 4 \\
1\ \ 6\ \overline{\big|\ 2\ \ 3\ \ 4} \\
1\ \ 6 \\
\overline{\ 7\ \ 4} \\
6\ \ 4 \\
\overline{\ 1\ \ 0}\quad = (A)_{16} = b_0
\end{array}
\qquad
\begin{array}{r}
0 \\
1\ \ 6\ \overline{\big|\ 1\ \ 4} \\
0 \\
\overline{\ 1\ \ 4}\quad = (E)_{16} = b_1
\end{array}
$$

Hence, $(234)_{10} = (EA)_{16}$. In the shorthand notation;

$$
\begin{array}{rrll}
16 & \big|\ 2\ \ 3\ \ 4 & 10 = (A)_{16} & \uparrow \\
& 16\ \big|\ 1\ \ 4 & 14 = (E)_{16} & \\
& & 0 &
\end{array}
$$

Radix Multiply Method

Base conversions for fractions can be accomplished by the *radix multiply* method. Let N_F be a fraction in base A. The fraction can be written in series form as follows.

$$(N_F)_A = b_{-1}B^{-1} + b_{-2}B^{-2} + \ldots + b_{-m}B^{-m} \tag{1.5}$$

The b_i's in Eqn. 1.5 represent the digits of $(N_F)_B$ in base A. The most significant digit $(b_{-1})_A$ can be obtained by multiplying $(N_F)_A$ by $(B)_A$ as follows:

$$B \times N_F = B \times (b_{-1}B^{-1} + b_{-2}B^{-2} + \ldots + b_{-m}B^{-m})$$

$$= \underbrace{b_{-1}}_{Integer, I_{-1}} + \underbrace{b_{-2}B^{-1} + \ldots + b_{-m}B^{-(m-1)}}_{Fraction, F_{-2}}$$

Thus, $(b_{-1})_A$ is the integer part of the product that results from the multiplication of $(N_F)_A$ by $(B)_A$. In general, $(b_{-i})_A$ is the integer part, I_{-i}, of the product that results from multiplying the fraction $F_{-(i+1)}$ by $(B)_A$. Therefore, the radix multiply procedure is summarized as follows:

1. Let $F_{-1} = (N_F)_A$.

2. Compute digits $(b_{-1})_A$, for $i = 1 \ldots m$, by multiplying F_i by $(B)_A$, producing integer I_{-i}, which represents digit $(b_{-i})_A$, and fraction $F_{-(i+1)}$.

3. Convert each digit $(b_{-i})_A$ to base B.

The following two examples illustrate this method.

EXAMPLE 1.21

Convert $(0.1285)_{10}$ to base 8.

0.1285	0.0280	0.2240	0.7920
$\times$ 8	$\times$ 8	$\times$ 8	$\times$ 8
1.0280	0.2240	1.7920	6.3360
$\uparrow$	$\uparrow$	$\uparrow$	$\uparrow$
b_{-1}	b_{-2}	b_{-3}	b_{-4}

0.3360	0.6880	0.5040	0.0320
$\times$ 8	$\times$ 8	$\times$ 8	$\times$ 8
2.6880	5.5040	4.0320	0.2560
$\uparrow$	$\uparrow$	$\uparrow$	$\uparrow$
b_{-5}	b_{-6}	b_{-7}	b_{-8}

Thus

$$0.1285_{10} = (0.10162540\ldots)_8$$

EXAMPLE 1.22

Convert $(0.828125)_{10}$ to base 2.

A shorthand notation will be used in this example when applying the radix multiply method. On each line, the fraction is multiplied by 2 to get the following line:

$$
\begin{array}{r|l}
\text{MSD} & 1.656250 \leftarrow 0.828125 \times 2 \\
& 1.312500 \leftarrow 0.656250 \times 2 \\
& 0.625000 \leftarrow 0.312500 \times 2 \\
& 1.250000 \leftarrow 0.625000 \times 2 \\
& 0.500000 \leftarrow 0.250000 \times 2 \\
\text{LSD} & 1.000000 \leftarrow 0.500000 \times 2
\end{array}
$$

$$0.828125_{10} = (0.110101)_2$$

1.3.2 General Conversion Algorithms

The examples presented so far demonstrate the principles of base conversion. It is often helpful to define generalized procedures for solving various problems so that basic steps can be applied in the proper sequence. The base conversion methods used will now be formulated into two generalized conversion algorithms.

Algorithm 1.1

To convert a number N from base A to base B, use

(a)   the series substitution method with base B arithmetic, or

(b)   the radix divide or multiply method with base A arithmetic.

Algorithm 1.1 can be used for conversion between any two bases. However, it may be necessary to perform arithmetic in an unfamiliar base when doing so. The following algorithm overcomes this difficulty at the expense of a longer procedure.

Algorithm 1.2

To convert a number N from base A to base B, use

(a)   the series substitution method with base 10 arithmetic to convert N from base A to base 10, and

(b)   the radix divide or multiply method with decimal arithmetic to convert N from base 10 to base B.

Algorithm 1.2 in general requires more steps than Algorithm 1.1. However, the latter is often easier, faster, and less error prone because all arithmetic is performed in decimal.

EXAMPLE 1.23

Convert $(18.6)_9 = (?)_{11}$

$$N_A = (18.6)_9$$

a. Converting to base 10 via series substitution yields

$$N_{10} = 1 \times 9^1 + 8 \times 9^0 + 6 \times 9^{-1}$$
$$= 9 + 8 + 0.666...$$
$$= (17.666...)_{10}$$

b. Converting from base 10 to base 11 via radix divide produces

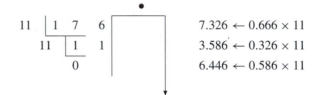

$$7.326 \leftarrow 0.666 \times 11$$
$$3.586 \leftarrow 0.326 \times 11$$
$$6.446 \leftarrow 0.586 \times 11$$

Putting the integer and fraction parts together,

$$N_{11} = (16.736...)_{11}.$$

1.3.3 Conversion between Base A and Base B When $B = A^k$

Simplified conversion procedures can be used when one base is a power of the other, for example, $B = A^k$. These procedures are very useful and are described next.

Algorithm 1.3

(a)   To convert a number N from base A to base B when $B = A^k$ and k is a positive integer, group the digits of N in groups of k digits in both directions from the radix point and then replace each group with the equivalent digit in base B.

(b)   To convert a number N from base B to base A when $B = A^k$ and k is a positive integer, replace each base B digit in N with the equivalent k digits in base A.

The following examples illustrate the power and speed of this algorithm for the case where $A = 2$.

EXAMPLE 1.24

Convert $(1011011.1010111)_2$ to base 8.

Algorithm 1.3a can be applied where $B = 8 = 2^3 = A^k$. Therefore, three binary digits are grouped for each octal digit.

$$\underbrace{001}_{1}\ \underbrace{011}_{3}\ \underbrace{011}_{3}\ .\ \underbrace{101}_{5}\ \underbrace{011}_{3}\ \underbrace{100}_{4}$$

$$1011011.1010111_2 = (133.534)_8$$

EXAMPLE 1.25

Convert $(AF.16C)_{16}$ to base 8.

Since both 16 and 8 are powers of 2, Algorithm 1.3 can be applied twice as follows.

- Use Algorithm 1.3b to convert $(AF.16C)_{16}$ to base 2, since $16 = 2^4$. Each hexadecimal digit is replaced by four binary digits.

$$\overbrace{1010}^{A}\ \overbrace{1111}^{F}\ .\ \overbrace{0001}^{1}\ \overbrace{0110}^{6}\ \overbrace{1100}^{C}$$

$$(AF.16C)_{16} = (10101111.0001011011)_2$$

- Use Algorithm 1.3a to covert the binary number to base 8.

$$\underbrace{010}_{2}\ \underbrace{101}_{5}\ \underbrace{111}_{7}\ .\ \underbrace{000}_{0}\ \underbrace{101}_{5}\ \underbrace{101}_{5}\ \underbrace{100}_{4}$$

Therefore;

$$(AF.16C)_{16} = (257.0554)_8$$

1.4 Signed Number Representation

The sign of numbers stored in digital systems is specified by a digit called the *sign digit,* which is usually placed in the leftmost digit position of the number, as illustrated in Fig. 1.2. Positive numbers are specified by a zero sign digit and negative numbers by a nonzero sign digit. The magnitude of a positive number is simply represented by its positional digits. However, several methods are available for representing the magnitude of negative numbers. Table 1.6 illustrates the sign magnitude, radix complement, and diminished radix complement methods. Each method is discussed in more detail next.

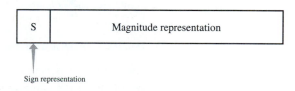

Figure 1.2   Signed number format.

1.4.1 Sign Magnitude Numbers

The simplest method of representing signed numbers is *sign magnitude*. However, the use of this method requires arithmetic circuitry and algorithms that are more costly in circuitry and computation time than for other methods. Hence, the sign magnitude representation is not commonly used in practice for representing integer numbers.

A signed number $N = \pm(a_{n-1} \ldots a_0.a_{-1} \ldots a_{-m})_r$ may be written in sign magnitude form as follows.

$$N = (sa_{n-1} \ldots a_0.a_{-1} \ldots a_{-m})_{rsm} \tag{1.6}$$

where $s = 0$ if N is positive and $s = r - 1$ if N is negative.

EXAMPLE 1.26

Determine the sign-magnitude code of
$N = -(13)_{10}$ in binary ($r = 2$) and decimal
($r = 10$).

In binary:

$$N = -(13)_{10}$$
$$= -(1101)_2$$
$$= (1, 1101)_{2sm}$$

In decimal:

$$N = -(13)_{10}$$
$$= (9, 13)_{10sm}$$

where 9 is used to represent the negative sign for $r = 10$.

See Table 1.6 for more examples of sign magnitude binary numbers. For the sake of clarity, commas will be used to delimit sign digits.

1.4.2 Complementary Number Systems

Complementary numbers form the basis of complementary arithmetic, which is a powerful method often used in digital systems for handling mathematical operations on signed numbers. In these systems, positive numbers are represented in the same fashion as in a sign magnitude system, while negative numbers are represented as the complement of the corresponding positive number. Radix complement and diminished radix complement are important number systems and are discussed next. Complementary arithmetic is illustrated by examples in this chapter as well.

Radix Complements

The *radix complement* $[N]_r$ of a number $(N)_r$ as defined in Eq. 1.2 is defined as

$$[N]_r = r^n - (N)_r \tag{1.7}$$

TABLE 1.6   SIGNED NUMBER REPRESENTATION EXAMPLES*

Signed Decimal	Sign Magnitude Binary	Two's Complement System	One's Complement System
+15	0,1111	0,1111	0,1111
+14	0,1110	0,1110	0,1110
+13	0,1101	0,1101	0,1101
+12	0,1100	0,1100	0,1100
+11	0,1011	0,1011	0,1011
+10	0,1010	0,1010	0,1010
+9	0,1001	0,1001	0,1001
+8	0,1000	0,1000	0,1000
+7	0,0111	0,0111	0,0111
+6	0,0110	0,0110	0,0110
+5	0,0101	0,0101	0,0101
+4	0,0100	0,0100	0,0100
+3	0,0011	0,0011	0,0011
+2	0,0010	0,0010	0,0010
+1	0,0001	0,0001	0,0001
0	0,0000	0,0000	0,0000
	(1,0000)		(1,1111)
-1	1,0001	1,1111	1,1110
-2	1,0010	1,1110	1,1101
-3	1,0011	1,1101	1,1100
-4	1,0100	1,1100	1,1011
-5	1,0101	1,1011	1,1010
-6	1,0110	1,1010	1,1001
-7	1,0111	1,1001	1,1000
-8	1,1000	1,1000	1,0111
-9	1,1001	1,0111	1,0110
-10	1,1010	1,0110	1,0101
-11	1,1011	1,0101	1,0100
-12	1,1100	1,0100	1,0011
-13	1,1101	1,0011	1,0010
-14	1,1110	1,0010	1,0001
-15	1,1111	1,0001	1,0000
-16	—	1,0000	—

*Note that sign bits are delimited by commas.

where n is the number of digits in $(N)_r$. The largest positive number (called *positive full scale*) that can be represented is $r^{n-1} - 1$, while the most negative number (called *negative full scale*) is $-r^{n-1}$.

The *two's complement* is a special case of radix complement for binary numbers ($r = 2$) and is given by

$$[N]_2 = 2^n - (N)_2 \qquad (1.8)$$

where n is the number of bits in $(N)_2$. Two's complement is the most commonly used format for signed numbers in digital systems and will therefore be the focus of most of the examples in this text.

The following examples illustrate how the two's complement of a given binary number can be found using Eq. 1.8.

EXAMPLE 1.27

Determine the two's complement of $(N)_2 = (01100101)_2$.

From Eq. 1.8,

$$\begin{aligned}
[N]_2 &= [01100101]_2 \\
&= 2^8 - (01100101)_2 \\
&= (100000000)_2 - (01100101)_2 \\
&= (10011011)_2.
\end{aligned}$$

EXAMPLE 1.28

Determine the two's complement of $(N)_2 = (11010100)_2$, and verify that it can be used to represent $-(N)_2$ by showing that $(N)_2 + [N]_2 = 0$.

First we determine the two's complement from Eq. 1.8:

$$\begin{aligned}
[N]_2 &= [11010100]_2 \\
&= 2^8 - (11010100)_2 \\
&= (100000000)_2 - (11010100)_2 \\
&= (00101100)_2.
\end{aligned}$$

To verify that $[N]_2$ can be used to represent $-(N)_2$, let us compute $(N)_2 + [N]_2$:

```
      1  1  0  1  0  1  0  0
  +   0  0  1  0  1  1  0  0
  1   0  0  0  0  0  0  0  0
  ↑
carry
```

If we discard the carry bit, we get $(N)_2 + [N]_2 = (00000000)_2$, that is, the sum of a binary number and its two's complement is 0. Therefore, it follows that $[N]_2$ can be used to represent $-(N)_2$.

EXAMPLE 1.29

Determine the two's complement of $[N]_2 = (00101100)_2$, computed in Example 1.28.

$$[[N]_2]_2 = [00101100]_2$$

$$= 2^8 - (00101100)_2$$
$$= (100000000)_2 - (00101100)_2$$
$$= (11010100)_2$$

Note that the result is the original value of $(N)_2$ given in Example 1.28.

From the last example, we see that applying the two's complement operation to a number twice simply produces its original value. This is readily verified for the general case by substituting $-(N)_2$ for $[N]_2$ as follows:

$$[[N]_2]_2 = [-(N)_2]_2$$
$$= -(-(N)_2)_2$$
$$= (N)_2$$

EXAMPLE 1.30

Determine the two's complement of
$(N)_2 = (10110)_2$ **for** $n = 8$.

From Eq. 1.8.

$$[N]_2 = [10110]_2$$
$$= 2^8 - (10110)_2$$
$$= (100000000)_2 - (10110)_2$$
$$= (11101010)_2$$

Note that we keep 8 bits in the result. The reader is encouraged to verify that this value of $[N]_2$ can be used to represent $-(N)_2$ and that $[[N]_2]_2 = (N)_2$.

The following example illustrates that the basic procedure for determining the radix complement of a number is the same for any radix.

EXAMPLE 1.31

Find the 10's complement of $(N)_{10} = (40960)_{10}$.

From Eq. 1.7,

$$[N]_{10} = [40960]_{10}$$
$$= 10^5 - (40960)_{10}$$
$$= (100000)_{10} - (40960)_{10}$$
$$= (59040)_{10}.$$

Note that we keep 5 digits in the result. The reader is encouraged to verify that $[N]_{10}$ can be used to represent $-(N)_{10}$ and that $[[N]_{10}]_{10} = (N)_{10}$.

While the radix complement of a number can always be determined by the definition given in Eq. 1.7, easier methods are available. The following two algorithms for computing $[N]_r$ given $(N)_r$ are presented without proof.

Algorithm 1.4   Find $[N]_r$ given $(N)_r$.

Copy the digits of N, beginning with the least significant and proceeding toward the most significant until the first nonzero digit has been reached. Replace this digit, a_i, with $r - a_i$. Then continue if necessary by replacing each remaining digit, a_j, of N by $(r - 1) - a_j$ until the most significant digit has been replaced.

For the special case of binary numbers ($r = 2$), the first nonzero digit, a_i, is by default a 1. Therefore, a_i is replaced by $r - a_i = 2 - 1 = 1$; hence a_i remains unchanged. Each remaining bit, a_j, is replaced by $(r - 1) - a_j = 1 - a_j = \bar{a}_j$. Therefore, Algorithm 1.4 is applied to binary numbers by simply copying down all bits up to and including the first 1 bit and then complementing the remaining bits.

EXAMPLE 1.32

Find the two's complement of $N = (01100101)_2$.

$$N = 0 \quad 1 \quad 1 \quad 0 \quad 0 \quad 1 \quad 0 \quad 1$$
$$\qquad\qquad\qquad\qquad\qquad\qquad\qquad\qquad\updownarrow \qquad \text{first nonzero digit}$$
$$[N]_2 = (1 \quad 0 \quad 0 \quad 1 \quad 1 \quad 0 \quad 1 \quad 1)_2$$

EXAMPLE 1.33

Find the two's complement of $N = (11010100)_2$.

$$N = 1 \quad 1 \quad 0 \quad 1 \quad 0 \quad 1 \quad 0 \quad 0$$
$$\qquad\qquad\qquad\qquad\qquad\qquad\updownarrow \qquad \text{first nonzero digit}$$
$$[N]_2 = (0 \quad 0 \quad 1 \quad 0 \quad 1 \quad 1 \quad 0 \quad 0)_2$$

EXAMPLE 1.34

Find the two's complement of $N = (10110)_2$ for $n = 8$.

First, since $n = 8$, three zeros must be concatenated in the most significant bit positions to form an 8-bit number. Then apply Algorithm 1.4.

$$N = 0 \quad 0 \quad 0 \quad 1 \quad 0 \quad 1 \quad 1 \quad 0$$
$$\qquad\qquad\qquad\qquad\qquad\qquad\updownarrow \qquad \text{first nonzero digit}$$
$$[N]_2 = (1 \quad 1 \quad 1 \quad 0 \quad 1 \quad 0 \quad 1 \quad 0)_2$$

EXAMPLE 1.35

Find the 10's complement of $(40960)_{10}$.

$$N = 4 \quad 0 \quad 9 \quad 6 \quad 0$$
$$\qquad\qquad\qquad\qquad\qquad\updownarrow \qquad \text{first nonzero digit}$$
$$[N]_{10} = (5 \quad 9 \quad 0 \quad 4 \quad 0)_{10}$$

Algorithm 1.5   Find $[N]_r$ given $(N)_r$.

First replace each digit, a_k, of $(N)_r$ by $(r - 1) - a_k$ and then add 1 to the resultant.

For the special case of binary numbers ($r = 2$), we replace each bit, a_k, by $(r - 1) - a_k = 1 - a_k = \bar{a}_k$. Therefore Algorithm 1.5 is applied by simply complementing each bit and then adding 1 to the result.

EXAMPLE 1.36

Find the two's complement of $N = (01100101)_2$.

$$N = \ 01100101$$
$$10011010 \quad \text{Complement the bits}$$
$$+1 \quad \text{Add 1}$$
$$[N]_2 = (10011011)_2$$

EXAMPLE 1.37

Find the two's complement of $N = (11010100)_2$.

$$N = \ 11010100$$
$$00101011 \quad \text{Complement the bits}$$
$$+1 \quad \text{Add 1}$$
$$[N]_2 = (00101100)_2$$

EXAMPLE 1.38

Find the 10's complement of $(40960)_{10}$.

$$N = \ 40960$$
$$59039 \quad \text{Complement the digits}$$
$$+1 \quad \text{Add 1}$$
$$[N]_{10} = (59040)_{10}$$

Note that Algorithm 1.4 is convenient for hand calculations, while Algorithm 1.5 is more useful for machine implementation since it does not require decision making.

Radix Complement Number Systems

Previously the radix complement was defined and several methods for finding the radix complement of a given number were presented and illustrated. We also suggested by example that the radix complement of a number can be used to represent the negative of that number. Next, we describe more precisely a number system that utilizes the two's complement to represent negative numbers. Similarly, systems could be defined for other bases.

In the *two's complement number system*, positive values are represented in the same fashion as in the sign magnitude system; a leading bit of 0 is used to represent the sign. Negative numbers are represented by the two's complements of the corresponding positive number representations. We shall use the notation $(N)_{2cns}$ to denote a number that is represented in the two's complement number system. Thus, $N = +(a_{n-2}, \ldots, a_0)_2 = (0, a_{n-2}, \ldots, a_0)_{2cns}$, where $0 \leq N \leq 2^{n-1} - 1$. If $N = (a_{n-1}, a_{n-2}, \ldots, a_0)_2$, then $-N$ is represented in the two's complement number system by $[a_{n-1}, \ldots, a_0]_2$, where $-1 \geq -N \geq -2^{n-1}$. All negative numbers in the two's complement number system have a sign bit of 1. Table 1.6 lists the two's complement number system codes for $n = 5$.

The following examples illustrate the encoding of positive and negative numbers in the two's complement number system. The reader is encouraged to verify the two's complement entries in Table 1.6 after studying the examples.

EXAMPLE 1.39

Given $(N)_2 = (1100101)_2$, determine the two's complement number system representations of $\pm(N)_2$ for $n = 8$.

By inspection,

$$+(N)_2 = (0, 1100101)_{2cns}$$

From Eq. 1.8,

$$-(N)_2 = [+(N)_2]_2$$
$$= [0, 1100101]_2$$
$$= 2^8 - (0, 1100101)_2$$
$$= (100000000)_2 - (0, 1100101)_2$$
$$= (1, 0011011)_{2cns}.$$

From their sign bits, we see that $(0, 1100101)_{2cns}$ represents a positive value and $(1, 0011011)_{2cns}$ is its negative. In this example and those that follow we shall use a comma to facilitate identifying the sign bit.

EXAMPLE 1.40

Find the two's complement number system representations of $\pm(110101)_2$ for $n = 8$.

By inspection,

$$+(110101)_2 = (0, 0110101)_{2cns}$$

From Eq. 1.8,

$$-(110101)_2 = [110101]_2$$
$$= 2^8 - (110101)_2$$
$$= (100000000)_2 - (110101)_2$$
$$= (1, 1001011)_{2cns}$$

EXAMPLE 1.41

Determine the two's complement number system encoding of $-(13)_{10}$ for $n = 8$.

We begin by converting $(13)_{10}$ from decimal to binary.

$$+(13)_{10} = +(1101)_2 = (0, 0001101)_{2cns}$$

Next we compute the two's complement of $(0, 0001101)_{2cns}$ to represent $-(13)_{10}$:

$$-(13)_{10} = -(0, 0001101)_{2cns}$$
$$= [0, 0001101]_2$$
$$= 2^8 - (0, 0001101)_2$$
$$= (1, 1110011)_{2cns}$$

EXAMPLE 1.42

Determine the decimal number represented by $N = (1, 1111010)_{2cns}$.

From the sign bit, we see that N is a negative number. Therefore, we determine the magnitude of N (the corresponding positive value) by computing its two's complement.

$$N = (1, 1111010)_{2cns}$$
$$= -[1, 1111010]_2$$
$$= -(2^8 - (1, 1111010)_2)$$
$$= -(0, 0000110)_{2cns}$$
$$= -(6)_{10}$$

where $(0, 0000110)_{2cns} = +(6)_{10}$. Therefore, $(1, 1111010)_{2cns}$ represents $-(6)_{10}$.

Now let us consider some examples of arithmetic with radix complement numbers.

Radix Complement Arithmetic

Most digital computers use a radix complement number system to minimize the amount of circuitry needed to perform integer arithmetic. For example, the operation $A - B$ can be performed by computing $A + (-B)$, where $(-B)$ is represented by the two's complement of B. Hence, the computer need only have binary adder and complementing circuits to handle both addition and subtraction. This point of view is convenient for discussing radix complement arithmetic and will therefore be taken in the paragraphs that follow. Since computer arithmetic is primarily performed in binary, we shall focus our discussion on two's complement arithmetic.

Before beginning our discussion in depth, let us consider a fundamental limitation of the machine representation of numbers. Machines such as digital computers operate with finite number systems imposed by the number of bits that can be used in the representation of numerical quantities. The number of bits available in the computer's arithmetic unit limits the range of numbers that can be represented in the machine. Numbers that fall outside this range cannot be handled by the system. Machines that use the two's complement number system (2cns) can represent integers in the range

$$-2^{n-1} \leq N \leq 2^{n-1} - 1 \tag{1.9}$$

where n is the number of bits available for representing N. Note that $2^{n-1} - 1 = (0, 11 \ldots 1)_{2cns}$ and that $-2^{n-1} = (1, 00 \ldots 0)_{2cns}$ (the leftmost bit represents the sign and the remaining $n - 1$ bits represent the magnitude).

If an operation produces a result that falls outside the available range as defined by Eq. 1.9, that is, if $N > 2^{n-1} - 1$ or $N < -2^{n-1}$, an *overflow condition* is said to occur. In such cases, the n-bit number produced by the operation will not be a valid representation of the result. Digital computers monitor their arithmetic operations when performing two's complement arithmetic and generate a warning signal when overflow occurs so that invalid numbers are not mistaken for correct results.

Three cases will now be considered for illustrating arithmetic in the two's complement number system: $A = B + C$, $A = B - C$, and $A = -B - C$. Each case will be described in general and then clarified by appropriate examples. For all cases, assume that $B \geq 0$ and $C \geq 0$. The results are easily generalized to include negative values of B and C.

Case 1. Compute $A = B + C$. Since both B and C are nonnegative, A will also be non negative, and this simply becomes

$$(A)_2 = (B)_2 + (C)_2$$

Since all three numbers are positive, there is no need to use the two's complement.

The only difficulty that can arise in this case is when $A > 2^{n-1} - 1$, that is when an overflow occurs. An overflow condition is easily detected because the sign bit of A will be incorrect. To show this, consider the sum of the two largest representable n-bit positive numbers:

$$0 \leq A \leq (2^{n-1} - 1) + (2^{n-1} - 1) = 2^n - 2$$

Since the largest representable n-bit positive value is $2^{n-1} - 1$, an overflow condition occurs for any sum in the range

$$A \geq 2^{n-1}$$

The nth bit of any binary number in this range will be set to 1. Unfortunately, this happens to be the bit that represents the sign in an n-bit two's complement number. Therefore, the result appears to be a negative number, thus indicating the overflow condition.

It should be noted that since $A < 2^n$ there will never be a carry out of the nth bit of the binary adder.

The following examples will utilize the 5-bit two's complement number system whose values are listed in Table 1.6;

EXAMPLE 1.43

Compute $(9)_{10} + (5)_{10}$ using 5-bit two's complement arithmetic.

We begin by writing $(9)_{10}$ and $(5)_{10}$ as 5-bit two's complement numbers. Since both numbers are positive, a zero sign bit is used for each. From Table 1.6,

$$+(9)_{10} = +(1001)_2 = (0, 1001)_{2cns}$$
$$+(5)_{10} = +(0101)_2 = (0, 0101)_{2cns}$$

Adding these two 5-bit codes gives

$$
\begin{array}{ccccc}
 & 0 & 1 & 0 & 0 & 1 \\
+ & 0 & 0 & 1 & 0 & 1 \\
\hline
 & 0 & 1 & 1 & 1 & 0 \\
\end{array}
$$

Since the result also has a zero sign bit, it correctly represents the desired positive sum, which is interpreted as

$$(0, 1110)_{2cns} = +(1110)_2 = +(14)_{10}$$

EXAMPLE 1.44

Compute $(12)_{10} + (7)_{10}$.

From Table 1.6,

$$(12)_{10} = +(1100)_2 = (0, 1100)_{2cns}$$
$$(7)_{10} = +(0111)_2 = (0, 0111)_{2cns}$$

Adding the two 5-bit codes gives

$$
\begin{array}{ccccc}
0 & 1 & 1 & 0 & 0 \\
+ \quad 0 & 0 & 1 & 1 & 1 \\
\hline
1 & 0 & 0 & 1 & 1
\end{array}
$$

The result is $(1, 0011)_{2cns}$, which from Table 1.6 is interpreted as

$$(1, 0011)_{2cns} = -(1101)_2 = -(13)_{10}$$

A closer look at this computation reveals that the addition of two positive numbers appears to have produced a negative result! However, this cannot be correct, so there must be an explanation. The answer is that the sum of the given two numbers requires more than the allotted 5 bits to represent it. The correct sum is $+(19)_{10}$, which is outside the 5-bit two's complement number range, since positive full scale is $(0, 1111)_{2cns} = +(15)_{10}$. The incorrect sign bit obtained in the computation indicates an incorrect result. Hence an overflow condition has occurred.

Case 2. Compute $A = B - C$. The computation is treated as $A = B + (-C)$ in the following manner. We desire to compute

$$A = (B)_2 + (-(C)_2)$$

Suppose we represent this operation by encoding the numbers in two's complement. The positive number $(B)_2$ is unchanged. However, $-(C)_2$ becomes $[C]_2$:

$$A = (B)_2 + [C]_2$$
$$= (B)_2 + 2^n - (C)_2$$
$$= 2^n + (B - C)_2$$

Hence the computation is equivalent to $2^n + (B - C)$. This is the answer we want, except that there is an extra 2^n term. Can we ignore it? If $B \geq C$, then $B - C \geq 0$, making $A \geq 2^n$. The 2^n term represents a carry bit and can be discarded, leaving $(B - C)_2$ (an n-bit binary adder will generate a carry for any sum $A \geq 2^n$). Therefore,

$$(A)_2 = (B)_2 + [C]_2|_{\text{carry discarded}}$$

If $B < C$, then $B - C < 0$, giving $A = 2^n - (C - B)_2 = [C - B]_2$, or $A = -(C - B)_2$ which is the desired answer. Note that there is no carry in this instance. All possible conditions will be summarized in tabular form later.

When B and C are both positive numbers, the magnitude of $B - C$ will always be less than either of the two numbers. This means that no overflow can occur when computing $B - C$.

EXAMPLE 1.45

Compute $(12)_{10} - (5)_{10}$.

We perform this computation as $(12)_{10} + (-(5)_{10})$

$$(12)_{10} = +(1100)_2 = (0, 1100)_{2cns}$$
$$-(5)_{10} = -(0101)_2 = (1, 1011)_{2cns}$$

Adding the two 5-bit codes gives

```
      0   1   1   0   0
  +   1   1   0   1   1
  ────────────────────
  1   0   0   1   1   1
  ↑
  Carry
```

Discarding the carry, the sign bit is seen to be 0, and therefore the result is interpreted as

$$(0, 0111)_{2cns} = +(0111)_2 = +(7)_{10}$$

EXAMPLE 1.46

Reversing the order of the operands from the previous example, compute $(5)_{10} - (12)_{10}$.

We perform the computation as $(5)_{10} + (-(12)_{10})$.

$$(5)_{10} = +(0101)_2 = (0, 0101)_{2cns}$$
$$-(12)_{10} = -(1100)_2 = (1, 0100)_{2cns}$$

Adding the two 5-bit codes gives

```
      0   0   1   0   1
  +   1   0   1   0   0
  ────────────────────
      1   1   0   0   1
```

In this case there is no carry, and the sign bit is 1, indicating a negative result, which is

$$(1, 1001)_{2cns} = -(0111)_2 = -(7)_{10}$$

EXAMPLE 1.47

Compute $(0, 0111)_{2cns} - (1, 1010)_{2cns}$.

We perform the computation as $(0, 0111)_{2cns} + (-(1, 1010)_{2cns})$. The left-hand operand is already in two's complement number system format. Since its sign bit is 1, the right-hand operand represents a negative number. To negate it, we take the two's complement of this negative number to get the corresponding positive value. Note from the definition of two's complement that

$$-[A]_2 = [[A]_2]_2$$
$$= 2^n - [A]_2$$
$$= 2^n - (2^n - A)$$
$$= A$$

Therefore,

$$-(1, 1010)_{2cns} = (0, 0110)_{2cns}$$

Adding the two 5-bit codes gives

$$
\begin{array}{ccccc}
 & 0 & 0 & 1 & 1 & 1 \\
+ & 0 & 0 & 1 & 1 & 0 \\
\hline
 & 0 & 1 & 1 & 0 & 1
\end{array}
$$

The result is positive, as indicated by the 0 sign bit, and is interpreted as

$$(0, 1101)_{2cns} = +(1101)_2 = +(13)_{10}$$

The reader should verify that this computation is equivalent to computing $(7)_{10} - (-(6)_{10}) = (13)_{10}$.

Case 3. Compute $A = -B - C$. The desired result is $A = -(B + C) = [B + C]_2$. Both $-B$ and $-C$ will be represented by the two's complements of their magnitudes, and the computation will be performed as $A = (-B) + (-C)$. Therefore,

$$
\begin{aligned}
A &= [B]_2 + [C]_2 \\
&= 2^n - (B)_2 + 2^n - (C)_2 \\
&= 2^n + 2^n - (B + C)_2 \\
&= 2^n + [B + C]_2
\end{aligned}
$$

If the carry bit (2^n) is discarded, the computation produces the correct result, the two's complement representation of $-(B + C)_2$.

EXAMPLE 1.48

Compute $-(9)_{10} - (5)_{10}$.

We perform the computation as $(-(9)_{10}) + (-(5)_{10})$.

$$-(9)_{10} = -(1001)_2 = (1, 0111)_{2cns}$$
$$-(5)_{10} = -(0101)_2 = (1, 1011)_{2cns}$$

Adding the two 5-bit codes gives

$$
\begin{array}{cccccc}
 & 1 & 0 & 1 & 1 & 1 \\
+ & 1 & 1 & 0 & 1 & 1 \\
\hline
1 & 1 & 0 & 0 & 1 & 0 \\
\uparrow \\
\text{Carry}
\end{array}
$$

Discarding the carry leaves a sign bit of 1. Therefore, the result is correct and is interpreted as

$$(1, 0010)_{2cns} = -(1110)_2 = -(14)_{10}$$

As is the case when adding two positive values, an overflow can occur when adding two negative values, producing a result in the range

$$A < -2^{n-1}$$

which is indicated by a result having an incorrect sign bit (that is, a result that appears to be positive). This is illustrated in the following example.

EXAMPLE 1.49

Compute $-(12)_{10} - (5)_{10}$.

We perform the computation as $(-(12)_{10}) + (-(5)_{10})$

$$-(12)_{10} = -(1100)_2 = (1, 0100)_{2cns}$$
$$-(5)_{10} = -(0101)_2 = (1, 1011)_{2cns}$$

Adding the two 5-bit codes gives

$$
\begin{array}{ccccccc}
 & 1 & 0 & 1 & 0 & 0 \\
+ & 1 & 1 & 0 & 1 & 1 \\
\hline
1 & 0 & 1 & 1 & 1 & 1 \\
\uparrow & & & & & \\
\end{array}
$$

Carry

Discarding the carry, the result is interpreted as

$$(0, 1111)_{2cns} = +(1111)_2 = +(15)_{10}$$

Note that the sign bit is incorrect, indicating an overflow. This result is "too negative"; it exceeds the number range in the negative direction by 1, since the desired result was $-(17_{10})$. Consequently, because of the overflow the result is incorrectly interpreted as $+(15)_{10}$.

The next example illustrates the utility of two's complement arithmetic in digital computers.

EXAMPLE 1.50

A and B are integer variables in a computer program, with $A = (25)_{10}$ and $B = -(46)_{10}$. Assuming that the computer uses 8-bit two's complement arithmetic, show how it would compute $A + B, A - B, B - A,$ and $-A - B$.

Variables A and B would be stored in the memory of the computer in 8-bit two's complement number system format:

$$A = +(25)_{10} = (0, 0011001)_{2cns}$$
$$B = -(46)_{10} = -(0, 0101110)_{2cns} = (1, 1010010)_{2cns}$$

First, let us compute the two's complements of A and B to represent $-A$ and $-B$, respectively:

$$-A = -(25)_{10} = -(0, 0011001)_{2cns} = (1, 1100111)_{2cns}$$
$$-B = -(-(46)_{10}) = -(1, 1010010)_{2cns} = (0, 0101110)_{2cns}$$

Performing the computations,

$$
A + B: \quad
\begin{array}{ccccccccc}
 & 0 & 0 & 0 & 1 & 1 & 0 & 0 & 1 \\
+ & 1 & 1 & 0 & 1 & 0 & 0 & 1 & 0 \\
\hline
 & 1 & 1 & 1 & 0 & 1 & 0 & 1 & 1 \\
\end{array}
$$

The result is $(1, 1101011)_{2cns} = -(0, 0010101)_{2cns} = -(21)_{10}.$

$$
\begin{array}{c}
0\ \ 0\ \ 0\ \ 1\ \ 1\ \ 0\ \ 0\ \ 1 \\
A - B = A + (-B): \quad +\ \ 0\ \ 0\ \ 1\ \ 0\ \ 1\ \ 1\ \ 1\ \ 0 \\
\hline
0\ \ 1\ \ 0\ \ 0\ \ 0\ \ 1\ \ 1\ \ 1
\end{array}
$$

The result is $(0, 1000111)_{2cns} = +(71)_{10}.$

$$
\begin{array}{c}
1\ \ 1\ \ 0\ \ 1\ \ 0\ \ 0\ \ 1\ \ 0 \\
B - A = B + (-A): \quad +\ \ 1\ \ 1\ \ 1\ \ 0\ \ 0\ \ 1\ \ 1\ \ 1 \\
\hline
1\ \ 1\ \ 0\ \ 1\ \ 1\ \ 1\ \ 0\ \ 0\ \ 1
\end{array}
$$

The result is $(1, 0111001)_{2cns} = -(0, 1000111)_{2cns} = -(71)_{10}.$

$$
\begin{array}{c}
1\ \ 1\ \ 1\ \ 0\ \ 0\ \ 1\ \ 1\ \ 1 \\
-A - B = (-A) + (-B): \quad +\ \ 0\ \ 0\ \ 1\ \ 0\ \ 1\ \ 1\ \ 1\ \ 0 \\
\hline
1\ \ 0\ \ 0\ \ 0\ \ 1\ \ 0\ \ 1\ \ 0\ \ 1
\end{array}
$$

The result is $(0, 0010101)_{2cns} = +(21)_{10}.$ Note that in the last two cases the carry bit is discarded.

A summary of two's complement addition and subtraction is given in Table 1.7.

TABLE 1.7   SUMMARY OF TWO'S COMPLEMENT ADDITION AND SUB-TRACTION

Case*	Carry	Sign Bit	Condition	Overflow?
$B + C$	0	0	$B + C \leq 2^{n-1} - 1$	No
	0	1	$B + C > 2^{n-1} - 1$	Yes
$B - C$	1	0	$B \leq C$	No
	0	1	$B > C$	No
$-B - C$	1	1	$-(B + C) \geq -2^{n-1}$	No
	1	0	$-(B + C) < -2^{n-1}$	Yes

* B and C are positive numbers.

Radix complement arithmetic can be utilized for any radix, and not just binary numbers. To illustrate, the next two examples will demonstrate ten's complement arithmetic using three-digit numbers.

EXAMPLE 1.51

Add $+(75)_{10}$ and $-(21)_{10}$ using 3-digit ten's complement arithmetic.

First, we determine the ten's complement codes for the two numbers from Eq. 1.7:

$$(75)_{10} = (0, 75)_{10cns}$$
$$-(21)_{10} = (9, 79)_{10cns}$$

Then we perform the computation as $(75)_{10} + (-(21)_{10})$. Adding the two 3-digit codes gives

$$
\begin{array}{r}
0 \quad 7 \quad 5 \\
+ \quad 9 \quad 7 \quad 9 \\
\hline
1 \quad 0 \quad 5 \quad 4 \\
\uparrow \\
\text{Carry}
\end{array}
$$

Discarding the carry digit, the result is $(0, 54)_{10cns} = (54)_{10}$, which is the correct result.

EXAMPLE 1.52

Add $+(21)_{10}$ and $-(75)_{10}$.

Again, we begin by determining the ten's complement codes for the two numbers via Eq. 1.7:

$$(21)_{10} = (0, 21)_{10cns}$$
$$-(75)_{10} = (9, 25)_{10cns}$$

Adding the two 3-digit codes gives

$$
\begin{array}{r}
0 \quad 2 \quad 1 \\
+ \quad 9 \quad 2 \quad 5 \\
\hline
9 \quad 4 \quad 6
\end{array}
$$

The result is $(9, 46)_{10cns}$, with the leading 9 indicating that this number represents a negative value. The reader should verify that $(9, 46)_{10cns}$ is the correct representation in a ten's complement number system for the desired result, $-(54)_{10}$.

Diminished Radix Complement Number Systems

The *diminished radix complement* $[N]_{r-1}$ of a number $(N)_r$ is defined as

$$[N]_{r-1} = r^n - (N)_r - 1 \qquad (1.10)$$

where n is the number of digits in $(N)_r$.

The *one's complement* is a special case of diminished radix complement for binary numbers $(r = 2)$ and is given by

$$[N]_{2-1} = 2^n - (N)_2 - 1 \qquad (1.11)$$

where n is the number of bits in $(N)_2$.

The one's complement of a given binary number can be found directly from Eq. 1.11 as illustrated in the following examples. The reader is encouraged to verify the one's complement entries in Table 1.6 after studying the examples.

EXAMPLE 1.53

Determine the one's complement of $(01100101)_2$.

From Eq. 1.11,

$$[N]_{2-1} = 2^8 - (01100101)_2 - 1$$
$$= (100000000)_2 - (01100101)_2 - (00000001)_2$$
$$= (10011011)_2 - (00000001)_2$$
$$= (10011010)_2.$$

EXAMPLE 1.54

Determine the one's complement of $(11010100)_2$.

From Eq. 1.11,

$$[N]_{2-1} = 2^8 - (11010100)_2 - (00000001)_2$$
$$= (100000000)_2 - (11010100)_2 - (00000001)_2$$
$$= (00101100)_2 - (00000001)_2$$
$$= (00101011)_2.$$

EXAMPLE 1.55

Find the nine's complement of $(40960)_{10}$.

From Eq. 1.10,

$$[N]_{10-1} = 10^5 - (40960)_{10} - (00001)_{10}$$
$$= (100000)_{10} - (40960)_{10} - (00001)_{10}$$
$$= (59040)_{10} - (00001)_{10}$$
$$= (59039)_{10}.$$

While the one's complement of a number can always be determined by the definition given in Eq. 1.11, easier methods are available. The following algorithm for computing $[N]_{r-1}$ given $(N)_r$ is suggested by the preceding examples and is presented without proof.

Algorithm 1.6   Find $[N]_{r-1}$ given $(N)_r$.

Replace each digit a_i of $(N)_r$ by $r - 1 - a_i$. Note that when $r = 2$ this simplifies to complementing each individual bit of $(N)_r$.

A comparison of Eqs. 1.7 and 1.10 indicates that the radix complement and the diminished radix complement of a number $(N)_r$ are related as follows.

$$[N]_r = [N]_{r-1} + 1 \qquad (1.12)$$

It should now be clear that Algorithm 1.5 for finding the radix complement follows from Algorithm 1.6.

Number systems that use the diminished radix complement for negative number representation can be formulated in a manner reminiscent of that used with radix complement. However, this will not be done here. Instead, we will simply illustrate the arithmetic.

Diminished Radix Complement Arithmetic

The key features of diminished radix complement arithmetic are illustrated in the following examples. The first three examples focus on one's complement addition for various combinations of positive and negative operands. The numbers used in these examples are from Table 1.6.

EXAMPLE 1.56

Add $+(1001)_2$ and $-(0100)_2$.

The positive number is represented by 01001 and the negative number by the one's complement of 00100, which is 11011. Hence $00100 + 11011 = 100100$. Note that this is *not* the correct result. However, the correct result is obtained if the carry-out of the most significant bit is added to the least significant bit position. That is, $00100 + 1 = 00101$. This procedure is referred to as an *end-around carry* and is a necessary correction step in diminished complement arithmetic.

EXAMPLE 1.57

Add $+(1001)_2$ and $-(1111)_2$.

The positive number is represented by 01001 and the negative by 10000. This results in $01001 + 10000 = 11001$. Note that in this case the end-around carry is 0 and therefore does not affect the result.

EXAMPLE 1.58

Add $-(1001)_2$ and $-(0011)_2$.

Representing each number by its one's complement yields $10110 + 11100 = 110010$. The end-around carry step yields the correct result, that is, $10010 + 1 = 10011$.

The next two examples illustrate nine's complement arithmetic.

EXAMPLE 1.59

Add $+(75)_{10}$ and $-(21)_{10}$.

The nine's complement of 021 is 978. Hence the operation proceeds as $075 + 978 = 1053$, which is the correct result after the end-around carry procedure. $053 + 1 = 054$.

EXAMPLE 1.60

Add $+(21)_{10}$ and $-(75)_{10}$.

The computation is given by $021 + 924 = 945$, which is correct since the end-around carry is 0.

1.5 Computer Codes

A *code* is a systematic and preferably standardized use of a given set of symbols for representing information. Simple forms of codes are encountered routinely in everyday life. For example, when a traffic light is approached, it is understood that a red signal means stop, a green signal means go, and a yellow signal means caution. In other words, the code is

Red light:	Stop
Yellow light:	Caution
Green light:	Go

Another familiar code is used in baseball. When an umpire raises his or her arms with two fingers showing on the right hand and three fingers showing on the left, it is understood that the count on the batter is two strikes and three balls. These two simple examples illustrate the idea of codes and no doubt the reader can think of many more.

Codes of a more complex nature are used in computers and other digital systems in the processing, storage, and exchange of information of various types. Three important types of computer codes are numeric, character, and error detection and correction. Some important codes in each of these categories are discussed briefly next.

1.5.1 Numeric Codes

Numeric codes are typically used to represent numbers for processing and/or storage. Fixed-point and floating-point numbers are examples of such codes.

Fixed-point Numbers

Fixed-point numbers are used to represent either signed integers or signed fractions. In both cases, either sign magnitude, two's complement, or one's complement systems are used for representing the signed values. Fixed-point integers have an implied binary point to the right of the least significant bit, as shown in Fig. 1.3a, and fixed-point fractions have the implied binary point between the sign bit and the most significant magnitude bit, as shown in Fig. 1.3b.

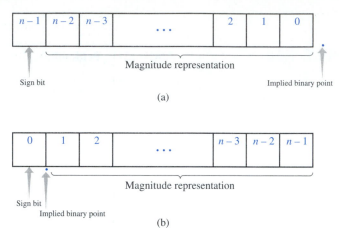

Figure 1.3 Fixed-point number representations. **(a)** Fixed-point integer. **(b)** Fixed-point fraction.

EXAMPLE 1.61

Give two possible interpretations of the 8-bit fixed-point number 01101010, using the two's complement system.

Since the sign bit is 0, the number represents either the positive integer 1101010. if the binary point is placed as in Fig. 1.3a or the positive fraction 0.1101010 if the binary point is placed as in Fig. 1.3b.

EXAMPLE 1.62

Give two possible interpretations of the 8-bit fixed-point number 11101010, using the two's complement system.

The sign bit is 1. Therefore, the number represents either $-0010110.$ or -0.0010110 depending on the convention used for placement of the binary point.

Excess or Biased Representations

An *excess$-K$ representation* of a code C is formed by adding the value K to each code word of C. Excess representations are frequently used in the representation of the exponents of floating-point numbers so that the smallest exponent value will be represented by all zeros. Note that the excess-2^n numbers are just the two's complement numbers with the sign bit reversed!

The excess-8 representation given in Table 1.8 is produced by adding $(1000)_2$ to the 4-bit two's complement code. Note that the result is the smallest number (-8) being represented by 0000 and the largest (+7) by 1111.

TABLE 1.8   EXCESS-8 CODE

Decimal	Two's Complement	Excess-8
+7	0111	1111
+6	0110	1110
+5	0101	1101
+4	0100	1100
+3	0011	1011
+2	0010	1010
+1	0001	1001
0	0000	1000
-1	1111	0111
-2	1110	0110
-3	1101	0101
-4	1100	0100
-5	1011	0011
-6	1010	0010
-7	1001	0001
-8	1000	0000

Floating-point Numbers

Floating-point numbers are similar in form to numbers written in scientific notation. In general, the floating-point form of a number N is written as

$$N = M \times r^E \tag{1.13}$$

where M, the *mantissa* or *significand*, is a fixed-point number containing the significant digits of N, and E, the *exponent* or *characteristic*, is a fixed-point integer. In the general case, given a fixed-point number N, where

$$N = \pm(a_{n-1} \ldots a_0.a_{-1} \ldots a_{-m})_r$$

then in floating-point form

$$N = \pm(.a_{n-1} \ldots a_{-m})_r \times r^n$$

When deriving a representation of a floating-point number, the mantissa and exponent are coded separately. The radix is implied and is thus not included in the representation.

The mantissa M is often coded in sign magnitude, usually as a fraction, and can be written as

$$M = (S_M.a_{n-1} \ldots a_{-m})_{rsm} \tag{1.14}$$

where $(.a_{n-1} \ldots a_{-m})_r$ represents the magnitude of M and S_M indicates the sign of the number. S_M is usually chosen so that

$$M = (-1)^{S_M} \times (.a_{n-1} \ldots a_{-m})_r \tag{1.15}$$

and thus $S_M = 0$ indicates a positive number, whereas $S_M = 1$ indicates a negative number.

The exponent E is most often coded in *excess-K two's complement*. The excess-K two's complement of an exponent is formed by adding a *bias* of K to the two's complement integer value of the exponent. For binary floating-point numbers (numbers for which radix $r = 2$), K is usually selected to be 2^{e-1}, where e is the number of bits in the exponent. Therefore,

$$-2^{e-1} \leq \quad E \quad < 2^{e-1}$$
$$0 \leq E + 2^{e-1} < 2^e$$

which indicates that the biased value of E is a number that ranges from 0 to $2^e - 1$ as E increases from its most negative to its most positive value. The excess-K form of E can be written as

$$E = (b_{e-1}, b_{e-2} \dots b_0)_{\text{excess}-K} \tag{1.16}$$

where b_{e-1} indicates the sign of E.

M and E, coded via Eqs. 1.14 and 1.16, are combined to produce the following floating-point number format:

$$N = (S_M b_{e-1} b_{e-2} \dots b_0 a_{n-1} \dots a_{-m})_r \tag{1.17}$$

representing the number

$$N = (-1)^{S_M} \times (.a_{n-1} \dots a_{-m})_r \times r^{(b_{e-1} b_{e-2} \dots b_0) - 2^{e-1}} \tag{1.18}$$

One exception to the format of Eq. 1.17 is the number 0, which is treated as a special case and is usually represented by an all-zero word.

Floating-point representations of a given number are not unique. Given a number N, as defined in Eq. 1.13, it can be seen that

$$N = M \times r^E \tag{1.19}$$

$$= (M \div r) \times r^{E+1} \tag{1.20}$$

$$= (M \times r) \times r^{E-1} \tag{1.21}$$

where $(M \div r)$ is performed by shifting the digits of M one position to the right, and $(M \times r)$ is performed by shifting the digits of M one position to the left. Therefore, more than one combination of mantissa and exponent represent the same number. For example, let $M = +(1101.0101)_2$. Representing M as a sign magnitude fraction in the format of Eq. 1.14 and repeatedly applying Eq. 1.20 gives

$$M = +(1101.0101)_2$$

$$= (0.11010101)_2 \times 2^4 \tag{1.22}$$

$$= (0.011010101)_2 \times 2^5 \tag{1.23}$$

$$= (0.0011010101)_2 \times 2^6 \tag{1.24}$$

$$\vdots$$

When performing computations in a computer, it is usually most convenient to have a unique representation for each number. *Normalization* is used to provide uniqueness for floating-point numbers. A floating-point number is said to be *normalized* if the exponent is adjusted so that the mantissa has a nonzero value in its most significant digit position. Therefore, Eq. 1.22 gives the normalized representation of N, while the numbers in Eqs. 1.23 and 1.24 are not normalized.

Note that the most significant bit of a normalized binary number is always 1. Therefore, if M is represented in sign magnitude form as a normalized fraction,

$$0.5 \le |M| < 1.$$

Floating-point formats used in computer systems from different manufacturers often differ in the numbers of bits used to represent the mantissa and exponent and the method of coding used for each. Almost all systems utilize the general format illustrated in Fig. 1.4, with the sign stored in the leftmost bit, followed by the exponent and then the mantissa. The one-word format of Fig. 1.4a is typically used in computers with word lengths of 32 bits or more. The two-word format of Fig. 1.4b is used in computers with "short" word lengths for single-precision floating-point numbers or in computers with long word lengths for extended-precision (also called double-precision) representation.

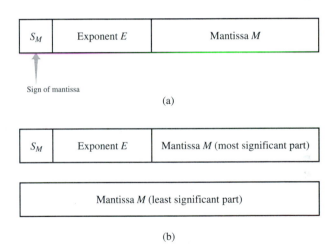

Figure 1.4   Floating-point number formats. **(a)** Typical single-precision format. **(b)** Typical extended-precision format.

Table 1.9 presents a summary of the single- and double-precision formats used by several computer systems, including the formats defined in the IEEE Standard 754-1985 [8]. Note that all of these formats use a biased exponent, with a varying number of bits. The DEC VAX formats and the IEEE Standard formats both suppress storage of the most significant bit of the mantissa. Since all numbers are binary values in normalized form, the most significant bit is known to be 1. Therefore, storage of this bit is unnecessary, and thus one additional bit of precision can be gained (denoted by the +1 in the third column of Table 1.9).

TABLE 1.9 SOME COMMON FLOATING POINT NUMBER FORMATS*

System/ Format	Total bits	Significand bits	Exponent bits	Exponent bias	Mantissa coding
IEEE Std. 754-1985:					Sign/Mag: (radix 2):
Single Precision	32	23 (+1)	8	127	$1 \leq \lvert M \rvert < 2$
Double Precision	64	52 (+1)	11	1023	$1 \leq \lvert M \rvert < 2$
IBM System/360:					Sign/Mag (radix 16):
Single Precision	32	24	7	64	$1/16 \leq \lvert M \rvert < 1$
Double Precision	64	56	7	64	$1/16 \leq \lvert M \rvert < 1$
DEC VAX 11/780:					Sign/Mag (radix 2):
F Format	32	23 (+1)	8	128	$1/2 \leq \lvert M \rvert < 1$
D Format	64	55 (+1)	8	128	$1/2 \leq \lvert M \rvert < 1$
G Format	64	52 (+1)	11	1024	$1/2 \leq \lvert M \rvert < 1$
CDC Cyber 70:	60	48	11	1024	1's Complement (radix 2) $1 \leq \lvert M \rvert < 2^{48}$

*(+1) $\Rightarrow$ most significant bit suppressed.

EXAMPLE 1.63

Write the binary number $N = (101101.101)_2$ in the floating-point format of Eq. 1.17, where $n + m = 10$ and $e = 5$. Assume that a normalized sign magnitude fraction is used to represent M and that Excess-16 two's complement is used for E.

$$N = (101101.101)_2 = (0.101101101)_2 \times 2^6$$

Writing the mantissa in the format of Eq. 1.14:

$$M = +(0.1011011010)_2$$
$$= (0.1011011010)_{2sm}$$

The exponent is coded by determining its two's complement form and then adding a bias of 16. (Note that the number of exponent bits $e = 5$ and that the bias value is $2^{e-1} = 2^4 = 16$). Therefore,

$$E = +(6)_{10}$$
$$= +(0110)_2$$
$$= (00110)_{2cns}$$

Adding the bias value of $16 = (10000)_2$ to the two's complement of E yields

$$
\begin{array}{r}
00110 \\
+ \quad 10000 \\
\hline
10110
\end{array}
$$

So,

$$E = (1, 0110)_{\text{excess-16}}$$

Note that the sign of the exponent, b_{e-1}, is 1, indicating a positive exponent value.

Combining M and E gives

$$N = (0, 1, 0110, 1011011010)_{fp}$$

Arithmetic operations on floating-point numbers require special algorithms to manipulate exponents and mantissas, which are beyond the scope of this text. The reader is referred to [9] for information on algorithms for floating-point arithmetic.

1.5.2 Character and Other Codes

It is often necessary or desirable to represent information as strings of alphabetical or numerical characters. Numerous character codes have been developed for this purpose and some of the most important ones will now be discussed.

Binary Coded Decimal (BCD)

The *binary coded decimal* or *BCD* code is used for representing the decimal digits 0 through 9 and is an example of a *weighted* code. That is, each bit position in the code has a fixed numerical value or weight associated with it. The digit represented by a given code word can be found by summing up the weighted bits. The BCD code uses 4 bits, with the weights chosen to be the same as those of a 4-bit binary integer. Hence, the BCD code for a given decimal digit is the same as the binary equivalent of the number with leading zeros. BCD codes are sometimes referred to as $8 - 4 - 2 - 1$ codes because of the weights used. The complete BCD code is given in Table 1.10.

TABLE 1.10 **BINARY CODED DECIMAL (BCD) CODES**

0:	0000	5:	0101
1:	0001	6:	0110
2:	0010	7:	0111
3:	0011	8:	1000
4:	0100	9:	1001

BCD codes are used to encode numbers for output to numerical displays and for representing numbers in processors that perform decimal arithmetic. The latter can be found in mainframe computers on one end of the spectrum and in hand-held calculators on the other.

EXAMPLE 1.64

Encode the decimal number $N = (9750)_{10}$ in BCD.

First, the individual digits are encoded from Table 1.10.
$$9 \to 1001, \ 7 \to 0111, \ 5 \to 0101, \ \text{and } 0 \to 0000$$
Then the individual codes are concatenated to give
$$N = (1001011101010000)_{\text{BCD}}$$

Extensions of the BCD code have been developed to cover not only the decimal digits but also alphabetical and other printing characters, as well as nonprinting control characters. These codes are typically 6 to 8 bits in length. They are used for representing data during input or output and for internally representing nonnumeric data such as text. One such code, used in several IBM mainframe computer models, is the *Extended Binary Coded Decimal Interchange Code* (*EBCDIC*).

ASCII

The most widely used character code in computer applications is the *ASCII* (American Standard Code for Information Interchange) code, pronounced "askey." The 7-bit ASCII code is given in Table 1.11. An eighth bit is often used with the ASCII code to provide error detection. This technique, parity coding, is discussed later in the chapter.

EXAMPLE 1.65

Encode the word *Digital* in ASCII code, representing each character by two hexadecimal digits.

Character	Binary Code	Hexadecimal Code
D	1000100	44
i	1101001	69
g	1100111	67
i	1101001	69
t	1110100	74
a	1100001	61
l	1101100	6C

Note that the hexadecimal form is more compact and readable than the binary form. For this reason, the former is often used when representing ASCII coded information.

Gray Codes

A *cyclic code* may be defined as any code in which, for any code word, a circular shift produces another code word. The *Gray code* is one of the most

TABLE 1.11   ASCII CHARACTER CODE

		$c_6 c_5 c_4$							
		000	001	010	011	100	101	110	111
$c_3 c_2 c_1 c_0$	0000	NUL	DLE	SP	0	@	P	`	p
	0001	SOH	DC1	!	1	A	Q	a	q
	0010	STX	DC2	"	2	B	R	b	r
	0011	ETX	DC3	#	3	C	S	c	s
	0100	EOT	DC4	$	4	D	T	d	t
	0101	ENQ	NAK	%	5	E	U	e	u
	0110	ACK	SYN	&	6	F	V	f	v
	0111	BEL	ETB	'	7	G	W	g	w
	1000	BS	CAN	(	8	H	X	h	x
	1001	HT	EM	)	9	I	Y	i	y
	1010	LF	SUB	*	;	J	Z	j	z
	1011	VT	ESC	+	;	K	[	k	{
	1100	FF	FS	`	<	L	\	l	|
	1101	CR	GS	-	=	M	]	m	}
	1110	S0	RS	.	>	N	^	n	~
	1111	S1	US	/	?	O	_	o	DEL

common types of cyclic codes and has the characteristic that the code words for two consecutive numbers differ in only 1 bit. That is, the distance between the two code words is 1. In general, the *distance* between two binary code words is equal to the number of bits in which the two words differ.

EXAMPLE 1.66

Define a Gray code for encoding the decimal numbers 0 through 15.

Four bits are needed to represent all the numbers, and the necessary code can be constructed by assigning bit i of the code word to be 0 if bits i and $i + 1$ of the corresponding binary number are the same and 1 otherwise. The most significant bit of the number must always be compared with 0 when using this technique. The resulting code is given in Table 1.12.

EXAMPLE 1.67

The need to observe or measure the position of a circular shaft occurs in many applications. This can be accomplished by mounting an encoded conducting disk on the shaft and electrically sensing the position of the disk. How can the disk be encoded so that incorrect position indications are not read when the sensors move from one sector of the disk to another?

The desired result can be obtained if the disk sectors are encoded in a Gray code since only one bit position in the code will change as the sensors move from one sector to the next. Figure 1.5 illustrates the solution.

TABLE 1.12 GRAY CODE FOR DECIMAL NUMBERS 0 THROUGH 15

Decimal	Binary	Gray
0	0000	0000
1	0001	0001
2	0010	0011
3	0011	0010
4	0100	0110
5	0101	0111
6	0110	0101
7	0111	0100
8	1000	1100
9	1001	1101
10	1010	1111
11	1011	1110
12	1100	1010
13	1101	1011
14	1110	1001
15	1111	1000

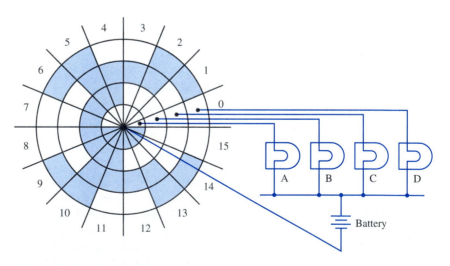

Figure 1.5 Gray-coded disk.

1.5.3 Error Detection Codes
and Correction Codes

An *error* in binary data is defined as an incorrect value in one or more bits. A *single error* refers to an incorrect value in only one bit, while a *multiple error* refers to one or more bits being incorrect. Errors may be introduced by hardware failures, external interference (noise), or other unwanted events. Information may be encoded using special codes that allow the detection and sometimes the correction of certain classes of errors. Some simple error detection and correction codes are illustrated next.

It will be useful to state some definitions and notations before presenting specific codes. Let I and J be n-bit binary information words. The *weight* of I, $w(I)$, is defined to be the number of bits of I equal to 1. The *distance between I and J*, $d(I, J)$, is equal to the number of bit positions in which I and J differ.

EXAMPLE 1.68

Determine the weights of I and J and the distance between them if $I = (01101100)$ and $J = (11000100)$.

Counting the 1 bits in each number, we get

$$w(I) = 4 \quad \text{and} \quad w(J) = 3$$

Next, we compare the two numbers bit by bit, noting where they differ as follows:

$$0 \quad 1 \quad 1 \quad 0 \quad 1 \quad 1 \quad 0 \quad 0$$
$$1 \quad 1 \quad 0 \quad 0 \quad 0 \quad 1 \quad 0 \quad 0$$
$$\uparrow \qquad \uparrow \qquad \uparrow$$

The numbers differ in three bit positions, therefore,

$$d(I, J) = 3$$

General Properties of Error Detection and Correction Codes

If the distance between any two code words of a code C is $\geq d_{min}$, the code is said to have *minimum distance* d_{min}. The error detection and correction properties of a code are determined in part by its minimum distance. This is illustrated in Figure 1.6, in which circled dots represent valid code words and uncircled dots represent words that contain errors. Two dots are connected if the corresponding words differ in exactly one bit position. For a given d_{min}, at least d_{min} errors are needed to transform one valid code word to another. If there are fewer than d_{min} errors, then a detectable noncode word results. If the noncode word is "closer" to one valid code word than to any other, the original code word can be deduced, and thus the error can be corrected.

In general, a code provides t *error correction* plus detection of s additional errors if and only if the following inequality is satisfied.

$$2t + s + 1 \leq d_{min} \tag{1.25}$$

It can be seen from a closer examination of Eq. 1.25 that a single-error detection code ($s = 1, t = 0$) requires a minimum distance of 2. A single-error correction code ($s = 0, t = 1$) requires a minimum distance of 3, and a code with both single-error correction and double-error detection ($s = t = 1$) requires a minimum distance of 4. Figure 1.6 illustrates these and several other combinations.

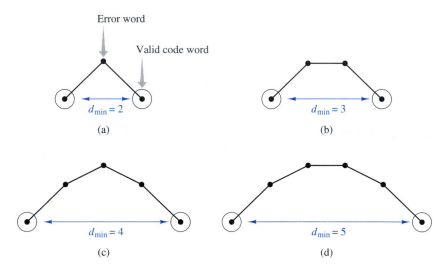

Figure 1.6 Relationship between the minimum distance between code words and the ability to detect and correct bit errors. (Connected words differ in exactly one bit position.) **(a)** Single-error detection (SED). **(b)** Single-error correction (SEC) or double-error correction (DED). **(c)** (SEC and DED) or TED. **(d)** DEC, (SEC and 3ED), or 4ED.

Simple Parity Codes

Parity codes are formed from a code C by concatenating ($|$) *a parity bit*, P, to each code word of C. Figure 1.7 illustrates the concept. In an *odd-parity code,* the parity bit is specified to be either 0 or 1 as necessary for $w(P|C)$ to be odd. The parity bit of an *even-parity code* is selected so that $w(P|C)$ will be even. Figure 1.8 shows how parity encoding is used on a nine-track magnetic tape.

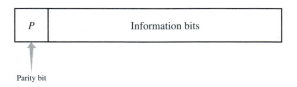

Figure 1.7 Parity-coded information.

01011000

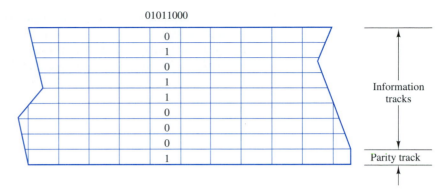

Figure 1.8   Parity coding on magnetic tape.

EXAMPLE 1.69

Concatenate a parity bit to the ASCII code of the characters $0, X, =,$ and BEL to produce an odd parity code.

Character	ASCII Code	Odd-Parity Code
0	0110000	10110000
X	1011000	01011000
=	0111100	10111100
BEL	0000111	00000111

EXAMPLE 1.70

Encode the message *CATCH 22* in ASCII code with even parity and group the coded word into 16-bit segments.

Segment 1: $(\underbrace{11000011}_{C}\ \underbrace{01000001}_{A})$ ASCII

Segment 2: $(\underbrace{11010100}_{T}\ \underbrace{11000011}_{C})$ ASCII

Segment 3: $(\underbrace{01001000}_{H}\ \underbrace{10100000}_{blank})$ ASCII

Segment 4: $(\underbrace{10110010}_{2}\ \underbrace{10110010}_{2})$ ASCII

Note that this message can be stored in four memory words of a 16-bit computer as

Word X:	1100001101000001
Word $X + 1$:	1101010011000011
Word $X + 2$:	0100100010100000
Word $X + 3$:	1011001010110010

Error detection on parity-encoded information is easily accomplished by checking to see if a code word has the correct parity. For example, if the parity of an odd-parity code word is actually even, then a detectable error has occurred. It is easy to build logic circuits to detect parity, as will be seen later in the text.

Parity codes are minimum-distance-2 codes and thus can be used to detect single errors. In fact, they can be used to detect any odd number of errors since such errors will always change the parity of the code word. On the other hand, errors in an even number of bits will not change the parity and are therefore not detectable using a parity code.

Two-out-of-Five Code

The *two-out-of-five code* is an error detection code having exactly 2 bits equal to 1 and 3 bits equal to 0 in each code word and is representative of *m*-out-of-*n* codes. Error detection is accomplished by counting the number of ones in a code word. An error is indicated anytime the number of ones is not exactly equal to 2. It follows that two-out-of-five codes permit the detection of single errors as well as multiple errors in adjacent bits. Table 1.13 presents a two-out-of-five code for the decimal digits.

Hamming Codes

Richard Hamming, in 1950, published the description of a class of error-correcting codes that have subsequently become widely used. *Hamming codes* may be viewed as an extension of simple parity codes in that multiple parity or *check bits* are employed. Each check bit is defined over a subset of the information bits in a word. The subsets overlap in such a manner that each information bit is in at least two subsets. *Single-error-correcting (SEC)*

TABLE 1.13   TWO-OUT-OF-FIVE CODES FOR THE DECIMAL DIGITS

Digit	Two-out-of-Five Code
0	00011
1	00101
2	01001
3	10001
4	00110
5	01010
6	10010
7	01100
8	10100
9	11000

codes permit the detection and correction of any single-bit error. *Single-error-correcting/ double-error-detecting (SEC/DED)* codes provide the detection but not correction of any double error, in addition to single-error detection and correction.

The error detection and correction properties of a Hamming code are determined by the number of check bits used and how the check bits are defined over the information bits. The minimum distance d_{min} is equal to the weight of the minimum-weight nonzero code word. In other words, d_{min} is equal to the number of ones in the codeword with the fewest ones. It is beyond the scope of this book to discuss the design of Hamming codes in depth. However, the two Hamming codes given in Table 1.14 will be used to illustrate code properties. Also, a method for designing simple SEC Hamming codes will be presented.

Hamming Code 1. The code provides single-error correction but no double-error detection since its minimum distance is 3. This can be seen more clearly in the following analysis. A single error in the leftmost bit of code word 0100110 produces the error word 1100110. Table 1.15 shows the difference and distance between each valid code word and the error word.

Note that only the code word in which the error occurred has distance 1 from the error word. This means that no single error in any other code word could have produced the error word. Hence, the detection of the error word

TABLE 1.14 TWO HAMMING CODES FOR 4-BIT INFORMATION WORDS

Information Words $(i_3i_2i_1i_0)$	Hamming Code 1 $(i_3i_2i_1i_0c_2c_1c_0)$	Hamming Code 2 $(i_3i_2i_1i_0c_3c_2c_1c_0)$
0000	0000000	00000000
0001	0001011	00011011
0010	0010101	00101101
0011	0011110	00110110
0100	0100110	01001110
0101	0101101	01010101
0110	0110011	01100011
0111	0111000	01111000
1000	1000111	10000111
1001	1001100	10011100
1010	1010010	10101010
1011	1011001	10110001
1100	1100001	11001001
1101	1101010	11010010
1110	1110100	11100100
1111	1111111	11111111

1100110 is equivalent to correcting the error, since the only possible single error that could have produced the pattern is an error in the leftmost bit of code word 0100110.

The above preceding analysis also suggests an error detection and correction procedure. That is, we could find the difference between a data word and each possible valid code word. A distance of 0 would indicate a valid match, a distance of 1 would indicate a single error in the corresponding code word in the bit position corresponding to the 1 bit of the difference, and a distance of 2 or more over all code words would indicate a multiple error. While this procedure works in theory, it would not be practical for codes with a large number of code words. Practical approaches will be discussed later.

Our analysis also reveals that several code words are distance 2 from the error word. Hence, a double error in each of these words could produce the same error word as the single error (examine Figure 1.6). This implies that double errors cannot in general be detected with this code. Single-error correction in conjunction with double-error detection requires a minimum-distance-4 code.

The check bits of the code are defined to provide even parity over a subset of the information bits, as follows:

$$c_2: \quad i_3, \quad i_2, \quad i_1$$
$$c_1: \quad i_3, \quad i_2, \quad i_0$$
$$c_0: \quad i_3, \quad i_1, \quad i_0$$

TABLE 1.15   EFFECTS OF ERRORS ON CODE WORDS

Code Words	Error Word	Difference	Distance
0000000	1100110	1100110	4
0001011	1100110	1101101	5
0010101	1100110	1110011	5
0011110	1100110	1111000	4
0100110	1100110	1000000	1
0101101	1100110	1001011	4
0110011	1100110	1010101	4
0111000	1100110	1011110	5
1000111	1100110	0100001	2
1001100	1100110	0101010	3
1010010	1100110	0110100	3
1011001	1100110	0111111	6
1100001	1100110	0000111	3
1101010	1100110	0001100	2
1110100	1100110	0010010	2
1111111	1100110	0011001	3

This relationship can be conveniently specified by a matrix known as the *generator matrix*, or G matrix, as shown next. Each column of the G matrix corresponds to a bit in the code word as indicated.

$$G = \begin{bmatrix} 1 & 0 & 0 & 0 & 1 & 1 & 1 \\ 0 & 1 & 0 & 0 & 1 & 1 & 0 \\ 0 & 0 & 1 & 0 & 1 & 0 & 1 \\ 0 & 0 & 0 & 1 & 0 & 1 & 1 \end{bmatrix} = \begin{bmatrix} 1 & 0 & 0 & 0 & p_{11} & p_{12} & p_{13} \\ 0 & 1 & 0 & 0 & p_{21} & p_{22} & p_{23} \\ 0 & 0 & 1 & 0 & p_{31} & p_{32} & p_{33} \\ 0 & 0 & 0 & 1 & p_{41} & p_{42} & p_{43} \end{bmatrix} \quad (1.26)$$

$$i_3 \ i_2 \ i_1 \ i_0 \ c_2 \ c_1 \ c_0$$

The encoding of an information word, i, to produce a code word, c, can be expressed in terms of the generator matrix, G, as follows.

$$c = iG \quad (1.27)$$

The decoding of a data word can best be expressed in terms of a matrix, H, known as the *parity-check matrix*. The H matrix can be derived from the G matrix as follows for the preceding code.

$$H = \begin{bmatrix} p_{11} & p_{21} & p_{31} & p_{41} & 1 & 0 & 0 \\ p_{12} & p_{22} & p_{32} & p_{42} & 0 & 1 & 0 \\ p_{13} & p_{23} & p_{33} & p_{43} & 0 & 0 & 1 \end{bmatrix} = \begin{bmatrix} 1 & 1 & 1 & 0 & 1 & 0 & 0 \\ 1 & 1 & 0 & 1 & 0 & 1 & 0 \\ 1 & 0 & 1 & 1 & 0 & 0 & 1 \end{bmatrix}$$

$$(1.28)$$

An n-tuple c is a code word generated by G if and only if

$$Hc^T = 0 \quad (1.29)$$

Let d represent a data word corresponding to a code word c, which has been corrupted by an error pattern e. Then

$$d = c + e \quad (1.30)$$

Decoding begins with the computation of the *syndrome, s*, of d in order to determine if an error is present. If no error is present, decoding concludes by removing the check bits, leaving only the original information bits. If a correctable error is found, the error is corrected before removing the check bits. If an uncorrectable error is found, the process terminates with an error signal so indicating.

The syndrome of d is computed as follows using H:

$$s = Hd^T \quad (1.31)$$
$$= H(c + e)^T$$
$$= Hc^T + He^T$$
$$= 0 + He^T$$
$$= He^T \quad (1.32)$$

The syndromes for the H matrix given in Eq. 1.28 are shown in Table 1.16. Note that the pattern of each syndrome is the same as the pattern of the column in the H matrix corresponding to the erroneous bit.

Hamming Code 2. The minimum distance is 4 since no nonzero code word has weight less than 4. Hence the code has both single-error correction and

TABLE 1.16   SYNDROMES AND ERROR PATTERNS

Error Pattern	Syndrome	Meaning
0 0 0 0 0 0 0	0 0 0	No error
0 0 0 0 0 0 1	0 0 1	Error in c_0
0 0 0 0 0 1 0	0 1 0	Error in c_1
0 0 0 0 1 0 0	1 0 0	Error in c_2
0 0 0 1 0 0 0	0 1 1	Error in i_0
0 0 1 0 0 0 0	1 0 1	Error in i_1
0 1 0 0 0 0 0	1 1 0	Error in i_2
1 0 0 0 0 0 0	1 1 1	Error in i_3

double-error detection properties. The generator and parity-check matrices are as follows:

$$G = \begin{bmatrix} 10000111 \\ 01001110 \\ 00101101 \\ 00011011 \end{bmatrix} \tag{1.33}$$

$$H = \begin{bmatrix} 01111000 \\ 11100100 \\ 11010010 \\ 10110001 \end{bmatrix} \tag{1.34}$$

Note that each column in the H matrix of Eq. 1.34 has an odd number of ones. Such Hamming codes are called *odd-weight-column* codes and have several desirable properties, including single-error correction, double-error detection, and detection of other multiple errors. Moreover, they allow relatively low cost and fast encoding and decoding circuitry. As a result, odd-weight-column codes are frequently used in practice.

Hamming codes are most easily designed by specifying the H matrix. For any positive integer $m \geq 3$, an (m, k) SEC code exists with the following properties.

- Code length: $n = 2^m - 1$

- Number of information bits: $k = 2^m - m - 1$

- Number of check bits: $n - k = m$

- Minimum distance: $d_{min} = 3$

The H matrix for such a code is an $n \times m$ matrix consisting of all the nonzero binary m-tuples as its columns. The matrix in Eq. 1.28 is an example of such a matrix for $m = 3$. Note that other H matrices for $m = 3$ can be found by reordering the columns.

A (15, 11) Hamming code is produced when $m = 4$. One possible H matrix for such a code is the following:

$$H = \begin{bmatrix} 111101110001000 \\ 111011001100100 \\ 110110100110010 \\ 101110011010001 \end{bmatrix} \qquad (1.35)$$

Any l columns may be deleted from an H matrix of a Hamming code to produce another Hamming code with the following properties.

- Code length: $n = 2^m - l - 1$
- Number of information bits: $k = 2^m - m - l - 1$
- Number of check bits: $n - k = m$
- Minimum distance: $d_{min} \geq 3$

These properties lead to the possibility of designing codes with improved error correction and detection properties and more useful code lengths.

EXAMPLE 1.71

Design a Hamming code for encoding five $(k = 5)$ information bits.

Four check bits $(m = 4)$ are required since for $m = 3, k = 2^3 - 3 - 1 = 4 < 5$. However, for $m = 4, k = 2^4 - 4 - 1 = 11 > 5$. But a $(9, 5)$ code can be found by deleting six columns from the H matrix of a (15, 11) code. Deleting six columns from Eq. 1.35 yields

$$H = \begin{bmatrix} 111101000 \\ 111010100 \\ 110110010 \\ 101110001 \end{bmatrix} \qquad (1.36)$$

The corresponding generator matrix is

$$G = \begin{bmatrix} 100001111 \\ 010001110 \\ 001001101 \\ 000101011 \\ 000010111 \end{bmatrix} \qquad (1.37)$$

This completes our coverage of error detection and correction codes. Readers wanting to learn more about codes are referred to reference [4].

1.6 Summary

Our introduction to number systems and computer codes is complete. The reader should now be familiar with decimal, binary, octal, and hexadecimal number systems and be able to convert numbers from any one of these bases to any other. Moreover, the reader should understand arithmetic operations in all the bases and should understand how negative numbers may be represented in computers. Also, familiarity with fixed-point and floating-point numbers should have been gained. An understanding of binary coded decimal (BCD) and ASCII character codes should have been obtained. Gray codes and excess or biased codes have also been introduced. Finally, a general knowledge of simple error detection and correction codes should have been obtained. A more in-depth understanding of these subjects can be gained by referring to the references.

REFERENCES

1. M. Y. HSIAO, "A Class of Optimal Minimum Odd-Weight-Column SEC-DED Codes," *IBM Journal of Research and Development,*, Vol. 14, No. 4, pp. 395-401, July 1970.

2. K. HWANG, *Computer Arithmetic*. New York: Wiley, 1979.

3. D. E. KNUTH, *Seminumerical Algorithms*. Reading, MA: Addison-Wesley, 1969.

4. S. LIN AND D. J. COSTELLO, *Error Control Coding: Fundamentals and Applications*. Englewood Cliffs, NJ: Prentice Hall, 1983.

5. W. W. PETERSON AND E. J. WELDON, JR., *Error-correcting Codes,* 2nd ed. Cambridge, MA: MIT Press, 1972.

6. J. F. WAKERLY, *Microcomputer Architecture and Programming*. New York: Wiley, 1981.

7. S. WASER AND M. J. FLYNN, *Introduction to Arithmetic for Digital Systems*. New York: Holt, Rinehart, and Winston, 1982.

8. *IEEE STANDARD FOR BINARY FLOATING-POINT ARITHMETIC,* ANSI/IEEE Std. 754-1985, Institute of Electrical and Electronic Engineers, 345 East 47th St., New York, NY, August 1985.

9. ISRAEL, KOREN, *Computer Arithmetic Algorithms*. Englewood Cliffs, NJ: Prentice Hall 1993.

PROBLEMS

1.1 Calculate $A + B$, $A - B$, $A \times B$, and $A \div B$ for the following pairs of binary numbers.

(a) 10101, 1011

(b) 1011010, 101111

(c) 101, 1011

(d) 10110110, 01011011

(e) 1101011, 1010

(f) 1010101, 101010

(g) 10000, 1001

(h) 1011.0101, 110.11

1.2 Calculate $A + B$, $A - B$, $A \times B$, and $A \div B$ for the following pairs of octal numbers.

(a) 372, 156

(b) 704, 230

(c) 1000, 777

(d) 423, 651

1.3 Calculate $A + B$, $A - B$, $A \times B$, and $A \div B$ for the following pairs of hexadecimal numbers.

(a) 2CF3, 2B

(b) FFFF, 1000

(c) 9A5, D17

(d) 372, 156

1.4 Convert each of the following decimal numbers to binary, octal, and hexadecimal numbers.

(a) 27

(b) 915

(c) 0.375

(d) 0.65

(e) 174.25

(f) 250.8

1.5 Convert each of the following binary numbers to octal, hexadecimal, and decimal numbers using the most appropriate conversion method.

(a) 1101

(b) 101110

(c) 0.101

(d) 0.01101

(e) 10101.11

(f) 10110110.001

1.6 Convert each of the following octal numbers to binary, hexadecimal, and decimal using the most appropriate conversion method.

(a) 65

(b) 371

(c) 240.51

(d) 2000

(e) 111111

(f) 177777

1.7 Convert each of the following hexadecimal numbers to binary, octal, and decimal using the most appropriate conversion method.

(a) 4F

(b) ABC

(c) F8.A7

(d) 2000

(e) 201.4

(f) 3D65E

1.8 Find the two's complement of each of the following binary numbers assuming $n = 8$.

(a) 101010

(b) 1101011

(c) 0

(d) 11111111

(e) 10000000

(f) 11000

1.9 Find the one's complement of each of the following binary numbers assuming $n = 8$.

(a) 110101

(b) 1010011

(c) 0

(d) 10000000

(e) 100001

(f) 01111111

1.10 Calculate $A + B, A - B, -A + B$, and $-A - B$ for each of the following pairs of numbers assuming a two's complement number system and $n = 8$. Check your results by decimal arithmetic. Explain any unusual results.

(a) 1010101, 1010

(b) 1101011, 0101010

(c) 11101010, 101111

(d) 10000000, 01111111

1.11 Repeat Problem 1.10 for the following numbers using a one's complement number system.

(a) 101011, 1101

(b) 10111010, 11010

(c) 1010101, 0101010

(d) 10000000, 01111111

1.12 Show how a 16-bit computer using a two's complement number system would perform the following computations.

(a) $(16850)_{10} + (2925)_{10} = (?)_{10}$

(b) $(16850)_{10} - (2925)_{10} = (?)_{10}$

(c) $(2925)_{10} - (16850)_{10} = (?)_{10}$

(d) $-(2925)_{10} - (16850)_{10} = (?)_{10}$

1.13 Encode each of the following numbers in BCD and in excess-3 codes.

(a) 39

(b) 1950

(c) 94704

(d) 625

1.14 Encode each of the following character strings in ASCII code. Represent the encoded strings by hexadecimal numbers.

(a) 1980

(b) A = b + C

(c) COMPUTER ENGINEERING

(d) The End.

1.15 Define a 4-bit code for representing the decimal digits that has the property that the code words for any two digits whose difference is 1 differ in only one bit position and that this property also holds for the digits 0 and 9.

1.16 How many bit errors can be detected in a two-out-of-five code? How many errors, if any, can be corrected in a two-out-of-five code? Prove your answers mathematically.

1.17 Examine the Gray-coded disk of Fig 1.5. Suppose the display lights give the following indications: A is off, B is on, C is on, and D is flickering on and off. Locate the position of the disk by sector numbers.

1.18 For the nine-track magnetic tape of Fig 1.7, the following 8-bit messages are to be recorded. Determine the parity bit to establish odd parity for each message.

(a) P10111010

(b) P00111000

(c) P10011001

(d) P01011010

1.19 Let 10111001 be an error word from Hamming code 2. Determine the correct code word by computing the difference and distance between the error word and each valid code word.

1.20 Develop a syndrome table for Hamming code 2 that covers the error-free case, all single errors, and all double errors. Is there a simple characterization of the double-error syndromes? Are there any error patterns of three or more errors that the code can detect?

1.21 Use the syndrome table developed in Problem 1.20 to decode the following words.

(a) 10010111

(b) 10011011

(c) 00111110

(d) 00000111

(e) 11101110

(f) 01011000

(g) 11100001

(h) 01101000

1.22 Develop the generator and parity-check matrices for a Hamming SEC code for encoding information words of 6 bits in length.

1.23   Encode all the information words for a code defined by the following parity-check matrix. Note that codes with a parity-check matrix in the form of Eq. 1.28 are called separable codes since the information bits may be separated in a block from the check bits. The code resulting from the following matrix will be nonseparable since information bits and the check bits are interspersed.

$$H = \begin{bmatrix} 1111000 \\ 1100110 \\ 1010101 \end{bmatrix}$$

1.24   What error detection and correction properties does the code defined in Problem 1.23 have? Develop a syndrome table for the code. Describe any interesting characteristics of the syndromes.

1.25   Describe the advantages and disadvantages of separable codes of the form represented by the matrix of Eq. 1.28 when compared to nonseparable codes of the form represented by the matrix in Problem 1.23.

2

In this chapter the basic mathematical tools for computer logic design and the underlying mathematical concepts are presented. The material itself is not only an important subject, but it also provides the foundation for the subsequent more advanced concepts discussed throughout the text. The discussion of this chapter is intended to be independent of any specific circuit elements to be used in the construction of digital circuits. Subsequent chapters will examine the application of these mathematical tools to various circuit element types.

Algebraic Methods for the Analysis and Synthesis of Logic Circuit

▶ 2.1 Fundamentals of Boolean Algebra

The analysis and synthesis tools presented in this chapter are based on the fundamental concepts of Boolean algebra, and hence this topic will now be examined. In 1849, George Boole presented an algebraic formulation of the processes of logical thought and reason [1]. This formulation has come to be known as Boolean algebra, a brief summary of which follows.

2.1.1 Basic Postulates

The basic description of the Boolean algebra formulation is based on concepts from set theory, in which a *Boolean algebra* is formally defined as a distributive, complemented lattice [2]. We present here a summary of this definition as a set of postulates that summarizes the basic elements and properties of a Boolean algebra.

Postulate 1. **Definition** A *Boolean algebra* is a closed algebraic system containing a set K of two or more elements and the two operators $\cdot$ and $+$; alternatively, for every a and b in set K, $a \cdot b$ belongs to K and $a + b$ belongs to K ($+$ is called OR and $\cdot$ is called AND).

Postulate 2. **Existence of 1 and 0 elements** There exist unique elements 1 (one) and 0 (zero) in set K such that for every a in K

    (a) $a + 0 = a$,

    (b) $a \cdot 1 = a$,

where 0 is the identity element for the $+$ operation and 1 is the identity element for the $\cdot$ operation.

Postulate 3. **Commutativity of the $+$ and $\cdot$ operations** For every a and b in K

    (a) $a + b = b + a$,

    (b) $a \cdot b = b \cdot a$.

Postulate 4.   Associativity of the $+$ and $\cdot$ operations   For every a, b, and c in K

(a) $a + (b + c) = (a + b) + c$,

(b) $a \cdot (b \cdot c) = (a \cdot b) \cdot c$.

Postulate 5.   Distributivity of $+$ over $\cdot$ and $\cdot$ over $+$ For every a, b, and c in K

(a) $a + (b \cdot c) = (a + b) \cdot (a + c)$,

(b) $a \cdot (b + c) = (a \cdot b) + (a \cdot c)$.

Postulate 6.   Existence of the complement   For every a in K there exists a unique element called $\bar{a}$ (*complement* of a) in K such that

(a) $a + \bar{a} = 1$,

(b) $a \cdot \bar{a} = 0$.

Upon this set of premises we may now develop other useful relationships, which we shall call theorems. To simplify notation in the remainder of the text, the dot ($\cdot$) will be suppressed when indicating the $\cdot$ operation.

EXAMPLE 2.1

$$a + b \cdot c = (a + b) \cdot (a + c)$$
$$a + bc = (a + b)(a + c)$$

Before proceeding to the theorem development, let us examine the postulates more closely to understand exactly what they mean.

2.1.2 Venn Diagrams for Postulates [2]

The postulates may be graphically presented in the form of Venn diagrams. This graphical description is possible since the algebra of sets is a Boolean algebra in which the sets correspond to elements, the intersection operation corresponds to $\cdot$, and the union operation corresponds to $+$. On the Venn diagram, sets are shown as closed contours, that is, circles, squares, ellipses, and the like. Venn diagrams for the sets a, b, $a \cdot b$, and $a + b$ are shown in Fig. 2.1. Alternative notation sometimes used for $a + b$ is $a \vee b$ or $a \cup b$, and for $a \cdot b$, ab or $a \wedge b$ or $a \cap b$.

The Venn diagrams can be used to illustrate the postulates. Let us select as an example Postulate 5.

EXAMPLE 2.2

Let us use the Venn diagram to illustrate Postulate 5.

From the analysis in Fig. 2.2, it is evident that the set $a + bc$ and the set $(a + b)(a + c)$ are two representations of the same shaded area, and hence $a + bc$ is equal to $(a + b)(a + c)$.

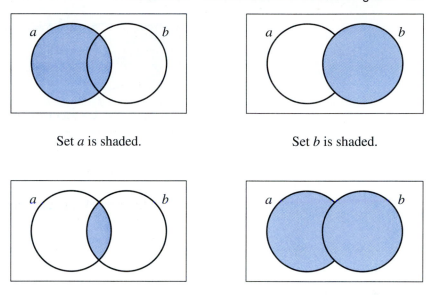

Set a is shaded.

Set b is shaded.

Set $a \cdot b$ is shaded.

Set $a + b$ is shaded.

Figure 2.1 Examples of Venn diagrams.

It is interesting to examine some facets of Postulate 6. This postulate refers to the complement of a. If a is the shaded set shown in Figure 2.3, the complement of $a, \bar{a}$, is that area outside a in the universal set. In other words, a and $\bar{a}$ are mutually exclusive and lie inside the universal set. Since they are mutually exclusive, they contain no area in common, and hence their intersection is the null set: $a \cdot \bar{a} = 0$. The union of a and $\bar{a}$ is by definition the universal set: $a + \bar{a} = 1$.

Furthermore, since the universal set, 1, contains all other sets, its complement must be the null set, 0. Therefore, $\bar{1} = 0$ and $\bar{0} = 1$.

The Venn diagram is a powerful tool for visualizing not only the postulates that have been presented but also the important theorems of Boolean algebra that follow.

2.1.3 Duality

The principle of *duality* is a very important concept in Boolean algebra. Briefly stated, the principle of duality pronounces that, if an expression is valid in Boolean algebra, the dual of the expression is also valid. The dual expression is found by replacing all $+$ operators with $\cdot$, all $\cdot$ operators with $+$, all ones with zeros, and all zeros with ones.

EXAMPLE 2.3

Find the dual of the expression

$$a + (bc) = (a + b)(a + c)$$

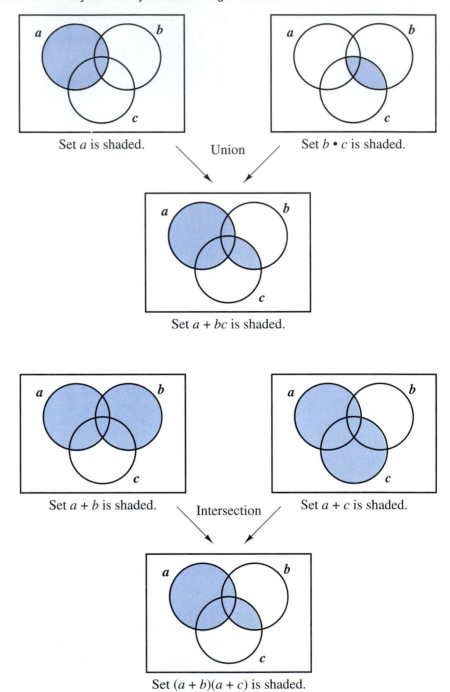

Set a is shaded.   Union   Set $b \cdot c$ is shaded.

Set $a + bc$ is shaded.

Set $a + b$ is shaded.   Intersection   Set $a + c$ is shaded.

Set $(a + b)(a + c)$ is shaded.

Figure 2.2   Venn diagrams for Postulate 5.

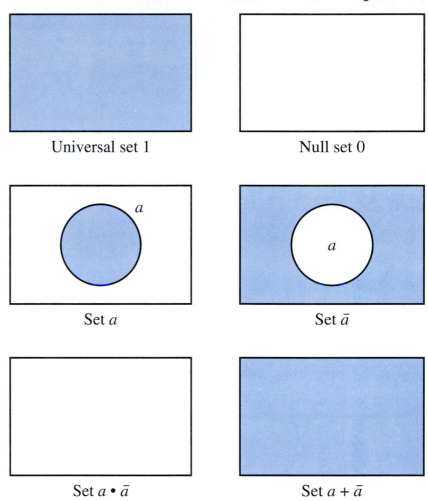

Figure 2.3 Venn diagrams illustrating Postulate 6.

Changing all $+$ operators to $\cdot$ and vice versa, the dual expression is

$$a(b + c) = ab + ac$$

When obtaining a dual, we must be careful not to alter the location of parentheses, if they are present. Note that the two expressions in the last example are parts (a) and (b) of Postulate 5. In fact, Postulates 2 through 6 are all listed as dual expressions.

The principle of duality will be used extensively in proving Boolean algebra theorems. In fact, once we have employed the postulates and previously proven theorems to demonstrate the validity of one expression, duality can be used to prove the validity of the dual expression.

2.1.4 Fundamental Theorems of Boolean Algebra

We shall now state several useful theorems in Boolean algebra. In these theorems, the letters $a, b, c, \ldots$ represent elements of a Boolean algebra. The first theorem describes the property of idempotency and is stated as follows.

Theorem 1. Idempotency

(a) $a + a = a.$

(b) $a \cdot a = a.$

Proof.   We may prove either part (a) or (b) of this theorem. Suppose we prove part (a):

$$
\begin{aligned}
a + a &= (a + a)1 & \text{[P2(b)]} \\
&= (a + a)(a + \bar{a}) & \text{[P6(a)]} \\
&= a + a\bar{a} & \text{[P5(a)]} \\
&= a + 0 & \text{[P6(b)]} \\
&= a & \text{[P2(a)]}
\end{aligned}
$$

The postulates used to justify a particular step are listed to the right. An important point to remember is that symbols on opposite sides of the equal sign may be used interchangeably; for example, Theorem 1 tells us that we may exchange $\{a\}$ for $\{\, a \cdot a \,\}$, and vice versa.

The next theorem further emphasizes the properties of the unique elements 1 and 0.

Theorem 2.   Null elements for + and · operators

(a) $a + 1 = 1.$

(b) $a \cdot 0 = 0.$

Proof.   Let us again prove part (a) of the theorem.

$$
\begin{aligned}
a + 1 &= (a + 1)1 & \text{[P2(b)]} \\
&= 1 \cdot (a + 1) & \text{[P3(b)]} \\
&= (a + \bar{a})(a + 1) & \text{[P6(a)]} \\
&= a + \bar{a} \cdot 1 & \text{[P5(a)]} \\
&= a + \bar{a} & \text{[P2(b)]} \\
&= 1 & \text{[P6(a)]}
\end{aligned}
$$

Since part (a) of this theorem is valid, it follows from the principle of duality that part (b) is valid also.

Theorem 3.   Involution

$$\bar{\bar{a}} = a.$$

Proof. From Postulate 5, $a \cdot \bar{a} = 0$ and $a + \bar{a} = 1$. Therefore, $\bar{a}$ is the complement of a, and also a is the complement of $\bar{a}$. Since the complement of $\bar{a}$ is unique, it follows that $\bar{\bar{a}} = a$.

At this point let us use the preceding material to summarize all the properties of the unique elements 1 and 0 in Table 2.1. The $\cdot$ (AND) properties of 1 and 0 remind us of the fundamental properties of multiplication in standard mathematics; however, the $+$ (OR) properties quickly indicate that we are not dealing with mathematics we previously have studied, and none of the mathematical properties that we employed there can be assumed for use in Boolean algebra. We may use only the postulates and theorems we are currently developing, since we are now working in a completely new and different system.

The Boolean algebra property of absorption is now stated in the next theorem. Absorption has no counterpart in "ordinary" algebra.

Theorem 4. Absorption

(a) $a + ab = a$.

(b) $a(a + b) = a$.

Proof. Let us prove part (a).

$$
\begin{aligned}
a + ab &= a \cdot 1 + ab & \text{[P2(b)]} \\
&= a(1 + b) & \text{[P5(b)]} \\
&= a(b + 1) & \text{[P3(b)]} \\
&= a \cdot 1 & \text{[T2(a)]} \\
&= a & \text{[P2(b)]}
\end{aligned}
$$

Theorem 4 can be easily visualized using a Venn diagram. The following examples illustrate the use of this theorem.

EXAMPLE 2.4

$$(X + Y) + (X + Y)Z = X + Y \qquad \text{[T4(a)]}$$

EXAMPLE 2.5

$$A\bar{B}(A\bar{B} + \bar{B}C) = A\bar{B} \qquad \text{[T4(b)]}$$

EXAMPLE 2.6

$$A\bar{B}C + \bar{B} = \bar{B} \qquad \text{[T4(a)]}$$

TABLE 2.1 PROPERTIES OF 0 AND 1 ELEMENTS

OR	AND	COMPLEMENT
$a + 0 = a$	$a \cdot 0 = 0$	$\bar{0} = 1$
$a + 1 = 1$	$a \cdot 1 = a$	$\bar{1} = 0$

The following three theorems are similar to absorption in that they can be employed to eliminate extra elements from a Boolean expression.

Theorem 5.

(a) $a + \bar{a}b = a + b$.

(b) $a(\bar{a} + b) = ab$.

Proof.   Part (a) of the theorem is proved as follows:

$$
\begin{aligned}
a + \bar{a}b &= (a + \bar{a})(a + b) &&\text{[P5(a)]}\\
&= 1 \cdot (a + b) &&\text{[P6(a)]}\\
&= (a + b) \cdot 1 &&\text{[P3(b)]}\\
&= (a + b) &&\text{[P2(b)]}
\end{aligned}
$$

The following examples illustrate the use of Theorem 5 in simplifying Boolean expressions.

EXAMPLE 2.7

$$B + A\bar{B}\bar{C}D = B + A\bar{C}D \qquad \text{[T5(a)]}$$

EXAMPLE 2.8

$$\bar{Y}(X + Y + Z) = \bar{Y}(X + Z) \qquad \text{[T5(b)]}$$

EXAMPLE 2.9

$$(X + Y)(\overline{(X + Y)} + Z) = (X + Y)Z \qquad \text{[T5(b)]}$$

EXAMPLE 2.10

$$AB + \overline{(AB)}C\bar{D} = AB + C\bar{D} \qquad \text{[T5(a)]}$$

Theorem 6.

(a) $ab + a\bar{b} = a$.

(b) $(a + b)(a + \bar{b}) = a$.

Proof.   Part (a) of the theorem is proved as follows:

$$
\begin{aligned}
ab + a\bar{b} &= a(b + \bar{b}) &&\text{[P5(b)]}\\
&= a \cdot 1 &&\text{[P6(a)]}\\
&= a &&\text{[P2(b)]}
\end{aligned}
$$

The following examples illustrate the use of Theorem 6 in simplifying Boolean expressions.

EXAMPLE 2.11

$$ABC + A\bar{B}C = AC \qquad \text{[T6(a)]}$$

EXAMPLE 2.12

$$(AD + B + C)(AD + \overline{(B + C)}) = AD \qquad \text{[T6(b)]}$$

EXAMPLE 2.13

Simplify $(\bar{W} + \bar{X} + \bar{Y} + \bar{Z})(\bar{W} + \bar{X} + \bar{Y} + Z)$
$(\bar{W} + \bar{X} + Y + \bar{Z})(\bar{W} + \bar{X} + Y + Z)$.

$$= (\bar{W} + \bar{X} + \bar{Y})(\bar{W} + \bar{X} + Y + \bar{Z})(\bar{W} + \bar{X} + Y + Z) \qquad [\text{T6(b)}]$$

$$= (\bar{W} + \bar{X} + \bar{Y})(\bar{W} + \bar{X} + Y) \qquad [\text{T6(b)}]$$

$$= (\bar{W} + \bar{X}) \qquad [\text{T6(b)}]$$

Theorem 7.

(a) $ab + a\bar{b}c = ab + ac$.

(b) $(a + b)(a + \bar{b} + c) = (a + b)(a + c)$.

Proof.   Part (a) of the theorem is proved as follows:

$$ab + a\bar{b}c = a(b + \bar{b}c) \qquad [\text{P5(b)}]$$
$$= a(b + c) \qquad [\text{T5(a)}]$$
$$= ab + ac \qquad [\text{P5(b)}]$$

The following examples illustrate the use of Theorem 7 in simplifying Boolean expressions.

EXAMPLE 2.14

$$xy + x\bar{y}(\bar{w} + \bar{z}) = xy + x(\bar{w} + \bar{z}) \qquad [\text{T7(a)}]$$

EXAMPLE 2.15

$$(\bar{x}\bar{y} + z)(w + \bar{x}\bar{y} + \bar{z}) = (\bar{x}\bar{y} + z)(w + \bar{x}\bar{y}) \qquad [\text{T7(b)}]$$

EXAMPLE 2.16

$$(\bar{A} + \bar{B} + \bar{C})(\bar{B} + C)(A + \bar{B}) = (\bar{A} + \bar{B})(\bar{B} + C)(A + \bar{B}) \qquad [\text{T7(b)}]$$
$$= \bar{B}(\bar{B} + C) \qquad [\text{T6(b)}]$$
$$= \bar{B} \qquad [\text{T4(b)}]$$

EXAMPLE 2.17

$$w\bar{y} + w\bar{x}y + wxyz + wx\bar{z} = w\bar{y} + w\bar{x}y + wxy + wx\bar{z} \qquad [\text{T7(a)}]$$
$$= w\bar{y} + wy + wx\bar{z} \qquad [\text{T6(a)}]$$
$$= w + wx\bar{z} \qquad [\text{T6(a)}]$$
$$= w \qquad [\text{T4(a)}]$$

We will find in the following chapters that these theorems form the basis for some of our standardized and computer-automated methods for simplifying Boolean expressions.

In working with Boolean algebra, we often need to determine the complement of a Boolean expression. The following theorem provides the basis for this operation.

Theorem 8.   DeMorgan's theorem

(a) $\overline{a + b} = \bar{a} \cdot \bar{b}.$

(b) $\overline{a \cdot b} = \bar{a} + \bar{b}.$

Proof.   Let us prove part (a).

If $X = a + b$, then $\bar{X} = \overline{(a + b)}$. By Postulate 6, $X \cdot \bar{X} = 0$ and $X + \bar{X} = 1$. If $X \cdot Y = 0$ and $X + Y = 1$, then $Y = \bar{X}$ because the complement of X is unique. Therefore, we let $Y = \bar{a}\bar{b}$ and test $X \cdot Y$ and $X + Y$:

$$
\begin{aligned}
X \cdot Y &= (a + b)(\bar{a}\bar{b}) \\
&= (\bar{a}\bar{b})(a + b)   && \text{[P3(b)]} \\
&= (\bar{a}\bar{b})a + (\bar{a}\bar{b})b   && \text{[P5(b)]} \\
&= a(\bar{a}\bar{b}) + (\bar{a}\bar{b})b   && \text{[P3(b)]} \\
&= (a\bar{a})\bar{b} + \bar{a}(\bar{b}b)   && \text{[P4(b)]} \\
&= 0 \cdot \bar{b} + \bar{a}(b \cdot \bar{b})   && \text{[P6(b), P3(b)]} \\
&= \bar{b} \cdot 0 + \bar{a} \cdot 0   && \text{[P3(b), P6(b)]} \\
&= 0 + 0   && \text{[T2(b)]} \\
&= 0   && \text{[P2(a)]}
\end{aligned}
$$

$$
\begin{aligned}
X + Y &= (a + b) + \bar{a}\bar{b} \\
&= (b + a) + \bar{a}\bar{b}   && \text{[P3(a)]} \\
&= b + (a + \bar{a}\bar{b})   && \text{[P4(a)]} \\
&= b + (a + \bar{b})   && \text{[T5(a)]} \\
&= (a + \bar{b}) + b   && \text{[P3(a)]} \\
&= a + (\bar{b} + b)   && \text{[P4(a)]} \\
&= a + (b + \bar{b})   && \text{[P3(a)]} \\
&= a + 1   && \text{[P6(a)]} \\
&= 1   && \text{[T2(a)]}
\end{aligned}
$$

Therefore, by the uniqueness of $\bar{X}$, $Y = \bar{X}$, and therefore

$$\bar{a}\bar{b} = \overline{a + b}$$

Theorem 8 may be generalized as follows.

(a) $\overline{a + b + \cdots + z} = \bar{a} \cdot \bar{b} \cdots \cdots \bar{z}.$

(b) $\overline{ab \ldots z} = \bar{a} + \bar{b} + \cdots + \bar{z}.$

The rule to follow when complementing an expression is to use relation (a) or (b), replacing each + (OR) operator with an · (AND) operator, and vice versa, and replacing each variable with its complement.

A note of caution is in order here. In applying DeMorgan's theorem, operator precedence must be observed: · takes precedence over +. The following example illustrates this important point.

EXAMPLE 2.18

Complement the expression $a + bc$.

$$\overline{a + b \cdot c} = \overline{a + (b \cdot c)}$$
$$= \bar{a} \cdot \overline{(b \cdot c)}$$
$$= \bar{a} \cdot (\bar{b} + \bar{c})$$
$$= \bar{a}\bar{b} + \bar{a}\bar{c}$$

Note that: $\overline{a + b \cdot c} \neq \bar{a} \cdot \bar{b} + \bar{c}$

The following examples illustrate the use of DeMorgan's theorem.

EXAMPLE 2.19

$$\overline{X + \bar{Y}} = \bar{X} \cdot \overline{\bar{Y}} \qquad \text{[T8(a)]}$$
$$= \bar{X} \cdot Y \qquad \text{[T3]}$$

EXAMPLE 2.20

Complement the expression $a(b + z(x + \bar{a}))$, and simplify the result so that the only complemented terms are individual variables.

$$\overline{a(b + z(x + \bar{a}))} = \bar{a} + \overline{(b + z(x + \bar{a}))} \qquad \text{[T8(b)]}$$
$$= \bar{a} + \bar{b}\,\overline{(z(x + \bar{a}))} \qquad \text{[T8(a)]}$$
$$= \bar{a} + \bar{b}(\bar{z} + \overline{(x + \bar{a})}) \qquad \text{[T8(b)]}$$
$$= \bar{a} + \bar{b}(\bar{z} + \bar{x} \cdot \overline{\bar{a}}) \qquad \text{[T8(a)]}$$
$$= \bar{a} + \bar{b}(\bar{z} + \bar{x}a) \qquad \text{[T3]}$$
$$= \bar{a} + \bar{b}(\bar{z} + \bar{x}) \qquad \text{[T5(a)]}$$

EXAMPLE 2.21

Repeat Example 2.20 for the expression $a(b + c) + \bar{a}b$.

$$\overline{a(b + c) + \bar{a}b} = \overline{ab + ac + \bar{a}b} \qquad \text{[P5(b)]}$$
$$= \overline{b + ac} \qquad \text{[T6(a)]}$$
$$= \bar{b}(\overline{ac}) \qquad \text{[T8(a)]}$$
$$= \bar{b}(\bar{a} + \bar{c}) \qquad \text{[T8(b)]}$$

As illustrated by this last example, the process of complementing an expression can often be simplified by reducing the expression prior to applying DeMorgan's theorem.

DeMorgan's theorem thus presents the general technique for complementing Boolean expressions. It will be especially useful in manipulating Boolean expressions into formats suitable for realization with specific types of logic gates.

The last fundamental theorem of Boolean algebra to be considered is the consensus theorem.

Theorem 9.   Consensus

(a) $ab + \bar{a}c + bc = ab + \bar{a}c$.

(b) $(a + b)(\bar{a} + c)(b + c) = (a + b)(\bar{a} + c)$.

Proof.   Henceforth, Postulates 3 and 4 will be used without reference.

$$ab + \bar{a}c + bc = ab + \bar{a}c + 1 \cdot bc \qquad [\text{P2(b)}]$$
$$= ab + \bar{a}c + (a + \bar{a})bc \qquad [\text{P6(a)}]$$
$$= ab + \bar{a}c + abc + \bar{a}bc \qquad [\text{P5(b)}]$$
$$= (ab + abc) + (\bar{a}c + \bar{a}cb)$$
$$= ab + \bar{a}c \qquad [\text{T4(a)}]$$

The key to using this theorem is to find an element and its complement, note the associated terms, and eliminate the included term (the "consensus" term), which is composed of the associated terms.

The consensus theorem is useful both in reducing Boolean expressions and expanding expressions in several of the automated minimization algorithms that will be described later.

EXAMPLE 2.22

$$AB + \bar{A}CD + BCD = AB + \bar{A}CD \qquad [\text{T9(a)}]$$

EXAMPLE 2.23

$$(a + \bar{b})(\bar{a} + c)(\bar{b} + c) = (a + \bar{b})(\bar{a} + c) \qquad [\text{T9(b)}]$$

EXAMPLE 2.24

$$ABC + \bar{A}D + \bar{B}D + CD = ABC + (\bar{A} + \bar{B})D + CD \qquad [\text{P5(b)}]$$
$$= ABC + \overline{AB}D + CD \qquad [\text{T8(b)}]$$
$$= ABC + \overline{AB}D \qquad [\text{T9(a)}]$$
$$= ABC + (\bar{A} + \bar{B})D \qquad [\text{T8(b)}]$$
$$= ABC + \bar{A}D + \bar{B}D \qquad [\text{P5(b)}]$$

In each of the preceding examples, an element or expression and its complement offer the key to reducing the expression.

It is important to note that the theorems presented can be quickly demonstrated via Venn diagrams. Hence readers are encouraged to use this graphical picture as an aid in remembering these important theorems. Table 2.2 summarizes the basic postulates and theorems of Boolean algebra. Theorem 10, which is included in this table, will be presented later.

TABLE 2.2   BOOLEAN ALGEBRA POSTULATES AND THEOREMS

Expression	Dual
$P2(a) : a + 0 = a$	$P2(b) : a \cdot 1 = a$
$P3(a) : a + b = b + a$	$P3(b) : ab = ba$
$P4(a) : a + (b + c) = (a + b) + c$	$P4(b) : a(bc) = (ab)c$
$P5(a) : a + bc = (a + b)(a + c)$	$P5(b) : a(b + c) = ab + ac$
$P6(a) : a + \bar{a} = 1$	$P6(b) : a \cdot \bar{a} = 0$
$T1(a) : a + a = a$	$T1(b) : a \cdot a = a$
$T2(a) : a + 1 = 1$	$T2(b) : a \cdot 0 = 0$
$T3 : \quad \bar{\bar{a}} = a$	
$T4(a) : a + ab = a$	$T4(b) : a(a + b) = a$
$T5(a) : a + \bar{a}b = a + b$	$T5(b) : a(\bar{a} + b) = ab$
$T6(a) : ab + a\bar{b} = a$	$T6(b) : (a + b)(a + \bar{b}) = a$
$T7(a) : ab + a\bar{b}c = ab + ac$	$T7(b) : (a + b)(a + \bar{b} + c) = (a + b)(a + c)$
$T8(a) : \overline{a + b} = \bar{a}\bar{b}$	$T8(b) : \overline{ab} = \bar{a} + \bar{b}$
$T9(a) : ab + \bar{a}c + bc = ab + \bar{a}c$	$T9(b) : (a + b)(\bar{a} + c)(b + c) = (a + b)(\bar{a} + c)$
$T10(a) : f(x_1, x_2, \ldots, x_n) = x_1 f(1, x_2, \ldots, x_n) + \bar{x}_1 f(0, x_2, \ldots, x_n)$	
$T10(b) : f(x_1, x_2, \ldots, x_n) = [x_1 + f(0, x_2, \ldots, x_n)][\bar{x}_1 + f(1, x_2, \ldots, x_n)]$	

◗ 2.2 Switching Functions

The postulates and theorems of Boolean algebra presented previously are given in general terms without the elements of the set K being specified. Hence, the results are valid for any Boolean algebra. In the discussions that follow, emphasis will focus on the Boolean algebra in which $K = \{0, 1\}$. This formulation is often referred to as *switching algebra*.

The concept of a function is well known to those familiar with ordinary algebra. Switching functions represent the corresponding concept for switching algebra and can be defined as follows. Let $X_1, X_2, \ldots, X_n$ be symbols called variables, each of which represents either the element 0 or 1 of a switching algebra (0 or 1 is said to be the *value* of the variable), and let $f(X_1, X_2, \ldots, X_n)$ represent a switching function of $X_1, X_2, \ldots, X_n$. The function f represents the value 0 or the value 1 depending on the set of values assigned to $X_1, X_2, \ldots, X_n$. Since there are n variables and each variable has two possible values, there are 2^n ways of assigning these values to the n variables. Furthermore, there are two possible values for the function $f(x_1, x_2, \ldots, x_n)$. Therefore, there are 2^{2^n} different switching functions of n variables.

For the case in which $n = 0$, the two switching functions of zero variables are

$$f_0 = 0 \qquad f_1 = 1$$

For $n = 1$, the four functions of the variable A are

$$f_0 = 0, \qquad f_2 = A$$
$$f_1 = \bar{A}, \qquad f_3 = 1$$

The 16 functions of the two variables A and B are derived next. Let $f_i(A, B)$ be defined as follows:

$$f_i(A, B) = i_3 AB + i_2 A\bar{B} + i_1 \bar{A}B + i_0 \bar{A}\bar{B}$$

where $(i)_{10} = (i_3 i_2 i_1 i_0)_2$ assumes the binary values $0000, 0001, 0010, \ldots 1111$. The resulting 16 functions are as follows:

$$f_0(A, B) = 0$$
$$f_1(A, B) = \bar{A}\bar{B}$$
$$f_2(A, B) = \bar{A}B$$
$$f_3(A, B) = \bar{A}B + \bar{A}\bar{B} = \bar{A}$$
$$f_4(A, B) = A\bar{B}$$
$$f_5(A, B) = A\bar{B} + \bar{A}\bar{B} = \bar{B}$$
$$f_6(A, B) = A\bar{B} + \bar{A}B$$
$$f_7(A, B) = A\bar{B} + \bar{A}B + \bar{A}\bar{B} = \bar{A} + \bar{B}$$
$$f_8(A, B) = AB$$
$$f_9(A, B) = AB + \bar{A}\bar{B}$$
$$f_{10}(A, B) = AB + \bar{A}B = B$$
$$f_{11}(A, B) = AB + \bar{A}B + \bar{A}\bar{B} = \bar{A} + B$$
$$f_{12}(A, B) = AB + A\bar{B} = A$$
$$f_{13}(A, B) = AB + A\bar{B} + \bar{A}\bar{B} = A + \bar{B}$$
$$f_{14}(A, B) = AB + A\bar{B} + \bar{A}B = A + B$$
$$f_{15}(A, B) = AB + A\bar{B} + \bar{A}B + \bar{A}\bar{B} = 1$$

By evaluating each of these functions for each combination of A and B, the preceding information can also be given in table form, as illustrated in Table 2.3.

TABLE 2.3 SIXTEEN FUNCTIONS OF TWO VARIABLES

AB	f_0	f_1	f_2	f_3	f_4	f_5	f_6	f_7	f_8	f_9	f_{10}	f_{11}	f_{12}	f_{13}	f_{14}	f_{15}
0 0	0	1	0	1	0	1	0	1	0	1	0	1	0	1	0	1
0 1	0	0	1	1	0	0	1	1	0	0	1	1	0	0	1	1
1 0	0	0	0	0	1	1	1	1	0	0	0	0	1	1	1	1
1 1	0	0	0	0	0	0	0	0	1	1	1	1	1	1	1	1

A switching function can be described by a switching expression as follows:

$$f(A, B, C) = AB + \bar{A}C + A\bar{C}$$

If $A = 1$ and $B = C = 0$, then the value of the function f is 1, which is verified as follows:

$$f(1, 0, 0) = 1 \cdot 0 + \bar{1} \cdot 0 + 1 \cdot \bar{0}$$

$$= 1 \cdot 0 + 0 \cdot 0 + 1 \cdot 1 \qquad \text{[T3]}$$

$$= 0 + 0 + 1 \cdot 1 \qquad \text{[T2(b)]}$$

$$= 1 \cdot 1 \qquad \text{[P2(a)]}$$

$$= 1 \qquad \text{[P2(b)]}$$

Other values can be computed in a similar manner; for example, when $A = 0$, $B = 1$, and $C = 0$, it can be seen that $f = 0$.

2.2.1 Truth Tables

A given switching function can be represented by a number of different, but equivalent, switching expressions. If we evaluate a switching function for all possible input combinations and list the results in tabular form, we obtain a unique representation of the function called a *truth table*.

For example, truth tables, as shown in Tables 2.4a, b, and c, can be used to demonstrate the basic OR, AND, and Complement operations employed in the switching algebra by considering each to be a switching function and displaying all possible combinations of the elements.

If we evaluate the function $f(A, B, C) = AB + \bar{A}C + A\bar{C}$ for all possible input combinations and list them in a tabular form, we obtain the truth table shown as Table 2.5a. Replacing each 0 in Table 2.5a with F(false) and

TABLE 2.4   TRUTH TABLES FOR THE OR, AND, AND NOT FUNCTIONS

$a\,b$	$f(a, b) = a + b$		$a\,b$	$f(a, b) = a \cdot b$		a	$f(a) = \bar{a}$
0 0	0		0 0	0		0	1
0 1	1		0 1	0		1	0
1 0	1		1 1	0			
1 1	1		1 0	1			
	(a)			(b)			(c)

TABLE 2.5   TRUTH TABLES FOR
$$f(A, B, C) = AB + \bar{A}C + A\bar{C}$$

$A\,B\,C$	$f(A, B, C)$		$A\,B\,C$	$f(A, B, C)$
0 0 0	0		$F\,F\,F$	F
0 0 1	1		$F\,F\,T$	T
0 1 0	0		$F\,T\,F$	F
0 1 1	1		$F\,T\,T$	T
1 0 0	1		$T\,F\,F$	T
1 0 1	0		$T\,F\,T$	F
1 1 0	1		$T\,T\,F$	T
1 1 1	1		$T\,T\,T$	T
	(a)			(b)

each 1 with T (true) yields an alternative form of the truth table, shown in Table 2.5b, and demonstrates the one-to-one correspondence that exists between the switching algebra and the truth-functional calculus [4].

The truth table can also be used as a convenient means of evaluating switching functions. For example, consider our previous function

$$f(A, B, C) = AB + \bar{A}C + A\bar{C}$$

The truth table may be obtained one term at a time as follows:

A, B, C	AB	$\bar{A}$	$\bar{A}C$	$AB + \bar{A}C$	$\bar{C}$	$A\bar{C}$	$(AB + \bar{A}C) + A\bar{C}$	$f(A, B, C)$
0 0 0	$0 \cdot 0 = 0$	$\bar{0} = 1$	$1 \cdot 0 = 0$	$0 + 0 = 0$	$\bar{0} = 1$	$0 \cdot 1 = 0$	$0 + 0 = 0$	0
0 0 1	$0 \cdot 0 = 0$	$\bar{0} = 1$	$1 \cdot 1 = 1$	$0 + 1 = 1$	$\bar{1} = 0$	$0 \cdot 0 = 0$	$1 + 0 = 1$	1
0 1 0	$0 \cdot 1 = 0$	$\bar{0} = 1$	$1 \cdot 0 = 0$	$0 + 0 = 0$	$\bar{0} = 1$	$0 \cdot 1 = 0$	$0 + 0 = 0$	0
0 1 1	$0 \cdot 1 = 0$	$\bar{0} = 1$	$1 \cdot 1 = 1$	$0 + 1 = 1$	$\bar{1} = 0$	$0 \cdot 0 = 0$	$1 + 0 = 1$	1
1 0 0	$1 \cdot 0 = 0$	$\bar{1} = 0$	$0 \cdot 0 = 0$	$0 + 0 = 0$	$\bar{0} = 1$	$1 \cdot 1 = 1$	$0 + 1 = 1$	1
1 0 1	$1 \cdot 0 = 0$	$\bar{1} = 0$	$0 \cdot 1 = 0$	$0 + 0 = 0$	$\bar{1} = 0$	$1 \cdot 0 = 0$	$0 + 0 = 0$	0
1 1 0	$1 \cdot 1 = 1$	$\bar{1} = 0$	$0 \cdot 0 = 0$	$1 + 0 = 1$	$\bar{0} = 1$	$1 \cdot 1 = 1$	$1 + 1 = 1$	1
1 1 1	$1 \cdot 1 = 1$	$\bar{1} = 0$	$0 \cdot 1 = 0$	$1 + 0 = 1$	$\bar{1} = 0$	$1 \cdot 0 = 0$	$1 + 0 = 1$	1

2.2.2 Algebraic Forms of Switching Functions

In our discussion thus far we have seen several different forms for switching functions, including algebraic expressions, truth tables, and Venn diagrams. We shall now define some other specific forms of functions that will prove to be very useful.

SOP and POS Forms

Switching functions in the *sum of products* (SOP) form are constructed by summing (ORing) product (ANDed) terms, where each product term is formed by ANDing a number of complemented or uncomplemented variables, each called a *literal*. An example SOP form of a function of four variables is

$$f(A, B, C, D) = A\bar{B}C + \bar{B}\bar{D} + \bar{A}C\bar{D}$$

Switching functions in *product of sums* (POS) form are constructed by taking the product of (ANDing) sum (ORed) terms, where each sum term is formed by ORing a number of literals. An example POS form of a function of four variables is

$$f(A, B, C, D) = (\bar{A} + B + C)(\bar{B} + C + \bar{D})(A + \bar{C} + D)$$

Canonical Forms

Canonical forms for switching functions are SOP and POS forms with special characteristics. As was shown earlier, a switching function can be represented by many different, but equivalent, switching expressions. The canonical SOP and POS forms, however, are unique for each function.

Minterms. For a function of n variables, if a product term contains each of the n variables exactly one time in complemented or uncomplemented form, the product term is called a *minterm*. If the function is represented as a sum of minterms only, the function is said to be in *canonical sum of products* (*canonical SOP*) form. For example,

$$f_\alpha(A, B, C) = \bar{A}B\bar{C} + AB\bar{C} + \bar{A}BC + ABC \qquad (2.1)$$

is the canonical SOP form of function $f_\alpha(A, B, C)$, which has four minterms.

To simplify writing the canonical SOP form, a special notation is commonly used in which each minterm is represented by an n-bit binary code. Each bit represents one of the variables of the minterm as follows:

[handwritten: opposite in Max Term]

Uncomplemented variable:	1
Complemented variable:	0

[handwritten: min term]

The variables are listed in the same order in each minterm. The significance of this notation is that, for a minterm to evaluate to 1, each uncomplemented variable in a minterm must be 1, and each complemented variable must be 0. Using this code, the minterms of $f_\alpha(A, B, C)$ may be written in one of the following equivalent forms:

Minterm	Minterm Code	Minterm Number
$\bar{A}B\bar{C}$	010	m_2
$AB\bar{C}$	110	m_6
$\bar{A}BC$	011	m_3
ABC	111	m_7

Each minterm is written in abbreviated form as m_i, where i is the decimal integer equal to the corresponding binary code for the minterm. Thus, $f_\alpha(A, B, C)$ may be written in compact form as

$$f_\alpha(A, B, C) = m_2 + m_3 + m_6 + m_7 \qquad (2.2)$$

A further simplification results if the function is written in *minterm list form* as follows:

$$f_\alpha(A, B, C) = \sum m(2, 3, 6, 7) \qquad (2.3)$$

The three Eqs. (2.1), (2.2), and (2.3) illustrate three different, but equivalent ways to represent the canonical SOP form for $f_\alpha(A, B, C)$.

The order of the variables in the functional notation in equations (2.2) and (2.3) is very important since it determines the order of the bits of the minterm numbers. This fact can be easily demonstrated by changing the order relation of the variables in the function $f_\alpha(A, B, C)$ to $f_\beta(B, C, A)$ as follows:

$$f_\beta(B, C, A) = \sum m(2, 3, 6, 7)$$
$$= \underbrace{m_2}_{010} + \underbrace{m_3}_{011} + \underbrace{m_6}_{110} + \underbrace{m_7}_{111}$$
$$= \bar{B}C\bar{A} + \bar{B}CA + BC\bar{A} + BCA$$
$$= \bar{A}\bar{B}C + A\bar{B}C + \bar{A}BC + ABC \qquad (2.4)$$

Note that Eq. (2.4) is not identical to Eq. (2.1) even though the minterm lists are the same. Further manipulation of Eq. (2.4) yields

$$f_\beta(A, B, C) = f_\beta(B, C, A)$$

$$= \underbrace{\bar{A}\bar{B}C}_{001} + \underbrace{\bar{A}BC}_{011} + \underbrace{A\bar{B}C}_{101} + \underbrace{ABC}_{111}$$

$$= m_1 + m_3 + m_5 + m_7$$

$$= \sum m(1, 3, 5, 7) \tag{2.5}$$

Equations (2.4) and (2.5) are equal; the difference in minterm lists reflects the ordering of the variables in the functional notation.

The truth table for $f_\beta(A, B, C)$ can easily be derived from its canonical SOP form:

Row No. (i)	Inputs ABC	m_1 $\bar{A}\bar{B}C$	m_3 $\bar{A}BC$	m_5 $A\bar{B}C$	m_7 ABC	Outputs $f_\beta(A, B, C)$
0	0 0 0	0	0	0	0	0
1	0 0 1	1	0	0	0	1
2	0 1 0	0	0	0	0	0
3	0 1 1	0	1	0	0	1
4	1 0 0	0	0	0	0	0
5	1 0 1	0	0	1	0	1
6	1 1 0	0	0	0	0	0
7	1 1 1	0	0	0	1	1

A careful examination of the table shows that each row is numbered according to its decimal code, and that the only ones that appear in the table are those in rows i, which correspond to minterms m_i. Hence, in general, we may eliminate all intermediate steps and simply write down the truth table directly from the minterm list, as shown next for the function $f_\alpha(A, B, C)$:

Row No. (i)	Inputs ABC	Outputs $f_\alpha(A, B, C)$	$= \sum m(2, 3, 6, 7)$	Complement $\bar{f}_\alpha(A, B, C)$	$= \sum m(0, 1, 4, 5)$
0	0 0 0	0		1	$\leftarrow m_0$
1	0 0 1	0		1	$\leftarrow m_1$
2	0 1 0	1	$\leftarrow m_2$	0	
3	0 1 1	1	$\leftarrow m_3$	0	
4	1 0 0	0		1	$\leftarrow m_4$
5	1 0 1	0		1	$\leftarrow m_5$
6	1 1 0	1	$\leftarrow m_6$	0	
7	1 1 1	1	$\leftarrow m_7$	0	

In addition, it can be seen that the truth table for $\bar{f}_\alpha(A, B, C)$ has ones in rows 0, 1, 4, and 5. Therefore,

$$f_\alpha(A, B, C) = \sum m(2, 3, 6, 7)$$

and

$$\bar{f}_\alpha(A, B, C) = \sum m(0, 1, 4, 5)$$

Notice that all the minterms that are composed of three variables (totaling $2^3 = 8$) are contained either in the minterm list for $f_\alpha(A, B, C)$ or that for $\bar{f}_\alpha(A, B, C)$. In general, each of the 2^n minterms of n variables will always appear in either the canonical SOP form for $f(x_1, x_2, \ldots, x_n)$ or that of $\bar{f}(x_1, x_2, \ldots, x_n)$.

EXAMPLE 2.25

Given the function
$$f(A, B, Q, Z) = \bar{A}\bar{B}\bar{Q}\bar{Z} + \bar{A}\bar{B}\bar{Q}Z + \bar{A}BQ\bar{Z} + \bar{A}BQZ,$$
let us express the functions $f(A, B, Q, Z)$ and $\bar{f}(A, B, Q, Z)$ in minterm list form.

$$f(A, B, Q, Z) = \bar{A}\bar{B}\bar{Q}\bar{Z} + \bar{A}\bar{B}\bar{Q}Z + \bar{A}BQ\bar{Z} + \bar{A}BQZ$$
$$= m_0 + m_1 + m_6 + m_7$$
$$= \sum m(0, 1, 6, 7)$$

$\bar{f}(A, B, Q, Z)$ will contain the remaining 12 ($2^4 - 4$) minterms. The minterm list for this function is

$$\bar{f}(A, B, Q, Z) = m_2 + m_3 + m_4 + m_5 + m_8 + m_9$$
$$+ m_{10} + m_{11} + m_{12} + m_{13} + m_{14} + m_{15}$$
$$= \sum m(2, 3, 4, 5, 8, 9, 10, 11, 12, 13, 14, 15)$$

At this point we should recall from switching algebra that

$$f(x_1, x_2, \ldots, x_n) + \bar{f}(x_1, x_2, \ldots, x_n) = 1$$

However, since

$$f(x_1, x_2, \ldots, x_n) + \bar{f}(x_1, x_2, \ldots, x_n) = \sum_{i=0}^{2^n - 1} m_i$$

then

$$\sum_{i=0}^{2^n - 1} m_i = 1 \tag{2.6}$$

In other words, the sum (OR) of all the minterms of n variables ($m_0, \ldots, m_{2^n - 1}$) is equal to 1. Finally, it is important to note that, although

$$AB + \overline{AB} = 1 \qquad\qquad [P6(a)]$$

and

$$AB + \bar{A} + \bar{B} = 1 \qquad\qquad [T7(b)]$$

are valid expressions,

$$AB + \bar{A}\bar{B} \neq 1.$$

Setting the last expression to 1 is a common mistake by students of switching algebra.

Maxterms. If a sum term of a function of n variables contains each of the n variables exactly one time in complemented or uncomplemented form, the sum term is called a *maxterm*. If a function is represented as a product of sum terms, each of which is a maxterm, the function is said to be in *canonical product of sums (canonical POS) form*. For example,

$$f_\gamma(A, B, C) = (A + B + C)(A + B + \bar{C})(\bar{A} + B + C)(\bar{A} + B + \bar{C}) \quad (2.7)$$

is the canonical POS form of function $f_\gamma(A, B, C)$, which has four maxterms.

We adopt a special notation for maxterms, as for minterms, with one major difference; the coding is interchanged as follows:

opposite in Min Term

| Uncomplemented variable: | 0 |
| Complemented variable: | 1 |

Max Term

The significance of this notation is that, for a maxterm to evaluate to 0, each uncomplemented variable in a maxterm must be 0 and each complemented variable must be 1. The maxterms of $f_\gamma(A, B, C)$ are thus represented as follows:

Maxterm	Maxterm Code	Maxterm List
$A + B + C$	000	M_0
$A + B + \bar{C}$	001	M_1
$\bar{A} + B + C$	100	M_4
$\bar{A} + B + \bar{C}$	101	M_5

Each maxterm is written in abbreviated form as M_i, where i is the decimal integer of the corresponding binary code for the maxterm. Thus,

$$f_\gamma(A, B, C) = M_0 M_1 M_4 M_5 \quad (2.8)$$

$$= \prod M(0, 1, 4, 5) \quad (2.9)$$

The latter form is called the *maxterm list form*. Equations (2.7), (2.8), and (2.9) are equivalent canonical POS forms for $f_\gamma(A, B, C)$. As was the case with Eqs. (2.2) and (2.3), the ordering of the variables in Eq. (2.8) and (2.9) is very important. The truth table for $f_\gamma(A, B, C)$ is

Row No. (i)	Inputs A B C	M_0 $A + B + C$	M_1 $A + B + \bar{C}$	M_4 $\bar{A} + B + C$	M_5 $\bar{A} + B + \bar{C}$	Outputs $f_\gamma(A, B, C)$
0	0 0 0	0	1	1	1	0
1	0 0 1	1	0	1	1	0
2	0 1 0	1	1	1	1	1
3	0 1 1	1	1	1	1	1
4	1 0 0	1	1	0	1	0
5	1 0 1	1	1	1	0	0
6	1 1 0	1	1	1	1	1
7	1 1 1	1	1	1	1	1

Each row in the table is numbered according to the decimal code, as was done before in the minterm case. Note that the only zeros that appear in the table are those in rows i, which correspond to maxterms M_i. Hence, as in the minterm case, the truth table can be generated by inspection directly from the maxterm list. Comparing the truth tables for $f_\alpha(A, B, C)$ and $f_\gamma(A, B, C)$ indicates that

$$f_\alpha(A, B, C) = \sum m(2, 3, 6, 7)$$
$$= f_\gamma(A, B, C)$$
$$= \prod M(0, 1, 4, 5) \qquad (2.10)$$

Hence the functions $f_\alpha(A, B, C)$ and $f_\gamma(A, B, C)$ are equal and therefore Eq.(2.10) shows both the canonical SOP and canonical POS forms for $f_\alpha(A, B, C)$.

EXAMPLE 2.26

Given the function $f(A, B, C) =$ $(A + B + \bar{C})(A + \bar{B} + \bar{C})(\bar{A} + B + \bar{C})(\bar{A} + \bar{B} + \bar{C})$, let us construct the truth table and express the function in both maxterm and minterm form.

$$f(A, B, C) = \underbrace{(A + B + \bar{C})}_{001} \underbrace{(A + \bar{B} + \bar{C})}_{011} \underbrace{(\bar{A} + B + \bar{C})}_{101} \underbrace{(\bar{A} + \bar{B} + \bar{C})}_{111}$$
$$= M_1 M_3 M_5 M_7$$
$$= \prod M(1, 3, 5, 7)$$

The maxterms place zeros in rows 1, 3, 5, and 7 of the truth table.

Row No. (i)	Inputs A B C	Outputs f(A, B, C)	$= \prod M(1, 3, 5, 7)$
0	0 0 0	1	
1	0 0 1	0	$\leftarrow M_1$ *(exist where the zero is)*
2	0 1 0	1	
3	0 1 1	0	$\leftarrow M_3$
4	1 0 0	1	
5	1 0 1	0	$\leftarrow M_5$
6	1 1 0	1	
7	1 1 1	0	$\leftarrow M_7$

From the truth table for $f(A, B, C)$, we observe that

$$f(A, B, C) = \sum m(0, 2, 4, 6)$$

Therefore,

$$\bar{f}(A, B, C) = \sum m(1, 3, 5, 7)$$
$$= \underbrace{m_1}_{001} + \underbrace{m_3}_{011} + \underbrace{m_5}_{101} + \underbrace{m_7}_{111}$$
$$= \bar{A}\bar{B}C + \bar{A}BC + A\bar{B}C + ABC$$

Consequently,

$$f(A, B, C) = \overline{\bar{A}\bar{B}C + \bar{A}BC + A\bar{B}C + ABC}$$
$$= \overline{\bar{A}\bar{B}C} \cdot \overline{\bar{A}BC} \cdot \overline{A\bar{B}C} \cdot \overline{ABC}$$

$$= \underbrace{(A + B + \bar{C})}_{001} \underbrace{(A + \bar{B} + \bar{C})}_{011} \underbrace{(\bar{A} + B + \bar{C})}_{101} \underbrace{(\bar{A} + \bar{B} + \bar{C})}_{111}$$

$$= M_1 M_3 M_5 M_7$$

$$= \prod M(1, 3, 5, 7)$$

Therefore, we have algebraically shown that

$$f(A, B, C) = \prod M(1, 3, 5, 7) = \sum m(0, 2, 4, 6)$$

which is clearly evident by inspection of the truth table.

In the manipulation of functions, a specific relationship between minterm m_i and maxterm M_i becomes apparent. As an example, for a function $f(A, B, C)$

$$\bar{m}_1 = \underbrace{\overline{\bar{A}\bar{B}C}}_{001} = \underbrace{A + B + \bar{C}}_{001} = M_1$$

(minterm code)   (maxterm code)

and vice versa. What is illustrated here is true in the general case; that is,

$$\boxed{\begin{array}{l} \bar{m}_i = M_i \\ \bar{M}_i = \bar{\bar{m}}_i = m_i \end{array}}$$

(2.11)
(2.12)

Therefore, minterms and maxterms are complements of one another.

EXAMPLE 2.27

Given the function $f(A, B, C)$ of Example 2.26, let us determine the relationship between the maxterms for the function and its complement.

The truth table is as follows.

Row No. (i)	Inputs ABC	Outputs $f(A, B, C)$	Outputs $\bar{f}(A, B, C)$	$= \prod M(0, 2, 4, 6)$
0	0 0 0	1	0	$\leftarrow M_0$
1	0 0 1	0	1	
2	0 1 0	1	0	$\leftarrow M_2$
3	0 1 1	0	1	
4	1 0 0	1	0	$\leftarrow M_4$
5	1 0 1	0	1	
6	1 1 0	1	0	$\leftarrow M_6$
7	1 1 1	0	1	

Since zeros appear in rows 0, 2, 4, and 6, the canonical form for $\bar{f}(A, B, C)$ is

$$\bar{f}(A, B, C) = \prod M(0, 2, 4, 6)$$

and therefore

$$f(A, B, C) = \prod M(1, 3, 5, 7)$$

The function $f(A, B, C)$ has three variables and hence eight maxterms, all of which appear in the list for either $f(A, B, C)$ or $\bar{f}(A, B, C)$. From switching algebra we know that

$$f(A, B, C) \cdot \bar{f}(A, B, C) = 0$$

and therefore

$$(M_0 M_2 M_4 M_6)(M_1 M_3 M_5 M_7) = 0$$

or

$$\prod_{i=0}^{2^3-1} M_i = 0$$

This example illustrates a relationship that is true in general, which is

$$\prod_{i=0}^{2^n-1} M_i = 0 \tag{2.13}$$

Finally, we note from the truth table that

$$f(A, B, C) = \sum m(0, 2, 4, 6) = \prod M(1, 3, 5, 7)$$

and

$$\bar{f}(A, B, C) = \sum m(1, 3, 5, 7) = \prod M(0, 2, 4, 6)$$

2.2.3 Derivation of Canonical Forms

In the preceding examples, it was shown how canonical POS and SOP forms of a function can be translated directly to truth tables, and vice versa. If a function is expressed in a noncanonical form, it is often more convenient to utilize switching algebra to convert it to canonical POS or SOP form, without having to first derive the truth table.

The following theorem is frequently utilized in the expansion of switching expressions to canonical form.

Theorem 10.   Shannon's expansion theorem

(a) $f(x_1, x_2, \ldots, x_n) = x_1 \cdot f(1, x_2, \ldots, x_n) + \bar{x}_1 \cdot f(0, x_2, \ldots, x_n)$

(b) $f(x_1, x_2, \ldots, x_n) = [x_1 + f(0, x_2, \ldots, x_n)][\bar{x}_1 + f(1, x_2, \ldots, x_n)]$

The foundation for this theorem is Postulate 2 and Theorem 1. Since $x_1 = x_1 \cdot x_1 = x_1 \cdot 1$, any x_1 inside the function in part (a) of the theorem may be replaced by 1, and likewise $x_1 = x_1 + x_1 = x_1 + 0$, allowing any x_1 inside the function in part (b) of the theorem to be replaced by 0. Theorem 10 is useful in expanding functions or adding literals to product terms.

EXAMPLE 2.28

Convert the following switching function to canonical SOP form.

$$f(A, B, C) = AB + A\bar{C} + \bar{A}C$$

Let us systematically apply Theorem 10a to this function for the three variables A, B, and C. For variable A, Theorem 10a yields

$$f(A, B, C) = AB + A\bar{C} + \bar{A}C$$
$$= A \cdot f(1, B, C) + \bar{A} \cdot f(0, B, C)$$

$$= A(1 \cdot B + 1 \cdot \bar{C} + \bar{1} \cdot C) + \bar{A}(0 \cdot B + 0 \cdot \bar{C} + \bar{0} \cdot C)$$
$$= A(B + \bar{C}) + \bar{A}C$$

Continuing for variable B, we obtain

$$f(A, B, C) = A(B + \bar{C}) + \bar{A}C$$
$$= B[A(1 + \bar{C}) + \bar{A}C] + \bar{B}[A(0 + \bar{C}) + \bar{A}C]$$
$$= B[A + \bar{A}C] + \bar{B}[A\bar{C} + \bar{A}C]$$
$$= AB + \bar{A}BC + A\bar{B}\bar{C} + \bar{A}\bar{B}C$$

Finally, using variable C,

$$f(A, B, C) = AB + \bar{A}BC + A\bar{B}\bar{C} + \bar{A}\bar{B}C$$
$$= C[AB + \bar{A}B \cdot 1 + A\bar{B} \cdot \bar{1} + \bar{A}\bar{B} \cdot 1]$$
$$+ \bar{C}[AB + \bar{A}B \cdot 0 + A\bar{B} \cdot \bar{0} + \bar{A}\bar{B} \cdot 0]$$
$$= ABC + \bar{A}BC + \bar{A}\bar{B}C + AB\bar{C} + A\bar{B}\bar{C}$$

An alternative method for converting expressions to canonical SOP or POS form is to apply Theorem 6 to add literals to product or sum terms until minterms or maxterms are produced. The following examples illustrate this procedure.

EXAMPLE 2.29

Convert the following function to canonical SOP form:

$$f(A, B, C) = AB + A\bar{C} + \bar{A}C$$

Let us apply Theorem 6a to each of the three product terms of this expression.

$$AB = AB\bar{C} + ABC = m_6 + m_7$$
$$A\bar{C} = A\bar{C}\bar{B} + A\bar{C}B = A\bar{B}\bar{C} + AB\bar{C} = m_4 + m_6$$
$$\bar{A}C = \bar{A}C\bar{B} + \bar{A}CB = \bar{A}\bar{B}C + \bar{A}BC = m_1 + m_3$$

Therefore,

$$f(A, B, C) = AB + A\bar{C} + \bar{A}C$$
$$= (m_6 + m_7) + (m_4 + m_6) + (m_1 + m_3)$$
$$= \sum m(1, 3, 4, 6, 7)$$

EXAMPLE 2.30

Expand the following function to canonical POS form:

$$f(A, B, C) = A(A + \bar{C})$$

Theorem 6b can be applied as follows to produce maxterms.

$$A = (A + \bar{B})(A + B)$$
$$M_3 \leftarrow \quad = (A + \bar{B} + \bar{C})(A + \bar{B} + C)(A + B + \bar{C})(A + B + C)$$
$$= M_3 M_2 M_1 M_0$$
$$(A + \bar{C}) = (A + \bar{C} + \bar{B})(A + \bar{C} + B)$$
$$= (A + \bar{B} + \bar{C})(A + B + \bar{C})$$

$$= M_3 M_1$$

Therefore,

$$A(A + C) = (M_3 M_2 M_1 M_0)(M_3 M_1)$$
$$= \prod M(0, 1, 2, 3)$$

2.2.4 Incompletely Specified Functions

In the design of digital circuits, we often encounter cases in which the switching function is not completely specified. In other words, a function may be required to contain certain minterms and omit others, with the remaining minterms optional. In this case, the optional minterms may be included in the logic design if they help simplify the logic circuit, or otherwise omitted. A minterm that is optional is called a *don't-care minterm*. If we express a function in terms of its maxterms, the don't-care minterms are usually written in the corresponding maxterm form, in which case they would be called *don't-care maxterms*.

Don't-cares arise in two ways. First, certain input combinations might never be applied to a particular switching network; hence, since they never occur, their minterms may be used in any manner we choose. Such don't-care conditions arise quite naturally in many practical applications. For example, suppose a switching network has inputs $a_3 a_2 a_1 a_0$, which represent binary coded decimal (BCD) digits as defined in Table 2.6. (Recall that BCD codes were discussed in Chapter 1.) Only 10 minterms, $m_0 \ldots m_9$, can occur, corresponding to the 10 decimal digits. The remaining six minterms, $m_{10} \ldots m_{15}$, cannot occur and are therefore don't-cares in every situation. Consequently, these terms may either be included or omitted as desired in switching expressions for any function $f(a_3 a_2 a_1 a_0)$ of these inputs.

TABLE 2.6   BINARY CODED DECIMAL (BCD) CODES

Decimal Digit	BCD Code $a_3 a_2 a_1 a_0$	Decimal Digit	BCD Code $a_3 a_2 a_1 a_0$
0	0000	5	0101
1	0001	6	0110
2	0010	7	0111
3	0011	8	1000
4	0100	9	1001

Don't-care conditions also arise where all input combinations do occur for a given network, but the output is required to be 1 or 0 only for certain combinations.

When writing switching expressions, the don't-care minterms will be labeled d_i instead of m_i, and don't-care maxterms as D_i instead of M_i, as shown in the following example.

EXAMPLE 2.31

Suppose that we are given a function $f(A, B, C)$ that has minterms m_0, m_3, and m_7 and don't-care conditions d_4 and d_5. We wish to express the function and its complement in both minterm and maxterm form and then reduce the function to its simplest form.

The minterm list form for this function is

$$f(A, B, C) = \sum m(0, 3, 7) + d(4, 5)$$

and the maxterm list is

$$f(A, B, C) = \prod M(1, 2, 6) \cdot D(4, 5)$$

Note that the don't-care maxterms D_i are simply the don't-care minterms since the terms may be either 1 or 0. Hence,

$$\bar{f}(A, B, C) = \sum m(1, 2, 6) + d(4, 5)$$
$$= \prod M(0, 3, 7) \cdot D(4, 5)$$

To simplify the expression $f(A, B, C)$, we list the terms as

$$f(A, B, C) = \bar{A}\bar{B}\bar{C} + \bar{A}BC + ABC + d(A\bar{B}\bar{C} + A\bar{B}C)$$

Note that the second and third terms differ in a single literal and hence may be grouped to produce

$$f(A, B, C) = \bar{A}\bar{B}\bar{C} + BC + d(A\bar{B}\bar{C} + A\bar{B}C)$$

Without the use of the don't-cares, no further simplification of the function is possible. However, recall that the don't-cares by definition can be either zero or one. Therefore, we can either use them or omit them, depending on whether they do or do not aid in the simplification. If in the preceding function we choose to use d_4 and omit d_5, the function becomes

$$f(A, B, C) = \bar{A}\bar{B}\bar{C} + BC + A\bar{B}\bar{C}$$
$$= \bar{B}\bar{C} + BC$$

which is the simplest form of the function. A similar analysis could be performed with the function in maxterm form.

2.3 Switching Circuits

Digital logic circuits, or *switching circuits* as they are often called, are composed of serial and parallel combinations of switching elements called *gates* or are implemented via programmable logic arrays or similar devices. From a mathematical standpoint, gates are simply open or closed signal paths. From a technological standpoint, they are high-speed electronic switching devices capable of turning on or off in a few nanoseconds. In this chapter we examine the use of gates to build logic circuits that realize switching functions. Design with programmable logic arrays will be discussed in Chapter 6.

2.3.1 Electronic Logic Gates

In digital logic circuits, switching variables may be associated with the input conditions on the gates, that is, high or low voltage levels applied to the gate inputs. Switching functions may correspond to the output of a gate or system of gates, represented by a high or low voltage level on the output.

Electrical Signals and Logic Values

Truth tables defining the operation of logic gate circuits are presented in data books in terms of high (H) and low (L) voltages. The designer may use these voltage levels to represent the logic values 0 and 1 in different ways. The *positive logic* convention uses a high voltage level (H) to represent logic 1 and a low voltage (L) to represent logic 0. The *negative logic* convention uses L to represent logic 1 and H to represent logic 0. In a *mixed-logic* system, positive logic is used for some signals and negative logic for others.

A signal that is set to logic 1 is said to be *asserted*, or *active*, or *true*. An *active-high* signal is asserted when it is high (positive logic), where as an *active-low* signal is asserted when it is low (negative logic). If not asserted, that is, if set to logic 0, a signal is said to be *deasserted*, or *negated*, or *false*. The term *polarity* is used to refer to the active-high or active-low nature of a logic signal.

When representing signals by logic variables, active-low signal names are written in complemented form (for example, $\bar{a}$, a', $a*$); active-high signal names are written in uncomplemented form (a). Each signal name should be selected so that the name suggests the purpose of that signal. For example, the signal name RUN suggests a signal that is asserted (high) to make a piece of equipment start running. If the signal is active low, the signal name $\overline{RUN}$ should be used to indicate that the equipment will be made to run when the signal is asserted low. In this text we will primarily use active-high signals. However, since many commercial circuit modules have active-low inputs and/or outputs, a number of examples will also be presented in which active-low signals are used.

Gate Symbols

Each gate is represented in a logic circuit diagram by a representative symbol, including inputs and outputs. The number of inputs to a gate is referred to as its *fan-in*. Standard circuit modules are available that contain AND, OR, NAND, and NOR gates with a limited number of fan-in options, usually gates with two, three, four, or eight inputs. Programmable logic devices and custom circuits typically provide a wider range of fan-in options, allowing each circuit to be matched more closely to the logic expression being realized.

The shape of the symbol body represents the basic logic function, or Boolean operator, realized by the gate (OR, AND, NOT, or other). *Bubbles* drawn at the inputs and/or outputs of a logic symbol indicate active-low signals. A bubble on an input indicates that the input is active low, that is, it must be asserted low to produce a logic 1 as an input to the function. The absence of a bubble indicates an active-high input; the input is asserted by setting it to logic 1. Likewise, a bubble on an output indicates an active-low output, which implies that if the function evaluates to 1 a logic 0 is produced on the output.

To understand logic circuits, we must master completely the operators shown in Fig. 2.4. Both sets of symbols illustrated are defined in IEEE/ANSI Standard 91-1984 [7]. Each of these operators, or *gates*, will be examined in the following section. In this text, when drawing circuits composed of discrete gates, we will primarily use symbol set 1, which identifies logic functions via distinctive symbol shapes. Symbol set 2 is used in later chapters for describing larger functional modules.

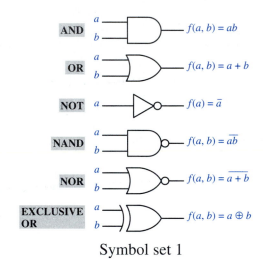

Symbol set 1

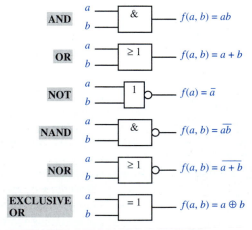

Symbol set 2 (ANSI/IEEE Standard 91-1984)

Figure 2.4 Symbols for switching devices.

Commercially available circuit modules containing specific configurations of discrete logic gates are presented in Fig. 2.5. These modules are used in building functioning circuits for practical applications. Groups of individual gates implemented in one logic module are called small scale integration (SSI) modules and contain between 10 and 100 transistors to build the total module. The modules described are available in dual-in-line packages (DIPs) with pin

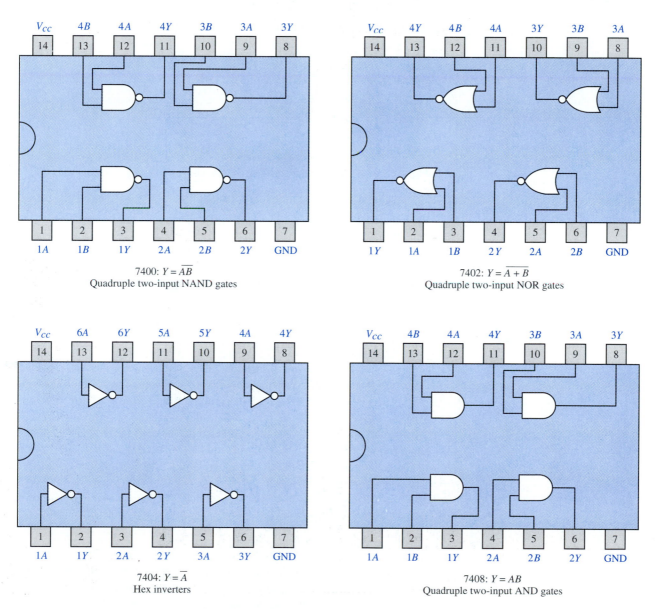

7400: $Y = \overline{AB}$
Quadruple two-input NAND gates

7402: $Y = \overline{A + B}$
Quadruple two-input NOR gates

7404: $Y = \overline{A}$
Hex inverters

7408: $Y = AB$
Quadruple two-input AND gates

Figure 2.5   Standard TTL small scale integrated circuit devices (top view).

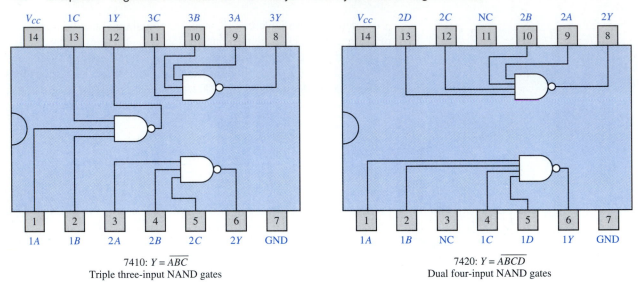

7410: $Y = \overline{ABC}$
Triple three-input NAND gates

7420: $Y = \overline{ABCD}$
Dual four-input NAND gates

Figure 2.5   Figure 2.5 standard TTL SSI devices (continued).

assignments as indicated in Fig. 2.5. Entire functions are often realized with a single, custom, very large scale integrated (VLSI) circuit device. In such cases, design is done with individual gates or with functional modules containing predefined patterns of gates. Modular design will be discussed in Chapter 4.

2.3.2 Basic Functional Components

AND

The truth table for the AND operator may be determined from switching algebra. The result is given in Fig. 2.6a. This truth table for the AND operator illustrates that its output is 1 if and only if both of its inputs are 1 simultaneously.

The electronic AND gate is designed to realize the AND operator in a positive logic system. The truth table of an AND gate is given in Fig. 2.6b, where L represents a low voltage and H represents a high voltage. Note that the AND operator of Fig. 2.6a is realized by substituting 0 for L and 1 for H in the AND gate truth table in Fig. 2.6b. The standard symbols for the AND gate are shown in Figs. 2.6c and d. In Fig. 2.6d, note that the standard IEEE block symbol uses an ampersand (&) to indicate that the AND operation is performed within the block.

OR

The OR function is identical to the OR operator of switching algebra. Its truth table is given in Fig. 2.7a. Note that the output is 0 if and only if both of the inputs are 0, and 1 if any one or more of the inputs are 1. The corresponding

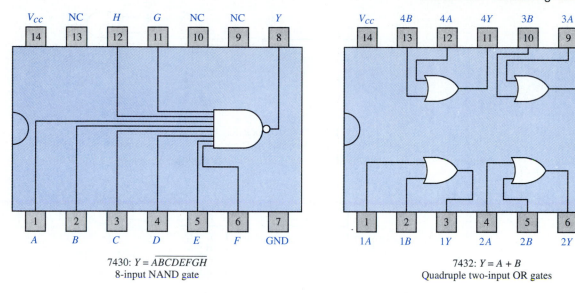

7430: $Y = \overline{ABCDEFGH}$
8-input NAND gate

7432: $Y = A + B$
Quadruple two-input OR gates

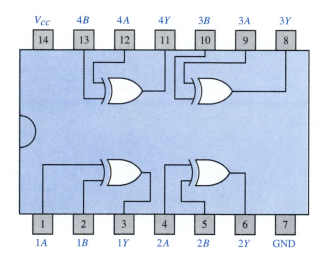

7486: $Y = A \oplus B$
Quadruple two-input exclusive-OR gates

Figure 2.5   Figure 2.5 standard TTL SSI devices (continued).

truth table of an electronic OR gate is given in Fig. 2.7b. It should be noted that the OR gate realizes the OR operator in a positive logic system. The standard OR gate symbols are shown in Figs. 2.7c and d. In Fig. 2.7d, note that the IEEE block symbol contains the designation ≥ 1. This means that the mathematical sum of the values of the input variables a and b determines the output of the

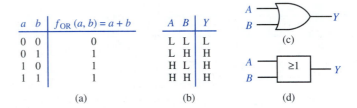

a b	$f_{AND}(a, b) = ab$
0 0	0
0 1	0
1 0	0
1 1	1

(a)

A	B	Y
L	L	L
L	H	L
H	L	L
H	H	H

(b)

(c)

(d)

Figure 2.6 The AND logic function and AND gate. **(a)** AND logic function. **(b)** Electronic AND gate. **(c)** Standard symbol. **(d)** IEEE block symbol.

a b	$f_{OR}(a, b) = a + b$
0 0	0
0 1	1
1 0	1
1 1	1

(a)

A	B	Y
L	L	L
L	H	H
H	L	H
H	H	H

(b)

(c)

(d)

Figure 2.7 The OR logic function and OR gate. **(a)** OR logic function. **(b)** Electronic OR gate. **(c)** Standard symbol. **(d)** IEEE block symbol.

gate. The output is 1 when the sum of a and b is greater than or equal to 1, as illustrated in the following table:

a b	$\text{sum}(a, b)$	$\text{sum}(a, b) \geq 1$?	$f_{OR}(a, b) = a + b$
0 0	0	False	0
0 1	1	True	1
1 0	1	True	1
1 1	2	True	1

NOT

A NOT gate (Fig. 2.8), or *inverter*, always has exactly one input and is used to implement the complement concept in switching algebra. Any variable has its true (uncomplemented) and false (complemented) forms, a and $\bar{a}$, respectively. A NOT gate is used to form one from the other.

The standard symbols for the NOT gate, shown in Figs. 2.8c and d, include a bubble drawn at the output of the gate. As described earlier, a bubble at the output of any logic circuit element indicates that an internal logic 1 produces an external logic 0, and likewise that an internal logic 0 produces an external logic 1. No other logic function is performed within a NOT gate. Hence, the logic value on the output of a NOT gate is simply the complement of the logic value on its input.

$$A \longrightarrow\!\!\!\triangleright\!\!\circ\!\!\longrightarrow Y$$

(c)

a	$f_{\text{NOT}}(a) = \bar{a}$
0	1
1	0

(a)

A	Y
L	H
H	L

(b)

$$A \longrightarrow\boxed{1}\!\circ\!\longrightarrow Y$$

(d)

Figure 2.8 The NOT logic function and NOT gate. **(a)** NOT logic function. **(b)** Electronic NOT gate. **(c)** Standard symbol. **(d)** IEEE block symbol.

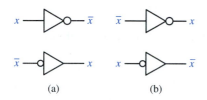

Figure 2.9 Matching signal polarity to NOT gate inputs/outputs. **(a)** Preferred usage. **(b)** Improper usage.

A NOT gate can be thought of as changing the polarity of a signal from active high to active low, or vice versa. Consequently, the NOT gate symbol can be drawn with the bubble at either the input or the output. By convention, the bubble is drawn at the gate input when the input signal is active low and at the gate output if the signal being driven is active low. Figure 2.9a shows the preferred usage of the NOT gate symbol, matching the bubbles to the active-low signal, $\bar{x}$. The diagrams in Fig. 2.9b, although not incorrect, are not considered proper usage.

Positive Versus Negative Logic

The AND and OR logic functions are realized by AND and OR gates, respectively, if the positive logic convention is used for all gate inputs and outputs, that is, if the signals connected to the gate inputs and outputs are all active high. When the signals connected to the gate inputs and output are all active low, the roles of these gates are reversed.

Recall that in the negative logic convention 1 is represented by a low voltage and 0 by a high voltage. Therefore, the function realized by an AND gate in a negative logic system can be derived by substituting 0 for H and 1 for L in the AND gate truth table of Fig. 2.6b. The resulting table, presented in Fig. 2.10a, is identical to the OR operator truth table of Fig. 2.7a. Thus, an AND gate with active-low inputs and output can be viewed as realizing the logical OR function.

This may be verified with switching algebra by applying involution (Theorem 3) and DeMorgan's theorem (Theorem 8) to the expression for the logical AND function as follows:

$$
\begin{aligned}
y &= a \cdot b \\
&= \overline{\overline{a \cdot b}} \\
&= \overline{\bar{a} + \bar{b}} \\
&= \bar{f}_{OR}(\bar{a}, \bar{b}) \quad\quad (2.14)
\end{aligned}
$$

Equation 2.14 indicates that an AND gate symbol can be drawn as an OR function with active-low inputs and output, as shown in Fig. 2.10b. While this might seem awkward at first, this symbol better illustrates the function realized

A	B	Y
1	1	1
1	0	1
0	1	1
0	0	0

(a)   (b)   (c)

(d)

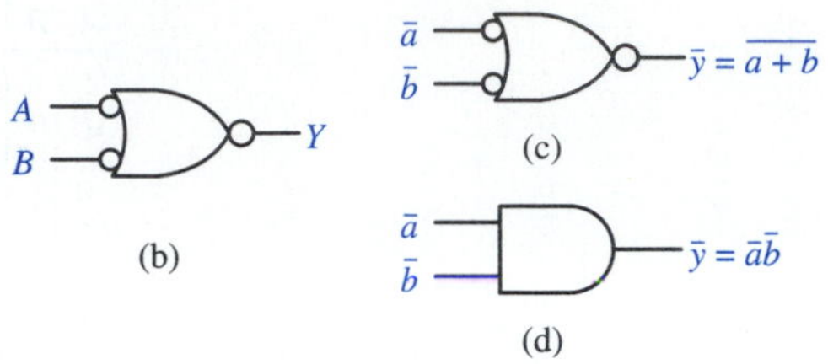

Figure 2.10 AND gate usage in a negative logic system.
(a) AND gate truth table ($L = 1$, $H = 0$). (b) Alternative AND gate symbol (negative logic). (c) Preferred usage. (d) Improper usage.

by an AND gate in a negative logic system than does the standard symbol of Fig. 2.6c.

For example, consider the gate shown in Fig. 2.10c. The gate inputs are connected to active-low signals $\bar{a}$ and $\bar{b}$ and the output to active-low signal $\bar{y}$. The logic expression for output $\bar{y}$ is formed by complementing each of the inputs, taking the OR, and then complementing the result, as follows:

$$\bar{y} = \overline{(\bar{a}) + (\bar{b})}$$
$$= \overline{a + b}$$
$$= \bar{f}_{OR}(a, b) \qquad (2.15)$$

Therefore, $\bar{y}$ is asserted (low) whenever one or both of the inputs are asserted. Note that the alternative form, shown in Fig. 2.10d, is not incorrect but is more difficult to analyze, and should therefore be avoided when negative logic is being used.

In a similar manner, an OR gate realizes the logical AND operator when its inputs and output are active-low signals. The function realized by an OR gate in a negative logic system can be derived by substituting 0 for H and 1 for L in the OR gate truth table of Fig. 2.7b. The resulting table, presented in Fig. 2.11a, is identical to the AND operator truth table of Fig. 2.6a. Therefore, an OR gate with active-low inputs and output can be viewed as realizing the logical AND function. This may be verified with switching algebra, as was done earlier for the AND gate.

$$y = a + b$$
$$= \overline{\overline{a + b}}$$
$$= \overline{\bar{a} \cdot \bar{b}}$$
$$= \bar{f}_{AND}(\bar{a}, \bar{b}) \qquad (2.16)$$

Equation 2.16 indicates that an OR gate symbol can be drawn as an AND function with active-low inputs and output, as shown in Fig. 2.11b. This alternative symbol better illustrates the function realized by an OR gate in a negative logic system than does the standard symbol of Fig. 2.7c.

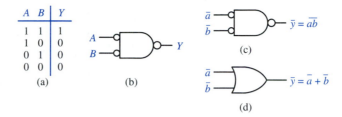

Figure 2.11 OR gate usage in a negative logic system. **(a)** OR gate truth table ($L = 1$, $H = 0$). **(b)** Alternate OR gate symbol (negative logic). **(c)** Preferred usage. **(d)** Improper usage.

For example, consider the gate in Fig. 2.11c. Writing the logic expression for active-low output $\bar{y}$ in terms of active-low inputs $\bar{a}$ and $\bar{b}$ gives

$$\bar{y} = \overline{(\bar{a}) \cdot (\bar{b})}$$
$$= \overline{a \cdot b}$$
$$= \bar{f}_{AND}(a, b) \tag{2.17}$$

Therefore, $\bar{y}$ is asserted only when both $\bar{a}$ and $\bar{b}$ are simultaneously asserted. This operation is more difficult to see if the gate is drawn as in Fig. 2.11d. Therefore, the form of Fig. 2.11c should always be used with negative logic.

The following example demonstrates the use of AND and OR gates with devices having active-low inputs and outputs.

EXAMPLE 2.32

Design a logic circuit to implement a building smoke alarm system.

The building is to be protected by a smoke alarm system that comprises two smoke detectors, a sprinkler, and an automatic telephone dialer that calls the fire department. The sprinkler is to be activated if either smoke detector detects smoke, and the fire department should be called whenever both smoke detectors detect smoke. The smoke detectors have active-low outputs, $\overline{D1}$ and $\overline{D2}$, that are asserted whenever they detect smoke particles. The sprinkler has an active-low input $\overline{SPK}$ that must be asserted to turn the sprinkler on. Likewise, the telephone dialer initiates a call when its active-low input signal $\overline{DIAL}$ is asserted.

The logic equations for the sprinkler and telephone dialer are derived by determining the conditions that should activate each device. The sprinkler is to be activated whenever either smoke detector output is asserted. The desired operation is $SPK = D1 + D2$. Since these signals are only available in active-low form, we write

$$\overline{SPK} = \overline{D1 + D2} \tag{2.18}$$

Likewise, the dialer is to be activated whenever both smoke detector outputs are asserted; thus, $DIAL = D1 \cdot D2$. Since these signals are only available in active-low form, we write

$$\overline{DIAL} = \overline{D1 \cdot D2} \tag{2.19}$$

Equations 2.18 and 2.19 are realized by the logic diagram in Fig. 2.12. Note that gate $G1$ is an AND gate used to realize the OR function of Eq. 2.18, while $G2$ is an OR gate used to realize the AND function of Eq. 2.19.

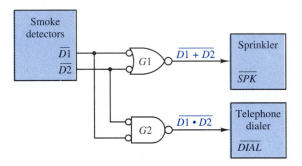

Figure 2.12   Smoke alarm system, illustrating negative logic.

AND and OR gates are used whenever the inputs and outputs have the same polarity. The next two gates to be presented, the NAND and NOR gates, are used in mixed-logic systems, that is, when the inputs are active high and the outputs active low, or vice versa.

NAND

The NAND gate is a combination of an AND gate followed by a NOT gate. The NAND function is defined as

$$f_{NAND}(a, b) = \overline{ab} \tag{2.20}$$

From Eq. 2.20, it can be seen that the NAND gate realizes the logical AND function when its input signals are active high and its output active low. The truth tables for the NAND function and NAND gate are derived by complementing the output columns of the AND function and AND gate truth tables, respectively. The resulting tables are given in Figs. 2.13a and b. The key to understanding the NAND function is to notice that the output is 0 if and only if its inputs are simultaneously 1.

The standard NAND gate symbols are shown in Figs. 2.13c, d, and e. The bubble on the output terminal in Fig. 2.13c indicates the NOT operation, differentiating it from the AND gate. The form in Fig. 2.13d is derived by applying DeMorgan's theorem to the NAND function switching expression of Eq. 2.20:

$$f_{\text{NAND}}(a, b) = \overline{ab} = \bar{a} + \bar{b} \tag{2.21}$$

a b	$f_{NAND}(a, b) = \overline{ab}$
0 0	1
0 1	1
1 0	1
1 1	0

(a)

A B	Y
L L	H
L H	H
H L	H
H H	L

(b)

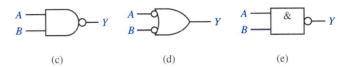

(c)   (d)   (e)

Figure 2.13   The NAND logic function and NAND gate. **(a)** NAND logic function. **(b)** Electronic NAND gate. **(c)** Standard symbol. **(d)** Alternate symbol. **(e)** IEEE block symbol.

Thus, a NAND gate is used to realize the OR function when the input signals are active low and the output active high. As discussed for the NOT gate earlier, the bubbles on the NAND gate symbol should always be matched to the active-low signals. Thus the symbol in Fig. 2.13c is used when the output signal is active low, and the symbol in Fig. 2.13d is used when the input signals are active low. Proper usage and improper usage of the two NAND gate symbols are illustrated in Figs. 2.14a and b, respectively.

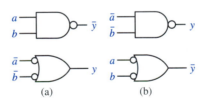

Figure 2.14   Matching signal polarity to NAND gate inputs/outputs. **(a)** Preferred usage. **(b)** Improper usage.

Several other interesting properties of the NAND gate are shown next:

$$f_{NAND}(a, a) = \overline{a \cdot a} = \overline{a} \qquad = f_{NOT}(a)$$
$$\overline{f_{NAND}(a, b)} = \overline{\overline{a \cdot b}} = a \cdot b = f_{AND}(a, b)$$
$$f_{NAND}(\overline{a}, \overline{b}) = \overline{\overline{a} \cdot \overline{b}} = a + b = f_{OR}(a, b)$$

Therefore, a NAND gate with both of its inputs driven by the same signal is equivalent to a NOT gate, a NAND gate whose output is complemented is equivalent to an AND gate, and a NAND gate with complemented inputs acts like an OR gate.

Hence NAND gates may be used to implement all three of the elementary operators (AND, OR, and NOT), as shown in Figure 2.15. Consequently, any switching function can be constructed using only NAND gates. Gates that have this property are called *primitive* or *functionally complete*.

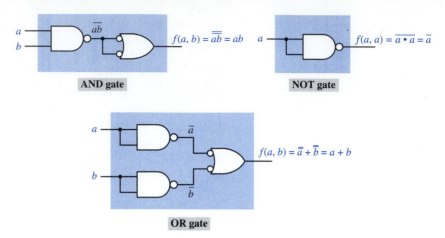

Figure 2.15   AND, OR, and NOT gates constructed exclusively from NAND gates.

NOR

The NOR gate is a combination of an OR gate followed by a NOT gate, representing the function

$$f_{NOR}(a, b) = \overline{a + b} \qquad (2.22)$$

The NOR gate realizes the logical OR function with active-high inputs and an active-low output. Hence, the truth table for the NOR function and NOR gate are derived by complementing the output columns of the OR function and OR gate truth tables, respectively. The resulting tables are given in Figs. 2.16a and b. The key to remembering the function of a NOR gate is the first row of the truth table; the output of a NOR gate is 1 if and only if both inputs are simultaneously 0.

a	b	$f_{NOR}(a, b) = \overline{a + b}$
0	0	1
0	1	0
1	0	0
1	1	0

(a)

A	B	Y
L	L	H
L	H	L
H	L	L
H	H	L

(b)

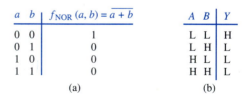

(c)   (d)   (e)

Figure 2.16   The NOR logic function and NOR gate. **(a)** NOR logic function. **(b)** Electronic NOR gate. **(c)** Standard symbol. **(d)** Alternate symbol. **(e)** IEEE block symbol.

The standard NOR gate symbols are given in Figs. 2.16c, d, and e. The bubble on the output terminal indicates the NOT operation, differentiating it from the OR gate. The form in Fig. 2.16d is derived by applying DeMorgan's theorem to the definition of the NOR function defined in Eq. 2.22:

$$f_{NOR}(a, b) = \overline{a + b} = \bar{a} \cdot \bar{b} \qquad (2.23)$$

Thus, a NOR gate may be used to realize the AND function with active-low inputs and an active-high output. As discussed for the NAND gate earlier, the symbol in Fig. 2.16c is used when the output signal is active low, and the symbol in Fig. 2.16d is used when the input signals are active low. Proper usage and improper usage of the NOR gate symbols are illustrated in Figs. 2.17a and b, respectively.

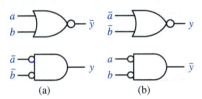

Figure 2.17   Matching signal polarity to NOR gate inputs/outputs. **(a)** Preferred usage. **(b)** Improper usage.

As is the case for NAND gates, NOR gates are also primitive elements in that they may be used to generate AND, OR, and NOT operations, as shown next.

$$f_{NOR}(a, a) = \overline{a + a} = \bar{a} \qquad\quad = f_{NOT}(a)$$
$$f_{NOR}(a, b) = \overline{\overline{a + b}} = a + b = f_{OR}(a, b)$$
$$f_{NOR}(\bar{a}, \bar{b}) = \overline{\bar{a} + \bar{b}} = a \cdot b \quad = f_{AND}(a, b)$$

Figure 2.18 presents these three operations in symbolic form.

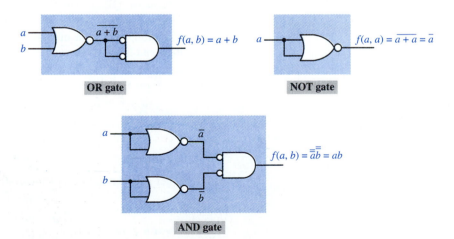

Figure 2.18   AND, OR, and NOT gates constructed exclusively from NOR gates.

Since both are functionally complete, NAND and NOR gates are valuable in that entire designs can be implemented with a single element type. It is easier to build an integrated circuit chip using all NAND gates (or all NOR gates), rather than combining AND, OR, and NOT gates. In addition, electronic NAND and NOR gate circuits are typically faster and easier to fabricate than equivalent AND and OR gates and are thus more cost effective to use.

Exclusive-OR (XOR)

The Exclusive-OR (or simply XOR) operation is defined functionally as

$$f_{XOR}(a, b) = a \oplus b = a\bar{b} + \bar{a}b \qquad (2.24)$$

The truth table derived from Eq. 2.24 is presented in Fig. 2.19a. The corresponding XOR gate truth table is given in Fig. 2.19b, and the standard logic symbols in Figs. 2.19c and d.

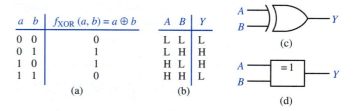

a	b	$f_{XOR}(a, b) = a \oplus b$
0	0	0
0	1	1
1	0	1
1	1	0

(a)

A	B	Y
L	L	L
L	H	H
H	L	H
H	H	L

(b)

(c)

(d)

Figure 2.19   The EXCLUSIVE-OR (XOR) logic function and XOR gate. **(a)** XOR logic function. **(b)** Electronic XOR gate. **(c)** Standard symbol. **(d)** IEEE block symbol.

The output of the Exclusive-OR gate is 1 if and only if its inputs are not simultaneously equal. In other words, when the inputs are different, the output is 1. The exclusive-OR is so named because of its relation to the OR gate. The two differ in the input combination $a = 1, b = 1$. The exclusive-OR excludes this combination, giving an output of 0, whereas the OR gate includes this combination and is therefore synonymously called the inclusive-OR.

The product of sums form for the exclusive-OR is derived from the sum of products form as follows:

$$a \oplus b = \bar{a}b + a\bar{b}$$
$$= \bar{a}a + \bar{a}b + a\bar{b} + b\bar{b} \qquad [\text{P2(a), P6(b)}]$$
$$= \bar{a}(a + b) + \bar{b}(a + b) \qquad [\text{P5(b)}]$$
$$a \oplus b = (\bar{a} + \bar{b})(a + b) \qquad [\text{P5(b)}]$$

Several other useful relationships involving the exclusive-OR are as follows:

$$a \oplus a = 0 \qquad (2.25)$$
$$a \oplus \bar{a} = 1 \qquad (2.26)$$
$$a \oplus 0 = a \qquad (2.27)$$
$$a \oplus 1 = \bar{a} \qquad (2.28)$$

$$\bar{a} \oplus \bar{b} = a \oplus b \tag{2.29}$$

$$a \oplus b = b \oplus a \tag{2.30}$$

$$a \oplus (b \oplus c) = (a \oplus b) \oplus c \tag{2.31}$$

The reader may verify that these relations are valid by constructing truth tables for them.

The IEEE standard block symbol for the exclusive-OR gate indicates that the output will be asserted when the mathematical sum of the inputs is equal to 1:

$a\ b$	$\text{sum}(a, b)$	$\text{sum}(a, b) = 1?$	$f(a, b) = a \oplus b$
0 0	0	False	0
0 1	1	True	1
1 0	1	True	1
1 1	2	False	0

From this table it can be seen that the output of an exclusive-OR gate is the modulo-2 sum of its inputs. Therefore, exclusive-OR gates are often used in the design of arithmetic circuits that perform binary addition and subtraction. This will be discussed in more detail in Chapter 4.

Exclusive-NOR (XNOR)

A common function that is related to the exclusive-OR is the coincidence operation, or exclusive-NOR (XNOR), which is merely the complement of the exclusive-OR. This function is defined as follows:

$$f_{\text{XNOR}}(a, b) = \overline{a \oplus b} = a \odot b \tag{2.32}$$

The XNOR gate truth tables and logic symbols are presented in Fig. 2.20. The

$a\ b$	$f_{\text{XNOR}}(a, b) = a \odot b$		$A\ B$	Y
0 0	1		L L	H
0 1	0		L H	L
1 0	0		H L	L
1 1	1		H H	H
	(a)		(b)	

(c)

(d)

Figure 2.20 The EXCLUSIVE-NOR (XNOR) logic function and XNOR gate. **(a)** XNOR logic function. **(b)** Electronic XNOR gate. **(c)** Standard symbol. **(d)** IEEE block symbol.

sum of products and product of sums forms of the coincidence operation are derived as follows:

$$a \odot b = \overline{a \oplus b}$$
$$= \bar{a}b + a\bar{b} \qquad \text{[P2]}$$
$$= \overline{\bar{a}b} \cdot \overline{a\bar{b}} \qquad \text{[T8(a)]}$$

$$= (a + \bar{b})(\bar{a} + b) \qquad \text{[T8(b)]}$$
$$= a\bar{a} + ab + \bar{a}\bar{b} + b\bar{b} \qquad \text{[P5(b)]}$$
$$= ab + \bar{a}\bar{b} \qquad \text{[P6(b), P2(a)]}$$

It can also be easily verified that

$$a \oplus \bar{b} = a \odot b \qquad (2.33)$$

2.4 Analysis of Combinational Circuits

Digital circuits are designed by transforming a word description of a function into a set of switching equations and then realizing the equations with gates, programmable logic devices (PLDs), or other logic elements. Digital circuit analysis is the inverse problem. Beginning with a hardware realization of a digital circuit, a description of the circuit is derived in the form of switching expressions, truth tables, timing diagrams, or other behavioral descriptions. Analysis is used to determine the behavior of a logic circuit, to verify that the behavior of a circuit matches its specifications, or to assist in converting the circuit to a different form, either to reduce the number of gates or to realize it with different elements.

This chapter will present the analysis and synthesis of digital circuits, including the design and use of building block modules that are used to implement larger designs. A number of more complex medium scale integration (MSI) modules will be discussed in Chapter 4. These modules are higher-level devices containing 100 to 1000 transistors. Chapter 5 will examine the use of programmable logic devices to develop digital circuit designs.

2.4.1 Algebraic Method

Logic networks may be built by interconnecting the gates presented in the previous section. These circuits are used to perform specific functions inside a digital computing system. Any given switching network may be completely represented by a switching expression or function, and, thus, all the power of switching algebra may be applied to manipulate the switching function into any form we desire.

An important point to remember is that all switching expressions may be written in terms of AND, OR, and NOT operations. Hence, any switching network may be constructed using only primitive elements such as NAND gates (or NOR gates), as shown in Fig. 2.15 (or Fig. 2.18).

EXAMPLE 2.33

Find a simplified switching expression and logic network for the logic circuit in Fig. 2.21a.

We proceed by writing a switching expression for the output of each gate.

$$P_1 = \overline{ab}$$
$$P_2 = \overline{\bar{a} + c}$$

$$P_3 = b \oplus \bar{c}$$

$$P_4 = P_1 \cdot P_2 = \overline{ab}\ \overline{(\bar{a} + c)}$$

The output is

$$f(a, b, c) = \overline{P_3 + P_4}$$

$$= \overline{(b \oplus \bar{c}) + \overline{ab}\ \overline{(\bar{a} + c)}}$$

To analyze this function, we may convert it to a simpler form using switching algebra:

$$\bar{f}(a, b, c) = (b \oplus \bar{c}) + \overline{ab}\ \overline{\bar{a} + c}$$

$$= bc + \bar{b}\bar{c} + \overline{ab}\ \overline{\bar{a}} + c \qquad \text{[Eq. 2.24]}$$

$$= bc + \bar{b}\bar{c} + (\bar{a} + \bar{b})a\bar{c} \qquad \text{[T8]}$$

$$= bc + \bar{b}\bar{c} + a\bar{b}\bar{c} \qquad \text{[T5(b)]}$$

$$= bc + \bar{b}\bar{c} \qquad \text{[T4(a)]}$$

$$\bar{f}(a, b, c) = b \odot c \qquad \text{[Eq. 2.32]}$$

Therefore, from Eq. 2.32,

$$f(a, b, c) = \overline{b \odot c} = b \oplus c$$

This function has been reduced to a single exclusive-OR gate, which is shown in Fig. 2.21b. Both switching networks shown in Fig. 2.21 have the same truth

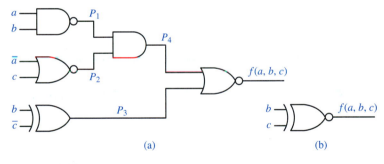

(a)   (b)

Figure 2.21   Equivalent switching networks.

table and are therefore equivalent. It is obvious that the one in Figure 2.21b is more desirable since it is less complex.

EXAMPLE 2.34

Find a simplified switching expression and circuit for the network of Fig. 2.22.

The logic expression for each gate output is shown on the logic diagram of Fig. 2.22. From these, we derive the output expression as

$$f(a, b, c)$$

$$= \overline{\overline{(a \oplus b)(b \oplus c)} \cdot \overline{(\bar{a} + \bar{b} + \overline{a + c})}}$$

$$= \overline{\overline{(a \oplus b)(b \oplus c)}} + \bar{a} + \bar{b} + \overline{a + c} \qquad \text{[T8(b)]}$$

$$= (a \oplus b)(b \oplus c) + (\bar{a} + \bar{b})(a + c) \qquad \text{[T8(a)]}$$
$$= (a\bar{b} + \bar{a}b)(b\bar{c} + \bar{b}c) + (\bar{a} + \bar{b})(a + c) \qquad \text{[Eq. 2.24]}$$
$$= a\bar{b}b\bar{c} + a\bar{b}\bar{b}c + \bar{a}bb\bar{c} + \bar{a}b\bar{b}c + \bar{a}a + \bar{a}c + a\bar{b} + \bar{b}c \qquad \text{[P5(b)]}$$
$$= a\bar{b}c + \bar{a}b\bar{c} + \bar{a}c + a\bar{b} + \bar{b}c \qquad \text{[P6(b),T4(a)]}$$
$$= \bar{a}b\bar{c} + \bar{a}c + a\bar{b} + \bar{b}c \qquad \text{[T4(a)]}$$
$$= \bar{a}b\bar{c} + \bar{a}c + a\bar{b} \qquad \text{[T9(a)]}$$
$$= \bar{a}b + \bar{a}c + a\bar{b} \qquad \text{[T7(a)]}$$
$$= \bar{a}c + a \oplus b \qquad \text{[Eq. 2.24]}$$

Notice that this is the form of the switching network in Fig. 2.22b.

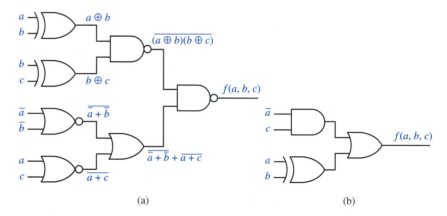

(a)   (b)

Figure 2.22 Equivalent switching networks.

Truth Table Method

We previously derived the truth table for a function from a switching expression by evaluating the expression one part at a time. The same approach may be taken with logic diagrams, deriving the truth table one gate at a time.

The truth table for the function derived in the last example may be found using the switching algebra technique previously described:

abc	$\bar{a}c$	$a \oplus b$	$f(a, b, c)$
0 0 0	0	0	0
0 0 1	1	0	1
0 1 0	0	1	1
0 1 1	1	1	1
1 0 0	0	1	1
1 0 1	0	1	1
1 1 0	0	0	0
1 1 1	0	0	0

Column $\bar{a}c$ is 1 whenever $\bar{a} = 1$ and $c = 1$ or whenever $a = 0$ and $c = 1$. Column $a \oplus b$ is 1 whenever $a \neq b$. These two columns are ORed to create $f(a, b, c)$; therefore, $f(a, b, c)$ is 0 whenever both $\bar{a}c$ and $a \oplus b$ are 0.

In this section we have taken a given switching network, analyzed it by writing down the switching function, simplified it using switching algebra, and obtained an equivalent, but less complicated network.

2.4.2 Analysis of Timing Diagrams

Thus far, we have analyzed logic circuit diagrams by deriving switching expressions and/or truth tables of the logic functions realized by the circuits. Another method of analysis is to apply a sequence of values to the inputs of a circuit over a period of time, either experimentally or with a logic simulation program, and to observe the relationship between the inputs and the corresponding sequence of outputs in the form of a timing diagram. From this timing diagram, we can derive the logic function realized by the circuit and study the effects of gate propagation delays on circuit operation.

Timing Diagrams

A *timing diagram* is a graphical representation of input and output signal relationships in a switching network, as might be seen on the display of an oscilloscope or logic analyzer or in a logic simulation program. Often, intermediate signals are also illustrated. In addition, timing diagrams may show propagation delays introduced by the switching devices as the signals propagate through the network. A properly chosen timing diagram can depict all the information contained in the truth table, as shown in the following example.

EXAMPLE 2.35

The circuit of Fig. 2.23a is stimulated with a sequence of inputs, producing the timing diagram of Fig. 2.23b. In this example, a 1 is represented by a high signal and a 0 by a low signal. Let us determine the truth table and minterm lists for the two functions $f_\alpha(A, B, C)$ and $f_\beta(A, B, C)$ realized by this circuit.

The input and output signals are drawn on the diagram for this circuit. The input patterns have been selected so that each possible combination of inputs A, B, and C occurs for one unit of time.

Examining the timing diagram at times $t_0, t_1, \ldots, t_7$, we determine the values of the inputs and outputs at each time and write them in truth table form as in Fig. 2.23c. From the truth table we can write the minterm list and then derive a simplified logic expression for each function, as follows:

$$f_\alpha(A, B, C) = \sum m(1, 2, 6, 7)$$
$$= \bar{A}\bar{B}C + \bar{A}B\bar{C} + AB\bar{C} + ABC$$
$$= \bar{A}\bar{B}C + B\bar{C} + AB$$

$$f_\beta(A, B, C) = \sum m(1, 3, 5, 6)$$
$$= \bar{A}\bar{B}C + \bar{A}BC + A\bar{B}C + AB\bar{C}$$
$$= \bar{A}C + A\bar{B}C + AB\bar{C}$$

In the previous example, all gate outputs were shown as changing instantaneously following an input change. In reality, there is always a delay between the time of an input change and the corresponding output change in a circuit. In the next section we consider the effects of gate propagation delays on circuit operation.

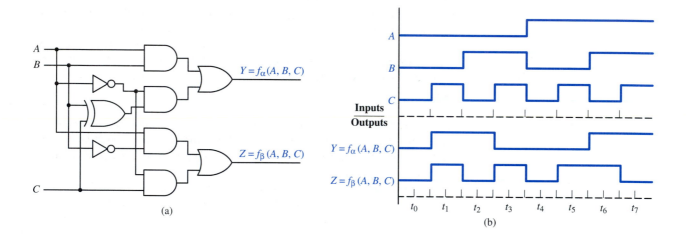

(a)

(b)

Time	Inputs ABC	Outputs $f_\alpha(A, B, C)$	$f_\beta(A, B, C)$
t_0	0 0 0	0	0
t_1	0 0 1	1	1
t_2	0 1 0	1	0
t_3	0 1 1	0	1
t_4	1 0 0	0	0
t_5	1 0 1	0	1
t_6	1 1 0	1	1
t_7	1 1 1	1	0

(c)

Figure 2.23 Derivation of a truth table from a timing diagram. **(a)** Logic circuit realizing two functions. **(b)** Timing diagram. **(c)** Truth table.

Propagation Delay

In addition to logic function, a designer must be concerned with a number of physical characteristics of digital logic circuits, including the following:

- Propagation delays
- Gate fan-in and fan-out restrictions
- Power consumption
- Size and weight

These characteristics are physical properties of the lower-level circuits used to create the logic gates, and the number and configuration of gates in a given circuit. Lower-level design is beyond the scope of this book; the reader is referred to Wakerly [9]. However, propagation delays and fan-in/fan-out restrictions have a significant impact on logic design, and must therefore be considered during any digital logic circuit analysis and/or design.

A physical logic gate requires a nonzero amount of time to react to input changes and produce changes in its output state. This delay between the time of an input change and the corresponding output change is called a *propagation delay*. Thus, if a logic circuit realizes a function $z = f(x_1, \ldots, x_n)$, the propagation delay is the time that it takes changes to "propagate" from some input x_i through the circuit to the output z. Propagation delays are functions of the circuit complexity, the electronic technology used, and such factors as gate fan-out (the number of other gate inputs driven by a single gate output), temperature, and chip voltage.

Following various input changes, the outputs of electronic logic gate circuits may take different amounts of time to switch from low to high than from high to low. Hence, two propagation delay parameters are typically specified for a given logic gate:

t_{PLH} = propagation delay time, low- to high-level output

t_{PHL} = propagation delay time, high- to low-level output

with t_{PLH} and t_{PHL} measured from the time of the input change to the time of the corresponding output change.

Where precise timing information is not needed, a single propagation delay parameter, denoted by t_{PD}, is used to approximate both t_{PLH} and t_{PHL}. Usually, t_{PD} is computed as the average of t_{PLH} and t_{PHL}.

$$t_{PD} = \frac{t_{PLH} + t_{PHL}}{2}$$

For the AND gate illustrated in Fig. 2.24a, Figs. 2.24b-d illustrate the response of the gate output to a sequence of changes in its input values. In Fig. 2.24b, the ideal case is shown, in which the outputs change instantaneously, that is, the propagation delay is 0. In Fig. 2.24c, all output changes are shown as being delayed by an average propagation delay, t_{PD}. Figure 2.24d presents a more precise picture of the timing, with separate parameters for t_{PLH} and t_{PHL}.

Table 2.7 lists t_{PD} values for two-input NAND gates from a number of different logic families, along with the power dissipation per gate for each.

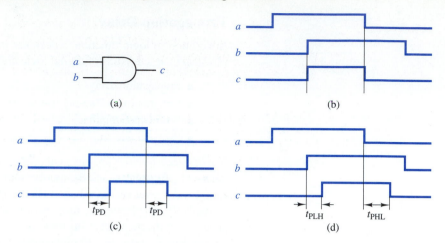

Figure 2.24 Propagation delay through a logic gate. **(a)** Two-input AND gate. **(b)** Ideal (zero) delay. **(c)** $t_{PD} = t_{PLH} = t_{PHL}$. **(d)** $t_{PLH} < t_{PHL}$.

Logic gates are available in a number of different technologies, eight of which are shown in the table. As can be seen in this table, there are trade-offs between speed and power dissipation among the different technologies. For example, the $74S\times\times$ devices are faster than the equivalent $74\times\times$ or $74LS\times\times$ devices, while the $74LS\times\times$ devices are slower, but consume less power. A designer often sacrifices speed for lower power consumption in applications for which power supply current will be limited, such as in battery-powered systems.

TABLE 2.7 **POWER DISSIPATION AND PROPAGATION DELAYS FOR SEVERAL LOGIC FAMILIES [8]**

Logic Family	Propagation Delay t_{PD} (ns)	Power Dissipation Per Gate (mW)	Technology
7400	10	10	Standard TTL
74H00	6	22	High-speed TTL
74L00	33	1	Low-power TTL
74LS00	9.5	2	Low-power Schottky TTL
74S00	3	19	Schottky TTL
74ALS00	3.5	1.3	Advanced low-power Schottky TTL
74AS00	3	8	Advanced Schottky TTL
74HC00	8	0.17	High-speed CMOS

Propagation delays also differ among different gates implemented with the same technology, since their transistor-level circuits are different. Table 2.8 lists t_{PHL} and t_{PLH} parameters for five primitive gates (AND, OR, NAND, NOR, and NOT) from the 74LS family. Note that a typical and a maximum value are given for each parameter. Propagation delays vary from one device to another, and are affected by the number of loads driven by the gate. Therefore, most device data sheets specify a maximum delay time, corresponding to worst case loading conditions, in addition to the typical delay time for each device.

TABLE 2.8   PROPAGATION DELAYS OF PRIMITIVE 74LS SERIES GATES [8]

Chip	Function	t_{PLH} Typical	t_{PLH} Maximum	t_{PHL} Typical	t_{PHL} Maximum
74LS04	NOT	9	15	10	15
74LS00	NAND	9	15	10	15
74LS02	NOR	10	15	10	15
74LS08	AND	8	15	10	20
74LS32	OR	14	22	14	22

EXAMPLE 2.36

A sequence of inputs is applied to the circuit of Fig. 2.25a, producing the timing diagram of Fig. 2.25b. Each gate has propagation delay t_{PD} of one time unit. We wish to find the truth table and minimum switching expression for this circuit.

From the timing diagram, the truth table of Fig. 2.25c is derived by examining the outputs of each gate following each of the input changes. Since signals take different amounts of time to propagate to each gate output, we must wait until all signal propagation is complete before determining the output corresponding to the current input. Note that no signal will propagate through more than three gates, therefore no more than three time units will elapse between an input change and a stable output.

For example, at time t_1 input C changes from 0 to 1, which causes inverter output D and AND gate output G to both change at time $t_1 + 1$. The change at G causes OR gate output Y to change from 0 to 1 at time $t_1 + 2$. Thus the input change required two time units to propagate from circuit input C to circuit output Y. Therefore, we should wait until after $t_1 + 2$ to determine the final value of Y. Note that the input change at time t_2 also required two time units to propagate to the output, whereas the changes at times t_4 and t_7 require three time units.

From the truth table we can write the list of minterms and derive a minimum switching expression as follows:

$$f(A, B, C) = \sum m(1, 4, 5, 6)$$
$$= \bar{A}\bar{B}C + A\bar{B}\bar{C} + A\bar{B}C + AB\bar{C}$$
$$= A\bar{C} + \bar{B}C$$

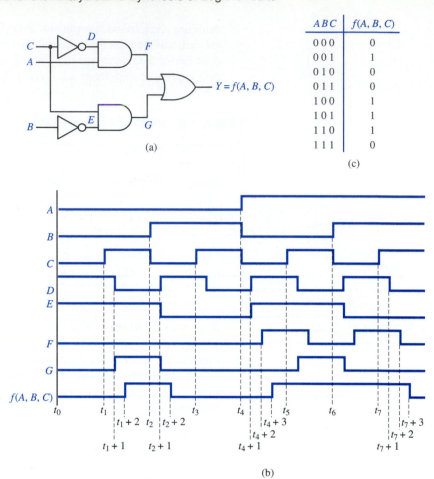

Figure 2.25 Derivation of a truth table from a timing diagram. **(a)** Circuit diagram.
(b) Timing diagram. **(c)** Truth table.

2.5 Synthesis of Combinational Logic Circuits

Thus far, we have introduced several tools that may be used in analyzing and synthesizing switching networks. These tools include switching algebra, switching devices, truth tables, and timing diagrams. In this section we shall employ some of these tools to design and implement switching networks.

2.5.1 AND–OR and NAND Networks

An AND-OR network employs AND gates to form product terms and an OR gate to form the sum of these products. Therefore, a given switching function that is to be implemented in AND-OR logic must be expressed in sum of products (SOP) form. For example, the function

$$f_\delta(p, q, r, s) = p\bar{r} + qrs + \bar{p}s$$

is directly implemented in AND-OR logic in Fig. 2.26a.

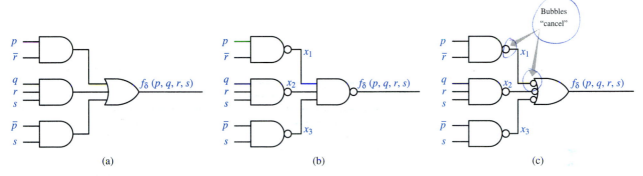

Figure 2.26   Implementations of $f_\delta(p, q, r, s) = p\bar{r} + qrs + \bar{p}s$. **(a)** AND-OR network. **(b)** NAND network. **(c)** NAND network (preferred form).

A simple translation using switching algebra may be employed to transform a sum of products expression into an appropriate form for direct NAND implementation. Place two bars over the entire SOP function; then use DeMorgan's theorem (Theorem 8) to find the NAND form for the function

$$f_\delta(p, q, r, s) = \overline{\overline{p\bar{r} + qrs + \bar{p}s}} \qquad [\text{T3}]$$

$$= \overline{\overline{p\bar{r}} \cdot \overline{qrs} \cdot \overline{\bar{p}s}} \qquad [\text{T8(a)}]$$

$$= \overline{x_1 \cdot x_2 \cdot x_3}$$

where $x_1 = \overline{p\bar{r}}$, $x_2 = \overline{qrs}$, and $x_3 = \overline{\bar{p}s}$. The NAND realization of this function is shown in Fig. 2.26b.

Fig. 2.26c presents the same circuit, but with the output NAND gate shown in its DeMorgan-equivalent form. Writing the logic expression for the output,

$$f_\delta(p, q, r, s) = \bar{x}_1 + \bar{x}_2 + \bar{x}_3$$

$$= \overline{\overline{p\bar{r}}} + \overline{\overline{qrs}} + \overline{\overline{\bar{p}s}}$$

$$= p\bar{r} + qrs + \bar{p}s$$

Note that the inversion bubbles on both ends of lines x_1, x_2, and x_3 in Fig. 2.26c effectively cancel each other, making the diagram resemble that of Fig. 2.26a, and thus clearly illustrating that a sum of products form is being implemented. Therefore, the format of Fig. 2.26c is preferred over that of Fig. 2.26b when drawing a NAND circuit.

The techniques employed here may be used on any sum of products function to derive an AND-OR or NAND network.

2.5.2 OR-AND and NOR Networks

An OR-AND network employs OR gates to form sum terms and an AND gate to form the product of these sums. Therefore, a specified switching function that is to be implemented in OR-AND logic must be expressed in product of sums (POS) form. For example, the function

$$f_\epsilon(A, B, C, D) = (\bar{A} + B + C)(B + C + D)(\bar{A} + D)$$

is realized directly in OR-AND logic in Fig. 2.27a.

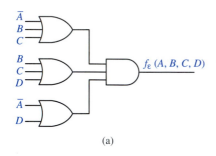

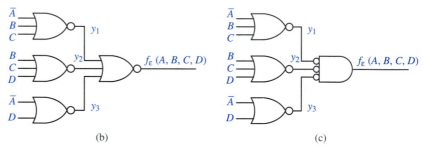

Figure 2.27   Implementations of $f_\epsilon(A, B, C, D) = (\bar{A} + B + C)(B + C + D)(\bar{A} + D)$. **(a)** OR-AND network. **(b)** NOR network. **(c)** NOR network (preferred form).

We may use the same switching algebra transformation that we employed previously to express $f_\epsilon(A, B, C, D)$ in an appropriate form for direct NOR implementation, again using DeMorgan's theorem:

$$f_\epsilon(A, B, C, D) = \overline{\overline{(\bar{A} + B + C)(B + C + D)(\bar{A} + D)}} \qquad \text{[T3]}$$

$$= \overline{\overline{\bar{A} + B + C} + \overline{B + C + D} + \overline{\bar{A} + D}} \qquad \text{[T8(b)]}$$

$$= \overline{y_1 + y_2 + y_3}$$

where $y_1 = \overline{\bar{A} + B + C}$, $y_2 = \overline{B + C + D}$, and $y_3 = \overline{\bar{A} + D}$. The NOR realization of this function is shown in Fig. 2.27b.

Fig. 2.27c presents the same circuit, but with the output NOR gate shown in its DeMorgan-equivalent form. Writing the output logic expression,

$$f_\epsilon(A, B, C, D) = \bar{y}_1 \cdot \bar{y}_2 \cdot \bar{y}_3$$

$$= \overline{\overline{(\bar{A} + B + C)}} \cdot \overline{\overline{(B + C + D)}} \cdot \overline{\overline{(\bar{A} + D)}}$$

$$= (\bar{A} + B + C)(B + C + D)(\bar{A} + D)$$

As was the case with two-level NAND circuits, the inversion bubbles effectively cancel out. This format more clearly illustrates that a function in product of sums form is being implemented and is therefore the preferred way to draw the two-level NOR circuit.

The preceding method may be generalized to implement any product of sums function in NOR logic.

2.5.3 Two-level Circuits

Networks that have a structure like those shown in Figs. 2.26 and 2.27 are referred to as *two-level networks*. Input signals must pass through two levels of gates before reaching the output. As illustrated in Fig. 2.28a, the first level is defined as the level containing the gate that produces the output. Gates that receive the circuit inputs are on the second level. When NOT gates are required on input lines, a three-level network is produced, as illustrated in Fig.2.28b. A network has *n* levels when at least one input signal must pass through *n* gates before reaching the output.

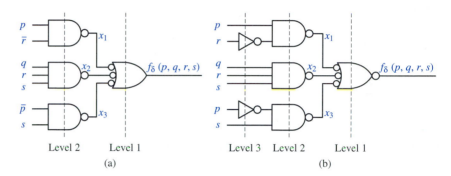

Figure 2.28   Two-level and three-level network structures. **(a)** Two-level network. **(b)** Three-level network.

Switching functions in the SOP or POS form can be implemented directly in two-level networks when the inputs are available in both complemented and uncomplemented form. A three-level network is required when only one form of the inputs is available. In the latter case, only NOT gates are needed on level 3.

Circuits with more than two levels are often needed where there are gate fan-in limits. For example, the function $f(a, b, c, d, e) = abcde$ can be realized with a single five-input AND gate as shown in Fig. 2.29a. However, if the designer is restricted to working with only two-input AND gates, then a three- or four-level circuit will be needed, as shown in Figs. 2.29b and c, respectively. The reader should verify that these circuits are equivalent.

At this point the reader has all the tools necessary to take a switching function expressed in minterm or maxterm list form and implement it in NAND or NOR logic, respectively. The implementation procedure for NAND logic is outlined next; the terms in parentheses are used if the implementation is to be in NOR logic.

Step 1. Express the function in minterm (maxterm) list form.

Step 2. Write out the minterms (maxterms) in algebraic form.

Step 3. Simplify the function in sum of products (product of sums) form using switching algebra.

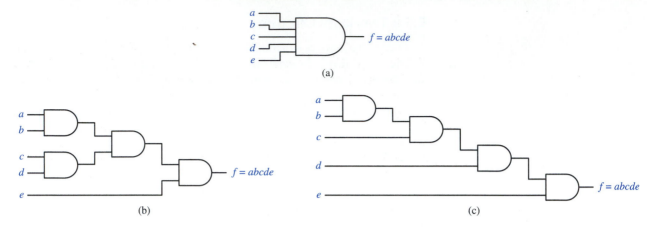

Figure 2.29 Multilevel circuit made necessary by fan-in restrictions. **(a)** A single five-input AND gate. **(b)** Three-level network of two-input gates. **(c)** Four-level network of two-input gates.

Step 4. Use Theorem 8a (8b) and Theorem 3 to transform the expression into the NAND (NOR) formulation.

Step 5. Draw the NAND (NOR) logic diagram.

This procedure will now be illustrated using $f_\phi(X, Y, Z) = \sum m(0, 3, 4, 5, 7)$

EXAMPLE 2.37

Implement $f_\phi(X, Y, Z) = \sum m(0, 3, 4, 5, 7)$ in NAND logic.

1. $f_\phi(X, Y, Z) = \sum m(0, 3, 4, 5, 7)$

2. $f_\phi(X, Y, Z) = m_0 + m_3 + m_4 + m_5 + m_7$
$$= \bar{X}\bar{Y}\bar{Z} + \bar{X}YZ + X\bar{Y}\bar{Z} + X\bar{Y}Z + XYZ$$

3. $f_\phi(X, Y, Z) = \bar{Y}\bar{Z} + YZ + XZ \qquad$ [T6(a)]

4a. $f_\phi(X, Y, Z) = \overline{\overline{\bar{Y}\bar{Z}} + \overline{YZ} + \overline{XZ}} \qquad$ [T3]

or

4b. $f_\phi(X, Y, Z) = \overline{\overline{\bar{Y}\bar{Z} + YZ + XZ}} \qquad$ [T3]
$$= \overline{\overline{\bar{Y}\bar{Z}} \cdot \overline{YZ} \cdot \overline{XZ}} \qquad \text{[T8(a)]}$$

The logic diagram of Fig. 2.30a is derived from the expression in step 4a and is said to be a *minimum two-level SOP realization* of the switching function. This example completely illustrates the design procedure.

EXAMPLE 2.38

Implement $f_\phi(X, Y, Z) = \sum m(0, 3, 4, 5, 7)$ in NOR logic.

1. $f_\phi(X, Y, Z) = \prod M(1, 2, 6)$

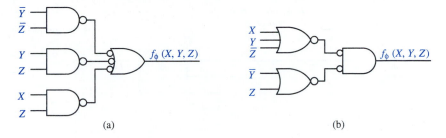

Figure 2.30   Canonical form of $f_\phi(X, Y, Z) = \sum m(0, 3, 4, 5, 7)$ to NAND and NOR networks. **(a)** NAND realization. **(b)** NOR realization.

2. $f_\phi(X, Y, Z) = M_1 \cdot M_2 \cdot M_6$
$$= (X + Y + \bar{Z})(X + \bar{Y} + Z)(\bar{X} + \bar{Y} + Z)$$

3. $f_\phi(X, Y, Z) = (X + Y + \bar{Z})(\bar{Y} + Z)$ [T6(b)]

4a. $f_\phi(X, Y, Z) = \overline{\overline{(X + Y + \bar{Z})} \cdot \overline{(\bar{Y} + Z)}}$ [T3]

or

4b. $f_\phi(X, Y, Z) = \overline{\overline{(X + Y + \bar{Z})(\bar{Y} + Z)}}$ [T3]
$$= \overline{\overline{(X + Y + \bar{Z})} + \overline{(\bar{Y} + Z)}}$$ [T8(b)]

The NOR network derived from step 4a is shown in Fig. 2.30b and is said to be a *minimum two-level POS realization* of the switching function. Each network shown in Fig. 2.30 implements the function $f_\phi(X, Y, Z)$.

2.5.4 AND–OR–invert Circuits

An AND–OR–invert (AOI) circuit consists of a set of AND gates, the outputs of which are fed into a NOR gate, and it hence can be used to readily realize two-level sum of products circuits. A typical configuration, such as that employed in the standard 7400 series logic (7454), is shown in Fig. 2.31. In general, the circuits are defined by the number of inputs to the AND gates. For example, a circuit employing three AND gates, one of which has two inputs, one of which has three inputs, and one of which has four inputs, would be referred to as a 2–3–4 AOI circuit.

The 7454 circuit shown in Figure 2.31 is a 2–2–2–2 AOI circuit, which realizes the function

$$F = \overline{AB + CD + EF + GH}$$

Although the AOI circuit may be used in a number of ways, we will illustrate only one application here. If B, D, F, and H are operated as enable (control) lines, and A, C, E, and G are information lines, then the preceding circuit can be used to funnel information from the four sources A, C, E, and G into a single channel (this circuit is called a *4-to-1 multiplexer*, and will be described in Chapter 4). For example, if $A = Y1$, $C = Y2$, $E = Y3$ and $G = Y4$ and $B = 1$ and $D = F = H = 0$, the output will be $F = \overline{Y1}$. If the enable lines are then changed so that $D = 1$ and $B = F = H = 0$, the output

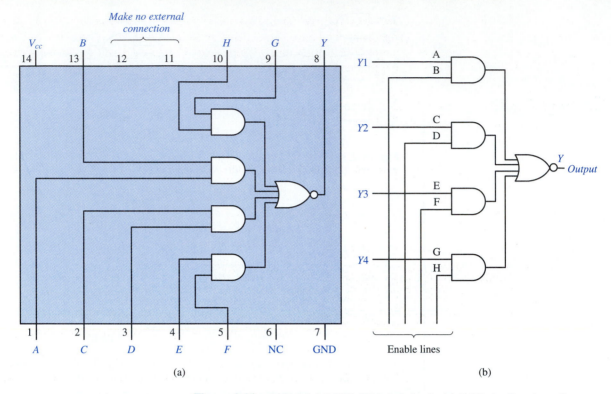

Figure 2.31   7454 2-2-2-2 AND-OR-invert circuit. **(a)** 7454 circuit package (top view). **(b)** 7454 used as a 4-to-1 multiplexer.

will be $F = \overline{Y2}$. Therefore, by sequentially setting the signals on the enable lines to logic 1 in the fashion illustrated, a set of data streams represented by A, C, E, and G may be funneled into a single stream represented by F.

2.5.5 Factoring

Factoring is a technique for obtaining higher-level forms of switching functions (which require circuits in which signals may propagate through more than two levels of logic gates). The importance of these higher-level forms stems from the fact that they often require less hardware and are therefore more economical to implement. Higher-level forms are also needed in situations in which gates with limited fan-in must be used. In these cases, factoring is used to reduce the number of literals in large product or sum terms to values less than or equal to the available number of gate inputs. However, higher-level forms are more difficult to design than simple SOP or POS forms, and are generally slower due to having more than two levels of logic gates.

Factoring, which normally involves the use of the distributive law (Postulate 5) of switching algebra, is essentially an art in which experience plays an important role. The technique is further complicated by the fact that re-dundancy may have to be added at an intermediate step in order to obtain a simpler realization through factoring. This method will be demonstrated via the following examples.

EXAMPLE 2.39

Suppose we are given the following four-variable function:

$$f_\lambda(A, B, C, D) = A\bar{B} + A\bar{D} + A\bar{C}$$

The two-level realization of this function using NAND gates is shown in Fig. 2.32a.

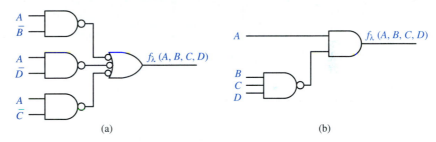

(a)   (b)

Figure 2.32   Realizations of $f_\lambda(A, B, C, D)$. **(a)** Original form. **(b)** After factoring.

Note that this second-order realization of the function requires four gates and nine gate inputs. However, if we apply factoring to the function, we can obtain a higher-order realization, as follows:

$$f_\lambda(A, B, C, D) = A\bar{B} + A\bar{D} + A\bar{C}$$
$$= A(\bar{B} + \bar{D} + \bar{C})$$
$$= A(\overline{BCD})$$

This realization of $f_\lambda(A, B, C, D)$, shown in Fig. 2.32b, requires only two gates and five gate inputs.

EXAMPLE 2.40

Realize the function $f(a, b, c, d) = \sum m(8, 13)$ using only two-input AND and OR gates.

We begin by writing the canonical SOP form:

$$f(a, b, c, d) = \sum m(8, 13)$$
$$= a\bar{b}\bar{c}\bar{d} + ab\bar{c}d \qquad (2.34)$$

The two product terms in Eq. 2.34 cannot be reduced using switching algebra. Therefore, two four-input AND gates and one two-input OR gate would be required to realize a two-level AND-OR circuit.

Since only two-input gates are available, we can use factoring to reduce the size of the product terms, as follows:

$$f(a, b, c, d) = ab\bar{c}\bar{d} + ab\bar{c}d$$

$$= (a\bar{c})(bd + \bar{b}\bar{d}) \tag{2.35}$$

In Eq. 2.35, no product or sum term contains more than two literals. Thus, this switching expression can be realized entirely with two-input gates, as shown in Fig. 2.33. Note that the circuit contains four levels of logic gates, including the input inverters.

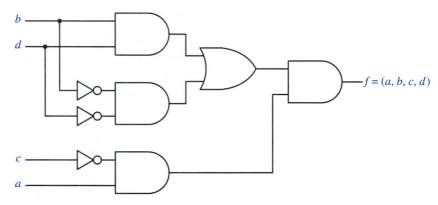

Figure 2.33   Factoring used to realize $f(a, b, c, d) = \sum m(8, 13)$ with two-input gates.

The algebraic approach demonstrated in this example can also be performed using various graphical and tabular methods, such as the Karnaugh map (K-map), which will be presented in Chapter 3. For more details on this subject, the reader is referred to [3].

2.6 Applications

Thus far, we have introduced several tools, such as switching algebra, truth tables, and Venn diagrams, that are basic to the analysis and synthesis of logic networks. In addition, the basic concepts of digital logic circuit analysis and design have been introduced. The following examples illustrate the use of these techniques in solving problems.

One area in which the basic tools find extensive use is in the areas of symbolic logic and truth functions. We will not treat these subjects in any detail, but rather illustrate the use of the logic in several very simple examples.

EXAMPLE 2.41

A burglar alarm for a bank is designed so that it senses four input signal lines. Line A is from the secret control switch, line B is from a pressure sensor under a steel safe in a locked closet, line C is from a battery-powered clock, and line D is connected to a switch on the locked closet door. The following conditions produce a logic 1 voltage on each line:

A : The control switch is closed.

B : The safe is in its normal position in the closet.

C : The clock is between 1000 and 1400 hours.

D : The closet door is closed.

Write the equations of the control logic for the burglar alarm that produces a logic 1 (rings a bell) when the safe is moved and the control switch is closed, or when the closet is opened after banking hours, or when the closet is opened with the control switch open.

The statement "when the safe is moved and the control switch is closed" is represented by $A\bar{B}$. "When the closet is opened after banking hours" is represented by $\bar{C}\bar{D}$. "When the closet is opened with the control switch open" is represented by $\bar{A}\bar{D}$. Therefore, the logic equation for the burglar alarm is

$$f(A, B, C, D) = A\bar{B} + \bar{C}\bar{D} + \bar{A}\bar{D}$$

EXAMPLE 2.42

John and Jane Doe have two children, Joe and Sue. When eating out they will go to a restaurant that serves only hamburgers or one that serves only chicken. Before going out, the family votes to decide on the restaurant. The majority wins, except when Mom and Dad agree, and in that case they win. Any other tie votes produce a trip to the chicken restaurant. We wish to design a logic circuit that will automatically select the restaurant when everyone votes.

If we let a 1 represent a vote cast for hamburgers and a 0 represent a vote cast for chicken, the truth table for the voting circuit is given in Table 2.9. The logic function is

$$f(A, B, C, D) = \bar{A}BCD + A\bar{B}CD + AB\bar{C}\bar{D}$$
$$+ AB\bar{C}D + ABC\bar{D} + ABCD$$

$$= \bar{A}BCD + A\bar{B}CD + AB$$
$$= AB + ACD + \bar{A}BCD$$
$$= AB + ACD + BCD$$

The logic circuit for this function is given in Fig. 2.34.

TABLE 2.9				TRUTH TABLE FOR DOE FAM-ILY VOTER
John A	Jane B	Joe C	Sue D	Vote for Hamburger f
0	0	0	0	0
0	0	0	1	0
0	0	1	0	0
0	0	1	1	0
0	1	0	0	0
0	1	0	1	0
0	1	1	0	0
0	1	1	1	1
1	0	0	0	0
1	0	0	1	0
1	0	1	0	0
1	0	1	1	1
1	1	0	0	1
1	1	0	1	1
1	1	1	0	1
1	1	1	1	1

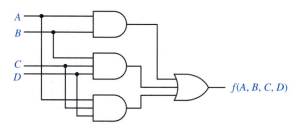

Figure 2.34   Logic circuit for restaurant voter example.

EXAMPLE 2.43

We wish to derive the logic equations for a circuit that will add the two 2-bit binary numbers $(A_1 A_0)_2$ and $(B_1 B_0)_2$ and produce the sum bits $(S_1 S_0)_2$ and the carry out bit C_1; that is,

$$A_1 A_0$$
$$+ B_1 B_0$$
$$\overline{C_1 S_1 S_0}$$

There are four inputs, A_1, A_0, B_1, and B_0, and three outputs C_1, S_1, and S_0. Therefore, the truth table is that shown in Table 2.10. Each line of the truth

TABLE 2.10 **TRUTH TABLE OF 2-BIT BINARY ADDER**

	A_1	A_0	B_1	B_0	C_1	S_1	S_0
	0	0	0	0	0	0	0
	0	0	0	1	0	0	1
	0	0	1	0	0	1	0
	0	0	1	1	0	1	1
	0	1	0	0	0	0	1
	0	1	0	1	0	1	0
	0	1	1	0	0	1	1
→	0	1	1	1	1	0	0
	1	0	0	0	0	1	0
	1	0	0	1	0	1	1
	1	0	1	0	1	0	0
	1	0	1	1	1	0	1
	1	1	0	0	0	1	1
	1	1	0	1	1	0	0
	1	1	1	0	1	0	1
	1	1	1	1	1	1	0

table is derived as shown in the following calculation for the eighth line.

$$\begin{array}{r} 1\;\;1\;\; \\ 0\;\;1 \\ +\;\;1\;\;1 \\ \hline 1\;\;0\;\;0 \end{array}$$

The logic equation for the terms C_1, S_1, and S_0 are obtained from the truth table as:

$$S_0 = \bar{A}_1\bar{A}_0\bar{B}_1B_0 + \bar{A}_1\bar{A}_0B_1B_0 + \bar{A}_1A_0\bar{B}_1\bar{B}_0 + \bar{A}_1A_0B_1\bar{B}_0$$
$$+A_1\bar{A}_0\bar{B}_1B_0 + A_1\bar{A}_0B_1B_0 + A_1A_0\bar{B}_1\bar{B}_0 + A_1A_0B_1\bar{B}_0$$

$$S_1 = \bar{A}_1\bar{A}_0B_1\bar{B}_0 + \bar{A}_1\bar{A}_0B_1B_0 + \bar{A}_1A_0\bar{B}_1B_0 + \bar{A}_1A_0B_1\bar{B}_0$$
$$+A_1\bar{A}_0\bar{B}_1\bar{B}_0 + A_1\bar{A}_0\bar{B}_1B_0 + A_1A_0\bar{B}_1\bar{B}_0 + A_1A_0B_1B_0$$

$$C_1 = \bar{A}_1A_0B_1B_0 + A_1\bar{A}_0B_1\bar{B}_0 + A_1\bar{A}_0B_1B_0 + A_1A_0\bar{B}_1B_0$$
$$+A_1A_0B_1\bar{B}_0 + A_1A_0B_1B_0$$

These expressions can be reduced to the following:

$$S_0 = A_0\bar{B}_0 + \bar{A}_0B_0$$

$$S_1 = \bar{A}_1\bar{A}_0B_1 + \bar{A}_1B_1\bar{B}_0 + \bar{A}_1A_0\bar{B}_1B_0 + A_1A_0B_1B_0 + A_1\bar{B}_1\bar{B}_0 + A_1\bar{A}_0\bar{B}_1$$

$$C_1 = A_0B_1B_0 + A_1A_0B_0 + A_1B_1$$

2.7 Computer-aided Design of Logic Circuits

2.7.1 The Design Cycle

Many of today's digital logic circuits contain the equivalent of thousands to hundreds of thousands of logic gates. Most of these circuits are fabricated on single integrated circuit chips (ICs). Designing and fabricating a VLSI (very large scale integrated) circuit chip is a complex and expensive process. Therefore, it is necessary to verify the correctness of the logic circuit design before beginning the design of the actual chip to ensure a high probability of correct operation the first time the chip is fabricated. The same is true when designing digital systems out of multiple ICs and circuit boards. Circuits and systems of this complexity are virtually impossible to develop and verify without the assistance of computer-aided design (CAD) tools.

The design cycle for a digital logic circuit comprises a number of steps between concept and physical implementation, including design synthesis, simulation, realization, and testing. This process is depicted in Fig. 2.35. From a statement of the problem, the designer begins by developing an abstract solution that is systematically transformed into a digital logic circuit. This transformation is aided by modeling and evaluating the circuit at each level of design abstraction. A design is evaluated by using its model to simulate its operation, allowing the circuit's response to various input stimuli to be verified. The model is revised and resimulated as needed until the correct responses are obtained. In addition to verifying correct operation, the effects of different design options on circuit performance can be evaluated to assist in making cost-effective design decisions. Once the modeled behavior of the design is acceptable, the physical design is developed and implemented. Finally, the finished circuit is tested, with the test results compared to the modeled behavior to detect faulty devices.

In this chapter we describe the CAD processes and tools used in the synthesis and analysis phases of digital circuit design. Each block in the synthesis and analysis phases of Fig. 2.35 will be examined. First, design modeling will be discussed. The next section will describe schematic capture and other CAD tools that capture digital circuit models and translate them into the format of the design database. Then digital logic simulation will be discussed as applied to verifying the logic behavior and timing of a design. Finally, CAD tools that derive minimum switching expressions for logic functions will be examined.

2.7.2 Digital Circuit Modeling

Modeling a digital logic circuit or system serves several purposes. First, the process of developing a model helps the designer formalize a solution. Second, a circuit model can be processed by a digital computer to check for design errors, verify correctness, and predict timing characteristics. In addition, a number of CAD tools are available that automatically perform all or some of

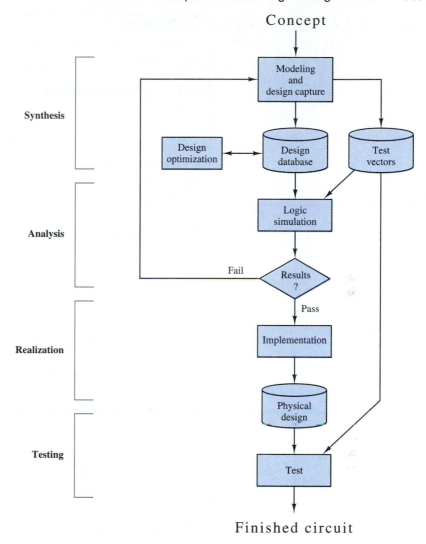

Figure 2.35   Computer-aided design of a digital logic circuit.

the synthesis steps, including design optimization and transformation of the design from an abstract form to a physical realization.

A model can represent a digital system at different levels of design abstraction, ranging from behavioral to structural. This is illustrated in Fig. 2.36. The designer often begins with a high-level abstract model that describes only the desired *behavior* to be realized by the circuit without specifying actual circuit components. This allows the essential features of the design to be worked out without becoming mired in implementation details, and also provides a readable description of the design that can assist in developing, documenting, and maintaining the circuit. Behavioral models are most often represented in

Level	Abstraction
Behavioral	Define the algorithms to be realized by the circuit.
Register Transfer	Define the circuit as a structure of modules and define the data flow between them, along with the control algorithm.
Gate	Define the circuit as a structure of primitive logic gates.
Transistor	Define the circuit as a structure of transistors and other low-level electronic components.
Layout	Describe the geometric patterns of materials that define the physical IC layout.

Figure 2.36   Levels of model abstraction for digital logic circuits.

a *hardware description language* (HDL), such as VHDL [10-12] or Verilog [13]. HDLs enable a designer to formally express the algorithms that describe the behavior of the circuit. Logic equations, truth tables, and minterm or max-term lists are other commonly-used mechanisms for describing circuit behavior without implying a particular circuit structure. Another approach is to write a computer program in a standard programming language, such as C or FOR-TRAN, to model the behavior of the circuit. However, the resulting models are typically not compatible with other simulation and other CAD tools, making this approach less attractive.

Figures 2.37 and 2.38 present three different forms of a behavioral model of a 1-bit full-adder circuit. As shown in the block diagram of Fig. 2.37a, a full adder has two operand inputs, addend a and augend b, a carry input, c_{in}, a sum output s, and a carry output c_{out}. Figures 2.37b and c list the truth table and logic equations, respectively, that define the sum and carry functions of the full adder.

Figure 2.38 lists a VHDL behavioral model of a full adder. A VHDL model consists of two parts: an entity and an architecture. The *entity* defines the interface between the circuit and the outside world. Corresponding to the block diagram of Fig. 2.37a, the VHDL entity description of the full adder lists three input "ports," a, b, and c_{in}, and two output ports, s and c_{out}, all declared

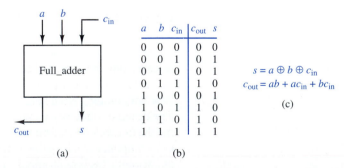

Figure 2.37   Behavioral models of a full-adder circuit. **(a)** Block diagram. **(b)** Truth table. **(c)** Logic equations.

```
entity full_adder is
  port{a,b,cin: in  bit;
       s,cout:  out bit}
end full_adder;

architecture behavior of full_adder is
begin
 process (a,b,cin)
   variable ai,bi,ci,si: integer;
   begin

     -- convert bit types to integers
     if a = '0' then ai := 0;    -- convert a to integer
               else ai := 1;
     end if;
     if b = '0' then bi := 0;    -- convert b to integer
               else bi := 1;
     end if;
     if cin = '0' then ci := 0; -- convert cin to integer
                else ci := 1;
     end if;

     -- compute the integer sum of the inputs
     si := ai + bi + ci;

     -- convert the result to separate sum and carry bits
     case si is
       when 0 =>  s <= '0';  cout <= '0';
       when 1 =>  s <= '1';  cout <= '0';
       when 2 =>  s <= '0';  cout <= '1';
       when 3 =>  s <= '1';  cout <= '1';
     end switch;
 end process;
 end full_adder;
```

Figure 2.38   VHDL behavioral model of a full adder circuit.

to be of data type "bit." The first line of the entity declaration defines the name of the model to be "full_adder."

While the entity describes the circuit from the viewpoint of the outside world, the *architecture* defines the function implemented within the circuit. A given circuit can be modeled and implemented in many ways, so VHDL allows multiple architectures to be defined for a given entity. A designer does not need to know the implementation details of a circuit in order to use it in a higher-level design. Only the definitions of the signals into and out of the circuit and their various timing and loading parameters are needed to be able to work with it. Thus, the entity description supplies all the information needed by a user of the module. In the full-adder architecture listed in Fig. 2.38, the first line indicates that this particular implementation of "full_adder" is called "behavior." The adder function is described here by a "process" in which the three inputs are converted to integer values and added to produce a sum. The result is the converted into two separate bits, a sum bit of 0 or 1, and a carry output if the sum is equal to 2. The phrases beginning with two dashes are comments and are not part of the model. The reader is referred to [11,12] for more information on modeling with VHDL.

A *structural model* is simply an interconnection of components, that is, a "structure," with no explicitly specified behavior. Behavior is deduced by analyzing the behavioral models of the individual components and their interconnection. The most common mechanism used to represent structural models of digital circuits is the logic or *schematic* diagram. Textual representations of schematic diagrams, called *netlists*, are also used frequently, as are HDL descriptions of circuit structures. Figures 2.39a and b present a structural model of the full-adder circuit defined earlier in schematic and netlist formats, respectively.

The netlist format is of particular interest since most CAD systems require a netlist in order to simulate the operation of a circuit. If schematic diagrams are used, they are typically translated to netlist form prior to simulation. A *net* is defined as a wire or logic signal line whose value can be controlled and/or monitored during circuit operation. In a netlist, each circuit element is typically defined as follows:

$$gate\_name \quad gate\_type \quad output \quad input1 \quad input2 \quad ... \quad inputN$$

where *gate_name* is a symbolic name assigned to this particular gate, *gate_type* is the type of logic gate (AND2, OR3, and so on), *output* is the name of a net connected to the gate output, and *input1* through *inputN* are the names of nets connected to the gate inputs. In this circuit and the following examples, gate

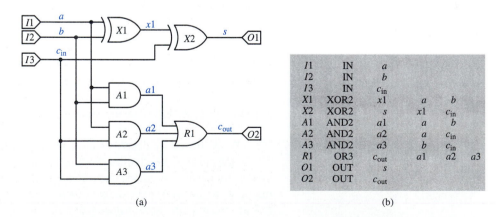

(a)

$I1$	IN	a		
$I2$	IN	b		
$I3$	IN	c_{in}		
$X1$	XOR2	$x1$	a	b
$X2$	XOR2	s	$x1$	c_{in}
$A1$	AND2	$a1$	a	b
$A2$	AND2	$a2$	a	c_{in}
$A3$	AND2	$a3$	b	c_{in}
$R1$	OR3	c_{out}	$a1$	$a2$	$a3$
$O1$	OUT	s		
$O2$	OUT	c_{out}		

(b)

Figure 2.39   Structural models of a full-adder circuit. **(a)** Schematic diagram. **(b)** Netlist.

type AND2 is a two-input AND gate, XOR2 a two-input exclusive-OR gate, and OR3 a three-input OR gate.

Figure 2.39b presents the netlist extracted from the schematic diagram of Fig. 2.39a. In this example there are six primitive logic gates and nine nets. Nets a, b, and c_{in} are designated as external inputs, while s and c_{out} are external outputs. Nets $a1$, $a2$, $a3$, and $x1$ are all internal to the circuit. Note that the IN and OUT gate types do not actually correspond to logic gates, but simply designate external connections.

Figure 2.40 lists a VHDL structural description of the full-adder schematic of Fig. 2.39a. Note that the VHDL descriptions of both the structural and behavioral models use the same entity definition. This is because the interface

```
entity full_adder is
  port{a,b,cin: in  bit;
       s,cout:  out bit}
end full_adder;

architecture structure of full_adder is
component XOR2       -- declare XOR gate
  port{z: out bit;
       x,y: in bit};
  end component;

component AND2       -- declare AND gate
  port{z: out bit;
       x,y: in bit};
  end component;

component OR3        -- declare OR gate
  port{z: out bit;
       w,x,y: in bit};
  end component;

signal x1,a1,a2,a3: bit;  -- internal signal wires

begin   -- define the schematic by connecting component ports
        -- to signal wires
  X1: XOR2 port map (x1,a,b);
  X2: XOR2 port map (s,x1,cin);
  A1: AND2 port map (a1,a,b);
  A2: AND2 port map (a2,a,cin);
  A3: AND2 port map (a3,b,cin);
  O1: OR3  port map (cout,a1,a2,a3);
end full_adder;
```

Figure 2.40   VHDL structural model of a full-adder circuit.

with the outside world is independent of the internal implementation of the function. The VHDL architecture of the structural model defines the implementation as simply an interconnection of components XOR2, AND2, and OR3. Each component to be used is declared by a "component" statement listing the entity name and port list of the component. When the model is compiled, the models of these components will be obtained from a component library. In the body of the architecture, each component to be used is instantiated in a separate statement, with each instance assigned a unique gate name. The circuit structure is defined by associating signals (wires) with input or output ports of the components. For example, signal $x1$ in the full-adder architecture of Fig. 2.40 is connected to output port z of XOR2 gate $X1$ and to the x input of XOR2 gate $X2$. Likewise, external inputs a and b are connected to input ports x and y of XOR2 gate $X1$. The reader may refer to [11,12] for further information on creating structural models with VHDL.

Digital circuit models need not be exclusively behavioral or structural. Most large designs are developed in a modular fashion, beginning with a behavioral model that is partitioned into modules. Digital circuits for each module are then designed separately until the entire circuit is realized. During this process, some of the modules may have behavioral models and some structural. Circuit models that contain both behavioral and structural components are referred to as *mixed-mode* models. As the logic circuit for each module is developed, it is inserted into the overall model in place of the behavior it realizes, and the entire model is verified to ensure that the overall behavior is correct. This allows each

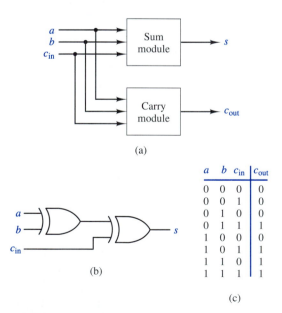

(a)

(b)

a	b	c_{in}	c_{out}
0	0	0	0
0	0	1	0
0	1	0	0
0	1	1	1
1	0	0	0
1	0	1	1
1	1	0	1
1	1	1	1

(c)

Figure 2.41   Mixed-mode model of the full-adder circuit. **(a)** Full-adder block diagram. **(b)** Circuit for the sum function. **(c)** Truth table of the carry function.

```
entity full_adder is
  port{a,b,cin: in  bit;
       s,cout:  out bit}
end full_adder;


architecture structure of full_adder is
component XOR2       -- declare XOR gate
  port{z: out bit;
       x,y: in bit};

signal x1,a1,a2,a3: bit;  -- internal signal wires

begin
  -- realize sum bit with XOR gate structure
  X1: XOR2 port map (x1,a,b);
  X2: XOR2 port map (s,x1,cin);

  -- describe behavior of carry
  process (a,b,cin)
  begin    -- carry out = 1 if at least two inputs = 1
    if a = '1' and b = '1' then
       cout <= '1';
    elsif  a = '1' and cin = '1' then
       cout <= '1';
    elsif  b = '1' and cin = '1' then
       cout <= '1';
    else
       cout <= '0';
    end if;
  end process;
end full_adder;
```

Figure 2.42   VHDL mixed-mode model of the full-adder circuit.

individual circuit to be tested within the context of the overall design without waiting for the entire logic circuit to be developed.

Figure 2.41a shows a mixed-mode model of the full adder, which has been partitioned into separate modules to compute the sum and carry bits. In Fig. 2.41b, the sum is realized by a structure of two XOR gates. The carry output, as shown in Fig. 2.41c, is modeled by its truth table. The next step in the design would be the design of the logic circuit for the carry output from its truth table.

Figure 2.42 presents the same mixed-mode full-adder model in VHDL. As in Fig. 2.41, the sum is realized by a structure of two XOR gates, while the carry output is described only by its behavior. It should be noted that VHDL, as well as a number of other HDLs, are capable of representing circuits and systems at any desired level of abstraction or any mixture of levels, allowing the designer to work within a single environment from concept to logic circuit realization.

2.7.3 Design Synthesis and Capture Tools

The Design Synthesis Process

As described earlier, *logic synthesis* is the process of designing a digital circuit from some initial specification of a problem. As illustrated in Fig. 2.43, a number of activities are associated with the synthesis of a logic circuit.

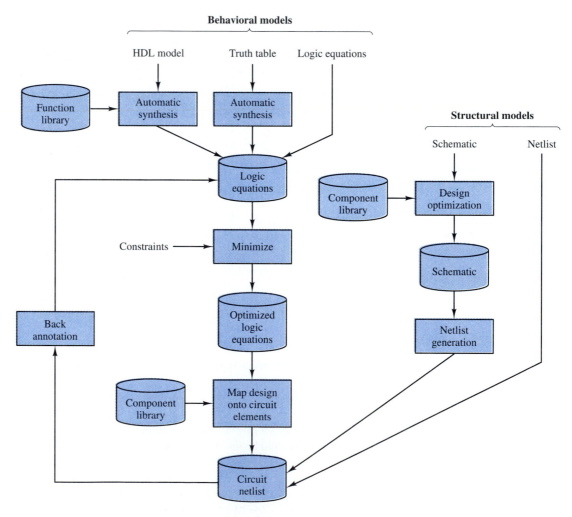

Figure 2.43   Synthesis of a logic circuit from a behavioral or structural model.

If the designer begins by developing a behavioral model, this model must be transformed to a structural model that can be realized with available components. This transformation begins by deriving a set of logic equations from the model. These equations are then reduced or otherwise manipulated to satisfy given constraints for the design. These constraints may include limitations on total cost, number or types of gates that may be used, gate fan-in and/or fan-out, physical space (restricting the number of gates or circuit packages), timing characteristics (restricting the design to, say, two versus three or more levels), power consumption, and design time. Finally, the reduced equations are mapped onto specific circuit elements. The final output is a logic circuit netlist which indicates the elements used and their interconnection.

Some or all of these steps in the transformation can be done automatically with special CAD tools. We will discuss design minimization in more detail later in this chapter. The reader is referred to [14] for further information on the automatic synthesis of logic circuits from behavioral models.

If the designer develops a structural model in schematic or netlist form, rather than beginning with a behavioral model, then the steps described above, that is, derivation and minimization of logic equations and mapping onto circuit components, must be performed manually. In this case, only the final circuit is stored in the final circuit database. However, many CAD systems include a function called *back annotation*, shown in Fig. 2.43, that extracts logic equations from a schematic netlist that can be fed back into the design process. This allows the design to be processed by the minimization tools and remapped onto selected circuit components to make whatever improvements or corrections are desired.

Each circuit model created in the design process must be captured in a format that can be stored and processed by a digital computer. CAD tools used in design capture vary according to the type of model. Schematic diagrams are created with a *schematic capture* or *schematic editor* program, which provides an interactive graphics environment in which the designer can draw and edit schematic drawings. Nonschematic model formats are created and stored in a CAD system as ASCII text files and can thus be developed with standard text editors. Some CAD systems provide special text editors that have been customized for a particular HDL, netlist, or other model format. These special editors aid in formatting the model and checking for errors, as well as providing shortcuts for model creation, such as model templates that can be filled in with element names and parameters.

Before a design can be processed by a computer, it must often be translated into an intermediate format that can be manipulated by the various CAD tools. This intermediate format would be independent of the method used to develop the model. During translation, the model is typically checked for errors. These errors include connectivity errors, such as dangling (unconnected) gate inputs, multiple gates driving a single line, and one gate output driving too many gate inputs, as well as such errors as unnamed nets and missing, improper, or inconsistent circuit parameters. These are often referred to as *design rule errors*, since they violate basic logic circuit design rules. However, these checks do not determine the logical correctness of the function. Logical correctness must be verified via logic simulation, as will be discussed later.

Designs represented with an HDL, such as VHDL, are likewise checked for errors while being translated to intermediate formats, much as a standard FORTRAN or C program would be checked for syntax errors while being compiled. Errors detected during translation include language syntax errors, as well as design rule errors similar to those just described.

Schematic Capture

A schematic capture program is an interactive graphics tool with which a designer "draws" a logic diagram to be processed by a CAD system. The basic steps in the schematic capture process are as follows:

1. Create (or "open") a drawing sheet.
2. Select components from a library and place them on the drawing sheet.
3. Draw nets (wires) to interconnect the components.
4. Assign symbolic names to each component and net.
5. Define or adjust component characteristic parameters.
6. Check the schematic for errors.
7. Save the schematic in the database.

In schematic capture, a single component symbol may represent a primitive logic element or an entire circuit module. A *primitive component* is defined as one that is not a composition of smaller components. Each primitive component is represented by a graphical symbol, to be used in drawing schematics, and an underlying model that describes its behavior, to be used during simulation. In digital logic circuit design, primitive components typically include basic logic gates, input and output connectors, and latches and flip-flops (latches and flip-flops will be defined in Chapter 6). Input and output connectors are not really circuit elements, but serve to identify connections to external signals.

Components are kept in one or more *libraries* in the CAD system database, from which they are retrieved as needed. Typically, one or more libraries of standard primitive components are supplied with the CAD system, providing the designer with a collection of commonly used logic gates and similar elements. In the full-adder schematic of Fig. 2.39a, the logic elements AND2 (two-input AND gate), XOR2 (two-input exclusive-OR gate), OR3 (three-input OR gate), IN (connector for an external input signal), and OUT (connector for an external output signal) were selected from a library of primitive logic gates.

Libraries of nonprimitive circuits are used in the creation of hierarchical, modular designs, as will be described in Chapter 4. These libraries may be supplied by the CAD system vendor or obtained from a third party, such as the manufacturer that will fabricate the VLSI chips or circuit boards designed with this system. Most CAD systems also support user-created libraries, allowing an individual designer to develop and store circuit designs in a special library for future use. The remainder of this chapter will focus on modeling combinational logic circuits with primitive gates.

Figure 2.44 illustrates the schematic capture process, using the full-adder circuit of Fig. 2.39a as an example. Figure 2.44a shows a typical schematic capture screen. A menu of operations is displayed to the left of the drawing area. An operation is performed by positioning a cursor on the menu selection with a mouse or similar pointing device and then clicking a mouse button or pressing a key to initiate the operation. For this discussion, we shall refer to this process as simply clicking on a selection. Most systems also allow commands to be entered from a keyboard.

A drawing sheet is opened by clicking on OPEN SHEET in the menu. Components are then selected from the library and positioned on the sheet.

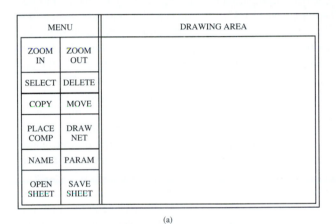

(a)

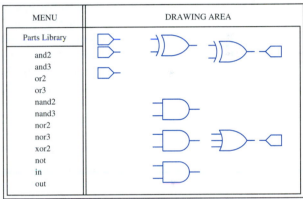

(b)

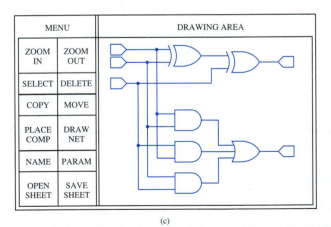

(c)

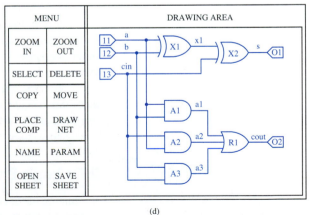

(d)

Figure 2.44   The schematic capture process. **(a)** Main menu and drawing area. **(b)** Gates selected from a library. **(c)** Nets drawn to connect gates. **(d)** Names added to gates and nets.

Clicking on PLACE COMP produces a menu of available components, as shown in Fig. 2.44b. A component is selected from the library by clicking on it in the menu. The selected component is then placed on the drawing sheet by moving the cursor to the desired location and clicking again. Once on the sheet, a component can be copied, moved around, or deleted as desired by clicking on the component to select it and then clicking on COPY, MOVE, or DELETE in the main menu. Other common operations include scaling and rotation of components. Figure 2.44b shows the full-adder drawing after all gates have been placed on the sheet.

After components have been placed on the sheet, they must be interconnected by nets (wires). One end of a net is connected to a component by clicking on one of the component's input or output terminals. The net is then drawn by moving the cursor; a segment of the net is drawn from the initial end point to the cursor. The net is completed by clicking on the gate terminal or net to which it should be connected. Nets with multiple segments are created one segment at a time by moving to and clicking at the end point of each segment. Some CAD systems automate this process, allowing the user to simply click on the two points to be connected. The computer then automatically routes the net between them. The completely wired full-adder circuit is shown in Fig. 2.44c.

The next step in creating a schematic drawing is to assign symbolic names to the components and nets, as shown in Fig. 2.44d. A component or net name is assigned or changed by clicking on NAME in the menu, clicking on the component or net in the drawing, and then entering the desired name from a keyboard. These symbolic names are used for several purposes. During simulation, each net is identified by its symbolic name to specify where to apply test stimuli and/or observe logic values. For testing, failures of selected gates are simulated and test vectors applied to detect the failures. The symbolic gate names are used to identify the locations of faults during this process. In addition to use during logic and fault simulation, the naming of components and nets helps to document the design.

In addition to assigning symbolic names, many CAD systems allow various parameters to be defined for each gate, including timing delays and other properties. Parameters are added and changed in the same manner as symbolic names, using the PARAM menu option.

After the schematic drawing has been completed, the final step is to check it for errors and then save it in the database by clicking on SAVE SHEET in the main menu. At this point, any connectivity or other design errors will be identified so they can be fixed during the next drawing session.

2.7.4 Logic Simulation

Simulating the operation of a digital logic circuit serves three primary purposes: logic verification, performance analysis, and test development. A block diagram of the simulation environment is illustrated in Fig. 2.45. The circuit model is typically given to the simulator in a flattened netlist form. *Flattening* is the process of replacing all nonprimitive circuit modules with the networks of primitive logic elements that they represent. To process a netlist, the simulator accesses a primitive component library to get the simulation models of the logic gates specified in the netlist.

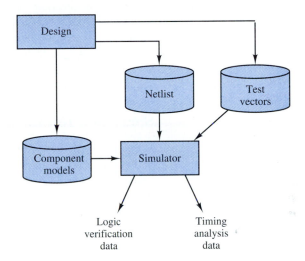

Figure 2.45   Digital logic simulation environment.

A logic circuit design is verified by applying test vectors to stimulate the circuit inputs. A *test vector* is an ordered list of ones and zeros, each corresponding to a stimulus value to be applied to a specified circuit input. The output responses of selected gates are then captured and checked for correctness by comparing them to the truth table, logic equations, or other specification from which the model was developed. At the early stages of the design cycle, logical correctness is the primary interest. Therefore, simplified or "ideal" component models are used, which do not exhibit time delays in their responses to input stimuli. This separates timing information from logic function to simplify the preliminary analyses.

To analyze the performance of a circuit, each component model must approximate with high fidelity the physical characteristics of its corresponding device. In particular, the amount of time a device takes to respond to input stimuli, referred to as its *propagation delay*, must be modeled accurately. With accurate models, simulation results can be analyzed to predict overall propagation delays between selected input and output pins of a circuit (called *pin-to-pin delay*). In addition, potential timing problems, including spikes and hazards as will be described in Chapter 3, can be detected. When the designer is faced with design options, simulation provides a method for evaluating the effects of each option on circuit performance, allowing the optimal choices to be made.

After a circuit has been fabricated, it must be tested to determine if it contains any faulty components or signal lines. For each potential fault, test vectors are applied that will produce outputs from the faulty circuit that will differ from those of the fault-free circuit, enabling the tester to determine if the fault is present. *Fault simulation* is the process of simulating the occurrence of various faults (called *fault injection*) and determining if they are detectable by a given set of test vectors. The results typically indicate the percentage of faults that can be detected by the test set. Thus, fault simulation assists in developing an optimal test set for a logic circuit, that is, a test that will detect an acceptable percentage of the potential faults in a minimum amount of testing time. Testing and design for testability will be discussed in Chapter 12. The remainder of this chapter will consider only logic verification and performance analysis. The reader is referred to [15] for further information on fault simulation and testing.

Simulation Test Inputs

Proper evaluation of a design requires a carefully designed set of test inputs, called a *test set*. If logic verification of a combinational logic circuit is the objective of the simulation, time may be ignored in the specification of test inputs. In this case, the test set comprises a list of input vectors to be applied, one after the other. As each input vector is applied, the circuit outputs are computed and recorded and then the next input is applied, and so on. A test set is listed in Fig. 2.46 for the full-adder circuit of Fig. 2.39a. This is an *exhaustive* test; that is, all possible input combinations are used, allowing the entire truth table to be verified. In general, 2^n vectors are required to exhaustively test an n-input combinational logic circuit, which might not be practical for circuits with many inputs. In such cases, test sets are designed that allow verification of the most common and critical circuit operations, leaving the designer with some degree of confidence that the design is error free. The number and nature of the test vectors used determine how high this degree of confidence is.

If circuit timing is to be studied, then test inputs must be applied at specific times, allowing the circuit sufficient time to respond to each vector. Therefore, the time of each input change must be specified with each vector in the test set. Figure 2.47a shows a set of waveforms to be applied to inputs a, b, and c of a circuit. Figures 2.47b and c illustrate two different formats commonly used to specify test input waveforms. In Fig. 2.47b, the test set is listed in tabular form, organized as one test vector per line. The first number on

a	b	c_{in}
0	0	0
0	0	1
0	1	0
0	1	1
1	0	0
1	0	1
1	1	0
1	1	1

Figure 2.46
Functional test set for the full-adder circuit.

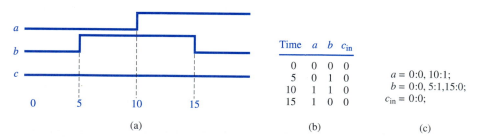

Time	a	b	c_{in}
0	0	0	0
5	0	1	0
10	1	1	0
15	1	0	0

$a = 0{:}0,\ 10{:}1;$
$b = 0{:}0,\ 5{:}1,15{:}0;$
$c_{in} = 0{:}0;$

(a)   (b)   (c)

Figure 2.47 Full-adder test set specifying input waveforms. **(a)** Test input waveforms. **(b)** Tabular format. **(c)** Waveform format.

each line is the simulation time at which the vector is to be applied. This same test is given in a different format in Fig. 2.47c. In this case, each line comprises an input name and the specification of a signal waveform to be applied to that input. A *waveform* is specified as a list of {time:value} pairs, each indicating a time at which the waveform is to be changed and the value to which the signal should be changed. The reader should verify that the test sets of Figs. 2.47b and c describe the same test.

Event-Driven Simulation

Some logic simulation programs compute the output of every logic gate during every interval of simulated time. However, most digital logic circuit simulators are *event driven*, where an *event* is defined as a change in the value of a signal at a given time. For example, consider the AND gate of Fig. 2.48a and the timing diagram of Fig. 2.48b. At time T_0 the AND gate inputs are $a = b = 1$, as illustrated in the timing diagram. At time T_1 the event $(T_1, a, 0)$ takes place, i.e. at time T_1, signal a changes to 0 from its present value. As a result of this event on input a, the AND gate output c will change from 1 to 0 at time $T_1 + \Delta t$, where Δt is the propagation delay through the AND gate. Therefore, the event $(T_1 + \Delta t, c, 0)$ results from event $(T_1, a, 0)$. Now assume that the event $(T_2, b, 0)$ occurs, i.e. input b changes from 1 to 0 at time T_2. Since the AND gate output c is already 0, it is not affected by the new value of b, and no additional events are triggered. In this manner, each input event propagates through the circuit until it either reaches an output of the circuit or until no further signal changes result, i.e. the events "drive" the simulation.

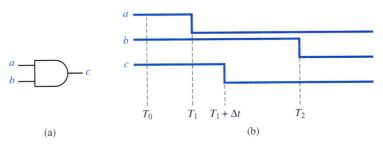

(a)   (b)

Figure 2.48   Event-driven simulation example. **(a)** AND gate model. **(b)** Timing diagram.

An event-driven simulator is organized around an *event queue* or *event list*, in which events are stored in order of their scheduled time of occurrence. In each simulation step, the first event is removed from the queue, i.e. the event that is scheduled to occur next. The event is made to occur by changing the value of the indicated net. If this net is an input to one or more gates, then the output of each affected gate is recomputed. For each computed output that differs from its present output, a new event is created for the net driven by that output and placed in the event queue. The time at which this event is scheduled is computed as the current time plus the gate delay. In this manner, simulation continues until the event queue is empty or until a specified time interval has elapsed.

Simulation is initiated by converting the input test set into a set of events and inserting them into the event queue at their scheduled times. During simulation, a record of all events is maintained from which simulation results can be generated and examined, either in tabular or timing diagram form. Figure 2.49 illustrates the event sequence that would occur during a simulation of the full-adder circuit of Fig. 2.39a using the test set of Fig. 2.47a. In this example, each gate was assumed to have a delay of one time unit. In the figure, the value x represents the initial unknown value of a logic signal.

The results of the simulation, showing only the external inputs and outputs, can be displayed as waveforms, as illustrated in Fig. 2.50a, or in tabular format, as in Figs. 2.50b and c, which list samples of the waveform taken at the indicated times. The designer usually specifies the signals that are to be

Event	Resulting Events	a	b	c_{in}	$a1$	$a2$	$a3$	$x1$	s	c_{out}
Initial state		x	x	x	x	x	x	x	x	x
$(0,a,0)$	$(1,a1,0),(1,a2,0)$	0	x	x	x	x	x	x	x	x
$(0,b,0)$	$(1,x1,0),(1,a3,0)$	0	0	x	x	x	x	x	x	x
$(0,c_{in},0)$	$(1,a1,0),(1,a2,0)$	0	0	0	x	x	x	x	x	x
$(1,a1,0)$		0	0	0	0	x	x	x	x	x
$(1,a2,0)$		0	0	0	0	0	x	x	x	x
$(1,x1,0)$	$(2,s,0)$	0	0	0	0	0	x	0	x	x
$(1,a3,0)$	$(2,c_{out},0)$	0	0	0	0	0	0	0	x	x
$(2,s,0)$		0	0	0	0	0	0	0	0	x
$(2,c_{out},0)$		0	0	0	0	0	0	0	0	0
$(5,b,1)$	$(6,x1,1)$	0	1	0	0	0	0	0	0	0
$(6,x1,1)$	$(7,s,1)$	0	1	0	0	0	0	1	0	0
$(7,s,1)$		0	1	0	0	0	0	1	1	0
$(10,a,1)$	$(11,x1,0),(11,a1,1)$	1	1	0	0	0	0	1	1	0
$(11,x1,0)$	$(12,s,0)$	1	1	0	0	0	0	0	1	0
$(11,a1,1)$	$(12,c_{out},1)$	1	1	0	1	0	0	0	1	0
$(12,s,0)$		1	1	0	1	0	0	0	0	0
$(12,c_{out},1)$		1	1	0	1	0	0	0	0	1
$(15,b,0)$	$(16,x1,1),(16,a1,0)$	1	0	0	1	0	0	0	0	1
$(16,x1,1)$	$(17,s,1)$	1	0	0	1	0	0	1	0	1
$(16,a1,0)$	$(17,c_{out},1)$	1	0	0	0	0	0	1	0	1
$(17,s,1)$		1	0	0	0	0	0	1	1	1
$(17,c_{out},1)$		1	0	0	0	0	0	1	0	1

Figure 2.49   Event sequence in the full-adder simulation.

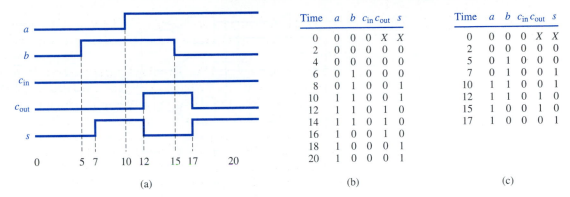

Time	a	b	c_{in}	c_{out}	s
0	0	0	0	X	X
2	0	0	0	0	0
4	0	0	0	0	0
6	0	1	0	0	0
8	0	1	0	0	1
10	1	1	0	0	1
12	1	1	0	1	0
14	1	1	0	1	0
16	1	0	0	1	0
18	1	0	0	0	1
20	1	0	0	0	1

Time	a	b	c_{in}	c_{out}	s
0	0	0	0	X	X
2	0	0	0	0	0
5	0	1	0	0	0
7	0	1	0	0	1
10	1	1	0	0	1
12	1	1	0	1	0
15	1	0	0	1	0
17	1	0	0	0	1

(a) (b) (c)

Figure 2.50 Full-adder simulation results. **(a)** Waveform format. **(b)** Samples at fixed intervals. **(c)** Samples at each event.

displayed and may often generate requests for multiple displays for a given simulation, displaying different information each time. The table in Fig. 2.50b lists the values of the selected signals taken every two time units, while Fig. 2.50c lists values only at those times at which events occurred. The latter form makes it easier for the designer to identify significant events during the simulation. However, if the number of events is large, sampling at fixed intervals might be preferred, with the sampling interval selected to limit the total number of samples.

To illustrate the use of simulation to verify a logic function, let us debug the full-adder circuit of Fig. 2.51a, which contains one error. Each gate and inverter is assumed to have a delay of one time unit. Applying the test set of Fig. 2.47 produces the simulation results shown in Fig. 2.51b. Comparing the results to the truth table of the full adder given in Fig. 2.37b, we see that the output s at time 3 is incorrect for input vector $abc_{in} = 000$ (output s should be 0 and not 1), but is correct for the other input vectors. To isolate the source of the error, we capture more information by adding signals n_1, n_2, n_3, and n_4 to the output trace, as shown in Fig. 2.51c. Examining this trace, we see that net $n_3 = 0$ at time 2 for input vector $abc_{in} = 000$, whereas the correct value should be $n_3 = 1$. This directs us to the input of that NAND gate, where we see that a connection is missing to this gate from input b, i.e. the gate realizes the expression $\bar{a}\bar{c}$ instead of $\bar{a}b\bar{c}$. Therefore, we have identified the error and can now correct it and resimulate to verify proper operation.

We can also use logic simulation to identify potential hazards/glitches in a logic circuit. For example, the logic circuit of Fig. 2.52a is suspected to contain a static hazard. If the inputs are initially all 1's and we apply test vector $(a, b, c) = 011$ at time t_1, the simulation produces the waveforms of Fig. 2.52b, where each gate is assumed to have a delay Δt. Output g was expected to remain constant, since $g = 1$ for both input vectors. However, it is obvious from the output waveform that there is a glitch in the output at time t_3. Looking at the inputs to the OR gate, we see that the glitch is caused by both e and f being 0 momentarily between times t_2 and t_3, until f finally changes to 1, returning

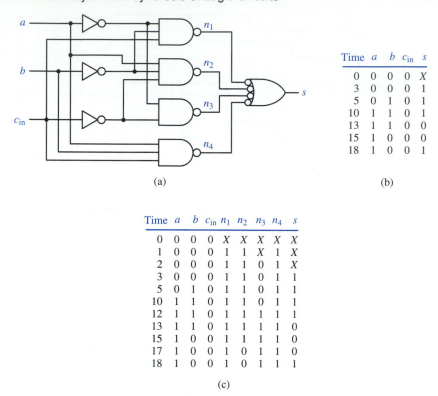

Time	a	b	c_{in}	s
0	0	0	0	X
3	0	0	0	1
5	0	1	0	1
10	1	1	0	1
13	1	1	0	0
15	1	0	0	0
18	1	0	0	1

(a) (b)

Time	a	b	c_{in}	n_1	n_2	n_3	n_4	s
0	0	0	0	0	X	X	X	X	X
1	0	0	0	0	1	1	X	1	X
2	0	0	0	0	1	1	0	1	X
3	0	0	0	0	1	1	0	1	1
5	0	1	0	0	1	1	0	1	1
10	1	1	0	0	1	1	0	1	1
12	1	1	0	0	1	1	1	1	1
13	1	1	0	0	1	1	1	1	0
15	1	0	0	0	1	1	1	1	0
17	1	0	0	0	1	0	1	1	0
18	1	0	0	0	1	0	1	1	1

(c)

Figure 2.51 Debugging a full-adder containing an error. **(a)** Erroneous full-adder circuit. **(b)** Simulation output showing error in s at time 3. **(c)** Expanded simulation results, isolating error to n_3.

output g to 1. Having identified the hazard, we can apply the procedures to be discussed in Chapter 3 in order to eliminate it.

Not all simulators are event driven. In some cases, the circuit model is transformed into a computer program which is then compiled and executed by the host computer, just as any other program. Instead of processing events, the output of each gate is recomputed during each time interval. During the model transformation, the gates are ordered so that the inputs of each gate depend only on the external inputs and the outputs of gates which have already been computed during the current time interval. The primary benefit of using a compiled model and careful gate ordering is that the speed of execution of a compiled simulation is typically much faster than that of an event-driven simulation in terms of the number of gate simulations performed per unit of time. However, since compiled simulators recompute each gate output during every simulation time interval, whether or not the gate inputs have changed, much time is used in evaluating *inert* gates, i.e. gates whose inputs have not changed

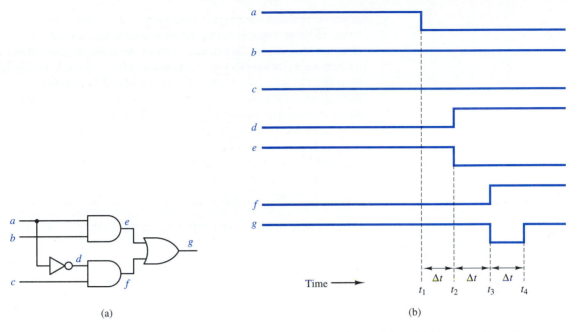

(a)

(b)

Figure 2.52   Static hazard detected via simulation. **(a)** Network with static hazard. **(b)** Simulation output waveforms.

and therefore whose output will not change. Note that overall simulation time can be computed as

$$T_{\text{simulation}} = \frac{\text{time}}{\text{gate}} \times \text{gates evaluated}$$

In event-driven simulation, only the outputs of those gates affected by input events are recomputed, improving overall performance in most cases by more than making up for the slower evaluation time for each gate. In addition, many compiled simulations impose limits on the types of delay models that can be used, which is not the case in event-driven simulation.

Symbolic Logic Signal Values

In Chapter 1 we defined 0 and 1 to be the only possible values of a digital logic signal. When evaluating a real electronic circuit, the designer may need information about a given signal other than its logic value, such as how strongly it is being driven or whether it is rising or falling. For this reason, logic simulators often provide signal "values" other than 0 and 1 to allow various conditions to be represented. In these simulators, the value of a logic signal is represented by a *state* and a *strength*, where the *state* represents a particular condition and the *strength* provides information about the gate which is supplying the signal.

The minimum set of states used in logic simulation is {0, 1}. Many simulators add a third state value, X, to represent an unknown state or a potential problem on a signal line, such as a voltage spike or multiple gates trying to drive a single net to different states. Signals are often initialized to X at the start of simulation, as shown in the example presented in Fig. 2.49, to indicate the unknown initial condition. These initial X values are replaced by normal logic values as the circuit is exercised. If a signal line remains at X throughout the simulation, it indicates potential problems to the designer, since that particular line was not affected by any of the test inputs.

With the addition of the X state, new truth tables for each of the primitive logic gates must be defined. Figure 2.53 gives the truth tables for AND, OR, and NOT gates. The reader should verify that these can be derived from the definitions of null and identity elements presented earlier in this chapter. States other than 0, 1, and X may also be used by simply defining new truth tables for the elements. Common states used in commercial simulators include rising/upward-changing (U), falling/downward-changing (D), and others.

AND	0	1	X
0	0	0	0
1	0	1	X
X	0	X	X

OR	0	1	X
0	0	1	X
1	1	1	1
X	X	1	X

NOT	0
0	1
1	0
X	X

Figure 2.53   Truth tables for three-valued logic.

In some circuits, the outputs of multiple gates can be connected to a single line, as illustrated in Fig. 2.54. In these cases, the *strength* with which

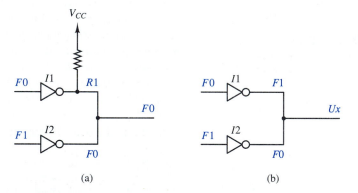

(a)   (b)

Figure 2.54   Signal strength used to resolve conflicting gate outputs.
(a) Output resolved in favor of stronger signal. **(b)** Output value unable to be resolved.

each gate drives the signal line must be considered so that the resulting signal value on the line can be determined, especially if the gates attempt to drive the same line to different states. Typical signal strength values used in simulation include the following:

Forcing (*F*): the signal line is strongly forced to a given state.

Resistive (*R*): the signal line is weakly forced to a given state.

Floating (*Z*): the signal line is not forced at all. This happens when a signal line is not driven by the output of any logic gate.

Unknown (*U*): the signal strength cannot be determined.

Each signal value is specified by a combination of a state and strength. For example, $F0$ indicates forced strongly to 0, $R1$ indicates weakly forced to 1, and so on. If the outputs of two different circuit elements are connected to the same signal line and try to force the line to different states, the strength values are used to resolve the conflict. For example, consider the circuit of Fig. 2.54a, in which the output of open-collector inverter $I1$ is $R1$ and output of normal inverter $I2$ is $F0$. In this case the resolved state would be $F0$. If a value cannot be resolved, say if one output is $F0$ and the other is $F1$, as shown in Fig. 2.54b, the value Ux would be assigned, indicating an unknown strength and state. This condition alerts the designer that there is a potential problem with this circuit.

If it is not important to monitor signal strength, state alone may be specified, with F usually assumed to be the default strength.

Primitive Device Delay Models

Every primitive logic gate is characterized by a logic function and an intrinsic delay, that is, the amount of time that it takes for its output to respond to an input event. Delays are functions of the circuit complexity, the electronic technology used, and such factors as gate fan-out (the number of other gate inputs driven by a single gate output), temperature, chip voltage, and so on. A typical model for a primitive AND gate is illustrated in Fig. 2.55, comprising an ideal (zero-delay) AND gate followed by a delay element. For each output change, the actual change is delayed by time Δt, which is the value assigned to the delay element.

In processing an event at time T at an input of the AND gate, the simulator would first compute the output of the ideal gate, $c*$, using a truth table or other model. The computed value of $c*$ would then be scheduled to appear at the output c of the delay element at time $T + \Delta t$. This behavior is often referred to as *transport delay*, since the output waveform at c appears to be transported, or shifted in time by Δt from the output of the ideal gate, $c*$.

The delay element may incorporate other delay models to represent different physical characteristics of the gate. The most commonly used delay models include unit, nominal, rise/fall, and min/max delays. These are described in the following sections.

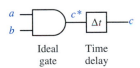

Figure 2.55 AND gate modeled as an ideal gate and a transport delay.

Unit/Nominal Delay

Verification of the logical correctness of a design does not require detailed timing information. In such cases, it is sufficient to assume that each gate has some fixed delay associated with it. The simplest approach is to assign to each

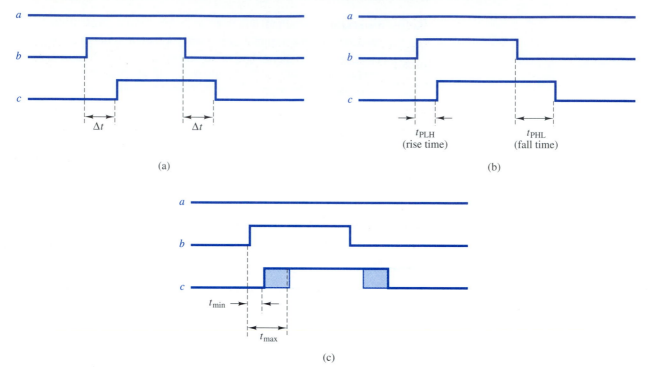

Figure 2.56 Effects of different transport delay models. **(a)** Unit/nominal delay. **(b)** Rise/fall delay. **(c)** Min/max delay.

gate in the circuit the same *unit delay*, that is, assume that each gate output responds to an input event in exactly one time unit. All simulation times are then measured in terms of an integral number of time units. The actual amount of time represented by one time unit is not important to the simulator; the designer can simply multiply a given number of time units by the physical time represented by a single unit.

Since different logic gates have different characteristics, more accuracy can be achieved by assigning *nominal delays*, which are transport delays that are determined separately for each type of gate. For example, a simple gate, such as a NAND or NOR gate, might be assigned a nominal delay of one time unit, while a more complex element, such as an XOR gate, might be assigned a nominal delay of two time units. Figure 2.56a illustrates the operation of the AND gate of Fig. 2.55, assuming a nominal delay of Δt for the gate.

A degenerate case of the unit and nominal delay models is the *zero delay* model, in which an input change is assumed to have an immediate effect on the output. The zero delay model, however, does not always provide a true picture of how a circuit operates, particularly in the case of sequential circuits, as will be described later in this text. Thus the use of zero delay models is primarily restricted to verifying the logic equations realized by a combinational circuit.

Rise/Fall Delay

The outputs of many electronic logic gate circuits take different amounts of time to rise from 0 to 1 than they do to fall from 1 to 0. This is modeled by replacing the single unit or nominal delay with a separate *rise time*, t_{PLH} (propagation delay from low to high), and *fall time*, t_{PHL} (propagation delay from high to low). When scheduling an output event, the simulator delays the signal by t_{PLH} on a $0 \rightarrow 1$ change, and by t_{PHL} for a $1 \rightarrow 0$ change. Thus, a $0 \rightarrow 1$ event occurring at time T would be scheduled at $T + t_{PLH}$, while a $1 \rightarrow 0$ event occurring at time T would be scheduled at $T + t_{PHL}$. This is illustrated in Fig. 2.56b for the AND gate model.

Ambiguous or Min/Max Delay

The characteristics of real electronic devices are affected by manufacturing process variations or by such factors as chip voltage, temperature, and fan-out. This makes it impossible to predict the exact rise or fall time of a signal. For applications in which timing is critical, designers often perform worst-case analyses of a circuit to determine the effects of gates performing at their fastest or slowest speeds. This is handled by specifying a range of values, $\{t_{min}, t_{max}\}$ for each timing parameter, where t_{min} is the minimum delay and t_{max} the maximum delay. Each shaded area in Fig. 2.56c indicates the time interval during which the output event might occur, with the interval beginning at time $T + t_{min}$ and ending at $T + t_{max}$. The output may change at any time within this interval.

One problem with using min/max delays is that the results tend to be pessimistic. This is because the very worst case of all gates operating with their slowest delays or all with their fastest delays is indicated in the results. This will rarely be the case in actual circuits.

Consider for example the circuit of Fig. 2.57a and assume that each gate has minimum delay $t_{min} = 2$ and maximum delay $t_{max} = 5$. The circuit will be simulated with initial conditions of the inputs set to $a = b = d = 0$ and $c = 1$, and then input d will change from 0 to 1 at time $t = 10$. Figure 2.57b shows the output waveforms produced by the simulator using the min/max delay models of the gates. Note that the width of the *ambiguity region*, that is, the region within which a change can occur, is wider at each successive level of the circuit. The minimum time at which output h can change is equal to the time of the input change plus the sum of the minimum delays for signals e, g, and h, or $10 + 3 \times t_{min} = 16$. Likewise, the maximum time that it could take for output h to change is determined by the maximum delays of the gates along the path from the input to the output, or $10 + 3 \times t_{max} = 25$. Thus, the output may change any time within the time interval [16, 25]. In reality, it is unlikely that all the gate delays will be either the extreme minimum or maximum. Therefore, the actual change can normally be expected to occur somewhere near the middle of this region. However, the designer must consider the two extremes to ensure proper circuit operation under all conditions.

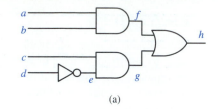

(a)

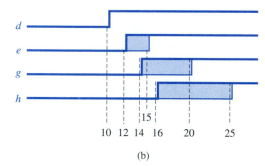

(b)

Figure 2.57 Simulation illustrating accumulation of min/max delays. **(a)** Circuit model. **(b)** Worst-case delays shown.

An alternative approach for examining minimum and maximum delays is to perform a *critical path analysis*. In critical path analysis, no simulation is performed. Instead, each possible signal path between the inputs and outputs of the circuit is identified. The minimum and maximum delays of all the gates along each path are then added to determine the minimum and maximum output responses. Paths whose minimum or maximum delays represent potential problems are identified as the *critical paths* through the circuit. The designer can then modify the design along the critical paths to prevent these problems.

Inertial Delay

The delay models described are all examples of *transport delay*; that is, a new value is "transported" to the output of the gate after the designated delay. This does not always model accurately the operation of a physical electronic device. For many devices, an input value must persist for some minimum duration of time to provide the output with the needed inertia to change. In such cases, short spikes at the inputs do not affect the output. The minimum input signal duration needed to produce an output change is referred to as *inertial delay*.

The effect of inertial delay on circuit operation is illustrated in the timing diagrams of Fig. 2.58. In Fig. 2.58a, a transport delay model is assumed. Any input change results in a corresponding output change after Δt seconds, no matter how brief the duration of the input value. In Fig. 2.58b an inertial delay of Δt seconds is assumed, which implies that any input change shorter than Δt seconds will not affect the output. In this case, two of the input changes do not produce corresponding output changes.

Inertial delays are often modeled as delays at the inputs of a gate, as illustrated in Fig. 2.59. For an input change on input a at time T, an event

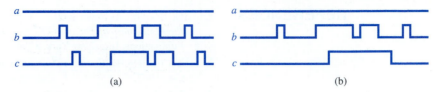

(a)   (b)

Figure 2.58 Transport versus inertial delay models. **(a)** Transport delay model.
(b) Inertial delay model.

is scheduled for line $a*$ at time $T + \Delta t$. If a second change in line a occurs before time $T + \Delta t$, then the event on line $a*$ is canceled by removing it from the event queue. The net result is that no changes have been scheduled for the output c of the gate.

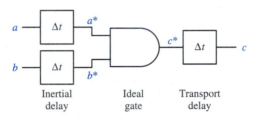

Inertial   Ideal   Transport
delay   gate   delay

Figure 2.59 Inertial delay model implemented with input delays.

2.8 Summary

Boolean algebra is the foundation upon which the analysis and synthesis of switching circuits rests; therefore, much time was spent in developing Boolean algebra as a familiar tool. In addition, the concepts of Venn diagrams, truth tables, minterms, maxterms, and the like have been discussed in order to provide the reader with the proper foundation necessary to attack the problems of combinational logic network analysis and synthesis.

In addition, this chapter has examined the basic elements of computer-aided design as they apply to combinational logic circuits. We have shown several methods for modeling digital circuits, capturing them into the database of a CAD system, and simulating their operation to verify the design and to predict timing and other characteristics of a circuit before actually constructing it. In addition, we have examined some of the automated synthesis operations that can be performed with CAD systems, including the generation of a circuit design from an abstract model.

The discussions of this chapter were not based on any one particular CAD system or program. Rather, the intent was to provide an overview of the basic processes involved in computer-aided design and analysis of digital logic circuits. The reader is encouraged to consult the documentation and tutorial material available with those CAD tools that are available for specific information on how to perform the operations described here.

REFERENCES

1.   G. BOOLE, *An Investigation of the Laws of Thought, on Which Are Founded the Mathematical Theories of Logic and Probability*, 1849. Reprinted by Dover Publications, Inc., New York, 1954.

2.   Y. CHU, *Digital Computer Design Fundamentals.* New York: McGraw-Hill Book Co., 1962.

3.   F. J. HILL, AND G. R. PETERSON, *Computer Aided Logical Design with Emphasis on VLSI, 4th ed.* New York: Wiley, 1993.

4.   G. A. MALEY, AND J. EARLE, *The Logic Design of Transistor Digital Computers.* Englewood Cliffs, NJ: Prentice Hall, 1963.

5.   E. J. MCCLUSKEY, JR., *Introduction to the Theory of Switching Circuits.* New York: McGraw-Hill Book Co., 1965.

6.   D. L. DIETMEYER, *Logic Design of Digital Systems, 3rd ed.* Boston: Allyn and Bacon, 1971.

7.   *STANDARD GRAPHIC SYMBOLS FOR LOGIC FUNCTIONS: IEEE/ANSI STANDARD 91-1984,* Institute of Electrical and Electronics Engineers, Inc., IEEE Standards Office, 345 East 47th St., New York, NY 10017, 1984.

8.   *THE TTL DATA BOOK, VOLUME 2,* Texas Instruments, Inc., Dallas, TX, 1985.

9.   J. F. WAKERLY, *Digital Design Principles and Practices, 2nd ed.*, Chapter 2. Englewood Cliffs, NJ: Prentice Hall, 1994.

10. *IEEE STANDARD VHDL LANGUAGE REFERENCE MANUAL,* IEEE Std. 1076-1987, March 1988, IEEE, 345 East 47th Street, New York, NY 10017.

11. R. LIPSETT, C. SCHAEFER, AND C. USSERY, *VHDL: Hardware Description and Design.* Kluwer Academic Publishers, 1989.

12. J. R. ARMSTRONG, *Chip-Level Modeling With VHDL.* Englewood Cliffs, NJ: Prentice Hall 1989.

13. DONALD E. THOMAS, AND PHILIP MOORBY, *The Verilog Hardware Description Language.* Norwell, Massachusetts: Kluwer Academic Publishers, 1991.

14. M. D. EDWARDS, *Automatic Logic Synthesis Techniques for Digital Systems.* New York: McGraw-Hill, 1992.

15. M. ABRAMOVICI, M. A. BREUER, AND A. D. FRIEDMAN, *Digital System Testing and Testable Design.* New York: IEEE Press, 1990.

PROBLEMS

2.1   Using switching algebra, simplify the following expressions:

(a) $f(w, x, y, z) = x + xyz + \bar{x}yz + wx + \bar{w}x + \bar{x}y$

(b) $f(A, B, C, D, E) = (AB + C + D)(\bar{C} + D)(\bar{C} + D + E)$

(c) $f(x, y, z) = y\bar{z}(\bar{z} + \bar{z}x) + (\bar{x} + \bar{z})(\bar{x}y + \bar{x}z)$

2.2   Simplify the following switching expressions.

(a) $f(A, B, C, D) = \overline{(A + \bar{C} + D)(\bar{B} + C)(A + \bar{B} + D)(\bar{B} + C)(\bar{B} + C + \bar{D})}$

(b) $f(A, B, C, D) = \overline{AB + \bar{A}\bar{D} + B\bar{D} + \bar{A}B + C\bar{D}A + \bar{A}D + CD + \bar{A}\bar{B}\bar{D}}$

(c) $f(A, B, C, D) = \overline{A\bar{B}C} + AB + \overline{\overline{ABC}} + A\bar{C} + AB\bar{C}$

(d) $f(A, B, C) = \overline{(B + \bar{A})(AB + C)} + AB\bar{A} + \bar{A}\bar{B}C + \overline{(A + B)(\bar{A} + C)}$

(e) $f(A, B, C) = \overline{\overline{(\bar{A} + \bar{B})(A + \bar{A}B)(\bar{A} + \bar{B} + \bar{A}\bar{B}C)} + \overline{(A + B)(\bar{A} + C)}}$

2.3   Prove part (b) of the Theorem 4 (absorption).

2.4 Prove part (b) of the Theorem 5 (absorption).

2.5 Prove part (b) of the Theorem 9 (consensus).

2.6 Simplify the following switching expressions.
 (a) $f(A, X, Z) = \bar{X}(X + Z) + \bar{A} + AZ$
 (b) $f(X, Y, Z) = (\bar{X}Y + XZ)(X + \bar{Y})$
 (c) $f(x, y, z) = \bar{x}y(z + \bar{y}x) + \bar{y}z$

2.7 Find the simplest switching expression for the following functions.
 (a) $f(A, B, C) = \sum m(1, 4, 5)$
 (b) $f(A, B, C, D) = \prod M(0, 2, 4, 5, 8, 11, 15)$
 (c) $f(A, B, C, D) = \sum m(0, 2, 5, 8, 9, 10, 13)$

2.8 Given the function $f(x, y, z) = x\bar{y} + x\bar{z}$ write $f(x, y, z)$ as a sum of minterms and as a product of maxterms.

2.9 Use Venn diagrams to determine which of the following switching functions are equivalent.
$$f_1(A, B, C) = A\bar{B}\bar{C} + B + \bar{A}\bar{B}C$$
$$f_2(A, B, C) = \bar{A}\bar{B}\bar{C} + B + A\bar{B}C$$
$$f_3(A, B, C) = \bar{A}\bar{C} + AC + B\bar{C} + \bar{A}B$$
$$f_4(A, B, C) = A\bar{C} + AB + B\bar{C} + \bar{A}C$$

2.10 Sketch the following functions on a Venn diagram.
 (a) $f(A, B) = AB + \bar{A}\bar{B}$
 (b) $f(A, B, C) = AB + \bar{A}\bar{C}$
 (c) $f(A, B, C, D) = A + \bar{B}CD + \bar{A}BD$
 (d) $f(A, B, C, D) = \bar{A}B + C\bar{D}$
 Hint: Each new variable is represented by a contour that divides each disjoint segment of the Venn diagram into two segments. A four-variable Venn diagram is shown in Fig. P2.10.

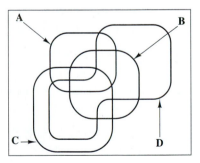

Figure P2.10

2.11 Prove that the following expressions are valid using Venn diagrams.
 (a) $A + B = A\bar{B} + \bar{A}B + AB = \overline{\bar{A}\bar{B}}$
 (b) $A\bar{C} + BC + A\bar{B} \neq \bar{B}\bar{C} + \bar{A}B + AC$
 (c) $\bar{A}C + AB + B\bar{C} = \bar{A}\bar{B} + BC + A\bar{C}$
 (d) $AD + A\bar{C}\bar{D} + AB + \bar{A}BD + \bar{A}\bar{B}\bar{C} = AB + BD + AD + \bar{B}\bar{C}$

2.12 Use Theorem 5 to simplify the following expressions:

(a) $\bar{X} + XAB\bar{C} + \bar{B}C$

(c) $Z(\bar{Z} + AB\bar{C}) + \bar{A}\bar{B}$

(b) $\bar{X}\bar{Y} + (X + Y)Z$

(d) $(\bar{X} + \bar{Y})(XY + Z)$

2.13 Use Theorem 8 (DeMorgan's) to complement the following expressions:

(a) $X(Y + \bar{Z}(Q + \bar{R}))$

(c) $XY + A\bar{C} + IQ$

(b) $X + Y(\bar{Z} + Q\bar{R})$

(d) $(A + B\bar{C})(\bar{A} + \bar{D}E)$

2.14 Apply switching algebra Theorem 9 (consensus) to simplify the following expressions:

(a) $QR + \bar{X}Q + RX$

(b) $(X + Y)Z + \bar{X}\bar{Y}W + ZW$

(c) $(\bar{X} + Y)WZ + X\bar{Y}V + VWZ$

(d) $(X + Y + Z + \bar{W})(V + X)(\bar{V} + Y + Z + \bar{W})$

2.15 Use Theorem 10 (Shannon's expansion theorem) to transform each of the following functions into the format
$$f(A, B, C, Q) = \bar{Q}f_\alpha(A, B, C) + Qf_\beta(A, B, C)$$
$$= [\bar{Q} + f_\gamma(A, B, C)][Q + f_\delta(A, B, C)]$$
Find $f_\alpha, f_\beta, f_\gamma$, and f_δ when

(a) $f(A, B, C, Q) = (Q + \bar{A})(\bar{B} + C) + \bar{Q}\bar{C}$

(b) $f(A, B, C, Q) = A\bar{B}\bar{C} + Q\bar{A} + \bar{Q}C$

(c) $f(A, B, C, Q) = (A + \bar{B} + Q)(\bar{A} + \bar{Q} + C)$

(d) $f(A, B, C, Q) = AB\bar{C} + \bar{A}C$

2.16 Find truth tables for the following switching functions.

(a) $f(A, B) = A + \bar{B}$

(c) $f(a, b, c) = a\bar{b}c + b\bar{c}$

(b) $f(A, B, C) = AB + \bar{A}C$

(d) $f(a, b, c) = a(b + \bar{c})(\bar{b} + c)$

2.17 Find truth tables for the following switching functions.

(a) $f(A, B, C, D) = AB\bar{C}D + ABC\bar{D}$

(b) $f(A, B, C, D) = AB + \bar{A}\bar{B} + C\bar{D}$

(c) $f(A, B, C, D) = A(\bar{B} + C\bar{D}) + \bar{A}B\bar{C}D$

2.18 Find the minterm and maxterm list forms for the switching functions of Problem 2.16. Use any method.

2.19 Find the canonical SOP form for the switching functions of Problem 2.17. Use any technique.

2.20 Expand the following function into canonical SOP form.
$$f(x_1, x_2, x_3) = x_1\bar{x}_3 + x_2\bar{x}_3 + x_1x_2x_3$$

2.21 Expand the following function into canonical POS form.
$$f(W, X, Q) = (Q + \bar{W})(X + \bar{Q})(W + X + Q)(\bar{W} + \bar{X})$$

2.22 A burglar alarm is designed so that it senses four input signal lines. Line A is from the secret control switch, line B is from a pressure sensor under a steel safe in a locked closet, line C is from a battery-powered clock, and line D

is connected to a switch on the locked closet door. The following conditions produce a logic 1 voltage on each line.

A : The control switch is closed.

B : The safe is in its normal position in the closet.

C : The clock is between 1000 and 1400 hours.

D : The closet door is closed.

Write the switching expression for the burglar alarm that produces a logic 1 (rings a bell) when the safe is moved and the control switch is closed, or when the closet is opened after banking hours, or when the closet is opened with the control switch open.

2.23 A long hallway has three doors, one at each end and one in the middle. A switch is located at each door to operate the incandescent lights along the hallway. Label the switches A, B, and C. Design a logic network to control the lights.

2.24 Find the minimum equivalent circuit for the one shown in Figure P2.24.

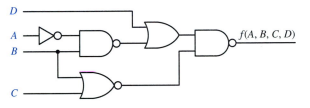

Figure P2.24

2.25 Given the timing diagram in Fig. P2.25, find the simplest switching expression for $f(A, B, C)$.

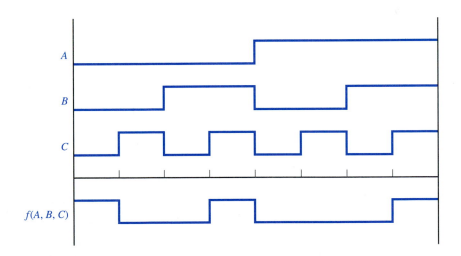

Figure P2.25

2.26 Find a minimum two-level NOR realization for the following switching function.
$$f(A, B, C) = \sum m(1, 2, 3, 5, 6, 7, 8, 9, 12, 14)$$

2.27 Given the network shown in Fig. P2.27, find the minimum two-level NOR realization.

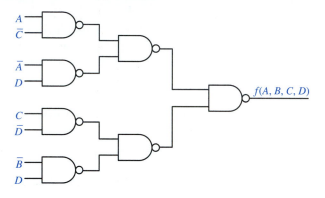

Figure P2.27

2.28 For the timing diagram shown in Fig. P2.28, find both a minimum NAND and a minimum NOR realization.

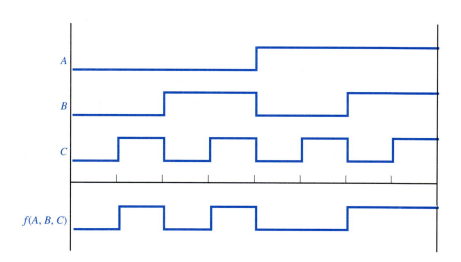

Figure P2.28

2.29 Find a minimal two-level NAND realization for each of the following switching functions.

(a) $f(A, B, C) = \sum m(0, 2, 3, 7)$

(b) $f(A, B, C, D) = \sum m(0, 2, 8, 10, 14, 15)$

(c) $f(A, B, C, D, E) = \sum m(4, 5, 6, 7, 25, 27, 29, 31)$

2.30 Obtain a minimal two-level NOR realization for the following switching functions.

(a) $f(A, B, C) = \sum m(0, 2, 3, 7)$

(b) $f(A, B, C, D) = \sum m(0, 2, 8, 10, 14, 15)$

(c) $f(A, B, C, D, E) = \sum m(0, 1, 2, 3, 8 \text{ to } 24, 26, 28, 30)$

2.31 Joe, Jack, and Jim get together once a week to either go to a movie or go bowling. To decide what to do, they vote and a simple majority wins. Assuming a vote for the movie is represented as a 1, design a logic circuit that automatically computes the decision.

2.32 Derive the logic equations for a circuit that will subtract two 2-bit binary numbers, $(X_1 X_0)_2 - (Y_1 Y_0)_2$, and produce as an output the resulting number $(D_1 D_0)_2$ and borrow condition B_1.

$$
\begin{array}{r}
X_1 X_0 \\
- Y_1 Y_0 \\
\hline
B_1 D_1 D_0
\end{array}
$$

2.33 Derive the logic equation and circuit diagram for a circuit with three inputs A, B, and C. The output is to be high only when exactly one of the three inputs is high. Use only NAND gates in the design.

2.34 We wish to design a logic circuit with four inputs A, B, C, and D. The output is to be high only when a majority of the inputs is high. Draw the final circuit using only NOR gates.

2.35 A logic circuit has four inputs A, B, C, and D. Find the logic equations for the circuit if the output is to be high only when an odd number of the inputs is high. Draw a circuit diagram using any desired logic gates.

2.36 The input to a logic circuit consists of four signal lines A, B, C, and D. These lines represent a 4-bit binary number, where A represents the most significant bit and D the least significant bit. Design the logic circuit such that the output is high only when the binary input is less than $(0111)_2 = 7_{10}$. Use any desired logic gates.

In Chapter 2 we learned how Boolean algebra can be used to eliminate unnecessary terms and literals from a switching expression, allowing it to be realized with a minimum number of logic gates. Unfortunately, algebraic manipulation relies heavily on the ability of the user to identify where the different postulates and theorems can be applied, making this process error-prone and impractical for all but the simplest switching functions. In this chapter we will examine several methods for automating the minimization of completely-specified and incompletely-specified switching functions. Karnaugh maps will be used to graphically derive minimal sum of products and product of sums expressions for switching functions, and the Quine-McCluskey tabular method will be used to simplify single- and multiple-output functions. We will then examine minimization algorithms that can be readily programmed and incorporated into computer-aided design systems.

Simplification of Switching Functions

3.1 Simplification Goals

The simplification of switching functions is a common and worthwhile goal. Its importance stems from the fact that the simpler the function, the easier it is to realize. The goal of simplification is to minimize the cost of realizing a function with physical circuit elements, where the definition of cost depends on the nature of the circuit elements to be used. In general, it is desirable to minimize the number of circuit elements and to make each element as simple as possible. In a two-level sum of products realization of a switching function, minimizing cost implies reducing the number of product terms in the expression representing the function (to reduce gate count) and minimizing the number of literals in each product term (to minimize gate complexity, measured here in terms of the number of gate inputs). When using some programmable logic devices (to be described in Chapter 5) the number of inputs to the logic forming the product terms is constant, so reducing the number of inputs to a gate provides no hardware savings, and thus only the number of terms is significant. In other cases, algebraic forms other than two-level sum of product or product of sums might be desirable if the gate count can be reduced. In designing printed circuit boards (the flat card-shaped modules used inside computer systems), the total number of integrated circuit (IC) devices may be a more limiting factor than the number of individual gates.

In all cases, a design must be made to fit within the constraints of the circuit elements to be used. The elements might have a limited number of inputs, or *fan-ins*, and may be limited in the number of output gates they can drive, or *fan-outs*. In some cases, the designer may be restricted to a specific type of circuit element. Finally, timing considerations may dictate that a faster two-level realization be utilized, rather than a slower, three-level or higher, one. In addition, steps may need to be taken to prevent undesirable momentary output changes, called *hazards*, from occurring due to uneven propagation delays through a circuit.

In this chapter, it will be assumed that we desire to minimize first the number of gates needed for a two-level realization (minimum number of products in a SOP form, or minimum number of sums in a POS form). If two or more expressions can be found containing the same number of terms, the expression with the fewest number of literals will be identified to allow gates with the lowest fan-in to be used. Remember, a *literal* is each appearance of a variable or its complement.

EXAMPLE 3.1

Determine the number of terms and literals in the following functions:

$$g(A, B, C) = A\bar{B} + \bar{A}B + AC$$
$$f(X, Y, Z) = \bar{X}Y(Z + \bar{Y}X) + \bar{Y}Z$$

$g(A, B, C)$ is a two-level form having three product terms and six literals. $f(X, Y, Z)$ is a four-level form having seven literals, combined via three products and two sums.

3.2 Characteristics of Minimization Methods

The postulates and theorems of switching algebra are the mechanisms we will employ to minimize the number of terms and literals in a switching function. Various algorithms have been developed to apply these postulates and theorems in a methodical fashion. The methods presented in this chapter are *heuristic*, that is, they utilize information derived from the problem to direct the solution, often allowing arbitrary decisions to be made when no optimal choice is readily apparent. As such, heuristic methods are not always guaranteed to find the minimum solution and are generally considered *suboptimal*, although they do find minimal solutions much of the time.

Optimal approaches exist in the form of formal algorithms that are always guaranteed to generate a minimum solution for a problem. However, most of these algorithms are more complex and more difficult to apply than heuristic methods. Therefore, many designers are content to utilize heuristic methods, trading complexity for optimality of the solution.

The following examples demonstrate the application of various postulates and theorems of switching algebra to simplify switching functions. The following sections will then examine methods to automate the simplification process.

EXAMPLE 3.2

Use switching algebra to find minimal SOP and POS forms for the function $f(X, Y, Z)$ of Example 3.1.

This expression can be minimized as follows.

$$
\begin{aligned}
f(X, Y, Z) &= \bar{X}Y(Z + \bar{Y}X) + \bar{Y}Z \\
&= \bar{X}YZ + \bar{X}Y\bar{Y}X + \bar{Y}Z & \text{[P5(b)]} \\
&= \bar{X}YZ + \bar{Y}Z & \text{[P6(b), P2(a)]} \\
&= \bar{X}Z + \bar{Y}Z & \text{[T7(a)]} \\
&= (\bar{X} + \bar{Y})Z & \text{[P5(b)]}
\end{aligned}
$$

The last two forms represent the minimum SOP and POS forms, respectively. The minimum SOP form has two terms and a total of four literals. It therefore requires two two-input AND gates and one two-input OR gate to realize. However, the POS form requires one two-input OR gate and one two-input AND gate to realize.

EXAMPLE 3.3

Use switching algebra to find a minimal SOP expression for the function

$$f(A,B,C,D) = ABC + ABD + \bar{A}B\bar{C} + CD + B\bar{D}$$

which has four variables and 13 literals.

$$
\begin{aligned}
f(A, B, C, D) &= ABC + ABD + \bar{A}B\bar{C} + CD + B\bar{D} \\
&= ABC + AB + \bar{A}B\bar{C} + CD + B\bar{D} \quad &[\text{T7(a)}] \\
&= ABC + AB + B\bar{C} + CD + B\bar{D} \quad &[\text{T7(a)}] \\
&= AB + B\bar{C} + CD + B\bar{D} \quad &[\text{T4(a)}] \\
&= AB + CD + B(\bar{C} + \bar{D}) \quad &[\text{P5(b)}] \\
&= AB + CD + B\overline{CD} \quad &[\text{T8(b)}] \\
&= AB + CD + B \quad &[\text{T5(a)}] \\
&= B + CD \quad &[\text{T4(a)}]
\end{aligned}
$$

Note that the number of literals has been reduced from 13 to 3.

In the preceding examples, the optimality of the final expression depends on the ability of the designer to determine the best postulate or theorem to apply at each step of the simplification. This becomes a difficult task as the complexity of the expressions to be simplified increases. The methods presented in this chapter are designed to automate these steps and thus increase the chances of finding optimal solutions for functions of arbitrary complexity.

3.3 Karnaugh Maps

In our previous work we found that the simplification of switching functions via the switching algebra is a difficult task, at best. In other words, in switching algebra no road map exists to be followed, and hence we must search for the best approach like a mountain climber relying on intuition and past experience. To perform the minimization of switching functions efficiently, we obviously must have at our disposal viable techniques that are standard and systematic and thus provide a road map to the desired answer. The Karnaugh map is such a tool for switching functions of up to six variables [1, 2].

3.3.1 Relationship to Venn Diagrams and Truth Tables

The Karnaugh map is actually nothing more than an extension of the concepts of truth tables, Venn diagrams, and minterms. To make the extension explicit, let us now transform a Venn diagram into a Karnaugh map. Consider the Venn diagram shown in Fig. 3.1a. The two variables A and B are represented by

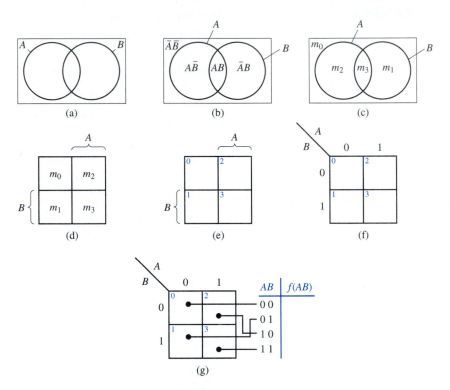

Figure 3.1 Venn diagram and equivalent K-map for two variables.

designated subdivisions of the universal set. Figure 3.1b illustrates that each unique disjoint subdivision of the Venn diagram is formed by the intersections AB, $\bar{A}B$, $A\bar{B}$, and $\bar{A}\bar{B}$. The reader should note that these intersections are just the minterms of two variables. The subdivisions of the Venn diagram are relabeled as minterms m_0, m_1, m_2, and m_3 in Figure 3.1c. This form of the Venn diagram has unequal areas for the four minterms. However, we may adjust the areas and make them all the same, as shown in Fig. 3.1d. Note that adjacent areas of the Venn diagram are also adjacent in Fig. 3.1d. However, now one half of the diagram represents the variable A and one half also represents B. Since the minterm notation is identified with each square on the diagram, we may omit the letter m and leave only the subscript, as seen in Fig. 3.1e. This is one form of the Karnaugh map. A second form for the Karnaugh map is shown in

Figure 3.1f. In this last form, the association of a map square with a particular variable, say A, is indicated by 0 for $\bar{A}$ and 1 for A.

It is important to note that the Karnaugh map is a graphical or pictorial representation of a truth table and hence there exists a one-to-one mapping between the two. The truth table has one row for each minterm while the Karnaugh map has one square per minterm. This is illustrated in Fig. 3.1g. Likewise, there is also a one-to-one correspondence between truth table rows and Karnaugh map squares if maxterms are being utilized.

The development of the Karnaugh map for three variables is shown in Fig. 3.2. An important point that requires careful analysis is the step between Fig. 3.2c and d. For example, consider the minterm m_0. This minterm is adjacent to m_1, m_2, and m_4 in Fig. 3.2c. However, in Fig. 3.2d, m_0 is not physically adjacent to m_4. To reconcile this inconsistency, the left and right edges of the map are considered to be the *same line*. In other words, the left edge can be folded over until it touches the right edge, making the Karnaugh map for three variables appear as a cylinder. In practice, the map is drawn as in Fig. 3.2e or f, and the left and right edges are imagined to be coincident.

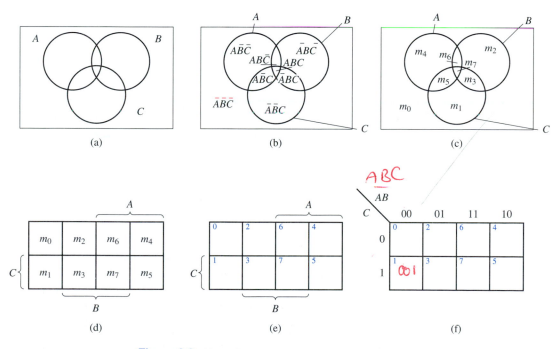

Figure 3.2   Venn diagram and equivalent K-map for three variables.

3.3.2 K-maps of Four or More Variables

The K-maps for four, five, and six variables are demonstrated in Figs. 3.3a through f. Note that the four-variable map is simply an extension of the three-

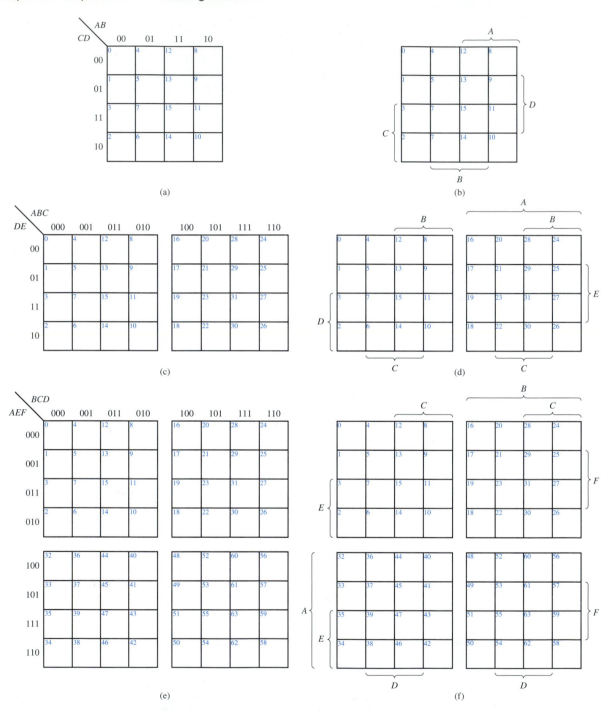

Figure 3.3 K-maps for four, five, and six variables. **(a)** $f(A, B, C, D)$ - form 1.
(b) $f(A, B, C, D)$ - form 2. **(c)** $f(A, B, C, D, E)$ - form 1. **(d)** $f(A, B, C, D, E)$ -
form 2. **(e)** $f(A, B, C, D, E, F)$ - form 1. **(f)** $f(A, B, C, D, E, F)$ - form 2.

variable map. The five-variable map for $f(A, B, C, D, E)$ is split into two halves, the left representing minterms containing $\bar{A}$ and the right representing minterms containing A. The two halves should be viewed as being stacked one on top of the other, with vertically adjacent cells differing only in variable A and thus adjacent. For example, the cells corresponding to minterms m_5 $(\bar{A}\bar{B}C\bar{D}E)$ and m_{21} $(A\bar{B}C\bar{D}E)$ are adjacent.

Likewise, the six-variable map is divided into four quadrants, each representing one combination of variables A and B. The quadrants should be viewed as being stacked on top of each other, with vertically adjacent cells being adjacent.

The maps presented in Figs. 3.1e and f, 3.2e and f, and 3.3a through f combine all the familiar features that logic designers use in switching circuit synthesis. Either of the two formats for an n-variable K-map may be used at the reader's discretion. K-maps of more than six variables are impractical for most problems.

3.4 Plotting Functions in Canonical Form on the K-map

Switching functions may be expressed in a wide variety of forms, ranging from minterm/maxterm lists to simple SOP/POS expressions to more complex expressions. However, each has a unique canonical POS/SOP form. In this section we will examine methods for plotting switching functions of different forms on a Karnaugh map.

Switching functions may be readily plotted on a K-map if they are expressed in canonical form, since each minterm/maxterm of the canonical form corresponds to one cell on the K-map. Suppose we wish to find the K-map for the following function:

$$f(A, B, C) = m(0, 3, 5) = m_0 + m_3 + m_5$$
$$= \prod M(1, 2, 4, 6, 7) = M_1 M_2 M_4 M_6 M_7$$

Recall from Chapter 2 that the maxterm list is readily derived from the minterm list, and vice versa. First, let us consider the representation of the function as the sum of minterms 0, 3, and 5. Using the Venn diagram form of the K-map, the function $f(A, B, C)$ represents the shaded areas shown in Fig. 3.4a. This same function plotted on a K-map is shown in Fig. 3.4b. Note that shaded areas are normally not used on K-maps. Instead, we employ the familiar 1 and 0 used in truth tables, with each shaded area (each minterm) represented by 1 and each unshaded area (each maxterm) represented by a 0. Under these conditions, the K-map of Fig. 3.4b corresponds directly to the truth table of the function, with each cell of the K-map corresponding to one row of the truth table. When the function is represented as a sum of minterms, we normally omit the maxterms from the map and represent the function as shown in Fig. 3.4c. Likewise, if the function is expressed as a product of maxterms, we omit the minterms and represent the function as shown in Fig. 3.4d.

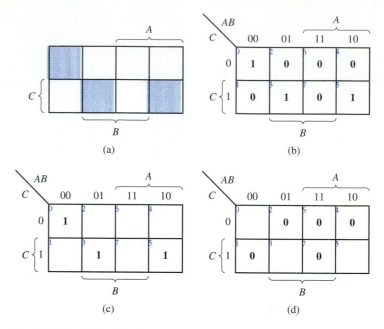

Figure 3.4 Plotting functions on K-maps. **(a)** Venn diagram form. **(b)** 1's represent minterms, 0's represent maxterms. **(c)** Plot of minterms only. **(d)** Plot of maxterms only.

EXAMPLE 3.4

Let us plot the following function on a K-map:
$$f(a,b,Q,G) = m(0,3,5,7,10,11,12,13,14,15) \longrightarrow ones \Rightarrow min\ term$$
$$= \prod M(1,2,4,6,8,9) \longrightarrow zeros \Rightarrow max\ term$$

The function, expressed as a sum of minterms, is plotted on a version of the K-map labeled with both conventions in Fig. 3.5a. The function, expressed as a product of maxterms, is shown on the K-map in Fig. 3.5b.

A most important point should be noted about the ordering of the variables. As was demonstrated in the last section, the minterm and maxterm numbers in the list change if the order of the variables is altered. Therefore, the order of the variables in the function fixes the order of the variables on the K-map.

EXAMPLE 3.5

Let us repeat Example 3.4 with the variables reordered to give $f(Q,G,b,a)$.

First, write the minterms of $f(a,b,Q,G)$:
$$f(a,b,Q,G) = \sum m(0,3,5,7,10,11,12,13,14,15)$$
$$= \bar{a}\bar{b}\bar{Q}\bar{G} + \bar{a}\bar{b}QG + \bar{a}bQ\bar{G} + \bar{a}bQG + a\bar{b}Q\bar{G}$$
$$+ a\bar{b}QG + ab\bar{Q}\bar{G} + ab\bar{Q}G + abQ\bar{G} + abQG$$

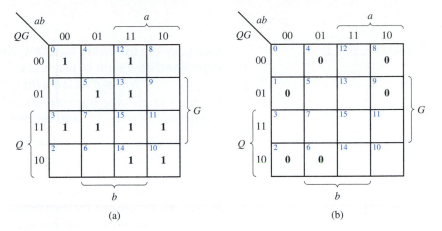

Figure 3.5 K-maps for $f(a, b, Q, G)$ in Example 3.4. **(a)** Minterm form . **(b)** Maxterm form.

Next, rearrange the variables:

$$f(Q, G, b, a) = \bar{Q}\bar{G}\bar{b}\bar{a} + QG\bar{b}\bar{a} + \bar{Q}G b\bar{a} + QGb\bar{a} + Q\bar{G}\bar{b}a$$
$$+ QG\bar{b}a + \bar{Q}\bar{G}ba + \bar{Q}Gba + Q\bar{G}ba + QGba$$
$$= \sum m(0, 12, 6, 14, 9, 13, 3, 7, 11, 15)$$
$$= \sum m(0, 3, 6, 7, 9, 11, 12, 13, 14, 15)$$

The function is plotted on the map of Fig. 3.6, which is equivalent to the one in Fig. 3.5a.

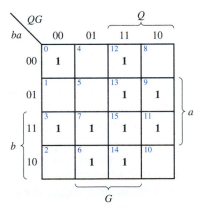

Figure 3.6 K-map of Figure 3.5(a) with variables reordered: $f(Q, G, b, a)$.

K-maps can also be conveniently used to expand a function into canonical form. To illustrate this technique, we shall continue to use a combination of the two K-map forms shown in Fig. 3.3.

EXAMPLE 3.6

Consider the following function, which is expressed as a sum of products.

AND (NAND)

$$f(A, B, C) = AB + B\bar{C}$$

We wish to plot the function on a K-map and determine its minterm and maxterm lists.

The map illustrating the two product terms is shown in Fig. 3.7a. The term AB represents the portion of the map where both A and B are 1, that is, minterms 6 and 7, as seen in Fig. 3.7b. The term $B\bar{C}$ represents the area on the map where B is 1 and C is 0, that is, minterms 2 and 6. Rather than shade in areas on the K-map, we usually plot the ones directly on the map, as shown in Fig. 3.7b. The map illustrating the maxterms of the function is derived directly from the minterm map and is shown in Fig. 3.7c.

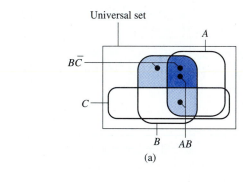

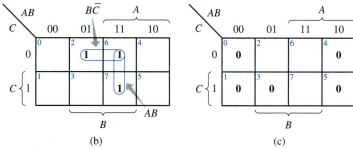

Figure 3.7 K-maps for Example 3.6. **(a)** Map drawn in Venn diagram form. **(b)** Sum of minterms. **(c)** Maxterms of the function.

From Figs. 3.7b and c, the function can be expressed in minterm and maxterm forms as

$$f(A, B, C) = m(2, 6, 7) = \prod M(0, 1, 3, 4, 5)$$

In this example we note that minterm 6 is used twice, that is, is "covered" by both of the original product terms. The multiple use of minterms and maxterms is often the rule, rather than the exception, in switching functions. Also, note that it was not really necessary to draw the K-map of Fig. 3.7c since the maxterms can be identified directly on the K-map of Fig. 3.7b by simply noting the cells not set to 1.

EXAMPLE 3.7

Let us plot the following function on the K-map and determine its minterm and maxterm lists.

$$f(A, B, C, D) = (A + C)(B + C)(\bar{B} + \bar{C} + D)$$

Since this expression is in POS form, we may plot the zeros (its maxterms) on the K-map. The map illustrating the maxterms is shown in Fig. 3.8a. The term $A + C$ will force the function to have a zero value when $A = C = 0$, so it represents the area of the map for which $A = 0$ and $C = 0$, representing, that

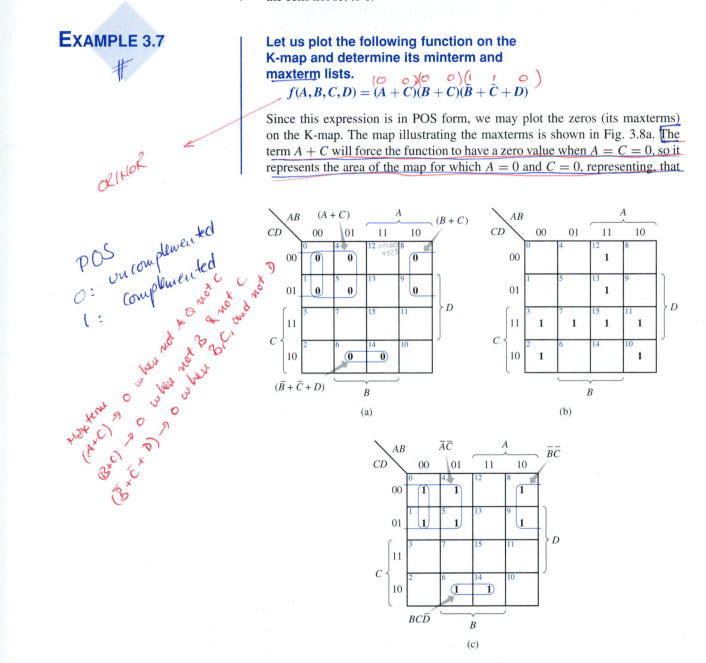

Figure 3.8   K-maps for Example 3.7. **(a)** K-map showing maxterms. **(b)** K-map showing minterms. **(c)** K-map showing minterms of $\bar{f}(A, B, C, D)$.

is, covering, maxterms 0, 1, 4, and 5. Likewise, $B + C$ represents maxterms 0, 1, 8, and 9. The term $\bar{B} + \bar{C} + D$ represents maxterms 6 and 14 because the term is 0 when $B = 1$, $C = 1$, and $D = 0$. The corresponding map illustrating the minterms is shown in Fig. 3.8b.

From Figs. 3.8a and b, the function can be expressed as

$$f(A, B, C, D) = \prod M(0, 1, 4, 5, 6, 8, 9, 14)$$
$$= \sum m(2, 3, 7, 10, 11, 12, 13, 15)$$

Some designers find plotting POS expressions to be awkward. An alternative method is to complement the function and apply DeMorgan's theorem to obtain a SOP expression for $\bar{f}(A, B, C, D)$.

$$\bar{f}(A, B, C, D) = \overline{(A + C)(B + C)(\bar{B} + \bar{C} + D)}$$
$$= \overline{(A + C)} + \overline{(B + C)} + \overline{(\bar{B} + \bar{C} + D)}$$
$$= \bar{A}\bar{C} + \bar{B}\bar{C} + BC\bar{D}$$

The SOP form of $\bar{f}(A, B, C, D)$ is then plotted on a K-map as shown in Fig. 3.8c. Recalling that the minterms of $\bar{f}(A, B, C, D)$ are the maxterms of $f(A, B, C, D)$, and vice versa, the K-map of Fig. 3.8a is produced by simply converting each 0 cell (maxterm) in the K-map of $\bar{f}(A, B, C, D)$ to a 1 cell (minterm) in the K-map of $f(A, B, C, D)$. Note, also, that the expression for each product term plotted in Fig. 3.8b is the complement of the expression of the corresponding sum term in Fig. 3.8c.

As was indicated in Example 3.5, it was not necessary to draw the K-map of Fig. 3.8b to determine the minterm list, since the minterms are simply the nonzero cells in the K-map of Fig. 3.8a.

An alternative procedure for plotting the POS form of a function f is to complement the function and apply DeMorgan's theorem to produce a SOP form for $\bar{f}$. Then $\bar{f}$ is plotted on the K-map, from which the minterm list of $\bar{f}$ can be read, with the minterms of f corresponding to the zero cells of $\bar{f}$.

EXAMPLE 3.8

Derive the minterm list of the function
$$f(A, B, C, D) = (\bar{A} + \bar{B})(\bar{A} + C + \bar{D})(\bar{B} + \bar{C} + \bar{D})$$

We begin by complementing the function and applying DeMorgan's theorem:

$$\bar{f}(A, B, C, D) = \overline{(\bar{A} + \bar{B})(\bar{A} + C + \bar{D})(\bar{B} + \bar{C} + \bar{D})}$$
$$= \overline{(\bar{A} + \bar{B})} + \overline{(\bar{A} + C + \bar{D})} + \overline{(\bar{B} + \bar{C} + \bar{D})}$$
$$= AB + A\bar{C}D + BCD$$

$\bar{f}(A, B, C, D) = AB + A\bar{C}D + BCD$ is plotted on the K-map as shown in Fig. 3.9a. From this K-map we can write

$$\bar{f}(A, B, C, D) = \sum m(7, 9, 12, 13, 14, 15)$$

Since the zero cells in the K-map of Fig. 3.9a represent $f(A, B, C, D)$, by inspection of the K-map we can write

$$f(A, B, C, D) = \sum m(0, 1, 2, 3, 4, 5, 6, 8, 10, 11)$$

The function is plotted on the K-map of Fig. 3.9b.

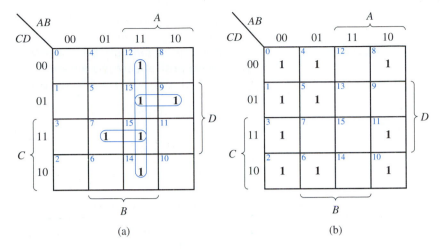

Figure 3.9 K-maps for Example 3.8. **(a)** K-map of $\bar{f}(A, B, C, D)$. **(b)** Corresponding K-map of $f(A, B, C, D)$.

3.5 Simplification of Switching Functions Using K-maps

In the previous section we derived a SOP or POS expression for a function from its K-map without consideration of whether the expression was the simplest possible for that function. The K-map will now be used to obtain a minimal sum of products expression for a switching function. By minimal sum of products we mean an expression that is equivalent to the original expression, but that contains a minimum number of product terms in which a minimum number of literals are present. Minimizing the number of product terms allows the fewest number of gates to be used to realize the function, while minimizing the number of literals allows gates with the smallest possible fan-in (and therefore the lowest cost) to be used to realize each term.

Simplification of functions on the K-map is expedited by the fact that on the map switching terms that are logically adjacent are also physically adjacent. Let us define *logically adjacent* minterms as follows: two minterms, m_i and m_j, are logically adjacent if they differ in only one variable position. For example, $AB\bar{C}\bar{D}$ and $AB\bar{C}D$ are logically adjacent minterms of four variables since they differ only in variable position D. From Theorem 6(a) we know that $AB\bar{C}\bar{D} + AB\bar{C}D = AB\bar{C}$; therefore, terms $AB\bar{C}\bar{D}$ and $AB\bar{C}D$ *combine*, eliminating variable D. In general, any two logically adjacent terms can be combined, eliminating one variable.

On the K-map we illustrate combining terms by drawing a ring around the terms that, when combined, yield a simpler expression, that is, one with fewer literals.

The following example illustrates the process of combining logically adjacent terms, using both switching algebra and K-map methods.

EXAMPLE 3.9

We wish to simplify the following function using both switching algebra and the K-map.

$$f(A, B, C, D) = \sum m(1, 2, 4, 6, 9)$$

The simplification of this function via switching algebra may be performed as follows:

Step 1. Combine m_1 and m_9.

$$f(A, B, C, D) = \bar{A}\bar{B}\bar{C}D + \bar{A}\bar{B}C\bar{D} + \bar{A}B\bar{C}\bar{D} + \bar{A}BC\bar{D} + A\bar{B}\bar{C}D$$
$$= (\bar{A}\bar{B}\bar{C}D + A\bar{B}\bar{C}D) + \bar{A}\bar{B}C\bar{D} + \bar{A}B\bar{C}\bar{D} + \bar{A}BC\bar{D}$$
$$= \bar{B}\bar{C}D + \bar{A}\bar{B}C\bar{D} + \bar{A}B\bar{C}\bar{D} + \bar{A}BC\bar{D}$$

Step 2. Combine m_2 and m_6, duplicating m_6 first.

$$f(A, B, C, D) = \bar{B}\bar{C}D + \bar{A}\bar{B}C\bar{D} + \bar{A}B\bar{C}\bar{D} + (\bar{A}BC\bar{D} + \bar{A}BC\bar{D})$$
$$= \bar{B}\bar{C}D + (\bar{A}\bar{B}C\bar{D} + \bar{A}BC\bar{D}) + \bar{A}B\bar{C}\bar{D} + \bar{A}BC\bar{D}$$
$$= \bar{B}\bar{C}D + \bar{A}C\bar{D} + \bar{A}B\bar{C}\bar{D} + \bar{A}BC\bar{D}$$

Step 3. Combine m_4 and m_6.

$$f(A, B, C, D) = \bar{B}\bar{C}D + \bar{A}C\bar{D} + (\bar{A}B\bar{C}\bar{D} + \bar{A}BC\bar{D})$$
$$= \bar{B}\bar{C}D + \bar{A}C\bar{D} + \bar{A}B\bar{D}$$

The corresponding K-map simplification is shown in Fig. 3.10. The simplification involves circling sets of physically adjacent squares, corresponding to groups of logically adjacent minterms. Note that, since opposite edges of the map are actually coincident, the horse shoe shapes in Fig. 3.10 are really circles. Each circle indicates the manner in which the circled minterms are combined to yield a simpler switching expression.

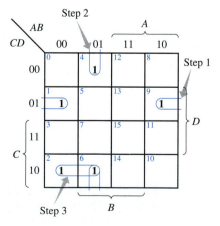

Figure 3.10   K-map for Example 3.9.

In step 1, minterms m_1 and m_9, which are adjacent on the K-map, are combined by circling the corresponding squares. Comparing these two squares, we see that the variable that changes from 0 in m_1 to 1 in m_9 is the variable A; hence, when the two minterms are combined, this variable is eliminated, as shown in step 1 of the switching algebra approach. Minterms m_4 and m_6 are combined on the K-map in step 2. Comparing these two squares we see that they differ only in the variable C; hence, this variable is eliminated when squares 4 and 6 are combined. Finally, in step 3, combining squares 2 and 6 eliminates the variable B. Thus, the three steps on the K-map are equivalent to the corresponding steps indicated in the switching algebra simplification. The reader is reminded, as is demonstrated in steps 2 and 3, that minterms can be used more than once because $X = X + X$ by idempotency (Theorem 1).

3.5.1 Guidelines for Simplifying Functions Using K-maps

There are five important points to keep in mind when simplifying functions on K-maps:

1. Each square (minterm) on a K-map of two variables has two squares (minterms) that are logically adjacent, each square on a K-map of three variables has three adjacent squares, and so on. In general, each square on a K-map of n variables has n logically adjacent squares, with each pair of adjacent squares differing in exactly one variable.

2. When combining terms (squares) on a K-map we always group squares in powers of 2, that is, two squares, four squares, eight squares, and so on. Grouping two squares eliminates one variable, grouping four squares eliminates two variables, and so on. In general, grouping 2^n squares eliminates n variables.

3. Group as many squares together as possible; the larger the group is, the fewer the number of literals in the resulting product term.

4. Make as few groups as possible to cover all the squares (minterms) of the function. A minterm is *covered* if it is included in at least one group. The fewer the groups, the fewer the number of product terms in the minimized function. Each minterm may be used as many times as it is needed in steps 4 and 5; however, it must be used at least once. As soon as all minterms are used once, stop. A minterm that has been used in at least one group is said to have been *covered*.

5. In combining squares on the map, always begin with those squares for which there are the fewest number of adjacent squares (the "loneliest" squares on the map). Minterms with multiple adjacent minterms (called *adjacencies*) offer more possible combinations and should therefore be combined later in the minimization process.

3.5.2 General Terminology for Switching Function Minimization

The previous discussion illustrated the relationship between the switching algebra and K-map procedures for simplifying a switching function. We now define four terms that are not only useful in K-map simplification, but also provide

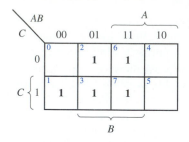

Figure 3.11 K-map illustrating implicants.

the basis for the more general switching function minimization techniques that will be presented later. These terms are *implicant*, *prime implicant*, *essential prime implicant*, and *cover*.

An *implicant* is a product term (that is, a product of one or more literals) that could be used to cover minterms of the function. In the K-map of Fig. 3.11 there are 11 implicants:

5 Minterms: $\{\bar{A}\bar{B}C, \bar{A}B\bar{C}, \bar{A}BC, AB\bar{C}, ABC\}$

5 Groups of two minterms: $\{\bar{A}B, AB, \bar{A}C, B\bar{C}, BC\}$

1 Group of four minterms: $\{B\}$

A *prime implicant* is an implicant that is not a part of (covered by) any other implicant of the function. Recall from the previous example that as we combine minterms (implicants) we eliminate variables. As we combine implicants (in powers of 2) into maximal groups, we form prime implicants. On the K-map a prime implicant is equivalent to a set of squares that is not a subset of any set containing a larger number of squares. Prime implicants represent the largest groupings of minterms that can be derived for the function. In the K-map of Fig. 3.11, there are only two prime implicants: B and $\bar{A}C$. Prime implicant B covers implicants $\bar{A}B\bar{C}$, $\bar{A}BC$, $AB\bar{C}$, ABC, $\bar{A}B$, AB, $B\bar{C}$, and BC. Prime implicant $\bar{A}C$ covers implicants $\bar{A}\bar{B}C$ and $\bar{A}BC$.

An *essential prime implicant* is a prime implicant that covers at least one minterm that is not covered by any other prime implicant. In the K-map of Fig. 3.11, prime implicant $\bar{A}C$ is essential because it is the only prime implicant that covers minterm 1, and prime implicant B is essential because it is the only prime implicant that covers minterms 2, 6, and 7. An essential prime implicant is easily identified on the K-map by noting that it covers at least one minterm that is circled only once.

Finally, a *cover* of a function is a set of prime implicants for which each minterm of the function is contained in (covered) by at least one prime implicant. All essential prime implicants of a function must be selected in any cover of a function. For the K-map of Fig. 3.11, the set of prime implicants $\{B, \bar{A}C\}$ represents a cover of the function.

3.5.3 Algorithms for Deriving Minimal SOP Forms from K-maps

Our primary goal in minimizing a function is to find a minimum set of prime implicants that covers a function, from which a minimum sum of products expression can be derived. With these points in mind, we now present two algorithms for finding a minimum cover of a function that is plotted on a K-map. These algorithms are designed to help the user follow the five guidelines presented previously, thereby simplifying the minimization process and ensuring a high likelihood of finding the minimum cover of any arbitrary function.

Algorithm 3.1

1. Count the number of adjacencies for each minterm on the K-map.

2. Select an uncovered minterm with the fewest number of adjacencies. Make an arbitrary choice if more than one choice is possible.

3. Generate a prime implicant for this minterm and put it in the cover. If this minterm is covered by more than one prime implicant, select the one that covers the most uncovered minterms.

4. Repeat steps 2 and 3 until all the minterms have been covered.

This algorithm is easy to apply and generally finds a minimal solution. However, since arbitrary choices are allowed in steps 1 and 2, it is not optimal. Therefore, it is not guaranteed to find the minimum cover for every function.

The following algorithm for generating a minimum cover of a function from a K-map is an efficient alternative to Algorithm 3.1 if the number of prime implicants is not too large.

Algorithm 3.2

1. Circle all prime implicants on the K-map.

2. Identify and select all essential prime implicants for the cover.

3. Select a minimum subset of the remaining prime implicants to complete the cover, that is, to cover those minterms not covered by the essential prime implicants.

This algorithm generates more terms and therefore requires more work than Algorithm 3.1. However, since all prime implicants are identified and considered, it is often better able to find a minimal cover. Again, arbitrary decisions may be needed in step 3, and thus the algorithm is not optimal. Once we have a minimum cover of the function, we derive the minimum SOP form by writing out the sum of the prime implicants in the cover.

We now illustrate the application of these two algorithms with the following examples.

EXAMPLE 3.10

Let us use the K-map and Algorithm 3.1 to simplify the following function.

$$f(A, B, C, D) = \sum m(2, 3, 4, 5, 7, 8, 10, 13, 15)$$

To initiate the simplification process, we first plot the function on the map as shown in Fig. 3.12a.

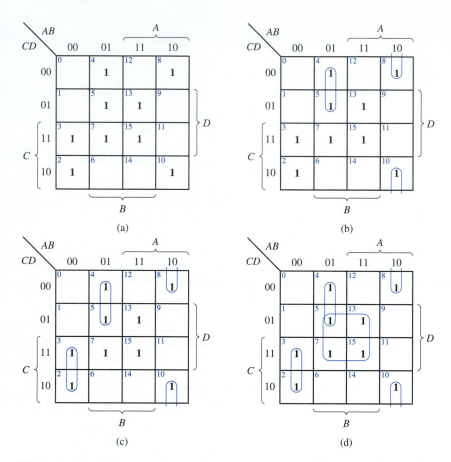

Figure 3.12 K-maps Illustrating Algorithm 3.1. **(a)** Plot of the function. **(b)** Prime implicants 4-5 and 8-10. **(c)** Prime implicant 2-3 covers m_2. **(d)** Prime implicant 5-7-13-15 completes the cover.

We now count the adjacencies for each minterm. From Fig. 3.12a we see that minterms m_4 and m_8 each have one adjacency, minterms m_2, m_3, m_{10}, m_{13}, and m_{15} each have two adjacencies, and minterms m_5 and m_7 each have three adjacencies.

Since m_4 and m_8 each have only one adjacency, we begin with them. Prime implicant 4–5 is the only prime implicant that covers m_4, and prime implicant 8–10 is the only cover of m_8. Therefore, we add these two prime implicants to the cover by circling them on the K-map as shown in Fig. 3.12b.

Examining the remaining uncovered minterms in Fig. 3.12b, we see that four of them have two adjacencies, therefore we make an arbitrary selection, say m_2. Minterm m_2 is covered by two prime implicants, 2–3 and 2–10. Since prime implicant 2–3 covers more of the remaining uncovered minterms, we select it for the cover by circling it as shown in Fig. 3.12c.

Since m_{13} and m_{15} each have two adjacencies, we again make an arbitrary selection, say m_{13}. Minterm m_{13} is covered only by prime implicant 5–7–13–15, so we add this prime implicant to the cover by circling it as shown in Fig. 3.12d.

From Fig. 3.12d we see that all minterms are now covered. Therefore, our minimum cover is {4–5, 8–10, 2–3, 5–7–13–15}.

The product terms that the prime implicants represent are obtained as follows. On the map, prime implicant 2–3 is located outside A and B and inside C; therefore, the term is $\bar{A}\bar{B}C$. The prime implicant 4–5 is outside A and C and inside B, therefore, the term is $\bar{A}B\bar{C}$. Prime implicant 5–7–13–15 is inside B and D; therefore, the term is BD. Finally, prime implicant 8–10 is located inside A and outside B and D; hence, the term is $A\bar{B}\bar{D}$. Therefore, the minimized function is

$$f(A, B, C, D) = \bar{A}\bar{B}C + \bar{A}B\bar{C} + BD + A\bar{B}\bar{D}$$

EXAMPLE 3.11

Repeat Example 3.10 using Algorithm 3.2.

We begin by circling all prime implicants on the K-map as shown in Fig. 3.13a. The prime implicants, listed according to the minterms covered, are {2–3, 3–7, 4–5, 5–7–13–15, 8–10, 2–10}.

In step 2 of the algorithm, we select essential prime implicants. From Fig. 3.13a, we can see that prime implicant 4–5 is essential because it covers m_4, which is not covered by any other prime implicant. A similar argument holds for prime implicants 8–10 and 5–7–13–15. Consequently, these essential prime implicants must be part of the cover for the function; they are plotted on the K-map of Fig. 3.13b.

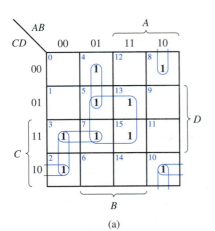

(a)

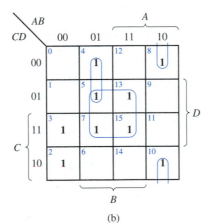

(b)

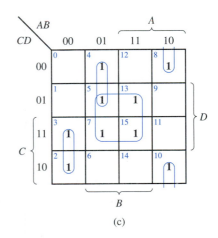

(c)

Figure 3.13 K-maps Illustrating Algorithm 3.2. **(a)** All prime implicants. **(b)** Essential prime implicants. **(c)** Minimum cover.

In step 3 of the algorithm we select a minimum number of prime implicants to cover the remaining minterms. The only minterms in Fig. 3.13b that remain uncovered are m_2 and m_3. Minterm m_2 is covered by prime implicants 2–3 and 2–10, while m_3 is covered by prime implicants 2–3 and 3–7. Selecting prime implicant 2–3 would cover both minterms, adding only one product term to the cover. Selecting 2–10 to cover m_2 would also require the selection of another prime implicant (3–7 or 2–3) to cover m_3; this would add two more product terms to the cover. Therefore, to obtain a minimum realization, we choose prime implicant 2–3, as plotted in Fig. 3.13c.

Hence our minimum cover contains the prime implicant 2–3 and the essential prime implicants 4–5, 5–7–13–15, and 8–10, which is the same result obtained in the previous example, as was plotted in Fig. 3.12d.

It is very important that the reader understand that the use of the K-map is simply a convenient method for performing switching algebra reductions. For example, if we had combined minterms 5–7–13–15 using algebra, we would in essence perform the following process.

$$
\begin{aligned}
m_5 + m_7 + m_{13} + m_{15} &= \bar{A}B\bar{C}D + \bar{A}BCD + AB\bar{C}D + ABCD \\
&= (\bar{A}B\bar{C}D + \bar{A}BCD) + (AB\bar{C}D + ABCD) \\
&= \bar{A}BD + ABD \\
&= BD
\end{aligned}
$$

Thus, we repeatedly combined terms using Theorem 6a, first to eliminate the variable C and then to eliminate the variable A. Thus, circling four squares eliminates two variables. The reader should verify that the same result would be obtained algebraically by eliminating variable A first, and then C.

EXAMPLE 3.12

Let us use the K-map to simplify the following function.
$$
f(A, B, C, D) = \sum m(0, 5, 7, 8, 10, 12, 14, 15)
$$

The function is plotted on the map in Fig. 3.14a.

Using Algorithm 3.1, we begin by selecting minterm m_0, which has only one adjacency, and generate prime implicant 0–8. Likewise, m_5 has only one adjacency and is covered by prime implicant 5–7. Looking at minterms with two adjacencies and selecting m_{10}, we generate prime implicant 8–10–12–14. At this point the only uncovered minterm is m_{15}, which is covered by prime implicants 7–15 and 14–15. Since these two prime implicants cover the same number of cells and are thus of equal complexity, we can choose either for the cover of the function. Figure 3.14b shows the resulting minimal cover if prime implicant 7–15 is chosen, and Fig. 3.14c shows the minimal cover if prime implicant 7–15 is chosen.

If Algorithm 3.2 is used, we would begin by circling all the prime implicants, as in Fig. 3.14d. From this map, we can identify as the essential prime implicants 0–8, 5–7, and 8–10–12–14. Selecting the essential prime implicants for the cover leaves only m_{15} uncovered. Therefore, to complete the minimum

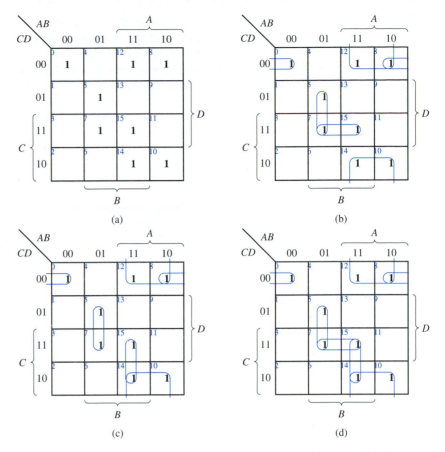

Figure 3.14   K-maps for $f(A, B, C, D) = \sum m(0, 5, 7, 8, 10, 12, 14, 15)$. **(a)** Plot of the function. **(b)** Minimal cover 1. **(c)** Minimal cover 2. **(d)** All prime implicants.

cover we select either prime implicant 7–15 or 14–15 to cover m_{15}, resulting in the same two solutions of Figs. 3.14b and c that were obtained with Algorithm 3.1.

Keep in mind that minterms may be covered any number of times. In this example, m_8 is covered twice in each of the two solutions. Multiple use of minterms occurs more often than not.

Now, from minimal cover 1 of Fig. 3.14b, the minimum SOP form of function $f(A, B, C, D)$ can be written as

$$f(A, B, C, D) = \bar{B}\bar{C}\bar{D} + \bar{A}BD + A\bar{D} + BCD$$

and from minimal cover 2 we get

$$f(A, B, C, D) = \bar{B}\bar{C}\bar{D} + \bar{A}BD + A\bar{D} + ABC$$

Since both SOP forms contain the same number of terms and literals, either represents a minimal SOP expression for the function.

Several other examples are now presented in rapid order. Each example contains, first, the function to be minimized, second, a K-map with the prime implicants of the minimum cover identified (circled), and, finally, an expression for the minimized function, which is a minimal covering of the function selected from the prime implicants.

EXAMPLE 3.13

Find a minimum SOP expression for
$f(A, B, C) = \sum m(1, 2, 3, 6).$

The function is plotted on the K-map of Fig. 3.15. Using Algorithm 3.1, we begin with minterms m_1 and m_6, which each have one adjacency and generate prime implicants 1–3 and 2–6, respectively. Since these cover all four minterms, no additional prime implicants are needed.

Using Algorithm 3.2, we see that this function has two essential prime implicants, 1–3 and 2–6, and one additional prime implicant, 2–3, which is not needed since the two essential prime implicants cover the function.

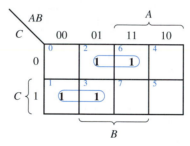

Figure 3.15 $f(A, B, C) = \sum m(1, 2, 3, 6) = \bar{A}C + B\bar{C}.$

The minimum SOP form is therefore the sum of the two prime implicants:
$$f(A, B, C) = \bar{A}C + B\bar{C}$$

EXAMPLE 3.14

Find a minimum SOP expression for
$f(A, B, C, D) = \sum m(0, 1, 2, 7, 8, 9, 10, 15).$

For this function, as seen in Fig. 3.16, there are three prime implicants, 7–15, 0–1–8–9, and 0–2–8–10, all of which are essential and therefore form the minimum cover of the function. Note that prime implicant 0–2–8–10 covers the four corners of the K-map. The four corners are adjacent by virtue of the fact the top and bottom rows are adjacent (differing in variable C), as are the leftmost and rightmost columns (differing in variable A).

EXAMPLE 3.15

Find a minimum SOP expression for
$f(A, B, C, D) = \sum m(0, 4, 5, 7, 8, 10, 14, 15).$

From the K-map of Fig. 3.17a, we can see that each minterm is covered by two prime implicants, and therefore none of the prime implicants is essential. In

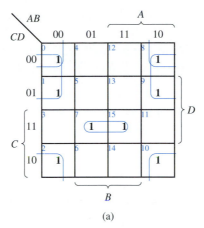

Figure 3.16 $f(A, B, C, D) = \bar{B}\bar{D} + \bar{B}\bar{C} + BCD$.

(a)

addition, each minterm has exactly two adjacencies. This condition is referred to as a *cycle* in the K-map. Whenever a cycle occurs, we must break it by making an arbitrary initial selection.

Let us begin by covering minterm m_0. We see that it can be covered with either of prime implicants 0–4 or 0–8. Selection of 0–4 leads to the minimum cover shown in Fig. 3.17b, for which the minimum SOP expression is

$$f(A, B, C, D) = \bar{A}\bar{C}\bar{D} + \bar{A}BD + ABC + A\bar{B}\bar{D}$$

Selection of prime implicant 0–8 to cover m_0 leads to the minimum cover shown in Fig. 3.17c, for which the minimum SOP expression is

$$f(A, B, C, D) = \bar{B}\bar{C}\bar{D} + \bar{A}B\bar{C} + BCD + AC\bar{D}$$

Thus, there are two totally different minimal SOP expressions for the function, which have the same number of terms and literals and therefore the same cost.

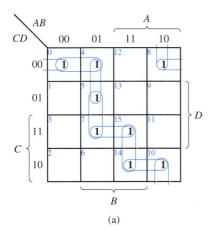

(a)

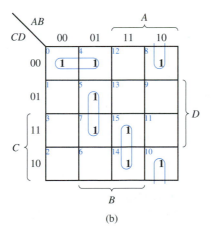

(b)

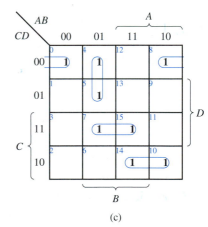

(c)

Figure 3.17   Function with no essential prime implicants. **(a)** All prime implicants. **(b)** Minimal cover 1. **(c)** Minimal cover 2.

EXAMPLE 3.16

Find a minimum SOP expression for
$$f(A,B,C,D,E) = \sum m(0,2,4,7,10,12,13,18,23,26,28,29)$$

Using Algorithm 3.1, we cover minterm m_0 with prime implicant 0–4, m_7 with prime implicant 7–23, m_{13} with prime implicant 12–13–28–29, and m_{10} with prime implicant 2–10–18–26. Plotting these on the K-map of Fig. 3.18, we see

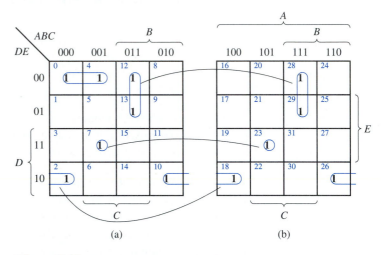

Figure 3.18   Minimizing a five-variable function.

that all four of these prime implicants are essential and form a complete cover of the function. The minimum SOP form of the function is
$$f(A, B, C, D, E) = \bar{A}\bar{B}\bar{D}\bar{E} + BC\bar{D} + \bar{B}CDE + \bar{C}D\bar{E}$$
Note that care must be taken to identify adjacencies between the two halves of a five-variable map. For example, implicant 12–13 is adjacent to implicant 28–29 and they thus combine to form prime implicant 12–13–28–29. The same is true for prime implicants 7–23 and 2–10–18–26.

For five-variable maps, as shown in Fig. 3.18, each minterm has only five possible adjacencies; for example, the adjacencies for m_8 are m_0, m_9, m_{10}, m_{12}, and m_{24}. Note that m_{16} is *not* adjacent to m_8; that is why we leave a space between halves of the map. Hence, minterms that appear in similar positions in the two parts of the map are adjacent and can be combined.

Another way to look at this is to imagine that the two halves of the map are transparent and stacked so that we look through squares 0–15 and see squares 16–31. In this configuration, similar minterms on each half are logically adjacent and hence combine. For example, the minterm combination m_{13} and m_{29} can be grouped to eliminate the variable A, as can minterms m_7 and m_{23}, m_2 and m_{18}, and others.

3.6 POS Form Using K-maps

Thus far we have concentrated our discussion on the use of the K-map in minimizing a function in SOP form. An identical procedure can be employed to minimize a function in POS (product of sums) form. Furthermore, all the techniques we have learned for combining minterms can be applied in the combination of maxterms to produce a minimum POS form.

3.6.1 General Terminology for POS Forms

In a manner analogous to the minimization of SOP forms, we define the terms *implicate*, *prime implicate*, *essential prime implicate*, and *cover* for use in deriving minimum POS forms.

An *implicate* is a sum term, that is, a sum of one or more literals, that could be used to cover maxterms of the function. Note that an implicate represents an input combination for which the function evaluates to 0. On the K-map, an implicate is a group of adjacent maxterms, or 0 squares. A *prime implicate* is an implicate that is not covered by any other implicate of the function. On the K-map, a prime implicate is a group of adjacent maxterms that is not covered by a larger group of maxterms. An *essential prime implicate* is a prime implicate that covers at least one maxterm that is not covered by any other prime implicate. On the K-map, an essential prime implicate covers at least one maxterm that is circled only once. A *cover* of a function is a set of implicates for which each maxterm of the function is contained in (covered by) at least one prime implicate.

3.6.2 Algorithms for Deriving Minimal POS Forms from K-maps

Algorithms 3.1 and 3.2 for generating minimum covers of a function, from which minimum SOP expressions are produced, are easily modified to produce minimum covers from which POS forms can be derived. The process of grouping cells into maximal groups and then selecting groups of cells to cover the function is identical, except that the cells represent maxterms rather than minterms, and the groups are called implicates rather than implicants. Therefore, we have the following two algorithms for generating a minimum cover of the maxterms of a function.

Algorithm 3.3

1. Count the number of adjacencies for each maxterm on the K-map.
2. Select an uncovered maxterm with the fewest number of adjacencies. Make an arbitrary choice if more than one choice is possible.

3. Generate a prime implicate for this maxterm and put it in the cover. If this maxterm is covered by more than one prime implicate, select the one that covers the most uncovered maxterms.
4. Repeat steps 2 and 3 until all the maxterms have been covered.

Algorithm 3.4

1. Circle all prime implicates on the K-map.
2. Identify and select all essential prime implicates for the cover.
3. Select a minimum subset of the remaining prime implicates to complete the cover, that is, to cover those maxterms not covered by the essential prime implicates.

After we have obtained a minimum cover of the function, we derive the minimum POS expression by writing each prime implicate as a sum term and then forming the product of the sum terms.

We will demonstrate the minimization process by considering one example in some detail and then provide several additional examples in rapid succession.

EXAMPLE 3.17

Let us find the minimum POS form for the function

$$f(A, B, C, D) = \prod M(0, 1, 2, 3, 6, 9, 14)$$

This function is plotted on the map as shown in Fig. 3.19a.

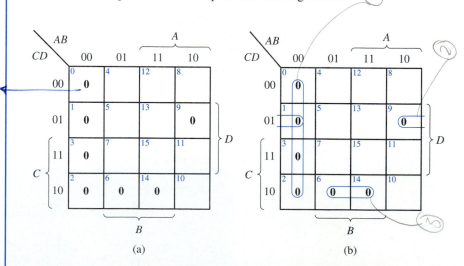

Figure 3.19   K-maps for Example 3.17. **(a)** Plot of the function. **(b)** Minimum cover.

Handwritten annotations:

complement:

where the max term is, there is a zero.

$\overline{A}\,\overline{B}$

$P_1 = \overline{A\overline{B}} = \overline{A}\,\overline{B}$

$P_1' = A + B = \overline{\overline{A}\,\overline{B}}$ $\overline{A}\,\overline{B}$

$P_2 = \overline{B}\,\overline{C}\,D$

$P_2' = B + C + \overline{D}$

$P_3 = B\,C\,\overline{D}$

$P_3' = \overline{B} + \overline{C} + D$

$P = P_1' + P_2' + P_3'$

MaxTerm

Using Algorithm 3.3, we begin by counting adjacencies, noting that maxterms M_9 and M_{14} each have one adjacency. Therefore, we cover M_9 with prime implicate 1–9, and we cover M_{14} with prime implicate 6–14. Next, looking at maxterms with two adjacencies, we select maxterm M_0 and cover it with prime implicate 0–1–2–3, which completes the cover. This minimum cover is plotted in Fig. 3.19b.

If we use Algorithm 3.4 to produce the minimum cover, the same result is obtained. Examining Fig. 3.19b, we can see that the three prime implicates 0–1–2–3, 1–9, and 6–14 are all essential and cover all the maxterms of the function. There is one additional prime implicate, 2–6, which is not needed for the cover.

The minimum POS form is derived from the minimum cover as follows. Prime implicate 0–1–2–3 represents the area on the map where A and B are 0. Therefore, the sum term for this essential prime implicate is $(A + B)$. In other words, $f(A, B, C, D) = 0$ when $(A + B) = 0$, which occurs when $A = 0$ and $B = 0$. Prime implicate 1–9 represents the portion of the map where B is 0, C is 0, and D is 1. Therefore, the sum term for this prime implicate is $(B + C + \bar{D})$. The last prime implicate is 6–14, which represents the area of the K-map where B is 1, C is 1, and D is 0. Therefore, the sum term for this prime implicate is $(\bar{B} + \bar{C} + D)$. Hence, the minimum POS form for this function is

$$f(A, B, C, D) = (A + B)(B + C + \bar{D})(\bar{B} + \bar{C} + D)$$

Some digital designers find working with maxterms and prime implicates awkward and prefer to perform K-map simplification using one of the algorithms for producing minimum SOP forms. SOP methods can be utilized to produce a minimum POS form of a function, f, by dealing with $\bar{f}$ instead of f. We begin by plotting the complement of the function $\bar{f}$ on the K-map. This converts the maxterms (zeros) into minterms (ones). We then use one of the SOP procedures to derive a minimum SOP expression for $\bar{f}$. Next, this SOP expression is complemented and DeMorgan's theorem (Theorem 8) is applied to produce the desired POS form of f. Thus we minimize $\bar{f}$ as a SOP function and then complement it to get f. This procedure is summarized as follows:

Algorithm 3.5

1. Plot the complement of the function $\bar{f}$ on the K-map.

2. Use Algorithm 3.1 or 3.2 to produce a minimum SOP expression for $\bar{f}$.

3. Complement the expression and apply DeMorgan's theorem to produce a minimum POS expression.

EXAMPLE 3.18

Repeat Example 3.17 using Algorithm 3.5.

Given the function
$$f(A, B, C, D) = \prod M(0, 1, 2, 3, 6, 9, 14)$$
as illustrated in Fig. 3.19a, we begin by plotting its complement on another K-map:
$$\bar{f}(A, B, C, D) = \sum m(0, 1, 2, 3, 6, 9, 14)$$
This is shown on the K-map of Fig. 3.20a. Note that this map is identical to that of Fig. 3.19a, but with the zeros replaced by ones.

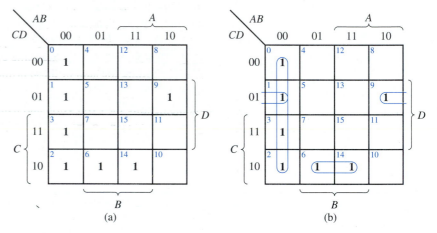

Figure 3.20 K-map of $\bar{f}(A, B, C, D)$ **(a)** Minterms of the function. **(b)** Minimal cover.

Using either Algorithm 3.1 or 3.2, we obtain the minimum cover {1–9, 6–14, 0–1–2–3}. Note that the order in which terms are considered and the resulting cover are the same as in Example 3.17, except that here the cover represents prime implicants of $\bar{f}$, rather than prime implicates of f.

We now write the minimum SOP expression for $\bar{f}$ from the prime implicants in the minimum cover:
$$\bar{f}(A, B, C, D) = \bar{A}\bar{B} + \bar{B}\bar{C}D + BC\bar{D}$$
Finally, we complement the expression and apply DeMorgan's theorem to obtain the minimum POS form of $f(A, B, C, D)$:
$$f(A, B, C, D) = \overline{\bar{A}\bar{B} + \bar{B}\bar{C}D + BC\bar{D}}$$
$$= (\overline{\bar{A}\bar{B}})(\overline{\bar{B}\bar{C}D})(\overline{BC\bar{D}})$$
$$= (A + B)(B + C + \bar{D})(\bar{B} + \bar{C} + D)$$

The primary advantage of this method is that we can use the SOP rules for K-map simplification on both SOP and POS functions. However, the additional steps of complementing the expression and applying DeMorgan's theorem are required to produce a minimum POS form. The following examples are done with both methods.

EXAMPLE 3.19

Find a minimum POS expression for
$f(A, B, C, D) = \prod M(3, 4, 6, 8, 9, 11, 12, 14).$

The maxterms of the function are plotted on the K-map of Fig. 3.21a. Using Algorithm 3.3, we first cover maxterm M_3 with prime implicate 3–11, M_4 with 4–6–12–14, and then M_8 with 8–9. The resulting minimum cover is shown in Fig. 3.21a. The minimum POS form is derived by writing the product of the sum terms corresponding to the prime implicates, where 3–11 represents $(B + \bar{C} + \bar{D})$, 4–6–12–14 represents $(\bar{B} + D)$, and 8–9 represents $(\bar{A} + B + C)$. The resulting POS expression is

$$f(A, B, C, D) = (\bar{B} + D)(B + \bar{C} + \bar{D})(\bar{A} + B + C)$$

To use Algorithm 3.5, we plot the complement of the function, as shown in Fig. 3.21b, and then form the same combination of cells: 3–11, 4–6–12–14, and 8–9. Writing the sum of these prime implicants,

$$\bar{f}(A, B, C, D) = B\bar{D} + \bar{B}CD + A\bar{B}\bar{C}$$

Complementing the expression and using DeMorgan's theorem,

$$f(A, B, C, D) = \overline{B\bar{D} + \bar{B}CD + A\bar{B}\bar{C}}$$
$$= (\overline{B\bar{D}})(\overline{\bar{B}CD})(\overline{A\bar{B}\bar{C}})$$
$$= (\bar{B} + D)(B + \bar{C} + \bar{D})(\bar{A} + B + C)$$

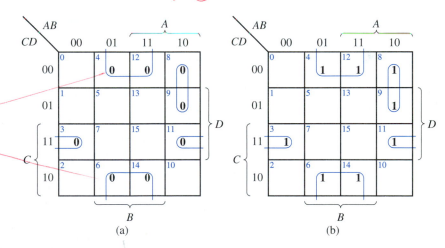

Figure 3.21   Minimum covers of $f(A, B, C, D) = \prod M(3, 4, 6, 8, 9, 11, 12, 14)$ and its complement. **(a)** $f(A, B, C, D)$. **(b)** $\bar{f}(A, B, C, D)$.

EXAMPLE 3.20

Derive a minimum POS expression for the function
$f(A, B, C, D, E) = \prod M(0, 2, 4, 11, 14, 15, 16, 20, 24, 30, 31)$

The function and its minimum cover are plotted on the K-map of Fig. 3.22. The minimum cover contains five prime implicates, all of which are essential.

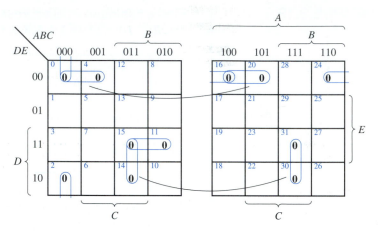

Figure 3.22 Finding a minimal POS expression for a 5-variable function.

Writing these prime implicates as sums and taking their product, we get

$$f(A, B, C, D, E) = (A + B + C + E)(B + D + E)(\bar{B} + \bar{C} + \bar{D})$$
$$(A + \bar{B} + \bar{D} + \bar{E})(\bar{A} + C + D + E)$$

The reader should verify that the same result is obtained by finding a minimum SOP expression for $\bar{f}$ and then complementing it to obtain f.

EXAMPLE 3.21

Find minimum POS and SOP expressions for the following function:

$$f(A, B, C, D) = \prod M(0, 2, 3, 9, 11, 12, 13, 15)$$

To find the minimum POS expression, we plot the maxterms of the function as shown in Fig. 3.23a. Using Algorithm 3.3, we generate prime implicate 0–2 to cover M_2, 12–13 to cover M_{12}, and 9–11–13–15 to cover M_9. This leaves M_3, which can be covered with either 3–11 or 2–3. Since each contains the same number of literals, let us arbitrarily select 2–3. The resulting POS expression is thus

$$f(A, B, C, D) = (A + B + D)(\bar{A} + \bar{B} + C)(\bar{A} + \bar{D})(A + B + \bar{C})$$

We can also generate the minimum POS form by plotting $\bar{f}$, as in Fig. 3.23b, and then deriving a minimum SOP expression for $\bar{f}$:

$$\bar{f}(A, B, C, D) = \bar{A}\bar{B}\bar{D} + AB\bar{C} + AD + \bar{A}\bar{B}C$$

Complementing, we get

$$f(A, B, C, D) = \overline{\bar{A}\bar{B}\bar{D} + AB\bar{C} + AD + \bar{A}\bar{B}C}$$
$$= (\overline{\bar{A}\bar{B}\bar{D}})(\overline{AB\bar{C}})(\overline{AD})(\overline{\bar{A}\bar{B}C})$$
$$= (A + B + D)(\bar{A} + \bar{B} + C)(\bar{A} + \bar{D})(A + B + \bar{C})$$

To generate a minimum SOP expression for $f(A, B, C, D)$, we plot the minterms of the function instead of the maxterms, as shown in Fig. 3.23c. Using Algorithm 3.1 or 3.2 produces the minimum cover shown in Fig. 3.23c. Taking the sum of the prime implicants gives

$$f(A, B, C, D) = \bar{A}\bar{C}D + A\bar{B}\bar{D} + \bar{A}B + BC\bar{D}$$

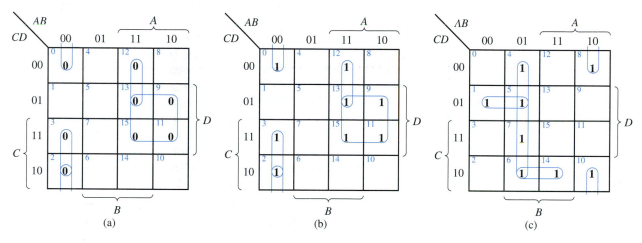

Figure 3.23   Deriving POS and SOP forms of a function. **(a)** Maxterms of f. **(b)** Minterms of $\bar{f}$. **(c)** Minterms of f.

Example 3.21 illustrates an important point. From any description of a function, we can generate either a minimal SOP or a minimal POS expression. To generate the minimal SOP expression, we work with the minterms of the function, whereas for a minimal POS expression we work with the maxterms. Once we have plotted the maxterms of a function on a K-map, as in Example 3.21, we automatically have a map of the minterms, and vice versa. Therefore, the initial function format need not affect whether we choose a SOP or POS form for the minimized function.

3.7 Incompletely Specified Functions

If don't-care terms are present, we adjoin one additional rule to those previously discussed for minimizing functions via maps. Recall that don't-cares by definition can be either 0 or 1. Hence, in minimizing terms in SOP or POS form, we choose the don't-cares to be 1 or 0 if, in doing so, the set of squares on the map that can be grouped together is larger than would otherwise be possible without including the don't-cares. Then, when deriving the minimum cover, we ignore the don't-cares and select only enough prime implicants/implicates to cover the specified terms. In other words, with regard to don't-cares, we can take them (or leave them) depending on whether they do (or do not) aid in the simplification of a function.

EXAMPLE 3.22

We wish to minimize the following function in both SOP and POS forms using K-maps.

$$f(A, B, C, D) = \sum m(1, 3, 4, 7, 11) + d(5, 12, 13, 14, 15)$$
$$= \prod M(0, 2, 6, 8, 9, 10) \cdot D(5, 12, 13, 14, 15)$$

The maps for the function $f(A, B, C, D)$ are shown in Figure 3.24a and b.

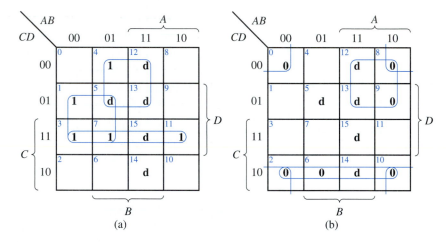

Figure 3.24   K-maps for Example 3.22. **(a)** Sum of products. **(b)** Product of sums.

The minimum SOP form derived from the map of Fig. 3.24a is

$$f(A, B, C, D) = B\bar{C} + \bar{A}D + CD$$

The minimum POS form derived from the map of Fig. 3.24b is

$$f(A, B, C, D) = (B + D)(\bar{C} + D)(\bar{A} + C)$$

Note that, if we use Boolean algebra on the minimum POS form to produce a POS form, we get

$$f(A, B, C, D) = \bar{A}B\bar{C} + \bar{A}D + CD$$

which is not identical to the minimum SOP form obtained from the map. This situation often occurs because of the presence of don't-cares, which can be used differently when optimizing each derived expression. In this case, several don't-care terms (5, 12, 13) were used as ones to derive the minimum SOP form and as zeros to derive the minimum POS form. However, in each case, the *required* minterms and maxterms have been implemented correctly.

The following example will serve to illustrate how don't-cares occur and how they are used.

EXAMPLE 3.23

We wish to design a 4-bit binary-coded decimal (BCD) input/single output logic circuit that will be used to distinguish digits that are greater than or equal to 5 from those that are less than 5. The input will be the BCD representation of the decimal digits $0, 1, \ldots, 9$, and the output should be 1 if the input is 5, 6, 7, 8, or 9 and 0 if the input is less than 5.

The block diagram of the circuit is shown in Fig. 3.25a, and the truth table for this operation is shown in Fig. 3.25b. Note that the don't cares appear in the table because these particular inputs do not represent BCD digits and hence cannot possibly occur. Therefore the output function f is

$$f(A, B, C, D) = \sum m(5, 6, 7, 8, 9) + d(10, 11, 12, 13, 14, 15)$$

This function is plotted on the map of Fig. 3.26a. From the map we obtain the minimum SOP form:

$$f(A, B, C, D) = A + BD + BC$$

The reader should verify that if we combine maxterms and don't-cares, as shown in Fig. 3.26b, we can obtain the minimum POS form:

$$f(A, B, C, D) = (A + B)(A + C + D).$$

Note that this function is much simpler than it would have been without the inclusion of the don't-cares. In addition, note in Fig. 3.26a that all the don't-cares were used, that is, chosen to be ones, whereas in Fig. 3.26b none of the don't cares was used, that is, chosen to be zeros. This will not always be the case.

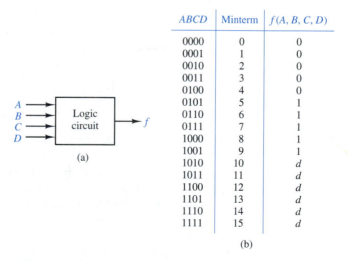

$ABCD$	Minterm	$f(A, B, C, D)$
0000	0	0
0001	1	0
0010	2	0
0011	3	0
0100	4	0
0101	5	1
0110	6	1
0111	7	1
1000	8	1
1001	9	1
1010	10	d
1011	11	d
1100	12	d
1101	13	d
1110	14	d
1111	15	d

(b)

Figure 3.25 Example 3.23 block diagram and truth table.
(a) Block diagram. **(b)** Truth table.

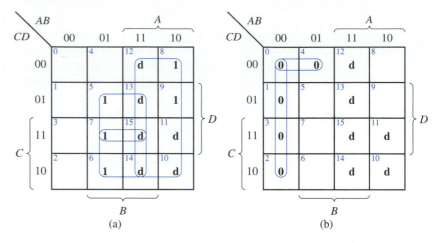

Figure 3.26   Use of don't cares for SOP and POS forms. **(a)** Minimum SOP cover.
(b) Minimum POS cover.

▶ 3.8 Using K-maps to Eliminate Timing Hazards

Thus far we have assumed that the optimum approach for designing each combinational logic circuit is to generate a minimum SOP or POS expression and then realize it with logic gates. Unfortunately, timing considerations often require that a less-than-minimum circuit be used.

As discussed in Chapter 2, every physical logic gate has a measurable response time or delay associated with it, which is the time it takes the gate output to change following an input change. This response time is denoted by T_{PHL} for an output change from high to low and T_{PLH} for a change from low to high.

The response time of most logic devices is very short (nanoseconds to fractions of a nanosecond, depending on the technology, fan-in, fan-out, and the like). However, the response time cannot be exactly the same for any two devices, even of the same type. Such relative differences in response time may cause undesirable events to occur in a switching network. These undesirable events are referred to as *hazards* [3].

To illustrate a hazard, consider the network shown in Fig. 3.27a. Let us first examine the ideal case by assuming that gates $G1$, $G2$, and $G3$ have identical response times $T_{\mathrm{PHL}} = T_{\mathrm{PLH}} = \Delta t$. Figure 3.27c gives the timing diagram of the circuit for a particular input sequence. Note that the change of x_3 at t_1 causes y_2 to change at $t_2 = t_1 + \Delta t$, which in turn produces a change in z at $t_3 = t_2 + \Delta t$. A change of x_2 at t_4 causes no change in output of any gate. At t_5 the change of x_1 initiates changes of y_2 from 1 to 0 and of y_3 from 0 to 1, both at $t_6 = t_5 + \Delta t$. Since $z = y_1 + y_2$, the result of y_1 and y_2 changing simultaneously is that there is no change in z.

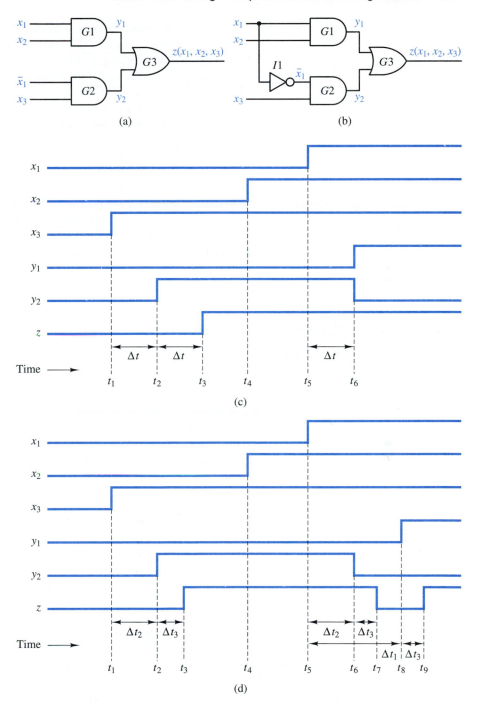

Figure 3.27   Illustration of a static hazard. **(a)** Network with static hazard.
(b) Equivalent network. **(c)** Timing diagram with identical delays Δt. **(d)** Timing
diagram with delays $\Delta t_1 > \Delta t_2 > \Delta t_3$.

Now let us examine a more realistic case in which the gate delays are not equal. Assume that gates $G1$, $G2$, and $G3$ have response times Δt_1, Δt_2, and Δt_3, respectively, with $\Delta t_1 > \Delta t_2 > \Delta t_3$. For convenience, let $\Delta t_1 = 2\Delta t_2$. This discrepancy in delays can be the result of gates having different physical characteristics. This situation can also arise in circuits having a different number of gates in each path, as in the circuit of Fig. 3.27b, which realizes the same function as the circuit of Fig. 3.27a. Let us assume that all four gates have identical response times. For a change in input x_1, the output of AND gate $G1$ changes after one gate delay, whereas the output of $G2$ does not change until after two gate delays, since the change in x_1 must propagate through inverter $I1$ and then through AND gate $G2$. The net result is that the overall delay at the output of $G2$ following a change in x_1 is two times the delay at the output of $G1$.

Figure 3.27d gives the timing diagram of the circuit for the same input sequence discussed previously. The change of x_3 at t_1 causes y_2 to change at t_2, which in turn produces a change in z at t_3. This is the expected sequence of events with $t_2 = t_1 + \Delta t_2$ and $t_3 = t_2 + \Delta t_3$. However, at t_5 the change of x_1 initiates an interesting sequence of events. First, since $\Delta t_2 < \Delta t_1$, the change in x_1 causes y_2 to change from 1 to 0 at t_6, prior to y_1 changing from 0 to 1 at t_8. As a result, z changes from 1 to 0 at t_7 and then from 0 to 1 at t_9. This change in z is different from that of the ideal case presented in Fig. 3.27b, and is not indicated by the logic description of the network. Hence, it is not the correct behavior of the network.

Momentary output changes such as the one illustrated are referred to as *static hazards* or *glitches*. In general, a static hazard is a condition for which a single variable change (x_1 in the example) may produce a momentary output change when no output change should occur. The reader should verify that no hazard would occur in the preceding example if the relative delays were such that $\Delta t_1 \le \Delta t_2$. As illustrated by this example, a static hazard is the result of unequal delays along different paths between one input of the circuit and an output gate.

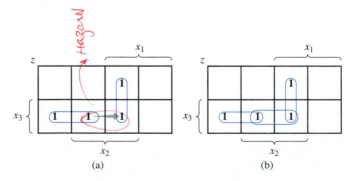

Figure 3.28 Identifying hazards on a K-map. **(a)** K-map with hazard condition. **(b)** K-map with hazard eliminated.

The cause of the preceding hazard condition can be seen by examining the K-map of the network in Fig. 3.28a. In the corresponding circuits of Figs. 3.27a and 3.27b, product term $x_1 x_2$ is produced by AND gate $G1$, and product term $\bar{x}_1 x_3$ is produced by AND gate $G2$. As illustrated in Fig. 3.27c, the hazard exists when a changing input (from $x_1 = 0, x_2 = 1, x_3 = 1$ to $x_1 = x_2 = x_3 = 1$) requires the corresponding minterms to be covered by different product terms. In the circuit, this means that the output of one AND gate changes from 1 to 0 while the output of the other AND gate changes from 0 to 1. The hazard occurs when the output of $G1$ goes to 0 before the output of $G2$ goes to 1.

Static hazards can be prevented by using careful logic design to make the output independent of the order in which the signals change. The hazard shown in Fig. 3.27c can be avoided by grouping the minterms as shown in Fig. 3.28b, adding a third product term to the sum of products expression that would not ordinarily be used. The resulting circuit is presented in Fig. 3.29. In this circuit the added product term, produced by AND gate $G4$, remains 1 while the outputs of $G1$ and $G2$ change. Therefore, the output of OR gate $G3$ remains constant at 1 regardless of whether $G1$ or $G2$ changes first.

In general, hazards can be removed by covering each pair of logically adjacent minterms with a common product term. Therefore, the removal of hazards requires the addition of redundant gates to a network, resulting in a nonminimum realization.

The preceding discussion was primarily concerned with static hazards known as *static 1 hazards*, for which the output should remain at logic 1 but temporarily drops to logic 0, producing a transient pulse, which is sometimes called a *glitch*. *Static 0 hazards* are also implied by the definition of static hazard and can occur. Static 1 hazards occur primarily in AND–OR circuits, which realize SOP expressions, while static 0 hazards occur in OR–AND circuits, which realize POS expressions.

For example, consider the circuit of Fig. 3.30a and its corresponding K-map in Fig. 3.30b. For input $B = 1, C = 0, D = 1$, a static 0 hazard occurs when input A changes from 0 to 1. Referring to the logic diagram, the hazard results if the output of OR gate $G1$ changes from 1 to 0 before the output of OR gate $G2$ changes from 0 to 1. Hence, although the output should remain 0, it momentarily changes to 1.

As with static 1 hazards, static 0 hazards are prevented by ensuring that each pair of adjacent maxterms is covered by a sum term. Figures 3.30c and d show a hazard-free realization of the circuit and the corresponding K-map created by adding the redundant sum term $(\bar{B} + C + \bar{D})$.

A second type of hazard known as a *dynamic hazard* may also exist in a network. A dynamic hazard is a condition in which an output is to change from $0 \rightarrow 1$ or $1 \rightarrow 0$ (that is, the output behavior is to be dynamic versus static), but changes more than once before settling into its new state. Like static hazards, a dynamic hazard is also caused by a special relative response time condition that occurs after an input transition that normally produces an output

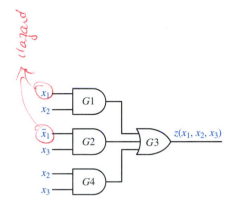

Figure 3.29   Hazard-free network.

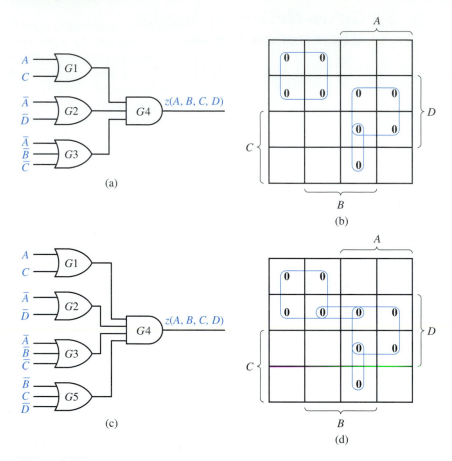

Figure 3.30 Example of a static-0 hazard. **(a)** Circuit with static-0 hazard. **(b)** K-map containing the hazard. **(c)** Hazard-free circuit. **(d)** K-map with hazard eliminated.

Figure 3.31 Dynamic hazards. **(a)** Dynamic hazard on 0 to 1 change. **(b)** Dynamic hazard on 1 to 0 change.

change. Such hazards cause output responses of $0 \to 1 \to 0 \to 1$ for normal $0 \to 1$ changes, as illustrated in Fig. 3.31a, or $1 \to 0 \to 1 \to 0$ for normal $1 \to 0$ changes, as shown in Fig. 3.31b. Dynamic hazards can be shown to be the result of static hazards that exist within the circuit. Consequently, networks that are free of static hazards are also free of dynamic hazards. The reader is referred to [4] for further discussion of detecting and eliminating static and dynamic hazards.

3.9 Quine–McCluskey Tabular Minimization Method

The *Quine–McCluskey (Q–M) method* is a tabular approach to Boolean function minimization [5, 6, 7]. Basically, the Q–M method has two advantages over the K-map. First, it is a straightforward, systematic method for producing a minimal function that is less dependent on the designer's ability to recognize patterns than the K-map method. Second, the method is a viable scheme for handling a large number of variables as opposed to the K-map, which, practically, is limited to about five or six variables. In general, the Q–M method performs an ordered linear search over the minterms in the function to find all combinations of logically adjacent minterms. As will be shown, the method can also be extended to functions with multiple outputs.

The Quine–McCluskey method begins with a list of the n-variable minterms of the function and successively derives all implicants with $n-1$ variables, implicants with $n-2$ variables, and so on, until all prime implicants are identified. A minimal covering of the function is then derived from the set of prime implicants. The four steps of the process are listed next. The exact meaning of each step will be illustrated by the examples that follow.

Step 1. List in a column all the minterms of the function to be minimized in their binary representation. Partition them into groups according to the number of 1 bits in their binary representations. This partitioning simplifies identification of logically adjacent minterms since, to be logically adjacent, two minterms must differ in exactly one literal, and therefore the binary representation of one minterm must have either one more or one fewer 1 bit than the other.

Step 2. Perform an exhaustive search between neighboring groups for adjacent minterms and combine them into a column of $(n-1)$-variable implicants, checking off each minterm that is combined. The binary representation of each new implicant contains a dash in the position of the eliminated variable. Repeat for each column, combining $(n-1)$-varible implicants into $(n-2)$-variable implicants, and so on, until no further implicants can be combined. Any term not checked off represents a prime implicant of the function, since it is not covered by a larger implicant. The final result is a list of prime implicants of the switching function.

Step 3. Construct a prime implicant chart that lists minterms along the horizontal and prime implicants along the vertical, with an $\times$ entry placed wherever a certain prime implicant (row) covers a given minterm (column).

Step 4. Select a minimum number of prime implicants that cover all the minterms of the switching function.

A complete example will now be presented that demonstrates these four steps.

EXAMPLE 3.24

Let us use the Q–M technique to minimize the function

$$f(A, B, C, D) = \sum m(2, 4, 6, 8, 9, 10, 12, 13, 15)$$

The K-map for this example is shown in Fig. 3.32, and the reader is encouraged to try his or her hand at obtaining a minimal function via the map method.

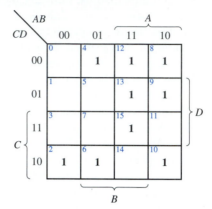

Figure 3.32 K-map for Example 3.30.

Step 1. To begin the Q–M minimization technique, the minterms are grouped according to the number of ones in the binary representation of the minterm number. This grouping of terms is illustrated in the following table:

Minterms	$ABCD$	
2	0010	
4	0100	Group 1 (a single 1)
8	1000	
6	0110	
9	1001	Group 2 (two 1's)
10	1010	
12	1100	
13	1101	Group 3 (three 1's)
15	1111	Group 4 (four 1's)

Step 2. Once this table has been formed, an exhaustive search for all combinations of logically adjacent terms is initiated. The method of performing this functional reduction is summarized here and explained in detail later. Consider the minimizing table shown next containing the three minterm lists. The two terms can be combined if and only if they differ in a single literal. Hence, in list 1 we can combine terms in group 1 only with those in group 2. When all the combinations between these two groups have been made and they have been entered in list 2, a line is drawn under these combinations, and we begin combining the terms in group 2 with those in group 3. This simple procedure is repeated from one list to another in order to generate the entire minimizing table.

List 1			List 2			List 3		
Minterm	$ABCD$		Minterms	$ABCD$		Minterms	$ABCD$	
2	0010	√	2, 6	0-10	PI$_2$	8, 9, 12, 13	1-0-	PI$_1$
4	0100	√	2, 10	-010	PI$_3$			
8	1000	√	4, 6	01-0	PI$_4$			
6	0110	√	4, 12	-100	PI$_5$			
9	1001	√	8, 9	100-	√			
10	1010	√	8, 10	10-0	PI$_6$			
12	1100	√	8, 12	1-00	√			
13	1101	√	9, 13	1-01	√			
15	1111	√	12, 13	110-	√			
			13, 15	11-1	PI$_7$			

There are a number of items in the table that beg for explanation. Note that the first element in list 2 indicates that minterms 2 and 6 have been combined since they differ in only a single literal. The terms differed in the variable B and hence a dash appears in that position in the combination 2, 6, indicating that variable B was eliminated when the two minterms were combined. This combination can easily be checked by Boolean algebra:

$$\text{minterm } 2 = \bar{A}\bar{B}C\bar{D}, \qquad \text{minterm } 6 = \bar{A}BC\bar{D}$$

and

$$\bar{A}\bar{B}C\bar{D} + \bar{A}BC\bar{D} = \bar{A}C\bar{D} \Rightarrow 0-10$$

Each minterm in list 1 that is combined with another is checked off with a √, indicating that it has been included in a larger set. Although a term may be combined more than once, it is only checked off once.

Once list 2 has been generated from list 1, an exhaustive search is made to combine the terms in list 2 to generate list 3. It is at this point that it becomes evident why it is important to indicate which of the variables has been eliminated. Since, as before, two terms in list 2 can be combined only if they differ in a single literal, only terms that have the same missing literal (a dash in the same position) can possibly be combined. Note that in list 2 minterm combinations 8, 12 and 9, 13 and also 8, 9 and 12, 13 can be combined to yield the combination 8, 9, 12, 13 in list 3.Inspection of list 2 shows that minterm combinations 8, 12 and 9, 13 both have the same missing literal and differ by one other literal. The same is true for the other combination. Hence all four terms are checked off in list 2 in the table. No other terms in list 2 in the table can be combined. Hence, all the terms that are not checked off in the entire table are prime implicants and are labeled PI$_1$ ... .PI$_7$. The function could now be realized as a sum of all the prime implicants; however, we are looking for a minimal realization, and hence we want to use only the smallest number that is actually required.

A convenient way to check for errors in lists 2, 3, 4, and so on, is to perform the following test on each entry: subtract the minterm numbers to verify that the proper variables have been omitted. For example, the entry (4, 6 01-0) in list 2 indicates that the variable with weight $6 - 4 = 2$ should be eliminated. In this example, the possible weights are 8, 4, 2, and 1. For the entry in list 3 (8, 9, 12, 13 $\Rightarrow$ 1-0-):

$$9 - 8 = 1 \qquad\qquad\qquad 12 - 8 = 4$$
$$13 - 12 = 1 \qquad\qquad\qquad 13 - 8 = 4$$

so variables with weights 1 and 4 should be eliminated.

Step 3. To determine the smallest number of prime implicants required to realize the function we form a prime implicant chart as follows:

	2	4	6	√ 8	√ 9	10	√ 12	√ 13	√ 15
**PI₁				×	⊗		×	×	
PI₂	×		×						
PI₃	×					×			
PI₄		×	×						
PI₅		×					×		
PI₆				×		×			
**PI₇								×	⊗

The double horizontal line through the chart between PI_1 and PI_2 is used to separate prime implicants that contain different numbers of literals.

Step 4. An examination of the minterm columns in the prime implicant chart indicates that minterms 9 and 15 are each covered by only one prime implicant (shown circled). Therefore, prime implicants 1 and 7 must be chosen, and hence they are essential prime implicants (as indicated by the double asterisks). Note that in choosing these two prime implicants we have *also* covered minterms 8, 12, and 13. All five of the covered minterms are checked in the table; the checks are placed above the minterm numbers.

  The problem now remaining is that of selecting as few additional (nonessential) prime implicants as are necessary to cover the minterms 2, 4, 6, and 10. In general, this is accomplished by forming a reduced prime implicant chart. This reduced chart is shown next; note that the chart contains only the minterms that remain to be covered and the remaining prime implicant candidates for inclusion in the cover.

	√ 2	√ 4	√ 6	√ 10
PI₂	×		×	
*PI₃	×			×
*PI₄		×	×	
PI₅		×		
PI₆				×

Which PIs should we select? Prime implicants PI_5 and PI_6 are obviously bad choices because they cover only one minterm, and that minterm is also covered by another PI that covers two minterms. Notice that the minterms 2, 4, 6, and 10 can be most efficiently covered (with the minimum number of prime implicants) by choosing PI_3 and PI_4. The single asterisk indicates our selection, and the checks above all the remaining minterms mean we have generated a complete cover. Therefore, a minimal realization of the original function would be

$$\begin{aligned} f(A, B, C, D) &= PI_1 + PI_3 + PI_4 + PI_7 \\ &= \text{1-0- } + \text{ -010 } + \text{ 01-0 } + \text{ 11-1} \\ &= A\bar{C} + \bar{B}C\bar{D} + \bar{A}B\bar{D} + ABD \end{aligned}$$

The corresponding groupings of the minterms on the K-map are shown in Fig. 3.33.

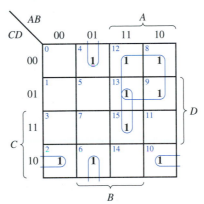

Figure 3.33 Grouping of terms.

3.9.1 Covering Procedure

The problem of selecting a minimum number of prime implicants to realize a switching function is sometimes called the *covering problem*. The following procedure may be employed to systematically choose a minimum number of nonessential prime implicants from the prime implicant chart.

The first step is to remove all essential prime implicant rows, as well as the minterm columns that they cover, from the chart, as in the last example. Then this reduced chart is further simplified as described next.

A row (column) i of a PI chart *covers* row (column) j if row (column) i contains an $\times$ in each column (row) in which j contains an $\times$. Each row represents a nonessential prime implicant PI_i, while each column represents a minterm m_i of the switching function. For example, consider the following PI chart for the switching function

$$f(A, B, C, D) = \sum m(0, 1, 5, 6, 7, 8, 9, 10, 11, 13, 14, 15)$$

	√	√		√	√	√	√				√	√
	0	1	5	6	7	8	9	10	11	13	14	15
**PI_1	⊗	×				×	×					
PI_2		×	×				×			×		
PI_3			×		×					×		×
PI_4						×	×	×	×			
PI_5							×		×	×		×
PI_6								×	×		×	×
**PI_7				⊗	×						×	×

For this PI chart, PI_1 and PI_7 are essential PI and are marked with double asterisks. Now we remove these two rows as well as all columns in which the rows have × entries. The following reduced PI chart is generated:

	5	10	11	13
PI_2	×			×
PI_3	×			×
PI_4		×	×	
PI_5			×	×
PI_6		×	×	

According to the definition of row and column covering stated earlier, row PI_2 covers row PI_3 (and vice versa), row PI_4 covers row PI_6 (and vice versa), column 11 covers column 10, and column 13 covers column 5.

In view of the previous discussion, the rules for PI chart reduction can be stated as follows:

Rule 1. A row that *is covered* by another row may be eliminated from the chart. When identical rows are present, all but one of the rows may be eliminated. In the example, rows PI_3 and PI_6 may be eliminated.

Rule 2. A column that *covers* another column may be eliminated. All but one column from a set of identical columns may be eliminated. In the example, columns 11 and 13 can be eliminated.

If we apply these rules to the previous PI chart, the following reduced PI chart is obtained:

	√	√
	5	10
*PI_2	×	
*PI_4		×

Hence we may choose PI_2 and PI_4 along with the essential PI_1 and PI_7 to obtain a minimum cover for the switching function.

A type of PI chart that requires a special approach to accomplish reduction will now be discussed. A *cyclic* PI chart is a chart that contains no essential PI and that cannot be reduced by rules 1 and 2. An example of a cyclic chart is shown next for the switching function

$$f(A, B, C) = \sum m(1, 2, 3, 4, 5, 6)$$

	√ 1	2	√ 3	4	5	6
*PI₁	×		×			
PI₂		×	×			
PI₃		×				×
PI₄				×		×
PI₅				×	×	
PI₆	×					×

Verify that no row or column covers another row or column. The procedure to follow for cyclic chart reduction is to arbitrarily select one PI from the chart. The row corresponding to this PI and the columns corresponding to the minterms covered by the PI are then removed from the chart. If the resulting reduced chart is not cyclic, then rules 1 and 2 may be applied. However, if another cyclic chart is produced, the procedure for a cyclic chart is repeated and another arbitrary choice is made. For example, arbitrarily choose PI_1 in the preceding cyclic chart. The following noncyclic chart is obtained by removing row PI_1 and columns 1 and 3.

	2	4	5	6
PI₂	×			
PI₃	×			×
PI₄		×		×
PI₅		×	×	
PI₆				×

Rules 1 and 2 may now be applied to further reduce this chart. PI_3 covers row PI_2; hence row PI_2 may be removed. Row PI_5 covers row PI_6, so we can eliminate PI_6. The resulting reduced chart is

	√ 2	√ 4	√ 5	√ 6
*PI₃	×			×
PI₄		×		×
*PI₅		×	×	

PI_3 and PI_5 must be chosen to cover the chart.

A minimum cover for the switching function is PI_1, PI_3, and PI_5. Other minimal covers also exist. The previous discussion can be summarized as follows:

Step 1. Identify any minterms covered by only one PI in the chart. Select these PIs for the cover. Note that this step identifies essential PIs on the first pass and nonessential PIs on subsequent passes (from step 4).

Step 2. Remove rows corresponding to the identified essential and nonessential PIs. Remove columns corresponding to minterms covered by the removed rows.

Step 3. If a cyclic chart results after completing step 2, go to step 5. Otherwise, apply the reduction procedure of rules 1 and 2.

Step 4. If a cyclic chart results from step 3, go to step 5. Otherwise, return to step 1.

Step 5. Apply the cyclic chart procedure. Repeat step 5 until a void chart occurs or until a noncyclic chart is produced. In the latter case, return to step 1.

The procedure terminates when step 2 or 5 produces a void chart. A void chart contains no rows or columns. On the first application of step 1, prime implicants are found that must be identified to cover minterms for which only one × appears in this column. They are identified by a double asterisk and are essential PIs. On the second and succeeding applications of step 1 (determined by step 4), nonessential prime implicants are identified by an asterisk from reduced PI charts.

3.9.2 Incompletely Specified Functions

The minimization of functions involving don't-cares proceeds exactly as shown in the preceding example with one important exception, which will be demonstrated by the next example.

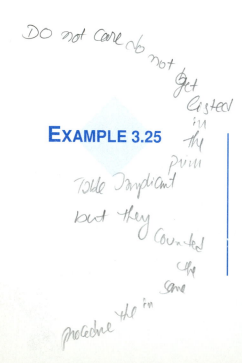

EXAMPLE 3.25

We want to use the Q–M approach to minimize the function

$$f(A,B,C,D,E) = m(2,3,7,10,12,15,27)$$
$$+ d(5,18,19,21,23)$$

Following the procedure demonstrated in the preceding example, all the minterms *and don't-cares* are listed in the minimizing table and combined in the manner previously illustrated. The results of this procedure are shown in the following table:

List 1			List 2			List 3		
Minterm	ABCDE		Minterms	ABCDE		Minterms	ABCDE	
2	00010	√	2, 3	0001-	√	2, 3, 18, 19	-001-	PI₁
3	00011	√	2, 10	0-010	PI₄	3, 7, 19, 23	-0-11	PI₂
5	00101	√	2, 18	-0010	√	5, 7, 21, 23	-01-1	PI₃
10	01010	√	3, 7	00-11	√			
12	01100	PI₇	3, 19	-0011	√			
18	10010	√	5, 7	001-1	√			
7	00111	√	5, 21	-0101	√			
19	10011	√	18, 19	1001-	√			
21	10101	√	7, 15	0-111	PI₅			
15	01111	√	7, 23	-0111	√			
23	10111	√	19, 23	10-11	√			
27	11011	√	19, 27	1-011	PI₆			
			21, 23	101-1	√			

A prime implicant chart for the example must now be obtained. It is at this point that the method differs from that described earlier. Since some of the terms in list 1 are don't-cares, there is no need to cover them. Only the specified minterms must be covered, and thus they are the only minterms that appear in the prime implicant chart shown next. Do *not* list don't-cares in the PI chart.

It can be seen from the chart that the essential prime implicants are PI_4, PI_5, PI_6, and PI_7. Since only minterm 3 is not covered by the essential prime implicants, a reduced prime implicant chart is not necessary. Minterm 3 can be covered using PI_1 or PI_2, so there are two minimal covers for this function. The minimal realizations for the function are

$$f(A, B, C, D, E) = PI_1 + PI_4 + PI_5 + PI_6 + PI_7$$

or

$$f(A, B, C, D, E) = PI_2 + PI_4 + PI_5 + PI_6 + PI_7$$

	2	3	7	10	12	15	27
PI₁	×	×					
PI₂		×	×				
PI₃			×				
** PI₄	×			⊗			
** PI₅			×			⊗	
** PI₆							⊗
** PI₇					⊗		

In terms of the variables,

$$f(A, B, C, D, E) = \bar{B}\bar{C}D + \bar{A}\bar{C}D\bar{E} + \bar{A}CDE + A\bar{C}DE + \bar{A}BC\bar{D}\bar{E}$$

or

$$f(A, B, C, D, E) = \bar{B}DE + \bar{A}\bar{C}D\bar{E} + \bar{A}CDE + A\bar{C}DE + \bar{A}BC\bar{D}\bar{E}$$

3.9.3 Systems with Multiple Outputs

In the design of digital systems, it is often necessary to implement more than one output function with some given set of input variables. Using the techniques developed thus far, the problem can be solved by treating each function individually. However, there exists a potential for sharing gates and thus obtaining a simpler and less expensive design.

The extension of the Q–M tabular method to the multiple-output case is performed like the singular case with the following exceptions:

1. To each minterm we must affix a flag to identify the function in which it appears.
2. Two terms (or minterms) can be combined only if they both possess one or more common flags and the term that results from the combination carries only flags that are common to both minterms.
3. Each term in the minimizing table can be checked off only if all the flags that the term possesses appear in the term resulting from the combination.

EXAMPLE 3.26

Let us use the tabular method to obtain a minimum realization for the functions

$$f_\alpha(A, B, C, D) = \sum m(0, 2, 7, 10) + d(12, 15)$$

$$f_\beta(A, B, C, D) = \sum m(2, 4, 5) + d(6, 7, 8, 10)$$

$$f_\gamma(A, B, C, D) = \sum m(2, 7, 8) + d(0, 5, 13)$$

Note that this example will also demonstrate a minimization with don't-cares present. The minimizing table is shown next.

Min term	List 1 $ABCD$	Flags		Min terms	List 2 $ABCD$	Flags		Min terms	List 3 $ABCD$	Flags	
0	0000	$\alpha\gamma$	✓	0, 2	00-0	$\alpha\gamma$	PI_2	4, 5, 6, 7	01--	β	PI_1
2	0010	$\alpha\beta\gamma$	PI_{10}	0, 8	-000	γ	PI_3				
4	0100	β	✓	2, 6	0-10	β	PI_4				
8	1000	$\beta\gamma$	PI_{11}	2, 10	-010	$\alpha\beta$	PI_5				
5	0101	$\beta\gamma$	✓	4, 5	010-	β	✓				
6	0110	β	✓	4, 6	01-0	β	✓				
10	1010	$\alpha\beta$	✓	8, 10	10-0	β	PI_6				
12	1100	α	PI_{12}	5, 7	01-1	$\beta\gamma$	PI_7				
7	0111	$\alpha\beta\gamma$	PI_{13}	5, 13	-101	γ	PI_8				
13	1101	γ	✓	6, 7	011-	β	✓				
15	1111	α	✓	7, 15	-111	α	PI_9				

Consider the combination 0, 8 in List 2. This term is generated for function $f_\gamma(A, B, C, D)$ from minterms 0 and 8 in list 1. Minterm 8 cannot be checked because its entire label $\beta\gamma$ is not included in the label for minterm 0. Minterm 0 has a check due to the term 0, 2 in List 2.

It is important to note at this point that although our minimizing tables thus far have had three lists, in general, the number of lists can be any integer less than or equal to $n + 1$, where n is the number of input variables for the switching function, or functions in the multiple-output case. The prime implicant chart for the minimizing table is shown next (remember, *no* don't-cares across the top):

	f_α				f_β			f_γ		
	√	√		√	√	√	√	√		
	0	2	7	10	2	4	5	2	7	8
**PI$_1$ β						⊗	×			
**PI$_2$ αγ	⊗	×						×		
PI$_3$ γ										×
PI$_4$ β						×				
**PI$_5$ αβ		×		⊗		×				
PI$_6$ β										
PI$_7$ βγ							×		×	
PI$_8$ γ										
PI$_9$ α			×							
PI$_{10}$ αβγ		×			×			×		
PI$_{11}$ βγ										×
PI$_{12}$ α										
PI$_{13}$ αβγ			×						×	

The chart illustrates that PI$_1$, PI$_2$, and PI$_5$ are essential prime implicants. The reduced prime implicant chart is shown next; note that all prime implicants covering only don't-cares have been omitted.

	f_α	f_γ	
	√	√	√
	7	7	8
*PI$_3$ γ			×
PI$_7$ βγ		×	
PI$_9$ α	×		
PI$_{11}$ βγ			×
*PI$_{13}$ αβγ	×	×	

It is obvious that the best set of remaining prime implicants is PI_3 and PI_{13}. We choose PI_3 rather than PI_{11} because it has fewer literals. Hence the minimum realizations for the three functions are

$$f_\alpha = PI_2 + PI_5 + PI_{13}$$
$$f_\beta = PI_1 + PI_5$$
$$f_\gamma = PI_2 + PI_3 + PI_{13}$$

or

$$f_\alpha = \bar{A}\bar{B}\bar{D} + \bar{B}C\bar{D} + \bar{A}BCD$$
$$f_\beta = \bar{A}B + \bar{B}C\bar{D}$$
$$f_\gamma = \bar{A}\bar{B}\bar{D} + \bar{B}\bar{C}\bar{D} + \bar{A}BCD$$

It is important to note that PI_2, PI_5, and PI_{13} are generated only once, but are used to implement two of the functions, as shown in Fig. 3.34.

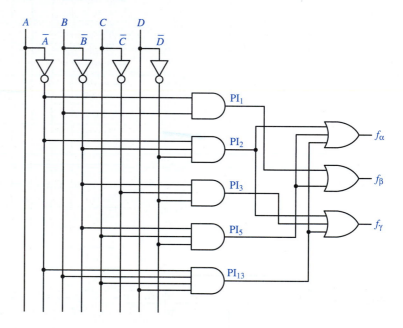

Figure 3.34   Reduced multiple-output circuit.

3.10 Petrick's Algorithm

As stated previously, the methods presented in the previous section for selecting a minimum cover are heuristic and therefore not guaranteed to find an optimum solution. In particular, the final steps of K-map Algorithms 3.2 and 3.4 and the final step of the Quine–McCluskey method all rely on heuristics and the talent of the designer to identify a minimum set of prime implicants to complete a cover after the essential prime implicants have been found. Often trial and error is used to identify and evaluate multiple possible covers.

A number of methods have been developed that can generate optimal solutions directly, at the expense of additional computation time. One such method is *Petrick's Algorithm* [8], which uses an algebraic approach to generate all possible covers of a function. The following algorithm for finding minimum covers is based on Petrick's algorithm.

Algorithm 3.6

1. Use Algorithm 3.2, Algorithm 3.4, or the Quine–McCluskey method to find all prime implicants of the function.

2. Create a prime implicant table and then identify and remove all essential prime implicants, as in step 3 of the Quine–McCluskey method.

3. For the remaining table, write a POS logic expression representing all possible covers as follows:

   a. For each minterm column m_i, write an expression for the sum (OR) of all PIs that cover m_i. This expression indicates that any one or more of these PIs can be selected to cover m_i.

   b. Form the product (AND) of all the sum terms from step a. This product indicates that all minterms must be covered.

4. Convert the logic expression from step 2 from POS to SOP format using distributive law, and then simplify the expression by using involution and absorption to remove redundant terms. Each product term in the resulting SOP expression represents one possible cover.

5. Select the cover with the lowest cost; here, "cost" is computed as the number of PIs in the product term and the number of literals in each PI.

The examples from the previous section will be used to illustrate Petrick's algorithm.

EXAMPLE 3.27

Use Algorithm 3.6 to derive a minimum cover for the function of Example 3.24.

After forming the prime implicant table and removing the essential PIs, the following reduced PI table was obtained.

	√	√	√	√
	2	4	6	10
PI$_2$	×		×	
*PI$_3$	×			×
*PI$_4$		×	×	
PI$_5$		×		
PI$_6$				×

We see that m_2 can be covered by PI_2 or PI_3, minterm m_4 by PI_4 or PI_5, minterm m_6 by PI_2 or PI_4, and minterm m_{10} by PI_3 or PI_6. The SOP expression representing all covers, C, of these minterms is

$$C = (PI_2 + PI_3)(PI_4 + PI_5)(PI_2 + PI_4)(PI_3 + PI_6)$$

Converting to minimum SOP form, we obtain

$$C = PI_2PI_3PI_5 + PI_3PI_4 + PI_2PI_4PI_6 + PI_2PI_5PI_6$$

From this expression, we see that there are four nonredundant covers of the remaining four minterms. Of these, the cover comprising PI_3 and PI_4 represents the lowest-cost solution, consisting of only two product terms, while the other three covers require three terms each.

The following example demonstrates the usefulness of Petrick's algorithm in dealing with PI tables that cannot be reduced by row or column dominance.

EXAMPLE 3.28

Use Algorithm 3.6 to find a minimal cover for the function $f(A, B, C) = \sum m(1, 2, 3, 4, 5, 6)$ from the following PI table.

	√		√			
	1	2	3	4	5	6
* PI_1	×		×			
PI_2		×	×			
PI_3		×				×
PI_4				×		×
PI_5				×	×	
PI_6	×				×	

Note that the table is cyclic; that is, there are no essential PIs. In addition, all PIs contain the same number of literals, so there is no obvious first choice in selecting a cover. Using Algorithm 3.6, the POS form of all covers, C, converted to minimal SOP form is

$$C = (PI_1 + PI_6)(PI_2 + PI_3)(PI_1 + PI_2)(PI_4 + PI_5)(PI_5 + PI_6)(PI_3 + PI_4)$$

$$= PI_1PI_3PI_5 + PI_2PI_3PI_5PI_6 + PI_1PI_2PI_4PI_5 + PI_2PI_4PI_6 + PI_2PI_3PI_5PI_6$$

From this expression we see that there are five nonredundant covers. Three of these contain four prime implicants, while covers $PI_1PI_3PI_5$ and $PI_2PI_4PI_6$ contain only three. For this function, all the prime implicants contain the same number of literals. Therefore, $PI_1PI_3PI_5$ and $PI_2PI_4PI_6$ both represent minimal solutions.

Although Petrick's algorithm identifies all possible nonredundant covers and therefore allows an optimal solution to be identified, its complexity increases considerably with the number of minterms and prime implicants, and it is therefore not practical for large functions. The next section discusses computer-aided methods that can be applied to arbitrarily large functions.

3.11 Computer-aided Minimization of Switching Functions

Although the Karnaugh map is one of the most efficient tools available for manually minimizing switching functions when the number of variables, n, is small, it becomes almost intractable for n greater than 4 or 5. Being a graphical technique, manipulation of K-maps is not easily implemented by computer programs.

Switching circuit minimization methods that manipulate tables, such as the Quine–McCluskey method, or methods that work directly with switching expressions are more readily extended to functions of arbitrary numbers of variables. Many of these methods can be automated by programming them on digital computers. Consequently, tabular and algebraic methods are used instead of K-maps for practical design work, and they form the basis for the switching function minimization algorithms incorporated into computer-aided design (CAD) systems. As described earlier for the K-map and Quine–McCluskey methods and illustrated in Fig. 3.35, there are four basic steps in deriving a minimum sum of products switching expression for a logic function.

1. Represent the function in a format suitable for the method to be used.
2. Determine the complete set of prime implicants of the function.
3. Determine the essential prime implicants from the prime implicant set.
4. Select nonessential prime implicants as necessary to complete a minimal cover of the function.

For incompletely specified functions, don't-care terms are treated as 1 terms in steps 1 and 2, to make the prime implicants as large as possible, and then ignored during steps 3 and 4, since they do not need to be covered when realizing the function.

Comparisons of different switching function minimization algorithms show trade-offs in memory utilization, execution time, and optimality of results [9, 10]. For this reason, many CAD systems make available several different algorithms to allow the designer to choose the one that best exploits the characteristics of the function to be minimized.

Factors that influence memory utilization and computation time include the number of minterms of the function, the number of prime implicants, the number of minterms that are not covered by the essential prime implicants of the function, and the number of circuit outputs, that is, the number of functions that must be simultaneously minimized. The nature of the algorithm itself will also influence computation time, including the method with which terms are represented, the efficiency with which individual steps are performed, the order in which terms are considered, and the degree to which the assumptions made in developing the heuristics of the algorithm fit the function being manipulated.

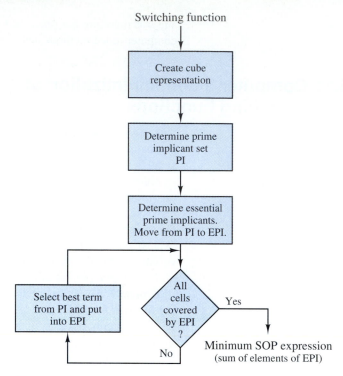

Figure 3.35   Minimization of switching functions.

For example, computer storage and computational requirements of tabular minimization algorithms increase rapidly as the number of function inputs and/or minterms increases. The Quine–McCluskey method requires generation of the entire minterm list of the function to be minimized. (Note that the total number of possible minterms may be as large as 2^n for an n-input function.) All these minterms must be stored individually in the memory of the computer, even though the function may be describable by a small number of product or sum terms. Then, to derive the prime implicants, all minterms must be pairwise compared to produce 1-cubes, all pairs of 1-cubes compared to form 2-cubes, and so on. Hence, the number of compare operations can be prohibitively large if the number of minterms is large. This is demonstrated by the following example.

EXAMPLE 3.29

Determine the number of minterms in the function

$$f(a,b,c,d,e,f) = a + abcdef$$

and determine the number of compare operations that are needed to reduce the expression via the Quine–McCluskey method.

Expansion of the function produces 32 minterms, which are combined via the Quine–McCluskey method into sixteen 1-cubes, eight 2-cubes, four 3-cubes, two 4-cubes, and one 5-cube, for a total of 63 cubes to be stored. All together, 651 compare operations must be performed to derive the single 5-cube, a.

Using switching algebra, the function can be reduced by one application of Theorem 4 (absorption):

$$f(a, b, c, d, e, f) = a + abcdef = a$$

This example illustrates that algebraic manipulation of the original product terms of a switching expression is often preferred to applying the Quine–McCluskey method, especially when the number of terms is small.

In the following section, we examine algebraic methods used in CAD systems for automating the steps of the minimization process. This is not an exhaustive list of techniques, but is intended to provide the reader with a general idea of the nature of the algorithms utilized. The reader is referred to [9, 10] for further discussions and examples of computer programs that implement several of the algorithms described in this chapter.

3.11.1 Cube Representation of Switching Functions

The notation most commonly used in CAD systems for representing switching expressions during design entry and printout, as well as for internal use, is *cube* notation. An n-dimensional geometric cube (n-*cube* for short) comprises 2^n vertices, each connected to n other vertices by lines (edges) along the n dimensions of the figure. Each vertex is uniquely identified by an n-bit binary number, represented by an n-tuple $x_1 x_2 \ldots x_n$. Each pair of adjacent vertices of an n-cube (vertices directly connected by an edge) differ in exactly one bit position, x_i, corresponding to the ith dimension along which the connecting edge lies. This is illustrated in Fig. 3.36a for a 3-cube.

A switching function of n variables, $f(x_1, \ldots, x_n)$, can be represented by a mapping of its minterms onto the vertices of an n-cube. This mapping uses the binary minterm coding described in Chapter 2, in which $x_i = 0$ indicates that x_i is complemented in the minterm, and $x_i = 1$ indicates an uncomplemented variable. For example, let

$$f_\delta(a, b, c) = \sum m(2, 4, 6) = \bar{a}b\bar{c} + a\bar{b}\bar{c} + ab\bar{c} = \{010, 100, 110\}$$

These three minterms map onto a 3-cube at vertices 010, 100, and 110, respectively, as shown in Fig. 3.36b. Each minterm is shown as one vertex (a heavy dot) in the figure.

An r-variable implicant of an n-variable function, formed by combining adjacent minterms, can be represented by a subcube (or r-cube) of the n-cube. For example, referring to Fig. 3.36, the edge (1-cube) connecting vertices 010 and 110 corresponds to implicant $b\bar{c}$ since, by Theorem 6(a),

$$\bar{a}b\bar{c} + ab\bar{c} = b\bar{c}$$

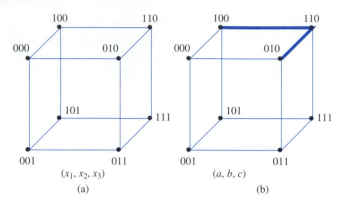

Figure 3.36 Mapping switching functions onto n-dimensional cubes. **(a)** 3-cube. **(b)** $f_\delta(a, b, c) = \sum m(2, 4, 6)$ mapped onto a 3-cube.

Implicants are represented in cube notation by using the dash (–) in place of each eliminated variable. For example, implicant $b\bar{c}$ of $f_\delta(a, b, c)$, is represented by -10. In general, an r-cube of an n-variable function is formed by combining 2^r adjacent minterms, which eliminates r variables. Thus an r-cube contains r – symbols. A sum of products form of an n-variable function $f(x_1, \ldots, x_n)$ can be expressed as a list of cubes, each representing one product term.

EXAMPLE 3.30

Determine the cube representation of
$f(x, y, z) = y + \bar{x}z.$

$$
\begin{array}{rcl}
y & \Rightarrow & -1- \\
\bar{x}z & \Rightarrow & 0-1
\end{array}
$$

Therefore, the function can be represented by the set of cubes $\{-1-, 0-1\}$.

When implementing logic minimization and simulation tools on a digital computer, variations of the basic cube representation are often used to allow programmers to exploit the inherent data structures and operations of the particular programming language used to implement the tools. Many of these programs allow switching expressions to be entered and/or printed out in the form of algebraic expressions, minterm lists, and so on, and then converted to cube representation for internal use. Examples can be found in [9, 10].

3.11.2 Algebraic Methods for Determining Prime Implicants

After a switching function has been represented in a suitable format, the minimization process begins by finding the prime implicants of the function. On a K-map, this involves identifying and circling the largest grouping of cells covering each minterm on the map. In the Quine–McCluskey method, pairs of cubes are compared, with cubes differing in exactly one literal combined to create larger cubes until no further combinations can be made.

Algebraic methods apply selected theorems of switching algebra to lists of product terms. These algorithms minimize memory requirements by working directly with supplied implicants (product terms) represented in cube notation, rather than requiring the function to be expanded into a minterm list. For functions described by a small number of implicants, computational efficiency is increased, even though the number of input variables may be large, since the number of operations will be minimized.

Most algebraic algorithms are based on the consensus theorem of Boolean algebra (Theorem 9) and are easily implemented in computer-aided design packages. In these algorithms the consensus theorem is used to combine adjacent implicants into larger ones and to identify new implicants that overlap implicants already in the list. These two operations are illustrated by the following example.

EXAMPLE 3.31

Use the consensus theorem to simplify the function
$$f(A, B, C, D) = \bar{A}BD + ABD + \bar{A}\bar{B}\bar{C}$$

The function, plotted in Fig. 3.37a, is covered by the set of three implicants: $\{\bar{A}BD, ABD, \bar{A}\bar{B}\bar{C}\}$. Let us begin by applying the consensus theorem to the first two terms in the list.

$$\bar{A}BD + ABD = \bar{A}BD + ABD + (BD)(BD) \qquad \text{[T9(a), consensus]}$$
$$= \bar{A}BD + ABD + BD \qquad \text{[T1(b), idempotency]}$$
$$= BD \qquad \text{[T4(a), absorption]}$$

The consensus term BD covers (absorbs) both $\bar{A}BD$ and ABD and can therefore replace both in the set of implicants. Note that this is equivalent to combining the two adjacent implicants $\bar{A}BD$ and ABD by Theorem 6(a).

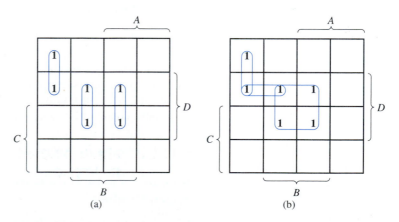

Figure 3.37   Determining prime implicants of $f(A, B, C, D) = \bar{A}BD + ABD + \bar{A}\bar{B}\bar{C}$. **(a)** Given terms. **(b)** Prime implicants.

Now, applying the consensus theorem to the remaining two terms in the implicant list, we obtain

$$\bar{A}\bar{B}\bar{C} + BD = \bar{A}\bar{B}\bar{C} + BD + \bar{A}\bar{C}D \quad \text{[T9(a), consensus]}$$

As shown in Fig. 3.37b, the consensus term $\bar{A}\bar{C}D$ covers neither $\bar{A}\bar{B}\bar{C}$ nor BD completely. $\bar{A}\bar{C}D$ thus represents another prime implicant of the function and is added to the list.

The final prime implicant list, $\{\bar{A}\bar{B}\bar{C}, BD, \bar{A}\bar{C}D\}$, is plotted in Fig. 3.37b.

Application of the consensus, idempotency, and absorption theorems to terms represented in cube notation are easily automated by special operators. The most commonly used is the *STAR product*, described in [11], which is an operator that identifies the bit positions in which two cubes differ.

In the *iterative consensus algorithm* [10, 11], a complete prime implicant list for a function is produced from any list of cubes that describes the function by appying the consensus theorem to all pairs of cubes in the list, using the STAR product, and identifying consensus cubes as shown in the previous examples. Each consensus cube is added to the list if it is not covered (absorbed) by any cube already in the list, and any cubes covered (absorbed) by a newly added consensus cube are eliminated from the list. This process of adding a new cube to a list is referred to as forming the *absorbed union* of the list and the cube. After all pairs of cubes in the list have been compared, only those representing the prime implicants remain.

The number of applications of the STAR product in the iterative consensus algorithm is large when the number of product terms is large. The *generalized consensus algorithm* [10, 12] uses the same basic principle, but reduces the total number of operations by systematically organizing the terms prior to applying the STAR operator, much as the minterms were grouped in step 1 of the Quine–McCluskey method to facilitate identification of logically adjacent terms.

3.11.3 Identifying Essential Prime Implicants

After finding the set of prime implicants, PI, of a function, selection of a minimal cover begins by identifying any essential prime implicants (EPIs) of the function. On a K-map, EPIs are easily spotted by locating each minterm cell on the map that is circled only by a single PI. In the Quine–McCluskey method a prime implicant table is utilized; EPIs are identified by noting minterm columns in the table containing a single check.

In this section we examine two algebraic methods for determining the EPIs of a function from its complete set of prime implicants.

Essential Prime Implicants Using the Sharp Product

Given a set PI of prime implicants of a function represented in cube notation, we wish to know if a selected prime implicant covers one or more minterms of the function that are not covered by the other prime implicants of PI. This can be determined using an operator called the *sharp product* as follows.

Let PI_i and PI_j be prime implicants of a function, each representing the set of minterms covered by that prime implicant. The *sharp product*, $PI_i \# PI_j$, is defined as the set of minterms covered by PI_i that are not covered by PI_j, that is, set PI_i with any minterms common to PI_i and PI_j removed. In terms of set operations,

$$PI_i \# PI_j = PI_i - (PI_i \cap PI_j). \tag{3.1}$$

Given a set of prime implicants $PI = \{P_1, \dots, P_n\}$ that cover a function, the sharp product

$$S = P_1 \# \{P_2, \dots, P_n\} = (\dots ((P_1 \# P_2) \# P_3) \dots \# P_n)$$

takes the set of minterms covered by P_1 and removes from it all minterms covered by at least one other prime implicant of PI. If S is nonempty, it contains those minterms that are covered by P_1 and by no other prime implicant in $\{P_2, \dots P_n\}$. P_1 is thus essential to the function and must be included in EPI. If S is empty, each minterm covered by P_1 is also covered by at least one other prime implicant in $\{P_2, \dots P_n\}$, making P_1 nonessential to the function.

For incompletely specified functions, where DC is the set of *don't-care* terms, the sharp product $S \# DC$ is also computed to remove any don't-care terms from S. If the result is an empty set, the only terms covered exclusively by P_1 are don't-care terms, and therefore P_1 is not essential to the function. This check ensures that only specified (non-don't-care) terms are considered for the cover of the function.

Essential Prime Implicants Using Iterative Consensus

The iterative and generalized consensus algorithms can be extended to identify essential prime implicants of a function from its prime implicant set. Given prime implicant set $PI = \{P_1, P_2 \dots, P_n\}$, each prime implicant, P_i, can be determined to be either essential or nonessential as follows.

P_i is removed from PI and one of the consensus algorithms applied to the remaining set of prime implicants $(PI - P_i)$. The two consensus algorithms are guaranteed to produce the entire set of prime implicants from any set of implicants that describe a function. Therefore, if P_i is regenerated, then $(PI - P_i)$ completely covers the function; that is, each minterm covered by P_i is also covered by at least one other prime implicant in $(PI - P_i)$. Therefore, P_i is not essential. If P_i is not regenerated, it covers at least one minterm that is not covered by any of the other prime implicants of PI and is therefore essential to the function and must be included in EPI.

3.11.4 Completing a Minimal Cover

If the essential prime implicants cover all of the minterms of a function, then set EPI of essential prime implicants is a unique minimum cover of the function.

Otherwise, one or more additional prime implicants must be selected to complete the cover.

Most minimization algorithms vary significantly in the methods used to extract a minimum cover from a prime implicant set after removing the essential prime implicants. Various *heuristics*, based on properties of the function or of the target circuit structure, are used to direct the solution process. The goal of a minimization algorithm is to find the minimum-cost solution, that is, the most cost effective set of nonessential prime implicants to complete a cover. However, given the cost of finding an optimal solution, especially for multiple-output functions, we are often willing to make trade-offs, settling for a near-optimum solution but one that can be generated in a reasonable amount of computation time.

The basic algorithm for determining the minimum cover of a function, given the essential prime implicant set EPI and the remaining set of nonessential prime implicants, PI, is illustrated in Fig. 3.38. Each step in this process is explained in the following.

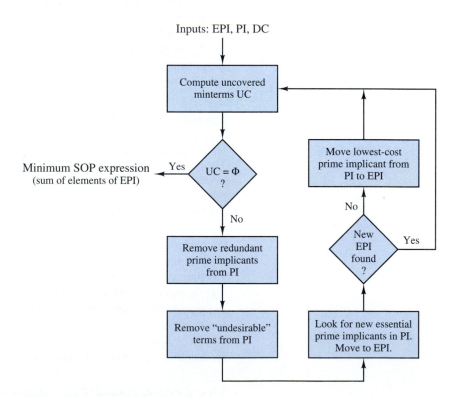

Figure 3.38   Selection of a minimum cover of a function.

Determining the Remaining Uncovered Minterms

After computing EPI, we must determine which minterms of the function, if any, are not yet covered by EPI. To do this, we can use the sharp product as follows to remove from PI any minterms covered by EPI and any don't-care terms.

$$UC = (PI\#EPI)\#DC \tag{3.2}$$

The resulting set, UC, contains all uncovered minterms of the function. If UC $= \Phi$, no minterms remain uncovered and EPI completely covers the function. Otherwise, one or more prime implicants from PI must be selected to cover the elements of UC.

Eliminating Redundant Prime Implicants

To simplify the selection of terms from PI to cover the remaining minterms in UC, we begin by removing from PI any prime implicants that are *redundant*; that is, they that do not cover any of the cubes in UC. If a prime implicant is determined to be redundant, it cannot contribute to the solution and should be eliminated from consideration by removing it from PI. A prime implicant P_i can be identified as redundant if

$$UC \cap P_i = \Phi \tag{3.3}$$

The intersection $UC \cap P_i$ can be computed by using the STAR product described earlier.

Eliminating Undesirable Prime Implicants

After removing any redundant prime implicants from PI, we should determine if any of the remaining prime implicants are more or less cost effective than others for completing the cover. A prime implicant P_i is *undesirable* as a choice for the solution if there exists some other prime implicant P_j such that P_j covers the same uncovered minterms as P_i and is of lower cost (contains fewer literals). In other words, selection of P_i cannot lead to a lower-cost solution than P_j and should therefore be eliminated from consideration by removing it from PI. P_i is undesirable if there can be found in set PI a prime implicant P_j such that

$$(UC \cap P_i)\#P_j = \Phi \tag{3.4}$$

and

$$\text{cost } P_i \geq \text{cost } P_j \tag{3.5}$$

Equation 3.4 indicates that P_j covers every minterm of UC that is covered by P_i, and Eq. 3.5 indicates that P_j is of lower or equal cost.

Selection of Nonessential Prime Implicants

After any redundant and/or undesirable prime implicants have been removed from PI, we must determine if the elimination of these terms has resulted in any of the remaining cubes in PI becoming essential. This will happen if all but one of the prime implicants covering an element of UC have been eliminated. Prime implicants made essential in this manner can be identified by reapplying to PI the algorithm described earlier for finding the essential prime implicants of a function.

If no prime implicant of PI is found to be essential, a *cycle* exists. In this case, the cycle is broken by selecting an arbitrary term from PI to add to EPI. The process of reducing set PI and selecting additional prime implicants to add to EPI continues until UC $= \Phi$. However, whenever an arbitrary selection is made, it is possible that the final solution might not be optimal. Many CAD programs are designed to compute all possible solutions and evaluate the results of each possible decision to determine the best choice for breaking each cycle. However, for large functions this might utilize more computation time than is practical, in which case we simply accept the results achieved by making a single choice to break each cycle.

3.11.5 Other Minimization Algorithms

Only single-output functions were discussed in this section. However, most of the algebraic algorithms presented have been extended to simultaneous minimization of several functions; this extension is needed for logic circuits with multiple outputs, which includes most practical applications. The reader is referred to [9–12] for information on extending the iterative and generalized consensus algorithms to multiple-output functions.

Minimization algorithms differ primarily in the methods used to extract a minimum cover of a function from a set of prime implicants. The heuristics used by many of these algorithms are targeted at particular circuit structures, taking advantage of the unique characteristics of these structures to guide the search for an optimal solution. A primary example is the programmable logic array (PLA), which will be described in Chapter 5. A PLA basically realizes sum of product expressions by forming product terms with a programmable AND array and then forming sums of these product terms with a programmable OR array. In general, PLA circuits are characterized by having a relatively large number of inputs and a relatively small number of product terms. Consequently, algorithms that require the generation and manipulation of all the minterms of the function are significantly less efficient than those that work directly with product terms.

One of the most widely-used minimization programs for PLAs is ESPRESSO-II, developed at the University of California at Berkeley [13]. ESPRESSO-II was developed after extensive study of two existing minimization algorithms: MINI, developed at IBM in 1974 [14] and PRESTO [15]. The development of ESPRESSO-II essentially took the best features of these predecessors, provided more efficient algorithms for the individual steps, and then worked with the final stages of the algorithm to more efficiently complete the minimum cover after the essential prime implicants have been found. Since the development of ESPRESSO-II, many additional minimization programs have been developed. The reader is referred to the documentation accompanying the CAD tools available at his or her site to identify the algorithm(s) available with those tools.

3.12 Summary

Graphical and tabular methods for the minimization of switching functions have been presented. The ramifications of each technique were discussed in detail. The graphical technique employs the Karnaugh map, which was shown to be nothing more than a convenient representation of the Venn diagram. The Quine–McCluskey method, which is a tabular approach, employs an efficient linear search in the minimization process. This minimization technique is also suitable for programming on a digital computer. Petrick's algorithm for deriving the minimum covers of a function from its prime implicant set was presented as an example of an optimal approach. Finally, minimization techniques that can be efficiently programmed for inclusion in computer-aided design systems were discussed, including the iterative and generalized consensus algorithms.

REFERENCES

1. M. KARNAUGH, "The Map Method of Combinational Logic Circuits," *AIEE Comm. Electronics*, November 1953, pp. 593–599.

2. E. W. VEITCH, "A Chart Method for Simplifying Truth Functions," *Proc. Computing Machinery Conf.*, May 2–3, 1952, pp. 127-133.

3. D. A. HUFFMAN, "The Design and Use of Hazard-free Switching Networks," *J. ACM*, Vol. 4, No. 1, January 1957, pp. 47–62.

4. Z. KOHAVI, *Switching and Finite Automata Theory*, 2nd ed., New York: McGraw-Hill Book Co., 1978.

5. E. J. MCCLUSKEY JR., *Introduction to the Theory of Switching Circuits*. New York: McGraw-Hill Book Co., 1965.

6. E. J. MCCLUSKEY JR., "Minimization of Boolean Functions," *Bell System Tech. J.*, November 1956, pp. 1417–1444.

7. W. V. QUINE, "The Problem of Simplifying Truth Functions," *Amer. Math. Monthly*, Vol. 59, 1952, pp. 521-531.

8. S. R. PETRICK, "On the Minimization of Boolean Functions," *Prof. Symp. Switching Theory*, ICIP, Paris, France, June 1959.

9. T. DOWNS, AND M. F. SCHULZ, *Logic Design with Pascal, Computer Aided Design Techniques*, New York: Van Nostrand Reinhold, 1988.

10. J. F. WAKERLY, *Digital Design Principles and Practices*, 2nd ed., Chapter 2. Englewood Cliffs, NJ: Prentice Hall, 1994.

11. T. H. MOTT, JR., "Determination of the Irredundant Normal Forms of a Truth Function by Iterated Consensus of the Prime Implicants", *IRE Trans. Electronic Computers*, Vol. EC-9, No. 2, 1960, pp. 245–252.

12. P. TISON, "Generalization of Consensus Theory and Application to the Minimization of Boolean Functions", *IEEE Trans. Electronic Computers*, Vol. EC-16, No. 4, 1967, pp. 446–456.

13. R. K. BRAYTON, G.C. HACHTEL, C.T. MCMULLEN, AND A.L. SANGIOVANNI-VINCENTELLI, *Logic Minimization Algorithms for VLSI Synthesis*, Boston: Kluwer Academic Publishers, 1984.

14. S. J. HONG, R.G. CAIN, AND D.L. OSTAPKO, "MINI: A Heuristic Approach for Logic Minimization", *IBM J. of Res. and Dev.*, Vol. 18, pp 443–458, September 1974.

15. D. W. BROWN, "A State Machine Synthesizer - SMS", *Proc. 18th Design Automation Conference*, pp 301–304, Nashville, June 1981.

PROBLEMS

3.1 Plot the following functions on the Karnaugh map.

(a) $f(A, B, C) = \bar{A}\bar{B} + \bar{B}C + \bar{A}C$

(b) $f(A, B, C, D) = \bar{B}\bar{C}D + \bar{A}B\bar{C} + AB\bar{D}$

(c) $f(A, B, C, D, E) = \bar{B}\bar{C}\bar{E} + \bar{B}CE + C\bar{D}E + \bar{A}BC\bar{D} + AB\bar{C}D\bar{E}$

3.2 Minimize the following functions using the K-map.

(a) $f(A, B, C) = \sum m(3, 5, 6, 7)$

(b) $f(A, B, C, D) = \sum m(0, 1, 4, 6, 9, 13, 14, 15)$

(c) $f(A, B, C, D) = \sum m(0, 1, 2, 8, 9, 10, 11, 12, 13, 14, 15)$

(d) $f(A, B, C, D, E) = \sum m(3, 4, 6, 9, 11, 13, 15, 18, 25, 26, 27, 29, 31)$

(e) $f(A, B, C, D, E) = \sum m(1, 5, 8, 10, 12, 13, 14, 15, 17, 21, 24, 26, 31)$

3.3 Minimize the following functions containing don't-cares using the K-map.

(a) $f(A, B, C, D) = \sum m(2, 9, 10, 12, 13) + d(1, 5, 14)$

(b) $f(A, B, C, D) = \sum m(1, 3, 6, 7) + d(4, 9, 11)$

(c) $f(A, B, C, D, E) = \sum m(3, 11, 12, 19, 23, 29) + d(5, 7, 13, 27, 28)$

3.4 The circuit in Fig. P3.1 accepts BCD inputs for the decimal digits 0 to 9. The output is to be 1 only if the input is odd. Design the minimum logic circuit to accomplish this.

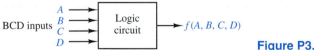

BCD inputs A B C D → Logic circuit → $f(A, B, C, D)$

Figure P3.1

3.5 Use the K-map to expand the following POS functions to canonical form.

(a) $f(A, B, C) = (A + \bar{B})(\bar{A} + B)(B + \bar{C})$

(b) $f(A, B, C, D) = (A + \bar{D})(\bar{A} + C)$

3.6 Minimize the following functions using a K-map.

(a) $f(A, B, C, D) = \sum m(3, 4, 6, 8, 9, 12, 14)$

(b) $f(A, B, C, D, E)$

$$= \sum m(1, 3, 4, 9, 11, 12, 13, 15, 17, 19, 22, 25, 27, 29, 30, 31)$$

3.7 Use K-maps to expand the following switching functions to canonical SOP form.

   (a) $f(A, B, C) = (\bar{A} + B)(A + B + \bar{C})(\bar{A} + C)$

   (b) $f(A, B, C, D) = A\bar{B} + \bar{A}CD + B\bar{C}\bar{D}$

   (c) $f(A, B, C, D) = (A + \bar{B})(C + \bar{D})(\bar{A} + C)$

   (d) $f(A, B, C, D, E) = \bar{A}E + BCD$

3.8 Determine which of the following functions are equivalent.

$$f_1(A, B, C, D) = AC + BD + A\bar{B}\bar{D}$$
$$f_2(A, B, C, D) = A\bar{B}\bar{D} + AB + \bar{A}B\bar{C}$$
$$f_3(A, B, C, D) = BD + A\bar{B}\bar{D} + ACD + ABC$$
$$f_4(A, B, C, D) = AC + A\bar{B}\bar{C}\bar{D} + \bar{A}BD + B\bar{C}D$$
$$f_5(A, B, C, D) = (B + \bar{D})(A + B)(A + \bar{C})$$

3.9 Use a K-map to find the following forms of the given switching function.

   (a) Canonical SOP form   **(b)** Canonical POS form

$$f(A, B, C, D, E) = B\bar{D}E + A\bar{B}D + \bar{A}C\bar{D}E + A\bar{C}E$$

3.10 Design a multiple-output combinational network that has two input signals x_0 and x_1, two control signals c_0 and c_1, and two output functions f_0 and f_1. The control signals have the following effect on the outputs:

c_0	c_1	f_0	f_1
0	0	0	0
0	1	x_0	0
1	0	0	x_1
1	1	x_0	x_1

      For example, when $c_0 = 0$ and $c_1 = 1$, then $f_0(x_0, x_1, c_0, c_1) = x_0$ and $f_1(x_0, x_1, c_0, c_1) = 0$.

3.11 Use K-maps to find the following functions.

$$f_1(A, B, C, D) = f_\alpha(A, B, C, D) \cdot f_\beta(A, B, C, D)$$
$$f_2(A, B, C, D) = f_\alpha(A, B, C, D) + f_\beta(A, B, C, D)$$
$$f_3(A, B, C, D) = \bar{f}_1(A, B, C, D) \cdot f_2(A, B, C, D)$$
$$f_4(A, B, C, D) = f_\alpha(A, B, C, D) \oplus f_\beta(A, B, C, D)$$

where

$$f_\alpha(A, B, C, D) = AB + BD + \bar{A}\bar{B}C$$
$$f_\beta(A, B, C, D) = \bar{A}B + B\bar{D}$$

3.12 **(a)** Use K-maps to generate all the prime implicants for the following output logic network.

$$f_\alpha(A, B, C, D) = AB + BD + \bar{A}\bar{B}C$$
$$f_\beta(A, B, C, D) = \bar{A}B + B\bar{D}$$

   (b) Repeat part (a) using the multiple-output Quine–McCluskey technique. Compare your prime implicant charts.

3.13 Minimize the following functions using the Quine–McCluskey method.

   (a) $f(A, B, C, D) = \sum m(0, 2, 4, 5, 7, 9, 11, 12)$

   (b) $f(A, B, C, D, E) = \sum m(0, 1, 2, 7, 9, 11, 12, 23, 27, 28)$

3.14 Use the Quine–McCluskey method to minimize the following functions with don't-cares.

(a) $f(A, B, C, D) = \sum m(0, 6, 9, 10, 13) + d(1, 3, 8)$

(b) $f(A, B, C, D) = \sum m(1, 4, 7, 10, 13) + d(5, 14, 15)$

3.15 Minimize the following multiple-output functions using the Q–M technique.

(a) $f_\alpha(A, B, C, D) = \sum m(0, 1, 2, 9, 15)$
$f_\beta(A, B, C, D) = \sum m(0, 2, 8, 12, 15)$

(b) $f_\alpha(A, B, C, D) = \sum m(3, 7, 9, 14) + d(1, 4, 6, 11)$
$f_\beta(A, B, C, D) = \sum m(6, 7, 12) + d(3, 14)$

3.16 Design a switching network that accepts BCD inputs and gives an output of logic 1 only when the input decimal digit is divisible by 3. Use a four-variable K-map to design your circuit.

3.17 Design a switching network that has five input variables and one output variable. Four of the input variables represent BCD digits, and the fifth is a control line. While the control line is at logic 0, the output should be logic 1 only if the BCD digit is greater than or equal to 5. While the control line is high, the output should be logic 1 only if the BCD digit is less than or equal to 5.

3.18 Design a multiple-output logic network whose input is a BCD digit and whose outputs are defined as follows: f_1: Detects input digits that are divisible by 4, f_2: Detects numbers greater than or equal to 3, f_3: Detects numbers less than 7.

3.19 Apply the covering procedure to obtain a minimum list of prime implicants for the function

$$f(A, B, C, D) = \sum m(1, 3, 4, 6, 7, 9, 13, 15)$$

3.20 Plot the following functions on the K-map and determine the minterm lists.

(a) $f(A, B, C) = \bar{B} + A\bar{C}$

(b) $f(A, B, C) = \bar{A}\bar{C} + \bar{A}B + BC$

3.21 Plot the following functions on the K-map and determine the minterm lists.

(a) $f(A, B, C) = \bar{A}B + BC + AC + A\bar{B}$

(b) $f(A, B, C) = \bar{B}C + \bar{A}B + B\bar{C}$

3.22 Plot the following functions on the K-map and determine the minterm lists.

(a) $f(A, B, C, D) = \bar{A}\bar{B}C + A\bar{C}\bar{D} + B\bar{C}D + AB\bar{D}$

(b) $f(A, B, C, D) = \bar{A}\bar{B}\bar{C} + \bar{B}CD + AB\bar{D} + ABC$

3.23 Plot the following functions on the K-map and determine the minterm lists.

(a) $f(A, B, C, D) = \bar{B}CD + \bar{A}B\bar{D} + B\bar{C}D + A\bar{B}D$

(b) $f(A, B, C, D) = \bar{B}\bar{C}\bar{D} + \bar{A}\bar{B}\bar{C} + \bar{A}\bar{C}D + BCD + ABC$

3.24 Plot the following functions on the K-map and determine the minterm lists.

(a) $f(A, B, C, D, E) = \bar{B}\bar{C}D + \bar{B}DE + \bar{A}BC\bar{D} + BC\bar{D}E + \bar{A}B\bar{D}\bar{E} + B\bar{C}\bar{D}\bar{E} + AB\bar{C}\bar{E}$

(b) $f(A, B, C, D, E) = \bar{A}\bar{B}D\bar{E} + \bar{A}B\bar{D} + BE + A\bar{B}\bar{C}\bar{D} + A\bar{C}\bar{D}E$

3.25 Plot the following functions on the K-map and determine the maxterm lists.

(a) $f(A, B, C) = (A + B)(\bar{B} + C)$

(b) $f(A, B, C) = \bar{B}(\bar{A} + C)$

3.26 Plot the following functions on the K-map and determine the maxterm lists.
    (a) $f(A, B, C) = A(B + \bar{C})$
    (b) $f(A, B, C) = (B + C)(A + \bar{B})$

3.27 Plot the following functions on the K-map and determine the maxterm list.
    (a) $f(A, B, C, D) = (\bar{C} + \bar{D})(\bar{A} + \bar{B} + D)(\bar{A} + \bar{C} + \bar{D})(\bar{A} + C + D)$
        $\cdot (B + C + D)$
    (b) $f(A, B, C, D) = (\bar{B} + C)(A + C + \bar{D})(A + B + \bar{D})(B + \bar{C} + \bar{D})$

3.28 Plot the following functions on the K-map and determine the maxterm list.
    (a) $f(A, B, C, D) = (A + \bar{D})(A + \bar{B})(\bar{B} + D)(\bar{A} + C + D)$
    (b) $f(A, B, C, D) = (A + \bar{B} + C)(\bar{A} + \bar{B} + \bar{D})(\bar{A} + \bar{C} + D)(B + \bar{C} + D)$

3.29 Plot the following function on the K-map and determine the maxterm list.
$$f(A, B, C, D, E) = (B + \bar{C} + \bar{D})(A + C + D)(A + \bar{B} + D)$$
$$\cdot (\bar{A} + B + D + E)(\bar{B} + D + \bar{E})$$

3.30 Use the K-map to simplify the following functions.
    (a) $f(A, B, C) = \sum m(1, 5, 6, 7)$
    (b) $f(A, B, C) = \sum m(0, 1, 2, 3, 4, 5)$

3.31 Use the K-map to simplify the following functions.
    (a) $f(A, B, C) = \sum m(0, 2, 3, 5)$
    (b) $f(A, B, C) = \sum m(0, 3, 4, 6, 7)$

3.32 Simplify the following functions using a K-map.
    (a) $f(A, B, C, D) = \sum m(0, 2, 5, 7, 8, 10, 13, 15)$
    (b) $f(A, B, C, D) = \sum m(1, 3, 4, 5, 6, 7, 9, 11, 12, 13, 14, 15)$

3.33 Use the K-map to simplify the following functions.
    (a) $f(A, B, C, D) = \sum m(0, 4, 5, 7, 8, 10, 11, 15)$
    (b) $f(A, B, C, D) = \sum m(1, 4, 5, 6, 9, 11, 15)$

3.34 Simplify the following functions using a K-map.
    (a) $f(A, B, C, D) = \sum m(1, 2, 5, 6, 7, 9, 11, 15)$
    (b) $f(A, B, C, D) = \sum m(0, 1, 2, 5, 12, 13, 14, 15)$

3.35 Use the K-map to simplify the following functions.
    (a) $f(A, B, C, D) = \sum m(1, 4, 5, 6, 8, 9, 11, 13, 15)$
    (b) $f(A, B, C, D) = \sum m(1, 2, 4, 5, 6, 9, 12, 14)$

3.36 Simplify the following functions using a K-map.
    (a) $f(A, B, C, D, E) = \sum m(0, 4, 6, 7, 8, 11, 15, 20, 22, 24, 26, 27, 31)$
    (b) $f(A, B, C, D, E) = \sum m(2, 7, 10, 12, 13, 22, 23, 26, 27, 28, 29)$

3.37 Use the K-map to simplify the following functions.
    (a) $f(A, B, C, D, E) = \sum m(1, 3, 8, 9, 11, 12, 14, 17, 19, 20, 22, 24, 25, 27)$
    (b) $f(A, B, C, D, E) = \sum m(0, 7, 8, 10, 13, 15, 16, 24, 28, 29, 31)$

3.38 Simplify the following functions using a K-map.
    (a) $f(A, B, C, D, E) = \sum m(1, 2, 5, 6, 13, 15, 16, 18, 22, 24, 29)$
    (b) $f(A, B, C, D, E) = \sum m(1, 7, 9, 12, 14, 15, 16, 23, 24, 28, 30)$

3.39 Use the K-map to simplify the following functions.

(a) $f(A, B, C, D, E) = \sum m(0, 5, 10, 11, 13, 15, 16, 18, 29, 31)$

(b) $f(A, B, C, D, E) = \sum m(4, 5, 7, 8, 9, 12, 13, 16, 18, 23, 24, 25, 28, 29)$

3.40 Find the minimum POS form for the following functions.
(a) $f(A, B, C) = \prod M(0, 2, 3, 4)$
(b) $f(A, B, C) = \prod M(0, 3, 4, 7)$

3.41 Find the minimum POS form for the following functions.
(a) $f(A, B, C) = \prod M(0, 1, 4, 5, 6)$
(b) $f(A, B, C) = \prod M(1, 2, 3, 6)$

3.42 Find the minimum POS form for the following functions.
(a) $f(A, B, C) = \prod M(1, 2, 5, 7)$
(b) $f(A, B, C) = \prod M(1, 2, 3, 4)$

3.43 Find the minimum POS form for the following functions.
(a) $f(A, B, C) = \prod M(0, 1, 3, 4, 6, 7)$
(b) $f(A, B, C) = \prod M(2, 3, 5, 7)$

3.44 Find the minimum POS form for the following functions.
(a) $f(A, B, C, D) = \prod M(0, 1, 5, 7, 8, 10, 11, 15)$
(b) $f(A, B, C, D) = \prod M(0, 1, 2, 4, 6, 7, 8, 10, 14)$

3.45 Find the minimum POS form for the following functions.
(a) $f(A, B, C, D) = \prod M(2, 3, 4, 5, 7, 12, 13)$
(b) $f(A, B, C, D) = \prod M(1, 2, 5, 7, 11, 13, 15)$

3.46 Find the minimum POS form for the following functions.
(a) $f(A, B, C, D) = \prod M(0, 2, 4, 5, 6, 9, 11, 13)$
(b) $f(A, B, C, D) = \prod M(1, 3, 4, 5, 6, 9, 11, 12, 13)$

3.47 Find the minimum POS form for the following functions.
(a) $f(A, B, C, D) = \prod M(0, 1, 5, 7, 9, 11, 12, 14)$
(b) $f(A, B, C, D) = \prod M(3, 4, 5, 7, 8, 9, 10)$

3.48 Find the minimum POS form for the following functions.
(a) $f(A, B, C, D, E) = \prod M(3, 4, 6, 13, 15, 16, 19, 24, 29, 31)$
(b) $f(A, B, C, D, E) = \prod M(1, 4, 7, 9, 15, 17, 20, 22, 25, 30)$

3.49 Find the minimum POS form for the following functions.
(a) $f(A, B, C, D, E) = \prod M(0, 1, 2, 5, 7, 8, 10, 15, 17, 21, 22, 24, 26, 29)$
(b) $f(A, B, C, D, E) = \prod M(0, 2, 4, 6, 9, 11, 13, 15, 16, 19, 20, 25, 27, 29, 31)$

3.50 Find the minimum SOP form for the following functions.
(a) $f(A, B, C, D) = \sum m(1, 2, 7, 12, 15) + d(5, 9, 10, 11, 13)$
(b) $f(A, B, C, D) = \sum m(0, 2, 5, 15) + d(8, 9, 12, 13)$

3.51 Determine the minimum SOP form for the following functions.
(a) $f(A, B, C, D) = \sum m(4, 7, 9, 15) + d(1, 2, 3, 6)$
(b) $f(A, B, C, D) = \sum m(0, 2, 3, 4, 5) + d(8, 9, 10, 11)$

3.52 Find the minimum SOP form for the following function.
$f(A, B, C, D, E) = \sum m(7, 9, 12, 13, 19, 22) + d(0, 3, 20, 25, 27, 28, 29)$

3.53 Determine the minimum POS form for the following functions.
(a) $f(A, B, C, D) = \prod M(4, 7, 9, 11, 12) \cdot D(0, 1, 2, 3)$
(b) $f(A, B, C, D) = \prod M(0, 3, 7, 12) \cdot D(2, 10, 11, 14)$

3.54 Find the minimum POS form for the following functions.
(a) $f(A, B, C, D) = \prod M(3, 4, 10, 13, 15) \cdot D(6, 7, 14)$
(b) $f(A, B, C, D) = \prod M(0, 7, 11, 13) \cdot D(1, 2, 3)$

3.55 Find the minimum POS form for the following function.
$f(A, B, C, D, E) = \prod M(0, 5, 6, 9, 21, 28, 31) \cdot D(2, 12, 13, 14, 15, 25, 26)$

3.56 Use the Quine–McCluskey method to minimize the following functions.
(a) $f(A, B, C, D) = \sum m(0, 2, 3, 5, 7, 11, 12, 14, 15)$
(b) $f(A, B, C, D) = \sum m(0, 1, 6, 8, 9, 13, 14, 15)$

3.57 Use the Quine–McCluskey method to minimize the following functions.
(a) $f(A, B, C, D) = \sum m(1, 4, 5, 6, 8, 9, 10, 12, 14)$
(b) $f(A, B, C, D) = \sum m(4, 5, 6, 8, 11, 13, 15)$

3.58 Minimize the following functions using the Quine–McCluskey method.
(a) $f(A, B, C, D) = \sum m(1, 3, 6, 7, 8, 9, 12, 14)$
(b) $f(A, B, C, D) = \sum m(0, 2, 4, 5, 10, 11, 13, 15)$

3.59 Use the Quine–McCluskey method to minimize the following functions with don't-cares.
(a) $f(A, B, C, D) = \sum m(1, 6, 7, 9, 12) + d(8, 11, 15)$
(b) $f(A, B, C, D) = \sum m(7, 8, 13, 15) + d(3, 4, 10, 14)$

3.60 Minimize the following functions with don't-cares using the Quine–McCluskey method.
(a) $f(A, B, C, D) = \sum m(5, 7, 11, 12, 27, 29) + d(14, 20, 21, 22, 23)$
(b) $f(A, B, C, D) = \sum m(1, 4, 6, 9, 14, 17, 22, 27, 28)$
$+ d(12, 15, 20, 30, 31)$

3.61 Minimize the following multiple-output functions using the Quine–McCluskey method.
(a) $f_\alpha(A, B, C, D) = \sum m(4, 5, 6, 15) + d(8, 11)$
$f_\beta(A, B, C, D) = \sum m(0, 2, 3, 4, 5) + d(8, 11)$
(b) $f_\alpha(A, B, C, D) = \sum m(3, 4, 6, 11, 12) + d(14, 15)$
$f_\beta(A, B, C, D) = \sum m(4, 5, 6, 11, 14) + d(8, 12)$

3.62 Minimize the following multiple-output function using the Quine–McCluskey method.
$$f_\alpha(A, B, C, D, E) = \sum m(0, 2, 8, 9, 20, 24) + d(4, 10, 14, 26, 30)$$
$$f_\beta(A, B, C, D, E) = \sum m(3, 4, 8, 11, 24) + d(10, 14, 20, 26, 30)$$

3.63 Use the Quine–McCluskey method to minimize the following multiple-output function.
$$f_\alpha(A, B, C, D, E) = \sum m(0, 4, 6, 20, 22) + d(2, 10, 18)$$
$$f_\beta(A, B, C, D, E) = \sum m(4, 6, 11, 19, 20, 27) + d(18, 22)$$

4

For small digital circuits, the design approaches presented in Chapters 2 and 3 are very effective. However, it is usually impractical to describe a large-scale circuit with a single truth table, minterm list, or set of logic equations. Structured top-down design methodologies must be utilized to effectively manage the complexity of large designs. In this chapter we introduce top-down modular design methods for combinational logic circuits. Then we will examine a number of common combinational logic modules. For each module type we will study its basic function, gate-level circuit realizations of the function, and how the module is used to create larger circuits. The top-down modular design process will then be illustrated by means of a comprehensive example in which a computer arithmetic/logic unit will be designed. The chapter will conclude with a discussion of computer-aided design support for modular design.

Modular Combinational Logic

4.1 Top-down Modular Design

Top-down design is a process in which a function is initially specified at a high level of abstraction and then decomposed into lower-level subfunctions, each of which is more concrete. The decomposition process continues until the design is reduced to a set of functions, each of which is well defined and can be realized with a relatively simple circuit. Hence, the design has been developed from the "top" level "down" to a level at which the individual modules are manageable.

After all functions have been defined, each is realized with a circuit module that is designed, implemented, and tested individually. The finished modules are then interconnected to complete the design. This implementation process is often referred to as a *bottom-up* process, since it begins with the bottommost elements of the design and works toward the topmost function.

The decomposition of a design is often represented in the form of a tree structure, as illustrated in Fig. 4.1a. Let us suppose that we wish to design a circuit for a data acquisition system in which data are read from two sensors, with one of the four computations listed in Table 4.1 performed on these values, as selected by a 2-bit code, $s_1 s_2$.

TABLE 4.1   DATA ACQUISITION SYSTEM FUNCTIONS

Select Code s_1	s_2	Output Function
0	0	$A + B$
0	1	$A - B$
1	0	$\min(A, B)$
1	1	$\max(A, B)$

The root of the design tree of Fig. 4.1a is the top-level function, B, which represents the complete system. Three basic functions are needed to implement the process control system: a circuit to create digital input signals from the two sensors, a circuit to perform the four computations on the two sensor values,

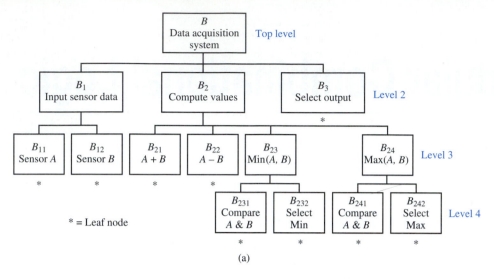

(a)

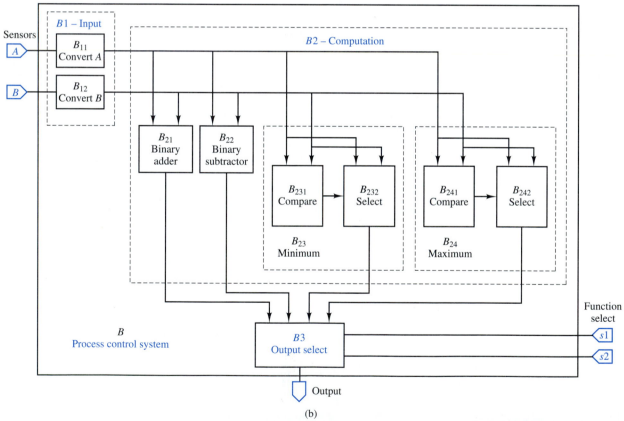

(b)

Figure 4.1 Top-down design of a function. **(a)** Hierarchical design tree. **(b)** Hierarchical block diagram.

and a circuit to select the desired result as the system output, according to the selection code $s_1 s_2$. Therefore, top-level block B is decomposed into second-level blocks B_1, B_2, and B_3, representing the input, computation, and output functions, respectively.

Next, each of the second-level functions is examined. Input function B_1 must convert data from the two sensors into binary numbers. Therefore, function B_1 is decomposed into two modules: conversion circuits B_{11} for *sensor A* and B_{12} for *sensor B*. Both of these functions represent modules that are not broken down into smaller circuits. Functions that are not further decomposed are called *leaf nodes* of the design tree.

The computation function B_2 must generate four values: $A + B$, $A - B$, Min(A, B), and Max(A, B). These four subfunctions are defined as B_{21}, B_{22}, B_{23}, and B_{24}, respectively. Subfunctions B_{21} and B_{22} can be implemented with simple binary adder and binary subtracter circuits, respectively, and are thus leaf nodes. Subfunction B_{23} is further decomposed into B_{231}, which compares A and B, and B_{232}, which selects one of A or B according to the result of the comparison. Subfunction B_{24} is similarly decomposed into B_{241} and B_{242}.

The output circuit is a function that selects one of four values, according to selection code $s_1 s_2$. This can be done with a standard circuit module. Therefore, block B_3 is a leaf node of the design tree.

From the design tree of Fig. 4.1a, a schematic diagram can be developed in block diagram form, as illustrated in Fig. 4.1b. Each block in this diagram represents one of the leaf nodes of the design tree, with all block inputs and outputs precisely defined. Each block output represents the function performed by that block, and the block inputs represent the arguments of the function.

After completion of the block diagram, the designer is faced with the decision of whether to use a previously-designed module or to develop a new one for each block. Many different modules have been developed and are available as standard functions that can be used as building blocks for complex digital circuits. In VLSI design, commonly-used modules, or *standard cells*, are maintained in libraries of functions from which they can be selected and incorporated into designs as needed. For developing circuit boards and other multi-chip systems, there is a number of standard modules available commercially as MSI circuit components.

In the following sections, we examine the design and applications of a number of standard combinational circuit modules. The modules described in this chapter correspond to standard 7400-series TTL functions, which are readily available off-the-shelf as MSI components in a variety of technologies, and are also available in most VLSI design libraries used in creating custom- and semi-custom VLSI circuits.

4.2 Decoders

An n-to-2^n *decoder* is a multiple-output combinational logic network with n input lines and 2^n output signals, as illustrated in Fig. 4.2. For each possible input condition, one and only one output signal will be at logic 1. Therefore, we may consider the n-to-2^n decoder as simply a minterm generator, with each output corresponding to exactly one minterm. Decoders are important tools in the logic designer's repertoire. They are used for such things as interrogating memory in order to select a particular word from the many that are available, code conversion (for example, binary to decimal), and routing of data.

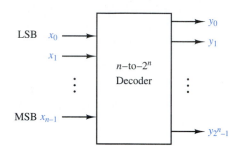

Figure 4.2 n-to2^n decoder module.

4.2.1 Decoder Circuit Structures

Before we look at applications of n-to-2^n decoders, let us examine some basic circuit structures used to implement these modules.

The logic circuit of a 2-bit *parallel decoder* is shown in Fig. 4.3a. In general, this decoder is very simple, but also expensive. As can be seen from the figure, an input combination or *vector* of $BA = 00$ selects the m_0 output line, $BA = 01$ selects the m_1 output line, and so on.

$$m_0 = \bar{B}\bar{A}$$
$$m_1 = \bar{B}A$$
$$m_2 = B\bar{A}$$
$$m_3 = BA \tag{4.1}$$

Figure 4.3b shows an alternative implementation of the 2-to-4 decoder, using only NAND gates. Figure 4.3c presents another configuration, using only NAND gates with no inverters. In both NAND gate designs, an output of 0 indicates the presence of the corresponding minterm. In this case, the outputs are said to be *active low* since an output value of 0 (the "active" level) signifies the occurrence of a "significant" input (the occurrence of a particular minterm). The output value is 1 (the "inactive" level) at all other times. An *active high* signal uses the value 1 to indicate a significant event and is 0 otherwise, such as in the decoder circuit of Fig. 4.3a. The output signals of the decoder in Fig. 4.3b may also be considered to be in complemented form.

Note that in the AND and NAND gate realizations of the n-to-2^n decoder shown in Figs. 4.3a and b there is only a single level of logic and that one n-input AND gate is required for each of the 2^n output lines. However, a problem is soon encountered in this configuration as n becomes large because the number of inputs to the AND gates (the *fan-in*) exceeds practical limits (five or six). This problem can be alleviated through the use of a *tree decoder*, such as that

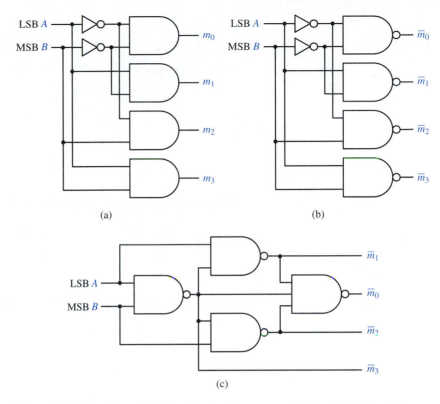

Figure 4.3 Two-bit parallel decoder circuit structures. **(a)** Parallel (active-high outputs). **(b)** Parallel (active-low outputs). **(c)** Alternate structure.

shown in Fig. 4.4b, which can be compared to the single-level decoder of Fig. 4.4a. This type of decoder employs multilevel logic with only two-input AND gates, independent of the number of input lines. A final structure, called the *dual tree*, is illustrated in Fig. 4.4c for a 4-to-16 decoder. In the dual-tree structure the n input lines are divided into j and k groups ($j + k = n$), and then two smaller decoders j-to-2^j and k-to-2^k are used to generate 2^j and 2^k internal signals. Then two-input AND gates are used to combine these signals to form the 2^n output lines for the total decoder network.

4.2.2 Implementing Logic Functions Using Decoders

Decoder output signals in complemented form are suitable for further processing using NAND logic. For example, if

$$f(A, B, \ldots, Z) = m_i + m_j + \cdots + m_k$$

then by DeMorgan's theorem

$$f(A, B, \ldots, Z) = \overline{\bar{m}_i \cdot \bar{m}_j \cdots \cdot \bar{m}_k} \tag{4.2}$$

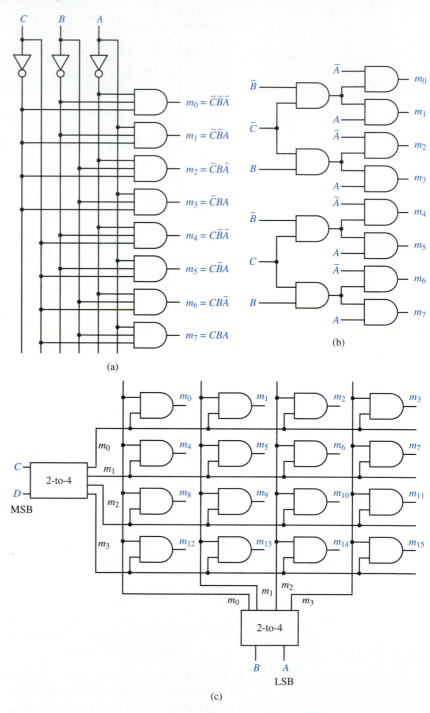

Figure 4.4 n-to-2^n decoder structures. **(a)** 3-bit parallel-type decoder. **(b)** 3-bit tree-type decoder. **(c)** 4-bit dual-tree type decoder.

This function can be implemented using a single k-input NAND gate and a decoder with active-low outputs.

Another way of using the decoder of Fig. 4.3b is to consider each output to represent a maxterm of a function, because

$$M_i = \bar{m}_i$$

Therefore, a function can be implemented from its maxterm list canonical form:

$$f(A, B, \ldots, Z) = M_i \cdot M_j \cdots \cdot M_k \tag{4.3}$$

using a decoder with active-low outputs and an AND gate.

The following example illustrates that a given function can be realized from its minterm or maxterm list in several ways with a decoder and one additional logic gate. Since these circuits are easily derived, we can examine all of them to identify the most cost effective.

EXAMPLE 4.1

Let us implement the following logic functions using decoders and logic gates.

$$f(Q, X, P) = \sum m(0, 1, 4, 6, 7)$$
$$= \prod M(2, 3, 5)$$

We may implement the function in several ways:

1. Use a decoder (with active-high outputs) with an OR gate:
$$f(Q, X, P) = m_0 + m_1 + m_4 + m_6 + m_7$$
2. Use a decoder (with active-low outputs) with a NAND gate:
$$f(Q, X, P) = \overline{\bar{m}_0 \cdot \bar{m}_1 \cdot \bar{m}_4 \cdot \bar{m}_6 \cdot \bar{m}_7}$$
3. Use a decoder (with active-high outputs) with a NOR gate:
$$f(Q, X, P) = \overline{m_2 + m_3 + m_5}$$
4. Use a decoder (with active-low outputs) with an AND gate:
$$f(Q, X, P) = \bar{m}_2 \cdot \bar{m}_3 \cdot \bar{m}_5$$

The four resulting implementations are shown in Figs. 4.5a through d, respectively.

4.2.3 Enable Control Inputs

Decoders and other functional modules often include one or more *enable* inputs, as shown in Fig. 4.6, which can be used to either inhibit (disable) the designated function or allow (enable) it to be performed. The decoding function of a decoder is inhibited by forcing all its outputs to the inactive state. For example, output y_0 of the 2-to-4 decoder in Fig. 4.6a is given by $y_0 = \bar{x}_1 \bar{x}_0 E = m_0 E$. In general,

$$y_k = m_k E \tag{4.4}$$

When $E = 0$, all outputs are forced to 0, whereas for $E = 1$, each output y_k is equal to m_k.

A common use of the enable function of a decoder is to extend the decoding capability by allowing multiple decoders to be cascaded as shown

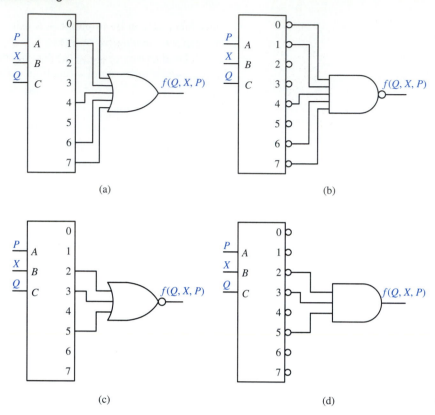

Figure 4.5 Using decoders to implement logic functions. **(a)** Active-high decoder with OR gate. **(b)** Active-low decoder with NAND gate. **(c)** Active-high decoder with NOR gate. **(d)** Active-low decoder with AND gate.

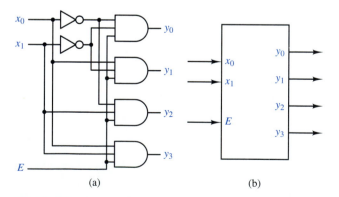

Figure 4.6 2-to-4 decoder with enable input E. **(a)** Schematic diagram. **(b)** MSI symbol.

in Fig. 4.7, which illustrates 3-to-8 and 4-to-16 decoders realized with the 2-to-4 decoder module of Fig. 4.6b. In Fig. 4.7a, input $I_2 = 0$ enables the top decoder, which is thus enabled for input codes $I_2 I_1 I_0$ equal to 000, 001, 010,

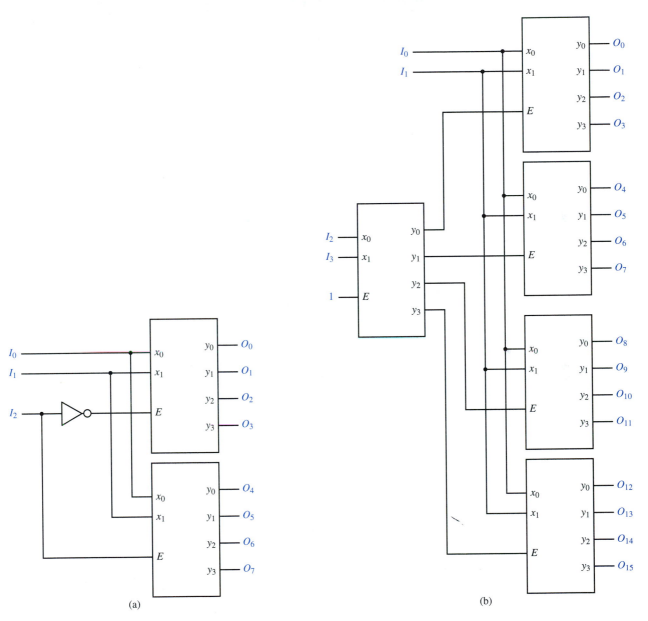

Figure 4.7 Use of 2-to-4 decoder modules to realize larger decoders. **(a)** 3-to-8 decoder. **(b)** 4-to-16 decoder.

and 011 (codes 0 through 3). The bottom decoder is enabled by $I_2 = 1$, enabling that module for input codes 4 through 7. Figure 4.7b illustrates a hierarchical decoding of a 4-bit number, with the first-level decoder enabling exactly one of the four second-level decoders.

4.2.4 Standard MSI Decoders

A number of standard MSI decoder modules are available that feature varying values of n and different configurations of enable control inputs. In this section we will examine a common 3-to-8 decoder, the 74138, and a 4-to-16 decoder, the 74154.

74138

The 73138, presented in Fig. 4.8, is a widely-used 3-to-8 decoder module. As seen in the logic diagram of Fig. 4.8a, the circuit has active-low outputs, and is enabled by a combination of three enable inputs: G1, G2A, and G2B. Examining a typical output, Y_i, the output equation is:

$$Y_i = \overline{m_i \cdot (G1 \cdot \overline{\overline{G2A}} \cdot \overline{\overline{G2B}})} \tag{4.5}$$

where m_i is the ith minterm of inputs C, B, and A. From this equation, note that the decoder is enabled only when $G1 = 1$, $\overline{G2A} = 0$, and $\overline{G2B} = 0$ ($G1$ is active high, and $\overline{G2A}$ and $\overline{G2B}$ are active low). For example,

$$Y_6 = \overline{m_6 \cdot (G1 \cdot \overline{\overline{G2A}} \cdot \overline{\overline{G2B}})}$$

where $m_6 = CB\bar{A}$, with C being the most significant bit in the minterm code.

The dual-in-line package pin layout for the 74138 is shown in Fig. 4.8b. A functional table describing its operation is presented in Fig. 4.8c. In the table, L (low) represents a logic 0 and H (high) represents a logic 1.

74154

Another commonly used module is the 4-to-16 decoder (74154) of Fig. 4.9. Let us examine the logic diagram of Fig. 4.9a. Consider a typical minterm, say m_{14}, of a four-variable function. The switching expression realized by output 14 of the 74154 is $DC B\bar{A}(\overline{\overline{G1} \cdot \overline{G2}}) = m_{14}(\overline{\overline{G1} \cdot \overline{G2}})$. So, in general,

$$Y_i = \overline{m_i(\overline{\overline{G1} \cdot \overline{G2}})} \tag{4.6}$$

It is important to note that D is the most significant bit and A is the least significant bit of the minterm code (D, C, B, A) and that the outputs are active low (that is, when the decoder is enabled, output 14 is simply $\bar{m}_{14}$). In this module, two gate control signals, $\overline{G1}$ and $\overline{G2}$, provide the enable function, that is, the decoder's outputs are enabled only when $\overline{G1}$ and $\overline{G2}$ are both equal to 0 ($\overline{\overline{G1} \cdot \overline{G2}} = 1$).

The dual-in-line package pin layout for the 74154 is shown in Fig. 4.9b. A functional table describing its operation is presented in Fig. 4.9c.

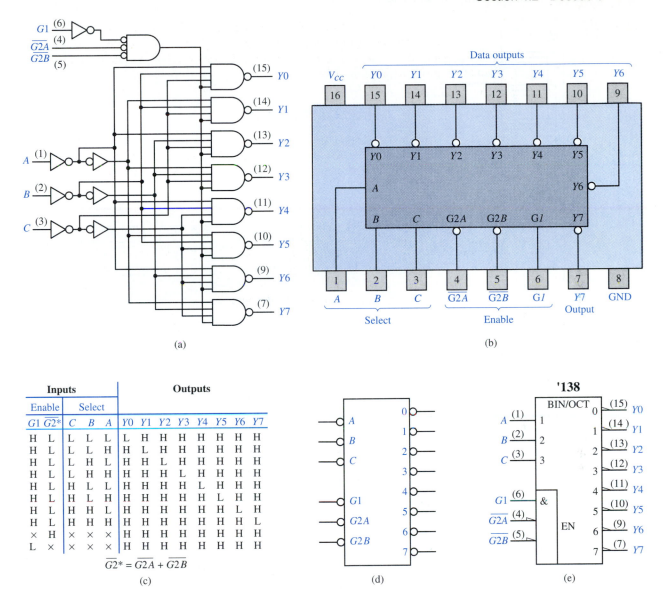

Figure 4.8 74138 decoder module. **(a)** Logic circuit. **(b)** Package pin configuration. **(c)** Function table. **(d)** Generic symbol. **(e)** IEEE standard logic symbol. *Source:* The TTL Data Book Volume 2, Texas Instruments Inc., 1985.

4.2.5 Decoder Applications

Address Decoding

Decoders find many applications in the synthesis of digital switching networks. However, their use as *address decoders* in computer memories and input/output

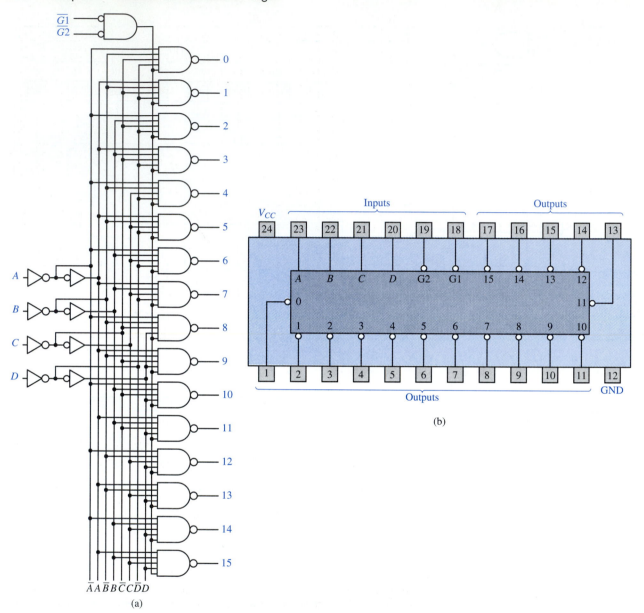

Figure 4.9   74154 decoder module. **(a)** Logic circuit. **(b)** Package pin configuration. *Source:* The TTL Data Book Volume 2, Texas Instruments Inc., 1985.

systems is perhaps one of the most important. In this application, each of 2^n devices (memory cells or input/output ports) is assigned a unique n-bit binary number, or *address*, that allows it to be distinguished from the other devices. A computer designates a specific device to take part in an operation by

Inputs						Outputs															
$\overline{G1}$	$\overline{G2}$	D	C	B	A	0	1	2	3	4	5	6	7	8	9	10	11	12	13	14	15
L	L	L	L	L	L	L	H	H	H	H	H	H	H	H	H	H	H	H	H	H	H
L	L	L	L	L	H	H	L	H	H	H	H	H	H	H	H	H	H	H	H	H	H
L	L	L	L	H	L	H	H	L	H	H	H	H	H	H	H	H	H	H	H	H	H
L	L	L	L	H	H	H	H	H	L	H	H	H	H	H	H	H	H	H	H	H	H
L	L	L	H	L	L	H	H	H	H	L	H	H	H	H	H	H	H	H	H	H	H
L	L	L	H	L	H	H	H	H	H	H	L	H	H	H	H	H	H	H	H	H	H
L	L	L	H	H	L	H	H	H	H	H	H	L	H	H	H	H	H	H	H	H	H
L	L	L	H	H	H	H	H	H	H	H	H	H	L	H	H	H	H	H	H	H	H
L	L	H	L	L	L	H	H	H	H	H	H	H	H	L	H	H	H	H	H	H	H
L	L	H	L	L	H	H	H	H	H	H	H	H	H	H	L	H	H	H	H	H	H
L	L	H	L	H	L	H	H	H	H	H	H	H	H	H	H	L	H	H	H	H	H
L	L	H	L	H	H	H	H	H	H	H	H	H	H	H	H	H	L	H	H	H	H
L	L	H	H	L	L	H	H	H	H	H	H	H	H	H	H	H	H	L	H	H	H
L	L	H	H	L	H	H	H	H	H	H	H	H	H	H	H	H	H	H	L	H	H
L	L	H	H	H	L	H	H	H	H	H	H	H	H	H	H	H	H	H	H	L	H
L	L	H	H	H	H	H	H	H	H	H	H	H	H	H	H	H	H	H	H	H	L
H	L	×	×	×	×	H	H	H	H	H	H	H	H	H	H	H	H	H	H	H	H
L	H	×	×	×	×	H	H	H	H	H	H	H	H	H	H	H	H	H	H	H	H
H	H	×	×	×	×	H	H	H	H	H	H	H	H	H	H	H	H	H	H	H	H

(c)

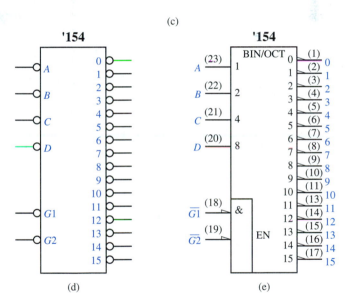

(d)   (e)

Figure 4.9   (Continued) 74154 decoder module. **(c)** Function table. **(d)** Generic symbol. **(e)** IEEE standard logic symbol. *Source:* The TTL Data Book Volume 2, Texas Instruments Inc., 1985.

broadcasting its address over n signal lines. As shown in Fig. 4.10, an n-to-2^n decoder decodes the n-bit address by activating one of 2^n select lines to access one of the devices. For example, in a computer memory, each address would correspond to one group of bits (binary digits) of information stored in the memory. In a simple 4K ($1K = 2^{10} = 1024$) memory, where $n = 12$, a total of 4096 select lines are required.

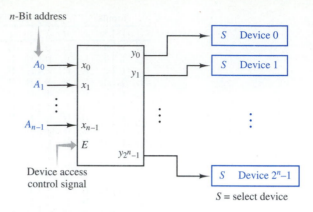

Figure 4.10   Address decoding in a digital system.

Minterm Generation

The n-to-2^n decoders also find many applications in the synthesis of digital switching networks by acting as minterm generators, since the outputs represent all possible minterms of the n input variables.

EXAMPLE 4.2

Realize the following functions using a 74154 and logic gates:

$$f_1(W, X, Y, Z) = \sum m(1, 9, 12, 15)$$

$$f_2(W, X, Y, Z) = \sum m(0, 1, 2, 3, 4, 5, 7, 8, 10, 11, 12, 13, 14, 15)$$

Using implementations 2 and 3 from Example 4.1:

$$f_1(W, X, Y, Z) = \overline{\bar{m}_1 \bar{m}_9 \bar{m}_{12} \bar{m}_{15}}$$

and

$$f_2(W, X, Y, Z) = \bar{m}_6 \cdot \bar{m}_9$$

Therefore, we may use the 74154 to generate the complemented minterms and the 7420 and 7408 to generate f_1 and f_2 as shown in Fig. 4.11. Note that we must connect $W = D$, $X = C$, $Y = B$, and $Z = A$.

BCD to Decimal Decoders

Combinational logic circuits are often used to convert data coded in one scheme into another format. Code converters are used for converting BCD to decimal, excess-3 to decimal, binary to excess-3, and so forth. For example, a BCD to decimal decoder is shown in Fig. 4.12a, with the BCD codes and their corresponding digits shown in Fig. 4.12b. This decoder is similar to the 4-to-16 binary decoder described earlier, but with only 10 outputs, one for each decimal digit.

To design the BCD to decimal decoder, we can draw a K-map for each of the 10 outputs and derive its logic equation. Each K-map contains exactly one minterm, corresponding to the decimal number of that output, and six don't-care terms, 10 to 15, since these numbers don't exist in BCD code. Three of

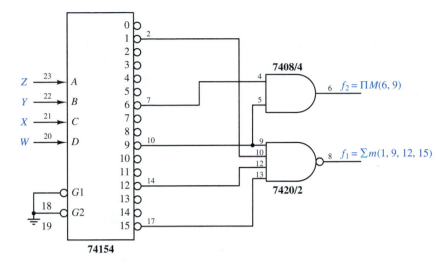

Figure 4.11   Realization of switching functions with a decoder.

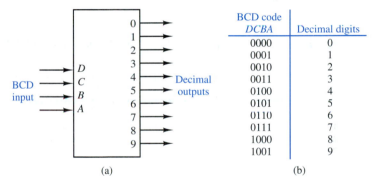

Figure 4.12   BCD to decimal decoder. **(a)** Logic symbol. **(b)** BCD codes and decimal digits.

the K-maps are shown in Fig. 4.13. The complete set of logic equations that describes the BCD decoder is:

Decimal 0	$\bar{D}\bar{C}\bar{B}\bar{A}$	Decimal 5	$C\bar{B}A$
1	$\bar{D}\bar{C}\bar{B}A$	6	$C B\bar{A}$
2	$\bar{C}B\bar{A}$	7	$C B A$
3	$\bar{C}B A$	8	$D\bar{A}$
4	$C\bar{B}\bar{A}$	9	$D A$

Since the binary and BCD codes are identical for the digits 0 to 9, a 74154 4-to-16 binary decoder can also be used to implement a BCD to decimal decoder by simply using outputs $\bar{m}_0$ through $\bar{m}_9$ and ignoring outputs $\bar{m}_{10}$ through $\bar{m}_{15}$. The 74154 may be more expensive than a minimum realization of the logic

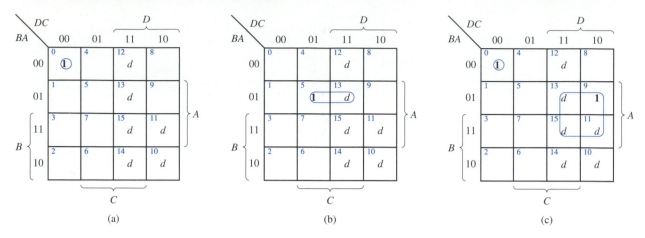

Figure 4.13 K-maps for outputs 0, 5, and 9 of a BCD to decimal code converter.
(a) Decimal $0 = \bar{D}\bar{C}\bar{B}\bar{A}$. **(b)** Decimal $5 = C\bar{B}A$. **(c)** Decimal $9 = DA$.

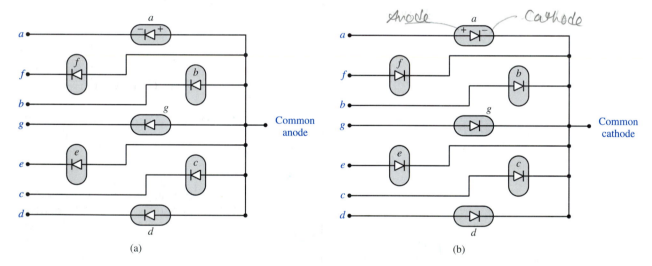

Figure 4.14 7-segment display elements. **(a)** Common anode (MAN 72A).
(b) Common cathode (MAN 74A).

equations for the BCD decoder listed here, but it would be a convenient solution if readily available.

Display Decoders

Another common decoding application is the conversion of encoded data to a format suitable for driving a numeric display. For example, digital watches and other electronic equipment often display BCD-encoded decimal digits on seven-segment displays. *Seven-segment LED displays* comprise seven light-emitting diodes (LEDs) arranged as shown in Fig. 4.14. Selected combinations of the LEDs are illuminated to create numeric digits and other symbols. For example, the segments normally activated to display the decimal digits are shown in Fig. 4.15.

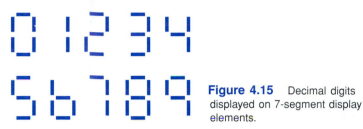

Figure 4.15 Decimal digits displayed on 7-segment display elements.

An LED emits light when the voltage at its anode is made sufficiently higher than the voltage at its cathode. This is illustrated on diode a in Figs. 4.14a and b, in which the anode is marked with a "$+$" and the cathode with a "$-$". In digital circuits, these voltages are created by applying a high voltage to the anode and a low voltage to the cathode.

To minimize the number of control signals, the anodes of the LEDs are usually connected at a common point, called the *common anode*, as shown in Fig. 4.14a, or else the cathodes are connected at a *common cathode*, as in Fig. 4.14b. In the common-anode configuration, the anodes are usually connected to a high voltage and the cathodes are controlled individually. Consequently, a logic 0 applied to a cathode illuminates that LED, whereas a logic 1 voltage disables the LED. The opposite conditions are used in the common-cathode configuration. Therefore, the inputs to the common-anode configuration may be considered active low, since low signals activate the LEDs, and the inputs to the common cathode configuration are active high.

To display a number encoded in BCD format, we can design a decoder to convert the BCD codes to the logic values needed for the seven segments. We begin by creating a truth table listing the segments to be activated for each decimal digit, as shown in Table 4.2. Using this table, a K-map can be drawn for each of the seven segments from which minimum logic equations can be derived. For example, Fig. 4.16 shows the K-maps for segments a and b, with product of sums expressions derived.

This design procedure can be generalized to design logic circuits for converting data from any arbitrary code format to another. Using the truth table format of Table 4.2, all input codes are simply listed as inputs to the circuit, with the corresponding output codes as circuit outputs. Then a K-map is drawn and a logic equation derived for each output, with any unspecified input codes mapped as don't-care conditions.

4.3 ENCODERS

An *encoder* is a combinational logic module that assigns a unique output code (a binary number) for each input signal applied to the device; as such, it is the

TABLE 4.2 BCD CODE TO SEVEN-SEGMENT CODE CONVERSION

Decimal Digit	BCD Code				Display Segments						
	D	C	B	A	a	b	c	d	e	f	g
0	0	0	0	0	1	1	1	1	1	1	0
1	0	0	0	1	0	1	1	0	0	0	0
2	0	0	1	0	1	1	0	1	1	0	1
3	0	0	1	1	1	1	1	1	0	0	1
4	0	1	0	0	0	1	1	0	0	1	1
5	0	1	0	1	1	0	1	1	0	1	1
6	0	1	1	0	0	0	1	1	1	1	1
7	0	1	1	1	1	1	1	0	0	0	0
8	1	0	0	0	1	1	1	1	1	1	1
9	1	0	0	1	1	1	1	0	0	1	1

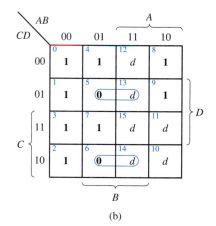

Figure 4.16 K-maps for a BCD to 7-segment code converter. **(a)** Segment $a = (\bar{B} + D)(A + B + C + \bar{D})$. **(b)** Segment $b = (\bar{B} + C + \bar{D})(\bar{B} + \bar{C} + D)$.

opposite of a decoder. If an encoder module has n inputs, the number of outputs s must satisfy the expression

$$2^s \geq n \tag{4.7}$$

or

$$s \geq \log_2 n$$

4.3.1 Encoder Circuit Structures

Encoders with Mutually Exclusive Inputs

Consider first the case in which the inputs are mutually exclusive; that is, one (and only one) of the input lines is active at any particular instant in time;

two or more input lines are never simultaneously active. In this case the input combinations that never occur may be used as don't-care conditions.

EXAMPLE 4.3

Design an encoder for four input lines if one and only one is active at any moment in time. See Fig. 4.17a.

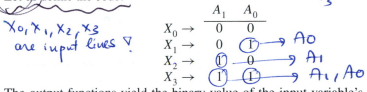

Let us define the code:

X_0, X_1, X_2, X_3
are input lines ▽

	A_1	A_0
$X_0 \rightarrow$	0	0
$X_1 \rightarrow$	0	1 → Ao
$X_2 \rightarrow$	1	0 → A1
$X_3 \rightarrow$	1	1 → A1, Ao

The output functions yield the binary value of the input variable's subscript. The truth table and K-maps for the encoder are presented in Figs. 4.17b and c. From the K-maps,

$$A_1 = X_3 + X_2$$
$$A_0 = X_3 + X_1$$

The logic circuit diagram for the encoder is given in Fig. 4.17d.

key word
let us!
← *we define a*
can define different code.

The preceding encoder requires that one (and only one) of the inputs be active at all times, a unique condition. Suppose that we relax the constraints somewhat and design an encoder that allows all input combinations to occur, but which outputs a nonzero code only if one of the input lines is active.

EXAMPLE 4.4

Design a four-line encoder that outputs a zero code unless one and only one input line is active.

Let us define the code:

	A_2	A_1	A_0
$X_1 \rightarrow$	0	0	1
$X_2 \rightarrow$	0	1	0
$X_3 \rightarrow$	0	1	1
$X_4 \rightarrow$	1	0	0
All others $\rightarrow$	0	0	0

This encoder also outputs the subscript of the active input line. However, it outputs the all-zero code if no input line is active or if multiple lines are active. Figure 4.18 details the design:

$$A_2 = X_4 \bar{X}_3 \bar{X}_2 \bar{X}_1$$
$$A_1 = \bar{X}_4 \bar{X}_3 X_2 \bar{X}_1 + \bar{X}_4 X_3 \bar{X}_2 \bar{X}_1$$
$$A_0 = \bar{X}_4 \bar{X}_3 \bar{X}_2 X_1 + \bar{X}_4 X_3 \bar{X}_2 \bar{X}_1$$

Note that the logic required to implement the second encoder is more complex than for the first.

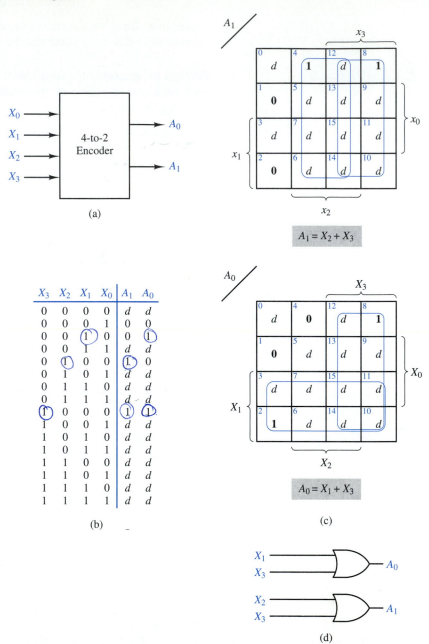

X_3	X_2	X_1	X_0	A_1	A_0
0	0	0	0	d	d
0	0	0	1	0	0
0	0	1	0	0	1
0	0	1	1	d	d
0	1	0	0	1	0
0	1	0	1	d	d
0	1	1	0	d	d
0	1	1	1	d	d
1	0	0	0	1	1
1	0	0	1	d	d
1	0	1	0	d	d
1	0	1	1	d	d
1	1	0	0	d	d
1	1	0	1	d	d
1	1	1	0	d	d
1	1	1	1	d	d

(b)

Figure 4.17 Four-to-two line encoder. **(a)** Functional diagram. **(b)** Truth table. **(c)** K-maps. **(d)** Logic diagram.

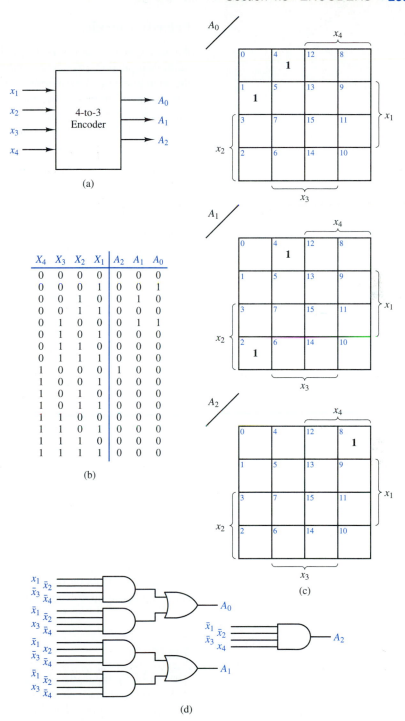

X_4	X_3	X_2	X_1	A_2	A_1	A_0
0	0	0	0	0	0	0
0	0	0	1	0	0	1
0	0	1	0	0	1	0
0	0	1	1	0	0	0
0	1	0	0	0	1	1
0	1	0	1	0	0	0
0	1	1	0	0	0	0
0	1	1	1	0	0	0
1	0	0	0	1	0	0
1	0	0	1	0	0	0
1	0	1	0	0	0	0
1	0	1	1	0	0	0
1	1	0	0	0	0	0
1	1	0	1	0	0	0
1	1	1	0	0	0	0
1	1	1	1	0	0	0

(b)

Figure 4.18   Four-to-three line encoder. **(a)** Functional diagram. **(b)** Truth table. **(c)** K-maps. **(d)** Logic diagram.

Priority Encoders

Another type of encoder is the *priority encoder*. The priority encoder allows multiple input lines to be active and sends out the binary value of the subscript of the input line with highest priority. To simplify the design, the highest priority is assigned to the highest subscript, the next highest priority to the second highest subscript, and so on. Consider the priority encoder of Fig. 4.19. The input lines are encoded

$$
\begin{array}{c|cc}
 & A_1 & A_0 \\
\hline
X_0 \rightarrow & 0 & 0 \\
X_1 \rightarrow & 0 & 1 \\
X_2 \rightarrow & 1 & 0 \\
X_3 \rightarrow & 1 & 1 \\
\end{array}
$$

If no input line is active, the priority encoder sends out $(A_1 A_0) = (00)$. If a single line is active, the encoder sends out the binary value of the subscript of the active line. If more than one input is active, the encoder sends out the binary value of the largest subscript of the active lines. Figure 4.19b displays the truth table for the encoder. Note that the two additional output lines indicate that no input line is active ($EO = 1$) and one or more inputs are active ($GS = 1$). Figures 4.19c and d present the K-map and logic diagram of the function, which reduces to

$$A_1 = X_2 + X_3 \tag{4.8}$$

$$A_0 = X_3 + X_1 \bar{X}_2 \tag{4.9}$$

and

$$EO = \overline{GS} = \overline{X_3 + X_2 + X_1 + X_0} \tag{4.10}$$

The two output functions A_1 and A_0 are independent of X_0. Note that the priority encoder can realize the truth table of Fig. 4.17b. Consequently, the priority encoder can also function as a minterm encoder.

4.3.2 Standard MSI Encoders

Two modular priority encoders (74147 and 74148) are demonstrated in Figs. 4.20 and 4.21. Both of these devices have active-low inputs and outputs. Look for this property in the logic diagram and function table for each device.

74147

The 74147, as shown in the logic circuit of Fig. 4.20a, takes 10 lines (0, 1, . . . , 9) and encodes them to 4 lines (D, C, B, A), as summarized in the function table of Fig. 4.20b. Notice that the input line 0 is not connected to the circuit, as suggested in Eqs. 4.8 and 4.9. The dual-in-line package pin layout of the 74147 is shown in Fig. 4.20c.

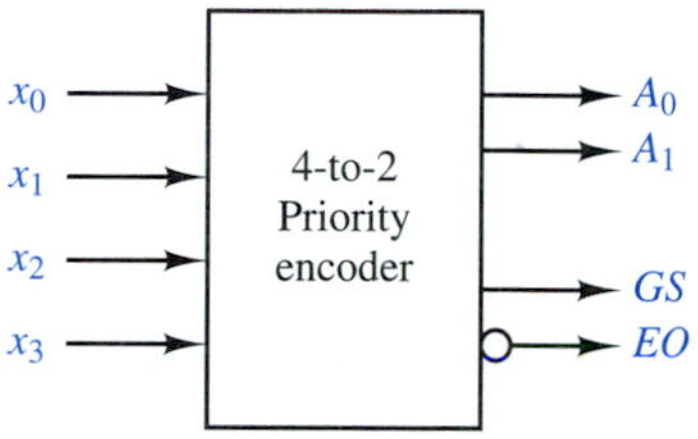

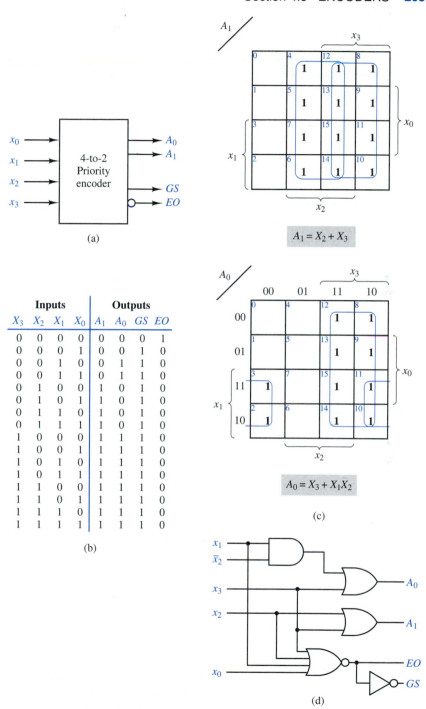

x_0
x_1
x_2
x_3
4-to-2
Priority
encoder
A_0
A_1
GS
EO

(a)

Inputs				Outputs			
X_3	X_2	X_1	X_0	A_1	A_0	GS	EO
0	0	0	0	0	0	0	1
0	0	0	1	0	0	1	0
0	0	1	0	0	1	1	0
0	0	1	1	0	1	1	0
0	1	0	0	1	0	1	0
0	1	0	1	1	0	1	0
0	1	1	0	1	0	1	0
0	1	1	1	1	0	1	0
1	0	0	0	1	1	1	0
1	0	0	1	1	1	1	0
1	0	1	0	1	1	1	0
1	0	1	1	1	1	1	0
1	1	0	0	1	1	1	0
1	1	0	1	1	1	1	0
1	1	1	0	1	1	1	0
1	1	1	1	1	1	1	0

(b)

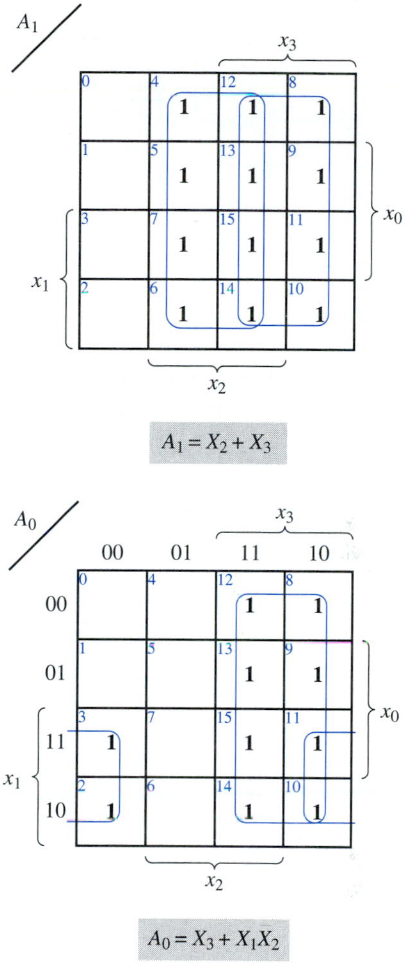

A_1
x_3
x_0
x_1
x_2
$A_1 = X_2 + X_3$
A_0
00
01
11
10
$A_0 = X_3 + X_1\overline{X}_2$

(c)

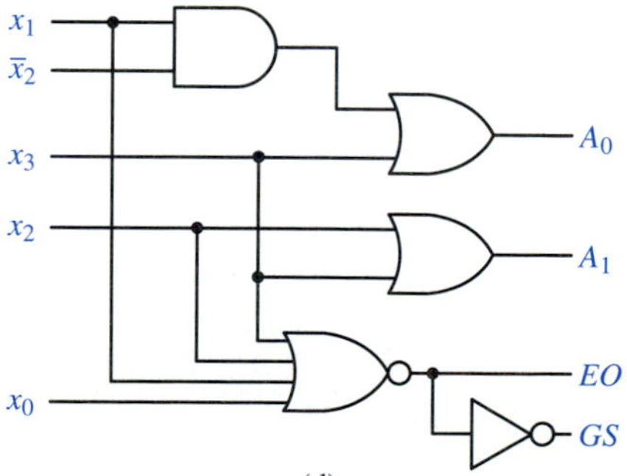

x_1
$\overline{x}_2$
x_3
x_2
x_0
A_0
A_1
EO
GS

(d)

Figure 4.19 Four-to-two line priority encoder. **(a)** Functional diagram. **(b)** Truth table. **(c)** K-maps. **(d)** Logic diagram.

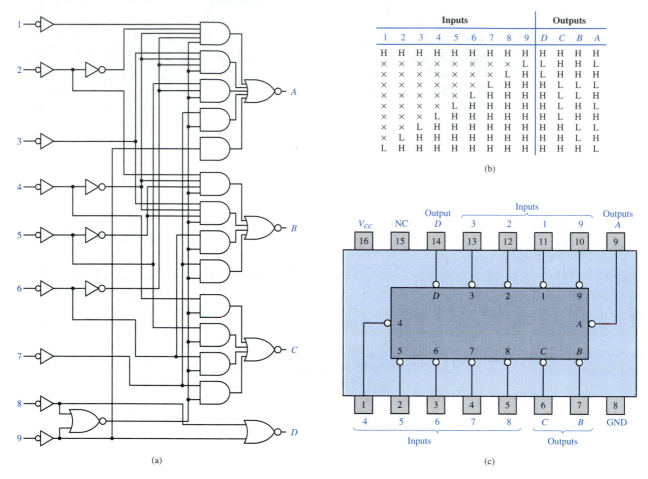

Inputs									Outputs			
1	2	3	4	5	6	7	8	9	D	C	B	A
H	H	H	H	H	H	H	H	H	H	H	H	H
×	×	×	×	×	×	×	×	L	L	H	H	L
×	×	×	×	×	×	×	L	H	L	H	H	H
×	×	×	×	×	×	L	H	H	H	L	L	L
×	×	×	×	×	L	H	H	H	H	L	L	H
×	×	×	×	L	H	H	H	H	H	L	H	L
×	×	×	L	H	H	H	H	H	H	L	H	H
×	×	L	H	H	H	H	H	H	H	H	L	L
×	L	H	H	H	H	H	H	H	H	H	L	H
L	H	H	H	H	H	H	H	H	H	H	H	L

(b)

(a)

(c)

Figure 4.20 74147 priority encoder module. **(a)** Logic diagram. **(b)** Function table. **(c)** Package configuration. *Source:* The TTL Data Book Volume 2, Texas Instruments Inc., 1985.

74148

The 74148 logic circuit, shown in Fig. 4.21a, takes eight lines $(0, 1, \ldots, 7)$ and encodes them to three lines $(A2, A1, A0)$ according to the function table in Fig. 4.21b. An input enable signal EI is connected to all the first-level logic gates to control their operation; when EI is active (low) the circuit operates. The 74148 also has two additional output signals, EO and GS. EO is active (low) when none of the input lines is active. GS is active (low) when one or more input lines are active. The dual-in-line package pin layout of the 74148 is shown in Fig. 4.21c.

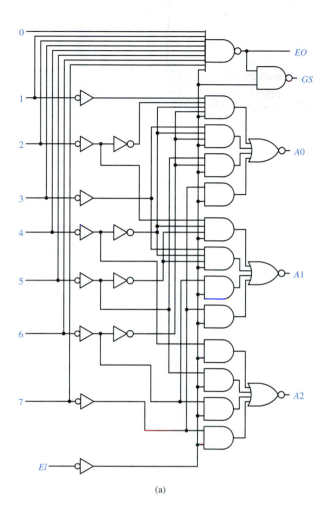

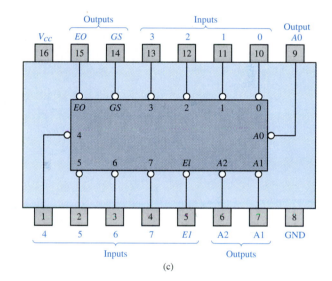

	Inputs								Outputs				
EI	0	1	2	3	4	5	6	7	A2	A1	A0	GS	EO
H	×	×	×	×	×	×	×	×	H	H	H	H	H
L	H	H	H	H	H	H	H	H	H	H	H	H	L
L	×	×	×	×	×	×	×	L	L	L	L	L	H
L	×	×	×	×	×	×	L	H	L	L	H	L	H
L	×	×	×	×	×	L	H	H	L	H	L	L	H
L	×	×	×	×	L	H	H	H	L	H	H	L	H
L	×	×	×	L	H	H	H	H	H	L	L	L	H
L	×	×	L	H	H	H	H	H	H	L	H	L	H
L	×	L	H	H	H	H	H	H	H	H	L	L	H
L	L	H	H	H	H	H	H	H	H	H	H	L	H

(b)

(a)

(c)

Figure 4.21 74148 priority encoder module. **(a)** Logic diagram. **(b)** Function table. **(c)** Package configuration. *Source:* The TTL Data Book Volume 2, Texas Instruments Inc., 1985.

EXAMPLE 4.5

For the 74148, what is the output code $(EO, GS, A2, A1, A0)$ under the following conditions:

$$(EI, 7, 6, 5, 4, 3, 2, 1, 0) = (0, 1, 0, 1, 0, 1, 0, 1, 1)$$

Since the device is enabled and three lines are active (inputs 6, 4, and 2), GS will be active low and $A2$, $A1$, $A0$ will encode line 6 (001):

$$(EO, GS, A2, A1, A0) = (1, 0, 0, 0, 1)$$

4.4 Multiplexers/Data Selectors

In general, a *multiplexer* (also called a *data selector*) is a modular device that selects one of many input lines to appear on a single output line. A *demultiplexer* performs the inverse operation; it takes a single input line and routes it to one of several output lines. A simplified diagram illustrating the general concept of multiplexing and demultiplexing is shown in Fig. 4.22a. The rotary switch SW_1 moves from input line A to B to C, and so on. The rotary switch SW_2 at the output of the channel is synchronized to SW_1 and it too moves from output line A to B to C, and so on. This multiplex/demultiplex configuration illustrates one manner in which data are selected and routed. The logic configuration is shown in Fig. 4.22b. Here the signals $a, b, \ldots k$ are control signals that select which set of inputs/outputs will be using the "single channel." The channel in this configuration could be contained within a computer system or could be a mechanism with which the computer communicates with the outside world.

4.4.1 Multiplexer Circuit Structures

In an n-to-1 line multiplexer, one of the n input data lines ($D_{n-1}, D_{n-2}, \ldots, D_0$) is designated for connection to the single output line (Y) by a selection code

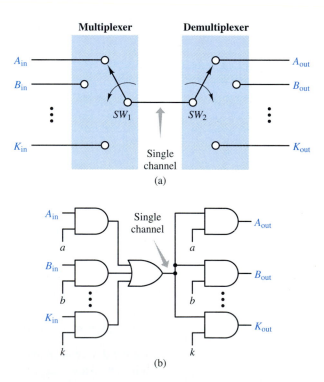

Figure 4.22 K-channel multiplexing/demultiplexing system. **(a)** Multiplex/demultiplex operation. **(b)** Simple logic configuration for (a).

$(S_{k-1}, \ldots, S_0)$, where $n = 2^k$. Examine Fig. 4.23a, which depicts a 4-to-1 line multiplexer, with $B = S_1$ and $A = S_0$. The circuit will connect data line D_i to the output Y when the code

$$i = (BA)_2 \qquad (4.11)$$

is applied to the selection terminals. Figure 4.23b displays the truth table of the multiplexer. From the truth table we may write

$$Y = (\bar{B}\bar{A})D_0 + (\bar{B}A)D_1 + (B\bar{A})D_2 + (BA)D_3 \qquad (4.12)$$

The selection code forms the minterms of two variables, B and A. Hence we may write

$$Y = \sum_{i=0}^{3} m_i D_i \qquad (4.13)$$

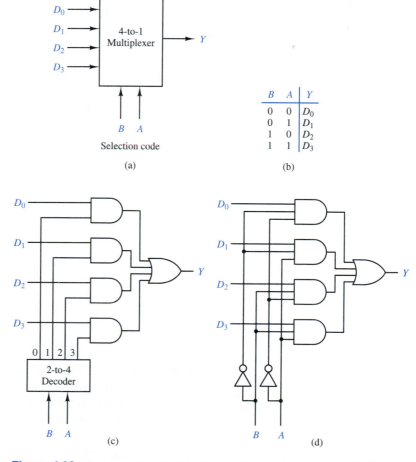

B	A	Y
0	0	D_0
0	1	D_1
1	0	D_2
1	1	D_3

Figure 4.23   Four-to-one multiplexer design. **(a)** Functional diagram. **(b)** Truth table. **(c)** Logic diagram. **(d)** Equivalent two-level circuit.

where the m_i are the minterms of the selection code. The logic diagram for the 4-to-1 multiplexer is shown in Fig. 4.23c. An equivalent circuit, using two-level AND–OR logic, is presented in Fig. 4.23d.

The 4-to-1 multiplexer of Fig. 4.23 can also be used in a tree-type network, as shown in Fig. 4.24 in which four multiplexers are used to feed another 4-to-1 multiplexer, thereby creating a 16-to-1 multiplexer. Even larger configurations can be generated in the same manner.

4.4.2 Standard MSI Multiplexers

74151A

The 8-to-1 multiplexer (74151A) is shown in Fig. 4.25. For this circuit we may write the output equation as

$$
\begin{aligned}
Y &= \big[(\bar{C}\bar{B}\bar{A})D_0 + (\bar{C}\bar{B}A)D_1 + (\bar{C}B\bar{A})D_2 + (\bar{C}BA)D_3 \\
&\quad + (C\bar{B}\bar{A})D_4 + (C\bar{B}A)D_5 + (CB\bar{A})D_6 + (CBA)D_7\big]\,\bar{\bar{G}} \\
&= \left(\sum_{i=0}^{7} m_i D_i\right)\overline{(\bar{G})}
\end{aligned}
\tag{4.14}
$$

The strobe $(\bar{G})$ acts as an enable signal (active low), forcing the output to 0 when $\bar{G} = 1$. The second output W is the complement of Y.

74150

The 74150 is the 16-to-1 multiplexer shown in Fig. 4.26. This is a 24-pin device with two lines for power and ground, 16 data input lines (E_i), a strobe $(\bar{G})$, four selection code lines (D, C, B, A), and one output line (W). The output of this device is

$$
W = \overline{\left(\sum_{i=0}^{15} m_i E_i\right)\overline{\bar{G}}}
\tag{4.15}
$$

where m_i is a minterm (D, C, B, A).

74153

Computer systems often require that several multibit sources of information be multiplexed over a single bus. To support such applications, two or more multiplexers are often combined in a single module with a common select code input. Figure 4.27 illustrates a module containing two 4-to-1 multiplexers, often referred to as a dual (2-bit) four-input multiplexer. The behavior of this module is illustrated by the rotary switch shown in Fig. 4.27b, in which one set of two inputs $\{1Ci, 2Ci\}$ is connected to the two output lines $\{1Y, 2Y\}$, when select lines $(BA)_2 = (i)_2$. An alternative symbol for the dual four-input multiplexer is shown in Fig. 4.27c. The logic diagram and IEEE standard symbol of the 74153 are given in Figs. 4.27d and e, respectively.

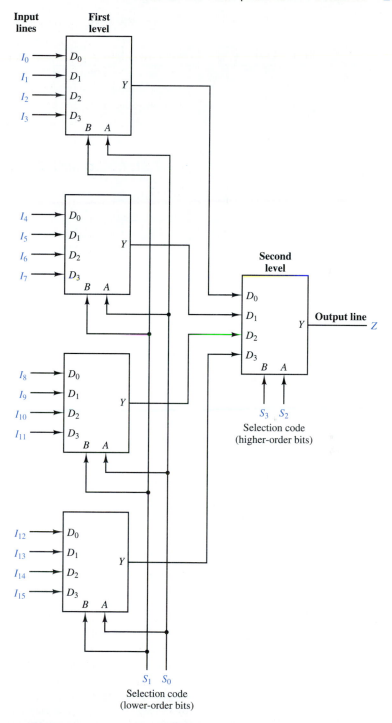

Figure 4.24   16-to-1 multiplexer realized with a tree-type network of 4-to-1 multiplexers.

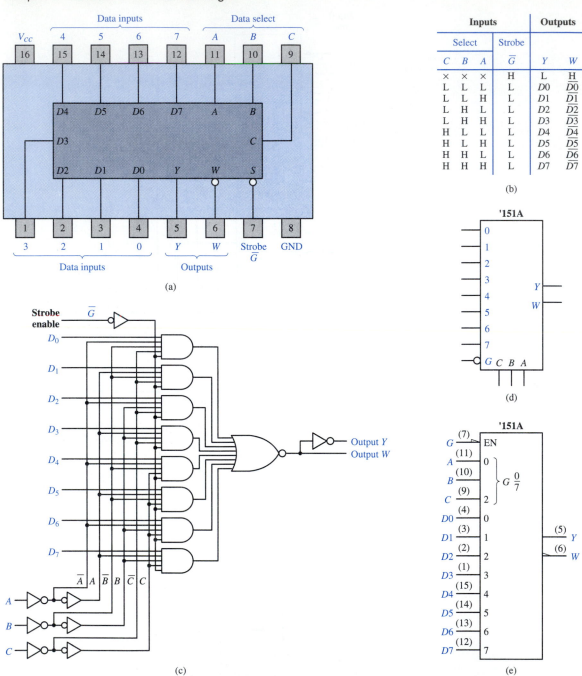

Inputs				Outputs	
Select			Strobe		
C	B	A	$\overline{G}$	Y	W
×	×	×	H	L	H
L	L	L	L	D0	$\overline{D0}$
L	L	H	L	D1	$\overline{D1}$
L	H	L	L	D2	$\overline{D2}$
L	H	H	L	D3	$\overline{D3}$
H	L	L	L	D4	$\overline{D4}$
H	L	H	L	D5	$\overline{D5}$
H	H	L	L	D6	$\overline{D6}$
H	H	H	L	D7	$\overline{D7}$

(b)

(a)

(c)

(d)

(e)

Figure 4.25 74151A 8-to-1 multiplexer. **(a)** Package configuration. **(b)** Function table. **(c)** Logic diagram. **(d)** Generic logic symbol. **(e)** IEEE standard logic symbol. *Source:* The TTL Data Book Volume 2, Texas Instruments Inc., 1985.

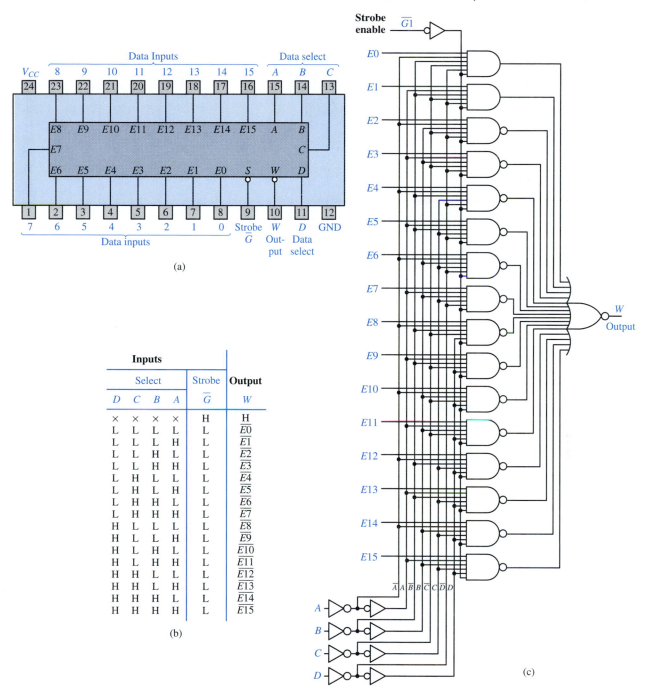

Figure 4.26 74150 16-to-1 multiplexer. **(a)** Package configuration.
(b) Function table. **(c)** Logic diagram. *Source:* The TTL Data Book Volume 2,
Texas Instruments Inc., 1985.

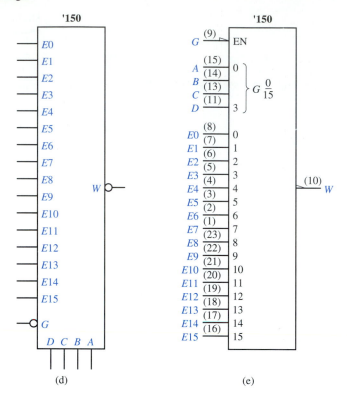

Figure 4.26 (Continued) 74150 16-to-1 multiplexer. **(d)** Generic logic symbol. **(e)** IEEE standard logic symbol. *Source:* The TTL Data Book Volume 2, Texas Instruments Inc., 1985.

74157

Figure 4.28 shows the 74157 quad (4-bit) two-input multiplexer module, which connects one of two 4-bit inputs to the 4-bit output as selected by control signal S. Control signal $\bar{G}$ enables and disables the output; the output lines are all forced to 0 if $\bar{G} = 1$.

Multiple 74157 modules can be utilized to create other multiplexer configurations of different path widths and numbers of inputs. In Fig. 4.29a, two 74157s are used to create an octal (8-bit) two-input multiplexer by controlling the select line S on both modules with the same select signal. In this case, the 8-bit input from source X is routed to the destination when select = 0, with the upper 4 bits routed through one module and the lower 4 bits through the other. Source W is routed to the destination in the same manner when select = 1.

Figure 4.29b shows a quad (4-bit) four-input multiplexer realized with two 74157 modules. Select signal $S1$ enables one of the two modules and disables the outputs of the other, forcing one of the two inputs to each of the OR gates in Fig. 4.29b to be 0. Select signal $S0$ selects one of the two 4-bit inputs of the enabled module, sending the 4 bits of the selected source

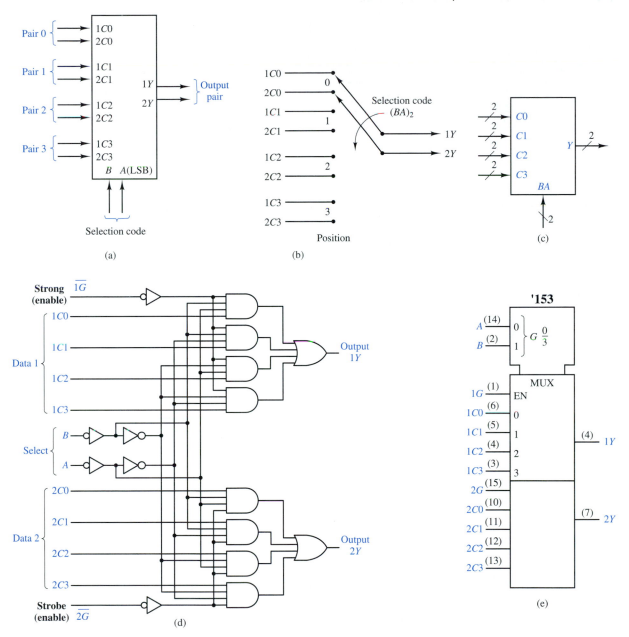

Figure 4.27 74153 dual (2-bit) four-input multiplexer. **(a)** Generic symbol.
(b) Equivalent switch. **(c)** Alternative symbol. **(d)** Logic diagram. **(e)** IEEE
standard logic symbol. *Source:* The TTL Data Book Volume 2, Texas Instruments
Inc., 1985.

to the other OR gate inputs. Consequently, each OR gate output is simply the
corresponding bit of the selected source.

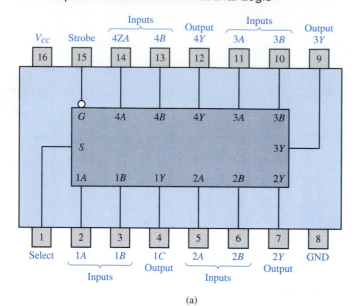

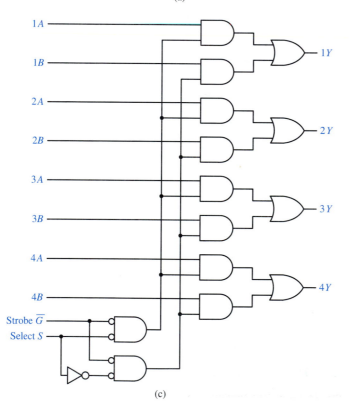

(a)

Inputs				Output
Strobe $\overline{G}$	Select S	Data A	B	Y
H	×	×	×	L
L	L	L	×	L
L	L	H	×	H
L	H	×	L	L
L	H	×	H	H

(b)

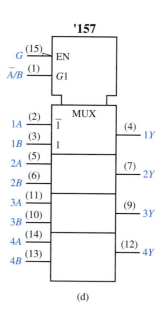

(c)

(d)

Figure 4.28 74157 quadruple 2-to-1 multiplexer. **(a)** Package configuration. **(b)** Function table. **(c)** Logic diagram. **(d)** IEEE standard logic symbol. *Source:* The TTL Data Book Volume 2, Texas Instruments Inc., 1985.

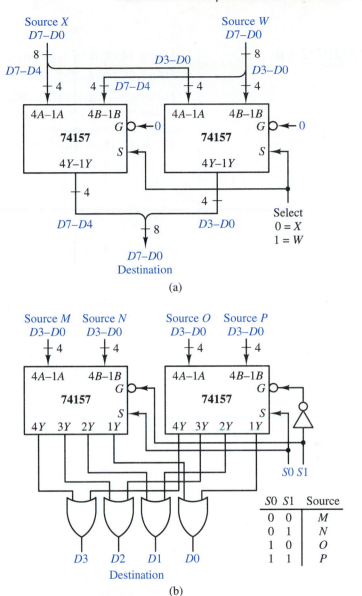

Figure 4.29   Using multiple 74157 4-bit two-input multiplexers.
(a) 8-bit two-input multiplexer. **(b)** 4-bit four-input multiplexer.

4.4.3 Applications of Multiplexers

The multiplexers/data selectors presented so far may also be used conveniently to implement switching functions. The fundamental idea is to use the *selection code to generate the minterms* of the function, and to use the data lines D_i to *enable the minterms* present in a specific case.

EXAMPLE 4.6

Use a 74151A to implement
$$f(x_1, x_2, x_3) = \sum m(0, 2, 3, 5).$$

Figure 4.30a lists the truth table for the function. The minterms are gated onto the output Y by setting $D_0 = D_2 = D_3 = D_5 = 1$. The remaining data lines are grounded as shown in Fig. 4.30b. Note that (x_1, x_2, x_3) are connected to (C, B, A). The order of the variables is very important.

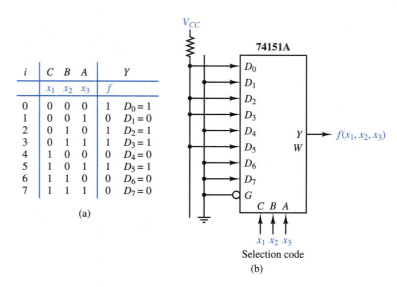

i	C	B	A	Y	
	x_1	x_2	x_3	f	
0	0	0	0	1	$D_0 = 1$
1	0	0	1	0	$D_1 = 0$
2	0	1	0	1	$D_2 = 1$
3	0	1	1	1	$D_3 = 1$
4	1	0	0	0	$D_4 = 0$
5	1	0	1	1	$D_5 = 1$
6	1	1	0	0	$D_6 = 0$
7	1	1	1	0	$D_7 = 0$

(a)

Figure 4.30 Realization of $f(x_1, x_2, x_3) = \sum m(0, 2, 3, 5)$. **(a)** Truth table. **(b)** Implementation with 74151A.

The concept demonstrated in Example 4.6 may be extended to implement higher-order functions. That is, an n-to-1 line multiplexer can be used to implement a $k + 1$ variable function ($n = 2^k$) by connecting k of the variables to the selection lines of the multiplexer, with the $(k + 1)$st variable used (along with ground and the power supply) to establish the data input lines.

EXAMPLE 4.7

Implement $f(a, b, c) = ab + \bar{b}c$ using the 4-to-1 multiplexer of Fig. 4.23.

In this case, there are three variables and two selection lines on the multiplexer. The first step is to express the function in canonical SOP form.

$$f(a, b, c) = ab + bc$$
$$= ab\bar{c} + abc + \bar{a}\bar{b}c + a\bar{b}c$$

The next step is to select two of the variables to connect to the multiplexer

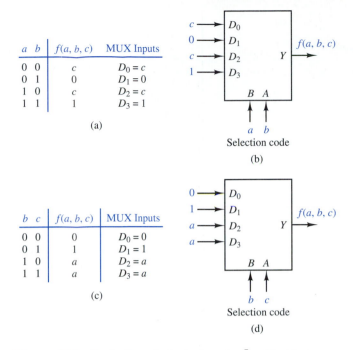

a	b	$f(a, b, c)$	MUX Inputs
0	0	c	$D_0 = c$
0	1	0	$D_1 = 0$
1	0	c	$D_2 = c$
1	1	1	$D_3 = 1$

(a)

b	c	$f(a, b, c)$	MUX Inputs
0	0	0	$D_0 = 0$
0	1	1	$D_1 = 1$
1	0	a	$D_2 = a$
1	1	a	$D_3 = a$

(c)

Figure 4.31 Realization of $f(a, b, c) = ab + \bar{b}c$ with 4-to-1 multiplexers. **(a)** Truth table; $f(a, b, c)$ evaluated for all values of a and b. **(b)** Multiplexer realization. **(c)** Alternate truth table; $f(a, b, c)$ evaluated for all values of b and c. **(d)** Alternate realization.

select lines and factor these terms out of the canonical SOP form. Let us use a and b for this example. Factoring out a and b gives

$$f(a, b, c) = \bar{a}\bar{b}(c) + a\bar{b}(c) + ab(\bar{c} + c)$$

From this expression, $f(a, b, c)$ can be evaluated for each combination of a and b. The result is listed in truth table form in Fig. 4.31a, which shows the expression for $f(a, b, c)$ for each combination of a and b. This truth table is implemented by the multiplexer of Fig. 4.31b. Note that each row of the truth table corresponds to one of the multiplexer inputs.

Any two variables can be connected to the multiplexer select lines. For example, if variables b and c are chosen, the truth table given in Fig. 4.31c results. This table is implemented by the multiplexer of Fig. 4.31d.

EXAMPLE 4.8

Implement
$$f(X_1, X_2, X_3, X_4) = \sum m(0, 1, 2, 3, 4, 9, 13, 14, 15)$$
using a 74151A.

In this case, the logic function has four input variables, while the multiplexer has only three selection code bits. One approach to use is to factor the minterms of the function using Postulate 5(b).

Since the canonical SOP form contains many terms, it is simpler to omit the factoring step and work directly from the function's truth table, which is given in Fig. 4.32a.

Note that the input variables have been divided into two groups, with X_1, X_2, X_3 being assigned to the selection code C, B, and A. The fourth variable is standing alone to be used as a data input variable. The three selection code bits effectively divide the truth table into eight parts, as indicated by the horizontal lines. When bits X_1, X_2, and X_3 are applied to the selection code, they designate one of the eight double rows of the table. Each double row may have the bit pattern

$$\left.\begin{matrix}0\\0\end{matrix}\right\} \text{logic } 0 \qquad\qquad \left.\begin{matrix}0\\1\end{matrix}\right\} \text{variable } X_4$$

$$\left.\begin{matrix}1\\1\end{matrix}\right\} \text{logic } 1 \qquad\qquad \left.\begin{matrix}1\\0\end{matrix}\right\} \text{variable } \bar{X}_4$$

So by choosing each data input to be one of these four conditions, we implement the function as shown in Fig. 4.32b.

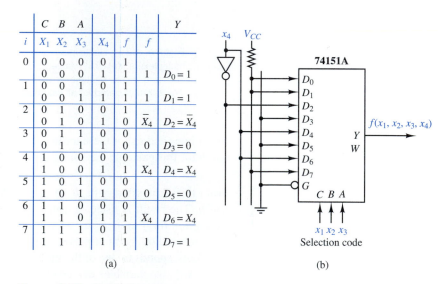

	C	B	A				Y
i	X_1	X_2	X_3	X_4	f	f	
0	0	0	0	0	1		
	0	0	0	1	1	1	$D_0 = 1$
1	0	0	1	0	1		
	0	0	1	1	1	1	$D_1 = 1$
2	0	1	0	0	1		
	0	1	0	1	0	$\bar{X}_4$	$D_2 = \bar{X}_4$
3	0	1	1	0	0		
	0	1	1	1	0	0	$D_3 = 0$
4	1	0	0	0	0		
	1	0	0	1	1	X_4	$D_4 = X_4$
5	1	0	1	0	0		
	1	0	1	1	0	0	$D_5 = 0$
6	1	1	0	0	0		
	1	1	0	1	1	X_4	$D_6 = X_4$
7	1	1	1	0	1		
	1	1	1	1	1	1	$D_7 = 1$

(a)   (b)

Figure 4.32 Realization of $f(x_1, x_2, x_3, x_4) = \sum m(0, 1, 2, 3, 4, 9, 13, 14, 15)$ with a 74151A multiplexer. **(a)** Truth table. **(b)** Logic diagram.

4.5 Demultiplexers/Data Distributors

In the last section we examined a combinational logic circuit that multiplexed n lines to one line by using a selection code to specify which input line to connect to the output line. In this section we will examine the inverse circuit, a *demultiplexer* or *data distributor*. A demultiplexer connects a single input line to one of n output lines, the specific output line being determined by an s-bit selection code, where

$$2^s \geq n \qquad (4.16)$$

A functional diagram for a 1-to-n demultiplexer is shown in Fig. 4.33a. The selection code is used to generate a minterm of s variables; that minterm then gates the input data to the proper output terminal. See Fig. 4.33b for a specific example. This 1-to-4 data distributor has an enable signal (E) that controls the operation of the circuit. When E is 1, the circuit is operational. We may thus describe the operation of the device by

$$Y_i = (m_i D) E \qquad (4.17)$$

where D is the input signal to be distributed to the n output lines. Compare Eq. 4.17 to Eq. 4.6. We see for the 74154 that

$$Y_i = m_i \overline{(\overline{\overline{G1}} \cdot \overline{\overline{G2}})}$$

If we specify that

1. the selection code inputs (D, C, B, A) to the 74154 generate m_i in Eqs. 4.17 and 4.6, and

2. $G2$ in Eq. 4.6 is the complement of the enable signal (E) in Eq. 4.17,

then we may use the 74154 4-to-16 decoder of Fig. 4.9 as a 1-to-16 demultiplexer.

Consider the operation of the 74154 with $\overline{G2} = 0$ and a specific selection code applied, say (D, C, B, A) = (1110):

$$Y_i = 1 \quad \text{for } i \neq 14$$

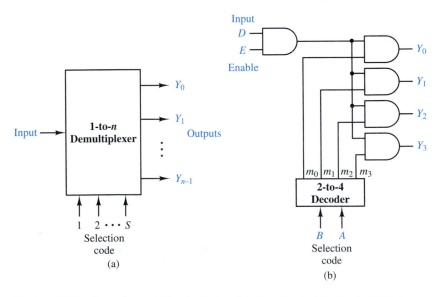

Figure 4.33   Demultiplexer/data distributor. **(a)** Functional diagram. **(b)** 1-to-4 demultiplexer with enable.

and

$$Y_{14} = \overline{m_{14}(\overline{\overline{G1}} \cdot \overline{\overline{G2}})}.$$

But $m_{14} = 1$ and $\overline{\overline{G2}} = 1$, so

$$Y_{14} = \overline{\overline{\overline{G1}}} = \overline{G1}$$

So if we set $\overline{G1} = D$, then the 74154 implements Eq. 4.17 for the demultiplexer.

EXAMPLE 4.9

Design a 16-line to 16-line multiplexer/demultiplexer system using a 74150 and a 74154.

The goal is to replace a cable of 16 lines with a smaller number of signals in order to save wire. Suppose the 16 signals are to be transported 1000 feet. Figure 4.34 displays a solution in which the 16 signals ($X_0, X_1, \ldots, X_{15}$) are multiplexed onto one line ($\bar{Q}$) using the signal channel code (C_3, C_2, C_1, C_0). At the distant end, the five lines are then used to demultiplex the data back to 16 parallel lines for further processing. It is important to note that the 16-to-5 line reduction has come at the expense of system utility since now, at any instant in time, one and only one of the 16 signal channels may be in use. That is, time slots must be assigned to each of the 16 lines, and a time schedule for line $\bar{Q}$ must be enforced. In this configuration, the 16 output lines will be high when they are not scheduled to use the single input channel Q.

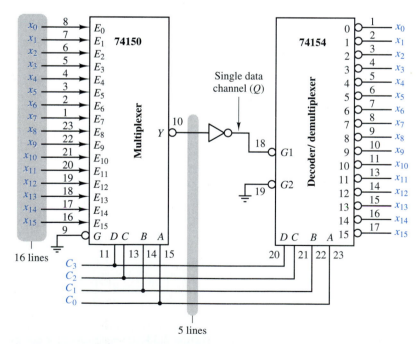

Figure 4.34   Demultiplexer/data distributor example.

4.6 Binary Arithmetic Elements

The basic fundamentals of performing arithmetic operations in various number systems were introduced in Chapter 1. All digital computers contain logic circuits to implement selected arithmetic operations in the particular number systems selected for use in those computers. The most commonly used number system for representing integers is the two's complement number system, because it simplifies the representation of both positive and negative values and the implementation of addition and subtraction circuits.

The following sections will examine the design of binary addition and subtraction circuits that can be used to manipulate two's complement numbers. Many other arithmetic modules are available for performing binary arithmetic operations, including multiplication, division, and others. The reader is referred to [1] for further information.

4.6.1 Basic Binary Adder Circuits

In many computer logic applications it is necessary to add binary numbers. In Chapter 1 it was demonstrated that addition of binary numbers in the two's complement number system is sufficient to perform the normal addition and subtraction operations of the digital computer. Of course, the adder circuits must be accompanied by the proper complementing network and arithmetic registers. Here we shall design several serial and parallel adder circuits.

Half-adder

A half-adder (HA) is a multiple-output combinational logic network that adds 2 bits of binary data, producing sum-bit and carry-bit output signals. See Fig. 4.35a. The input bits x_i and y_i are added mathematically in binary, as shown in the truth table of Fig. 4.35b. From the truth table we observe

$$s_i = x_i \oplus y_i \tag{4.18}$$
$$c_i = x_i y_i$$

A two-input NAND gate realization of these switching functions is presented in Fig. 4.35c.

Full-Adder

In performing binary addition, it was shown in Chapter 1 that at each bit position we, in general, will be adding two data bits and one carry bit. Hence, a full-adder (FA) is a multiple-output combinational logic network that adds 3 binary bits. See Fig. 4.35d. The truth table for the full-adder is shown in Fig. 4.35e. From the truth table or a K-map, we can show that

$$s_i = x_i \oplus y_i \oplus c_{i-1} \tag{4.19}$$
$$c_i = x_i y_i + x_i c_{i-1} + y_i c_{i-1}$$

A NAND implementation for a full-adder is shown in Fig. 4.35f. This implementation uses nine gates and two levels of logic. An exclusive-OR circuit for the same output s_i is shown in Fig. 4.35g.

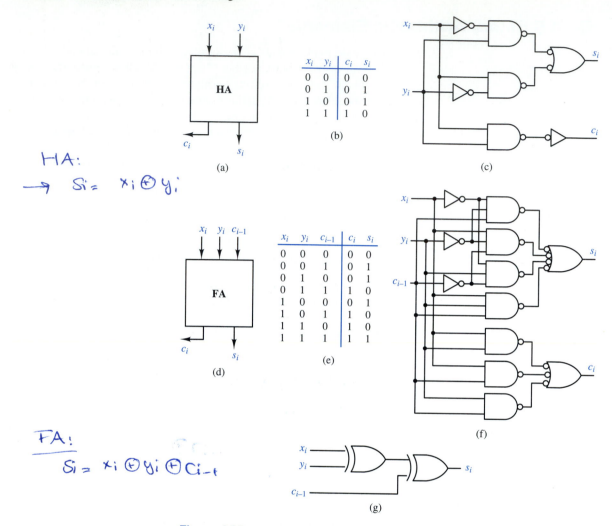

HA:

$$\rightarrow S_i = x_i \oplus y_i$$

FA:

$$S_i = x_i \oplus y_i \oplus c_{i-t}$$

Figure 4.35 Binary half-adder and full-adder circuits. **(a)** Half-adder. **(b)** HA truth table. **(c)** NAND gate HA circuit. **(d)** Full-adder. **(e)** FA truth table. **(f)** NAND gate FA circuit. **(g)** XOR gate realization of FA s_i output.

The digital logic designer uses the full-adder as a module to create large circuits, using the logic symbol shown in Fig. 4.35d. Two applications of the module will now be illustrated.

Pseudoparallel Adder Unit

An adder unit that employs $n - 1$ full-adders and one half-adder is illustrated in Fig. 4.36. This configuration uses one adder circuit for each bit position of

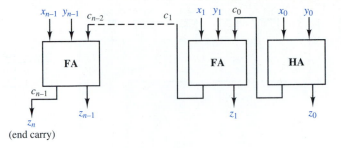

Figure 4.36 Pseudoparallel (ripple carry) adder.

the two input data words. The operation to be performed is

$$
\begin{array}{cc}
X & (x_{n-1}x_{n-2}\cdots x_1x_0)_2 \\
+\quad Y & +(y_{n-1}y_{n-2}\cdots y_1y_0)_2 \\
\hline
Z & (z_nz_{n-1}z_{n-2}\cdots z_1z_0)_2
\end{array}
$$

The configuration is called *pseudoparallel* because carries must propagate, or ripple, through the length of the adder unit. This configuration is also referred to as a *ripple-carry adder*. In general, the worst-case propagation path is through one half-adder and $n-1$ full-adders from the inputs x_0 and y_0 to the end sum and carry positions z_{n-1} and z_n.

4.6.2 MSI Binary Adder Modules

7482 Two-bit Adder

The 7482 is the 2-bit, pseudoparallel adder module shown in Fig. 4.37. The signal C_0 is a carry-in and C_2 a carry-out. The internal signal $\bar{C}_1$ is the carry from FA_1 to FA_2. By examining the logic diagram we may write

$$C_1 = C_0 \cdot A_1 + C_0 \cdot B_1 + A_1 \cdot B_1 \qquad (4.20)$$

$$
\begin{aligned}
\Sigma_1 &= C_0 \cdot \bar{C}_1 + A_1 \cdot \bar{C}_1 + B_1 \cdot \bar{C}_1 + A_1 \cdot B_1 \cdot C_0 \\
&= \bar{C}_1(C_0 + A_1 + B_1) + A_1 \cdot B_1 \cdot C_0 \\
&= (\bar{C}_0 + \bar{A}_1)(\bar{C}_0 + \bar{B}_1)(\bar{A}_1 + \bar{B}_1)(C_0 + A_1 + B_1) + A_1 \cdot B_1 \cdot C_0 \\
&= (\bar{C}_0 + \bar{A}_1 \cdot \bar{B}_1)(\bar{A}_1 + \bar{B}_1)(C_0 + A_1 + B_1) + A_1 \cdot B_1 \cdot C_0 \qquad (4.21) \\
&= [\bar{C}_0(A_1 + B_1) + C_0 \cdot \bar{A}_1 \cdot \bar{B}_1](\bar{A}_1 + \bar{B}_1) + A_1 \cdot B_1 \cdot C_0 \\
&= \bar{C}_0 \cdot \bar{A}_1 \cdot B_1 + \bar{C}_0 \cdot A_1 \cdot \bar{B}_1 + C_0 \cdot \bar{A}_1 \cdot \bar{B}_1 + A_1 \cdot B_1 \cdot C_0 \\
&= C_0 \oplus A_1 \oplus B_1
\end{aligned}
$$

In a similar manner,

$$C_2 = C_1 \cdot A_2 + C_1 \cdot B_2 + A_2 \cdot B_2 \qquad (4.22)$$

$$\Sigma_2 = C_1 \oplus A_2 \oplus B_2$$

In each full adder, the carry is generated by two levels of logic. The carry is then combined with the input signals to generate the sum with two additional levels of logic. Carry propagation requires only two levels of logic at each full

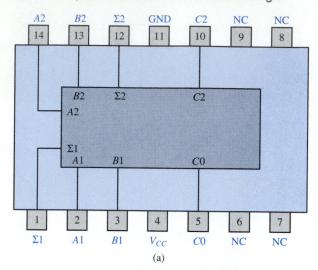

(a)

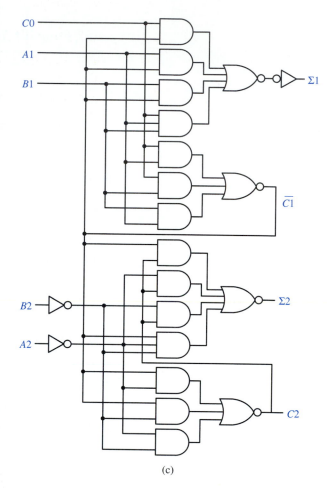

(c)

Inputs				Outputs					
				When $C0 = $ L			When $C0 = $ H		
$A2$	$A1$	$B2$	$B1$	$C2$	$\Sigma2$	$\Sigma1$	$C2$	$\Sigma2$	$\Sigma1$
L	L	L	L	L	L	L	L	L	H
L	L	L	H	L	L	H	L	H	L
L	L	H	L	L	H	L	L	H	H
L	L	H	H	L	H	H	H	L	L
L	H	L	L	L	L	H	L	H	L
L	H	L	H	L	H	L	L	H	H
L	H	H	L	L	H	H	H	L	L
L	H	H	H	H	L	L	H	L	H
H	L	L	L	L	H	L	L	H	H
H	L	L	H	L	H	H	H	L	L
H	L	H	L	H	L	L	H	L	H
H	L	H	H	H	L	H	H	H	L
H	H	L	L	L	H	H	H	L	L
H	H	L	H	H	L	L	H	L	H
H	H	H	L	H	L	H	H	H	L
H	H	H	H	H	H	L	H	H	H

(b)

Figure 4.37 The 7482 pseudo-parallel adder module. **(a)** Package pin configuration. **(b)** Function table. **(c)** Logic diagram. *Source:* The TTL Data Book Volume 2, Texas Instruments Inc., 1985.

adder. Hence we may say, in general, that the worst-case delay, t_{delay}, for a pseudoparallel adder constructed from these modules is

$$t_{\text{delay}} = (2n + 2)t_{\text{gate}} \qquad (4.23)$$

where n is the word length of the adder unit. Here, t_{delay} is measured in terms of the total number of levels of logic through which the carries must propagate, each level delaying the signal by an amount of time t_{gate}. The worst-case path is from the carry-in of the least significant bit to the sum output of the most significant bit.

7483 Four-bit Adder

Another adder module that can be used to build long-word-length adder units is the 7483, shown in Fig. 4.38. For this 4-bit module, C_0 is the carry-in and C_4 the carry-out. The internal carries (C_1, C_2, C_3) are not propagated explicitly; that is, within the adder module the output bits (Σ_1, Σ_2, Σ_3, Σ_4) are formed in parallel. From the logic diagram we may write

$$\begin{aligned} P_i &= (\overline{B_i \cdot A_i})(A_i + B_i) \\ &= (\bar{A}_i + \bar{B}_i)(A_i + B_i) \\ &= A_i \oplus B_i \end{aligned} \quad (4.24)$$

$$\begin{aligned} \Sigma_i &= P_i \oplus C_{i-1} \\ &= A_i \oplus B_i \oplus C_{i-1} \end{aligned} \quad (4.25)$$

and

$$\begin{aligned} C_1 &= \overline{(\bar{C}_0 \cdot \overline{A_1 \cdot B_1}) + \overline{(A_1 + B_1)}} \\ &= \overline{(\bar{C}_0 \cdot \overline{A_1 \cdot B_1})} \cdot (A_1 + B_1) \\ &= (C_0 + (A_1 \cdot B_1)) \cdot (A_1 + B_1) \\ &= C_0 \cdot A_1 + C_0 \cdot B_1 + A_1 \cdot B_1 \end{aligned} \quad (4.26)$$

In a similar manner, we may find

$$C_i = C_{i-1} \cdot A_i + C_{i-1} \cdot B_i + A_i \cdot B_i \quad (4.27)$$

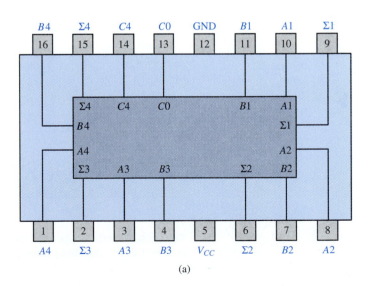

(a)

Figure 4.38 The 7483 four-bit adder module. **(a)** Package pin configuration. *Source:* The TTL Data Book Volume 2, Texas Instruments Inc., 1985.

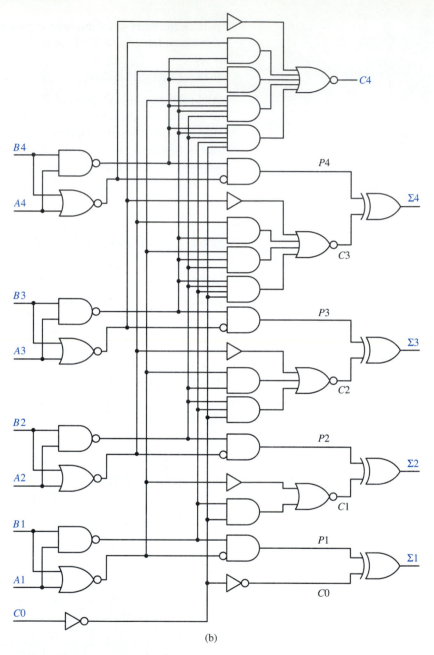

(b)

Figure 4.38   (Continued) the 7483 four-bit adder module. **(b)** Logic diagram.
Source: The TTL Data Book Volume 2, Texas Instruments Inc., 1985.

which agrees with Eq. 4.19. Within the 7483, the P_i signals are valid in two gate delays, the C_i signals in three gate delays, and the Σ_i outputs one XOR gate delay after the C_i terms. Since the 7483 generates four sum terms, we can build an n-bit pseudoparallel adder of

$$m = \lceil n/4 \rceil \qquad (4.28)$$

modules, where the notation $\lceil x \rceil$ means the smallest integer greater than x. Thus, the resulting unit will have an overall worst-case delay of three gate delays for the carry out of each module except the last, which will have four gate delays to its sum outputs:

$$t_{\text{delay}} = (3m + 1)t_{\text{gate}} \qquad (4.29)$$

The pseudoparallel adders are simple to build and are reasonably fast. However, these designs are unsatisfactory in some high-speed applications because of the increased delay as n becomes large.

4.6.3 High-speed Adder Units

In the design of arithmetic circuits, we often strive to improve circuit performance by increasing the speed with which different operations, such as binary addition, can be done. The speed of a circuit can be improved by selecting a technology in which the individual logic gates have shorter propagation delays or by designing the circuit to minimize the number of gate delays required to complete the operation. In most cases, the number of gates needed to realize a design must be increased to reduce the total propagation delay, resulting in a trade-off of cost for performance. In the following sections we examine a number of methods used to reduce the number of propagation delays in binary adder circuits. In each case we will evaluate the number of gates needed for the design and the total number of gate delays needed to produce the sum of two numbers.

Fully Parallel Adders

The fastest adder design would be strictly parallel. That is, all the inputs would be applied simultaneously and propagate through two levels of logic to obtain the result. However, this approach would require an enormous amount of logic circuitry and is not practical to employ. Consider the generation of the first three carry bits of a pseudoparallel adder:

$$c_0 = x_0 y_0 \qquad (4.30)$$

$$
\begin{aligned}
c_1 &= x_1 y_1 \bar{c}_0 + x_1 y_1 c_0 + x_1 \bar{y}_1 c_0 + \bar{x}_1 y_1 c_0 \\
&= x_1 y_1 + (x_1 \oplus y_1) c_0 \\
&= x_1 y_1 + (x_1 \oplus y_1)(x_0 y_0) \qquad (4.31)
\end{aligned}
$$

$$
\begin{aligned}
c_2 &= x_2 y_2 + (x_2 \oplus y_2) c_1 \\
&= x_2 y_2 + (x_2 \oplus y_2)[x_1 y_1 + (x_1 \oplus y_1)(x_0 y_0)] \\
&= x_2 y_2 + (x_2 \oplus y_2)(x_1 y_1) + (x_2 \oplus y_2)(x_1 \oplus y_1)(x_0 y_0) \qquad (4.32)
\end{aligned}
$$

These equations can be further simplified into sum of products form, allowing each to be realized with two levels of logic, independent of the word width of the adder. However, the gate count increases considerably with each higher bit position.

Carry Look-ahead Adders

Several compromises are employed between the pseudoparallel and strictly parallel alternatives. *Carry look-ahead adders* divide the full adders into groups and employ carry bypass logic to speed up the carry propagation. This technique is reasonable to employ when numerical data are to be added at high-speed fixed intervals. Examining Eqs. 4.30 through 4.32, let us define the two terms

$$g_i = x_i y_i \tag{4.33}$$

and

$$p_i = x_i \oplus y_i \tag{4.34}$$

Using these terms, Eqs. 4.30 through 4.32 can be rewritten as follows:

$$c_0 = g_0 \tag{4.35}$$

$$c_1 = g_1 + p_1 c_0$$
$$= g_1 + p_1 g_0 \tag{4.36}$$

$$c_2 = g_2 + p_2 c_1$$
$$= g_2 + p_2 g_1 + p_2 p_1 g_0 \tag{4.37}$$

Within each bit position, if $g_i = 1$ a carry is *generated*, independent of the carry input c_{i-1}. Likewise, a carry input of 1 will be *propagated* from the input to the output of stage i if $p_i = 1$. Hence, the terms g_i and p_i are referred to as the *carry generate* and *carry propagate* terms, respectively, for stage i. Note that these terms can be derived in parallel for all bit positions in a single gate delay and that the carry bits can be computed in parallel from the generate and propagate terms in two additional gate delays. A circuit realizing Eqs. 4.33 and 4.34 is given in Fig. 4.39a, and a circuit realizing Eqs. 4.35 through 4.37 is given in Fig. 4.39b.

The sum term realized by a full adder, as defined by Eq. 4.19, can be rewritten in terms of the carry and propagate terms as follows:

$$s_i = x_i \oplus y_i \oplus c_{i-1}$$
$$= p_i \oplus c_{i-1} \tag{4.38}$$

Therefore, once the carry terms are available, the sum terms can be computed in one additional gate delay, resulting in a total adder delay of

$$t_{cla} = 4t_{gate}$$

independent of the word width of the adder. Circuits for a single adder module and a complete 3-bit carry look-ahead adder are presented in Figs. 4.39a and c. It should be noted that the delays of exclusive-OR gates may be almost twice those of simple NAND/NOR gates. Therefore, a more realistic delay estimate is

$$4t_{gate} \leq t_{cla} \leq 6t_{gate}$$

where t_{gate} is the delay through a typical NAND gate.

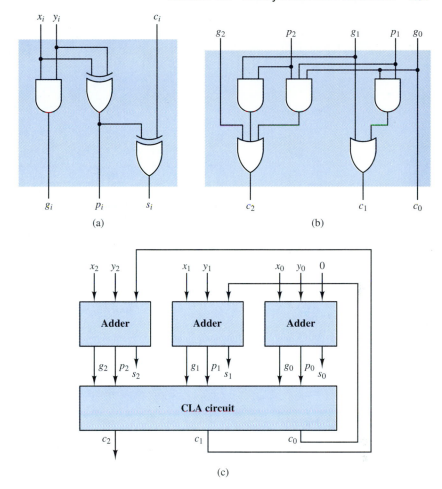

Figure 4.39   Carry look-ahead adder design. **(a)** Adder module producing g_i and p_i. **(b)** Carry look-ahead (CLA) circuit. **(c)** Complete carry look-ahead adder.

74182 MSI Carry Look-ahead Generator

Carry look-ahead generators are also available as standard MSI modules, such as the 74182 module shown in Fig. 4.40, which produces three carry terms from four sets of P_i and G_i terms and is cascadable by producing P and G outputs that can be supplied to additional 74182 modules.

Carry-completion-detection Adders

For asynchronous applications a *carry-completion-detection* adding scheme can speed up the addition process remarkably. This scheme adds logic circuitry to each full adder, which signals to a control circuit when it has finished adding. On average, the carries will propagate only about one-fifth the length of the adder unit; so, rather than wait for the worst-case propagation delay each time

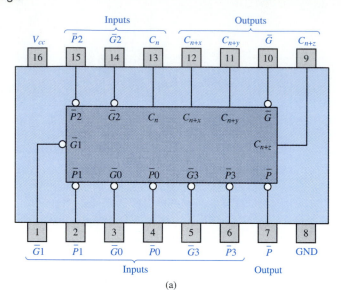

(a)

Inputs							Output
$\bar{G}3$	$\bar{G}2$	$\bar{G}1$	$\bar{G}0$	$\bar{P}3$	$\bar{P}2$	$\bar{P}1$	$\bar{G}$
L	×	×	×	×	×	×	L
×	L	×	×	L	×	×	L
×	×	L	×	L	L	×	L
×	×	×	L	L	L	L	L
All other combinations							H

(b)

Inputs				Output
$\bar{P}3$	$\bar{P}2$	$\bar{P}1$	$\bar{P}0$	$\bar{P}$
L	L	L	L	L
All other combinations				H

(c)

Inputs			Output
$\bar{G}0$	$\bar{P}0$	C_n	C_{n+x}
L	×	×	H
×	L	H	H
All other combinations			L

(d)

Inputs					Output
$\bar{G}1$	$\bar{G}0$	$\bar{P}1$	$\bar{P}0$	C_n	C_{n+y}
L	×	×	×	×	H
×	L	L	×	×	H
×	×	L	L	H	H
All other combinations					L

(e)

Inputs							Output
$\bar{G}2$	$\bar{G}1$	$\bar{G}0$	$\bar{P}2$	$\bar{P}1$	$\bar{P}0$	C_n	C_{n+z}
L	×	×	×	×	×	×	H
×	L	×	L	×	×	×	H
×	×	L	L	L	×	×	H
×	×	×	L	L	L	H	H
All other combinations							L

(f)

Figure 4.40 The 74182 look-ahead carry generator. **(a)** Package pin configuration. **(b)** Function table for $\bar{G}$ output. **(c)** Function table for $\bar{P}$ output. **(d)** Function table for C_{n+x} output. **(e)** Function table for C_{n+y} output. **(f)** Function table for C_{n+z} output. *Source:* The TTL Data Book Volume 2, Texas Instruments Inc., 1985.

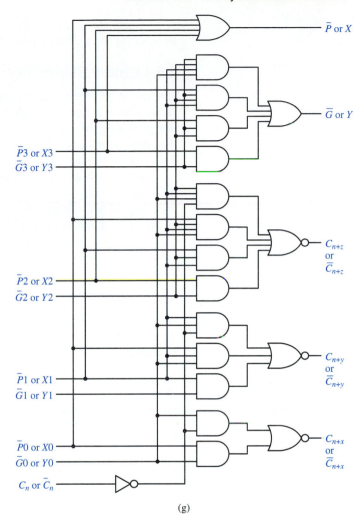

(g)

Figure 4.40 (Continued) the 74182 look-ahead carry generator.
(g) Logic diagram. *Source:* The TTL Data Book Volume 2, Texas
Instruments Inc., 1985.

two numbers are added, the carry completion signal allows new additions to
begin as soon as the last addition is finished.

Carry-save Adders

Still another speedup technique is useful when a string of numbers is to be
totaled, or accumulated. A carry-save technique inhibits carry propagation by
saving the carries between stages in storage elements called flip-flops. Then,
on the last addition, the carries are allowed to propagate in the pseudoparallel
manner. Circuits with flip-flops will be introduced in Chapter 6.

Complete details on these techniques are available in references [4] through [6] and are beyond the scope of this chapter.

4.6.4 Binary Subtraction Circuits

Circuits to perform subtraction of binary numbers can be developed in the same manner as for binary addition. Half- and full-subtracter modules can be designed using the procedure illustrated for half and full adders in Fig. 4.35, and then these modules can be cascaded to form n-bit pseudoparallel subtracters. This procedure is left as an exercise for the reader.

When both addition and subtraction must be performed, such as in the arithmetic circuitry of a digital computer, the overall design can be simplified by the use of two's complement arithmetic. Recall that subtraction in the two's complement number system is performed as follows:

$$(R)_2 = (P)_2 - (Q)_2$$
$$= (P)_2 + (-Q)_2$$
$$= (P)_2 + [Q]_2$$
$$= (P)_2 + (\bar{Q})_2 + 1$$

where $[Q]_2 = (\bar{Q})_2 + 1$ from Algorithm 1.4. Figure 4.41 illustrates the use of a binary adder to perform both addition and subtraction. The adder module realizes the function

$$(\Sigma)_2 = (A)_2 + (B)_2 + C_0 \tag{4.39}$$

When the select line is 0, the multiplexer routes its inputs A to its outputs Y, so $(Q)_2$ is connected to the B inputs of the adder module. Since the select line is also connected to $C0$ of the adder, $C0 = 0$. Under these conditions, the adder performs the following operation:

$$(\Sigma)_2 = (A)_2 + (B)_2 + C0$$

where

$$(A)_2 = (P)_2$$
$$(B)_2 = (Q)_2$$
$$C0 = 0$$

So

$$(R)_2 = (\Sigma)_2$$
$$= (P)_2 + (Q)_2 + 0$$
$$= (P)_2 + (Q)_2$$

This is the addition operation.

Now consider the case when $S = 1$. For $S = 1$, the multiplexer module routes its B inputs to its Y outputs, so the complement of $(Q)_2$ is connected to the B inputs of the adder module. The select line S also drives the $C0$ input of the adder module, so

$$(R)_2 = (\Sigma)_2$$
$$= (A)_2 + (B)_2 + C0$$

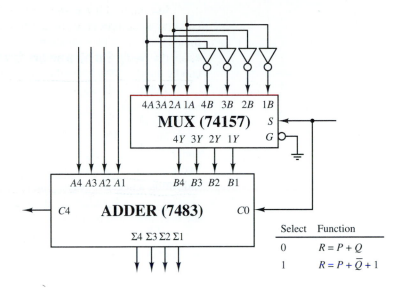

Select	Function
0	$R = P + Q$
1	$R = P + \bar{Q} + 1$

Figure 4.41   Two's complement adder/subtracter.

where

$$(A)_2 = (P)_2$$
$$(B)_2 = (\bar{Q})_2$$
$$C0 = 1$$

So

$$R = (P)_2 + (\bar{Q})_2 + 1$$
$$= (P)_2 + [Q]_2$$
$$= (P)_2 - (Q)_2$$

This is the subtraction operation.

Therefore, both addition and subtraction functions can be implemented with a single adder module and a multiplexer, as illustrated in Fig. 4.41.

4.6.5 Arithmetic Overflow Detection

As discussed in Chapter 1, the range of values that can be represented by n-bit numbers in the two's complement number system is

$$-2^{n-1} \le N \le 2^{n-1} - 1$$

Any arithmetic operation that attempts to generate a value outside this range is said to produce an *overflow* condition. In these cases the resulting n-bit number is not a valid representation of the result. Therefore, all overflow conditions should be detected so that invalid results are not used inadvertently.

In Chapter 1 it was shown that, in two's complement arithmetic, overflow conditions are produced by adding two positive values whose sum is greater than $2^{n-1} - 1$ or two negative values whose sum is less than -2^{n-1}. In both cases the result will have an incorrect sign bit. Therefore, overflow detection can be done by observing the sign bits of the operands and the result.

Table 4.3 shows the eight possible situations that can occur in the most significant stage of an n-bit adder. Bits a_{n-1} and b_{n-1} represent the sign bits of the numbers being added and are therefore inputs to the stage, along with carry bit c_{n-2}. The outputs of the stage are the carry-out and sum bits c_{n-1} and s_{n-1}, respectively. As seen in the table, an overflow condition occurs in two cases: the addition of two positive values producing sign bit $s_{n-1} = 1$, indicating a negative result, and the addition of two negative values producing sign bit $s_{n-1} = 0$, indicating a positive result. Therefore, a logic expression for the overflow condition V is

$$V = \bar{a}_{n-1}\bar{b}_{n-1}s_{n-1} + a_{n-1}b_{n-1}\bar{s}_{n-1} \tag{4.40}$$

An AND/OR logic circuit realization of Eq. 4.40 is presented in Fig. 4.42a.

TABLE 4.3   **MOST SIGNIFICANT STAGE OF AN n-BIT ADDER**

Adder Inputs			Adder Outputs		Overflow
a_{n-1}	b_{n-1}	c_{n-2}	c_{n-1}	s_{n-1}	V
0	0	0	0	0	0
0	0	1	0	1	1
0	1	0	0	1	0
0	1	1	1	0	0
1	0	0	0	1	0
1	0	1	1	0	0
1	1	0	1	0	1
1	1	1	1	1	0

Overflows can also be detected by observing the carry-in and carry-out bits, c_{n-2} and c_{n-1}, respectively, of the most significant full-adder stage. Looking at the two rows of Table 4.3 in which overflows occur, it can be seen that these are the only two situations in which $c_{n-2} \neq c_{n-1}$. As seen in the first two rows of Table 4.3, the addition of two positive numbers always results in a carry output $c_{n-1} = 0$. Therefore, the carry input to the most significant bit, c_{n-2}, must also be 0 to produce a correct positive sum. A carry of 1 into this bit results in $s_{n-1} = 1$, which is incorrect. A similar situation exists in row 7 of Table 4.3. The sum of two negative numbers produces $c_{n-1} = 1$. The absence of a carry into this bit results in an incorrect sign bit $s_{n-1} = 0$. Thus, the overflow condition is signaled by $c_{n-2} \neq c_{n-1}$ or $c_{n-2} \oplus c_{n-1} = 1$. Therefore,

$$V = c_{n-2} \oplus c_{n-1} \tag{4.41}$$

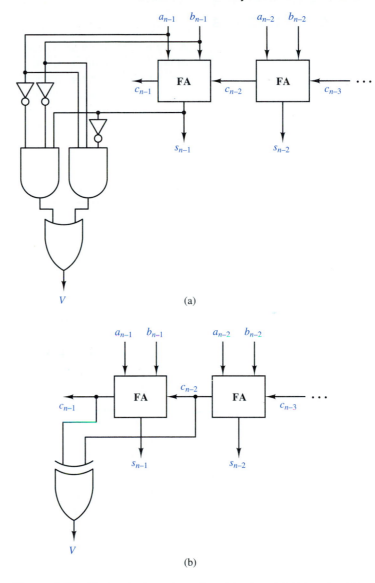

Figure 4.42 Two's complement overflow detection. **(a)** Using sign bits. **(b)** Using carry bits.

The corresponding logic circuit requires a single XOR gate, as shown in Fig. 4.42b. This circuit is simpler than than of Fig. 4.42a, but requires access to the carry bit c_{n-2} between the last two adder stages. This bit is not always accessible, as is the case when using the 7482 or 7483 MSI adder modules and a number of other parallel-adder designs. In these cases, overflows must be detected by examining sign bits, using Eq. 4.40.

4.7 Comparators

A *comparator* is an arithmetic device that determines the relative magnitude of two binary numbers and finds applications in numerous digital systems. In general, a comparator can perform a magnitude comparison of two words A and B in either straight binary or BCD codes. Three fully decoded decisions about the two words are made and are available at the outputs; that is, $A > B$, $A < B$, and $A = B$. See Fig. 4.43a. If

$$A = (A_{n-1}A_{n-2}\cdots A_0)_2 \qquad (4.42)$$
$$B = (B_{n-1}B_{n-2}\cdots B_0)_2$$

then the comparator will generate three output signals as follows:

$$\begin{aligned} f_1 &= 1, &\text{if } A < B \\ f_2 &= 1, &\text{if } A = B \qquad (4.43) \\ f_3 &= 1, &\text{if } A > B \end{aligned}$$

In other words, a comparator is a $2n$-input, 3-output combinational logic module.

EXAMPLE 4.10

Design a comparator that will compare the two words $A = (A_1A_0)_2$ and $B = (B_1B_0)_2$ in binary code.

The truth table for the output signals defined by Eqs. 4.43 is shown in Fig. 4.43b, and the K-map for the output function $(A_1A_0)_2 < (B_1B_0)_2$ is shown in Fig. 4.43c. Note that a 1 appears in every block where the binary value of $(A_1A_0)_2$ is less than that of $(B_1B_0)_2$. The K-maps for the outputs $(A_1A_0)_2 = (B_1B_0)_2$ and $(A_1A_0)_2 > (B_1B_0)_2$ are also shown in Fig. 4.43c. The output functions for these maps are

$$\begin{aligned} f_1 &= \bar{A}_1 B_1 + \bar{A}_1 \bar{A}_0 B_0 + \bar{A}_0 B_1 B_0 &\text{for } (A_1A_0)_2 < (B_1B_0)_2 \\ f_2 &= \bar{A}_1 \bar{A}_0 \bar{B}_1 \bar{B}_0 + \bar{A}_1 A_0 \bar{B}_1 B_0 \\ &\quad + A_1 \bar{A}_0 B_1 \bar{B}_0 + A_1 A_0 B_1 B_0 &\text{for } (A_1A_0)_2 = (B_1B_0)_2 \\ f_3 &= A_1 \bar{B}_1 + A_0 \bar{B}_1 \bar{B}_0 + A_1 A_0 \bar{B}_0 &\text{for } (A_1A_0)_2 > (B_1B_0)_2 \end{aligned}$$

One logic gate realization of this circuit is shown in Fig. 4.44.

7485

A comparable 4-bit magnitude comparator similar to the one derived in Example 4.10 is the 7485 circuit shown in Fig. 4.45. Note that this circuit can be put in block diagram form as shown in Fig. 4.46a. The module data inputs are

$$A = (A_3, A_2, A_1, A_0)_2 \qquad (4.44)$$
$$B = (B_3, B_2, B_1, B_0)_2$$

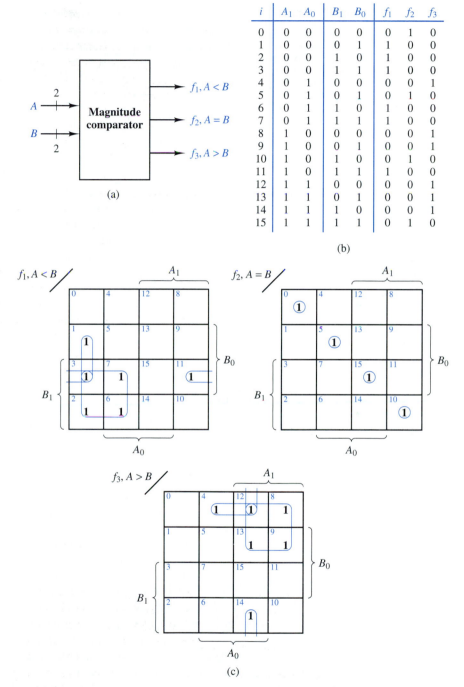

i	A_1	A_0	B_1	B_0	f_1	f_2	f_3
0	0	0	0	0	0	1	0
1	0	0	0	1	1	0	0
2	0	0	1	0	1	0	0
3	0	0	1	1	1	0	0
4	0	1	0	0	0	0	1
5	0	1	0	1	0	1	0
6	0	1	1	0	1	0	0
7	0	1	1	1	1	0	0
8	1	0	0	0	0	0	1
9	1	0	0	1	0	0	1
10	1	0	1	0	0	1	0
11	1	0	1	1	1	0	0
12	1	1	0	0	0	0	1
13	1	1	0	1	0	0	1
14	1	1	1	0	0	0	1
15	1	1	1	1	0	1	0

(b)

Figure 4.43   Two-bit comparator design. **(a)** Functional diagram. **(b)** Truth table. **(c)** K-maps.

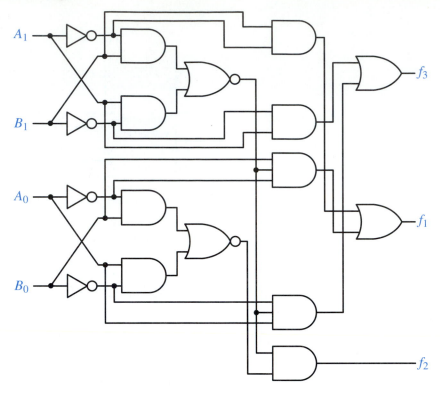

Figure 4.44   Logic realization of a 2-bit comparator.

and it also has cascade inputs

$$C1 \rightarrow A < B \qquad\qquad (4.45)$$
$$C2 \rightarrow A = B$$
$$C3 \rightarrow A > B$$

In this form it is clear that words of length greater than 4 bits may be compared by cascading these units. For example, the outputs of a stage handling the 4 least significant bits can be connected to the input terminals $A < B$, $A = B$, and $A > B$ of the next stage, together with the 4 most significant bits to generate an 8-bit comparator. In a similar manner, these units can be fully expanded to any number of bits.

EXAMPLE 4.11

Use the 7485 to construct a 16-bit magnitude comparator.

Four 7485 modules may be cascaded as shown in Fig. 4.46b to produce a 16-bit comparator. Note that the initial conditions on the first state must be

$$(C_1, C_2, C_3) = (0, 1, 0) \qquad\qquad (4.46)$$

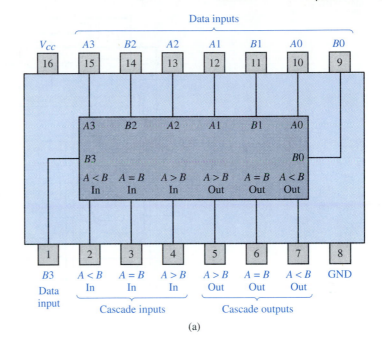

Figure 4.45 The 7485 4-bit magnitude comparator. (a) Package pin configuration. (b) Function table. *Source:* The TTL Data Book Volume 2, Texas Instruments Inc., 1985.

Comparing inputs				Cascading inputs			Outputs		
A3, B3	A2, B2	A1, B1	A0, B0	$A > B$	$A < B$	$A = B$	$A > B$	$A < B$	$A = B$
A3 > B3	×	×	×	×	×	×	H	L	L
A3 < B3	×	×	×	×	×	×	L	H	L
A3 = B3	A2 > B2	×	×	×	×	×	H	L	L
A3 = B3	A2 < B2	×	×	×	×	×	L	H	L
A3 = B3	A2 = B2	A1 > B1	×	×	×	×	H	L	L
A3 = B3	A2 = B2	A1 < B1	×	×	×	×	L	H	L
A3 = B3	A2 = B2	A1 = B1	A0 > B0	×	×	×	H	L	L
A3 = B3	A2 = B2	A1 = B1	A0 < B0	×	×	×	L	H	L
A3 = B3	A2 = B2	A1 = B1	A0 = B0	H	L	L	H	L	L
A3 = B3	A2 = B2	A1 = B1	A0 = B0	L	H	L	L	H	L
A3 = B3	A2 = B2	A1 = B1	A0 = B0	L	L	H	L	L	H
A3 = B3	A2 = B2	A1 = B1	A0 = B0	×	×	H	L	L	H
A3 = B3	A2 = B2	A1 = B1	A0 = B0	H	H	L	L	L	L
A3 = B3	A2 = B2	A1 = B1	A0 = B0	L	L	L	H	H	L

(b)

indicating $A = B$. The circuit output is f_1, f_2, f_3 from the most significant stage. The circuit compares the numbers

$$A = (A_{15}, A_{14}, \ldots, A_0)_2 \tag{4.47}$$
$$B = (B_{15}, B_{14}, \ldots, B_0)_2$$

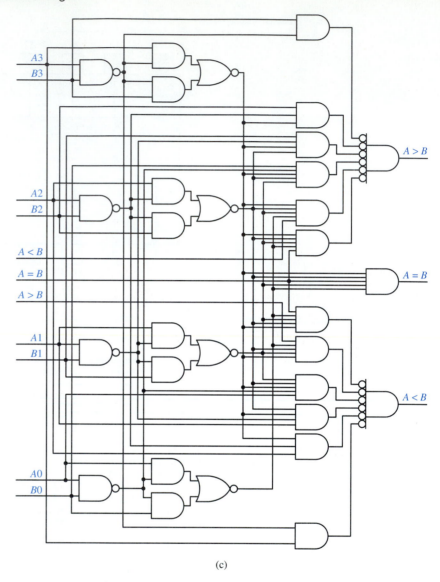

(c)

Figure 4.45 (Continued) the 7485 4-bit magnitude comparator. **(c)** Logic diagram. *Source:* The TTL Data Book Volume 2, Texas Instruments Inc., 1985.

▶ 4.8 Design Example: A Computer Arithmetic Logic Unit

Designs of most computer systems combine the arithmetic and logical operations, which we have described in Chapter 2 and earlier in this chapter, into a single functional unit called an *arithmetic logic unit*, or ALU. The standard logic symbol for an ALU is shown in Fig. 4.47. The output of the ALU is

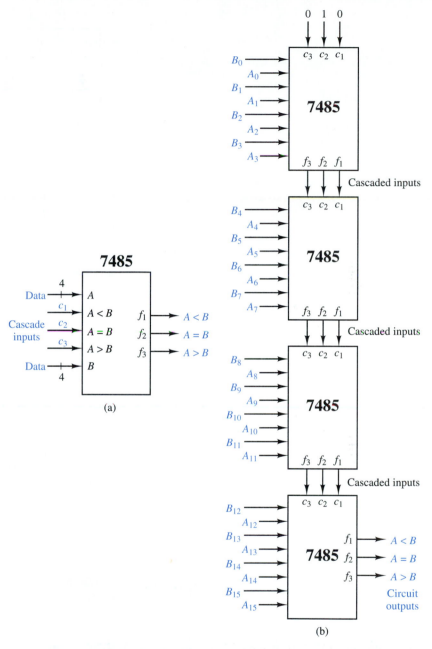

Figure 4.46   Cascading the 7485 4-bit magnitude comparator. **(a)** Functional diagram.
(b) 16-bit comparator.

an n-bit binary number, $F = (f_{n-1} \ldots f_0)_2$, which is the result produced by
performing some arithmetic or logical operation on two n-bit binary numbers,

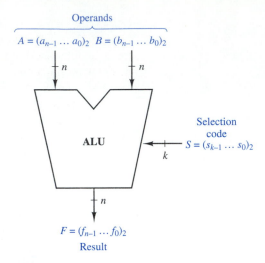

Operands

$A = (a_{n-1} \ldots a_0)_2$ $B = (b_{n-1} \ldots b_0)_2$

n n

ALU

Selection
code
$S = (s_{k-1} \ldots s_0)_2$

k

n

$F = (f_{n-1} \ldots f_0)_2$

Result

Figure 4.47   ALU logic symbol.

or operands, $A = (a_{n-1} \ldots a_0)_2$ and $B = (b_{n-1} \ldots b_0)_2$. The operation to be performed is determined by a k-bit selection code $S = (S_{k-1} \ldots S_0)$, where the number of possible ALU operations is 2^k.

Let us design an ALU module that will realize eight functions: the four standard arithmetic operations add $(A + B)$, subtract $(A - B)$, increment $(A + 1)$, and decrement $(A - 1)$, and the four logical operations AND $(A \cap B)$, OR $(A \cup B)$, XOR $(A \oplus B)$, and NOT $(\bar{A})$. Since there are a total of eight operations, the selection code must contain 3 bits; that is, $S = S_2 S_1 S_0$. Let us define the selection codes as given in Table 4.4 for the eight ALU functions.

We wish to develop the design in a *hierarchical*, *top-down* fashion. This means that the top-level ALU design should initially be decomposed into a small number of modules. These modules are subsequently decomposed

TABLE 4.4   **ALU FUNCTION TABLE**

Selection Code			ALU	
S_2	S_1	S_0	**Function**	**Description**
0	0	0	$F = A + B$	Add
0	0	1	$F = A - B$	Subtract
0	1	0	$F = A + 1$	Increment
0	1	1	$F = A - 1$	Decrement
1	0	0	$F = A \cap B$	AND
1	0	1	$F = A \cup B$	OR
1	1	0	$F = \bar{A}$	NOT
1	1	1	$F = A \oplus B$	XOR

further until the entire design can finally be represented by an interconnected hierarchy of small, well-defined functional modules. Then the logic circuits for these modules are designed, implemented, and tested individually. Finally, the modules are interconnected to form the complete ALU circuit.

The desired range of numbers to be manipulated by the ALU for an intended application determines the number of bits, n, in the binary numbers A, B, and F. To facilitate the development of an ALU circuit design that can be used for arbitrary values of n, let us begin our top-down design by decomposing the ALU into one-bit slices, where slice i performs the desired functions on bits a_i and b_i of the operands and produces result bit f_i, as illustrated in Fig. 4.48a. For the arithmetic functions, note that each slice has a carry input C_{i-1} and a carry output C_i. Once we have designed the circuit for the basic 1-bit slice, we then create an n-bit ALU (that is, an ALU for which A, B, and F are n-bit numbers) by simply cascading n of the 1-bit slices as illustrated in Fig. 4.48b, with a special circuit to generate the initial carry input C_{-1}.

Now let us consider the design of the basic one-bit ALU slice. Since the four arithmetic operations are somewhat related, as are the four logical operations, we can partition the ALU slice into three separate modules: an arithmetic unit (AU), a logic unit (LU), and an output multiplexer. This is illustrated in the block diagram of Fig. 4.49. The selection codes in Table 4.4 were defined so that bit S_2 determines whether the output f_i is to be an

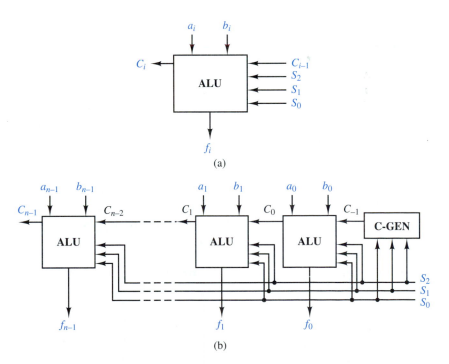

(a)

(b)

Figure 4.48   Partitioning an ALU into 1-bit slices. **(a)** 1-bit ALU slice. **(b)** n-bit ALU as a cascade of n one-bit slices.

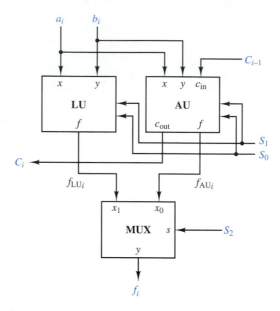

Figure 4.49   One-bit ALU partitioned into separate arithmetic and logic units.

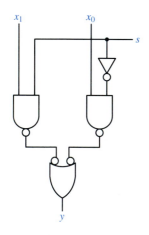

Figure 4.50   2-to-1 multiplexer.

arithmetic or logical result. Therefore, the output multiplexer selects the AU output ($f_i = f_{AU_i}$) for $S_2 = 0$, and the LU output ($f_i = f_{LU_i}$) for $S_2 = 1$.

We now develop the designs of each of the three modules of Fig. 4.49. The output multiplexer is a standard 2-to-1 multiplexer module, as discussed earlier in this chapter. Since this is a simple, straightforward design, it is not decomposed further. A two-level NAND gate circuit for the 2-to-1 multiplexer is given in Fig. 4.50.

Now let us turn our attention to the design of the logic unit. The logic functions of a digital computer system are parallel, bit-wise operations. This means that bit i of the result, f_{LU_i}, is a logic function of input bits a_i and b_i, as summarized in Table 4.5. One approach to implementing the LU module is to use a single primitive logic gate to realize each of the four logic functions, with the output of the desired gate selected using a 4-to-1 multiplexer, according to the selection code $S_1 S_0$. This circuit is shown in Fig. 4.51a, where LU inputs

TABLE 4.5   LOGIC UNIT FUNCTIONS

	Function	S_1	S_0	f_{LU_i}
AND:	$F = A \cap B$	0	0	$a_i b_i$
OR:	$F = A \cup B$	0	1	$a_i + b_i$
NOT:	$F = \bar{A}$	1	0	$\bar{a}_i$
XOR:	$F = A \oplus B$	1	1	$a_i \oplus b_i$

x and y are connected to ALU inputs a_i and b_i, respectively, and LU output f is connected to f_{LU_i}. The 4-to-1 multiplexer module can be realized by the circuit of Fig. 4.23d, which was described earlier.

If minimization of the number of gates in the LU module is important, the information in Table 4.5 can be plotted on a K-map, as shown in Figs. 4.51b and c, with the following reduced logic equation derived from the K-map:

$$f = \bar{S}_1 xy + S_0 x\bar{y} + S_0 \bar{x} y + S_1 \bar{S}_0 \bar{x} \tag{4.48}$$

A two-level NAND gate implementation of Eq. 4.48 is given in Fig. 4.51d.

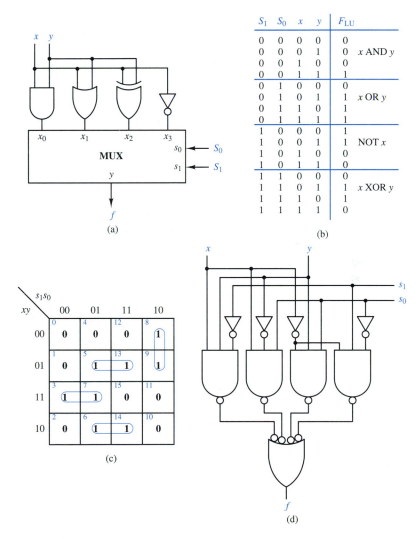

S_1	S_0	x	y	F_{LU}	
0	0	0	0	0	
0	0	0	1	0	x AND y
0	0	1	0	0	
0	0	1	1	1	
0	1	0	0	0	
0	1	0	1	1	x OR y
0	1	1	0	1	
0	1	1	1	1	
1	0	0	0	1	
1	0	0	1	1	NOT x
1	0	1	0	0	
1	0	1	1	0	
1	1	0	0	0	
1	1	0	1	1	x XOR y
1	1	1	0	1	
1	1	1	1	0	

(a)

(b)

(c)

(d)

Figure 4.51   Realizations of the logic unit. **(a)** Simple multiplexer realization. **(b)** Truth table. **(c)** K-map of the LU. **(d)** Minimized LU circuit.

The arithmetic unit of our ALU can be designed using the method described earlier in this chapter. Addition and subtraction will be performed by a single full-adder circuit, using two's complement arithmetic. For this design, let us use the full-adder (FA) circuit of Figs. 4.35f and g. When the ALU slices are cascaded, the FA stages will be connected in the ripple-carry adder configuration of Fig. 4.36. Now, recall that an n-bit full adder realizes the expression

$$F = X + Y + C_{-1} \qquad (4.49)$$

where F, X, and Y are n-bit binary numbers, and C_{-1} is the carry input. The four desired arithmetic operations can be easily implemented by manipulating the values of Y and C_{-1} in Eq. 4.49. Therefore, we will design a circuit that will produce the y_i input for each FA module, according to the selection code bits S_1 and S_0, and another circuit to derive C_{-1}. The overall 1-bit AU slice configuration is shown in Fig. 4.52. Note that FA input x_i is simply connected to ALU input a_i.

Let us consider each of the four arithmetic operations separately.

Add: $F = A + B$. Here, for the FA module, we simply set $X = A$, $Y = B$, and $C_{-1} = 0$. Therefore, the Y-GEN module should connect input b_i to the y_i input of the FA.

Subtract: $F = A - B$. Recalling the definition of two's complement,

$$
\begin{aligned}
F &= A - B \\
&= A + [B]_2 \\
&= A + (\bar{b}_{n-1} \dots \bar{b}_1 \bar{b}_0) + 1 \qquad (4.50)
\end{aligned}
$$

Therefore, the subtract function is implemented by setting $y_i = \bar{b}_i$ and $C_{-1} = 1$. Consequently, the Y-GEN module should connect the complement of b_i to the y_i input of the FA.

Increment: $A = A + 1$. In this case we simply set $Y = 0$ and $C_{-1} = 1$ in Eq. 4.49. Therefore, the Y-GEN module should supply 0 to the y_i input of the FA.

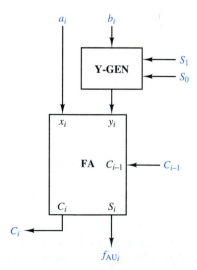

Figure 4.52   Block diagram of the AU slice.

Decrement: $A = A - 1$. Again, we call on the definition of two's complement as follows:

$$F = A - 1$$
$$= A + (-1)$$
$$= A + [00\ldots01]_2$$
$$= A + (11\ldots11)$$
$$= A + (11\ldots11) + 0 \tag{4.51}$$

Therefore, we realize the decrement function by setting the FA inputs $y_i = 1$ and $C_{-1} = 0$.

Table 4.6 summarizes the preceding discussion by listing the required values of FA inputs y_i and C_{-1} for each of the four arithmetic operations. From this table, we can derive logic circuits for the Y-GEN module of Fig. 4.52 and the C-GEN module of Fig. 4.48b.

TABLE 4.6   VALUES OF y_i AND C_{-1} FOR THE ARITHMETIC FUNCTIONS

Function	S_1	S_0	y_i	C_{-1}
Add	0	0	b_i	0
Subtract	0	1	$\bar{b}_i$	1
Increment	1	0	0	1
Decrement	1	1	1	0

For the Y-GEN circuit, we plot y_i on a K-map as shown in Figs. 4.53a and b. The logic equation for the output, y_i, is derived as follows:

$$y_i = \bar{S}_1\bar{S}_0 b_i + S_0\bar{b}_i + S_1 S_0$$
$$= \bar{S}_0(\bar{S}_1 b_i) + S_0(S_1 + \bar{b}_i)$$
$$= S_0 \oplus (\bar{S}_1 b_i) \tag{4.52}$$

A logic circuit realizing Eq. 4.52 is given in Fig. 4.53c.

For the C-GEN circuit, we plot C_{-1} on a K-map, as shown in Figs. 4.54a and b and derive the following logic equation:

$$C_{-1} = S_1\bar{S}_0 + \bar{S}_1 S_0$$
$$= S_1 \oplus S_0 \tag{4.53}$$

Equation 4.53 is realized with a single XOR gate, as shown in Fig. 4.54c.

The 1-bit ALU slice is now formed by interconnecting the individual modules developed previously (LU, FA, YGEN, and MUX). The complete circuit for the 1-bit ALU slice is shown in Fig. 4.55.

The final step of the design process is to create our n-bit ALU by cascading n of the 1-bit ALU slices and connecting the C-GEN module, as shown in Fig. 4.48b.

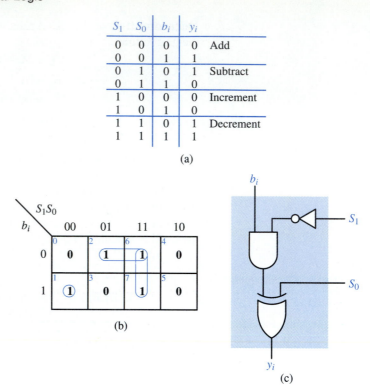

S_1	S_0	b_i	y_i	
0	0	0	0	Add
0	0	1	1	
0	1	0	1	Subtract
0	1	1	0	
1	0	0	0	Increment
1	0	1	0	
1	1	0	1	Decrement
1	1	1	1	

(a)

(b)

(c)

Figure 4.53 Y-GEN circuit module design. **(a)** Truth table. **(b)** K-map. **(c)** Logic circuit.

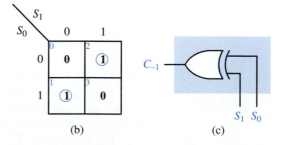

S_1	S_0	C_{-1}	
0	0	0	Add
0	1	1	Subtract
1	0	1	Increment
1	1	0	Decrement

(a)

(b)   (c)

Figure 4.54 C-GEN circuit module design. **(a)** Truth table. **(b)** K-map. **(c)** Logic circuit.

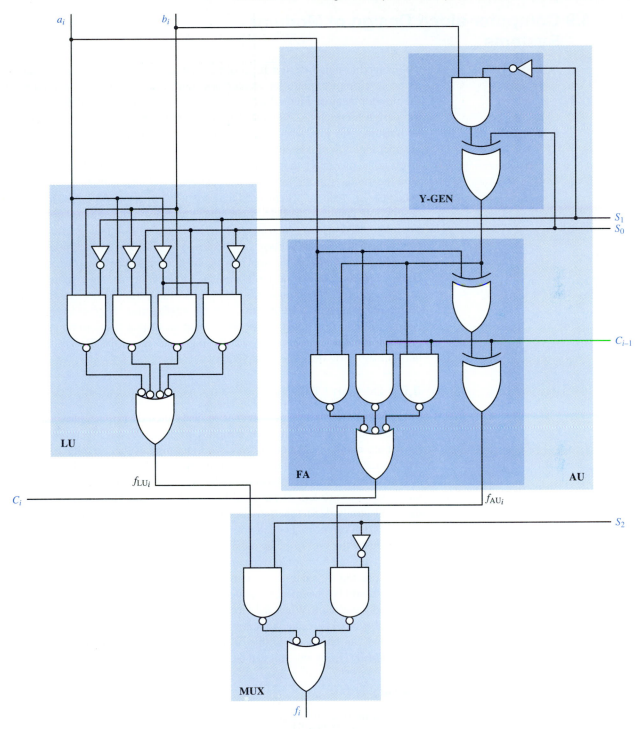

Figure 4.55   Complete 1-bit ALU slice.

4.9 Computer-aided Design of Modular Systems

The computer-aided design (CAD) methods and tools described in Chapter 2 for developing circuits of elementary logic gates are readily extended to the development of hierarchical, modular designs. At the topmost levels of the design hierarchy, schematic diagrams are drawn in block diagram form, as illustrated in Fig. 4.56. Each block in the diagram represents a specific abstract function that is defined by one or more lower-level models. At lower levels in the hierarchy, the functional blocks become successively less abstract, with the modules at the lowest levels realized by elements that are not further decomposed, such as schematic diagrams of primitive logic gates, hardware description language models, switching equations, truth tables, and so on. Therefore, CAD systems that support large designs allow block diagrams, gate-level schematics, and other types of models to be mixed within a single project.

Implementation of a design is typically done in a *bottom-up* fashion. Each component of a modular design is evaluated independently. An existing design may be used for that component if applicable. Such designs are maintained in design libraries, which are discussed in the next section. If no existing design is applicable, a new design must be developed. In this case, components are interconnected to create modules at the higher levels of the design hierarchy until the top-level design is complete.

4.9.1 Design Libraries

Modules used in hierarchical design projects include pre-designed standard functions and modules that are custom-designed for specific projects. The former are maintained in one or more *design libraries* that are either supplied with the CAD system, obtained from a third party, or developed by the user. Each design library contains a number of predefined modules that can be incorporated into designs as needed. These modules may be off-the shelf devices, such as the 7400-family MSI functions described in this chapter, industry-standard functions that can be embedded within other circuits, or other unique functions developed by the user or by an outside vendor.

If a desired function is not available in a design library, a custom module must be created as a gate-level circuit or modeled in some other manner. This module should be designed, simulated, and debugged as if it were to be used as a stand-alone circuit. When the circuit design and debugging are complete, a graphical symbol is created to represent it in higher-level designs. If the design is one that can be reused in this or other projects, it may be saved in a *user design library*, from which it can be extracted as needed.

Library Modules

As with primitive logic gates, each higher-level module in a design library has two components: a graphical symbol for use in creating schematic drawings and

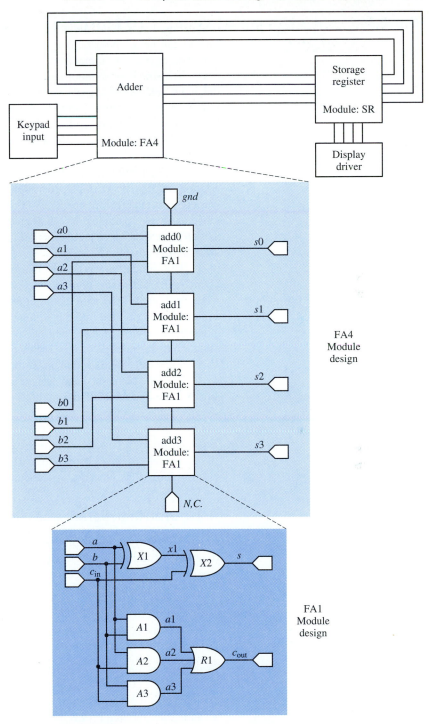

Figure 4.56   Hierarchical design.

a functional model for use in logic simulation and verification. The functional model can be a schematic diagram, hardware description language model, or some other simulation model.

The graphical symbol may be a simple block or a complex shape, with all input and output signals shown as *pins*. Each pin is characterized by the direction of the corresponding signal and the number of bits in the signal. In many cases special lines called *whiskers* are drawn on the symbol to represent the pin locations. Inversion bubbles may also be used to indicate active-low inputs or outputs.

A given graphical symbol is often used to represent more than one simulation model. For example, two-input NAND gates are available in a wide variety of standard components: 7400, 74S00, 74LS00, and so on. These parts differ in various parameters such as propagation delay and power consumption, but all realize the same logic function. Therefore, the same symbol can be used to represent any of these devices.

The simulation model may be in any of the formats described in Chapter 2, including schematic, hardware description language, truth table, logic equations, and others. The various timing and other parameters of the module may either be incorporated into the simulation model or left undefined, to be supplied by the user. The latter approach allows a single technology-independent function to be supplied in a library that can be adapted to the target technology that is ultimately used to implement the circuit.

It should be noted that a designer can incorporate a module from a design library into a hierarchical design without having access to the implementation details of the module. For example, if a full-adder module is to be used, it is not necessary to know the specific circuit structure used to realize the adder. Each design library module can be treated as a black box. All that is needed is the graphical symbol of the module, which defines its input and output signals, a description of its function, and selected timing and other parameters.

4.9.2 Drawing Hierarchical Schematics

In most CAD systems, the process of drawing a block-diagram-level schematic diagram is similar to that of drawing a gate-level diagram, as described in Chapter 2. The process begins by selecting and placing module and connector symbols on the drawing sheet, interconnecting these elements with wires, and assigning symbolic names to the modules and nets.

Naming Conventions

Each copy of a module used in a drawing is referred to as an *instance* of that module. Each instance is assigned a unique reference name to be used during simulation and documentation of the design. For example, in Fig. 4.56, the 4-bit full-adder module FA4 is assigned the reference name *Adder*. This module is realized using four instances of the one-bit full adder module FA1. These instances have been assigned names *add0*, *add1*, *add2*, and *add3*. Likewise, each individual logic gate and signal line in module FA1 has been assigned a reference name.

For debugging purposes, it is often necessary to examine a signal within a specified instance of a module. For example, suppose that the operation of the 1-bit full-adder module FA1 of Fig. 4.56 is suspect and that it is desired to monitor the value of signal $x1$ of this circuit during simulation of the complete system. Since there are four instances of FA1, the instance name is incorporated into the signal name as follows:

top_level_module_name/level2_module_name:signal_name

Therefore, to monitor signal line $x1$ within instance *add2* of the full adder of Fig. 4.56, the signal name would be *Adder/add2:x1*, which indicates signal $x1$ within module *add2*, within module *Adder* of the top-level design. This naming convention may be extended to any number of levels in a design hierarchy.

Hierarchical Connectors

To create hierarchical schematic drawings, the input and output pins of a module at one level of abstraction must be uniquely associated with the corresponding signals of the lower-level schematic. This is handled in the lower-level schematic by terminating each signal with a *hierarchical connector*, which signifies that the signal is to be visible in a higher-level drawing. This connector is associated with the corresponding input or output pin on the module symbol by assigning the same reference name to the pin and the signal line attached to the connector.

For example, Fig. 4.57a shows the graphical symbol for a 1-bit full adder and Fig. 4.57b shows the corresponding schematic diagram. Each pin on the graphical symbol has a reference name corresponding to one of the signal lines terminated by hierarchical connectors in the schematic. Note that, since the associations are made by names, the physical locations of the hierarchical connectors in the schematic need not match those of the corresponding pin on the symbol.

Many CAD systems provide a tool for automatically generating graphical symbols from schematic drawings. Typically, each symbol is similar to that shown in Fig. 4.57a, that is, a simple block figure with a separate pin for each hierarchical connector in the schematic drawing, input pins on the left and output pins on the right.

Buses

Many modules have multiple related input/output signals. In these cases, interconnections are often drawn as *buses*. A *bus* is a collection, or bundle, of related signal wires. Each bus is assigned a symbolic name to allow the bundle of wires to be referenced as a single unit during simulation and documentation of the circuit design.

For example, Fig. 4.56 shows a 4-bit full-adder module FA4 having eight inputs and four outputs, representing three 4-bit numbers. In this case it would

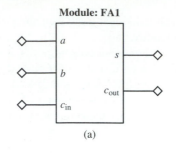

(a)

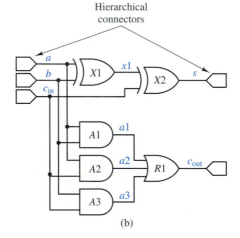

(b)

Figure 4.57 Hierarchical connectors between a full adder symbol and schematic. **(a)** Graphical symbol. **(b)** Schematic model.

be more convenient to represent the four wires carrying each of the three numbers as a 4-bit bus, defined as follows.

$$A(3:0) = \{A(3), A(2), A(1), A(0)\}$$
$$B(3:0) = \{B(3), B(2), B(1), B(0)\}$$
$$S(3:0) = \{S(3), S(2), S(1), S(0)\}$$

Each individual wire retains a unique name [for example, $A(3)$] to allow it to be connected to a device pin or selected for stimulation and/or monitoring during logic simulation. The simplified block diagram, with $A(3:0)$, $B(3:0)$, and $S(3:0)$ drawn as buses, is shown in Fig. 4.58a. This simplification is even more pronounced in modern computer systems in which buses of 32 to 64 bits are frequently used to interconnect components.

In most schematic capture programs, buses are drawn in the same way as individual wires. In some cases a normal wire is drawn and then subsequently defined to be a bus by assigning an indexed signal name, such as $A(3:0)$. In other cases, a separate *bus* tool is provided to draw the wire bundle, with the bus drawn as a thicker line or with a different color to distinguish it from single wires. The former is illustrated in Fig. 4.58a.

Figure 4.58a also illustrates the use of a *bus ripper*, which is a mechanism for splitting individual wires or groups of wires out of a bus to make connections

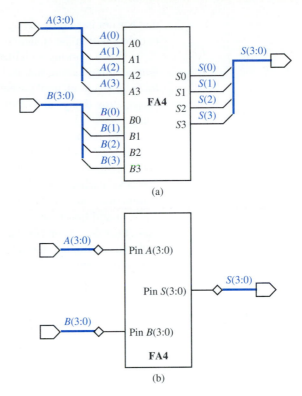

Figure 4.58 Use of buses to simplify logic diagrams.
(a) Bus with bus ripper. **(b)** Module with multibit pins.

to device pins and other connectors. In this figure, each of the three buses is separated into individual wires for connection to the 12 pins on the FA4 symbol.

Further simplification of modular schematic drawings is often made by defining multibit pins on modules, for which each pin represents a collection of related signal connections in the same manner as a bus represents a collection of related wires. This allows a bus to be connected directly to the pins of a module without having to separate it into individual wires. For example, Fig. 4.58b presents another version of the circuit of Fig. 4.58a, but with each pin on the module representing four signal connections.

4.10 Simulation of Hierarchical Systems

Design verification and debugging of a system are most often done using a *bottom-up* approach. The bottommost components in a design hierarchy are simulated and evaluated first, using the methods described in Chapter 2. When correct operation of these modules has been fully verified, circuits at the next level of abstraction that instantiate these components can be verified. A design that has not been fully debugged as a stand-alone circuit is much more difficult to debug within the context of a higher-level design.

When working with hierarchical designs, most simulation tools begin by *flattening* the circuit, that is, by replacing each module with its corresponding lower-level circuit until the entire circuit contains only primitive logic gates. All propagation delays and other parameters are then derived from the individual gates.

The process of working with signals in a hierarchical design is similar to that used with a flat design. However, during the flattening process, all components and all signal wires are assigned their full hierarchical names, as described earlier. These hierarchical names are used when selecting signals for stimulation and/or monitoring.

In addition to simplifying schematic drawings, buses are often used to make the selection and display of signals easier during simulation. Figures 4.59a and b show simulation results for a 4-bit binary adder, displayed in tabular and waveform formats, respectively. Note that in the waveform display each bus is

Time	$a(3:0)$	$b(3:0)$	$s(3:0)$
0	0000	0000	0000
5	0110	0101	0000
7	0110	0101	1011
10	0110	0001	1011
12	0110	0001	0111

(a)

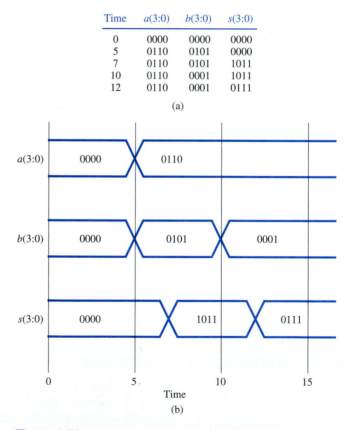

(b)

Figure 4.59 Simulation values for buses. **(a)** Tabular format. **(b)** Waveform format.

shown as a pair of lines in the logic 0 and 1 states, with the individual values displayed between them. This is done since some of the bus lines may be logic 1 and others logic 0. The crisscrossing of signal lines is used to indicate that one or more of the signals within the bus have changed.

Many simulators support mixtures of schematic diagrams, hardware description language models, and other modeling methods. In these cases, the stimulation and monitoring of signal lines is still done as described above. However, different design debugging tools may be provided for each type of model.

4.11 Summary

This chapter has treated the subject of modular combinational logic circuits. An attempt has been made to cover the important aspects involved in the analysis and synthesis of these circuits. In addition, a number of special circuits that find extensive use in all facets of digital computer organization and design have been presented and discussed.

REFERENCES

1.   *THE TTL DATA BOOK, Volume 2.* Dallas, Texas, Texas Instruments, Inc., 1988.

PROBLEMS

4.1   Derive switching expressions for outputs 5 and 11 of the 74154 decoder module. Using these expressions, describe the operation of the decoder and the function of the enable inputs.

4.2   Design a 4-to-16 decoder using logic gates. The encoded inputs are $\{D, C, B, A\}$ and the outputs are active low: $\{\bar{O}_0, \bar{O}_1, \ldots, \bar{O}_{15}\}$. The decoder should have one active-high enable line, E.

4.3   Design a 5-to-32 decoder using only 3-to-8 decoder modules. Assume that each 3-to-8 decoder has one active-low enable input, $\bar{E}_1$, and one active-high enable input, E_2.

4.4   Realize each of the following sets of functions using only a single 74154 decoder module and output logic gates (choose NAND or AND gates to minimize the fan-in of the output gates).

(a) $$f_1(a, b, c, d) = \sum m(2, 4, 10, 11, 12, 13)$$
$$f_2(a, b, c, d) = \prod M(0\,\text{to}\,3,\, 6\,\text{to}\,9,\, 12,\, 14,\, 15)$$
$$f_3(a, b, c, d) = \bar{b}c + \bar{a}\bar{b}d$$

(b) $$f_1(a, b, c, d) = \sum m(0, 1, 7, 13)$$
$$f_2(a, b, c, d) = ab\bar{c} + acd$$
$$f_3(a, b, c, d) = \prod M(0, 1, 2, 5, 6, 7, 8, 9, 11, 12, 15)$$

(c) Repeat part (a) for the complements of the three functions.

(d) Repeat part (b) for the complements of the three functions.

4.5   Given the circuit of Fig. P4.5, with the decoder having active-low outputs as shown, find the minimum switching expression for $f(W, X, Y, Z)$ in SOP form.

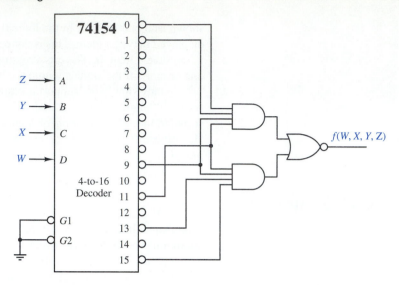

Figure P4.5

4.6   Design a binary-to-decimal decoder whose inputs are active-high, 4-bit, BCD-encoded numbers $(x_3x_2x_1x_0)$ and whose outputs are the active-low lines $(d_9, d_8, \ldots, d_1, d_0)$. The circuit should be minimized as much as possible.

4.7   Design a code converter whose input is a 4-bit code $(c_3c_2c_1c_0)$ representing the hexadecimal digits {0 to 9,A,b,C,d,E,F}, with the outputs driving a seven-segment display digit to display the corresponding character. (The letters B and D are normally displayed in lowercase to distinguish them from the numerals 8 and 0, respectively.)

4.8   Design a logic circuit that converts a 4-bit number from sign magnitude format to two's complement format. Use a two-level AND–OR circuit for each of the four outputs.

4.9   Design a code converter that converts a 4-bit number from Gray code to binary code.

4.10 Design a 4-to-2 bit priority encoder circuit using only NOR gates. The inputs are $a_3a_2a_1a_0$, with a_3 having the highest priority and a_0 the lowest. The outputs are y_1y_0, indicating the highest-priority active input, and G, which indicates that at least one input is active.

4.11 The 74147 ten-line priority encoder has active-low inputs and outputs. Determine the output, $DCBA$, of the module for the following input combinations.
    (a) $(0, 1, \ldots, 9) = (1, 0, 0, 0, 0, 0, 0, 1, 1, 1, 1)$
    (b) $(0, 1, \ldots, 9) = (1, 0, 0, 0, 1, 0, 0, 0, 1, 0)$

4.12 Derive switching expressions for the outputs of the AND gates driven by inputs D_3 and D_6 of the 74151A multiplexer module. Using these expressions, describe the operation of the multiplexer and the function of the strobe (enable) input.

4.13 Design a 5-to-1 multiplexer circuit, minimizing the circuit as much as possible.

4.14   Design a three-input/3-bit multiplexer. Use only NAND gates.

4.15   Design an 8-to-1 multiplexer using only 4-to-1 multiplexer modules without enable lines. (Do not use any additional gates.)

4.16   Design a 32-to-1 multiplexer using:
  (a)   Only 74151A modules. (Do not use any additional gates.)
  (b)   Two 74150 modules and one 4-to-1 multiplexer.
  (c)   Two 74150 modules, one inverter, and one NAND gate.

4.17   Design a dual (2-bit) 16-input multiplexer using only 74151A modules, OR gates, and inverters.

4.18   Realize the following functions with a 4-to-1 multiplexer module.
  (a) $f_1(a, b, c) = \sum m(2, 4, 5, 7)$
  (b) $f_2(a, b, c) = \prod M(0, 6, 7)$
  (c) $f_3(a, b, c) = (a + \bar{b})(\bar{b} + c)$

4.19   Realize the following functions with a 74151A multiplexer module.
  (a) $f(b, c, d) = \sum m(0, 2, 3, 5, 7)$
  (b) $f(b, c, d) = \bar{c} + b$
  (c) $f(a, b, c, d) = \prod M(0, 1, 2, 3, 6, 7, 8, 9, 12, 14, 15)$

4.20   Find the minterm list of the function $f(A, B, C, D)$ realized by the circuit of Fig. P4.20.

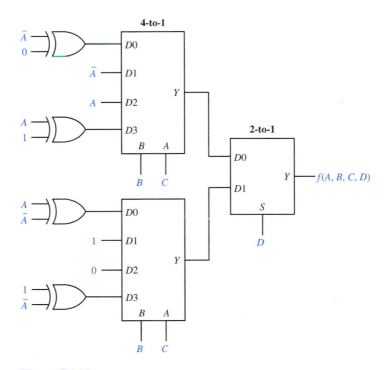

Figure P4.20

4.21 For the circuit of Fig. P4.21, which contains only 2-to-1 multiplexers (with all inputs and outputs active high), find the minterms of the output function $f(A, B, C, D)$.

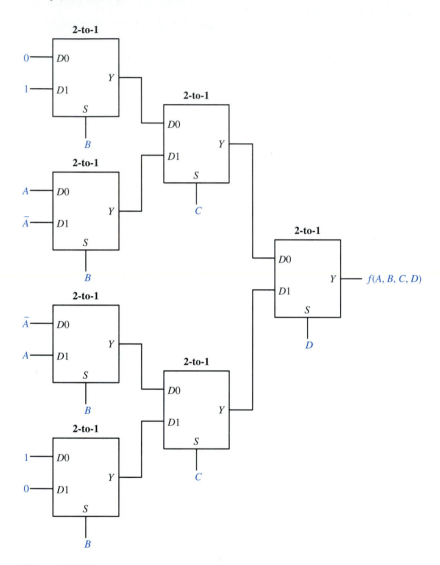

Figure P4.21

4.22 Find the minterms of the function realized by the circuit in Fig. P4.22.

4.23 Given the function $f(Q, R, S, T) = \sum m(4, 5, 6, 7, 8, 13, 14, 15)$. Using the circuits given in Fig. P4.23, implement the function by appropriately connecting the inputs Q, R, S, T to the NAND gates and to the 4-to-1 multiplexer and by

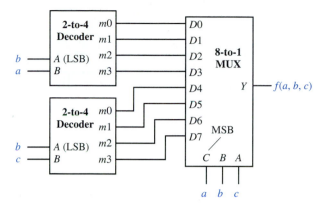

Figure P4.22

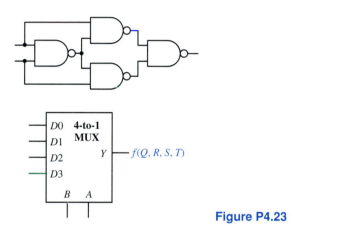

Figure P4.23

connecting the NAND gate output to the appropriate input(s) of the multiplexer. The only inputs available are Q, R, S, T; no 0 nor 1 nor $\bar{Q}$, $\bar{R}$, $\bar{S}$, $\bar{T}$ is available as an input. (Nine connections are required: three for the NAND circuit and six for the MUX.) Consider B to be the MSB for the multiplexer.

4.24   Determine the function realized by the circuit of Fig. P4.24 in minterm list form. Consider B to be the MSB for the multiplexer.

4.25   Given the circuit of Fig. P4.25, give the result $f(a, b, c, d)$ in minterm list form. Consider B to be the MSB for both the decoder and the multiplexer. Assume positive logic (active-high inputs and outputs).

4.26   Design a full adder module with data inputs A and B, carry input C_{in}, sum output S, and carry output C_{out}.
   (a)   Use a 3-to-8 decoder and NAND gates
   (b)   Use a four-input, 2-bit multiplexer

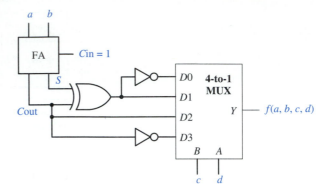

Figure P4.24

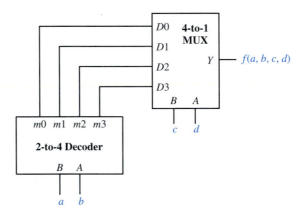

Figure P4.25

4.27 Three temperature sensors, shown in Fig. P4.27, indicate measured temperature with 8-bit binary values on their output lines, T_7 to T_0. Show with a block diagram how to use multiplexer modules to allow an 8-bit microprocessor to read any one of these sensors using its data input lines, D_7 to D_0, by issuing a 2-bit address, $A_1 A_0$.

4.28 Show how correctly encoded results are produced for the operation $A + B$, where A and B are encoded in the two's complement number system (n-bit values), and where
  (a) $A \geq 0$ and $B \geq 0$
  (b) $A \geq 0$ and $B < 0$
  (c) $A < 0$ and $B < 0$

4.29 Design a 2-bit adder circuit using a two-level NAND gate circuit for each output. The inputs are the 2-bit binary numbers $a_1 a_0$ and $b_1 b_0$. The outputs are the 2-bit binary sum $s_1 s_0$ and the carry output c_1.

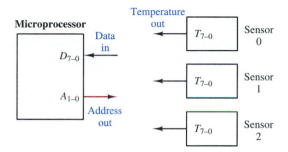

Figure P4.27

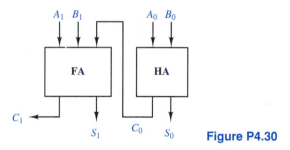

Figure P4.30

4.30   In the design of Problem 4.29, show that the resulting circuit is effectively a cascade of a 1-bit half-adder and a 1-bit full-adder, as shown in Fig. P4.30.

4.31   Design a 16-bit ripple-carry adder using only 7483 adder modules.

4.32   The circuit of Fig. P4.32, which is composed of five half-adders, will add 4 bits together as shown in the truth table. What function appears at the outputs labeled with question marks?

4.33   Using only half-adders, draw a circuit that will add 3 bits, x_i, y_i, z_i, together, producing carry and sum bits c_i, s_i as shown in the following table.

x_i	y_i	z_i	c_i	s_i
0	0	0	0	0
0	0	1	0	1
0	1	0	0	1
0	1	1	1	0
1	0	0	0	1
1	0	1	1	0
1	1	0	1	0
1	1	1	1	1

4.34   Design a 3-bit full-adder using carry look-ahead, rather than a ripple carry.

4.35   Design a 1-bit full-subtracter module, using only NOR gates, and then construct a 4-bit subtracter using only these modules.

4.36   Describe the overflow condition as applied to two's complement addition and subtraction.

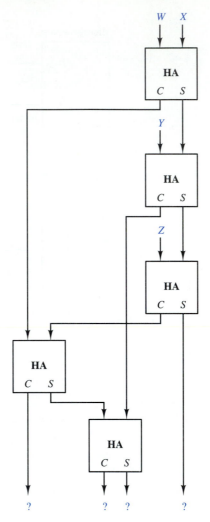

Figure P4.32

4.37   Design an overflow detection circuit for Fig. 4.41, assuming that the unit is to be used to add and subtract numbers in a 4-bit two's complement number system.

4.38   The 7483 adder module is faster than the 7482 adder module because the carry for each stage is calculated from all the inputs, rather than being propagated through each stage.

    (a)   Find the equation for the 7483 internal carry $C2$ in terms of only the $A(i)$, $B(i)$, and $C0$ inputs.

    (b)   Using $A2A1$, $B2B1$, and $C0$ as the numbers being added together to determine the carry (with $A2$ and $B2$ as MSBs), find the combinations of $(A2, A1, B2, B1, C0)$ that result in $C2 = 1$. (Find the minterms for $C2$.)

4.39   Design a BCD adder that adds two BCD digits and produces a BCD result and a carry output.

4.40 Design a 3-bit magnitude comparator with inputs $A = (a_2a_1a_0)_2$ and $B = (b_2b_1b_0)_2$ and with three outputs: $EQ(A = B)$, $GT(A > B)$, and $LT(A < B)$.

4.41 With appropriate gating and *one* 7485 comparator, design a circuit that compares two 5-bit binary numbers $A = (a_4 \ldots a_0)$ and $B = (b_4 \ldots b_0)$ with $f_3 = 1$ when $A > B$, $f_2 = 1$ when $A = B$, and $f_1 = 1$ when $A < B$. (*Hint:* Use the cascade inputs and additional gates to compare the two least significant digits.)

4.42 It is necessary to compare three 4-bit numbers $X = (x_3x_2x_1x_0)_2$, $Y = (y_3y_2y_1y_0)_2$, and $Z = (z_3z_2z_1z_0)_2$. Using 7485 magnitude comparators and associated logic gates, draw a circuit that will implement the following truth table.

Condition	f_0	f_1	f_2	f_3	f_4	f_5	f_6	f_7
$X > Y > Z$	1	0	0	0	0	0	0	0
$X > Z > Y$	0	1	0	0	0	0	0	0
$Y > X > Z$	0	0	1	0	0	0	0	0
$Y > Z > X$	0	0	0	1	0	0	0	0
$Z > X > Y$	0	0	0	0	1	0	0	0
$Z > Y > X$	0	0	0	0	0	1	0	0
$X = Y = Z$	0	0	0	0	0	0	1	0
Any other case	0	0	0	0	0	0	0	1

4.43 Design a logic circuit that multiplies two 2-bit numbers, $(a_1a_0)_2$ and $(b_1b_0)_2$, using only NAND gates. The product should be a 4-bit number $(p_3p_2p_1p_0)_2$.

4.44 Design a logic circuit that multiplies two 4-bit numbers, $(a_3a_2a_1a_0)_2$ and $(b_3b_2b_1b_0)_2$, using only AND gates and half- and full-adder modules. The product should be an 8-bit number $(p_7p_6p_5p_4p_3p_2p_1p_0)_2$.

4.45 For the 1-bit ALU slice of Fig. 4.55, find the minterm list form for $f_i(S_2, S_1, S_0, a_i, b_i, c_{i-1})$. Use the Quine–McCluskey tabular minimization method to find a minimal two-level NAND implementation for f_i.

4.46 Repeat problem 4.45 for output C_i.

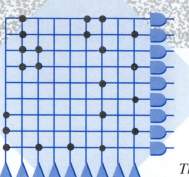

5

The total cost of a digital system can be dominated by circuit boards, power supplies, interconnections, and packaging, as well as design, testing, and other production costs. Digital logic devices often represent only a fraction of the total cost of a system. Consequently, digital system designers strive to minimize the total number of circuit packages, which in turn minimizes circuit board space, power requirements, and other related costs.

In this chapter we examine programmable logic devices (PLDs), which are digital logic chips containing circuitry that can be configured, or programmed, by a designer to realize logic functions that might ordinarily take dozens of SSI circuit packages to implement. We shall examine the basic circuit structures and operation of the three most commonly used PLD configurations, and look at how they are used to realize combinational logic circuits. Computer-aided design tools for PLD development will also be examined.

Combinational Circuit Design with Programmable Logic Devices

5.1 Semicustom Logic Devices

The number of circuit packages (integrated circuit chips, or ICs) is reduced by increasing the level of integration, that is, the number of gates per chip. Over the past 20 years, the number of gates on a single chip has increased from a few gates in standard 7400 series SSI logic devices to over 1 million devices in current high-performance VLSI chips. Higher levels of integration usually result in reduced printed circuit board (PCB) space and power requirements.

There are three basic approaches to implementing a digital LSI logic circuit: with standard SSI, MSI, and LSI components, with full-custom VLSI devices, or with semicustom devices. Standard SSI, MSI, and LSI functions are convenient, in that a circuit can be assembled quickly with readily available off-the-shelf parts. However, the total parts count, and thus the cost per gate, can become unacceptably large. Consolidating a design into one or more custom or semicustom devices can reduce the parts count and therefore the total cost significantly.

In a full-custom design, an IC is designed gate by gate, with the physical electrical component layouts and their interconnections also developed. By using computer-aided design (CAD) tools, both the circuit performance and the use of silicon area can be optimized, although the design process is expensive and lengthy. Using semicustom circuit devices reduces design time by utilizing predesigned gate arrays, standard cells, or programmable logic devices. *A gate array* is an IC that contains a number of unconnected logic gates. A designer need only specify how to interconnect the gates on the array. Manufacturing of the device is divided into two phases. In the initial phase, the unconnected gates are processed and the chips are stockpiled. The final phase requires only that the last few interconnection layers of the IC be fabricated, rather than the entire chip, reducing manufacturing time considerably. Large numbers of arrays are processed up to the final few interconnection layers and then are stored awaiting personalization for a particular application.

A *standard cell* is a circuit that is developed and stored in a *design library* with other standard cells. A designer creates an IC by selecting cells from the library, specifying where they should be placed on the IC, and then dictating how they should be interconnected. This process is not unlike designing a printed circuit board with SSI/MSI/LSI packages. The complexity of the functions in a standard cell library can range from discrete logic gates to entire microprocessors and other complex circuits. A standard cell design is often less optimal than a full-custom design, but design time is reduced considerably. The resulting IC must still be fabricated from scratch as if it were a full-custom design; that is, all the processing layers are needed to personalize the chip for a particular application.

The fabrication steps to personalize a device can be bypassed by using *programmable logic devices* (PLDs). PLDs are prefabricated ICs in which flexible interconnection layers are also included. The interconnection layers are personalized by electronic means for a specific application. This electronic personalization can be done by the end user in many cases. PLDs contain the resources necessary to realize basic two-level switching expressions and often include other logic elements as well, with the equivalent of as many as several thousand logic gates on a single PLD. A PLD circuit is developed by designing logic expressions, translating them into the format of the target PLD, and then installing them into the PLD using a PLD programmer. Thus, a working device can be produced from a design in only a few minutes, rather than the days or weeks that are required to manufacture a gate array or standard cell IC. If needed, design changes can be quickly and inexpensively implemented within hours or even minutes, whereas with standard cells or gate arrays design changes require complete refabrication and thus can take days or weeks.

5.2 Logic Array Circuits

Programmable logic array circuits are built around homogeneous arrays of elementary components that can be configured to perform logical AND and OR operations. In this section we examine the basic structures and operation of these circuits, including mechanisms to enable them to be programmed by a designer to realize switching functions.

5.2.1 Diode Operation in Digital Circuits

Programmable logic devices are built with different configurations of semiconductor diodes, transistor switches, or similar elements. A *PN diode* is an electronic device formed by creating a junction of two types of semiconductor materials, *p* type and *n* type, as illustrated in Figure 5.1. A *semiconductor* is a material that conducts current better than an insulator (such as rubber), but poorer than a conductor (such as copper). The *n* and *p* types indicate negative or positive charge conducting mechanisms. The operation of a diode can be made to approximate that of an "ideal" switch. When a voltage is applied across the diode to make the *p* side (the anode) significantly more positive than the *n* side (the cathode), the diode is said to be *forward-biased*. In this mode, it behaves as a closed switch or short circuit and maintains this forward bias at a very small value (that is, the voltage is approximately zero). When the cathode is significantly more positive than the anode, the diode is said to be

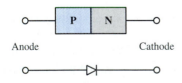

Figure 5.1 PN junction diode and schematic symbol.

reverse-biased, and effectively behaves as an open circuit (with the full amount of voltage appearing across the diode).

In digital circuit applications, one terminal of each diode is connected to either the power supply or ground through a resistor, as shown in Figures 5.2a and d. The other terminal is controlled by a digital logic signal that either forward or reverse-biases the diode. Let us consider the operation of the circuit in Figure 5.2a. When signal A is logic 1 (a positive voltage), the diode is reverse-biased and behaves as an open circuit, as illustrated in Figure 5.2b. In this case, signal line B is pulled up by the resistor toward the power supply voltage V, making signal B equal to logic 1. When A is logic 0 (0 volts), the diode becomes forward-biased and thus begins conducting, behaving as a short circuit as shown in Figure 5.2c, forcing the voltage at B to logic 0. Figures 5.2d, e, and f illustrate the equivalent effects when the resistor is connected to ground.

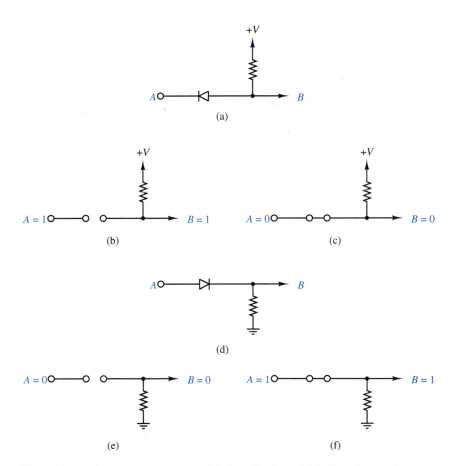

Figure 5.2   PN diode operation for digital applications. **(a)** With pull-up resistor. **(b)** Reverse-biased: diode open; B pulled up to 1. **(c)** Forward-biased: diode shorted, forcing B to 0. **(d)** With pull-down resistor. **(e)** Reverse biased: diode open; B pulled down to 0. **(f)** Forward biased: diode shorted, forcing B to 1.

A number of other electronic devices, including transistor switches, are commonly used instead of diodes in programmable logic applications. While this chapter will specifically discuss logic circuits constructed from diodes, the digital logic design concepts are the same for the other devices. The reader is referred to texts on electronics [1] or programmable logic devices [2,3] for further information on these devices.

5.2.2 AND and OR Logic Arrays

The behavior described above allows switching functions to be readily implemented with PN diodes. For example, the circuit of Figure 5.3a realizes an AND function with three inputs, A, B, and C. Let us verify this by deriving the truth table of this circuit. When $ABC = 111$, all three diodes are open, and the output is pulled up to logic 1 as shown in Figure 5.3b. If A is changed to 0, the corresponding diode becomes a short, forcing the output voltage to logic 0 as shown in Figure 5.3c. Since the other two diodes remain open, they do not affect the output. By symmetry, the same is true for $ABC = 101$, and $ABC = 110$. When multiple inputs are logic 0, each of the corresponding diodes is shorted, and the output is likewise forced to logic 0, as shown in Figure 5.3d. Therefore, the circuit implements a three-input AND function. The reader should verify that this circuit can readily be extended to K diodes to realize a K-input AND function.

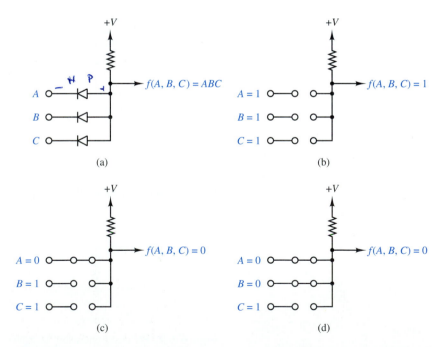

Figure 5.3 AND function realized with a diode array. **(a)** Basic configuration. **(b)** All diodes open; f pulled up to 1. **(c)** One diode shorted, forcing f to 0. **(d)** Multiple diodes shorted, forcing f to 0.

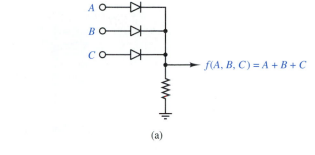

(a)

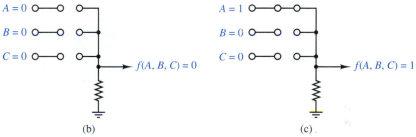

(b)   (c)

Figure 5.4 OR function realized with a diode array. **(a)** Basic configuration. **(b)** All diodes open; f pulled down to 0. **(c)** One diode shorted, forcing f to 1.

An OR function is realized by the circuit of Figure 5.4a. In this circuit, when $ABC = 000$ all three diodes are open and the output is pulled down to logic 0 as shown in Figure 5.4b. When $ABC = 100$, as shown in Figure 5.4c, the diode connected to A conducts (behaves as a short), forcing the output to logic 1. Since the other two diodes remain open, they do not affect the output. Likewise, the output will be logic 1 when any other input, or any combination of inputs, is equal to logic 1. Thus, the circuit realizes a three-input OR function. Again, note that this circuit may be readily extended to a K-input function by using K diodes.

5.2.3 Two-Level AND-OR Arrays

The AND and OR circuits described above can be interconnected in the same manner as logic gates to realize any arbitrary switching function. For example, consider the function

$$f(a, b, c) = ab\bar{c} + \bar{b}c$$

which is in two-level sum of products form. A realization of this function with diode logic arrays is shown in Figure 5.5a. Figure 5.5b illustrates a more compact format, which is commonly used to draw diode logic array circuits. The AND functions are represented by vertical lines with AND gate symbols representing the pull-up resistors, and the OR function is represented by a horizontal line with an OR gate symbol representing the pull-down resistor. The × symbols represent the diodes. Sometimes we omit the AND symbols for brevity.

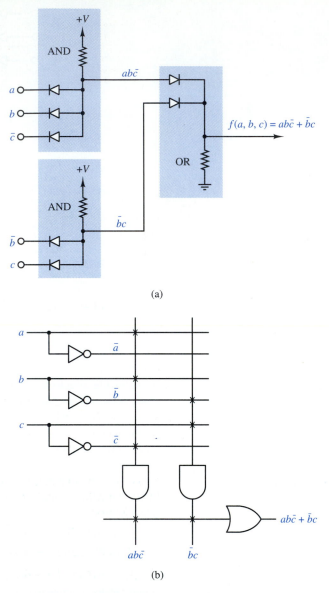

Figure 5.5 Sum of product forms realized with AND–OR arrays.
(a) Connecting AND and OR arrays. **(b)** Compact form.

Figure 5.6 illustrates how multiple functions can be realized with a single logic array by adding additional OR circuits. In this example, the following two functions are realized:

$$f_1(a, b, c) = ab + \bar{c}$$
$$f_2(a, b, c) = ab + \bar{b}c$$

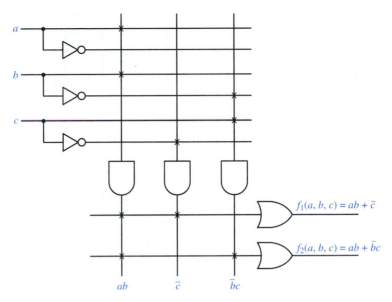

Figure 5.6 Multiple functions realized by an AND–OR array.

Note that the product term *ab* is used in both functions, that is, is "shared" by both OR operations. Specifying the locations of the diodes in the array personalizes, or programs, the array for a specific logic function.

The combination of a programmable AND array followed by a programmable OR array is commonly referred to as a *programmable logic array* (*PLA*), since arbitrary logic functions can be realized by specifying (programming) the configuration of the diodes.

EXAMPLE 5.1

Design a PLA to realize the following three logic functions and show the internal connections.

$$f_1(A,B,C,D,E) = \bar{A}\bar{B}\bar{D} + \bar{B}C\bar{D} + \bar{A}BCD\bar{E}$$
$$f_2(A,B,C,D,E) = \bar{A}BE + \bar{B}C\bar{D}E$$
$$f_3(A,B,C,D,E) = \bar{A}\bar{B}\bar{D} + \bar{B}\bar{C}DE + \bar{A}BCD$$

Since there are five variables, there must be five inputs to the PLA, each of which must be both complemented and uncomplemented. There are a total of seven unique product terms in the preceding three expressions. Therefore, the PLA must generate at least seven product terms. Finally, since three functions are being realized, there must be three sum (OR) terms generated.

The PLA organization is shown in Fig. 5.7. Table 5.1 shows the connections that must be made in the AND and OR arrays. In the table, the product term numbers correspond to the AND gate numbers in Fig. 5.7, each connected to one vertical *product line*, on which a product term is generated. In the AND array portion of the table, a 0 indicates that the complement of the variable is

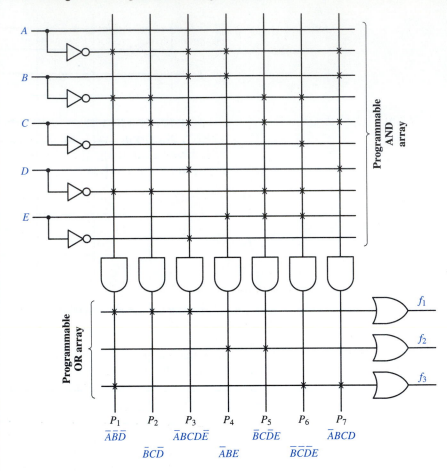

Figure 5.7 PLA for Example 5.1.

TABLE 5.1 PLA TABLE FOR EXAMPLE 5.1

Product Term	AND Array Inputs $ABCDE$	OR Array Outputs $f_1 f_2 f_3$
1 $\bar{A}\bar{B}\bar{D}$	00×0×	1 0 1
2 $\bar{B}C\bar{D}$	×010×	1 0 0
3 $\bar{A}BCD\bar{E}$	01110	1 0 0
4 $\bar{A}BE$	01××1	0 1 0
5 $\bar{B}C\bar{D}E$	×0101	0 1 0
6 $\bar{B}\bar{C}\bar{D}E$	×0001	0 0 1
7 $\bar{A}BCD$	0111×	0 0 1

connected to the product line, a 1 indicates that the uncomplemented input is connected to the product line, and an × indicates that neither is connected to the product line. For the OR array, a 1 indicates a connection and a 0 indicates no connection.

EXAMPLE 5.2

The output of a five-input "majority voter" circuit, shown in Fig. 5.8a, is to be 1 whenever a majority of its inputs is 1. Design this circuit with a PLA.

The output is 1 for all minterms containing three or more ones. The corresponding function is

$$f(a, b, c, d, e) = \sum m(7, 11, 13, 14, 15, 19, 21, 22, 23, 25 - 31)$$

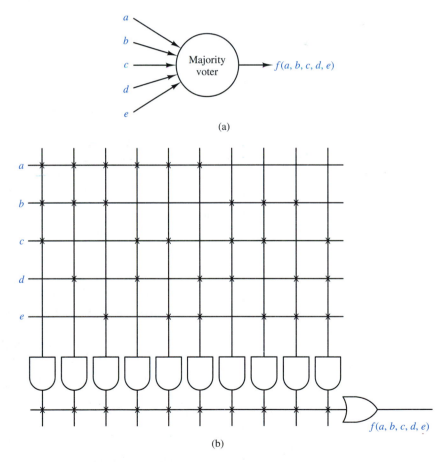

(a)

(b)

Figure 5.8   Majority voter of Example 5.2. **(a)** Output $= 1$ if majority of inputs $= 1$. **(b)** PLA realization.

Using a *K*-map, or other suitable method, the function can be expressed in minimum sum of products form as

$$f(a, b, c, d, e) = abc + abd + abe + acd + ace + ade$$
$$+ bcd + bce + bde + cde$$

This function is realized in the PLA shown in Fig. 5.8b.

Designers of custom and standard-cell VLSI circuits often utilize programmable logic arrays in lieu of discrete logic gates for the combinational logic portions of their designs. The connections in the AND and OR arrays are created during the device fabrication process (that is, are "mask programmed"). The configuration of each PLA, that is, the number of inputs, product terms, and sum terms, is tailored to the specific circuit being realized. There are a number of advantages to using PLAs. First, PLAs can be made more compact than equivalent circuits of discrete logic gates, thus utilizing less chip area. Second, computer-aided design tools are available that can automatically generate physical PLA layouts directly from logic equations, reducing overall design time. Finally, test algorithms have been developed for PLAs that are more efficient than equivalent testing algorithms for discrete logic gate circuits.

5.2.4 Field-programmable AND and OR Arrays

Field-programmable logic elements are devices that contain uncommitted AND/OR arrays that are programmed (configured) by the *designer*, rather than by their manufacturer. Most standard field-programmable (or simply "programmable") AND/OR arrays are capable of realizing arbitrary switching functions by allowing the designer to specify, or program, how to connect the diodes within the arrays to form product and sum terms.

To make a device programmable, a metal fuse (nickel–chromium, titanium–tungsten, or similar alloy) is placed in series with each diode between the diode and the output line, as shown in Fig. 5.9a. An intact fuse behaves as a short circuit, connecting the corresponding diode to the output. A fuse can be removed ("blown") by passing a high current through it, making the output independent of the corresponding input.

A programmable AND array is shown in Fig. 5.9a. Each input variable and its complement are connected by diodes and fuses to the output. By removing selected fuses, any product of variables A, $\bar{A}$, B, $\bar{B}$, C, and $\bar{C}$ can be realized. For example, consider the switching function

$$f(A, B, C) = \bar{A}B\bar{C}$$

As shown in Fig. 5.9b, this product is realized by removing the diodes in series with inputs A, $\bar{B}$, and C and leaving intact the diodes in series with inputs $\bar{A}$, B, and $\bar{C}$. Likewise, the function

$$f(A, B, C) = A\bar{B}$$

is realized by removing four fuses, as shown in Fig. 5.9c.

Instead of drawing each individual diode and fuse, a shorthand notation is commonly used to represent programmable logic configurations, as illustrated

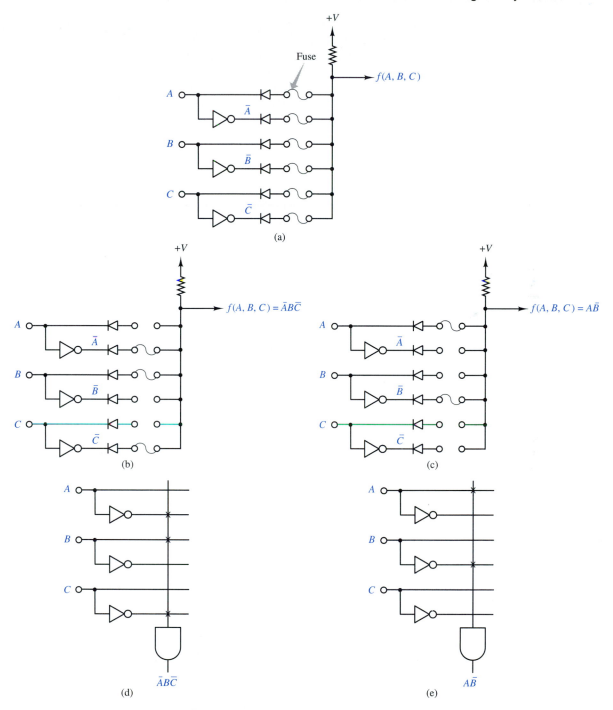

Figure 5.9   Fuse-programmable AND arrays. **(a)** Unprogrammed AND array.
(b) $f(A, B, C) = \bar{A}B\bar{C}$. **(c)** $f(A, B, C) = A\bar{B}$. **(d)** Compact notation for (b).
(e) Compact notation for (c).

in Figs. 5.9d and e. An $\times$ placed on a junction represents the presence of a fuse, and the absence of an $\times$ represents the absence of a fuse, that is, a blown fuse. The reader should verify that the circuits of Figs. 5.9d and e represent those of Figs. 5.9b and c, respectively.

Figure 5.10a illustrates a programmable OR array, which is created in the same manner as the programmable AND array described previously. The inputs to the OR array, P_1, P_2, and P_3, are usually product terms created in an AND array. The function

$$f(P_1, P_2, P_3) = P_1 + P_3$$

is produced as shown in Fig. 5.10b, and the corresponding shorthand notation is given in Fig. 5.10c.

The process of removing selected fuses from a programmable logic device is referred to as *programming* the device. This is most often done by using a computer-aided design (CAD) program to translate a description of a desired logic function (typically a switching expression) into a *map* of the fuses to be blown and then transferring this fuse map to a special instrument called a

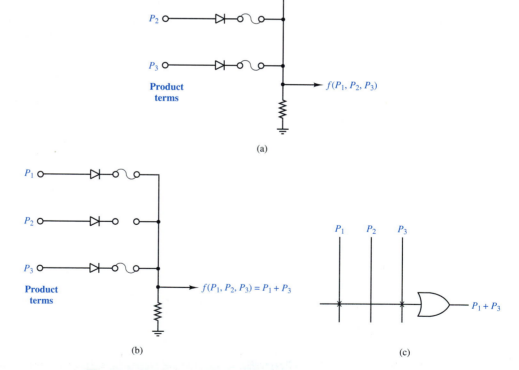

Figure 5.10   Fuse-programmable OR arrays. **(a)** Unprogrammed OR array. **(b)** $f(P_1, P_2, P_3) = P_1 + P_3$. **(c)** Compact form.

device programmer, which selects and then supplies the currents to blow the fuses specified in the map.

5.2.5 Output Polarity Options

In addition to product and sum terms, a number of other features are often provided in standard programmable logic devices, including programmable output polarity, feedback signals, and bidirectional signal pins. Figure 5.11a illustrates the common output-polarity options available on PLDs: active high, active low, complementary, and programmable polarity.

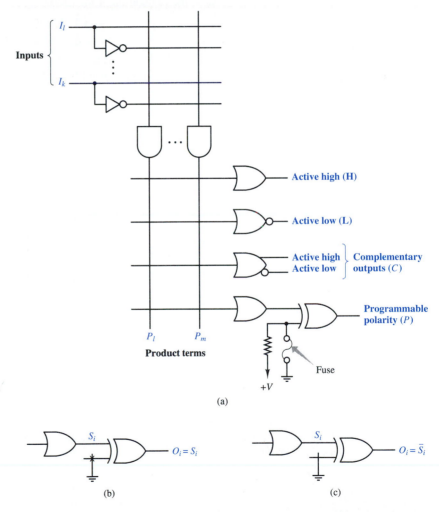

(a)

(b)   (c)

Figure 5.11   Output polarity options for field-programmable logic devices. **(a)** Output polarity options. **(b)** Fuse intact: O_i is active high, $O_i = S_i \otimes 0 = S_i$. **(c)** Fuse blown: O_i is active low, $O_i = S_i \otimes 1 = \bar{S}_i$.

A programmable-polarity output is created with an Exclusive-OR (XOR) gate with one fused input. This input is forced to logic 0 when the fuse is left intact or to logic 1 when the fuse is blown. Recalling the operation of an XOR gate, when the fuse is intact, as illustrated in Fig. 5.11b, output $O_i = S_i \oplus 0 = S_i$, and thus the output is active high. When the fuse is blown, as illustrated in Fig. 5.11c, output $O_i = S_i \oplus 1 = \bar{S}_i$, and thus the output is active low. Note that an $\times$ indicates an intact fuse, and the absence of an $\times$ indicates a blown fuse, as is the convention for the AND/OR arrays.

In addition to providing the capability to produce active-high and active-low outputs, programmable output polarity allows both sum of products (SOP) and product of sums (POS) forms to be realized. For example, Fig. 5.12 illustrates the realization of the following two functions:

$$f_1(A, B, C) = AB + \bar{A}C$$
$$f_2(A, B, C) = (A + B)(\bar{A} + C)$$

where f_1 is in SOP form and f_2 in POS form. As shown in the figure, the SOP form is implemented by making the output active high. The POS form is

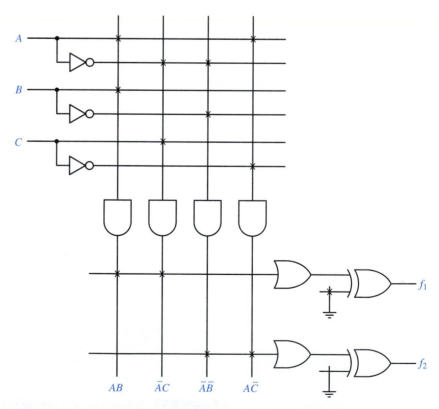

Figure 5.12 Implementation of SOP and POS forms using programmable output polarity.

realized by performing the following algebraic manipulation.

$$(A + B)(\bar{A} + C) = \overline{\overline{(A + B)(\bar{A} + C)}}$$
$$= \overline{\overline{(A + B)} + \overline{(\bar{A} + C)}}$$
$$= \overline{\bar{A}\bar{B} + A\bar{C}}$$

Thus, a POS form can be realized indirectly by inverting an SOP expression. Thus, product terms and programmable output polarity allow any of the primitive logic gates (AND, OR, NAND, NOR, or NOT) to be realized.

5.2.6 Bidirectional Pins and Feedback Lines

Another feature provided in many field-programmable logical devices is a bidirectional input/output pin, as illustrated in Fig. 5.13a. A bidirectional pin

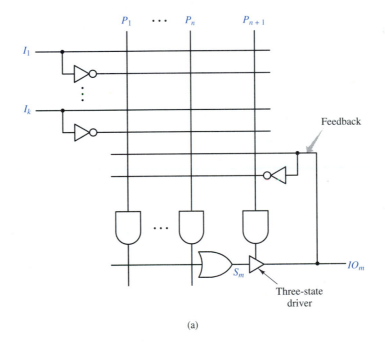

(a)

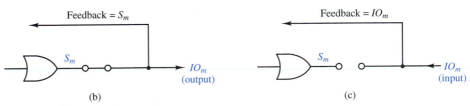

(b)   (c)

Figure 5.13 Bidirectional pins in programmable logic devices. **(a)** IO_m is a bidirectional I/O pin. **(b)** Three-state driver enabled ($P_{n+1} = 1$). **(c)** Three-state driver disabled ($P_{n+1} = 0$).

is driven by a *three-state driver* (sometimes called a *tristate driver*), whose control line is connected to one of the product terms. When the control line is 1, the driver is said to be *enabled* and functions as a short circuit (or closed switch), as shown in Fig. 5.13b. In this case the sum term is driven onto the pin, which therefore functions as an output. In addition, this value is fed back to the AND array, where it can be used to form product terms. In this manner, multilevel (greater than 2) circuits can be realized.

When the driver control line is 0, the driver is *disabled* and functions as an open circuit (or open switch), as shown in Fig. 5.13c. This disconnects

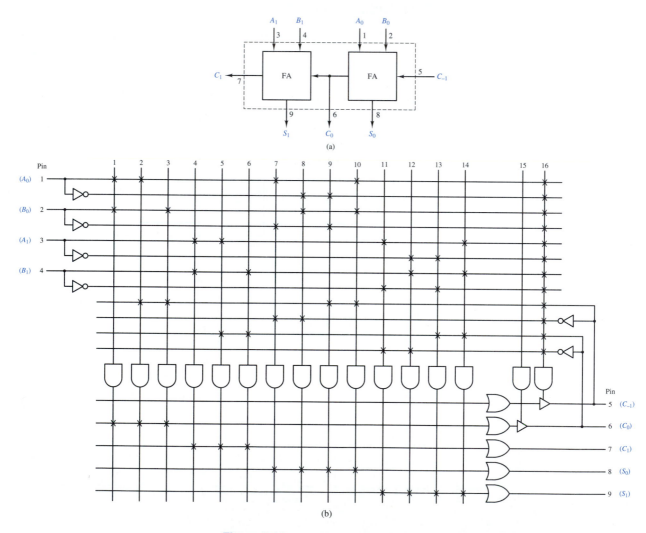

Figure 5.14 Two-bit ripple-carry adder, using I/O and feedback lines. **(a)** Block diagram with pin numbers. **(b)** Programmable logic realization.

the sum term from the pin, which, through the feedback line, now becomes an input to the AND array. The operation of these bidirectional pins and feedback lines is illustrated by the following example.

EXAMPLE 5.3

Implement a 2-bit ripple-carry adder, as shown in Fig. 5.14a, using a programmable logic array having four dedicated input pins, three dedicated output pins, and two bidirectional pins.

From Chapter 4, the standard logic equations for one stage, i, of an n-bit full-adder are the following:

$$S_i = A_i \bar{B}_i \bar{C}_{i-1} + \bar{A}_i B_i \bar{C}_{i-1} + \bar{A}_i \bar{B}_i C_{i-1} + A_i B_i C_{i-1}$$
$$C_i = A_i B_i + A_i C_{i-1} + B_i C_{i-1}$$

where A_i and B_i are the data inputs and C_{i-1} the carry input to stage i, S_i is its sum output, and C_i the carry output. For a ripple-carry adder, the carry-out of one stage is connected to the carry input of the next stage, as shown in Fig. 5.14a.

Figure 5.14b shows the PLA implementation of the block diagram of Fig. 5.14a. Since the adder requires five inputs, and there are only four dedicated input pins, bidirectional pin 5 is used as another input. Thus, the driver of pin 5 is disabled by product line 16 by leaving all its fuses intact. Note that product line 16 is forced to 0 since it is the product of all inputs and their complements. We could have used any variable pair, but leaving them all intact makes the device more reliable.

Carry term C_0 is used to compute terms S_1 and C_1 through the feedback line from pin 6, allowing C_0 to be combined with A_1 and B_1 by the preceding equations.

5.2.7 Commercial Devices

Most commercial programmable logic devices are organized as shown in Fig. 5.15, with the inputs applied to an AND array in both complemented and uncomplemented form, and the AND array outputs applied to an OR array, enabling multiple sum of products expressions to be realized. The outputs of the OR array may optionally be manipulated to derive a particular polarity. To reduce device complexity and cost and increase speed, the fuses can be omitted from either the AND array or the OR array, leaving that array in a fixed configuration. When the AND array is fixed, only the provided combinations of inputs (the product terms) are available. When the OR array is fixed, each output is a sum of selected product terms. Devices with fixed-AND arrays and programmable-OR arrays are referred to as *programmable read-only memories* (PROMs), while programmable-AND-array, fixed-OR-array devices are referred to as *programmable array logic* (PAL) devices. Devices in which both arrays are programmable are termed *field-programmable logic arrays* (FPLAs). The following sections will examine each of these three programmable device configurations and will present a number of typical examples of standard devices. The devices that will be examined are listed in Table 5.2.

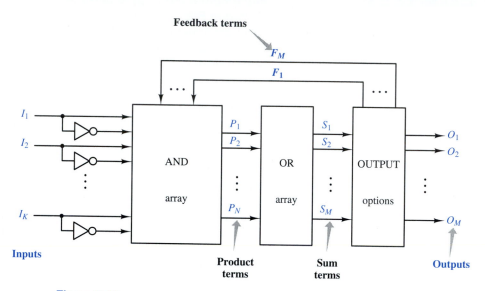

Figure 5.15 Basic programmable device organization.

TABLE 5.2 TYPICAL COMMERCIALLY AVAILABLE PLDS

Device	Description	Inputs	Product Terms	Outputs	Output Polarity
PLS100	PLA	16	48	8	Programmable
PLS153	PLA	16	42	10	Programmable
82S123	PROM	5	32	8	Active high
82S129	PROM	8	256	4	Active high
82S131	PROM	9	512	4	Active high
82S135	PROM	8	256	8	Active high
82S137	PROM	10	1024	4	Active high
82S147	PROM	9	512	8	Active high
82S181	PROM	10	1024	8	Active high
82S185	PROM	11	2048	4	Active high
82S191	PROM	11	2048	8	Active high
82S321	PROM	12	4096	8	Active high
PAL16L8	PAL	16	8	8	Active low
PAL14H4	PAL	14	4	4	Active high
PAL16C1	PAL	16	16	1	Complementary
PAL18P8	PAL	18	8	8	Programmable

5.3 Field-programmable Logic Arrays

5.3.1 FPLA Circuit Structures

Field-programmable logic arrays (FPLAs) are packaged PLA components that contain fuses in series with each diode in both the AND and OR arrays that can be removed by the user. Standard FPLA devices were introduced in 1975 by Signetics Corporation (now Philips Semiconductors), including the PLS100 [4], shown in Figure 5.16, and later followed by a variety of other parts, including the PLS153 [4], shown in Figure 5.17. These parts differ in the number of inputs, product terms, and outputs available, and also in the availability of programmable output polarity, feedback, and other features.

The configuration of a FPLA is typically given as $i \times p \times o$, where i is the number of inputs to the AND array, p is the number of product terms generated in the AND array, and o is the number of outputs from the OR array. The complement of each input is also supplied to the AND array, making a total of $2i$ inputs that can be used in product terms. In many FPLA devices, the outputs are also fed back to the AND array (complemented and uncomplemented), making a total of $i + o$ variables and their complements available for creating product terms.

For example, the PLS100 shown in Fig. 5.16 is organized as ($16 \times 48 \times 8$), having 16 dedicated inputs, 48 product terms, and 8 outputs with programmable polarity that are driven by tristate drivers that are enabled with a separate input. Since each input is supplied to the AND array in both complemented and uncomplemented form, any product of up to 16 variables can be created.

The PLS153A shown in Fig. 5.17 is organized as $18 \times 42 \times 10$. Only 8 of the 18 input pins are dedicated inputs. The other 10 "input pins" are bidirectional lines controlled by tristate drivers. When the driver is disabled, the pin is an input to the AND array. When the driver is enabled, the pin is an output, which is also fed back to the AND array. Each tristate driver is controlled by a separate product term. Thus, 10 of the product terms are used to enable tristate drivers, while the other 32 product terms are inputs to the OR array. Hence, each output can be a sum of up to 32 product terms. As with the PLS100, the polarity of each output is programmable through an XOR gate.

5.3.2 Realizing Logic Functions with FPLAs

It should be noted that an FPLA is simply a combinational logic function generator that provides sums of partial products for a given set of inputs. Hence, a single FPLA can reduce the total parts count in a design by realizing several logic functions in a single package.

When designing logic expressions for implementation in an FPLA, it should be noted that any or all of the input literals can be used in each product term and any or all of the product terms can be included in each sum term. The primary limitation is the total number of available product terms. Thus, when

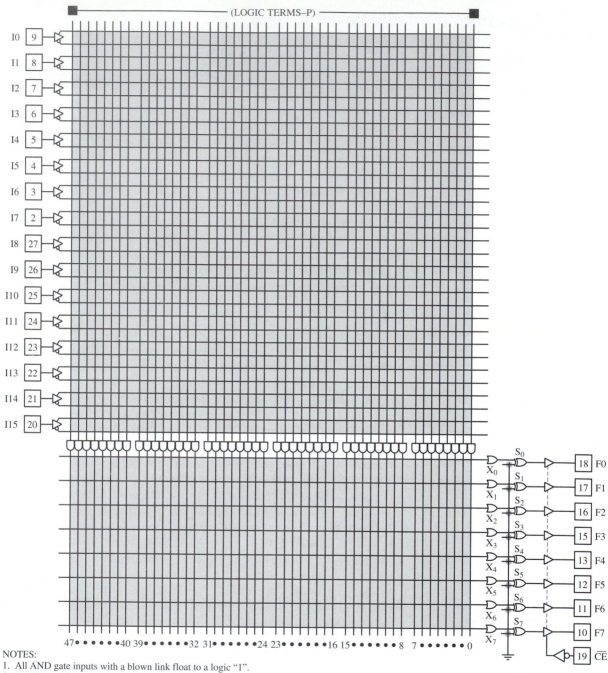

NOTES:
1. All AND gate inputs with a blown link float to a logic "1".
2. All OR gate inputs with a blown fuse float to logic "0".
3. ● Programmable connection.

Figure 5.16 Philips PLS100/101 FPLA [4]. *Source*: Philips, "Programmable Logic Devices (PLD) Data Handbook," Philips Semiconductor, Sunnyvale, CA, 1994.

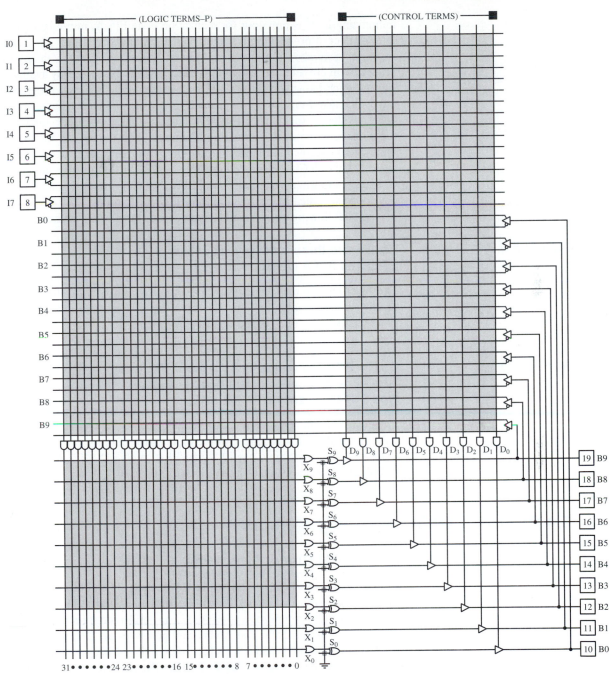

NOTES:
1. All programmed 'AND' gate locations are pulled to logic "1".
2. All programmed 'OR' gate locations are pulled to logic "0".
3. ● Programmable connection.

Figure 5.17   Philips PLS153A FPLA [4]. *Source*: Philips, "Programmable Logic Devices (PLD) Data Handbook," Philips Semiconductor, Sunnyvale, CA, 1994.

minimizing logic expressions for realization in an FPLA, minimization of the total number of product terms should be the primary objective. Unless it leads to a smaller number of products, reducing the number of literals in any single product term provides no cost savings, since all literals are already available for each product. In fact, extra time to blow the fuses actually makes programming the device take longer. For this reason, special minimization algorithms have been developed specifically for PLA devices that concentrate on reducing the number of products. In addition, since product terms can be shared by multiple sum terms in FPLAs, multiple-output minimization algorithms, such as the Quine–McCluskey procedure or the ESPRESSO algorithm mentioned in Chapter 3, are frequently used. The ESPRESSO algorithm, in particular, was developed specifically for use in minimizing PLA circuits.

The following examples illustrate the use of the FPLA devices described.

EXAMPLE 5.4

Realize the three functions of Example 5.1 in a PLS100 FPLA device.

The functions are realized as shown in Fig. 5.18. This figure shows the connections corresponding to Table 5.1 derived in Example 5.1. Note that all the other inputs to the PLS100 are don't-cares.

EXAMPLE 5.5

Use an FPLA to realize the standard TTL dual 4-to-1-line data selector/multiplexer (circuit type SN74153) shown in Fig. 5.19.

The PLA diagram that is organized to match the circuit layout is shown in Fig. 5.20. Since this PLA requires twelve inputs, two outputs, and eight product terms, it will easily fit into one PLS100 FPLA. A PLS153 FPLA, with four of its bidirectional lines used as inputs, can also be used.

5.4 Programmable Read-only Memory

5.4.1 PROM Circuit Structures

Programmable read-only memory (PROM) is the oldest of the programmable logic devices, dating back to 1970, because of its use in computer memory applications. A PROM comprises a fixed AND array and a programmable OR array, as illustrated in Fig. 5.21. The AND array generates all 2^n possible minterm products of its n inputs and is therefore often referred to as an *n-to-2^n decoder* (decoders were described in Chapter 4). The OR array allows any combination of product terms to be included in each sum term. Hence, the canonical sum of products form of any function can be realized directly from its truth table or minterm list. The number of sum terms varies between devices, according to chip size, number of pins on the package, and other cost considerations. PROM devices do not typically include output polarity or feedback options.

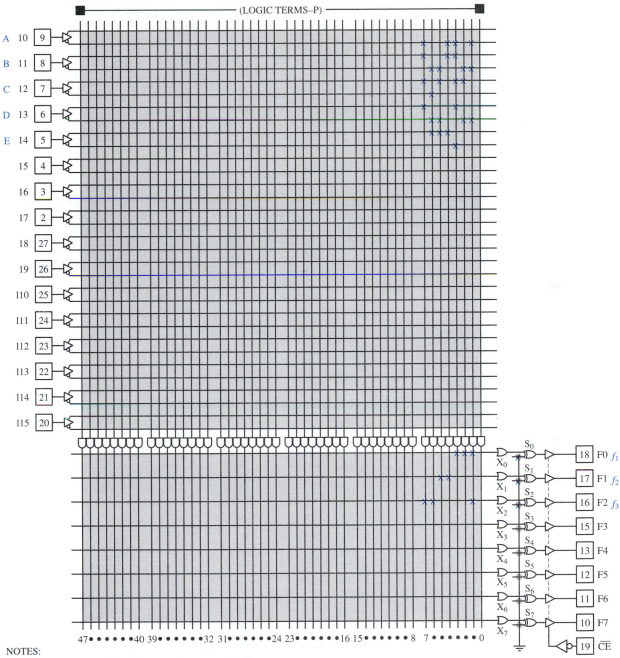

NOTES:
1. All AND gate inputs with a blown link float to a logic "1".
2. All OR gate inputs with a blown fuse float to logic "0".
3. ● Programmable connection.

Figure 5.18 Realization of Table 5.1 with a Philips PLS100 FPLA [4].
Source: Philips, "Programmable Logic Devices (PLD) Data Handbook," Philips Semiconductor, Sunnyvale, CA, 1994.

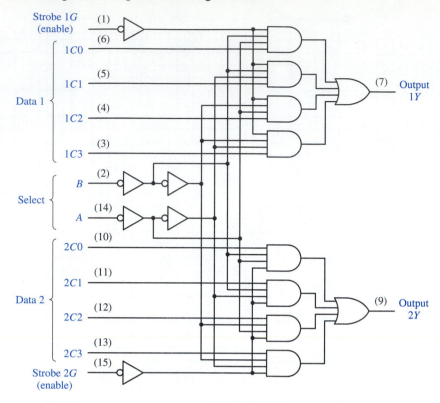

Figure 5.19   SN74153 dual 4-to-1 multiplexer.

Figure 5.22 illustrates the typical configuration of most typical commercially-available PROM devices. This particular configuration includes tristate output drivers that are controlled by a *Chip-Enable* control signal. Table 5.2 gives the configurations of a number of Signetics bipolar PROMs, illustrating the differences in number of inputs and outputs.

5.4.2 Realizing Logic Functions with PROMs

Recall that a given switching function can be represented by a unique canonical sum of products form. Hence, each output of a PROM is capable of realizing any arbitrary switching function by simply connecting that output to the minterms of the function. Therefore, to realize a given switching function with a PROM, one must first express the function in canonical sum of products form or else derive the truth table of the function. Then, each of the minterms of the function is connected to the desired OR term to produce the canonical SOP form. Note that there is *no advantage* to minimizing the function when using a PROM, since its canonical form must be used to generate the PROM fuse map. It should

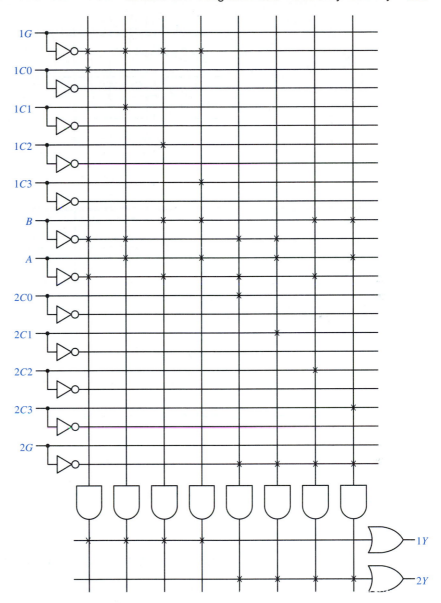

Figure 5.20   PLA realization of the SN74153 dual 4-to-1 multiplexer.

also be noted that the use of a commercially-available PROM would be very inefficient when only a small number of minterms is needed, unless minimizing chip count is the primary goal.

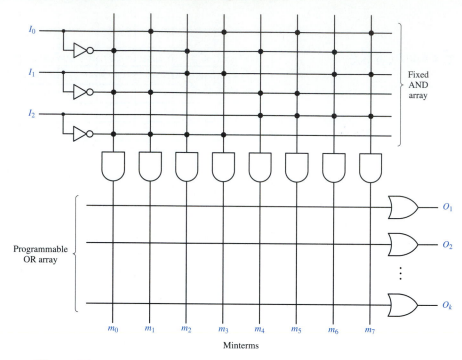

Figure 5.21 Programmable read-only memory (PROM) can realize K functions $f(I_2, I_1, I_0)$.

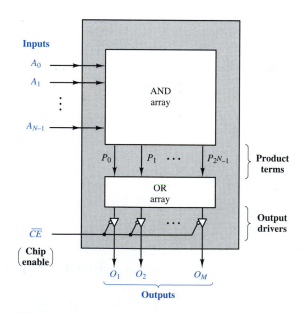

Figure 5.22 General configuration of a commercial PROM.

EXAMPLE 5.6

min term
SOP
(AND + Programable
OR)

Realize the following three switching functions with a three-input, three-output PROM.

$$f_1(A, B, C) = AB + \bar{B}C$$
$$f_2(A, B, C) = (A + \bar{B} + C)(\bar{A} + B)$$
$$f_3(A, B, C) = A + BC$$

First, we convert each function to canonical SOP form.

$$f_1(A, B, C) = AB + \bar{B}C$$
$$= AB\bar{C} + ABC + \bar{A}\bar{B}C + A\bar{B}C$$
$$= \sum m(1, 5, 6, 7)$$
$$f_2(A, B, C) = (A + \bar{B} + C)(\bar{A} + B)$$
$$= (A + \bar{B} + C)(\bar{A} + B + \bar{C})(\bar{A} + B + C)$$
$$= \prod M(2, 4, 5)$$
$$= \sum m(0, 1, 3, 6, 7)$$
$$f_3(A, B, C) = A + BC$$
$$= A\bar{B}\bar{C} + A\bar{B}C + AB\bar{C} + ABC + \bar{A}BC$$
$$= \sum m(3, 4, 5, 6, 7)$$

Therefore, output 1 is connected to product terms (1, 5, 6, 7), output 2 is connected to product terms (0, 1, 3, 6, 7), and output 3 is connected to product terms (3, 4, 5, 6, 7). The final circuit is shown in Fig. 5.23.

EXAMPLE 5.7

Use a PROM to realize a 1-bit full-adder module.

The truth table of a full adder is given in Table 5.3. From this table, the PROM is programmed by removing the fuses corresponding to each zero in the two functions, as shown in Fig. 5.24. Note that a three-input, two-output PROM is needed for this circuit.

PROMs are especially efficient solutions to problems that require that most of the minterms of a function be utilized. Examples include code converters, decoders, and lookup tables.

EXAMPLE 5.8

Design a binary to Gray code converter using a four-input, four-output PROM.

The truth table of the code converter is given in Table 5.4. Note that 15 of the 16 possible minterms are present in the output (only minterm 0 is not contained in any of the four outputs.) The truth table is mapped onto a PROM as illustrated in Fig. 5.25.

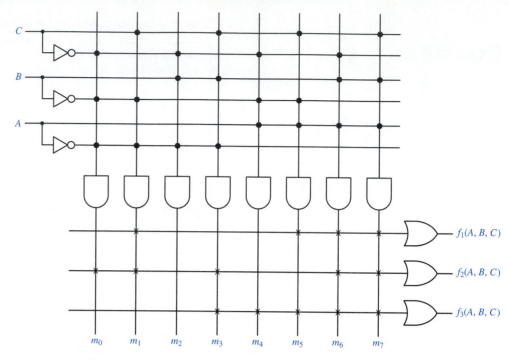

Figure 5.23   PROM solution for Example 5.6.

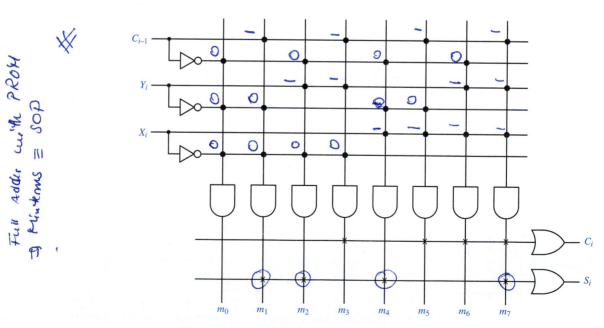

Full Adder with PROM
9 Minterms = SOP

Figure 5.24   PROM realization of a full adder.

TABLE 5.3   FULL-ADDER TRUTH TABLE

X_i	Y_i	C_{i-1}	C_i	S_i
0	0	0	0	0
0	0	1	0	1
0	1	0	0	1
0	1	1	1	0
1	0	0	0	1
1	0	1	1	0
1	1	0	1	0
1	1	1	1	1

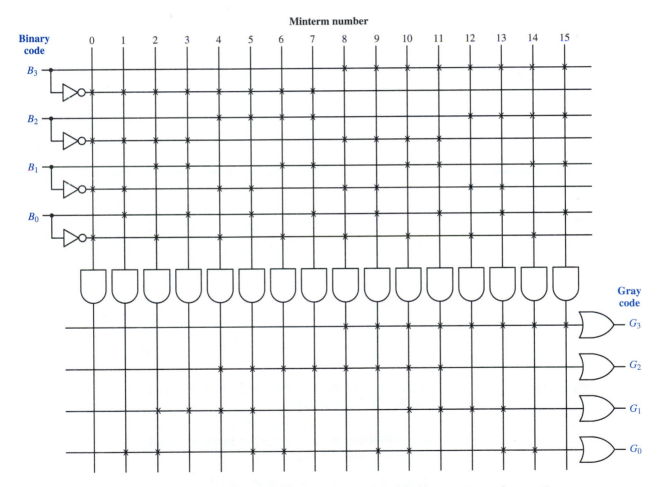

Figure 5.25   PROM realization of the binary-to-gray code converter.

TABLE 5.4 BINARY-TO-GRAY CODE TRUTH TABLE

Decimal Number	Binary $B_3B_2B_1B_0$	Gray Code $G_3G_2G_1G_0$
0	0000	0000
1	0001	0001
2	0010	0011
3	0011	0010
4	0100	0110
5	0101	0111
6	0110	0101
7	0111	0100
8	1000	1100
9	1001	1101
10	1010	1111
11	1011	1110
12	1100	1010
13	1101	1011
14	1110	1001
15	1111	1000

5.4.3 Lookup Tables

A common application of PROMs is the *lookup table*, in which a function is stored in tabular form with its arguments used as an index into the table to retrieve the value of the function for those arguments. Since truth tables can be readily realized by PROMs, lookup tables are implemented by writing them in truth table format and then realizing the truth table with a PROM. Tables of trigonometric functions, logarithms, exponentials, and other functions can thus be easily implemented. In addition, numerical calculations that can be tabularized, such as addition, subtraction, and multiplication, can also be readily implemented with PROMs, as illustrated in the following example.

EXAMPLE 5.9

Implement an 8-bit by 8-bit high-speed binary multiplier to compute

$$P_{15-0} = A_{7-0} \times B_{7-0}$$

using PROMs as lookup tables to perform all arithmetic operations.

Rather than using a single large PROM with 16 inputs and 16 outputs to implement a multiplication table with 2^{16} rows, let us partition the two operands into 4-bit quantities as follows.

$$P_{15-0} = A_{7-0} \times B_{7-0}$$
$$= ((A_{7-4} \times 2^4) + A_{3-0}) \times ((B_{7-4} \times 2^4) + B_{3-0})$$
$$= (A_{7-4} \times B_{7-4}) \times 2^8 + ((A_{7-4} \times B_{3-0}) + (A_{3-0} \times B_{7-4})) \times 2^4$$
$$+ A_{3-0} \times B_{3-0}$$

This operation can be done with four 4-bit by 4-bit multipliers to compute partial products and three binary adders to add the partial products. The multiplications by 2^4 and 2^8 can be done by simply shifting the corresponding terms 4 and 8 bits, respectively, to the left. Note that the multiplication table for a 4-bit by 4-bit multiplication has only 16 rows.

The block diagram of Fig. 5.26 is a system of PROMs used to implement the multiplier. PROMs 1 to 4 are programmed as multiplication lookup tables

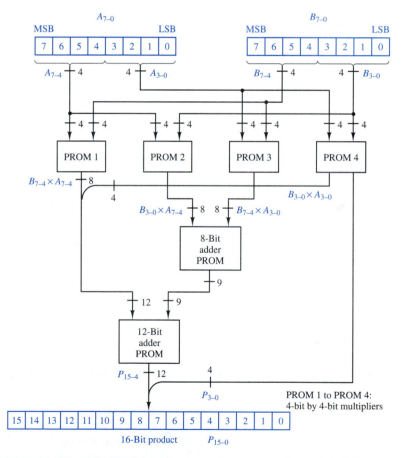

Figure 5.26   Implementation of a high-speed binary multiplier with PROMs. (PROMs 1 to 4 are 4 × 4 multipliers).

to form 4-bit by 4-bit partial products. The partial products are summed by adders, also implemented in PROMs, to form the final product.

5.4.4 General Read-only Memory Applications

One of the most common uses of PROM devices in computers and other digital systems is as read-only memories (ROMs) for permanent, nonvolatile storage of such information as computer programs, tables of constant data values, and code translation tables. Referring to Fig. 5.22, information can be read from a ROM by specifying its row number in the table, called its *address*, on the inputs $A_{n-1} \ldots A_0$. The selected data word appears on the outputs $O_m \ldots O_1$ after a short time delay, called the *access time* of the device.

An n-input, m-output PROM can store a table of up to 2^n m-bit data words. Consider the PROM diagram illustrated in Fig. 5.27. The AND array is effectively an n-to-2^n decoder, each decoder output corresponding to one minterm of the inputs $A_{n-1} \ldots A_0$. The OR array can be viewed as 2^n m-bit storage cells, each storing one m-bit data word. A supplied address is decoded, with the activated decoder output selecting its corresponding storage cell to drive the outputs $O_m \ldots O_1$.

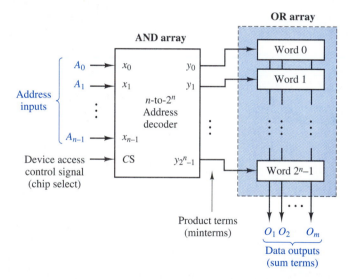

Figure 5.27   PROM device as a $2^n \times m$ read-only memory.

Information is arranged for storage in a PROM by determining the addresses at which each data word will be located. In most cases, information is simply placed at contiguous locations, beginning at the first address within the PROM. In some situations, however, information is arranged in lookup table form, with each address being a specific data code that is in some manner related to the information stored in the PROM.

5.4.5 Read-only Memory Technologies

In addition to the fusible link PROMs described previously, read-only memory and other programmable devices are available in a number of other technologies, providing trade-offs in cost, speed, flexibility, and reusability.

The complexity of a PROM device is determined by the number of diodes and fuses it contains. An n-input PROM has $2n$ diodes connecting the inputs to each product term (n uncomplemented and n complemented variables). Since there are 2^n possible product terms of n variables, the AND array includes $2n \times 2^n$ diodes. If there are k outputs, there are $k \times 2^n$ diodes and fuses in the OR array, since each of the 2^n product terms can be connected to each output. Therefore, the total cost is $(2n + k) \times 2^n$ diodes plus $k \times 2^n$ fuses.

For high-volume applications, *mask-programmed read-only memories*, or simply ROMs, are typically used. In ROM devices, there are no user-programmable fuses. Instead, during the final steps of the chip fabrication process at the factory, the OR array is permanently configured by placing or omitting simple wires in series with the diodes to represent unblown and blown fuses, respectively. A custom *mask* designates where the wires are to be placed during this fabrication step and therefore determines which cells are to be ones and which zeros. Each ROM mask is custom designed from a table supplied by the customer and therefore has a relatively high development cost, usually several thousand dollars. While the absence of programmable fuses in the OR array makes the cost of a mask-programmed ROM chip less than that of a comparable PROM device, this cost savings is partially offset by the mask charge. Therefore, ROMs are cost effective only when ordering many devices containing the same information, whereas for small numbers of parts, it is more cost effective to use PROM devices that can be programmed individually by the customer.

During the development of a logic circuit, the information to be stored in each PROM undergoes frequent changes until the design has been completely debugged. Unfortunately, ROMs and PROMs cannot be altered once they are programmed. They must be discarded and new devices programmed to replace them. *Erasable programmable read-only memories* (EPROMs) are often used in these situations. The OR array of an EPROM is programmed by using a special programming voltage to trap electrical charge in selected storage cells. The presence or absence of charge in a cell indicates a logic 0 or 1. Although not as permanent as a blown fuse, this charge will remain trapped for up to 10 years. However, it can be quickly dissipated by irradiating the chip with an ultraviolet light through a quartz window on the chip, restoring the OR array to its initial unprogrammed condition. The EPROM may then be reprogrammed with new information. This cycle of erasing and reprogramming may be repeated until the design is correct, allowing a single EPROM to be used throughout development.

An EEPROM (*electrically erasable, programmable read-only memory*) is similar to an EPROM in that it also represents ones and zeros in its memory cells by the presence or absence of trapped electrical charge. Like the EPROM, this charge can be dissipated and the chip reprogrammed. However, in an EEPROM the erasure is done electrically by applying a special voltage to the chip. This allows erasure and reprogramming of a chip without removing it from the product. Therefore, EEPROMs are attractive for applications in which the information needs to be changed without physically handling the chip. Many EEPROM devices support selective erasure of the chip; that is, they allow specified locations to be erased without disturbing others. Lower-cost EEPROM devices, called *flash memories*, are also available that support erasure only of the entire chip, thus trading flexibility for cost.

EPROM and EEPROM devices are more complex than PROM devices and are therefore more expensive per bit than comparable PROMs. In addition, most EPROMs and EEPROMs have longer propagation delays than comparably sized PROMs and ROMs, primarily since the former are fabricated using NMOS or CMOS transistor technologies, whereas PROMs and ROMs typically use bipolar TTL. However, higher cost and lower performance are often outweighed by the convenience of being able to erase and reprogram a chip. In some cases, the EPROMs or EEPROMs used during prototyping are kept for the final product. In situations where a product is to be manufactured in volume, however, product cost is often reduced by replacing the EPROMs or EEPROMs with equivalent PROMs or ROMs after the design has been finalized.

5.5 Programmable Array Logic

5.5.1 PAL Circuit Structures

PAL devices (or simply PALs) were introduced in the late 1970s by Monolithic Memories, Inc., as a lower-cost replacement for discrete logic gates, PROMs, and PLAs [5]. A PAL, as illustrated in Fig. 5.28, comprises a programmable AND array and a fixed OR array. In the fixed OR array, each output line is permanently connected to a specific set of product terms. In the PAL of Fig. 5.28, for example, each output line is connected to three product lines and therefore represents a sum of three product terms. Because of the fixed OR array, the PAL representation shown in Fig. 5.29 is more commonly used than that of Fig. 5.28.

Unlike a PROM, in which all 2^n possible products of n variables are generated, a PAL generates only a limited number of product terms, leaving it to the designer to select those products to be generated for each sum. Therefore, the overall cost of a PAL is considerably lower than those of comparable PROMs and FPLAs.

As is the case with read-only memories, PALs are available in a variety of circuit technologies, in addition to fuse-programmable bipolar TTL. In particular, the EPROM and EEPROM technologies described earlier, which utilize NMOS and CMOS transistor technologies, are often used for the programmable AND arrays of various PAL devices to provide the capability to erase and reprogram them. These chips are referred to as *erasable programmable logic devices* or EPLDs. As with read-only memories, CMOS and NMOS technology EPLDs are typically more costly and have longer propagation delays than comparable

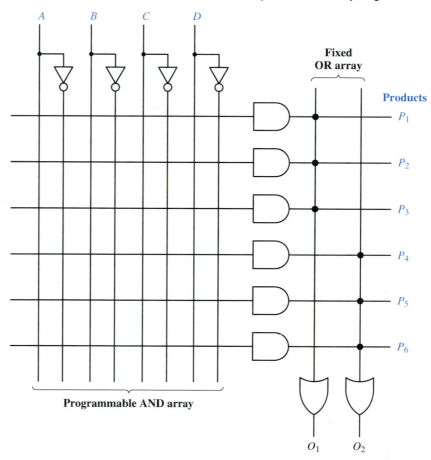

Figure 5.28 Programmable array logic (PAL) device.

bipolar TTL fuse-programmable PALs. However, the benefits of being able to erase and reprogram chips make EPLDs attractive for many applications.

5.5.2 Realizing Logic Functions with PALs

Because each output is restricted to being the sum of a fixed set of product terms, PALs are more limited than PROMs and FPLAs in the number of switching functions that can be realized. Therefore, the selection of a PAL device for a particular application must ensure that the number of product terms per output is sufficient for the worst-case number of products in that application. A further limitation is that a single product term cannot be shared between two sum terms. If two sums contain a common product term, that product must be generated twice. Fortunately, many switching functions can be represented by sums of limited numbers of product terms. Consequently, PALs are more cost effective than PROMs or FPLAs for functions that contain many input variables, but only a small number of product terms.

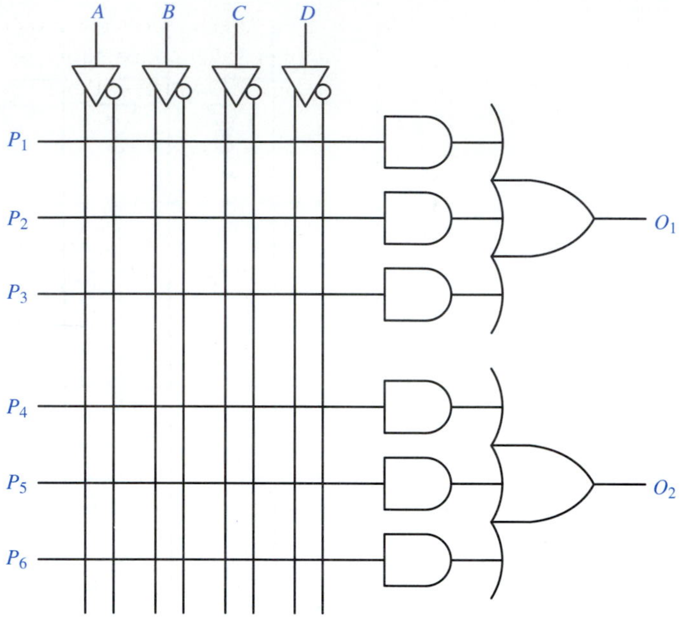

Figure 5.29 Standard PAL representation.

To realize a set of switching functions in a PAL, their minimum sum of products representations should be derived. Since the set of product terms available for each function is limited, the primary design objective should be to minimize the number of product terms in each SOP expression, rather than the total number of literals. Each input and its complement are available for every product term. Therefore, there is no real cost advantage to reducing the number of literals in any single product term. In addition, since product terms cannot be shared between outputs, as they can in PROMs and FPLAs, there is no need to use a multiple-output minimization algorithm, such as that presented in Chapter 3, to minimize the multiple functions collectively. For a PAL realization, each sum should be minimized independently.

EXAMPLE 5.10

Example 3.24 illustrated the simultaneous minimization of three functions:

$$f_\alpha(A, B, C, D) = \sum m(0, 2, 7, 10) + d(12, 15)$$
$$f_\beta(A, B, C, D) = \sum m(2, 4, 5) + d(6, 7, 8, 10)$$
$$f_\gamma(A, B, C, D) = \sum m(2, 7, 8) + d(0, 5, 13)$$

The result was the following three expressions:

$$f_\alpha(A, B, C, D) = \bar{A}\bar{B}\bar{D} + \bar{B}C\bar{D} + \bar{A}BCD$$
$$f_\beta(A, B, C, D) = \bar{A}B + \bar{B}C\bar{D}$$
$$f_\gamma(A, B, C, D) = \bar{A}\bar{B}\bar{D} + \bar{B}\bar{C}\bar{D} + \bar{A}BCD$$

These three expressions require a total of eight product terms, although there are only five unique terms, with three terms shared between multiple outputs. A PAL realization of these expressions is shown in Fig. 5.30.

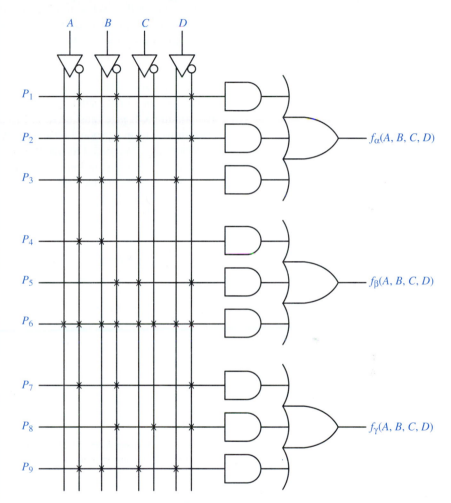

Figure 5.30 PAL realization of $f_\alpha(A, B, C, D)$, $f_\beta(A, B, C, D)$, and $f_\gamma(A, B, C, D)$.

Independently minimizing each function would produce the following expressions.

$$f_\alpha(A, B, C, D) = \bar{A}\bar{B}\bar{D} + \bar{B}C\bar{D} + BCD$$
$$f_\beta(A, B, C, D) = \bar{A}B + \bar{B}C\bar{D}$$
$$f_\gamma(A, B, C, D) = \bar{A}\bar{B}\bar{D} + \bar{B}\bar{C}\bar{D} + \bar{A}BD$$

These also contain a total of eight products, six of them unique, with two fewer literals than the previous set of expressions.

PAL realizations of these functions require a total of four inputs and eight product terms in each case, with no cost savings due to reduced literals or shared products. The cost of an FPLA realization, however, can be reduced by utilizing the first set of expressions since only five product terms need to be generated, rather than six as required for the second set of expressions. Thus, FPLA design benefits from the use of algorithms that simultaneously minimize multiple functions, whereas PAL design does not.

In the PAL of Fig. 5.30, note that function $f_\beta(A, B, C, D)$ contains only two product terms. Therefore, one of the three products connected to the corresponding OR gate must be forced to 0. As shown in Fig. 5.31, a variable, A, is removed from a product term (P_3) by removing both fuses (A and $\bar{A}$). A product term (P_4) is forced to 0 by leaving both fuses intact, since $A \cdot \bar{A} = 0$. Typically, all the fuses are left intact for each product line that is to be forced to 0, as is shown for product P_6 in Fig. 5.30.

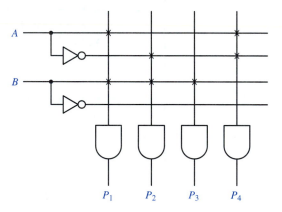

Figure 5.31 Product terms involving variable A and its complement.

5.5.3 PAL Output and Feedback Options

Standard TTL and CMOS PALs are classified by their number of inputs, outputs, product terms per output, and output options. Many PAL devices include output polarity options and internal feedback from the outputs back to the AND array. Other characteristics that vary between PAL devices include switching speed and power consumption.

The configuration of a PAL device is typically specified by its part number as follows:

$$\text{PAL } I A O$$

where I is the number of inputs, O is the number of outputs, and A specifies the architecture (output polarity) of the outputs, as follows:

A	output architecture
L	active low
H	active high
P	programmable polarity
C	complementary outputs

For example, the PAL16L8 device shown in Fig. 5.32 is a PAL with 16 inputs and 8 active-low outputs [5]. Each output is the sum of seven product terms and is driven by a tristate buffer controlled by an additional product term. Six of the outputs are fed back to the AND array, while the other two are not. The PAL18P8 device, shown in Fig. 5.33, has 8 bidirectional pins, which include programmable-polarity outputs, and 10 dedicated inputs [5]. The tristate drivers on the bidirectional lines are not shown explicitly in this diagram, but instead are included in the XNOR gate. Other PAL device configurations can be found in [5].

EXAMPLE 5.11

Design a PAL circuit that compares two 4-bit unsigned binary numbers, $A = (a_3a_2a_1a_0)_2$ and $B = (b_3b_2b_1b_0)_2$, and produces three outputs: $X = 1$ if $A = B$, $Y = 1$ if $A > B$, and $Z = 1$ if $A < B$.

From Chapter 4, the following equations can be derived for the three outputs.

$$X = (a_3 \odot b_3)(a_2 \odot b_2)(a_1 \odot b_1)(a_0 \odot b_0)$$
$$Y = a_3\bar{b}_3 + (a_3 \odot b_3)a_2\bar{b}_2 + (a_3 \odot b_3)(a_2 \odot b_2)a_1\bar{b}_1$$
$$+ (a_3 \odot b_3)(a_2 \odot b_2)(a_1 \odot b_1)a_0\bar{b}_0$$
$$Z = \bar{a}_3b_3 + (a_3 \odot b_3)\bar{a}_2b_2 + (a_3 \odot b_3)(a_2 \odot b_2)\bar{a}_1b_1$$
$$+ (a_3 \odot b_3)(a_2 \odot b_2)(a_1 \odot b_1)\bar{a}_0b_0$$

where $a_i \odot b_i = \bar{a}_i\bar{b}_i + a_ib_i$.

Expanding these equations to SOP form would produce 16 product terms for X and 15 products each for Y and Z. Since the number of product terms available for the sums of typical PAL devices is typically much less than this, let us instead generate the four terms

$$E_i = a_i \odot b_i, \qquad \text{for } i = 0, 3$$

and feed these terms back to the AND array. The set of equations then becomes

$$X = E_3E_2E_1E_0$$
$$Y = a_3\bar{b}_3 + E_3a_2\bar{b}_2 + E_3E_2a_1\bar{b}_1 + E_3E_2E_1a_0\bar{b}_0$$
$$Z = \bar{a}_3b_3 + E_3\bar{a}_2b_2 + E_3E_2\bar{a}_1b_1 + E_3E_2E_1\bar{a}_0b_0$$

The worst case is now four product terms per output. This will conveniently fit into a PAL18P8 device, as shown in Fig. 5.34, using eight of the ten dedicated inputs for A and B, four of the eight outputs for the E_i feedback terms, and three of the outputs for X, Y, and Z. Note that eight product terms are available per output, which is more than sufficient for the comparator function.

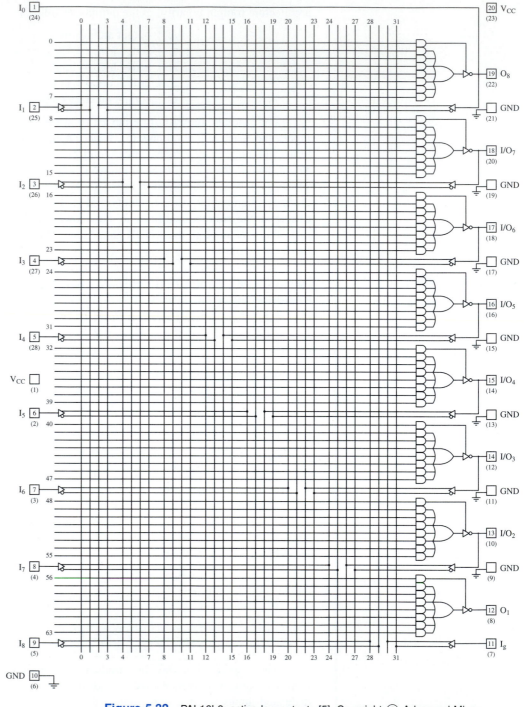

Figure 5.32 PAL16L8: active low outputs [5]. Copyright © Advanced Micro Devices, Inc., 1993. Reprinted with permission of copyright owner. All rights reserved.

Inputs (0 – 35)

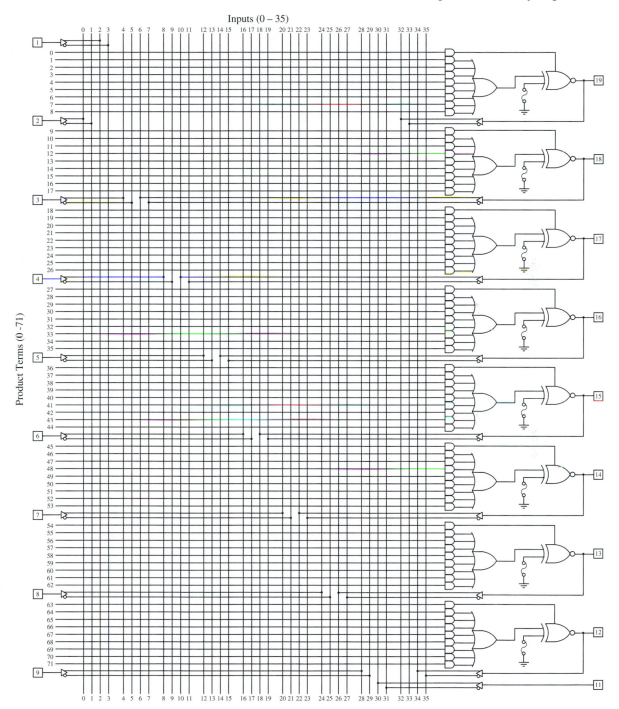

Figure 5.33 PAL18P8: programmable-polarity outputs [5]. Copyright ©
Advanced Micro Devices, Inc., 1993. Reprinted with permission of copyright
owner. All rights reserved.

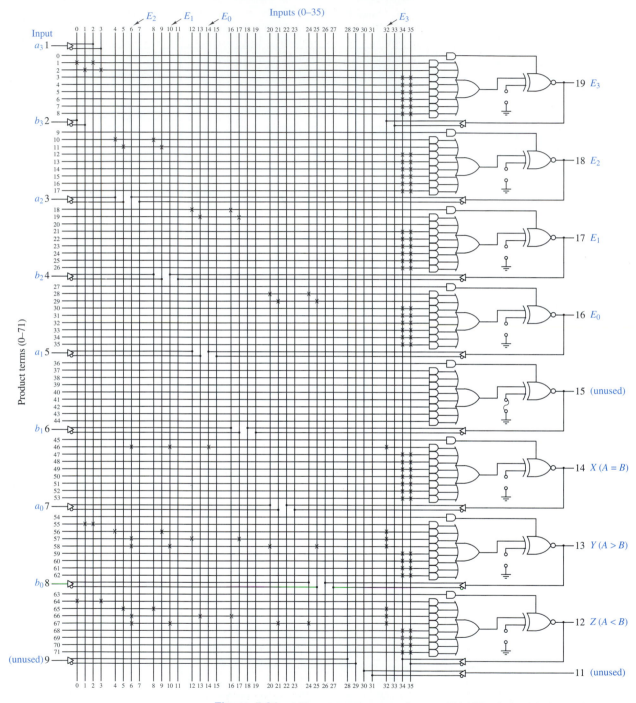

Figure 5.34 4-bit comparator mapped onto a PAL18P8 device [5]. Copyright © Advanced Micro Devices, Inc., 1993 (adapted). Reprinted with permission of copyright owner. All rights reserved.

Other PAL output options include memory elements, called flip-flops and latches, to support sequential circuit designs. Flip-flops and latches will be introduced in Chapter 6, and PAL devices that include these elements will be discussed in Chapter 11.

5.6 Computer-aided Design Tools for PLD Design

There are two general classes of commercially available PLD computer-aided design (CAD) tools, vendor specific and universal. Many vendors provide CAD tools to develop designs exclusively for their own PLDs. Examples include MAX + PLUS II from Altera and AMAZE from Signetics. A number of CAD systems, however, support development of PLD-based designs in a device independent manner and then map designs onto devices selected from various libraries. Typical examples of universal design packages include PALASM from Advanced Micro Devices, CUPL from Logical Devices, Inc., ABLE from DATA I/O Corporation, and PLDesigner from Minc, Inc.

Most PLD CAD packages allow designs to be created and entered in several formats, including schematic diagrams, logic equations, truth tables, and sequential circuit state diagrams and state tables. As shown in Fig. 5.35, each design is translated, or *compiled*, into logic equation form and then minimized, using methods similar to those described in Chapter 3. Often the designer has a choice of minimization algorithms, which provide trade-offs of computation time for optimality of results. The compiled design may then be simulated to verify its correctness and to evaluate timing and other parameters.

When the design is correct, the logic equations are mapped onto a selected PLD device. If the design cannot be made to fit the selected PLD, the designer must either modify the design, choose another device, or partition the design into modules that can be realized in separate PLDs. Some CAD systems automatically search through libraries of devices and identify those PLDs that provide the best fit while meeting specified criteria. Some of these systems are capable of automatically partitioning a design for mapping into multiple PLDs or combining smaller designs to fit into a single PLD. The output of the device-fitting step is a *fuse map*, which is a map of the fuses in the PLD, indicating which are to be blown and which are to be left intact to realize the design. In most cases, a standard, such as the JEDEC standard [5], is used for the fuse map. The fuse map is then downloaded into a special PLD programmer to program the fuse pattern into the chip.

Most PLD design packages utilize a high-level language to express designs in logic equation, truth table, or sequential circuit state machine format. Many of them also accept designs created with schematic capture programs. In these cases, the schematic is translated into logic equation form in the language used by that package.

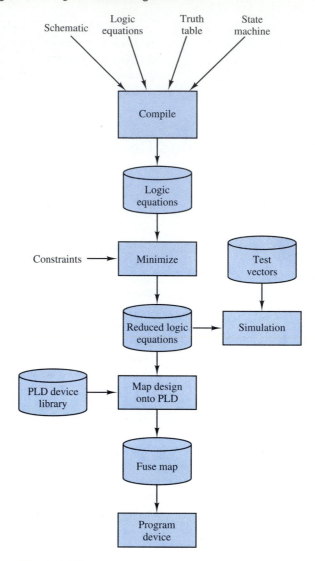

Figure 5.35 PLD design process.

For example, Fig. 5.36 shows a schematic diagram for a 1-bit full adder. This diagram was created with the Mentor Graphics *Design Architect* schematic editor and then translated by the Minc *PLDesigner* program into the PDL language. The resulting PDL listing is given in Fig. 5.37, and the reduced logic equations produced by the PDL compiler are given in Fig. 5.38.

The next section presents an overview of the PDL language. Other PLD design languages are similar to PDL. The reader is referred to [6,7,8] for more details.

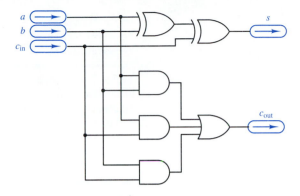

Figure 5.36   1-bit full adder schematic diagram.

5.6.1 Design Representation with PDL

PDL (PLDesigner Design Language) is typical of the high-level languages used by most PLD design tools. Designs can be entered in equation, truth table, state diagram, state table, and other behavioral forms. As illustrated by the example in Fig. 5.37, a PDL file includes a header section, which provides a verbal description of the design, an optional macro definition section, which allows symbolic representations of functions and expressions, and a function definition section containing input and output signal declarations and the logic equations, truth tables, and/or state machine descriptions that describe the function to be realized. Note that comments may be used throughout the design file, each beginning with double quotes.

Input and Output Signal Declarations

Every design has some number of external inputs and outputs and, in some cases, bidirectional input/output lines. In a PDL file these signals are defined, or *declared*, prior to listing the functional description of the design. In programmable logic devices, external inputs can either be dedicated input pins or else I/O lines whose output drivers are disabled. The following examples illustrate a number of input and output signal declaration formats.

```
INPUT x,y,[I3..I0];           "dedicated inputs:
OUTPUT x,[c3..c0];            "combinational outputs
OUTPUT x,y ENABLED_BY oe;     "combinational outputs with
                               tristate drivers

BIPUT x1,x2 ENABLED_BY oe;    "I/O line
```

In these examples, note that sequentially numbered signals may be defined using range notation. For example, $[c3..c0]$ represents the four signals $c3$, $c2$, $c1$, and $c0$. The ENABLED_BY keyword indicates a tristate driver associated

```
"========================================
" Header Section
"========================================
TITLE     schematic.vpt ;
ENGINEER  Joe E. Student;
COMPANY   State University ;
PROJECT   EE401 Homework Project ;
REVISION  1.0 ;
COMMENT   One-bit full adder circuit ;


"========================================
" Macro Definition Section
"========================================
"Macros for AND, OR, and XOR gates

MACRO AND2(i0,i1) (i0 * i1) ;
MACRO OR3(i0,i1,i2) (i0 + i1 + i2) ;
MACRO XOR(i0,i1)  (i0 (+) i1) ;


"========================================
" Function Definition Section
"========================================
FUNCTION schematic ;

" Declare external input and output signals
    INPUT    A,B,CIN ;
    OUTPUT   COUT,S ;

" Instantiate three AND gates
    MACRO  N$11  AND2(A,B) ;
    MACRO  N$12  AND2(A,CIN) ;
    MACRO  N$13  AND2(B,CIN) ;

" Instantiate one OR gate
    MACRO   COUT  OR3(N$11,N$12,N$13) ;

" Instantiate two XOR gates
    MACRO  N$14  XOR(A,B) ;
    MACRO  S     XOR(N$14,CIN) ;

END schematic ;
```

Figure 5.37   1-bit full adder PDL description generated from the schematic.

with an output and defines the control signal for the driver. The keyword ENABLED_BY may be used or omitted as needed to match the actual outputs of a particular logic device.

```
S.EQN          = CIN*/B*/A
               + /CIN*B*/A
               + /CIN*/B*A
               + CIN*B*A ; "(4 terms)


COUT.EQN       = A*CIN
               + B*CIN
               + B*A ; "(3 terms)
```

Figure 5.38   PDL equations for the 1-bit full adder generated by the PDL compiler.

TABLE 5.5   PLD LANGUAGE LOGICAL OPERATORS

Symbol	Logical Operation	Example
/	NOT	/a
/*	NAND	a /* b
/+	NOR	a /+ b
*	AND	a * b
+	OR	a /+ b
(+)	XOR	a (+) b
/(+)	XNOR	a /(+) b
[+]	Hardware XOR	a [+] b

Logic Equations

Logic equations are expressed in PDL exactly as they would be written on paper. The available PDL logic operators are listed in Table 5.5 in order of descending precedence. Parentheses may also be used as needed. Figure 5.39a shows the logic equations of 1-bit full-adder circuit, as they would be entered in PDL.

Equations in PDL can be expressed in any format, ranging from simple SOP or POS expressions to complex multi-level expressions. When a design is compiled, all equations are converted to the two-level SOP form needed to fit

```
s      = (a(+)b)(+)cin;
cout   = (a*b) + (a*cin) + (b*cin);

            (a)
```

```
S.EQN       = CIN*/B*/A
            + /CIN*B*/A
            + /CIN*/B*A
            + CIN*B*A ;
COUT.EQN    = A*CIN
            + B*CIN
            + B*A ;

            (b)
```

Figure 5.39   Full adder represented in PDL with logic equations. **(a)** PDL logic equations. **(b)** Equations produced by the PDL compiler.

the AND/OR arrays of PAL and PLA devices. For example, Fig. 5.39b shows the output of the PDL compiler for the full adder equations of Fig. 5.39a.

To aid in developing logic equations and mapping them onto a particular device, any input, output, or biput (bidirectional input/output) line may be defined as active low. For logic device outputs with inverting drivers, it is often

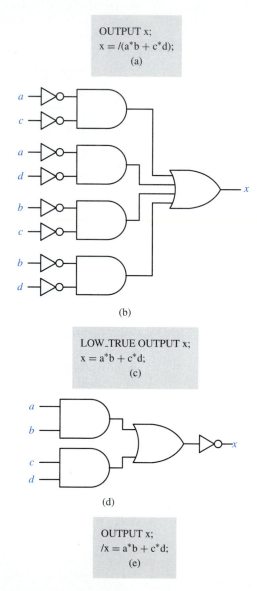

OUTPUT x;
x = /(a*b + c*d);
(a)

(b)

LOW_TRUE OUTPUT x;
x = a*b + c*d;
(c)

(d)

OUTPUT x;
/x = a*b + c*d;
(e)

Figure 5.40 Use of active-high and active-low device outputs. **(a)** PDL description of $x = \overline{ab + cd}$. **(b)** Schematic diagram (active-high output). **(c)** PDL description of $\bar{x} = ab + cd$. **(d)** Schematic digram (inverted output). **(e)** Alternate PDL form of $\bar{x} = ab + cd$.

convenient to define the output as active low. For example, Fig. 5.40 illustrates multiple representations of the same switching expression.

$$x = \overline{ab + cd} = (\bar{a} + \bar{b})(\bar{c} + \bar{d})$$

The form of Fig. 5.40a would direct the compiler to transform the expression to simple SOP form by DeMorgan's theorem, producing the AND/OR circuit of Fig. 5.40b. If the target logic device has an inverting driver on the output, the form of Fig. 5.40c would direct the compiler to use the AND/OR array to form the SOP expression $ab + cd$ and assume that an output driver will invert it, as shown in Fig. 5.40d. A signal may also be designated as active low within a signal assignment statement, as illustrated by Fig. 5.40e, which produces the same result as the listing in Fig. 5.40c.

Macros

A *macro* is a mechanism for symbolically representing functions that are to be used repeatedly, such as the switching expressions realized by various logic gates, and for assigning symbols to replace various patterns to improve the readability of a PDL description. Each instance of a macro is replaced by its definition during compilation of a design, with any formal parameters replaced by actual values. The format of a macro definition is the following:

MACRO macro-name [(parameters)] text;

The listing of Fig. 5.37 contains three macro definitions, each describing one of the circuit elements in the schematic diagram of Fig. 5.36. For example, the two-input AND gate is defined by

```
MACRO AND2(i0,i1) (i0 * i1 ) ;
```

defining function AND2 to be the AND of two parameters $i0$ and $i1$. Three copies of the AND2 macro are instantiated in the functional description of the full adder.

```
MACRO   N$11   AND2(A,B) ;
MACRO   N$12   AND2(A,CIN) ;
MACRO   N$13   AND2(B,CIN) ;
```

These define three 2-input AND gates whose equivalent logic expressions expand to

```
N$11 = A * B ;
N$12 = A * CIN ;
N$13 = B * CIN ;
```

The OR and XOR gates used in Fig. 5.36 are likewise described by macro definitions, which are then instantiated and expanded in the function definition section, creating logic gates $COUT$, $N\$14$, and S, whose inputs are driven by the circuit inputs and by the outputs of AND gates $N\$11$, $N\$12$, and $N\$13$. This is illustrated in Fig. 5.38, which shows the expanded equations generated from the PDL listing of Fig. 5.37.

Truth Tables

As described in Chapter 2, a truth table lists all combinations of the input variables of a logic function and the value of the function for each combination. To save time, multiple functions are often listed in the same truth table. For example, the truth table of the full adder of Fig. 5.39a is listed in Fig. 5.41a.

a	b	c_{in}	c_{out}	s
0	0	0	0	0
0	0	1	0	1
0	1	0	0	1
0	1	1	1	0
1	0	0	0	1
1	0	1	1	0
1	1	0	1	0
1	1	1	1	1

(a)

```
TRUTH_TABLE
   a,   b,   cin   ::   cout,   s;
   0,   0,   0     ::   0,      0;
   0,   0,   1     ::   0,      1;
   0,   1,   0     ::   0,      1;
   0,   1,   1     ::   1,      0;
   1,   0,   0     ::   0,      1;
   1,   0,   1     ::   1,      0;
   1,   1,   0     ::   1,      0;
   1,   1,   1     ::   1,      1;
END;
```

(b)

Figure 5.41   Full adder truth table. **(a)** Truth table. **(b)** PDL truth table format.

The PDL description of the full-adder truth table is shown in Fig. 5.41b. The first line defines the input and output variables, separated by a double colon (::). On each subsequent line, one input variable combination is listed, followed by a double colon and then the corresponding output values.

If needed, a don't-care condition is designated in the truth table by an × and a high impedance value by a Z. Output values can also be replaced by logic expressions of the input variables.

5.6.2 Processing a PDL Design File

After a PDL description of a design has been prepared, the PDL compiler is invoked to translate and reduce the design. This involves several steps. For a behavioral description, such as a truth table, a state table, or other state machine description, the compiler first synthesizes the machine by converting the state machine description to logic equations for all outputs and flip-flop excitation inputs. Once the design is in logic equation form, the equations are simplified to two-level SOP form, which can be mapped onto the AND/OR array of a selected PAL or PLA device.

In the process of simplifying equations, the equations are minimized by one of four options that can be specified by the user. The first is to do no reduction at all, but to simply leave the equations in SOP format. The second option is to apply the *ESPRESSO* algorithm, which reduces the equations quickly and with little memory usage, but without necessarily producing an optimum solution. The third option is to use the *ESPRESSO* algorithm with some of the *Quine–McCluskey* techniques applied to derive a better cover. The fourth option is to use the full *Quine–McCluskey* method, which produces an optimum solution, but at the expense of longer computation time and more memory usage.

For example, from the truth table of Fig. 5.41, the PDL compiler generated the logic equations given in Fig. 5.42 using the espresso algorithm for minimization.

COUT.EQN $= A^*CIN$
             $+ B^*CIN$
             $+ B^*A$; ”(3 terms)

S.EQN $= CIN^*/B^*/A$
             $+ /CIN^*B^*/A$
             $+ /CIN^*/B^*A$
             $+ CIN^*B^*A$; ”(4 terms)

Figure 5.42   Reduced excitation and output equations for a full adder.

After a design has been compiled, the next step is to verify its correctness using functional simulation. The PDL language allows test vectors and simulation controls to be specified within the design file, so compilation can be followed immediately by simulation with the *PLDsim* tool of the PLDsynthesis system. When PLDsynthesis is integrated into another design environment, such as the Mentor Graphics *Falcon Framework*, other simulators may also be used, such as the Mentor Graphics *QuickSim II* logic simulator. The reader is referred to [7] for further details on simulation within the PLDesigner and Falcon Framework environments.

The next step in the process is mapping the reduced equations onto a selected device. The PLDesigner system includes a library of devices from which those devices can be selected that best fit a design while meeting any user-specified criteria.

In PLDsynthesis, these user-specified criteria, or constraint values, include package type, logic family, manufacturer, temperature rating, maximum current, maximum frequency, maximum delay, and component price. Each constraint is assigned a weighting factor so that the selection of a device can be made by placing more importance on those constraint values considered most critical by the designer.

The output of the device-fitting operation is a fuse map, which can then be downloaded to a device programmer to program the chip. In some cases, simulation information can be supplied to the device programmer to allow it to exercise the device and compare actual operations to simulated results.

5.7 Summary

In this chapter we have examined the use of programmable logic devices in implementing combinational logic circuits. The basic circuit structures of the three types of PLDs were presented, and the process of mapping logic functions onto each was described, along with a number of examples. Finally, computer-aided design tools used to develop PLD circuits were described. In Chapter 11, we will discuss other programmable logic devices that support both combinational and sequential circuit design.

REFERENCES

1. PAUL M. CHIRLIAN, *Analysis and Design of Integrated Electronic Circuits*, 2nd ed. New York: Harper & Row, 1987.

2. ROGER C. ALFORD, *Programmable Logic Designer's Guide*. Indianapolis, IN: Howard W. Sams, 1989.

3. PARAG K. LALA, *Digital System Design Using Programmable Logic Devices*. Englewood Cliffs, NJ: Prentice Hall, 1990.

4. PHILIPS, *Programmable Logic Devices (PLD) Data Handbook*. Sunnyville, CA: Philips Semiconductor, 1994.

5. MONOLITHIC MEMORIES, *PAL Programmable Array Logic Handbook*, 2nd ed. Monolithic Memories, Inc., 1981.

6. MINC, INC., *PLDesigner Student Version Manual*. New York: McGraw-Hill Publishing Co., 1990.

7. *PLDsynthesis User's Manual*, Wilsonville, OR: Mentor Graphics Corp.

8. *PDL Language Reference Manual*, Wilsonville, OR: Mentor Graphics Corp.

PROBLEMS

5.1 Design a BCD to excess-3 code converter using:
   (a) Logic network (two-level NAND gates)
   (b) PLA (as in Fig. 5.7)
   (c) ROM (as in Fig. 5.25)
   (d) PAL (as in Fig. 5.30)
   Remember to specify the input and output dimensions of your PLA, ROM, and PAL.

5.2   Implement the following functions using:

(a)   4-to-16 decoder and logic gates

(b)   PLA (as in Fig. 5.7)

(c)   ROM (as in Fig. 5.25)

(d)   PAL (as in Fig. 5.30)

$$f_1(A, B, C, D) = \sum m(0, 1, 2, 3, 6, 9, 11)$$
$$f_2(A, B, C, D) = \sum m(0, 1, 6, 8, 9)$$
$$f_3(A, B, C, D) = \sum m(2, 3, 8, 9, 11)$$

5.3   Use a 32×6 ROM to convert a 6-bit binary number to its corresponding 2-digit BCD representation.

$$(a_5 a_4 a_3 a_2 a_1 a_0)_2 = [(x_3 x_2 x_1 x_0)_{BCD} (y_3 y_2 y_1 y_0)_{BCD}]_{10}$$

Show the ROM's contents in a truth table format. (*Hint:* $x_3 = 0$, and $y_0 = a_0$.)

5.4   Show the implementation of the functions in Problem 5.2 using:

(a)   PLS100 FPLA

(b)   PAL16L8

5.5   Show how a binary subtracter could be implemented using:

(a)   PLS100 FPLA

(b)   PAL16L8

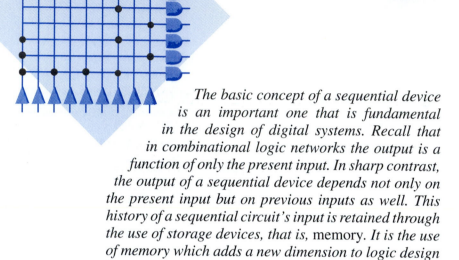

6

The basic concept of a sequential device is an important one that is fundamental in the design of digital systems. Recall that in combinational logic networks the output is a function of only the present input. In sharp contrast, the output of a sequential device depends not only on the present input but on previous inputs as well. This history of a sequential circuit's input is retained through the use of storage devices, that is, memory. It is the use of memory which adds a new dimension to logic design by providing the capability to solve numerous problems that cannot be handled by combinational logic alone.

In this chapter we introduce the basic sequential circuit model, and then describe the design and operation of a number of common memory elements, including latches and flip-flops.

Introduction to Sequential Devices

6.1 Models for Sequential Circuits

The sequential concept is not restricted to digital systems. For example, consider the operation of an elevator in a four-story building. The elevator acts as a sequential device because its actions are determined by input signals from its control panels (both on board and on each floor) and its present position at floor 1, 2, 3, or 4. The elevator must in some way "remember" its present position in order to determine its next floor transition. Therefore we define the *present state* of the elevator as a description of its present floor position, including a history of its past floor transitions. For example, the elevator may be "at floor 3 and going up." This present state must be differentiated from "at floor 3 and going down." The *next state* (and hence the next floor position) of the elevator is determined by its present state and its *input*, which consists of the condition of the control buttons on the control panels located in the elevator and stationed on each floor. If the elevator is "at floor 3 and going down," it will respond to a floor 2 request to go down, but ignore a floor 2 request to go up! Once the next state is determined, a *state transition* is ordered by sending a command to the pulley motor, which drives the elevator to a new floor. The concepts of present state, next state, input, and state transition are fundamental in the study of sequential logic circuits.

Another simple example of a sequential device, and one that finds wide application in digital systems, is a counter. This device can be employed to perform such functions as totaling the number of cars entering a parking lot or keeping track of certain functions being performed within a large computer system. Counters are covered in detail in the next chapter.

6.1.1 Block Diagram Representation

In our study of combinational logic networks we found that we could represent these circuits as shown in Fig. 6.1a. The mathematical relationship that describes this network is

$$z_i = f_i(x_1, x_2, \ldots, x_n), \qquad i = 1, \ldots, m \tag{6.1}$$

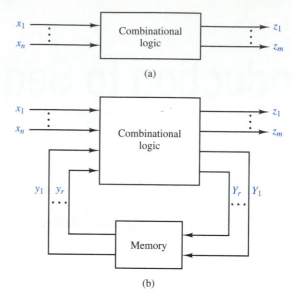

Figure 6.1 The sequential circuit model.
(a) Combinational logic circuit. **(b)** Sequential logic circuit.

This equation simply states that the output is a function of only the present input. All the signals in Eq. 6.1 are assumed to be either of the two values, 0 or 1.

The model for a sequential circuit is shown in Fig. 6.1b. The n-tuples $(x_1, \ldots, x_n)$ will be referred to as the *input*, the m-tuples $(z_1, \ldots, z_m)$ will be called the *output*, and the r-tuples $(y_1, \ldots, y_r)$ and $(Y_1, \ldots, Y_r)$ represent the *present state* and *next state*, respectively. The relationships that exist among these variables may be expressed mathematically as

$$z_i = g_i(x_1, \ldots, x_n, y_1, \ldots, y_r), \qquad i = 1, \ldots, m \qquad (6.2)$$

$$Y_i = h_i(x_1, \ldots, x_n, y_1, \ldots, y_r), \qquad i = 1, \ldots, r \qquad (6.3)$$

where g_i and h_i are Boolean functions. Equations 6.2 and 6.3 may be written in vector notation as

$$\mathbf{z} = \mathbf{g}(\mathbf{x}, \mathbf{y}) \qquad (6.4)$$

$$\mathbf{Y} = \mathbf{h}(\mathbf{x}, \mathbf{y}) \qquad (6.5)$$

where

$$\mathbf{z} = \begin{bmatrix} z_1 \\ z_2 \\ \vdots \\ z_m \end{bmatrix}, \qquad \mathbf{x} = \begin{bmatrix} x_1 \\ x_2 \\ \vdots \\ x_n \end{bmatrix}, \qquad \mathbf{y} = \begin{bmatrix} y_1 \\ y_2 \\ \vdots \\ y_r \end{bmatrix}, \qquad \mathbf{Y} = \begin{bmatrix} Y_1 \\ Y_2 \\ \vdots \\ Y_r \end{bmatrix} \qquad (6.6)$$

Note that z_i, x_i, y_i, and Y_i are all binary variables (their values are logic 0 or logic 1).

All the vectors in Eq. 6.6 are time dependent; we shall adopt the convention that vector $\mathbf{y}$ has the value $\mathbf{y}(t_k)$ at time t_k. Occasionally, we shall examine a signal $\mathbf{y}(t)$ at evenly spaced points in time. If $t_k = k\Delta t$ (k an integer), then

$$\mathbf{y}(t_k) = \mathbf{y}(k\Delta t) \triangleq \mathbf{y}^k \qquad (6.7)$$

where Δt is some fixed increment of time.

The memory devices in the block diagram of Fig. 6.1b may be of several types: semiconductor flip-flops, magnetic devices, delay lines, mechanical relays, rotation switches, and many others. Many of the semiconductor memory devices will be examined later.

The input signals x_i and output signals z_j for Fig. 6.1 may also assume a variety of forms. Several of these forms will be explored later.

6.1.2 State Tables and Diagrams

The logic equations 6.2 and 6.3 and vector equations 6.4 and 6.5 completely define the behavior of the sequential circuit modeled in Fig. 6.1b for a given memory device. However, the description, although complete, does not present a very lucid picture of the relationships that exist among the pertinent variables. The functional relationship that exists among the input, output, present state, and next state is very vividly illustrated by either the state table or the state diagram. The *state diagram* is a graphical representation of a sequential circuit in which the states of the circuit are represented by circles and the state transitions (the transfer from the present state $\mathbf{y}$ to the next state $\mathbf{Y}$) are shown by arrows. Each arrow is labeled with the input $\mathbf{x}$ and the resulting circuit output $\mathbf{z}$, as shown in Fig. 6.2a.

Figure 6.2b illustrates the *state table* representation. All circuit input vectors $\mathbf{x}$ are listed across the top, while all state vectors $\mathbf{y}$ are listed down the left side. Entries in the table are the next state $\mathbf{Y}$ and the output $\mathbf{z}$. The table is read as follows: For an input $\mathbf{x}$ with the sequential circuit in state $\mathbf{y}$, the circuit will proceed to the next state $\mathbf{Y}$ with an output $\mathbf{z}$.

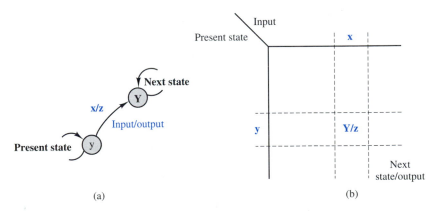

(a)   (b)

Figure 6.2   State tables and diagrams. **(a)** State diagram. **(b)** State table.

In practice, the state diagrams and tables are usually labeled using symbols rather than vectors. For example, consider a sequential circuit with two present-state variables y_1 and y_2. Then

$$\mathbf{y} = \begin{bmatrix} y_1 \\ y_2 \end{bmatrix}$$

Therefore, the vector $\mathbf{y}$ can have any of the four possible values:

$$\mathbf{y} = \begin{bmatrix} 0 \\ 0 \end{bmatrix} = A, \qquad \mathbf{y} = \begin{bmatrix} 1 \\ 0 \end{bmatrix} = C$$

$$\mathbf{y} = \begin{bmatrix} 0 \\ 1 \end{bmatrix} = B, \qquad \mathbf{y} = \begin{bmatrix} 1 \\ 1 \end{bmatrix} = D$$

(6.8)

Thus, the sequential circuit has only four possible states, which may be labeled A, B, C, and D. In general, if r represents the number of memory devices in a circuit with N_s states, these two quantities are related by the expression

$$2^{r-1} < N_s \le 2^r$$

(6.9)

This expression will be used in later chapters.

EXAMPLE 6.1

Consider a sequential circuit having one input variable x, two state variables y_1 and y_2, and one output variable z.

Inputs: $x = 0$
             $x = 1$
States: $[y_1, y_2] = [00] \equiv A$
             $[y_1, y_2] = [01] \equiv B$
             $[y_1, y_2] = [10] \equiv C$
             $[y_1, y_2] = [11] \equiv D$
Outputs: $z = 0$
             $z = 1$

The state diagram for this sequential circuit is defined by Fig. 6.3. Let us now assume that the circuit is initially in state A; if an input of $x = 0$ is now applied, the next state is D and the output is $z = 0$. This information may be read from either the state diagram or the state table. Now consider the application of the following input sequence to the circuit:

$$x = 0110101100$$

The circuit will behave as follows when the initial state is A:

Time:	0	1	2	3	4	5	6	7	8	9	10
Present state:	A	D	B	A	D	B	B	A	C	C	C
Input:	0	1	1	0	1	0	1	1	0	0	
Next state:	D	B	A	D	B	B	A	C	C	C	
Output:	0	1	0	0	1	1	0	1	1	1	

Hence, this input sequence applied to the machine in state A causes the output sequence

$$z = 0100110111$$

and leaves the circuit in final state C.

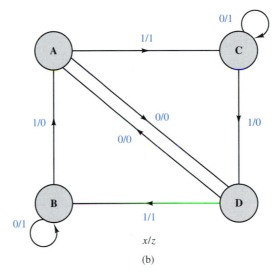

	Input x	
	0	1
A	D/0	C/1
Present B	B/1	A/0
state C	C/1	D/0
D	A/0	B/1

(a)

(b)

Figure 6.3   Example sequential circuit. **(a)** State table. **(b)** State diagram.

6.2 Memory Devices

As indicated earlier, an integral part of a sequential machine is the memory unit. Our discussion will be concerned primarily with the external characteristics of the memory devices and not their detailed internal functions. In other words, our analysis will be confined to the use of these elements in the design of digital systems.

In switching circuit applications, most memory elements are *bistable* electronic circuits; that is, they exist indefinitely in one of two possible stable states, 0 and 1. Binary data are stored in a memory element by placing the element into the 0 state to store a 0 and into the 1 state to store a 1. The output Q of the circuit indicates the present state of the memory. Each memory circuit has one or more *excitation inputs*, so called because they are used to "excite" or drive the circuit into a desired state. The different memory devices are typically named in accordance with their particular excitation inputs, which differ from device to device.

The two memory element types most commonly used in switching circuits are latches and flip-flops. A *latch* is a memory element whose excitation input signals control the state of the device. If a latch has an excitation input signal that forces the output of the device to 1, it is called a *set latch*. If it has an excitation input signal that forces the device output to 0, it is called a *reset latch*. If the device has both set and reset excitation signals, it is called a *set-reset latch*. Latch operation is illustrated in Fig. 6.4a.

A *flip-flop* differs from a latch in that it has a control signal called a *clock*. The clock signal issues a command to the flip-flop, allowing it to change states in accordance with its excitation input signals. In both latches and flip-flops, the next state is determined by the excitation inputs. However, as illustrated in Fig. 6.4, a latch changes state immediately in accordance with its input excitation signals, while a flip-flop waits for its clock signal before changing states. The final state of a flip-flop is determined by its excitation values at the time the clock signal occurs. In this manner, multiple flip-flops in a sequential circuit can be synchronized to a common clock signal so that they all change states together.

Formal procedures for designing flip-flop and latch circuits will be presented in Chapter 10. In this chapter, generic flip-flop and latch circuits will be described and several TTL modules that contain flip-flops and latches will be discussed. Table 6.1 gives a listing of the devices to be covered. Many other devices are commercially available. We have selected these to give the reader an introduction to the various features available. You must understand these features so that you can choose a proper device for each situation as you design sequential circuits.

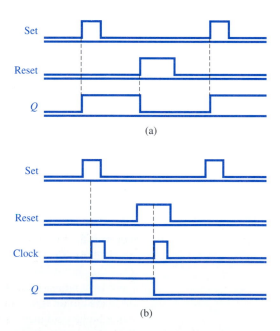

Figure 6.4 Latch and flip-flop timing. **(a)** Latch responds immediately to excitation. **(b)** Flip-flop responds only on a clock signal.

TABLE 6.1   **TTL MEMORY ELEMENTS [1]**

Device	Number of Elements	Element Description
74LS73A	2	Negative-edge triggered JK flip-flop with clear
7474	2	Positive-edge-triggered D flip-flop with preset and clear
74LS75	4	D latch with enable
7476	2	Pulse-triggered JK flip-flop with preset and clear
74111	2	Master–slave JK flip-flop with preset, clear, and data lockout
74116	2	4-Bit hazard-free D latch with clear and dual enable
74175	4	Positive-edge triggered D flip-flop with clear
74273	8	Positive-edge triggered D flip-flop with clear
74276	4	Negative-edge triggered J$\bar{\text{K}}$ flip-flop with preset and clear
74279	4	SR latch with active-low inputs

6.3 Latches

6.3.1 Set–Reset Latch

Using Feedback to Create Simple Latches

Consider the OR gate of Fig. 6.5a. Assume both inputs are at logic 0. If the output is connected back to one of the inputs as shown in Fig. 6.5b, the gate remains stable with an output of 0. Suppose a logic 1 is applied to the unconnected input S, as shown in Fig. 6.5c. What happens to the output of the OR gate? It changes to logic 1. Thus the device output Q has been *set* to logic 1. Changing the input S back to logic 0 leaves the output Q at logic 1 because of the feedback to the other OR gate input, as shown in Fig. 6.5d. So this device is permanently set to logic 1 and is therefore called a *set latch*.

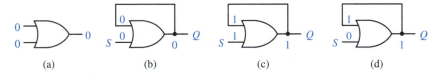

(a)   (b)   (c)   (d)

Figure 6.5   Set latch. **(a)** OR gate. **(b)** Feedback added. **(c)** Output set to 1. **(d)** Feedback holds Q = 1.

Let us replace the OR gate of Fig. 6.5 by a NOR and NOT gate cascade, as shown in Fig. 6.6a. This is an equivalent set latch circuit. If we use the output of the NOR gate as the output Q of the latch, we generate the circuit of Fig. 6.6b. Examine the operation of these cascaded gates. The output of the NOR gate is initially at logic 1 if logic 0 is present on both its inputs. The NOT gate feedback signal is logic 0, yielding a stable condition. Placing a logic 1 on the unconnected input R of the NOR gate forces its output to logic 0, as shown in Fig. 6.6c and forces the feedback signal to logic 1. Thus the latch output Q is reset to logic 0. If R returns to logic 0, as shown in Fig. 6.6d, no change occurs at the output because of the feedback signal. Therefore, the Q output will remain at logic 0 permanently, ignoring further changes in input R. Hence this circuit is called a *reset latch*. Figure 6.6e presents another view of the circuit.

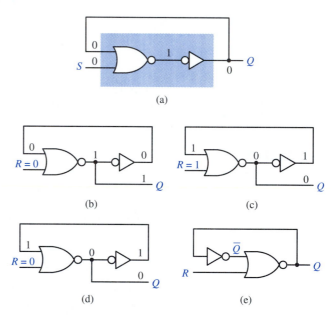

Figure 6.6 Reset latch. **(a)** Set latch redrawn. **(b)** Reset latch stable with $Q = 1$. **(c)** $R = 1$ resets latch to $Q = 0$. **(d)** Further changes inhibited. **(e)** Alternative view of reset latch.

Set–Reset Latch: NOR Structure

Devices that stay permanently in one logic state are not very useful except in very unusual design situations. If we combine the features of both latches described previously into one circuit, we can set or reset the latch circuit as needed. Let us replace the NOT gate in the circuit of Fig. 6.6a with a two-input NOR gate, $N2$, connected to operate as a NOT gate as shown in Fig. 6.7a. The device still operates as a set latch. Now, if we disconnect the lower input of NOR gate $N2$ as shown in Fig. 6.7b, this input will function as a reset excitation for the device (the same function as in Fig. 6.6e). Thus we have created a *set–reset latch* (*SR latch*) with two 2-input NOR gates. The more traditional view of the circuit is the cross-coupled form of Fig. 6.7c. Let us adopt the logic symbol of Fig. 6.7d to represent the SR latch. We will use it as a building block for other circuits in this section.

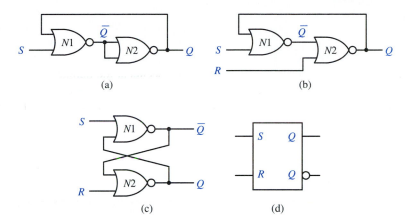

Figure 6.7   Set-reset latch (SR latch). **(a)** S latch redrawn. **(b)** SR latch.
(c) Traditional view of SR latch. **(d)** Logic symbol of SR latch.

SR Latch: NAND Structure

Can we produce the same functional devices that we derived with NOR gates
by using NAND gates? Consider the cross-coupled NAND gates of Fig. 6.8a. If
both the S and R inputs are held at logic 0, the NOT gates apply logic 1 signals
to the cross-coupled NAND gates. But if one input of a two-input NAND gate
is held at logic 1, it acts like a NOT gate; that is,

$$\text{Gate } N1 \ (S = 0): \quad \overline{\overline{S} \cdot \overline{Q}} = \overline{1 \cdot \overline{Q}} = \overline{\overline{Q}} = Q$$

$$\text{Gate } N2 \ (R = 0): \quad \overline{\overline{R} \cdot Q} = \overline{1 \cdot Q} = \overline{Q}$$

So the cross-coupled gates of Fig. 6.8a assume the function of a pair of
NOT gates when the inputs are $S = R = 0$, as shown in Fig. 6.8b. (The NOT
gates are drawn with dotted lines within the NAND gates to illustrate that the
NAND gates are effectively acting as inverters.) This NOT gate loop of Fig. 6.8b
forms the bistable storage cell for the latch. Output Q feeds through one NOT
gate to generate $\overline{Q}$, and $\overline{Q}$ feeds through the second NOT gate to regenerate Q.

If either of the inputs S or R is activated, that is, set to logic 1, while the
other is held at 0, one portion of the symmetric cross-coupled configuration is
altered by a logic 0 being applied to the input of one of the NAND gates; that is,

$$\text{Gate } N1 \ (S = 1): \quad \overline{\overline{S} \cdot \overline{Q}} = \overline{0 \cdot \overline{Q}} = \overline{0} = 1$$

or

$$\text{Gate } N2 \ (R = 1): \quad \overline{\overline{R} \cdot Q} = \overline{0 \cdot Q} = \overline{0} = 1$$

Thus, a logic 0 input to the NAND gate drives its output to logic 1. The logic
1 on the output of the active NAND gate then forces the output of the other
NAND in the pair to logic 0, since

$$\text{Gate } N2 \ (S = 1, \ R = 0): \quad \overline{Q} = \overline{\overline{R} \cdot Q} = \overline{\overline{0} \cdot 1} = \overline{1 \cdot 1} = \overline{1} = 0$$

or

$$\text{Gate } N1 \ (S = 0, \ R = 1): \quad Q = \overline{\overline{S} \cdot \overline{Q}} = \overline{\overline{0} \cdot 1} = \overline{1 \cdot 1} = \overline{1} = 0$$

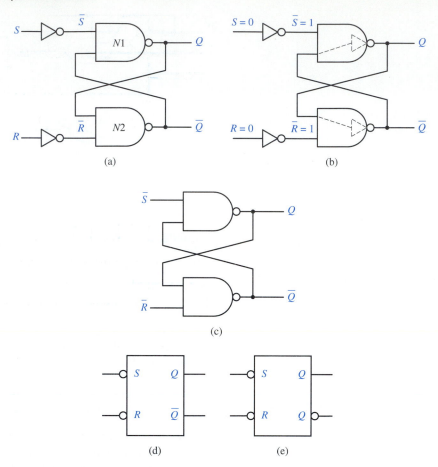

Figure 6.8 NAND SR latch. **(a)** Logic diagram. **(b)** Storage mode. **(c)** Reduced logic. **(d)** Logic symbol 1. **(e)** Logic symbol 2.

So a logic 1 on S will set Q to logic 1, which forces $\bar{Q}$ to logic 0. In other words, a logic 1 on S *sets* the latch. In the same manner, a logic 1 on input R will set $\bar{Q}$ to logic 1, which will subsequently drive output Q to logic 0, *resetting* the latch.

Suppose we drop the two NOT gates from the circuit inputs as shown in Fig. 6.8c. The inputs to the device become $\bar{S}$ and $\bar{R}$. In other words, the inputs to the latch are active low (normally high in the active state and transition to low to activate the device). Let us adopt the logic symbols illustrated in Figs. 6.8d and e to represent an SR latch with active-low inputs.

SR Latch Timing Diagrams and Delay Parameters

The operation of any latch circuit may be described using a timing diagram. Figure 6.9a illustrates the action induced in the cross-coupled NOR latch of

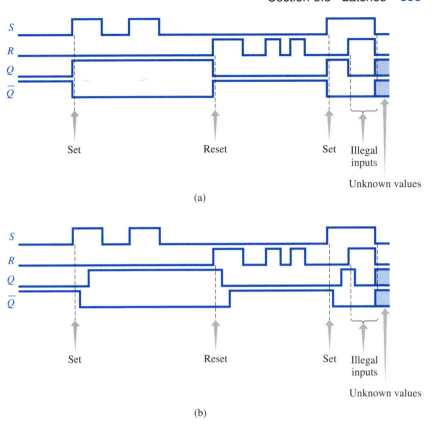

(a)

(b)

Figure 6.9   Set-reset latch timing diagram. **(a)** Ideal (zero-gate-delay) case.
(b) Actual timing with non-zero gate delays.

Fig. 6.7c by applying sequences of pulses to the set and reset inputs, S and R.
The waveforms for S and R have been selected to illustrate the various features
of the latch. The initial state of the latch is assumed to be logic 0 ($Q = 0$). The
device responds to the first of a series of pulses on one of its inputs, but ignores
subsequent ones until a pulse on the other input has intervened.

Note that placing logic 1 signals on both the R and S inputs forces both
outputs, Q and $\bar{Q}$, to logic 0. When the two inputs are returned to logic 0, a
race condition is created, and therefore we cannot be certain which state the
device will assume. In the real world, it is virtually impossible for two events
to occur at exactly the same time, even if we want them to! If the R signal is
returned to logic 0 before S, the final state of Q will be a logic 1. If S is returned
to logic 0 first, the device will be reset to logic 0. If R and S are returned to
logic 0 at exactly or very nearly the same time, the two NOR gates will race
to gain control of the output Q. If both are exactly equivalent electrically, the
output will oscillate! In practical circuits, one of the gates will win the race, but

we can't predict which one. Consequently, we restrict the use of the SR latch to exclude the input combination $S = R = 1$.

The timing diagram of Fig. 6.9a represents an ideal situation in which all gate propagation delays are considered to be 0. In reality, every circuit output requires a nonzero amount of time to respond to changes on its inputs, as specified by delay parameters t_{PLH} and t_{PHL} which we defined in Chapter 2. Recall that the mnemonic t_{PLH} designates the delay time between an input change and a corresponding low-to-high transition of an output. Likewise, t_{PHL} is the delay between an input change and a corresponding high-to-low output transition. For a latch circuit, t_{PLH} and t_{PHL} parameters represent the sum of the propagation delays through the gates between a given latch input and output, with separate delay parameters usually specified for each input/output pair.

For example, Fig. 6.10 illustrates the timing behavior of the SR latch of Fig. 6.7c. Following a change in S from $0 \rightarrow 1$, note that output $\bar{Q}$ changes from $1 \rightarrow 0$ after propagation delay t_{PHL} through NOR gate $N1$, and then the feedback signal causes the Q output to change from $0 \rightarrow 1$ after propagation time t_{PLH} through gate $N2$. Thus, output $\bar{Q}$ always changes before output Q when setting an SR latch built from cross-coupled NOR gates. Therefore, t_{PHL} from input S to output $\bar{Q}$ of the latch involves a single gate delay, whereas t_{PLH} from input S to output Q includes two gate delays. A similar relationship exists between input R and the two outputs. When resetting the latch with a pulse on input R, output Q changes before output $\bar{Q}$, as illustrated in Fig. 6.10. As a result of these non-zero propagation delays through the gates of the latch circuit, Fig. 6.9b presents a more realistic picture of the operation of the latch than the ideal timing diagram presented in Fig. 6.9a.

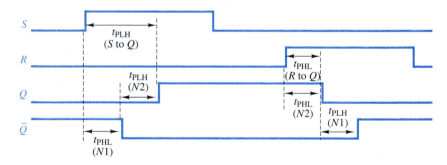

Figure 6.10 SR latch propagation delays.

SR Latch Excitation Table and Characteristic Equation

The logical operation of the SR latch is summarized in the *excitation table* of Fig. 6.11a. The excitation table is simply the state table of the latch, showing the state transitions for each combination of excitation inputs. Columns S and

Excitation inputs		Present state	Next state	
S	R	Q	Q^*	
0	0	0	0	No change
0	0	1	1	
0	1	0	0	Reset
0	1	1	0	
1	0	0	1	Set
1	0	1	1	
1	1	0	×	Not allowed
1	1	1	×	

(a)

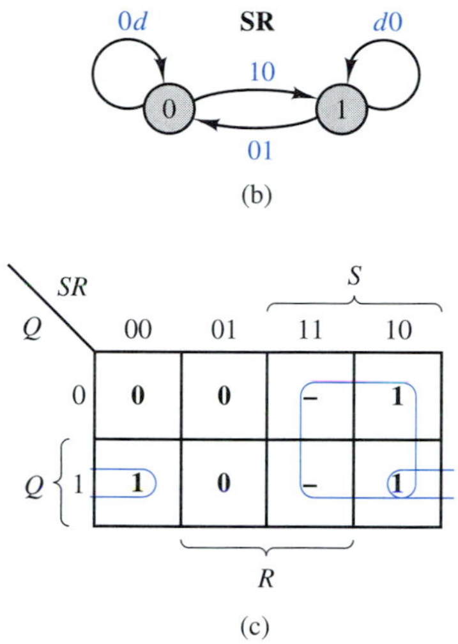

(b)

(c)

Figure 6.11 SR latch characteristics. **(a)** Excitation table. **(b)** State diagram. **(c)** K-map of latch output Q^*.

R are the inputs applied to an SR latch while it is in state Q. The column labeled Q is the state of the SR latch *before* an input combination is applied to S and R. The column labeled Q^* is the state of the SR latch *after* the SR inputs have been applied and a steady-state result has been achieved. We call column Q the *present state* of the SR latch and column Q^* the *next state*.

The information of Fig. 6.11a can be represented as a state diagram, as shown in Fig. 6.11b, and plotted in K-map form, as shown in Fig. 6.11c, where the value of the next state Q^* is plotted as a function of the inputs, S and R, and the present state Q. From this K-map can be derived the following logic expression for Q^*, called the *characteristic equation* of the SR latch:

$$Q^* = S + \bar{R}Q \tag{6.10}$$

The characteristic equation is so called because it characterizes the operation of the latch. For example, we can classify the operation of the latch into three cases.

Case 1: $S = R = 0$. Equation 6.10 reduces to $Q^* = Q$, which indicates that the state does not change.

Case 2: $S = 1$, $R = 0$. Equation 6.10 reduces to $Q^* = 1$, representing the set operation.

Case 3: $S = 0$, $R = 1$. Equation 6.10 reduces to $Q^* = 0$, representing the reset operation.

74279 Quad SR Latch Module

SR latches are commercially available as the SN74279 [1] module, as listed in Table 6.1. The 74279 module has four latch units, two as illustrated in Fig. 6.8 and two as shown in Fig. 6.12a. The latter pair of latches each include an extra

$\bar{S}$ input, with both active-low inputs $\bar{S}_1$ and $\bar{S}_2$ connected to the same NAND gate, as shown in Fig. 6.12b, so activating either of them will set the latch. To minimize the overall size of the module, only the true outputs, Q, are brought out to external pins on the package.

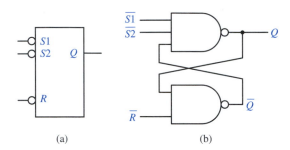

Figure 6.12 74279 latch with two set inputs. **(a)** Logic symbol. **(b)** Logic diagram. *Source:* The TTL Data Book Volume 2, Texas Instruments Inc., 1985.

Typical propagation delays for the 74279 are 12 ns for t_{PLH} from any input $\bar{S}$ to output Q and 15 ns from input $\bar{R}$ to output Q [1]. Note that the change in R must propagate through two gates to affect the output and therefore exhibits a longer propagation delay than changes due to $\bar{S}$.

6.3.2 Gated SR Latch

It is often desirable to use a special control signal to inhibit state changes in an SR latch while S and R are changing. When S and R are ready, this control signal is activated to enable the latch to respond to the new S and R values. This device is commonly referred to as a *gated SR latch*, since the control signal can be thought of as opening a gate through which signals on the S and R inputs propagate to the output.

Circuit Structure

In Fig. 6.13a, a control signal, C, is added to an SR latch to apply the inputs S and R. The two AND gates apply the control signals S and R during time intervals when the enable signal C is high (logic 1). When C is logic 0, the inputs of the SR latch are held in the $S = R = 0$ (no change) state. So the operation of the latch is as follows: when $C = 0$, no change occurs and thus the device is stable; when $C = 1$, the SR latch excitation table of Fig. 6.11a and the SR latch characteristic equation, Eq. 6.10, describe its function.

If we change the AND gates to NAND gates and use cross-coupled NAND gates for the SR latch, the circuit of Fig. 6.13b results. Substitution of the circuit of Fig. 6.8c for the latch symbol in Fig. 6.13b produces the NAND gate implementation of the gated SR latch shown in Fig. 6.13c. The generic logic symbol for the gated SR latch is presented in Fig. 6.13d.

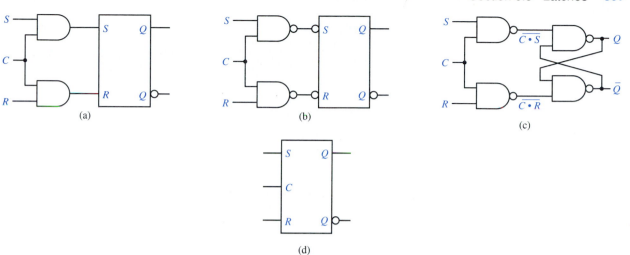

Figure 6.13 Gated SR latch. **(a)** With NOR SR latch. **(b)** With NAND SR latch. **(c)** NAND logic diagram. **(d)** Logic symbol.

Enable inputs	Excitation inputs		Present state	Next state	
C	S	R	Q	Q^*	
0	×	×	0	0	Hold
0	×	×	1	1	
1	0	0	0	0	No change
1	0	0	1	1	
1	0	1	0	0	Reset
1	0	1	1	0	
1	1	0	0	1	Set
1	1	0	1	1	
1	1	1	0	×	Not allowed
1	1	1	1	×	

(a)

(b)

Figure 6.14 Gated SR latch characteristics. **(a)** Excitation table. **(b)** State diagram.

Characteristic Equation

The complete excitation table and state diagram of the gated SR latch are given in Figs. 6.14a and b, respectively. From the excitation table we can derive the following characteristic equation for the gated SR latch:

$$Q^* = SC + \bar{R}Q + \bar{C}Q \qquad (6.11)$$

Note that when $C = 0$, Eq. 6.11 reduces to $Q^* = Q$, which means that the present state is *held*. Substituting $C = 1$ in Eq. 6.11 converts it to $Q^* = S + \bar{R}Q$, the characteristic equation of the simple SR latch, and thus the latch is *enabled*.

6.3.3 Delay Latch

One of the most frequent operations used in digital systems is storing data. Bits are moved from place to place and stored for varying periods of time. In these applications, the memory element excitation input is simply the data to be stored. In other words, we need a device that transfers a logic value on its excitation input D into the cross-coupled storage cell of a latch.

Circuit Structure and Characteristic Equation

The logic symbol of the *delay latch*, or simply *D latch*, is shown in Fig. 6.15a. We can make such a device from a gated SR latch. Examine Fig. 6.14a, the excitation table of the gated SR latch. If we assign $S = D$ and $R = \bar{D}$, then when enabled we restrict the operation of the latch to the four rows in Fig. 6.14a in which $S = 1$ and $R = 0$, the set condition, or $S = 0$ and $R = 1$, the reset condition. The gated SR latch excitation table can therefore be reduced to the D latch excitation table given in Fig. 6.16a. The corresponding state diagram is shown in Fig. 6.16b.

A NAND implementation of the D latch is shown in Fig. 6.16b. Note that this circuit is simply a gated SR latch with inputs $S = D$ and $R = \bar{D}$. An

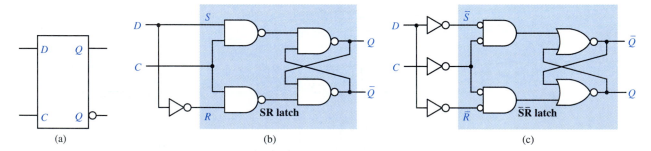

Figure 6.15   Delay latch (D latch). **(a)** Logic symbol. **(b)** NAND implementation. **(c)** NOR implementation

Enable input	Excitation input	Present state	Next state	
C	D	Q	Q^*	
0	×	0	0	Hold
0	×	1	1	
1	0	0	0	Store 0
1	0	1	0	
1	1	0	1	Store 1
1	1	1	1	

(a)

(b)

Figure 6.16   D latch characteristics. **(a)** Excitation table. **(b)** State diagram.

equivalent D latch implementation using NOR gates is given in Fig. 6.15c. In this circuit, an $\bar{S}\bar{R}$ latch is used, with inverters on the D and C inputs to make both inputs active high. Therefore, the functional operation of this NOR implementation is identical to that of the NAND implementation of Fig. 6.15b.

The characteristic equation of the D latch can be derived from that of the gated SR latch by substituting D for S and $\bar{D}$ for R in Eq. 6.11, as follows:

$$Q^* = SC + \bar{R}Q + \bar{C}Q$$
$$= DC + (\bar{\bar{D}})Q + \bar{C}Q$$
$$= DC + DQ + \bar{C}Q$$
$$= DC + \bar{C}Q \tag{6.12}$$

Characteristic equation 6.12 describes the operation of the D latch. When the enable signal is low, ($C = 0$), Eq. 6.12 reduces to $Q^* = Q$. In this case, the latch is placed in the *hold*, that is, no change, operating mode, and it holds the last value of D that was entered. In other words, when $C = 0$, data are held, or stored, in the latch. Substituting $C = 1$ in Eq. 6.12 gives $Q^* = D$. Thus, the next state Q^* is forced to be the value of the input excitation D whenever the enable signal C is high; that is, the excitation input D is gated directly to output Q. In this case, the D latch is said to be in the *gated* or *enabled* mode.

The operation of the D latch is illustrated in the timing diagram of Fig. 6.17. Note that, when C is high, any and all changes on D will pass through to the latch's output. So the latch stores the last value of D that is present on its input when the enable signal transitions from high to low, that is, for a $1 \rightarrow 0$ transition on signal C.

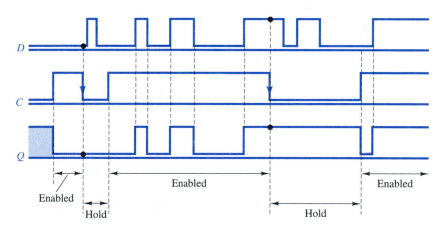

Figure 6.17   D Latch Timing Diagram

Setup Time, Hold Time, and Pulse-width Constraints

To ensure that a specific value on excitation input D will determine the final state of the latch, D must not be allowed to change too near the time at which

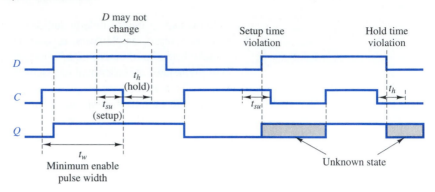

Figure 6.18 D Latch Timing Constraints

the enable signal makes its transition from high to low. Two time constraint parameters are defined for every latch device to identify when the excitation input must be held constant to guarantee correct operation.

The latch *setup time*, denoted t_{su}, is defined as the period of time immediately preceding the enable signal transition during which the excitation input must be stable; that is, the excitation input must be "set up" at least t_{su} prior to the enable signal transition and should not change until well after the transition.

The latch *hold time*, denoted t_h, is defined as the period of time immediately following the enable signal transition during which D should not change. Therefore, the excitation input must be held constant for at least t_h following the enable signal transition to ensure that the correct value has been latched.

Setup and hold times are illustrated in the diagram of Fig. 6.18. Here we have shown $t_{PLH} = t_{PHL} = 0$ to make the diagram easier to understand. Note the two constraint violations on the timing diagram. The change in D from $0 \rightarrow 1$ too close to the clock edge represents a setup time violation, and therefore the latch output may or may not change from $0 \rightarrow 1$ as desired. Likewise, the change in D from $1 \rightarrow 0$ too soon after the clock edge may result in an unpredictable state.

In addition to setup and hold time constraints, most gated latches require a minimum pulse width on the enable input to guarantee a correct state change. This minimum pulse width is denoted by t_w, as shown on Fig. 6.18. Any pulse whose width is shorter than the specified minimum t_w may not be sufficient to initiate a desired state change.

Consequently, for a given gated latch circuit, it is the responsibility of the designer to ensure that all enable pulses are of sufficient width to cause state changes and that, for any enable input transition at time T, no excitation input changes occur within the time period $[T - t_{su}, T + t_h]$.

74LS75 Quad D Latch Module

A number of standard TTL modules contain D latches. Four bistable D latches with enable inputs are available in the SN74LS75. The logic circuit for the D latch circuit used in this device, displayed in Fig. 6.19a, is a direct implementation of the D latch characteristic equation, Eq. 6.12.

The operating modes for this circuit are controlled by the enable signal C. When C is held at logic 0 as illustrated in Fig. 6.19b, the upper AND gate is disabled, so its output sends a logic 0 to the NOR gate. A NOR gate with one of its inputs held at logic 0 acts like a NOT gate for its other input line, as shown in Fig. 6.19b. Note also that holding C at logic 0 places a logic 1 on the lower AND gate, making it behave as a transparent gate for the latch feedback signal Q. In this mode of operation, the device resembles two NOT gates configured as a bistable storage element. We call this the *hold* or *storage* mode.

Now suppose we change the enable input C to logic 1 as shown in Fig. 6.19c. This mode of operation enables a path from input D through the upper AND gate and the NOR gate to the latch's output Q ($Q = D$). In this mode the input is gated directly to the output, as shown in Fig. 6.19c. We call this the *gated* operating mode. Note that the SN74LS75 gives the same operating modes as the previous D latch design in Fig. 6.15.

Correct operation of the latch requires that there be a delay between changes in D or C and any corresponding changes in the feedback signal Q, so that next state, Q^*, will indeed be determined by the present state, Q, and the inputs. This delay is provided by the propagation delays through the gates of the two-level latch circuit. We often show this delay as illustrated in the sequential circuit model for the latch shown in Fig. 6.19d, in which the the delays of the

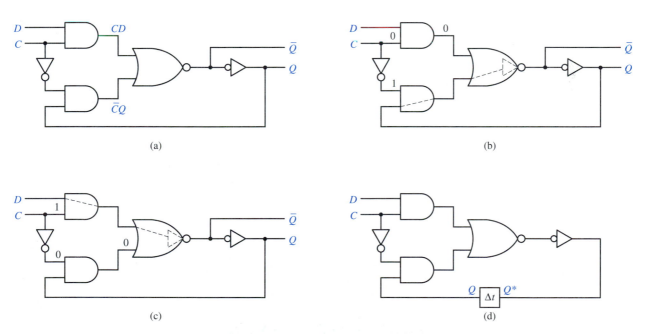

(a)

(b)

(c)

(d)

Figure 6.19   A second D latch configuration, the 74LS75. **(a)** Logic diagram.
(b) Hold, or storage, mode. **(c)** Gated mode. **(d)** Sequential circuit model.
Source: The TTL Data Book Volume 2, Texas Instruments Inc., 1985.

logic gates are modeled as a single lumped parameter, Δt. Typical delay times and timing constraint values for the 74LS75 are listed in Table 6.2.

TABLE 6.2   PROPAGATION DELAYS AND TIME CONSTRAINTS FOR THE SN74LS75 [1]

Timing Parameter	Typical Value (ns)
$t_{\mathrm{PLH}}\,(D \rightarrow Q)$	15
$t_{\mathrm{PHL}}\,(D \rightarrow Q)$	9
$t_{\mathrm{PLH}}\,(D \rightarrow \bar{Q})$	12
$t_{\mathrm{PHL}}\,(D \rightarrow \bar{Q})$	7
$t_{\mathrm{PLH}}\,(C \rightarrow Q)$	15
$t_{\mathrm{PHL}}\,(C \rightarrow Q)$	14
$t_{\mathrm{PLH}}\,(C \rightarrow \bar{Q})$	16
$t_{\mathrm{PHL}}\,(C \rightarrow \bar{Q})$	7
t_{su} (minimum setup time for D)	20
t_{h} (minimum hold time for D)	5
t_{w} (minimum pulse width on C)	20

74116 Dual 4-Bit Hazard-free D Latch Module

The D latch circuit of Fig. 6.19a uses a minimum number of logic gates. However, it contains a static 1 hazard, making it subject to output glitches; that is, its output may momentarily change to 0 when it should be a constant 1 level during certain input changes. A hazard-free design for this D latch may be needed in some applications to eliminate these glitches at the output. We can design a hazard-free version of this circuit by examining a K-map of its characteristic equation, presented in Fig. 6.20a. The static 1 hazard occurs in traversing from the product term DC to product term $Q\bar{C}$ on this map.

We can eliminate the static 1 hazard by adding a third product term DQ as shown in the K-map of Fig. 6.20b, making the logic equation

$$Q^* = DC + \bar{C}Q + DC$$

The resulting logic diagram for the hazard-free design thus requires three AND gates, as shown in Fig. 6.20c.

This design gives the principal features of the SN74116, a dual 4-bit D latch TTL module. The SN74116 also adds a clear feature and uses an active-low enable. Its operation is described by the functional diagram of Fig. 6.20d. Note that the device has two active-low enable signals $\overline{C1}$ and $\overline{C2}$, and thus the *hold* mode for the chip requires either or both of these enable signals to be high. For the *gated* mode, both enable signals must be low.

Note also that a reset signal, labeled $\overline{CLR}$, has been provided by changing the output NOT gate to a NOR gate. A logic 0 on the $\overline{CLR}$ line forces the output

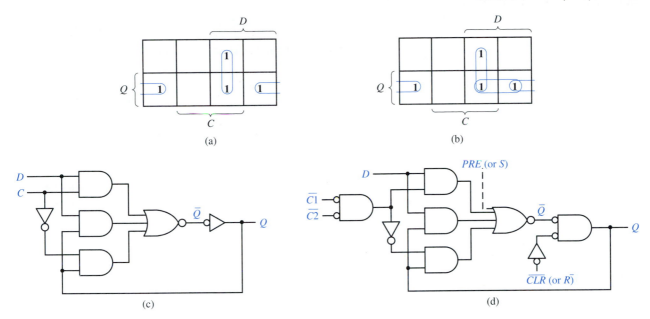

Figure 6.20   Hazard-free D latch, the SN74116. **(a)** K-map for Q^* of a D latch. **(b)** K-map for hazard-free D latch. **(c)** Hazard-free D latch logic diagram. **(d)** SN74116 functional diagram.

Q to logic 0. In addition, a set control input *PRE*, for preset, capable of forcing the output Q to logic 1, could have been added as shown by the dashed line if an extra pin were available. The $\overline{CLR}$ and *PRE* control inputs in Fig. 6.20d are referred to as *asynchronous* control lines, since they affect the state of the latch directly, without being synchronized with the enable signal. Groups of latches are commonly forced to a desired initial state by sending a pulse to their $\overline{CLR}$ or *PRE* control inputs by a single RESET signal line.

6.4 Flip-flops

The latch circuits presented thus far are not appropriate for use in synchronous sequential logic circuits. When the enable signal C is active, the excitation inputs are gated directly to the output Q. Thus, any change in the excitation input immediately causes a change in the latch output. Recall our model for the synchronous sequential circuit, presented in Fig. 6.1. The output signals from the memory elements are the input signals to the combinational logic, and vice versa. When its enable is active, a latch acts like a combinational circuit, too! Thus we have the possibility of two cascaded combinational circuits feeding each other, generating oscillations and unstable transient behavior. This problem is solved by using a special timing control signal called a *clock* to restrict the times at which the states of the memory elements may change.

6.4.1 Master–Slave SR Flip-Flops

Circuit Structure and Operation

One method to prevent the unstable behavior just described is to employ two latches in a *master–slave* configuration, as shown in Fig. 6.21a. The enable signals of the two latches are driven by complementary versions of a clock signal. When the clock signal C is low, the master latch is in the gated mode and the slave, in the hold mode. Changes on the excitation input signals S and R are gated into the master latch while the slave latch ignores any changes on its inputs. When the clock changes to logic 1, the two latches exchange roles. The slave latch enters the gated mode, sending the output of the master latch to the flip-flop output Q, while the master latch enters the hold mode and ignores any further changes on its inputs.

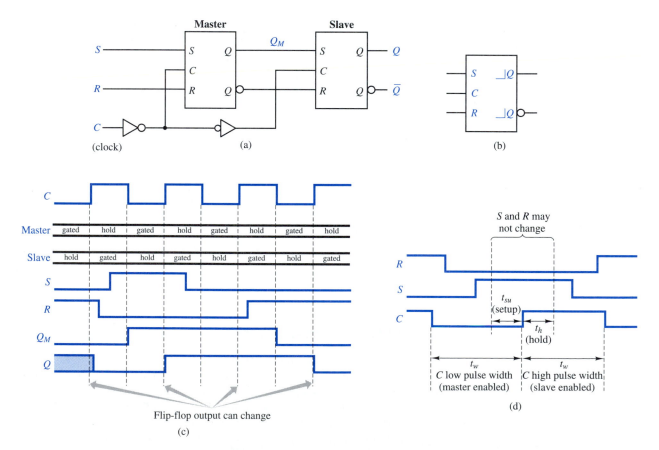

Figure 6.21   Master-slave SR flip-flop. **(a)** Logic diagram. **(b)** Pulse-triggered device logic symbol. **(c)** Timing behavior. **(d)** Timing constraints

Master–slave flip-flops like the one in Fig. 6.21a are sometimes called *pulse triggered* because they require both logic $0 \rightarrow 1$ and $1 \rightarrow 0$ transitions on the clock input in order to operate properly. On one transition the master operates, that is, enters the enabled mode; on the other transition, the slave operates. The logic symbol of Fig. 6.21b indicates the pulse-triggered nature of the device by showing the clock edge transition that enables the slave at the flip-flop output terminals Q and $\bar{Q}$. In Fig. 6.21b, the rising transition indicates that the flip-flop outputs Q and $\bar{Q}$ change on the positive edge of a pulse on the clock signal.

Timing Characteristics

If the SR flip-flop is used in a synchronous sequential circuit, an unstable oscillation cannot occur because, at all times, either the master latch or the slave latch is in the hold mode, effectively blocking all unstable transient behavior. This timing behavior is illustrated in Fig. 6.21c.

Note that the S and R inputs to the master latch should be stable before the clock transition that puts the master into the hold mode. Therefore, the flip-flop inputs are subject to the same setup and hold time constraints described earlier for gated latches. Figure 6.21d illustrates the setup and hold times for the SR flip-flop of Fig. 6.21a. Since the excitation inputs affect only the master latch, the setup and hold times are defined relative to the rising edge of the clock signal, which is the clock transition that changes the master latch from the gated mode to the hold mode. The excitation inputs of the slave latch are connected to the outputs of the master latch and are therefore not directly affected by the external excitation inputs.

Figure 6.21d also illustrates minimum clock pulse-width constraints for the master–slave flip-flop. The low pulse-width parameter is the minimum pulse width required for proper operation of the master latch, while the high pulse-width parameter is the minimum pulse width required for the slave latch. The sum of these two pulse widths determines the minimum period of any clock signal to be used for the flip-flop.

Excitation Table
and Characteristic Equation

The excitation table and state diagram for the SR master–slave flip-flop are presented in Figs. 6.22a and b, respectively. Note that the columns S, R, and Q of the excitation table denote the conditions on the flip-flop signals *before* the clock pulse is applied. The column Q^* denotes the flip-flop output *after* the clock pulse has been applied. Comparing this table to Fig. 6.11a, we see that the operation of the master–slave SR flip-flop is similar to that of the simple SR latch. Likewise, the state diagrams are identical, although the latch changes states immediately when S or R changes, whereas all flip-flop state changes are triggered by clock pulses. Consequently, the same characteristic equation describes the operation of both devices:

$$Q^* = S + \bar{R}Q \tag{6.13}$$

The difference is that the latch output reacts immediately to any input changes, while the flip-flop output changes are controlled by the clock pulse C. Note that both negative and positive edges are required for C.

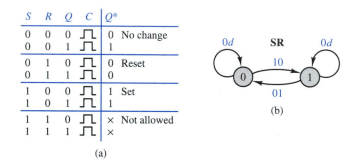

S	R	Q	C	Q^*	
0	0	0	⊓	0	No change
0	0	1	⊓	1	
0	1	0	⊓	0	Reset
0	1	1	⊓	0	
1	0	0	⊓	1	Set
1	0	1	⊓	1	
1	1	0	⊓	×	Not allowed
1	1	1	⊓	×	

(a)

(b)

Figure 6.22 SR master-slave flip-flop characteristics. **(a)** Excitation table. **(b)** State diagram.

6.4.2 Master–Slave D Flip-flops

We can build a master–slave D flip-flop from two D latches as shown in Fig. 6.23a. Note that this flip-flop operates in the same manner as the SR version of Fig. 6.22. The master latch is gated when the clock is low and the slave, when the clock is high. The logic symbol for this pulse-triggered device is shown in Fig. 6.23b. Note that the logic symbol indicates that the outputs change on the positive edge of a pulse on the clock signal.

The excitation table of the master–slave D flip-flop is given in Fig. 6.24a and the state diagram in Fig. 6.24b. The behavior of this device is illustrated on the timing diagram of Fig. 6.24c. At the top of the diagram, the gated latch is indicated by the symbols M and S for master and slave. When $C = 0$, the master is gated so that its input is passed to the slave. On the $0 \rightarrow 1$ transition of C, the master "latches" the input value on D (designated by the × symbol) and holds this value. Since the slave is gated while $C = 1$, the latched value in the master is passed to the flip-flop output Q. On the falling edge of the clock C, the slave "latches" the data from the master, as shown by the symbols × on signal Q_M in the diagram. Note that delays t_{PLH} and t_{PHL} have been included in the timing diagram.

The overall behavior of the D flip-flop output Q can be summarized by noting that Q will assume the value of D on the rising edge of the clock C. Therefore, the characteristic equation for a master–slave D flip-flop is simply

$$Q^* = D \tag{6.14}$$

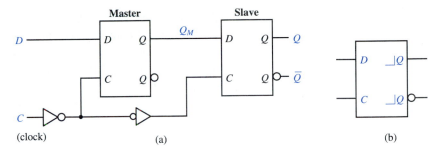

Figure 6.23   Master-slave D flip-flop. **(a)** Logic diagram. **(b)** Logic symbol.

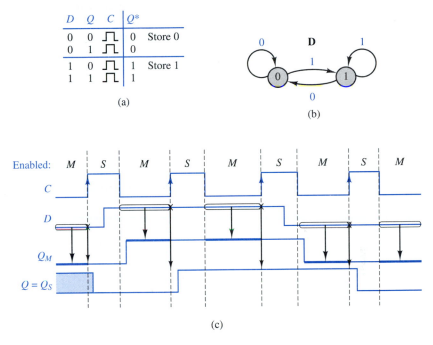

Figure 6.24   Master-slave D flip-flop characteristics. **(a)** Excitation table. **(b)** State diagram. **(c)** Timing diagram.

6.4.3 Master–Slave JK Flip-flops

Circuit Structure and Operation

The JK flip-flop may be considered an extension of the SR design examined earlier. The JK operates as an SR flip-flop whose inputs are assigned $J = S$ and $K = R$. However, whereas the $S = R = 1$ input combination is not allowed, the JK uses this special case to incorporate a very useful mode of operation. The additional feature of the JK device is that its state *toggles*, that is, changes from $0 \rightarrow 1$ or from $1 \rightarrow 0$ when $J = K = 1$. The four modes of operation (hold, set, reset, and toggle) are summarized in the excitation table presented in Fig. 6.25a and the corresponding state diagram in Fig. 6.25b.

By plotting the next state Q^* on a K-map, as shown in Fig. 6.25c, the characteristic equation of the JK flip-flop can be derived:

$$Q^* = \bar{K}Q + J\bar{Q} \tag{6.15}$$

From this equation, the logic diagram for the flip-flop can be derived, as presented in Fig. 6.26a. The logic symbol for this device is shown in Fig. 6.26b. Note that the clock input signal is inverted within the device itself so that the slave will change on the falling edge of the clock.

Examine the state diagram of Fig. 6.25b. The JK flip-flop will change from the 0 state to the 1 state with an input of $J = 1$ and $K = 0$ (set) or $J = 1$ and $K = 1$ (toggle). That is, a logic 1 on J will force the device into the 1 state no matter what value is placed on input K. Therefore, K is a don't-care condition, denoted on the state diagram by a value of d. The remainder of the diagram may be derived from the excitation table.

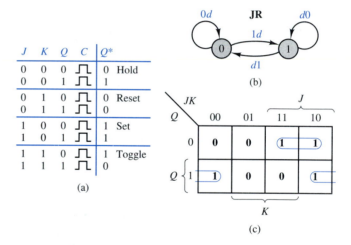

J	K	Q	C	Q*	
0	0	0	⊓	0	Hold
0	0	1	⊓	1	
0	1	0	⊓	0	Reset
0	1	1	⊓	0	
1	0	0	⊓	1	Set
1	0	1	⊓	1	
1	1	0	⊓	1	Toggle
1	1	1	⊓	0	

(a)

Figure 6.25 Pulse-triggered JK flip-flop characteristics. **(a)** Excitation table. **(b)** State diagram. **(c)** K-map for Q^*.

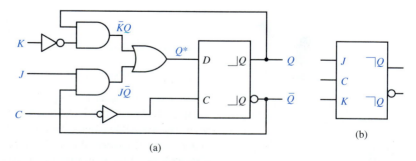

(a)

(b)

Figure 6.26 Pulse-triggered JK flip-flop. **(a)** Logic diagram. **(b)** Logic symbol.

7476 Dual Pulse-triggered JK Flip-flop Module

Several pulse-triggered JK flip-flops are available as standard TTL modules [1]. Figure 6.27 shows the logic symbol of the SN7476. This device packages two flip-flops that operate in the manner displayed in Fig. 6.26. Included in the configuration are asynchronous set signals $\overline{PRE}$ and reset signals $\overline{CLR}$. The $\overline{PRE}$ and $\overline{CLR}$ signals override the operation of the pulse-triggered inputs J, K, and CLK; that is, if $\overline{CLR} = 0$, then the state Q^* goes to 0, or if $\overline{PRE} = 0$, the state Q^* sets to 1, independent of the values of the clock and the excitation inputs.

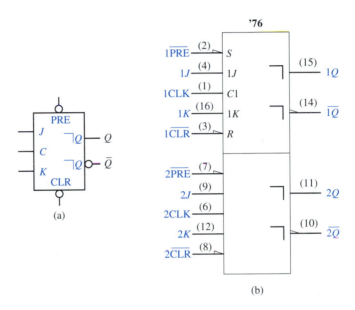

Figure 6.27 Dual pulse-triggered JK flip-flops, the 7476. **(a)** Generic logic symbol. **(b)** IEEE standard logic symbol. *Source:* The TTL Data Book Volume 2, Texas Instruments Inc., 1985.

6.4.4 Edge-triggered D Flip-flops

All the pulse-triggered flip-flops described in Section 6.4.3 require both a rising and falling edge on the clock for proper operation. The master–slave arrangement introduced a buffering mechanism to eliminate unstable transient conditions in sequential circuits with feedback elements. Another approach to solving the problem of unstable transients is to design the flip-flop circuitry so that it is sensitive to its excitation inputs only during rising or falling transitions of the clock. A circuit with this design feature is called *positive edge triggered* if it responds to a $0 \rightarrow 1$ clock transition or *negative edge triggered* if it responds to a $1 \rightarrow 0$ clock transition. The edge-sensitive feature eliminates unstable transients by drastically reducing the period during which the input excitation signals are applied to the internal latches.

Commercially available D flip-flop modules normally have a positive-edge-triggered clock control signal. Several of these devices, as listed in Table 6.1, are described next.

7474 Dual Positive-edge-triggered D Flip-flop Module

Consider the logic diagram of the SN7474 dual positive-edge-triggered D flip-flop shown in Fig. 6.28a. This circuit examines the excitation input signal D during the rising edge of the clock input CLK. The generic and IEEE standard symbols for the SN7474 are shown in Figs. 6.28b and c, respectively. It is important to note that the small triangle at the $C1$ input to the device is the standard notation to indicate that it is positive edge triggered.

The modes of operation of the SN7474 are shown in the excitation table of Fig. 6.29. Note that the asynchronous preset and clear signals, $\overline{CLR}$ and

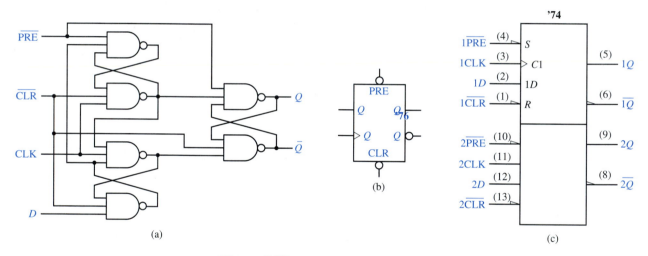

Figure 6.28   SN7474 dual positive-edge-triggered D flip-flop. **(a)** Logic diagram. **(b)** Generic logic symbol. **(c)** IEEE standard logic symbol. *Source:* The TTL Data Book Volume 2, Texas Instruments Inc., 1985.

Inputs				Outputs		
$\overline{PRE}$	$\overline{CLR}$	D	CLK	Q	$\overline{Q}$	Mode
L	H	×	×	H	L	Set
H	L	×	×	L	H	Clear
L	L	×	×	H	H	Not allowed
H	H	H	↑	H	L	Clocked operation
H	H	L	↑	L	H	Clocked operation
H	H	×	L	Q_0	$\overline{Q}_0$	Hold

Figure 6.29   SN7474 excitation table. *Source:* The TTL Data Book Volume 2, Texas Instruments Inc., 1985.

$\overline{PRE}$, override the clocked operation of the circuit. When both $\overline{CLR}$ and $\overline{PRE}$ are inactive (high), the clock *CLK* takes control of the device. While *CLK* is low, the flip-flop is in the hold mode. However, on a $0 \rightarrow 1$ transition of the clock, denoted by ↑, the data input *D* is transferred to the flip-flop output *Q*.

Edge-triggered Flip-flop Timing Characteristics

To insure proper operation of any edge-triggered flip-flop, the excitation inputs should not change immediately before or after the clock transition. The precise limitations on these time periods for each flip-flop type are specified in the TTL manual [1]. As defined earlier for latches and pulse-triggered flip-flops, the period before the clock transition for an edge-triggered flip-flop is defined to be the *setup time* (t_{su}); the period after the transition is the *hold time* (t_h). In general, if we violate these specified constraints for an edge-triggered TTL device, the device's behavior is not guaranteed. The relationships of these timing specifications to the clock transition and flip-flop propagation delay times for a generic positive-edge-triggered D flip-flop are illustrated in Fig. 6.30. Notice that the propagation delays from the time the clock crosses its rising-edge threshold until the output *Q* changes are called t_{PHL} and t_{PLH}, as defined earlier.

Let us examine the specific case of the SN7474. For this device, the values for both t_{PHL} and t_{PLH}, from the TTL manual [1], are listed in Fig. 6.30b as 0 ns.

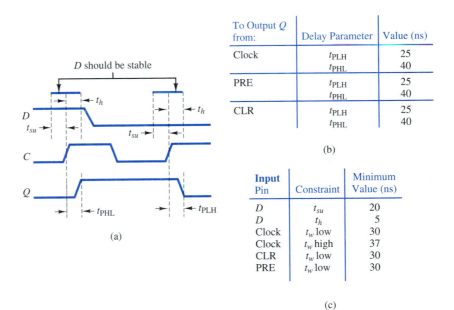

To Output Q from:	Delay Parameter	Value (ns)
Clock	t_{PLH}	25
	t_{PHL}	40
PRE	t_{PLH}	25
	t_{PHL}	40
CLR	t_{PLH}	25
	t_{PHL}	40

(b)

Input Pin	Constraint	Minimum Value (ns)
D	t_{su}	20
D	t_h	5
Clock	t_w low	30
Clock	t_w high	37
CLR	t_w low	30
PRE	t_w low	30

(c)

Figure 6.30 SN7474 flip-flop timing specifications [1]. **(a)** Timing diagram. **(b)** Propagation delays. **(c)** Timing constraints. *Source:* The TTL Data Book Volume 2, Texas Instruments Inc., 1985.

In other words, for the SN7474, the value of D is sampled and transferred to the flip-flop output Q at the exact instant the clock reaches its threshold value. You should always make sure that the input is either logic 1 or 0 at this instant in time so that the flip-flop's output Q will be the value you have planned in your system design. Timing constraints for the SN7474 are listed in Fig. 6.30c.

74175 and 74273 Positive-edge-triggered D Flip-flop Modules

Two other members of the TTL family of positive-edge-triggered D flip-flops are illustrated in Fig. 6.31. The SN74175 quad D flip-flop, shown in Fig. 6.31a,

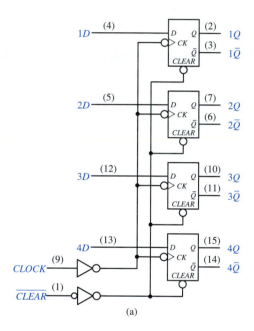

(a)

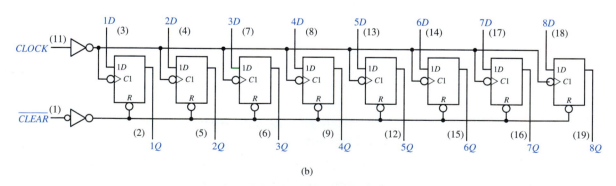

(b)

Figure 6.31 Positive-edge-triggered D flip-flop packages. **(a)** SN74175. **(b)** SN74273. *Source:* The TTL Data Book Volume 2, Texas Instruments Inc., 1985.

has common clock and clear controls, as well as both true (Q) and comple-mented ($\bar{Q}$) outputs. The SN74273 octal D flip-flop, shown in Fig. 6.31b, has the same common clock and clear lines, but brings only the true outputs (Q) to the outside world through the package pins. In the logic diagrams for these two devices, note the logic symbols used for the D flip-flops. The clock input *CK* displays the small triangle that signifies that the flip-flop is edge triggered. The inversion bubble in front of the triangle indicates a negative-edge-triggered device. But since the input signal *CLOCK* is inverted by the NOT gate at the bottom of the logic diagram, from the standpoint of the external package pins, the flip-flops appear to be positive edge triggered.

The SN74273 has setup and hold time requirements of 20 and 5 ns, re-spectively. These values are well within the tolerances needed to avoid unstable transients in most synchronous sequential logic circuit designs.

6.4.5 Edge-triggered JK Flip-flops

Edge-triggered JK flip-flops are common in the TTL family. The majority of them are negative edge triggered. Consider the following examples.

74LS73A Dual Negative-edge-triggered JK Flip-flop

Let us examine the logic diagram of a SN74LS73A shown in Fig. 6.32a. This dual negative-edge-triggered device requires setup and hold times of 20 and 0 ns, respectively. Its generic and IEEE standard logic symbols are given in Figs. 6.32b and c. Note that this 14-pin device features individual asynchronous clear lines $\overline{1CLR}$ and $\overline{2CLR}$. The inversion bubble in front of the triangle on the generic logic symbol of Fig. 6.32b indicates a negative-edge-triggered device. Likewise, the small triangle at each clock input in Fig. 6.32c is the IEEE standard notation for a negative-edge-triggered flip-flop.

74276 Quad Negative-edge-triggered JK Flip-flop

Suppose your design requires four JK flip-flops. Consider using the SN74276 shown in Fig. 6.32d. It features common preset and clear control signals. Each flip-flop brings its true output signal Q to a device package pin. Each flip-flop features individual excitation inputs J and $\bar{K}$, as well as its own negative-edge-triggered clock.

74111 Dual JK Flip-flop with Data Lockout

The SN74111 shown in Fig. 6.32e is a special implementation of the JK flip-flop. It contains a *data-lockout* feature that combines a positive-edge-triggered master latch followed by a negative pulse-triggered slave. That is, the master latch operates on the leading edge of the clock. While the clock remains high,

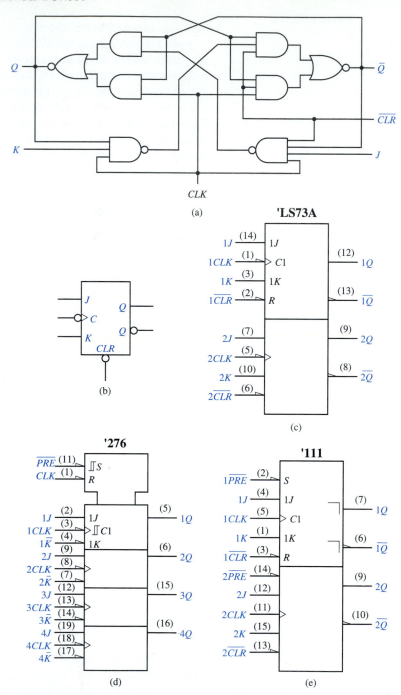

Figure 6.32 Edge-triggered JK flip-flops. **(a)** Logic diagram (SN74LS73A). **(b)** Generic logic symbol (SN74LS73A). **(c)** IEEE standard symbol (SN74LS73A). **(d)** SN74276. **(e)** SN74111. *Source:* The TTL Data Book Volume 2, Texas Instruments Inc., 1985.

further changes to the excitation inputs of the master are ignored. During this time, the slave latch is in the hold mode, holding the previous value of the master. When the clock signal falls, the new value in the master is gated to the slave. Note that this combination of clock controls is denoted by the presence of both a small triangle in front of the clock input $C1$, denoting a positive-edge-triggered master latch, and a falling edge symbol adjacent to the Q and $\bar{Q}$ flip-flop outputs, denoting that the slave is pulse triggered and changes on the falling edge of the clock. This device finds application in complicated designs where clock distribution networks introduce time delays called *clock skew*. The SN74111 can be used to minimize the effect of clock skew in digital system design.

6.4.6 T Flip-flops

Edge-triggered T Flip-flop

A common building block used in sequential logic circuits that counts pulses on a signal line is the T (*trigger* or *toggle*), flip-flop. Although this device is not available as a stand-alone TTL device, it is frequently used in building counting modules. The T flip-flop has only one excitation input signal, T, as shown on the logic symbol for the device pictured in Fig. 6.33a. The function of this device is to change (toggle) its state upon each negative-going transition of its excitation input signal, as shown in the excitation table and state diagram presented in Figs. 6.34a and b, respectively. Therefore, the characteristic equation of the edge-triggered T flip-flop is simply

$$Q^* = \bar{Q} \tag{6.16}$$

One way to visualize the construction of this device is to consider a negative-edge-triggered JK flip-flop with its J and K inputs set high. The device in Fig. 6.33a behaves as if it were a JK flip-flop connected as shown in Fig. 6.33b. This is the most commonly used implementation, since a wide variety of JK flip-flops are readily available.

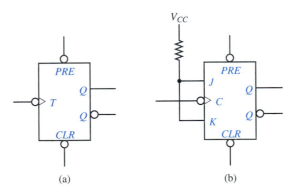

Figure 6.33   Negative-edge-triggered T flip-flop.
(a) Logic symbol. **(b)** Functional equivalent.

T	Q	Q^*	
↓	0	1	Toggle
↓	1	0	Toggle

(a)

(b)

Figure 6.34   Edge-triggered T flip-flop characteristics.
(a) Excitation table. **(b)** State diagram.

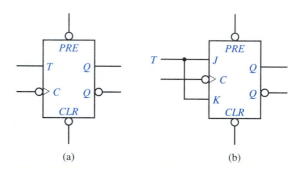

(a)

(b)

Figure 6.35   Clocked T flip-flop. **(a)** Logic symbol.
(b) Functional equivalent.

T	Q	C	Q^*	
0	0	↓	0	Hold
0	1	↓	1	
1	0	↓	1	Toggle
1	1	↓	0	

Figure 6.36   Excitation
table of clocked T flip-flop.

Clocked T Flip-flops

Some versions of the T flip-flop operate under clock pulse control, as illustrated in Fig. 6.35a. In this case, the flip-flop toggles if $T = 1$ when the clock makes a high-to-low transition and holds its present state if $T = 0$ when the flip-flop is clocked. The operation of a clocked T flip-flop is described by the excitation table given in Fig. 6.36.

The equivalent circuit of the clocked T flip-flop, shown in Fig. 6.35b, is simply a JK flip-flop with inputs $J = K = T$, and its C input driven by the clock signal. The characteristic equation of the clocked T flip-flop can be derived from that of the JK flip-flop by substituting T for J and K as follows:

$$Q^* = J\bar{Q} + \bar{K}Q$$
$$= T\bar{Q} + \bar{T}Q \tag{6.17}$$

For $T = 0$, the characteristic equation reduces to $Q^* = Q$, which is the hold condition, while for $T = 1$, the characteristic equation becomes $Q^* = \bar{Q}$, which represents the toggle condition.

Another variation of the clocked T flip-flop circuit is illustrated in Fig. 6.37a. In this circuit the control signal T_c allows the clock pulses to be selectively applied to the input terminal T, with each clock pulse that arrives at T causing the flip-flop to change state. A detailed timing diagram is offered in Fig. 6.37b.

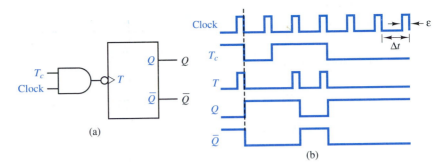

Figure 6.37 The clocked T flip-flop. **(a)** Logic symbol. **(b)** Timing diagram.

6.4.7 Latch and Flip-flop Summary

In the previous sections we have examined latch and flip-flop memory devices. Latch circuits are used primarily in situations where data are to be captured from signal lines and stored. The simple SR latch captures random pulses on its S and R inputs, since each pulse sets or resets the state of the latch. The gated SR and D latches change state only during times in which the latch is enabled. Therefore, gated latches are used to capture data that arrive and stabilize before the end of an enable pulse.

Flip-flops are used primarily for sequential circuit designs in which all state changes are to be synchronized to transitions of a clock signal. Most of these circuits utilize JK or D flip-flops, depending on which requires the smallest number of gates to derive the excitation inputs for each given design. SR flip-flops are rarely used, since JK flip-flops provide the same operating modes and add the additional toggle mode, eliminating the problem of having to avoid the condition $S = R = 1$. T flip-flops are used mainly in counter designs.

Table 6.3 summarizes the characteristic equations of the different latch and flip-flop devices discussed in this chapter. Since pulse-triggered flip-flops

TABLE 6.3 SUMMARY OF LATCH AND FLIP-FLOP CHARACTERISTICS

Device	Characteristic Equation
SR latch	$Q^* = S + \bar{R}Q$
Gated SR latch	$Q^* = SC + \bar{Q}R + \bar{C}Q$
D latch	$Q^* = DC + \bar{C}Q$
SR flip-flop	$Q^* = S + \bar{R}Q$
D flip-flop	$Q^* = D$
JK flip-flop	$Q^* = \bar{K}Q + J\bar{Q}$
T flip-flop (edge-triggered)	$Q^* = \bar{Q}$
T flip-flop (clocked)	$Q^* = T\bar{Q} + \bar{T}Q$

have the same characteristic equation as corresponding edge-triggered flip-flops, there is a single entry in the table for the D and JK flip-flops. We will use these characteristic equations in later chapters as we analyze and design various sequential circuits. The reader is referred to [2] through [5] for further information on the design and characteristics of latches and flip-flops.

6.5 Other Memory Devices

Many other kinds of storage devices may be used for the memory elements in Fig. 6.1b, several of which are magnetic cores, capacitors, magnetic films, superconductive cryotron elements, and electromechanical relays. Since these other types of memories are rarely used in today's computers, their explanation is beyond the scope of this text. The reader is referred to [5] and [6] for further information on various memory technologies and devices.

6.6 Timing Circuits

Another class of frequently used devices that are closely related to flip-flops are one-shots and timer modules. These important circuits are briefly summarized next.

6.6.1 One-shots

One-shots are monostable multivibrators, that is, digital storage circuits with only one stable state. They are temporarily driven into a transient state by a $0 \to 1$ and/or $1 \to 0$ transition on their inputs. They remain in this transient state for an amount of time specified by the timing constant of an RC network at the device's package pins. The generic operation of these devices is described in a number of digital electronics textbooks; for example, see [5]. Specific characteristics of the TTL family of devices can be found in the TTL Manual [1]. See, for example, the SN74121, SN74122, and SN74123. The SN74122 and SN74123 are retriggerable. This means that their transient timing cycle is restarted each time its inputs experience a transition. The SN74121 is not retriggerable; after it initiates a timing cycle, it ignores further changes on its inputs until that timing cycle has been completed.

6.6.2 The 555 Timer Module

The 555 timer module is a memory device that is used in a wide variety of applications since it can be configured for use as a one-shot or as an astable, or oscillating, multivibrator [7]. The 555 contains an SR latch, as illustrated in Fig. 6.38. The S and R latch inputs are controlled by the outputs of two analog comparators $C1$ and $C2$. A second reset input, $R1$, can be controlled directly. The output of either comparator is a logic 1 whenever its upper input is at a higher voltage than its lower input. One input of each comparator is held at a

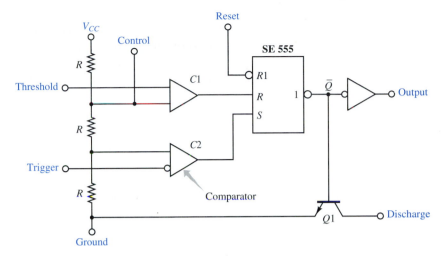

Figure 6.38   555 precision timing module.

fixed voltage by a three-resistor voltage divider. The lower input of comparator $C1$ is held at $2/3 V_{CC}$, while the upper input of comparator $C2$ is at $1/3 V_{CC}$.

The latch is *set* (*Output* $= 1$) by applying a logic 1 signal to the trigger. This signal is inverted to logic 0 before entering comparator $C2$, making the voltage at the lower input less than the $1/3 V_{CC}$ at the upper input, causing comparator $C2$ to apply a logic 1 to the S input of the latch. The latch is *reset* by forcing the threshold input to a voltage higher than $2/3 V_{CC}$, causing comparator $C1$ to apply a logic 1 to the R input of the latch. As with any SR latch, care must be taken not to allow $S = R = 1$.

Astable Operation

Astable operation is achieved by making the 555 self-triggering, that is, by alternately changing the trigger and threshold inputs using an RC circuit, as shown in Fig. 6.39. The frequency of oscillation is a function of resistors R_A and R_B and capacitor C and is computed as follows. The time for the capacitor to charge up through R_A and R_B, and thus the time for which $Out = 1$ is:

$$t_H = 0.693(R_A + R_B)(C) \tag{6.18}$$

Likewise, the time it takes the capacitor to discharge determines the time for which $Out = 0$ and is given by

$$t_L = 0.693(R_B)(C) \tag{6.19}$$

Combining Eqs. 6.18 and 6.19 gives the period of oscillation T as

$$T = t_H + t_L$$
$$= 0.693(R_A + 2R_B)(C) \tag{6.20}$$

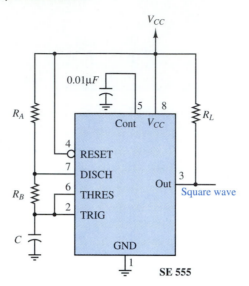

Figure 6.39   555 timing module configured for astable operation.

The frequency of oscillation f is simply the inverse of the period T as defined in Eq. 6.20, which is

$$f = \frac{1.44}{(R_A + 2R_B)C} \tag{6.21}$$

For example, to obtain $f = 45$ Hz, the following component values would be selected:

$$R_A = 100 \, K\Omega$$
$$R_B = 100 \, K\Omega$$
$$C = 3.125 \, \mu F$$

For those readers who understand analog circuits, the device works as follows. When output $= 1$, $\bar{Q} = 0$ and transistor $Q1$ is *cut off*, that is, behaves as an open circuit. This causes capacitor C to charge up through resistors R_A and R_B until the voltage at *Trigger/Threshold* is sufficiently high that the two comparators produce $S = 0$ and $R = 1$. This resets the latch, forcing output $= 0$ and $\bar{Q} = 1$. In this condition, transistor $Q1$ is turned on, that is, behaves as a short circuit, causing capacitor C to discharge through R_B and $Q1$ until the voltage at *Trigger/Threshold* is sufficiently low that the comparators produce $R = 0$ and $S = 1$, setting the latch. This operation continues indefinitely.

One-shot Operation

For one-shot operation, we want a storage element that can be triggered to a given state, with the state automatically returning to its default value after a given time. This can be done with a 555 timer module configured as shown in Fig. 6.40 for *monostable* (one-shot) operation. The 555 will be triggered by a pulse on its *Trigger* input, generating a pulse on its output.

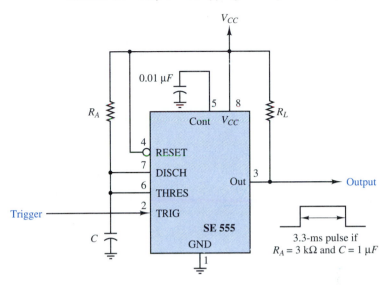

Figure 6.40 555 one-shot logic diagram.

The 555 circuit is configured for monostable operation by using one resistor, R_A, and one capacitor, C, as shown in Fig. 6.40. Referring to the 555 diagram in Fig. 6.38, *Output* is set to 1 whenever a logic 0 pulse is applied to the trigger input. In the configuration of Fig. 6.40, this causes the capacitor C to charge through resistor R_A until the voltage at the *Threshold* input is sufficiently high to reset the latch, returning output to 0. It is assumed that the *Trigger* input has returned to logic 1 prior to *Threshold* resetting the latch.

The values of resistor R_A and capacitor C determine the time it takes the capacitor to charge and thus determine the duration of the output pulse. The pulse width is given by

$$t_W = 1.1(R_A)(C) \tag{6.22}$$

Therefore, as an example, the values $R_A = 3\,k\Omega$ and $C = 1\,\mu F$ would produce a pulse of approximately 3.3-ms duration.

6.7 Rapid Prototyping of Sequential Circuits

Now that we have examined memory devices, let us conclude this chapter by looking briefly at their use in realizing sequential circuits. The Implementation of a sequential logic circuit requires the design of the combinational logic and memory blocks of the sequential circuit model of Fig. 6.1b, given a state table describing the circuit. We will examine design methods to minimize the hardware of these blocks in Chapters 8 and 9. However, a simple implementation of any arbitrary sequential circuit can be done by using a memory register to realize the memory block in conjunction with programmable read-only memory (PROM) devices, described in Chapter 5, to realize the combinational logic block. A typical PROM implementation is illustrated in Fig. 6.41a. This method is very useful if a prototype circuit is needed rapidly.

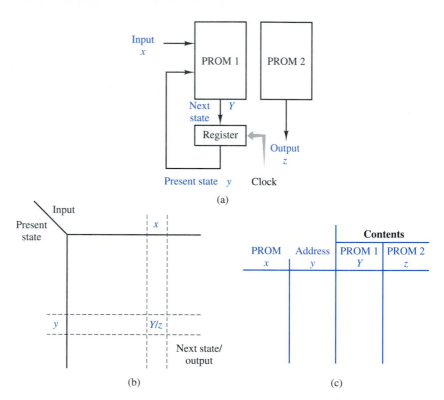

Figure 6.41   PROM sequential circuits. **(a)** PROM sequential circuit structure. **(b)** State table format. **(c)** PROM sequential circuit format.

Given a sequential circuit with n inputs $x_1, \ldots, x_n$, m outputs $z_1, \ldots, z_m$, and r state variables $y_1, \ldots, y_r$, recall from Eqs. 6.2 and 6.3 that the combination logic block must realize the equations

$$z_i = g_i(x_1, \ldots, x_n, y_1, \ldots, y_r) \qquad i = 1, \ldots, m \qquad (6.23)$$

$$Y_i = h_i(x_1, \ldots, x_n, y_1, \ldots, y_r) \qquad i = 1, \ldots, r \qquad (6.24)$$

where g_i and h_i are switching functions. The r next-state variables, Y_i, represent the values to be stored in the r memory elements when the state changes.

Referring to Fig. 6.41a, the first PROM implements the next-state combinational logic functions, h_i, while the second PROM is devoted to the output logic functions, g_i. For many applications, both PROMs may be implemented in a single chip.

The power of this type of design is in the programmability of the PROM devices. If we want to change the state behavior, then one or both of the PROMs are simply erased and reprogrammed. If we place the PROMs in sockets, no rewiring of our circuit has to be done to make these changes. Designers appreciate this feature when they must prototype the design themselves!

How do we specify the contents of the PROMs? Consider the state table of Fig. 6.41b, which is in the general format presented earlier in Fig. 6.2b. If we simply rearrange the information as shown in Fig. 6.41c, the state table may be used to generate the truth table for the PROMs.

EXAMPLE 6.2

Let us implement with a PROM the sequential circuit whose state table is shown in Fig. 6.42a.

The combinational logic has one input line (x) and two present-state flip-flop inputs (y_2 and y_1). The output of the combinational logic will be two next-state signals (Y_2 and Y_1) and the output line (z). We can rearrange this state table into the truth table of Fig. 6.42b. This truth table defines the combinational logic needed to implement the example sequential circuit.

	x	
y_2y_1	0	1
00	10/1	00/1
01	11/0	11/1
10	01/1	00/0
11	00/0	11/0
	Y_2Y_1/z	

(a)

x	y_2	y_1	Y_2	Y_1	z
0	0	0	1	0	1
0	0	1	1	1	0
0	1	0	0	1	1
0	1	1	0	0	0
1	0	0	0	0	1
1	0	1	1	1	1
1	1	0	0	0	0
1	1	1	1	1	0

(b)

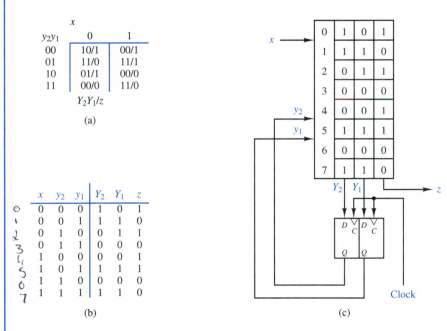

(c)

Figure 6.42 PROM sequential circuit example. **(a)** Example state table. **(b)** PROM truth table. **(c)** PROM implementation.

A single PROM containing eight words of 3 bits each may be used to implement the circuit as shown in Fig. 6.42c. Two D flip-flops complete the implementation.

EXAMPLE 6.3

Let us build a circuit that sequences through the prime numbers that are less than 256.

The PROM implementation for this sequencer is given in Fig. 6.43. Notice that the sequencer only uses certain rows in the PROM's structure. If the sequencer begins in state 2, it is sent to state 3, then 5, then 7, then 11, then 13, then 17, and so forth, until it reaches state 251. The next prime number above 251 is greater than 256, so the sequencer sends the unit back to state 2 to repeat the loop. But how can we start in state 2? One way is to program state 2 into all the unused locations in the PROM. When power is applied to the device, it will start in an unknown state. If it is an illegal state, that is, not a prime number, the first clock pulse will send the unit to state 2 and the sequence begins.

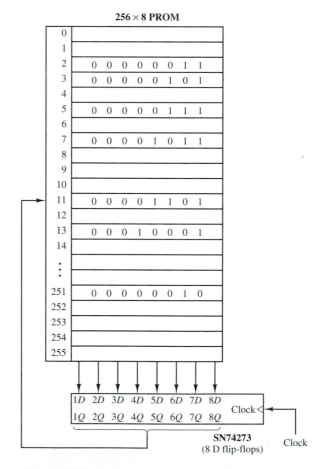

Figure 6.43 PROM implementation of a prime number sequencer.

Note that the eight flip-flops in the feedback loop of this unit can be implemented using one SN74273 chip. So we have implemented the prime sequencer unit with only two chips.

The preceding examples illustrated the use of PROM devices in creating sequential logic circuits. Other programmable logic devices are also utilized in sequential circuit design. These will be discussed in Chapter 11.

6.8 Summary

In this chapter we have introduced models for sequential circuits including logic diagrams, state tables, and state diagrams. A number of practical memory elements, including latches and flip-flops, have been described in detail. In Chapter 7 we shall examine sequential modules constructed from these elements. In Chapters 8 and 9 we will examine methods for analyzing and synthesizing synchronous and asynchronous sequential circuits that are built from these memory elements.

REFERENCES

1.   TEXAS INSTRUMENTS, *The TTL Data Book*, *Volume 2*. Dallas, Texas: Texas Instruments, Inc., 1988.

2.   J. F. WAKERLY, *Digital Design Principles and Practices*. Englewood Cliffs, NJ: Prentice Hall, 1990, pp. 349–369.

3.   R. H. KATZ, *Contemporary Logic Design*. Menlo Park, CA: Benjamin/Cummings, 1994, pp. 282–321.

4.   J. P. HAYES, *Introduction to Digital Logic Design*. Reading, MA: Addison-Wesley, 1993, pp. 405–447.

5.   G E. WILLIAMS, *Digital Technology*. Chicago: Science Research Associates, 1977, pp. 166–169.

6.   E. R. HNATEK, *A User's Handbook of Semiconductor Memories*. New York: Wiley, 1977.

7.   S. A. R. GARROD AND R. J. BORNS, *Digital Logic: Analysis*, *Application & Design*. Philadelphia: Saunders College Publishing, 1991, pp. 412–423.

PROBLEMS

6.1   Construct a state diagram from the following state table: What is the logic equation for the output variable z?

	x	
	0	1
A	$D/1$	$B/0$
B	$D/1$	$C/0$
C	$D/1$	$A/0$
D	$B/1$	$C/0$

6.2   Given the following state table, find the output and state sequences for the input sequence

$$x = 010101$$

if the circuit starts in state A:

	x	
	0	1
A	$D/0$	$B/0$
B	$C/0$	$B/0$
C	$B/0$	$C/0$
D	$B/0$	$C/1$

6.3 For the following sequential circuit, determine the output sequence for the input sequence

$$x = 0010110101$$

if the starting state is A. Draw a state diagram for the circuit.

	x	
	0	1
A	$B/0$	$C/1$
B	$C/1$	$B/0$
C	$A/0$	$A/1$

6.4 Derive the state diagram and characteristic equation of the latch circuit in Fig. P6.4.

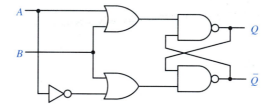

Figure P6.4

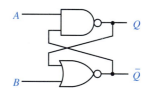

Figure P6.5

6.5 Find the excitation table of the latch circuit in Fig. P6.5 and describe its behavior in words.

6.6 Is the circuit of Fig. P6.6a a valid latch design? Explain. If it is a latch, complete the excitation table of Fig. P6.6b. Can it be used as a gated SR latch? If so, how?

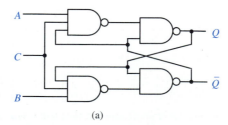

(a)

A	B	C	Q	Q^*	Mode
0	0	0	0	0	No change
0	0	0	1	1	No change

(b)

Figure P6.6

6.7 Construct state diagrams for the following:
   (a) D flip-flop   **(c)** T flip-flop
   (b) SR flip-flop   **(d)** JK flip-flop

6.8 Derive the characteristic state equations shown in:
   (a) Equation 6.10 for SR latches
   (b) Equation 6.12 for clocked D latches
   (c) Equation 6.15 for JK flip-flops
   (d) Equation 6.17 for clocked T flip-flops

6.9 Given the JK flip-flop of Fig. P6.9a, complete the timing diagram of Fig. P6.9b by determining the waveform of the output Q.

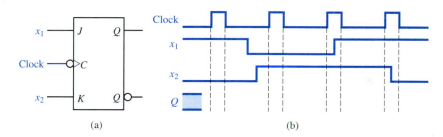

Figure P6.9 **(a)** Flip-flop. **(b)** Timing diagram.

6.10 Given the SR flip-flop of Fig. P6.10a, complete the timing diagram of Fig. P6.10b by determining the waveform of the output Q. Note that the flip-flop is triggered on the positive edge of the clock signal. The condition $S = R = 1$ is produced twice by the inputs. Will this lead to unstable operation? Explain.

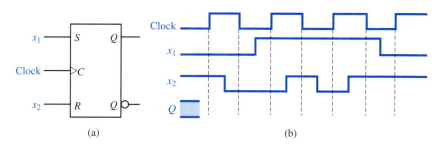

Figure P6.10 **(a)** Flip-flop. **(b)** Timing diagram.

6.11 The waveforms of Fig. P6.11 are applied to the inputs of an SN7476 JK flip-flop. Complete the timing diagram by drawing the waveforms of flip-flop outputs Q and $\bar{Q}$.

6.12 The circuit of Fig. P6.12a contains a D latch, a positive-edge-triggered D flip-flop, and a negative-edge-triggered D flip-flop. Complete the timing diagram of Fig. P6.12b by drawing the waveforms of signals y_1, y_2, and y_3.

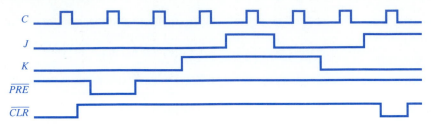

Figure P6.11

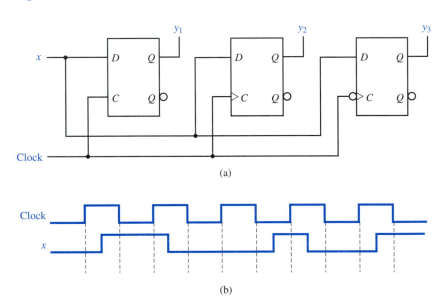

Figure P6.12 **(a)** Logic diagram. **(b)** Timing diagram.

6.13 The circuit of Fig. P6.13a contains a JK flip-flop and a D flip-flop. Complete the timing diagram of Fig. P6.13b by drawing the waveforms of signals Q_1 and Q_2, assuming that:
(a) The JK flip-flop is negative edge triggered.
(b) The JK flip-flop has data lockout.

6.14 Complete the following table of flip-flop excitation values required to produce the indicated flip-flop state changes, where y indicates the present state and Y the desired next state of the flip-flop.

Present State	Next State	JK flip-flop		D flip-flop	SR flip-flop		T flip-flop
y	Y	J	K	D	S	R	T
0	0						
0	1						
1	0						
1	1						

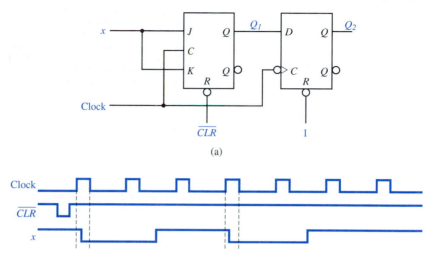

(a)

(b)

Figure P6.13 **(a)** Logic diagram. **(b)** Timing diagram.

6.15 Discuss why the condition $S = R = 1$ leads to an unstable condition for an SR latch.

6.16 Describe how the unstable condition $S = R = 1$ is avoided in the storage latch of the following:

    (a) D latch   **(c)** T flip-flop

    (b) JK flip-flop

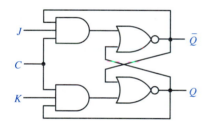

Figure P6.17

6.17 The circuit of Fig. P6.17 is intended to operate as a JK latch. Discuss whether or not this circuit is stable for the condition $J = K = C = 1$. If the circuit is unstable, discuss what could be done to the clock signal, C, to make the circuit operate as expected.

6.18 Design a master–slave JK flip-flop with asynchronous present and clear inputs using only NOR gates.

6.19 Describe the operational difference between a clocked D-type *latch* and a D-type master–slave *flip-flop* as observed from the outputs of the devices.

6.20 Describe how a master–slave flip-flop appears to operate as an *edge-triggered* device when observed from its external outputs.

6.21 Using the hazard-free D latch circuit of the SN74116 shown in Fig. 6.20c, design a master–slave D flip-flop with asynchronous preset and clear inputs, $\overline{PRE}$ and $\overline{CLR}$, respectively.

6.22 Examine the SN7474 D flip-flop circuit of Fig. 6.28a and describe how it operates as an edge-triggered device.

6.23 Examine the SN7476 JK flip-flop circuit of Fig. 6.27. Discuss why the $\overline{PRE}$ and $\overline{CLR}$ inputs are referred to as *asynchronous* inputs, while J and K are called *synchronous* inputs.

6.24   Connect a D flip-flop in such a manner that it will perform like a clocked T flip-flop.

6.25   Construct a D flip-flop using only a JK flip-flop and no additional gates.

6.26   The circuit of Fig. P6.26 is similar to that used in commercial programmable logic sequencer chips. It is designed to operate as either a JK flip-flop or as a D flip-flop according to the settings of switches SW_1 and SW_2. Determine the settings (open or closed) of the two switches required for JK and D flip-flop operation, and describe how this operation is achieved.

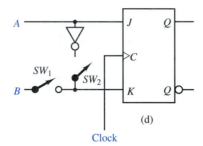

(d)

Clock   **Figure P6.26**

6.27   Design a synchronous sequential circuit, using EPROMs and edge-triggered D flip-flops, to implement the following state table:

	$x_1 x_2$			
	00	**01**	**11**	**10**
$A = 00$	A	B	D	C
$B = 01$	B	C	A	D
$C = 10$	C	D	B	A
$D = 11$	D	A	C	B

Specify the contents of your EPROM in a table of hexadecimal numbers.

6.28   Design a synchronous sequential circuit, using EPROMs and edge-triggered D flip-flops, to implement the following state table:

	$x_1 x_2 x_3$							
	000	**001**	**010**	**011**	**100**	**101**	**110**	**111**
$A = 000$	A	B	H	C	B	B	B	D
$B = 001$	B	C	A	A	A	D	C	A
$C = 010$	C	D	B	E	D	B	D	B
$D = 011$	D	E	C	A	C	F	A	C
$E = 100$	E	F	D	G	F	B	F	H
$F = 101$	F	G	E	A	E	H	G	E
$G = 110$	G	H	F	A	H	B	H	F
$H = 111$	H	A	G	A	G	B	E	G

Specify the contents of your EPROM in a table of hexadecimal numbers.

6.29 Design a synchronous sequential circuit, using EPROMs and edge-triggered D flip-flops, to implement the following state table:

	00	01	11	10
			$x_1 x_2$	
A	A	A	B	M
B	B	A	C	A
C	C	A	D	B
D	D	A	E	C
E	E	A	F	D
F	F	A	G	E
G	G	A	H	F
H	H	A	I	G
I	I	A	J	H
J	J	A	K	I
K	K	A	L	J
L	L	A	M	K
M	M	A	A	L

Specify the contents of your EPROM in a table of hexadecimal numbers.

7

In Chapter 6 we examined various binary memory elements in the form of latches and flip-flops. In this chapter, we now investigate sequential logic modules, in which combinational logic elements are combined with latches and flip-flops to realize several commonly-used functions. These modules are available as standard TTL components and as functions in VLSI design libraries. Each contains flip-flops that are grouped together to form a register, which is the basic building block of a digital computer. First we will look at shift registers, which are used for storing and manipulating binary data. Then we will combine shift registers with a binary adder to produce an accumulator. Finally, we will examine counters, which are configurations of flip-flops that generate sequences of binary numbers.

All of the modules in this chapter can be designed with straightforward interconnections of gates and memory elements. In the next chapter we will examine formal methods for designing sequential circuits.

Modular Sequential Logic

▶ 7.1 Shift Registers

A *shift register* is a sequential logic module constructed from flip-flops that manipulates the bit positions of binary data by shifting the data bits to the left or right. A typical shift register is illustrated in Fig. 7.1. The n-bit shift register in Fig. 7.1a holds n bits of binary data and is constructed using master–slave flip-flops. The design and operation of master–slave flip-flops has been presented in Chapter 6. Each master–slave flip-flop forms a *cell* of the shift register. Each cell has a master latch and a slave latch and holds 1 bit of binary data. The shift control pulse for the register is normally low and experiences a rapid low–high–low ($0 \rightarrow 1 \rightarrow 0$) transition to move, or shift, the binary data one position to the right. The binary data bits normally reside in the slave latches. On the rising ($0 \rightarrow 1$) edge of the shift control pulse, data from the slave latch in each cell are transferred to the master latch in the next cell to the right. Note that the data in a single cell at this moment consist of their old values (the binary output values before the shift pulse) residing in the slave latch and their new values (the binary output values after the completion of the shift pulse) residing in its master latch. On the falling edge ($1 \rightarrow 0$) of the shift-control pulse, the master latch in each cell is transferred to its slave, bringing its new value to its output terminal. Thus, after both rising and falling transitions of the shift control pulse, the binary bit in cell X_i has been transferred to cell X_{i-1}. In other words, the binary number in the shift register has been transferred one position to the right. Consequently, we call this register a *serial-in, serial-out* shift register. The serial-in and serial-out terminals have been labeled in Fig. 7.1a.

Fig. 7.1b illustrates an implementation of the serial-in, serial-out shift register using edge-triggered SR flip-flops. Note the logic symbol for the flip-flop. The clock terminal is labeled CK. The triangle denotes that it is an edge-triggered input, and the bubble in front indicates that it is sensitive to a falling ($1 \rightarrow 0$) transition. So we call this a *negative-edge triggered* SR flip-flop. The shift-control pulse (labeled *Shift*) is inverted by the NOT gate and applied to all the CK inputs simultaneously. These flip-flops change in unison when *Shift* changes from low to high ($0 \rightarrow 1$). On this transition, the data in flip-flop X_i are transferred to flip-flop X_{i-1}. Consequently, this configuration performs the same serial-in, serial-out function of the register in Fig. 7.1a.

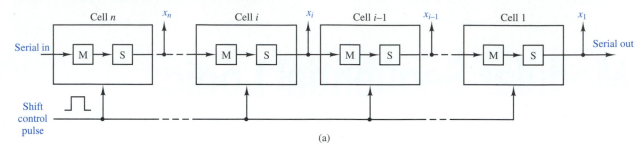

(a)

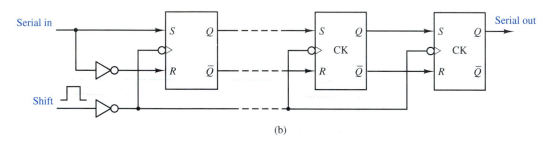

(b)

Figure 7.1   Serial-in, serial-out shift register. **(a)** Shift register with master–slave cells. **(b)** Shift register with edge-triggered SR flip-flops.

7.1.1 A Generic Shift Register

Now let us consider a *generic* shift register element. See Fig. 7.2. The labels on the diagram indicate the following:

> **Parallel in** $(Y_i, i = 1, n)$: one input line for each flip-flop with data to be entered into the register
>
> **Parallel out** $(X_i, i = 1, n)$: one output line coming from each flip-flop Q terminal
>
> **Shift pulse** (sometimes labeled **CLOCK**): a pulse on this control line makes the binary data in the register move over one cell in unison
>
> **Serial in**: data line feeding the first cell in the shift register; a bit enters on each *Shift* pulse
>
> **Serial out**: data line from the Q terminal of the last flip-flop in the register; a bit exits on each *Shift* pulse
>
> **Clear control**: a pulse on this line drives all the flip-flops in the register to logic 0
>
> **Preset control**: a pulse on this control line presets certain flip-flops to logic 1, those with a logic 1 on their parallel input line Y_i

The shift register of Fig. 7.2a may be operated in four modes: serial in and serial out, parallel in and serial out, serial in and parallel out, or parallel in and parallel out. The all-serial mode requires that the data in be in a serial

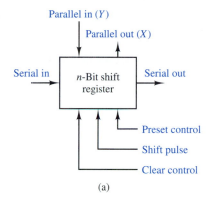

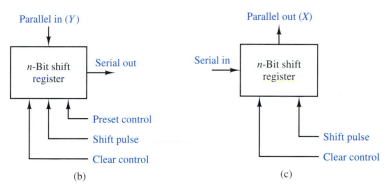

Figure 7.2   Generic shift register. **(a)** Logic symbol. **(b)** Parallel-in, serial-out. **(c)** Serial-in, parallel-out.

format synchronized with the *Shift pulse*. The shift register then serves as an n-pulse time delay for a stream of serial data.

The parallel-in with serial-out mode is shown in Fig. 7.2b. Proper operation in this mode requires the following control pulse sequence. First, a *Clear control* pulse must be applied to drive all shift register cells to logic 0. Second, the parallel data must be connected to the input lines Y_i, $i = 1, n$. Then a *Preset control* pulse is applied to drive certain shift register stages to the logic 1 state as specified by the parallel input data. Last, n *Shift pulse* signals are furnished to the unit to generate a serial stream of output data.

Finally, let us consider the serial-in, parallel-out mode of operation, illustrated in Fig. 7.2c. For proper operation in this mode, a *Clear control* pulse may be applied to zero all cells of the shift register. Then the *Serial-in* data are applied to the register synchronized with n *Shift pulse* signals. After the last *Shift pulse* has returned to zero, the *Parallel-out* data are available at the flip-flop outputs X_i, $i = 1, n$.

7.1.2 Standard TTL Shift Register Modules

The generic shift register module depicted in Fig. 7.2 finds very widespread usage in digital systems design. Digital designers employ shift registers in many different applications. How does one decide which shift register to use? A wide variety of shift register devices are commercially available. Now let us examine some typical examples from the SN7400 series. The modules that we will discuss are listed in Table 7.1. These specific models have been chosen to illustrate how many of the different features are implemented. For example, do you need a bidirectional device? What is the difference between synchronous data hold and clock inhibit? Will your design need synchronous load or asynchronous preset? These features are examined in detail in this chapter. The user is referred to *The TTL Data Book* [1] for complete information on these and similar devices.

TABLE 7.1   **SN7400 SERIES SHIFT REGISTERS [1]**

Device	Features
7491A	8-Bit, serial in, serial out
7496	5-Bit, serial in, serial out, asynchronous preset, parallel out, common clear
74164	8-Bit, serial in, serial out or parallel out, common clear
74165	8-Bit, serial in, serial out, asynchronous load, clock inhibit
74179	4-Bit, serial in, serial out, common clear, synchronous load, parallel out, synchronous data hold
74194	4-Bit, bidirectional, serial in, serial out, synchronous load, parallel out, clock inhibit, common clear

SN7491A

The SN7491A is an 8-bit, serial-in, serial-out shift register. It is an 8-bit version of Fig. 7.1b with one additional feature, a gated serial input. Examine the logic diagram of the device shown in Fig. 7.3a. Inputs A and B are ANDed into the S terminal of the first SR flip-flop. This allows one input to be used as a serial data source and the other as a data enable control line. Note that the shift control line is labeled *Clock* for this device. We can clear the register by holding the enable line to zero and pulsing the *Clock* line eight times. Observe that both true and complemented data are available at the output of the eighth flip-flop.

Figure 7.3b displays the function table for the device. When both inputs A and B are held high, logic-1 data bits enter the device. After eight clock pulses (at time t_{n+8}), the high data reach the output terminals (Q_H and $\bar{Q}_H$). If either input A or B is held low, the data reaching the output at time t_{n+8} will be logic 0.

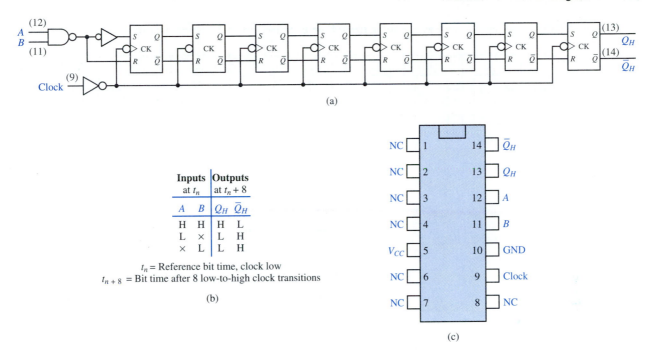

Figure 7.3 SN7491A serial-in, serial-out shift register. **(a)** Logic diagram. **(b)** Function table. **(c)** Package pins. *Source:* The TTL Data Book Volume 2, Texas Instruments Inc., 1985.

The pin configuration for the dual-in-line package is shown in Fig. 7.3c. This figure displays a top view of the device. The notation NC by a pin means that it is not connected (unused).

SN74164

The SN74164 is an 8-bit, serial-in, serial- or parallel-out shift register with a common clear control signal. Figure 7.4a presents the logic diagram of the device. Compare this diagram to the one for the SN7491A in Fig. 7.3a. Note that a $\overline{Clear}$ line has been added so that the device can be driven to the all-zero state by one active-low pulse $(1 \rightarrow 0 \rightarrow 1)$. Another feature of the SN74164 is its eight parallel output lines, one for each of the eight flip-flops in the device. In this device, the complement of the last cell of the register is not available as it was in the SN7491A.

One way of showing the behavior of this device is through an example timing diagram. See Fig. 7.4b. The sequence begins with a negative-going pulse on the $\overline{Clear}$ input line to drive the device to the all-zero state. Next the clock is supplied with a series of pulses. The device looks at the values on the A and B serial input lines every time the clock signal makes a $0 \rightarrow 1$ transition. If A and B are both high on this transition, a logic 1 is shifted into the device. Otherwise,

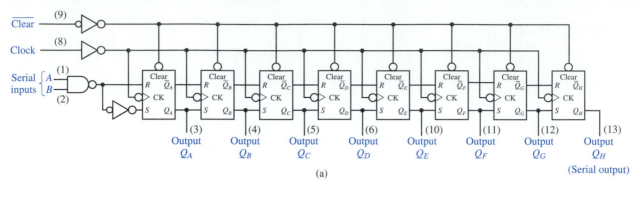

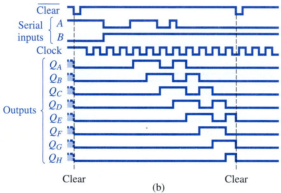

(a)

(b)

Inputs				Outputs			
Clear	Clock	A	B	Q_A	Q_B	$\cdots$	Q_H
L	$\times$	$\times$	$\times$	L	L		L
H	L	$\times$	$\times$	Q_{A0}	Q_{B0}		Q_{H0}
H	$\uparrow$	H	H	H	Q_{An}		Q_{Gn}
H	$\uparrow$	L	$\times$	L	Q_{An}		Q_{Gn}
H	$\uparrow$	$\times$	L	L	Q_{An}		Q_{Gn}

Q_{A0}, Q_{B0}, Q_{H0} = levels of Q_A, Q_B, Q_H, respectively,
before the indicated steady-state input conditions are established.
Q_{An}, Q_{Gn} = levels of Q_A, Q_G, respectively, before the most
recent $\uparrow$ transition of the clock (1-bit shift)

(c)

(d)

Figure 7.4 SN74164 serial-in, serial/parallel-out shift register. **(a)** Logic diagram. **(b)** Timing diagram. **(c)** Function table. **(d)** Package pins. *Source:* The TTL Data Book Volume 2, Texas Instruments Inc., 1985.

a logic 0 is entered. Note that a 1 or a 0 is entered on every $0 \rightarrow 1$ transition of the clock. Finally, another $\overline{Clear}$ signal drives all the flip-flop outputs to 0. An interesting pattern of delayed signals is generated at the flip-flop outputs of this device. Each pattern is delayed from its predecessor by one clock pulse interval (the time between $0 \rightarrow 1$ transitions on the clock).

Figure 7.4c displays the function table. Examine the table and interpret its rows and columns as follows. A low signal on the $\overline{Clear}$ line holds all eight outputs at logic 0. The $\overline{Clear}$ line must be held high for the shift register to operate. With the $\overline{Clear}$ line high and the *Clock* line low, the eight flip-flops in the device hold their initial values (Q_{i0}, for $i = A, \ldots, H$). In this state the device is looking for positive-going transitions ($0 \rightarrow 1$) on the clock to shift data down the chain of flip-flops. If a positive-edge transition (a $0 \rightarrow 1$ transition, denoted by an upward arrow in the table) occurs at time t_{n+1}, the outputs of flip-flops $Q_B, Q_C, \ldots, Q_H$, will assume the values of their neighboring flip-flips to the left at time t_n. For example, Q_B at time t_{n+1} equals Q_A at time t_n, or $Q_B = Q_{An}$. The value of output Q_A at time t_{n+1} is determined by the serial inputs A and B. If both A and B are high, then Q_A is high. Otherwise, Q_A is low.

Finally, the pin connections for the SN74164 are illustrated in Fig. 7.4d. Note that all 14 pins have been used in the device. The pin numbers in Fig. 7.4d have also been inserted into the logic diagram of Fig. 7.4a for the convenience of the device user.

SN7496

This is a 5-bit, serial-in, serial-out/parallel-out shift register with asynchronous common clear and asynchronous preset. See the logic diagram of Fig. 7.5a. The SN7496 has only one *Serial input* line. It has all the other features of the SN74164 plus one additional feature—asynchronous preset. Notice that each SR flip-flop has a gated *Preset i* input ($i = A, \ldots, E$). The common *Preset enable* line is ANDed with each external *Preset i* signal to gate it to each flip-flop. This feature may be used in conjunction with the $\overline{Clear}$ line to parallel load the shift register with data. First an active-low $\overline{Clear}$ pulse ($1 \rightarrow 0 \rightarrow 1$) is applied to the device to drive all five flip-flops to the logic 0 state. Then the individual *Preset i* signals with the data to be transferred into the register are applied to the flip-flops by an active-high *Preset enable* pulse ($0 \rightarrow 1 \rightarrow 0$). Note that the flip-flop outputs will be held at the values on their preset i lines if the *Preset enable* line is held high. Therefore, the preset enable pulse should be returned to logic 0 before any shift control pulses are applied to the *clock* line.

Some typical operations of the SN7496 are illustrated in Fig. 7.5b. First the serial-in, serial-out feature is illustrated. An active-low $\overline{Clear}$ pulse is applied to drive all the flip-flops to logic 0. Then an active-high signal is applied to the *Serial input* line, which is entered into flip-flop A on the first $0 \rightarrow 1$ transition of the clock. The serial input signal is then removed so that each succeeding $0 \rightarrow 1$ transition of the clock will shift the logic 1 down the chain of five-flip-flops. After the fifth clock pulse, all five flip-flops have returned to the all-zero state. Next an example of parallel loading the register is given. An active-high *Preset enable* pulse loads the register with binary data,

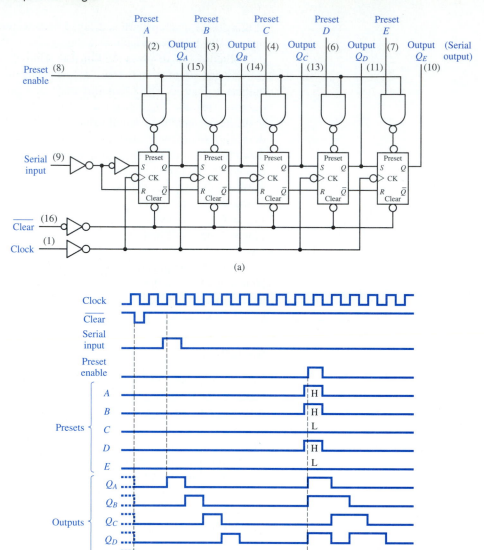

Figure 7.5 SN7496 5-bit serial-in, serial/parallel-out shift register. **(a)** Logic diagram. **(b)** Timing diagram.

$(Q_E Q_D Q_C Q_B Q_A) = (01011)$. Finally, the data entered into the register are converted from parallel to serial form by applying four additional clock pulses to drive all five bits out the register's Q_E output pin.

		Inputs							Outputs				
$\overline{\text{Clear}}$	Preset Enable	Preset					Clock	Serial	Q_A	Q_B	Q_C	Q_D	Q_E
		A	B	C	D	E							
L	L	×	×	×	×	×	×	×	L	L	L	L	L
L	×	L	L	L	L	L	×	×	L	L	L	L	L
H	H	H	H	H	H	H	×	×	H	H	H	H	H
H	H	L	L	L	L	L	L	×	Q_{A0}	Q_{B0}	Q_{C0}	Q_{D0}	Q_{E0}
H	H	H	L	H	L	H	L	×	H	Q_{B0}	H	Q_{D0}	H
H	L	×	×	×	×	×	L	×	Q_{A0}	Q_{B0}	Q_{C0}	Q_{D0}	Q_{E0}
H	L	×	×	×	×	×	↑	H	H	Q_{An}	Q_{Bn}	Q_{Cn}	Q_{Dn}
H	L	×	×	×	×	×	↑	L	L	Q_{An}	Q_{Bn}	Q_{Cn}	Q_{Dn}

Q_{A0}, Q_{B0}, etc. = levels of Q_A, Q_B, etc., respectively, before the indicated steady-state input conditions are established. Q_{An}, Q_{Bn}, etc. = levels of Q_A, Q_B, etc., respectively, before the most recent ↑ transition of the clock.

(c)

(d)

Figure 7.5 (Continued) SN7496 5-bit serial-in parallel-out shift register. **(c)** Function table. **(d)** Package pins (top view). *Source:* The TTL Data Book Volume 2, Texas Instruments Inc., 1985.

The function table for the SN7496 is given in Fig. 7.5c. Since the $\overline{Clear}$ signal is active low and *Preset enable* is active high, this combination is not normally applied to the device. If we apply $(\overline{Clear}, \textit{Preset enable}) = (0, 1)$, the SR flip-flops will assume the all-zero state as illustrated in row 2 of the table. Consider row 1 in the table: $(\overline{Clear}, \textit{Preset enable}) = (0, 0)$. This is the clear function. Rows 3, 4, and 5 demonstrate various presetting examples. In row 3, all the individual *Preset i* signals are high, so all the flip-flop outputs Q_i are driven high. In rows 4 and 5, selected *Preset i* signals are low, thus leaving those flip-flops Q_i unchanged by the action of the *Preset enable* signal. The last three rows of the table demonstrate shifting operations. Row 6 illustrates that no shifting occurs while the clock signal is held low. Rows 7 and 8 illustrate that the *Serial input* is entered into the register and all data bits are shifted one position to the right as each $0 \rightarrow 1$ clock transition occurs.

Figure 7.5d displays the pin configuration for this 16-pin dual in-line package.

SN74165

This device is an 8-bit, serial-in, serial-out shift register with asynchronous load and clock inhibit features. Inspect the logic diagram of Fig. 7.6a. Note that this chip has 12 inputs and only 2 outputs. To explain its function, we have enlarged the first cell of the register in Fig. 7.6b. First note that there is no clear signal. The logic symbol for each flip-flop indicates that it operates as a positive-edge-triggered D flip-flop with preset (labeled S) and clear (labeled R) terminals. Both the S and R terminals of the flip-flop are controlled by the inputs A and $Shift/\overline{load}$. *Shift* represents the operation "shift," and $\overline{Load}$ represents "not-load." In other words, *Shift* and *Not-load* are the same signal, so *Shift* and *Load* are complementary signals. Using Boolean algebra to solve for the logic equations for S and R, we find

$$S = A\,\overline{(Shift/\overline{Load})} \tag{7.1}$$

$$\begin{aligned}
R &= \overline{S}\,\overline{(Shift/\overline{Load})} \\
&= \overline{[A\,\overline{(Shift/\overline{Load})}]}\,\overline{(Shift/\overline{Load})} \\
&= [\bar{A} + (Shift/\overline{Load})]\overline{(Shift/\overline{Load})} \\
&= \bar{A}\,\overline{(Shift/\overline{Load})} \tag{7.2}
\end{aligned}$$

When $Shift/\overline{Load}$ is high, both S and R flip-flop inputs are low, so the flip-flop operates in its clocked mode. But when $Shift/\overline{Load}$ is low, then $S = A$ and $R = \bar{A}$, so the flip-flop output will assume the value of input A; this is the *parallel-load* mode of operation for the device.

Next examine the *Clock* and *Clock inhibit* signals. When *Clock inhibit* is high, the output of the OR gate is held high and blocks (inhibits) any $0 \rightarrow 1$ transitions of the clock input, *Clock*, from reaching the flip-flop clock input terminal, $C1$. So *Clock inhibit* = *1* is the *hold-data* mode of operation for this device.

The operation of the SN74165 is summarized in the function table of Fig. 7.6c. Row 1 of the table describes the parallel-load mode of operation just discussed. The last line in the table describes the hold mode in which the *Clock inhibit* signal blocks any activity on the clock input. The other three lines (with *Clock inhibit* held low) describe the shifting modes of operation. The second line of the table illustrates the device in its initial state with the clock input low waiting for a transition. All flip-flops are in a stable condition. On the rising edge of the clock pulse, the third and fourth rows of the table indicate that the serial input data are entered into the first cell while the remaining cells shift their data to the right.

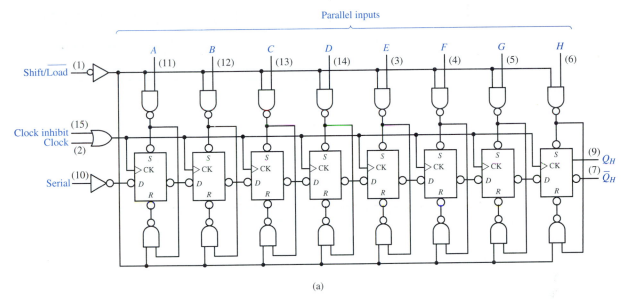

(a)

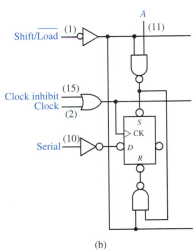

(b)

Inputs					Internal outputs		Output
Shift/ load	Clock inhibit	Clock	Serial	Parallel A...H	Q_A	Q_B	Q_H
L	×	×	×	a...h	a	b	h
H	L	L	×	×	Q_{A0}	Q_{B0}	Q_{H0}
H	L	↑	H	×	H	Q_{An}	Q_{Gn}
H	L	↑	L	×	L	Q_{An}	Q_{Gn}
H	H	×	×	×	Q_{A0}	Q_{B0}	Q_{H0}

(c)

Figure 7.6   SN74165 8-bit serial-in, serial-out shift register. **(a)** Logic diagram. **(b)** Cell A. **(c)** Function table.

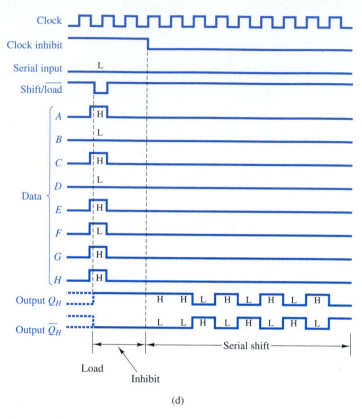

(d)

Figure 7.6 (Continued) SN74165 8-bit serial-in, serial-out shift register. **(d)** Timing diagram. *Source:* The TTL Data Book Volume 2, Texas Instruments Inc., 1985.

An example timing diagram for this device is shown in Fig. 7.6d. Here, an active-low pulse on the *Shift/Load* input performs an asynchronous parallel-load operation. It is called asynchronous because it is activated on the falling edge of the *Shift/Load* pulse instead of being synchronized with the rising edge of the *Clock signal*. The data loaded into the register are $(Q_H Q_G Q_F Q_E Q_D Q_C Q_B Q_A) = (11010101)$. After the *Clock inhibit* signal is returned to zero, the next seven pulses on *Clock* send the data serially out of the register (Q_H first and Q_A last). This demonstrates the parallel to serial conversion function of this register type.

SN74179

The module is a 4-bit, serial-in, serial-out, parallel-out shift register with asynchronous common clear, synchronous load, and synchronous data hold. Examine the logic diagram of Fig. 7.7a. The SR flip-flops have a $\overline{Clear}$ terminal but no preset function. The asynchronous common $\overline{Clear}$ control line forces all the

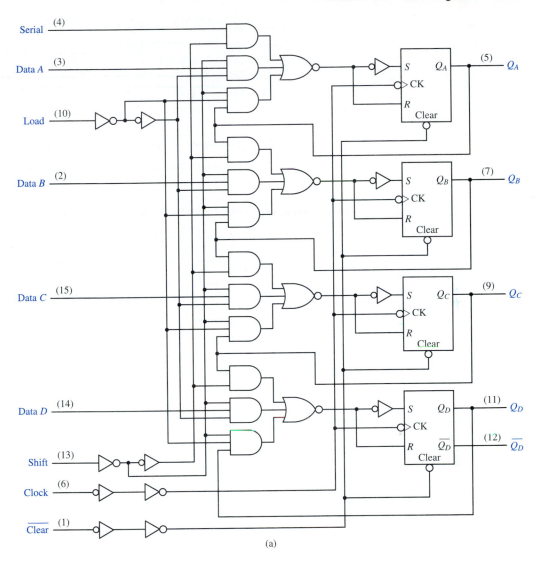

(a)

	Inputs		
$\overline{\text{Clear}}$	Shift	Load	Mode
L	×	×	Asynchronous clear
H	H	×	Shift
H	L	H	Synchronous load
H	L	L	Data hold

(b)

Figure 7.7 SN74179 4-bit serial-in, serial/parallel-out shift register. **(a)** Logic diagram. **(b)** Function table. *Source:* The TTL Data Book Volume 2, Texas Instruments Inc., 1985.

flip-flops in the register to the logic 0 state when it is held low. When $\overline{Clear}$ is high, three other modes of the register are possible. These operating modes are summarized in the function table of Fig. 7.7b.

Trace the logic inputs to the S and R flip-flop terminals. Note that $S = \bar{R}$ so that the flip-flop functions as a negative-edge-triggered D flip-flop, with $S = D$. Take a close look at flip-flop Q_B. The logic equation for its S input is

$$S_B = Q_A(Shift) + Data_B(\overline{Shift \cdot Load}) + Q_B(\overline{Shift} \cdot \overline{Load}) \qquad (7.3)$$

From this equation, it is apparent that when *Shift* is high, the device operates as a shift register with *Serial* being the serial-in pin and Q_D being serial out. From the second and third terms of the logic equation, we can see that when *Shift* is low, the *Load* signal controls the device operation. *Load* being high enables the *parallel synchronous load* mode of operation: *Data i* are entered into each flip-flop Q_i on the falling edge (negative edge) of the clock signal. Since this loading occurs under clock control, it is said to be synchronous.

The fourth operating mode of this device is established by holding both the *Shift* and *Load* lines low. This condition forces the output of each flip-flop to be gated back to its input terminals so that the data stored in the register "recirculates" or is held constant. This is called the *synchronous data hold* mode.

SN74194

This module is a 4-bit, bidirectional, serial-in, serial-out, parallel-out shift register with clock inhibit, asynchronous common clear, and synchronous load. The interesting new feature of this device is its bidirectional mode of operation. The logic diagram for the SN74194 is shown in Fig. 7.8a. Note the two mode control bits, $S0$ and $S1$. Examine the logic equations for CK (the clock input to each flip-flop) and S_B (the equivalent D input of flip-flop Q_B):

$$CK = Clock + \overline{S0} \cdot \overline{S1} \qquad (7.4)$$

$$S_B = Q_C \cdot \overline{S0} + Q_A \cdot \overline{S1} + B \cdot S0 \cdot S1 \qquad (7.5)$$

From Eq. 7.4 for CK, we see that when $S0$ and $S1$ are both low the clock is inhibited because its activity is masked by a constant logic 1 out of the second term in the equation. So the clocked modes of operation requires that either $S0$ or $S1$ (or both) be high.

Let us examine the clocked modes of operation. From Eq. 7.5, if $S1$ is high and $S0$ is low, then $S_B = Q_C$; that is, the output of flip-flop Q_C is applied to the input terminals of flip-flop B; this is the *shift left* operation. Exchanging the values of the mode control bits ($S0$ high and $S1$ low) reduces Eq. 7.5 to $S_B = Q_A$, applying the data in Q_A to flip-flop B; this is the *shift right* mode of operation. The fourth condition of the mode control bits ($S0$ and $S1$ both high) gates the module's external parallel data input bit B to the S and R inputs of flip-flop B; that is, Eq. 7.5 reduces to $S_B = B$; this is the *synchronous*,

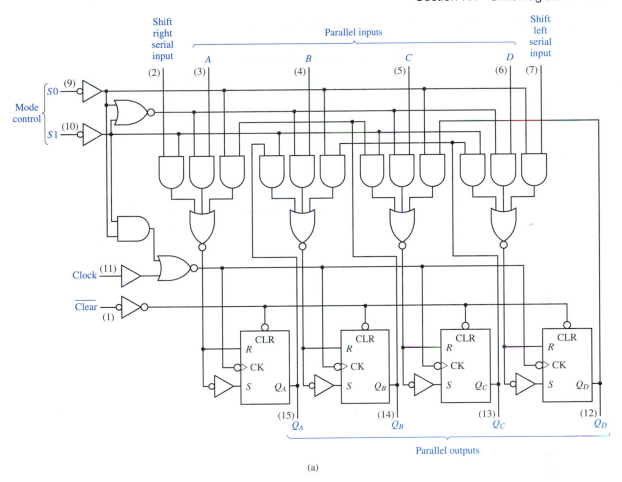

(a)

Inputs				Internal signals $(i = A, B, C, D)$	
$\overline{Clear}$	$S0$	$S1$	Clock	S_i	Mode
L	×	×	×	×	Asynchronous clear
H	L	L	×	×	Clock inhibit (data hold)
H	L	H	↑	Q_{i+1}	Shift left
H	H	L	↑	Q_{i-1}	Shift right
H	H	H	↑	i	Parallel load

(b)

Figure 7.8   SN74194 bidirectional serial-in, serial/parallel-out shift register. **(a)** Logic Diagram. **(b)** Function table. *Source:* The TTL Data Book Volume 2, Texas Instruments Inc., 1985.

parallel-load mode of operation. All four modes of operation are summarized in the function table of Fig. 7.8b.

The SN74194 is a 16-pin device.

7.2 Design Examples Using Registers

7.2.1 Serial Adder Unit

Shift registers may be used in conjunction with combinational circuit modules to produce some interesting functional units. Consider the full adder (presented in Chapter 4) and shift registers illustrated in Fig. 7.9. This unit may be used to add the binary numbers represented by parallel data signals X and Y, with the result being generated in register Z. This configuration uses two parallel-in, serial-out shift registers to accept the parallel data words X and Y and apply them 1 bit at a time to the full adder (FA). A serial-in, parallel-out shift register is used to convert the serial sum generated by the full adder to the parallel data word Z. The inputs X and Y are fed to the FA's least significant bit first. One D flip-flop is employed to time delay the carry bits so that they are added to X and Y in the proper position. The operation of the units is controlled by the *clear*, *Preset*, and *Shift* signals. First, a clear pulse forces a logic-0 into all the flip-flops of the three registers as well as the carry-delay flip-flop. Then a preset pulse enters the logic 1 data bits into the proper positions in the X and Y registers. The full adder will now generate the sum and carry for the least significant bits of X and Y. A control pulse on the *Shift* line causes the sum bit to enter the Z register and the carry to be stored in the carry-delay flip-flop. The

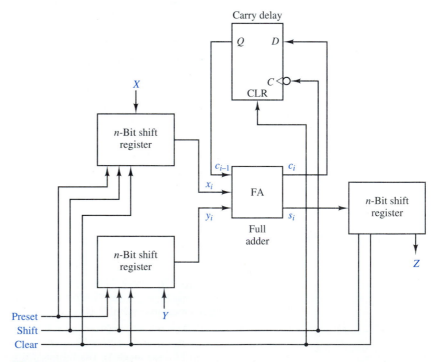

Figure 7.9   Serial adder unit.

full adder again generates the sum and carry output for the next most significant bits of X and Y. With each shift pulse, the addition of another bit position is performed. This process is repeated until the nth shift pulse enters the most significant bit of the sum of X and Y into the Z register. Now the operation is complete and the parallel sum is available at the outputs of the Z register.

7.2.2 Serial Accumulators

An *accumulator* is an adder unit that totals a series of binary data. It functions like a cash register in that any number of binary data items may be added while the accumulator keeps the current total sum. Just as with the cash register, we can exceed the operating range of the accumulator and produce overflow.

A serial accumulator may be designed using the serial adder unit of Fig. 7.9 by eliminating the register Y and allowing register Z to feed back to the inputs of the full adder. See Fig. 7.10a. For proper operation, the following control sequence should be employed. First, pulse the *Clear* control line to initialize all flip-flops to logic 0. Then apply a *Preset* pulse, followed by n *Shift* pulses. Now the first piece of binary data is in register Z, and register X will again be in the all-zero state. At this point, new data are supplied to the parallel input lines of register X and another preset pulse is applied. After n additional shift pulse signals, the sum of two data items appears in register Z. Any number of data items may be added as long as the n-bit range of register Z is not exceeded by the total sum. A serial accumulator is satisfactory for many low-speed digital system designs.

7.2.3 Parallel Accumulators

For higher-speed operation, the parallel accumulator design of Fig. 7.10b is more suitable. This design is based on a pseudoparallel adder unit with a feedback storage register Z. The proper operation of this circuit requires that the *Clear* control be pulsed to initialize the circuit. Afterward one *Accumulate* pulse is necessary to add each new data item. This unit is faster than the serial design and is much less complicated to operate. Accumulator modules find frequent application in digital logic design.

▶ 7.3 Counters

Counters are a class of sequential logic circuits that tally a series of input pulses; the input pulses may be regular or irregular in nature. The counter is a fundamental part of most digital logic applications. It is used in timing units, control circuits, signal generators, and numerous other devices.

Counters may be categorized as binary/nonbinary and asynchronous/synchronous. Several example counter designs are described next. Selected SN7400 series counter devices will be used as examples in this chapter to illustrate the wide variety of choices that are available to the logic designer. Synchronous

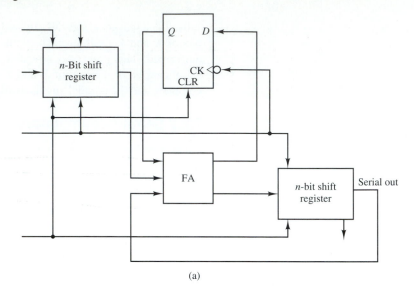

(a)

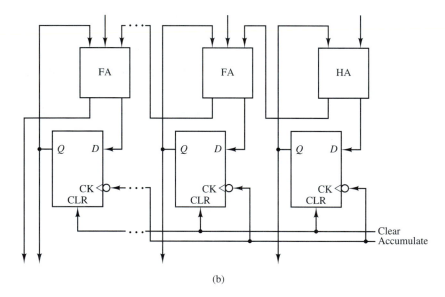

(b)

Figure 7.10 Accumulators. **(a)** Serial unit. **(b)** Parallel unit.

and asynchronous designs are covered. Such features as synchronous and asynchronous clear, enable, synchronous and asynchronous load, and ripple carry output are discussed. Binary and modulo-N counters are illustrated. Table 7.2 summarizes the counters that will be discussed. The features of each device will be defined as it is presented.

TABLE 7.2 SN7400 SERIES COUNTERS

Device	Type	Features
7492A	Asynchronous mod-12	$\div 2$, $\div 6$, $\div 12$, common clear
74160	Synchronous decade	4-Bit, synchronous load, asynchronous clear, enable, ripple carry-out
74163	Synchronous binary	4-Bit, synchronous load, synchronous clear, enable, ripple carry-out
74176	Asynchronous decade	$\div 2$, $\div 5$, $\div 10$, common clear, asynchronous load
74177	Asynchronous binary	$\div 2$, $\div 8$, $\div 16$, common clear, asynchronous load
74191	Synchronous up/down	4-Bit, asynchronous load, enable, maximum, and ripple clock outputs
74293	Asynchronous binary	$\div 2$, $\div 8$, $\div 16$, common clear

7.3.1 Synchronous Binary Counters

A synchronous n-bit binary counter constructed of clocked JK flip-flops is illustrated in Fig. 7.11a. A binary counter of n flip-flops should begin in the all-zero state and sequence through the numbers $0, 1, 2, 3, \ldots, 2^n - 1, 0, 1, 2, \ldots$, and so forth. In other words, the counter will have 2^n unique states as shown in Fig. 7.11b and will repeat the states as long as clock pulses are applied. The design of Fig. 7.11a is suggested by the state sequence listed in Fig. 7.11b. Note that each bit X_i should be complemented on the next count pulse if all bits X_k for $k = 1, \ldots, i - 1$ are at logic 1; bit X_1 is always complemented on each count pulse. Hence, a two-input AND gate may be used at each counter flip-flop to generate a toggle control signal for the next more significant bit in the counter chain. A counter flip-flop and its associated control circuitry are sometimes call a *counter stage*.

Under normal operating conditions, the J and K inputs to each flip-flop should remain stable at either logic 1 or 0 while the count pulse undergoes its $0 \rightarrow 1 \rightarrow 0$ transitions. A logic 1 on the clear control line will force all counter outputs to logic 0 and hold them there until the clear line is returned to logic 0 (its normal logic value). The *Inhibit* control signal is used to block the count pulses and leave the counter in some nonzero state, if such data-hold behavior is required for a particular application.

When the counter reaches the all-one state, the *overflow* signal will go high. In some counter designs, this overflow signal is used to drive cascaded counter modules to produce larger counter word lengths. In these cases, the overflow signal is commonly called the *ripple carry-out* (RCO).

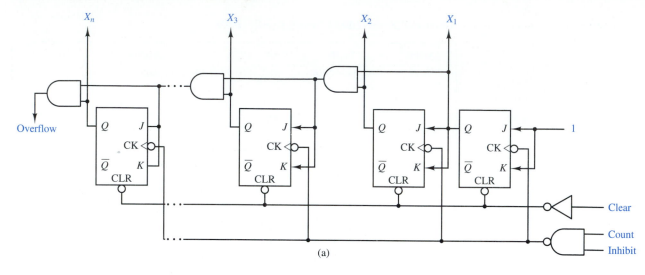

Figure 7.11 Synchronous binary counter. **(a)** Logic diagram. **(b)** State sequence.

SN74163

This is a 4-bit synchronous counter with synchronous load, synchronous clear, enable, and ripple carry-out. The logic diagram for the device is presented in Fig. 7.12a. Notice that all data changes in the JK flip-flops will occur on the rising edge of the external clock labeled *Clock*. Therefore, the clear and load operations are synchronized with the clock in this device.

Let us examine the operation of a typical counter stage, say C. The K input to the flip-flop may be written

$$K_C = \overline{[\overline{(\overline{Load})} + \overline{(\overline{Clear})} + Q_B \cdot Q_A \cdot ENT \cdot ENP]}$$
$$\cdot [((\overline{Load}) + \overline{(\overline{Clear})}) \cdot \overline{Clear} \cdot Data_C]$$

(7.6)

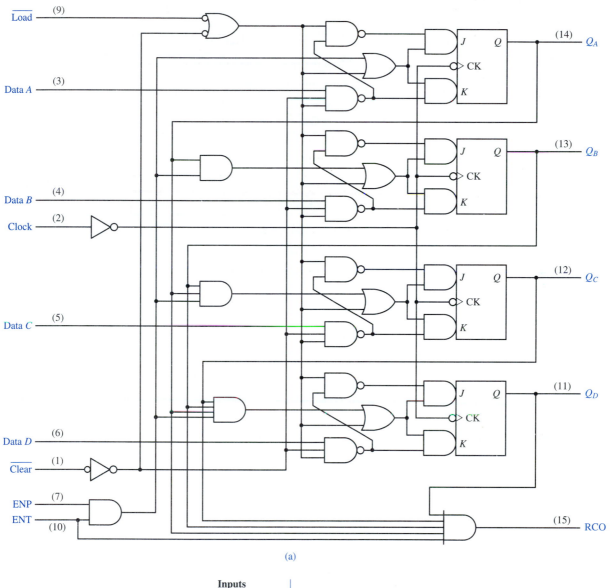

(a)

Inputs				
Clear	Load	ENT	ENP	Mode
L	×	×	×	Synchronous clear
H	L	×	×	Synchronous load
H	H	H	H	Count
H	H	L	×	Hold
H	H	×	L	Hold

(b)

Figure 7.12   SN74163 synchronous binary counter. **(a)** Logic diagram.
(b) Function table. *Source:* The TTL Data Book Volume 2, Texas Instruments Inc.,
1985.

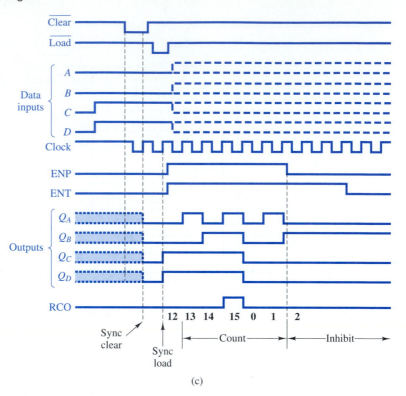

(c)

Figure 7.12 (Continued) SN74163 synchronous binary counter. **(c)** Timing diagram. *Source:* The TTL Data Book Volume 2, Texas Instruments Inc., 1985.

where $Data_C$ is the data C input in the logic diagram. Using Boolean algebra to reduce Eq. 7.6 produces

$$K_C = \overline{(\overline{Clear})} + \overline{Load} \cdot Q_B \cdot Q_A \cdot ENT \cdot ENP + \overline{(\overline{Load})} \cdot \overline{Data_C} \qquad (7.7)$$

The logic equation for the J input to the flip-flop is

$$J_C = \overline{[(\overline{Load}) + (\overline{Clear})} + \overline{Q_B \cdot Q_A \cdot ENT \cdot ENP]} \qquad (7.8)$$

$$\overline{\{[(\overline{(\overline{Load})} + \overline{(\overline{Clear})}) \cdot \overline{Clear} \cdot Data_C](\overline{(\overline{Load})} + \overline{(\overline{Clear})})\}}$$

or

$$J_C = \overline{Clear} \, [\overline{Load} \cdot Q_B \cdot Q_A \cdot ENT \cdot ENP + \overline{(\overline{Load})} \cdot Data_C] \qquad (7.9)$$

From logic equations 7.9 and 7.7, we can determine the function table for the counter. When $\overline{Clear}$ is low, $J_C = 0$ and $K_C = 1$ so the flip-flop will be reset on the next rising edge of a pulse on the *Clock* input signal. This is the *synchronous clear* mode of operation. When $\overline{Clear}$ is high, the other terms in the equations control the operation of the flip-flop. For example, if $\overline{Load}$ is low, $J_C = Data_C$ and $K_C = \overline{Data_C}$ so that the value of $Data_C$ will be entered into the flip-flop on the next rising edge of the signal *Clock*. This is the *synchronous load* mode.

The last case to consider is when both $\overline{Clear}$ and $\overline{Load}$ are high. In this case,

$$J_C = K_C = Q_B \cdot Q_A \cdot ENT \cdot ENP \qquad (7.10)$$

When the enable signals *ENT* and *ENP* are both high, this is the *count* mode of operation. In this mode, the counter operates like the one in Fig. 7.11a. Flip-flop Q_C is toggled when all counter bits that are less significant that Q_C (in this case Q_B and Q_A) are high. The output *RCO* (ripple carry-out) is used in the count mode. The logic equation for *RCO* is

$$RCO = ENT \cdot Q_D \cdot Q_C \cdot Q_B \cdot Q_A \qquad (7.11)$$

Consequently, when enable signal *ENT* is high, *RCO* is an all-ones-state decoder signal; *RCO* is high when the counter is in state $(Q_D Q_C Q_B Q_A)_2 = (1111)_2$ or $(15)_{10}$. Sometimes the *RCO* signal is used to warn that the counter is about to *overflow* its dynamic range (exceed its maximum value and return to the all-zero state).

When either of the enable signals (ENT and ENP) is low, $J_C = K_C = 0$, and this is the *data-hold* (or *inhibit*) mode of operation. All the operating modes are summarized in the function table of Fig. 7.12b.

An example timing diagram for the device is shown in Fig. 7.12c. First a *Clear* pulse is applied to force all the flip-flops to the logic 0 state. Then a *Load* pulse is applied to enter a binary number into the device. In this case the number is $(Q_D Q_C Q_B Q_A)_2 = (1100)_2$. Note that the *Clear* pulse is not required for loading a number into this device. The load pulse will accomplish its function without first applying the *Clear* pulse. Next, the enable signals *ENT* and *ENP* are activated and a series of count pulses are applied to the *Clock* input. The counter cycles through its states (in decimal) as follows: 12, 13, 14, 15, 0, 1, and 2. At this point, the *ENP* and later the *ENT* signals drop to 0 and inhibit any further changes to the state of the counter. Note that the signal *RCO* is high while the counter is in the all-ones state.

7.3.2 Asynchronous Binary Counters

An asynchronous binary counter is one whose state changes are not controlled by a synchronizing clock pulse. By eliminating the requirement for clock synchronization, a reduced amount of circuitry can be used to implement a binary counter. Consider the synchronous design of Fig. 7.11a. One may eliminate the AND gates in the synchronous design by observing the counter state transitions from another viewpoint; see Fig. 7.13a. Counter stage X_i is complemented each time state X_{i-1} makes a $1 \rightarrow 0$ transition; stage X_1 is always complemented. A counter based on these observations is demonstrated in Fig. 7.13b. An asynchronous common *Clear* command may be used to initialize the counter to the 0 state, and the *Count* control command is held at logic 1 for counting; logic 0 on *Count* inhibits all counting and leaves the counter in a constant state; this is the data-hold mode.

Let us examine the behavior of the asynchronous binary counter as overflow occurs. Just before overflow, all counter stages are at logic 1 as shown in

X_n	$\ldots$	X_3	X_2	X_1
0	$\ldots$	0	0	0
0	$\ldots$	0	0	1
0	$\ldots$	0	1	$\leftarrow$ 0
0	$\ldots$	0	1	1
0	$\ldots$	1 $\leftarrow$	0 $\leftarrow$	0

(a)

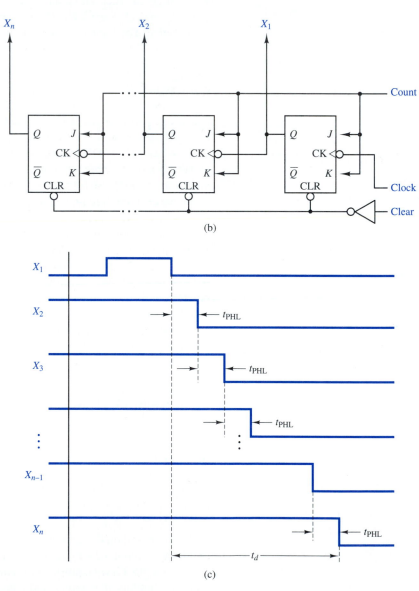

(b)

(c)

Figure 7.13 Asynchronous binary counter. **(a)** State sequence. **(b)** Logic diagram. **(c)** Timing diagram.

Fig. 7.13c. After the clock pulse falls, the flip-flop of counter stage X_1 responds in t_{PHL} seconds. Each stage then follows in a similar manner until the entire counter has reached the logic 0 state. It is important that the reader note the transient condition produced by this count sequence. Instead of the desired state change $(2^n - 1)_{10}$ to $(0)_{10}$, the counter has passed through the following state sequence:

$$(2^n - 1)_{10} (2^n - 2)_{10} (2^n - 4)_{10} (2^n - 8)_{10} \ldots (2^{n-1})_{10} (0)_{10}$$

Although these transitions are rapid, they can generate unwanted transient conditions if the counter outputs are used to drive a combinational logic circuit. See the discussions of hazards in Chapter 3. Because of the transient behavior described here, an asynchronous counter is sometimes call a *ripple* counter.

SN74293

This module is a SN7400 series implementation of the asynchronous binary counter of Fig. 7.13. Its logic diagram is shown in Fig. 7.14a. Note the two common clear lines $R_{0(1)}$ and $R_{O(2)}$. When both these lines are high, the device is forced to the all-zero state. The counter is divided into two segments, a 1-bit counter and a 3-bit counter. They may be cascaded (connect Q_A to input B) to make a 4-bit counter. The J and K inputs to each flip-flip are connected high within the device to make the flip-flops act like toggle (T) flip-flops.

Figure 7.14b displays the state diagram for the SN74293. The larger circles represent stable states for the device. The smaller circles represent rapid, transient behavior. Notice that the transition from state 15 to state 0 exhibits the behavior described in Fig. 7.13c.

Several comments about this transient behavior are in order. First, if the count pulses are much slower than the time delay of the clocked JK flip-flops, the counter will pass through the transient states rapidly and reside in the desired stable states most of the time. A second observation is that all the transient states have even numbers; therefore, the odd-numbered states exhibit stable behavior even in ripple-type counters.

SN74177

This module is an expanded function version of the SN74293. See Fig. 7.15a. In this device input A has been renamed *Clock* 1 and input B has been called *Clock* 2. The added feature is the *asynchronous load* mode of operation. Examine the logic equations for the *Preset* and *Clear* terminals of a typical flip-flop, say B:

$$Preset_B = Data_B \cdot [\overline{(Count/Load)} + \overline{(Clear)}] \cdot \overline{Clear} \qquad (7.12)$$

or

$$Preset_B = Data_B \cdot \overline{(Count/Load)} \cdot \overline{Clear} \qquad (7.13)$$

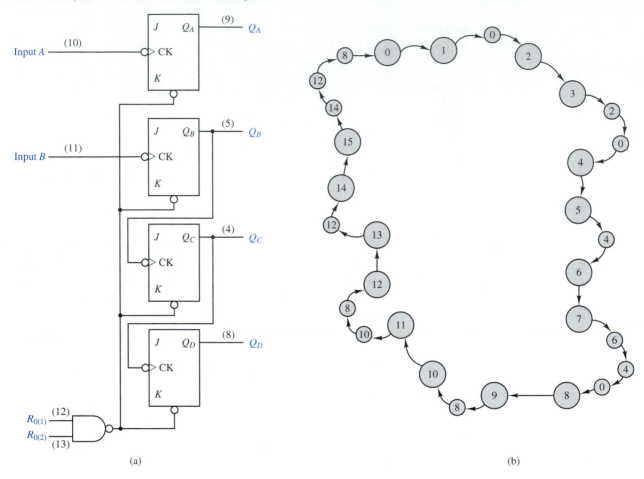

Figure 7.14 SN74293 asynchronous binary counter. **(a)** Logic diagram.
(b) State diagram. *Source:* The TTL Data Book Volume 2, Texas Instruments Inc.,
1985.

Do not confuse the external $\overline{\text{clear}}$ input line and the clear signals for each flip-
flip. The flip-flop clear signals are given subscripts in the following equations.
For the clear terminal of flip-flop B,

$$Clear_B = \overline{[(Count/\overline{Load}) + (\overline{Clear})]}$$
$$\cdot \overline{[Data_B \cdot \overline{(Count/\overline{Load})} \cdot \overline{Clear}]} \qquad (7.14)$$

or

$$Clear_B = \overline{(\overline{Clear})} + \overline{(Count/\overline{Load})} \cdot \overline{(Data_B)} \qquad (7.15)$$

Examining equations 7.13 and 7.15, we find that when external input line
$\overline{Clear}$ is low, inside the flip-flop, $Preset_B$ is low and $Clear_B$ is high. This is
the *asynchronous common clear* mode of operation. Setting the external $\overline{Clear}$
line high (inactive) allows the $Count/\overline{Load}$ external line to control the device.

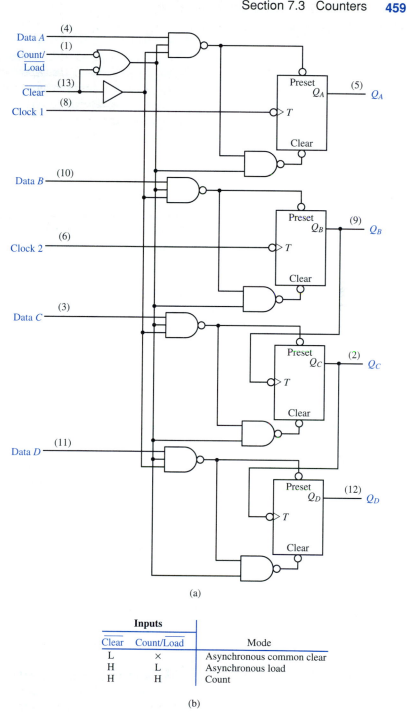

(a)

Inputs		
$\overline{\text{Clear}}$	Count/$\overline{\text{Load}}$	Mode
L	×	Asynchronous common clear
H	L	Asynchronous load
H	H	Count

(b)

Figure 7.15 SN74177 asynchronous binary counter. **(a)** Logic diagram. **(b)** Function table. *Source:* The TTL Data Book Volume 2, Texas Instruments Inc., 1985.

If the $\overline{Clear}$ line is high and $Count/\overline{Load}$ is low, then $Preset_B = Data_B$ and $Clear_B = \overline{(Data_B)}$. This is the *asynchronous load* mode of operation because the value of $Data_B$ will be forced into the flip-flop. If the external $\overline{Clear}$ and $Count/\overline{Load}$ lines are both high, then $Preset_B = Clear_B = 0$; this is the *count* mode for the device. The operating modes for the SN74177 are summarized in the function table of Fig. 7.15b.

7.3.3 Down Counters

A *down*, or *backward*, counter is one whose state transitions are reversed from those of the standard counter, which is also known as an *up*, or *forward*, counter. Examine the state tables of Fig. 7.16a. The down counter behaves as a complemented up counter; hence, an asynchronous down counter may be constructed using clocked JK flip-flops, as indicated in Fig. 7.16b. The *Clear* control signal drives the counter to the 0 state, and the *Count* control signal must be logic 1 in order for the clock pulses to cause counter state changes. Again this asynchronous design produces the rippling effect, which can be dangerous in some applications.

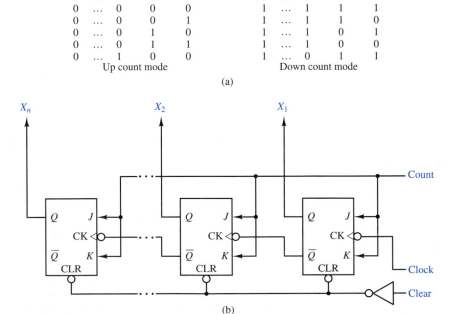

X_n	...	X_3	X_2	X_1
1	...	1	1	1
0	...	0	0	0
0	...	0	0	1
0	...	0	1	0
0	...	0	1	1
0	...	1	0	0

Up count mode

X_n	...	X_3	X_2	X_1
0	...	0	0	0
1	...	1	1	1
1	...	1	1	0
1	...	1	0	1
1	...	1	0	0
1	...	0	1	1

Down count mode

(a)

(b)

Figure 7.16   Asynchronous down counter. **(a)** State sequences. **(b)** Logic diagram.

7.3.4 Up/Down Counters

Many digital systems require a counter design that can function in both the up and down modes of operation. A combination up/down synchronous counter appears in Fig. 7.17. This counter is either in the up or down mode since the down control signal is the complement of the up control signal. Therefore, we labeled the up/down control line $Up/\overline{down}$. In the up mode, the Q outputs of the flip-flops control the J and K terminals of flip-flops higher in the chain. In the down mode, the $\bar{Q}$ outputs of the flip-flops fill this role.

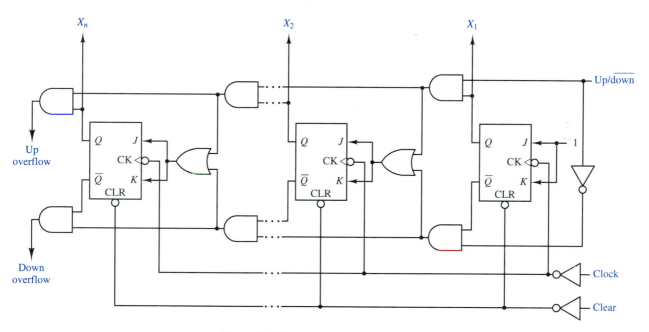

Figure 7.17 Synchronous up/down counter.

SN74191

This is the most complex chip that we have discussed so far in this chapter. It is a 4-bit, up/down, synchronous counter with asynchronous load, enable, ripple clock, and maximum state outputs. The logic diagram is displayed in Fig. 7.18a. Inspect the S and R terminals of the four flip-flops. These correspond to the *Preset* and *Clear* terminals in previous example chips. The logic driving the S and R terminals resembles the logic for *Preset* and *Clear* in the SN74177 of Fig. 7.15a. For flip-flop C in Fig. 7.18a,

$$S_C = Data_C \cdot \overline{(Load)} \tag{7.16}$$

$$R_C = \overline{[Data_C \cdot \overline{(Load)}] \cdot \overline{(Load)}]}$$

$$= \overline{Data_C} \cdot \overline{(Load)} \tag{7.17}$$

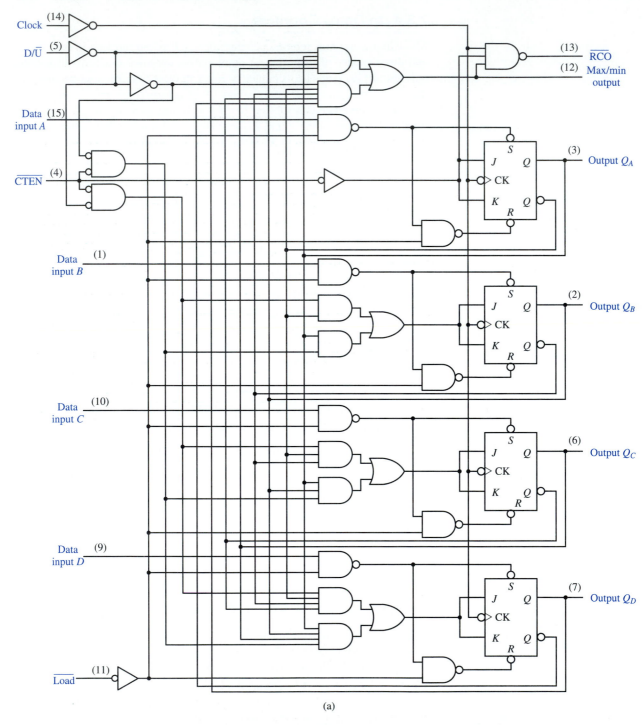

(a)

Figure 7.18 SN74191 up/down counter. **(a)** Logic diagram.

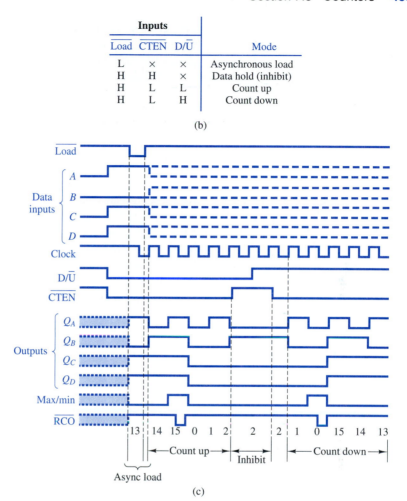

Inputs			
$\overline{\text{Load}}$	$\overline{\text{CTEN}}$	D/$\overline{\text{U}}$	Mode
L	×	×	Asynchronous load
H	H	×	Data hold (inhibit)
H	L	L	Count up
H	L	H	Count down

(b)

(c)

Figure 7.18   (Continued) SN74191 up/down counter. **(b)** Function table. **(c)** Timing diagram. *Source:* The TTL Data Book Volume 2, Texas Instruments Inc., 1985.

When $\overline{Load}$ is low, then $S_C = Data_C$ and $R_C = \overline{(Data_C)}$, so the value of $Data_C$ is loaded into the flip-flop asynchronously. When $\overline{Load}$ is high, $S_C = R_C = 0$, so the counter is controlled by its other inputs, $\overline{CTEN}$, D/$\overline{U}$, and *Clock*.

Next examine the J and K inputs of flip-flop C:

$$J_C = K_C = \overline{(\overline{CTEN})} \cdot [Q_B \cdot Q_A \cdot \overline{(D/\overline{U})} + \bar{Q}_B \cdot \bar{Q}_A \cdot (D/\overline{U})] \qquad (7.18)$$

When the count enable input signal $\overline{CTEN}$ is high, both J_C and K_C are logic 0, so no changes will occur in the flip-flop outputs. When $\overline{CTEN}$ is low, the counter enters the up or down counting mode depending on the value of D/$\overline{U}$. If D/$\overline{U}$ is low, then Q_B and Q_A determine the toggling of Q_C so that the counter is in the *up* mode. When $D/\bar{U}$ is high, $\bar{Q}_B$ and $\bar{Q}_A$ determine the toggling of Q_C, and so the counter sequences backward, or *down*, through its states. The function table for the device is given in Fig. 7.18b.

An additional feature of this counter is its *Max/min* output signal. In the up mode, this signal goes high on state 15. In the down mode it goes high on state 0. The *Max/min* output signal also feeds the $\overline{RCO}$ output:

$$\overline{RCO} = [\overline{Clock \cdot (Max/min) \cdot (\overline{CTEN})}] \tag{7.19}$$

$\overline{RCO}$ goes low when the device is counting ($\overline{CTEN}$ is low) and the *Max/min output* goes high.

An example timing diagram for the device is depicted in Fig. 7.18c. An asynchronous load operation drives the counter to the $(Q_D Q_C Q_B Q_A)_2 = (1101)_2 = (13)_{10}$ state. Then since $D/\bar{U}$ and $\overline{CTEN}$ are low, the device sequences up through states 14, 15, 0, 1, and 2. Then the $\overline{CTEN}$ signal goes high, inhibiting any further upward changes. Changing $D/\bar{U}$ to high and then bringing $\overline{CTEN}$ low puts the device in the down counting mode, so the state sequence reverses: 2, 1, 0, 15, 14, 13, and so forth. Note the behavior of *Max/min* and $\overline{RCO}$ on the timing diagram.

7.4 Modulo-N Counters

Many occasions arise in the design of digital systems in which a counter is needed that can count from state 0 through state $N - 1$ and then cycle back to state 0; such counters are said to be *modulo-N* counters. The most common modulo-N counters are the binary ones previously discussed. For binary counters, N is equal to 2^n, where n is the number of counter stages. Counters with other values for N are also very useful. For example, $N = 10$ (decade) counters are frequently encountered in digital systems design.

7.4.1 Synchronous BCD Counters

A synchronous BCD (binary coded decimal) counter is a modulo-10, or *decade*, counter. The BCD counter must behave like a binary counter until state 9 is reached. At this point the control circuitry must prepare the flip-flop inputs so that the next clock pulse will force the counter back to state (0000) instead of allowing the next binary-counter state (1010) to be reached. A synchronous BCD counter design is available in the SN74160 module.

SN74160

This is a synchronous decade counter with synchronous load, asynchronous clear, enable, and ripple carry-out. See Fig. 7.19.

The asynchronous clear control signal $\overline{Clear}$ is active low. The load control signal $\overline{Load}$ is also active low. How does this counter operate? We can analyze its operating characteristics by examining a typical flip-flop and then

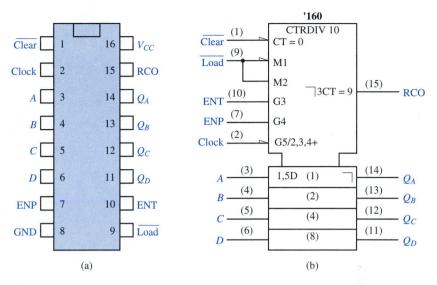

Figure 7.19   SN74160 synchronous decade counter. **(a)** Package pins. **(b)** Logic symbol.

generalizing the results to the 4-bit counter. Suppose we choose counter stage Q_B and examine its J and K inputs. The logic equations for these inputs are

$$J_B = \overline{(Load)} \cdot Data_B + \overline{Load} \cdot Q_A \cdot \bar{Q}_D \cdot ENT \cdot ENP$$

$$K_B = \overline{(Load)} \cdot \overline{Data_B} + \overline{Load} \cdot Q_A \cdot \bar{Q}_D \cdot ENT \cdot ENP$$

Note that when the load control signal $\overline{Load}$ is low, the true and complemented values of the data input signal ($Data_B$) for the counter stage are placed on J_B and K_B, respectively. Consequently, the flip-flop will act like a clocked-D flip-flop and, on the next clock pulse, the value on input line $Data_B$ will be synchronously loaded into the counter and will appear at the flip-flop output Q_B. When $\overline{Load}$ is high, the second product term in each logic equation controls J_B and K_B. This is the synchronous counting mode of operation. Both the enable signals ENP and ENT must be high before the counter will cycle through is states. All four flip-flops change states on the rising edge of the clock input $Clock$. Now examine the logic equation for the ripple carry-out RCO signal

$$RCO = Q_D \cdot Q_A \cdot ENT$$

Since the counter cycles through states 0, 1, 2,..., 9, the states 10, 11,..., 15 will never occur. Hence, the maximum state of the counter (1001) can be detected by an AND gate with inputs Q_D and Q_A. The input signal ENT must be high to enable RCO.

A timing diagram for a typical sequence of operations for the SN74160 is illustrated in Fig. 7.19d. First an asynchronous clear signal has been applied to drive the counter to the all-zero state. Next a synchronous load operation forces the counter to state 7 (0111). Then both enable signals, ENT and ENP, are applied to start the synchronous counting mode of operation. On the rising

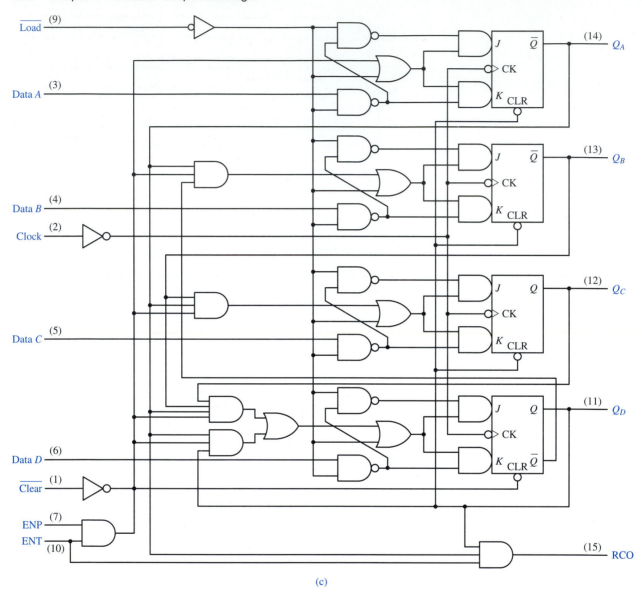

(c)

Figure 7.19 (Continued) SN74160 decade counter. **(c)** Logic diagram. *Source:* The TTL Data Book Volume 2, Texas Instruments Inc., 1985.

edge of each clock pulse *Clock*, the counter progresses to state 8, then 9, then recycles to state 0, and continues with states 1, 2, and 3. At this point in the sequence, the enable signal *ENP* is brought low and inhibits further sequencing of the counter. Notice that either signal *ENP* or *ENT* may be used to inhibit the counter (place it in the data-hold mode). Also note that the signal *RCO* is high during the period of time in which the counter is in state 9, its maximum state.

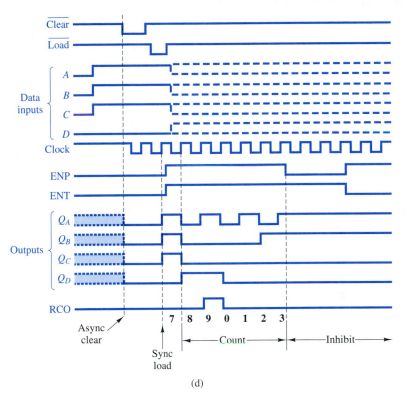

(d)

Figure 7.19 (Continued) SN74160 decade counter. **(d)** Timing diagram.
Source: The TTL Data Book Volume 2, Texas Instruments Inc., 1985.

7.4.2 Asynchronous BCD Counters

The synchronous decade counter of Fig. 7.19 can be replaced by an asynchronous counter in many applications. An asynchronous, or *ripple*, decade counter can be designed by modifying the binary counter of Fig. 7.13b. Suppose we add a logic circuit to detect state 10 and use this signal to drive the counter immediately to state 0 via the common reset line. State 10 has the binary value $(X_3X_2X_1X_0) = (1010)$. We can decode state 10 using a two-input AND gate with inputs X_3 and X_1. The condition $X_3 = X_1 = 1$ is unique since the counter will cycle through states 0, 1, 2,..., 9 before reaching state 10. No other state in the sequence satisfies the condition $X_3 = X_1 = 1$. The logic diagram for the asynchronous decade counter is shown in Fig. 7.20a. Let us now examine the transient behavior of this ripple counter design.

In Fig. 7.20b, a state diagram is used to describe the behavior of this circuit. The transient behavior of the counter from states 0 through 9 has been described earlier in this chapter. (See Fig. 7.14b.) In this figure the smaller circles represent transient states. The worst-case transient condition occurs on the transition from state 7 to state 8. Due to the rippling effect, three intermediate states are observed. Now consider the transition from state 9 to state 0. The

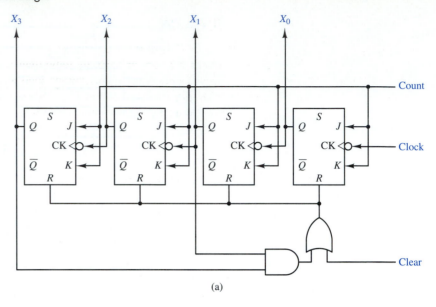

(a)

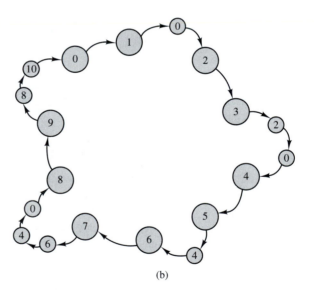

(b)

Figure 7.20 Asynchronous BCD counter. **(a)** Logic diagram. **(b)** State diagram.

ripple effect will cause the counter to enter state 8 and then state 10. However, the feedback circuit will detect state 10 and generate a common clear signal to reset all the counter stages to logic 0.

SN74176

The SN74176 is an asynchronous counter module that can perform the operations $\div 2$, $\div 5$, or $\div 10$. Its logic diagram is shown in Fig. 7.21. The module features common asynchronous load and clear controls. The load and clear operations for the counter may be explained by examining the logic equations for the set and reset inputs for a typical stage, say Q_C:

$$S_C = \overline{Clear} \cdot \overline{(\overline{Load})} \cdot Data_C$$

$$R_C = \overline{(\overline{Clear})} + \overline{(\overline{Load})} \cdot \overline{Data}_C$$

When the clear control signal $\overline{Clear}$ is low, $(S_C, R_C) = (0, 1)$ and the counter stage is reset to the logic 0 state. When $\overline{Clear}$ is high (inactive), a low signal on control line $\overline{Load}$ creates the condition $(S_C, R_C) = (Data_C, \overline{Data}_C)$ which forces the binary value of $Data_C$ into the counter stage, thus loading the flip-flop. When both $\overline{Clear}$ and $\overline{Load}$ are high (inactive), the device acts as an asynchronous counter.

In the count mode of operation, stage Q_A acts as a $\div 2$ counter stage. The other three flip-flops (Q_D, Q_C, Q_B) form a $\div 5$ counter stage, with Q_D being the most significant bit. The logic symbol for the counter is illustrated in Fig. 7.21b. Look at the inputs to flip-flops Q_D and Q_B. These two JK flip-flops operate synchronously! Flip-flop Q_C toggles when Q_B changes from high to low. So the proper operation of the three counter stages may be described as follows:

1. Clear the flip-flops to the all-zero state with a low signal on input $\overline{Clear}$.

2. Begin a sequence of clock pulses on input $Clock$ 2.

3. $\bar{Q}_D$ is driven high by the clear pulse, so the J and K inputs to flip-flop Q_B will be high, making Q_B act like a toggle flip-flop.

4. On the first few clock pulses, Q_D remains low while the flip-flop pair (Q_C, Q_B) acts like a binary counter sequencing through states 0, 1, 2, and 3. On the next clock pulse, both flip-flops Q_C and Q_B are high, so the J input to Q_D is also high due to the action of the AND gate. Now let us examine the K input for Q_D at this point in the state sequence. Since the K input of Q_D is tied to Q_D, the flip-flop output, it has a low value, so $(J_D, K_D) = (1, 0)$, the set condition. When the next clock pulse occurs, Q_D goes high while Q_B and Q_C toggle low in their normal binary count sequence. To this point in the sequence, the 3-bit counter began in state 0, and then changed to states 1, 2, and 3 and now rests in state 4.

5. Since Q_D is now high, $\bar{Q}_D$ is low so the J and K inputs to Q_B are low and inhibit any change on the next clock pulse on $Clock$ 2. Since Q_C and Q_B are low, the J input to Q_D is low, while the K input that is tied to Q_D is high, $(J_D, K_D) = (0, 1)$. This is the reset condition, so Q_D will change to 0 on the next clock pulse. Hence the next state after state 4 for the 3-bit counter will be the all-zero state.

6. The state sequence for the 3-bit counter is $(Q_D, Q_C, Q_B) = 0, 1, 2, 3, 4, 0, 1, \ldots$.

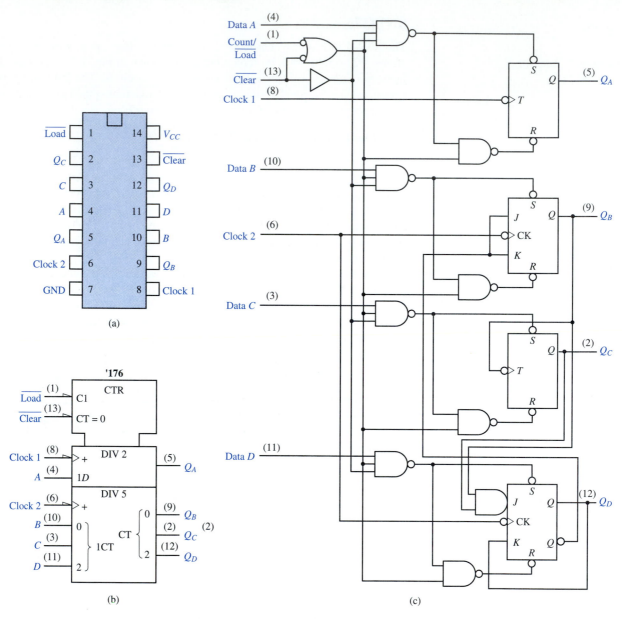

Figure 7.21 SN74176 asynchronous decade counter. **(a)** Package pins. **(b)** Logic symbol. **(c)** Logic diagram. *Source:* The TTL Data Book Volume 2, Texas Instruments Inc., 1985.

Suppose we connect the output Q_A to input *Clock* 2 and supply a sequence of count pulses to input *Clock* 1. Flip-flop Q_D will be the most significant bit, while flip-flop Q_A will be least significant. The following count sequence will be generated: $(Q_D, Q_C, Q_B, Q_A) = 0, 1, 2, 3, 4, 5, 6, 7, 8, 9, 0, 1, \ldots$. In this mode of operation the module is said to be a decade counter. But if we, instead, connect output Q_D to input *Clock* 1 and supply a sequence of count pulses to input *Clock* 2, Q_A will become the most significant bit and the following count sequence will be generated: $(Q_A, Q_D, Q_C, Q_B) = 0, 1, 2, 3, 4, 8, 9, 10, 11, 12, 0, 1,\ldots$. This counting sequence is called the *biquinary* mode of operation. The counter still has 10 states, but the sequence is no longer the decimal digits.

7.4.3 Modulo-6 and Modulo-12 Counters

Two other modulo-N counters find frequent application in digital design. They are the modulo-6 and modulo-12 counters. Have you ever wondered how a digital timer operates? A high-frequency oscillator (or the 60-hertz power line) furnishes a periodic clock signal that is fed into a sequence of counters. A *modulo-10* counter can be used to get tens of seconds (or minutes) from a 1-second (or 1-minute) count pulse. A *modulo-6* counter can be used to generate a sequence of 1-minute pulses from the "tens of seconds" signal. Figure 7.22 illustrates the block diagram for a simple digital timer that uses the power line for a clock signal generator. The *Clear* control signal is used to initialize the timer. The *Start/$\overline{Stop}$* signal may then be used to apply or inhibit the count pulses coming from the pulse generator connected to the power line. The pulses

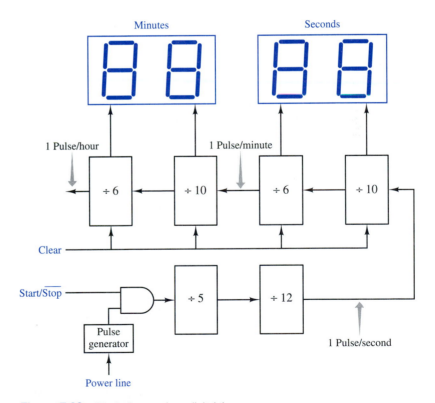

Figure 7.22   Block diagram for a digital timer.

from the pulse generator are being produced at a rate of 60 per second. So a modulo-60 counter is used to reduce the frequency of the pulses to 1 per second. The modulo-60 counter is implemented by a modulo-5 counter cascaded with a modulo-12. We could have used a ÷6 and ÷10 combination just as effectively. Two additional modulo-60 counters are used to produce seconds and minutes displays. If you need hours in your design, simply add another ÷10 and ÷6 stage. The modulo-5 and modulo-10 counters can be implemented using the SN74176. The modulo-6 and modulo-12 counters can be implemented using the SN7492A counter described next.

SN7492A

The SN7492A is an asynchronous modulo-6 or modulo-12 counter with a common asynchronous clear. The device is described in Fig. 7.23. Its operation may be determined from the logic diagram of Fig. 7.23c.

First examine counter stage Q_A. This is a simple ÷2 flip-flop. Next examine the operation of flip-flops (Q_C, Q_B). This 2-bit counter is the key to the SN7492A. These 2 bits form a synchronous modulo-3 counter. Note the J and K input logic equations for the two flip-flops:

$$J_C = Q_B$$
$$K_C = 1$$
$$J_B = \overline{Q_C}$$
$$K_B = 1$$

Suppose we apply a clear pulse $[R_{0(1)} = R_{0(2)} = 1]$ to initialize the two counter flip-flops, as shown in Fig. 7.23d. This action sets (Q_C, Q_B) = (0, 0). The J and K inputs to the flip-flops become (J_C, K_C) = (0, 1) and (J_B, K_B) = (1, 1). On the next clock pulse applied to input *Clock B*, Q_C will be reset to logic 0 and Q_B will toggle to logic 1, or (Q_C, Q_B) = (0, 1). After the clock pulse, the J and K inputs to the two flip-flops will change to the following conditions: (J_C, K_C) = (1, 1) and (J_B, K_B) = (1, 1). These input conditions direct Q_C to toggle to logic 1 and Q_B to toggle to logic 0 during the next clock pulse; so the next state of the 2-bit counter will be (Q_C, Q_B) = (1, 0). This state change will again change the J and K inputs on the two flip-flops: (J_C, K_C) = (0, 1) and (J_B, K_B) = (0, 1). These input conditions direct the two flip-flops to reset on the next clock pulse, driving the counter to (Q_C, Q_B) = (0, 0), the original starting state. So the entire state sequence in base 2 is (Q_C, Q_B) ⇒ (0, 0), (0, 1), (1, 0), (0, 0),. . .. In base 10 the sequence is 0, 1, 2, 0,. . ..

The most significant stage of the counter Q_D is another simple ÷2 flip-flop. The logic symbol for the module is illustrated in Fig. 7.23b. The following are several different counter sequences that may be produced by the module:

1. Connect Q_A to input *Clock B* and supply a sequence of count pulses to input *Clock A*. Flip-flop Q_D will be the most significant bit, while flip-flop Q_A will be the least significant. The following count sequence will be generated: (Q_D, Q_C, Q_B, Q_A) = 0, 1, 2, 3, 4, 5, 8, 9, 10, 11, 12, 13, 0,. . .. See the state diagram of Fig. 7.23e.

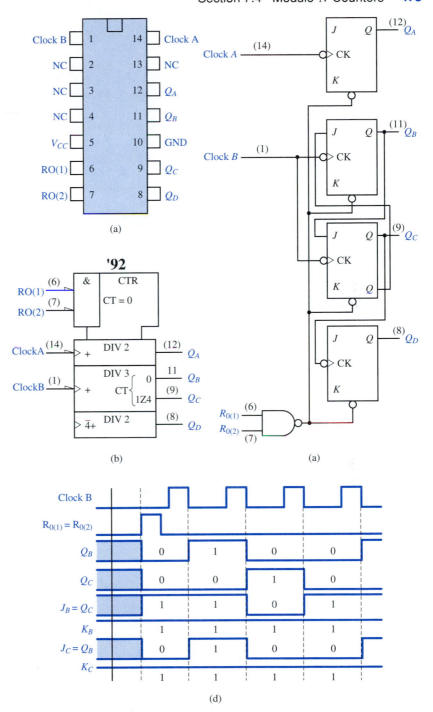

Figure 7.23 SN7492A asynchronous counter. **(a)** Package pins. **(b)** Logic symbol. **(c)** Logic diagram. **(d)** Timing diagram. *Source:* The TTL Data Book Volume 2, Texas Instruments Inc., 1985.

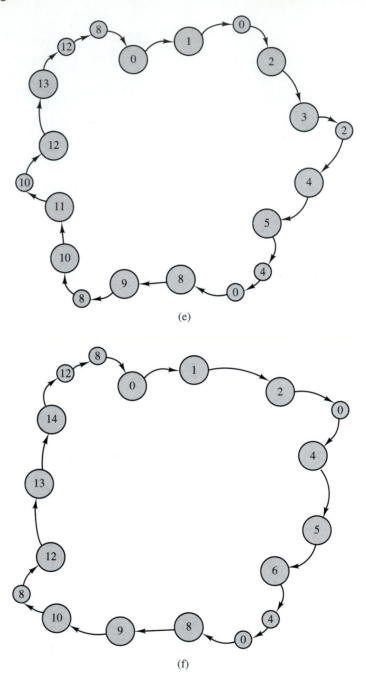

Figure 7.23 (Continued) SN7492A asynchronous counter. **(e)** State diagram $(CKB = Q_A)$. **(f)** State diagram $(CKA = Q_D)$. *Source:* The TTL Data Book Volume 2, Texas Instruments Inc., 1985.

2. Connect output Q_D to input *Clock A* and supply a sequence of count pulses to input *Clock B*. Q_A becomes the most significant bit, and the following count sequence will be generated: $(Q_A, Q_D, Q_C, Q_B) = 0, 1, 2, 4, 5, 6, 8, 9, 10, 12, 13, 14, 0, \ldots$ See the state diagram of Fig. 7.23f.

3. If we use the first connection scheme (connect Q_A to input *Clock B* and supply a sequence of count pulses to input *Clock A*) and ignore counter stage Q_D, the following count sequence will be generated: $(Q_C, Q_B, Q_A) = 0, 1, 2, 3, 4, 5, 0, \ldots$ Note that this is exactly the sequence we need for the timer design of Fig. 7.22.

7.4.4 Asynchronously Resetting Modulo-N Counters

The design technique used in the asynchronous BCD counter of Fig. 7.20 may be generalized for exploitation in any general modulo-N counter, as shown in Fig. 7.24. The state-detection logic consists of an AND gate with appropriate inputs to detect the state N, the modulus of the counter. The number n of counter stages needed is determined by the relation

$$2^{n-1} < N < 2^n$$

This relation assumes that N is not a power of 2 because the feedback network is not needed in those cases. The generalized counter of Fig. 7.24 requires an asynchronous common clear control signal. The stable states of the counter

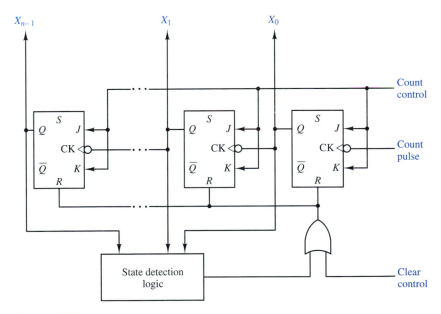

Figure 7.24   General modulo-N asynchronous counter.

will be 0, 1, 2, ..., $N - 1$. The state detection logic will sense state N and immediately force the counter past state N to state 0. Thus, these asynchronously resetting counters will always have a transient state N.

EXAMPLE 7.1

Design a modulo-13 counter using SN7400 series modules. Since

$$2^3 < N = 13 < 2^4$$

the number of counter stages must be $n = 4$.

Let us choose the SN74293 4-bit asynchronous binary counter and design a decoder for state $N = 13$. State 13 represents the counter value

$$(Q_D, \ Q_C, \ Q_B, \ Q_A) = (1, 1, 0, 1)$$

In normal operation, the counter will sequence through states 0, 1, ..., 12 before reaching state 13. Therefore, we can use the fact that state 13 will be the first occurrence of the logic condition $Q_D = Q_C = Q_A = 1$. Therefore, we can use a 3-input AND gate to decode state 13 as shown in Fig. 7.25a. When state 13 occurs, the AND gate generates a clear control signal and applies it to the reset terminals $R_{0(1)}$ and $R_{0(2)}$ through the OR gate. When the counter has stabilized in state 0, the reset control signal is returned to its inactive condition, logic 0.

The state diagram of Fig. 7.25b illustrates the transition states for this counter. Compare Fig. 7.25b with Fig. 7.14b. Note that the state detection logic has changed stable state 13 of Fig. 7.14b into a transient state and bypassed the remaining states, jumping directly to state 0.

7.4.5 Synchronously Resetting Modulo-N Counters

In many applications, the transient states in Fig. 7.25b cause spikes (or *glitches*) in a digital system. This worrisome behavior can be eliminated by using a synchronous counter in the circuit of Fig. 7.24. The counter should also have the synchronous clear feature. One important difference for the synchronous case is that the state detection logic must be designed to sense state $N - 1$, because the counter must reset on the *next* clock pulse after the detection logic has activated the clear control signal.

EXAMPLE 7.2

Design a synchronous modulo-13 counter.

We may use the SN74163 4-bit synchronous counter in the circuit of Fig. 7.26. Notice that the detection logic will activate the $\overline{Clear}$ input to the counter during state 12, so the *next* state after state 12 will be state 0. This synchronous circuit transitions through the stable states of Fig. 7.25b while eliminating all the transient state activity.

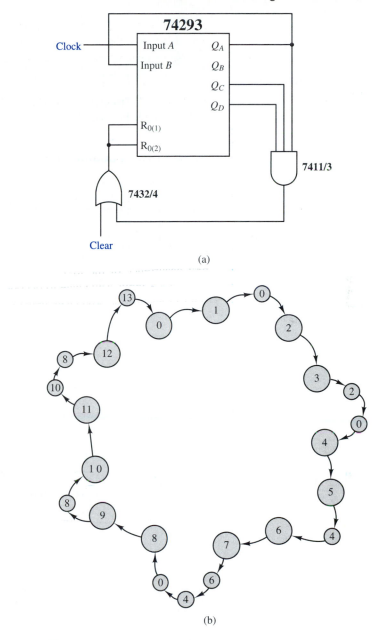

Figure 7.25   Asynchronously-resetting modulo-13 counter.
(a) Logic diagram. **(b)** State diagram.

7.5 Shift Registers as Counters

Now let us examine another class of counters. The shift registers that we covered earlier in this chapter may be used as counters in special circumstances.

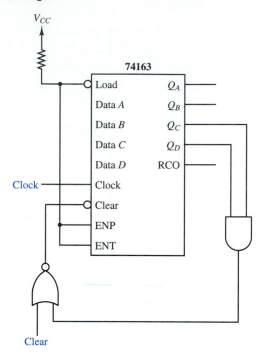

Figure 7.26 Synchronously resetting modulo-13 counter.

Counters constructed using shift registers with feedback are commonly called ring counters and twisted-ring counters. We will now investigate the behavior of these devices.

7.5.1 Ring Counters

A *ring counter* is a sequential device that has one shift-register flip-flop per counter state. The output of the shift register's serial output is fed back to the register's serial input pin. The resulting circuit circulates a bit pattern around the register. If we initialize the register so that it has a single logic 1 in its first flip-flop and logic 0 in all the others, the device will circulate the single logic 1 around its loop of flip-flops as illustrated in Fig. 7.27. Let n be the number of flip-flops and hence the number of states in the counter. The shift-register flip-flops are labeled $X_1, X_2, \ldots, X_n$. The operation of the counter begins with a pulse in control line *Initialize*. This drives flip-flop X_1 high and $X_2, X_3, \ldots, X_{n-1}$, and X_n low. At this point a single logic 1 is residing in flip-flop X_1. On the next falling edge of the input signal *Clock*, the logic 1 is transferred from flip-flop X_1 to flip-flop X_2. The process continues until the logic 1 reaches the end of the shift register, flip-flop X_n. On the falling edge of the next clock pulse, the logic 1 is transferred by the feedback line to the first flip-flop in the shift register, X_1. And then the process is repeated. In other words, the logic 1 circles through the shift register every n clock pulses. So the ring counter has one unique state for each flip-flop. The state sequence may be described

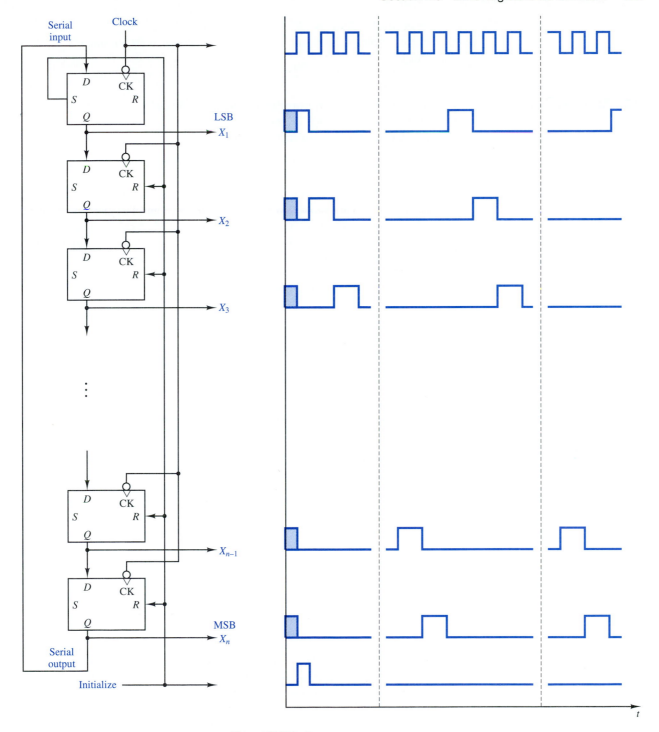

Figure 7.27   Ring counter.

in decimal values as $(X_n, X_{n-1}, \ldots, X_1)_2 = 1_{10}, 2_{10}, 4_{10}, 8_{10}, \ldots, (2^{n-1})_{10}$. For example, a 5-bit ring counter will sequence through states 1, 2, 4, 8, and 16.

EXAMPLE 7.3

Design a 5-bit ring counter using the SN7496 shift register of Fig. 7.5 and illustrate its operation using a timing diagram.

The SN7496 is a 5-bit parallel-input, parallel-output shift register with common clear and common preset. To load a logic 1 into its least significant bit Q_A, we must first clear all the flip-flops and then preset a logic 1 into Q_A using the *Preset A* data input and the *Preset enable* control signal. Examine the logic diagram of Fig. 7.28a. The serial output Q_E has been connected to the serial input data line. The *Preset A* line is tied high to the power supply, while the other preset inputs are tied low to ground. The operation of the device is illustrated in the timing diagram of Fig. 7.28b. First the device is cleared to the all-zero state. Then *Preset enable* forces a logic 1 into the first flip-flop Q_A. Each clock pulse then transfers the logic 1 to the next flip-flop until it reaches Q_E. Since Q_E is connected to *Serial input*, the logic 1 is transferred back to Q_A and the process is repeated. Two full cycles of the ring counter state sequence are shown. Note that the counter state sequence is $(Q_E, Q_D, Q_C, Q_B, Q_A) = 1, 2, 4, 8, 16, 1$, and so on.

Now let us contrast the ring counter to a k-bit binary counter connected to a k-to-2^k decoder as diagrammed in Fig. 7.29. This circuit is equivalent to the ring counter of Fig. 7.27 when the number of flip-flops in the ring is a power of 2, that is, $n = 2^k$. The *Initialize* signal clears the binary counter to state 0. Since a decoder is a minterm generator, one and only one of its outputs will be active high at any given moment in time. So when the counter is in state 0, the decoder's output line 0 will be high (signal X_1 on the timing diagram). The next clock pulse will drive the counter to state 1, causing the decoder's output line 1 to go high. As each new clock pulse arrives, the binary counter changes state and moves the logic 1 down to the next decoder output. When the counter reaches its maximum state, the last decoder output line will go high, placing the logic 1 on signal X_n. The next clock pulse will then cycle the counter to state 0 and hence send the logic 1 back to the first output line X_1. So the binary counter and decoder act like a ring counter.

What if a designer needs a ring counter for $n \neq 2^k$? The counter–decoder equivalent configuration of Fig. 7.29 can still be used by replacing the binary counter with a modulo-n counter. The decoder must satisfy the relationship

$$2^k > n > 2^{k-1}$$

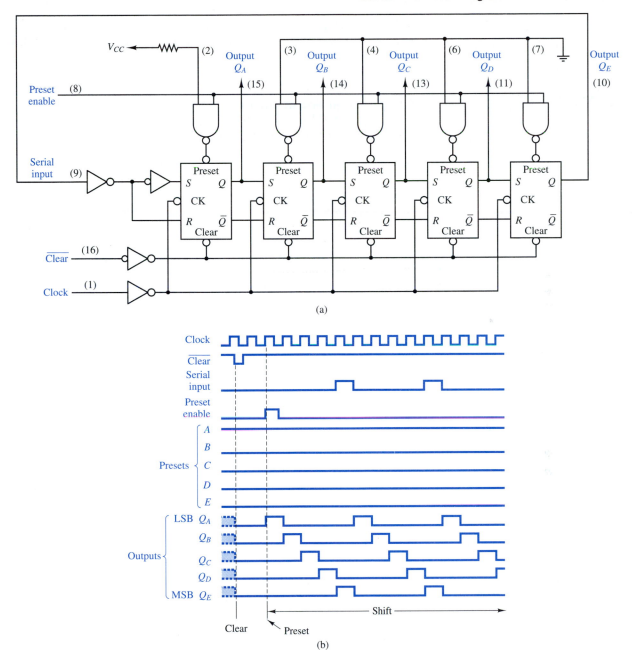

Figure 7.28   Ring counter example. **(a)** Logic diagram. **(b)** Timing diagram.

The decoder outputs labeled 0, 1, 2,..., $n-2$, $n-1$ will be used as the ring counter output lines X_1, X_2, X_3, ..., X_{n-1}, X_n. The decoder output lines labeled n, $n+1$, ..., $2^k - 1$ will not be used.

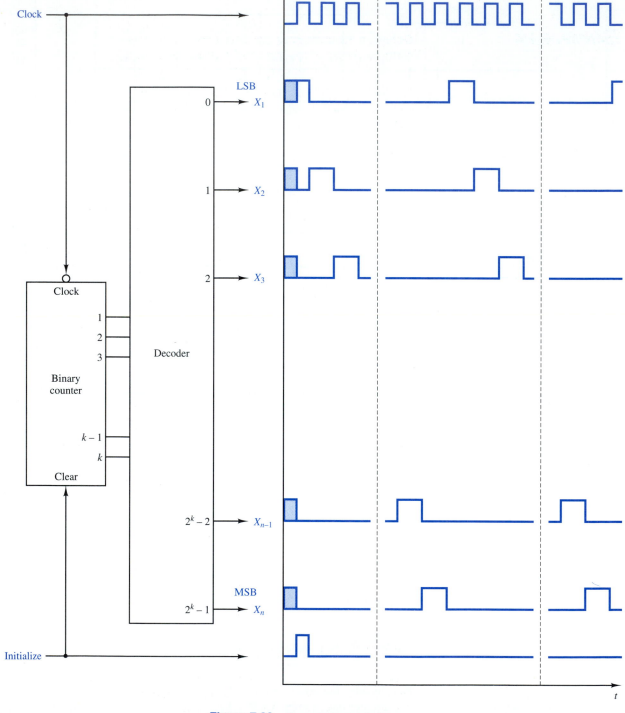

Figure 7.29 Ring counter equivalent.

EXAMPLE 7.4

Design a 13-state ring counter with active low outputs using a counter and a decoder. Since

$$2^4 > 13 > 2^3$$

the desired ring counter can be constructed from a modulo-13 counter and a 4-to-16 decoder.

Let us use the modulo-13 counter from Fig. 7.25 and a 74154 decoder. The logic diagram for the design is illustrated in Fig. 7.30.

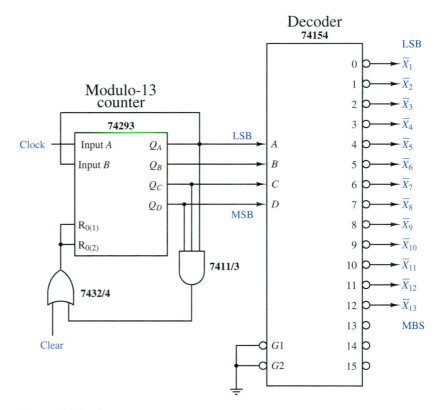

Figure 7.30   Thirteen-state ring counter equivalent.

7.5.2 Twisted-ring Counters

A ring counter with a NOT gate in the feedback loop is called a *twisted-ring counter*. Sometimes this circuit is also called a *Johnson counter*. Take a look at the logic diagram in Fig. 7.31. Here we have inserted a NOT gate between the most significant counter bit X_n and the shift register's *Serial input* line. Also

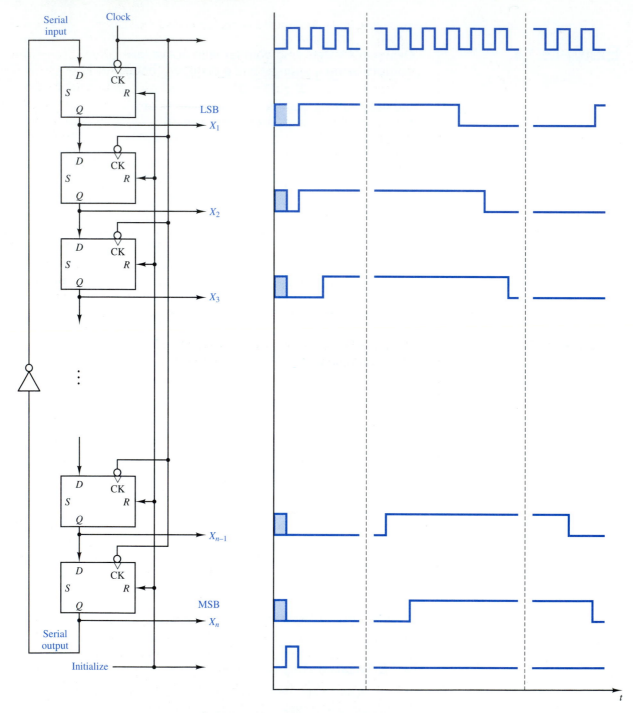

Figure 7.31 Twisted-ring counter.

notice that the *Initialize* signal connections have been altered to force the shift register to the all-zero state.

Let us examine the operation of the shift register in this configuration. First the *Initialize* signal clears the register. The NOT gate will therefore initially be supplying a logic 1 into the *Serial input* of the shift register (to the *D* input of the first shift-register flip-flop). As a matter of fact, this logic 1 feedback will continue until X_n goes high later in the counting sequence. So, as each pulse is applied to the *Clock* input of the shift register, the logic 1 moves down the register one position (like a wave front) until it reaches the last shift-register flip-flop X_n. When the logic 1 arrives at X_n, it changes the feedback signal on *Serial input* to logic 0 so that a logic 0 wavefront now moves down the register as additional clock pulses are applied. The timing diagram of Fig. 7.31 shows a complete cycle of the twisted-ring counter. Each output signal X_i $(i = 1, n)$ is a square wave, each delayed from its neighbors by one time period of the clock signal.

How many unique states does this counter possess? Since it takes n clock pulses to propagate the logic 1 down the register and then another n clock pulses to return the register to the all-zero state, the twisted-ring counter has $2n$ unique states, where n is the number of flip-flops in the shift register.

EXAMPLE 7.5

Design a twisted-ring counter that has 10 unique states using SN7400 series logic modules.

The number of flip-flops needed will be

$$n = \frac{10}{2} = 5$$

Let us choose the SN7496 and place a NOT gate in the feedback loop as shown in Fig. 7.32a. Although the *Preset i* $(i = A, B, \ldots, E)$ signals are not used, they are tied to ground to increase the noise immunity of the implementation.

The timing diagram illustrates the proper use of the circuit. An active-low $\overline{Clear}$ signal initializes the register to state 0, forcing a logic 1 on the *Serial input* signal. On the rising edge of each clock pulse, the logic 1 moves from left to right through the register until Q_E goes high. The NOT gate then forces logic 0 into the register on the next five clock pulses to return the register to state 0. Applying 10 clock pulses drives the twisted-ring counter through all 10 of its unique states.

The states of the twisted-ring counter may be decoded using AND gates as shown in Fig. 7.33. The twisted-ring counter output signals are listed in tabular form. A unique logic condition for each state is shown in the column labeled State Decoder Logic Equations. For example, look at the third line in the table. When $X_3 = 0$ and $X_2 = 1$, this twisted-ring counter state is uniquely indicated. Scan the X_3 and X_2 columns to satisfy yourself that no other row (or counter state) has this bit pattern for X_3 and X_2. All the other rows may also

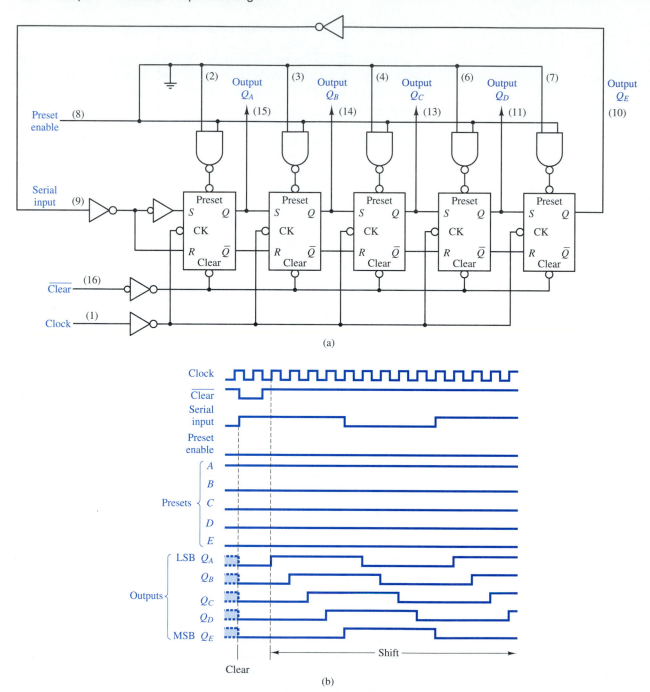

Figure 7.32 Ten-state twisted ring counter. **(a)** Logic diagram. **(b)** Timing diagram.

	Twisted-ring counter ouput signals							State decoder logic equations
X_n	X_{n-1}	X_{n-2}	X_{n-3}	$\cdots$ X_3	X_2	X_1	
0	0	0	0	0	0	0	$\bar{X}_n \cdot \bar{X}_1$
0	0	0	0	0	0	1	$\bar{X}_2 \cdot X_1$
0	0	0	0	0	1	1	$\bar{X}_3 \cdot X_2$
0	0	0	0	1	1	1	$\bar{X}_4 \cdot X_3$
0	0	0	0	1	1	1	$\bar{X}_{n-3} \cdot X_{n-4}$
0	0	0	1	1	1	1	$\bar{X}_{n-2} \cdot X_{n-3}$
0	0	1	1	1	1	1	$\bar{X}_{n-1} \cdot X_{n-2}$
0	1	1	1	1	1	1	$\bar{X}_n \cdot X_{n-1}$
1	1	1	1	1	1	1	$X_n \cdot X_1$
1	1	1	1	1	1	0	$X_2 \cdot \bar{X}_1$
1	1	1	1	1	0	0	$X_3 \cdot \bar{X}_2$
1	1	1	1	0	0	0	$X_4 \cdot \bar{X}_3$
1	1	1	1	0	0	0	$X_{n-3} \cdot \bar{X}_{n-4}$
1	1	1	0	0	0	0	$X_{n-2} \cdot \bar{X}_{n-3}$
1	1	0	0	0	0	0	$X_{n-1} \cdot \bar{X}_{n-2}$
1	0	0	0	0	0	0	$X_n \cdot \bar{X}_{n-1}$
0	0	0	0	0	0	0	$\bar{X}_n \cdot \bar{X}_1$
0	0	0	0	0	0	1	$\bar{X}_2 \cdot X_1$
0	0	0	0	0	1	1	$\bar{X}_3 \cdot X_2$

Figure 7.33   Twisted-ring counter state decoding.

be uniquely identified by using only two appropriate logic signals, as indicated in the last column of the table. If the twisted-ring counter has both true and complemented output signals, a 2-input AND gate may be used to decode each output state. If both are not available, NOT gates will be required.

EXAMPLE 7.6

Design a timing signal generator using a twisted-ring counter and state-decoding logic that meets the following specifications:

1. The timing signals will be active high during one period of the clock signal (go high on the rising edge of one clock pulse and then go low on the rising edge of the next clock pulse).

2. An initialization signal will be used to synchronize the timing generator with the other system components. The signal *Initialize* will be active high.

3. The first timing control signal (f_1) will generate a pulse that will go high on the leading edge of the second clock pulse applied after the initialize command.

4. The second timing control signal (f_2) will generate a pulse that will go high on the leading edge of the eighth clock pulse applied after the initialize command.

5. The third timing control signal (f_3) will generate a pulse that will go high on the leading edge of the eleventh clock pulse applied after the initialize command.

6. The timing waveforms (f_1, f_2, f_3) will be repeated every 16 clock pulses.

First let us generate the state sequence for a 16-state twisted-ring counter since the sequence of signals is to be repeated every 16 clock pulses. Since a twisted-ring counter has $2n$ states, where n is the number of flip-flops, let us select the SN74164 serial-in, parallel-out shift register of Fig. 7.4 for our implementation. The outputs of the shift register are (Q_H, Q_G, Q_F, Q_E, Q_D, Q_C, Q_B, Q_A). If we use a NOT gate to feed back the complement of Q_H to the serial inputs, the state behavior of the twisted-ring counter may be described in the table of Fig. 7.34a.

When the shift register is initialized to the all-zero state, it assumes the values in the first row of the table (labeled clock pulse 0). The first clock pulse will drive the register to the second row (labeled clock pulse 1). The second clock pulse forces the register into the third row (labeled clock pulse 2). This twisted-ring counter state is to be decoded as timing signal f_1, as shown in the last column of the table. We may continue this same procedure to identify the counter states to be decoded for timing signals f_2 and f_3. The decoding logic for the three timing signals is

$$f_1 = \bar{Q}_C \cdot Q_B$$
$$f_2 = Q_H \cdot Q_A$$
$$f_3 = Q_D \cdot \bar{Q}_C$$

These signals will be repeated every 16 clock pulses. The logic timing diagrams for the design are illustrated in Fig. 7.34b and c.

Clock pulse No.	State (decimal)	Q_H	Q_G	Q_F	Q_E	Q_D	Q_C	Q_B	Q_A	State (decoder)
0	0	0	0	0	0	0	0	0	0	$\bar{Q}_H \cdot \bar{Q}_A$
1	1	0	0	0	0	0	0	0	1	$\bar{Q}_B \cdot Q_A$
2	3	0	0	0	0	0	0	1	1	$f_1 = \bar{Q}_C \cdot Q_B$
3	7	0	0	0	0	0	1	1	1	$\bar{Q}_D \cdot Q_C$
4	15	0	0	0	0	1	1	1	1	$\bar{Q}_E \cdot Q_D$
5	31	0	0	0	1	1	1	1	1	$\bar{Q}_F \cdot Q_E$
6	63	0	0	1	1	1	1	1	1	$\bar{Q}_G \cdot Q_F$
7	127	0	1	1	1	1	1	1	1	$\bar{Q}_H \cdot Q_G$
8	255	1	1	1	1	1	1	1	1	$f_2 = Q_H \cdot Q_A$
9	254	1	1	1	1	1	1	1	0	$Q_B \cdot \bar{Q}_A$
10	252	1	1	1	1	1	1	0	0	$Q_C \cdot \bar{Q}_B$
11	248	1	1	1	1	1	0	0	0	$f_3 = Q_D \cdot \bar{Q}_C$
12	240	1	1	1	1	0	0	0	0	$Q_E \cdot \bar{Q}_D$
13	224	1	1	1	0	0	0	0	0	$Q_F \cdot \bar{Q}_E$
14	192	1	1	0	0	0	0	0	0	$Q_G \cdot \bar{Q}_F$
15	128	1	0	0	0	0	0	0	0	$Q_H \cdot \bar{Q}_G$
0	0	0	0	0	0	0	0	0	0	$\bar{Q}_H \cdot \bar{Q}_A$
1	1	0	0	0	0	0	0	0	1	$\bar{Q}_B \cdot Q_A$
2	3	0	0	0	0	0	0	1	1	$f_1 = \bar{Q}_C \cdot Q_B$

(a)

Figure 7.34 Sixteen-state twisted-ring counter example. **(a)** State sequence.

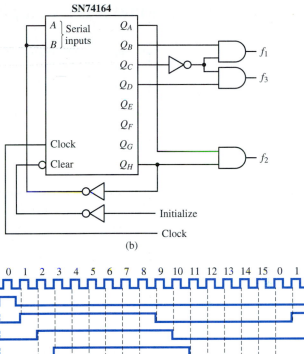

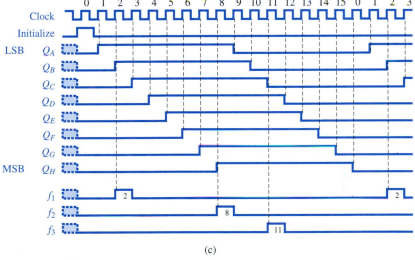

Figure 7.34 (Continued) Sixteen-state twisted-ring counter example. **(b)** Logic diagram. **(c)** Timing diagram.

7.6 Multiple-sequence Counters

Earlier in this chapter we presented one type of multiple-sequence counter, the up/down counter. Occasionally, a digital system requires a counter that possesses the ability to count in several other ways under the command of some input control signals. Methods for synthesizing synchronous and asynchronous sequential circuits that can count in any arbitrary sequence will be presented in Chapters 8 and 10, respectively. Some of the examples in those chapters will demonstrate these concepts.

7.7 Digital Fractional Rate Multipliers

A *digital fractional rate multiplier* is a device that transforms a stream of input clock pulses (call the input *Clock*) into a controlled stream of output pulses (call the output line *Y*). Let N_i be the number of input pulses for a particular time period, and let N_o be the number of output pulses. A binary fractional rate multiplier produces output pulses according to the following relation:

$$N_o = \frac{B}{2^n} N_i$$

where

$$B = (B_{n-1}, B_{n-2}, \ldots, B_2, B_1, B_0)_2$$

is the rate constant input to the device and n is the number of binary counter stages controlling the module. See Fig. 7.35. The *Clock* input drives an n-bit binary counter whose outputs are labeled $(X_n, X_{n-1}, \ldots, X_3, X_2, X_1)$. The counter outputs are ANDed with the incoming *Clock* signal to form intermediate pulse trains P_i $(i = 1, n)$:

$$P_n = X_1 \cdot Clock$$
$$P_{n-1} = \bar{X}_1 \cdot X_2 \cdot Clock$$
$$P_{n-2} = \bar{X}_1 \cdot \bar{X}_2 \cdot X_3 \cdot Clock$$

$$\cdots$$

$$P_2 = \bar{X}_1 \cdot \bar{X}_2 \cdot \bar{X}_3 \cdot \ldots \cdot \bar{X}_{n-2} \cdot X_{n-1} \cdot Clock$$
$$P_1 = \bar{X}_1 \cdot \bar{X}_2 \cdot \bar{X}_3 \cdot \ldots \cdot \bar{X}_{n-2} \cdot \bar{X}_{n-1} \cdot X_n \cdot Clock$$

The logic output Y uses the rate constant M and the pulse train signals P_i to implement the output equation as follows:

$$Y = \sum B_{i-1} \cdot P_i$$

This output configuration will deliver the proper number of output pulses (N_o) as specified by the rate constant B.

From the timing diagram of Fig. 7.35b, note that each of the pulse trains P_i generates 2^{i-1} pulses during one counter sequence period (2^n clock pulses). That is, P_1 generates 1 pulse, P_2 generates 2 pulses, P_3 generates 4 pulses, P_4 generates 8 pulses, and so on. It is also important to note that these pulse trains do not overlap in time. Consequently, we may use the bits of the rate constant B_i to gate these pulse trains into the OR gate as shown in the logic diagram.

Another important characteristic of these devices is the irregularity of the output pulse stream. The pulse-to-pulse separation on the output Y can vary widely. The output pulses are synchronized with the incoming clock.

EXAMPLE 7.7

Consider the application of a 3-bit binary rate multiplier. Let the rate constant $B = (7)_{10}$. In other words, the rate multiplier will output seven pulses for every eight input clock pulses. One of the input pulses will be eliminated. Which one?

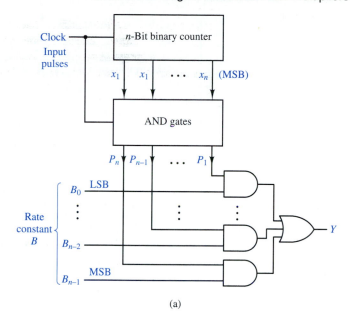

(a)

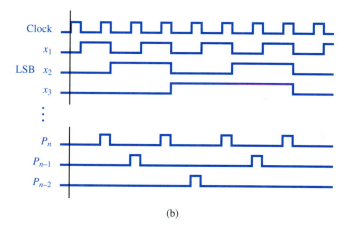

(b)

Figure 7.35   Binary fractional rate multiplier. **(a)** Logic diagram.
(b) Timing diagram.

If we examine the output equation for this device,

$$Y = B_2 \cdot P_3 + B_1 \cdot P_2 + B_0 \cdot P_1$$

where

$$P_3 = X_1 \cdot Clock$$
$$P_2 = \bar{X}_1 \cdot X_2 \cdot Clock$$
$$P_1 = \bar{X}_1 \cdot \bar{X}_2 \cdot X_3 \cdot Clock$$

and
$$B = (B_2, B_1, B_0)_2 = (1, 1, 1)_2$$
Substituting into the output equation yields
$$Y = (X_1 + \bar{X}_1 \cdot X_2 + \bar{X}_1 \cdot \bar{X}_2 \cdot X_3) \cdot Clock$$
In terms of the counter output variables (X_3, X_2, X_1),
$$\text{product term } X_1 \Rightarrow \sum m(1, 3, 5, 7)$$
$$\text{product term } X_2 \cdot \bar{X}_1 \Rightarrow \sum m(2, 6)$$
$$\text{product term } X_3 \cdot \bar{X}_2 \cdot \bar{X}_1 \Rightarrow \sum m(4)$$
so that
$$Y(X_3, X_2, X_1) = \left(\sum m(1, 2, 3, 4, 5, 6, 7)\right) \cdot Clock$$
which indicates that the first clock pulse of each sequence of eight will be eliminated since minterm 0 is missing from the list.

7.7.1 TTL Modules

Several of these digital fractional rate multipliers are commercially available. We will discuss the 6-bit binary rate multiplier (SN7497) and the decade rate multiplier (SN74167).

SN7497

The SN7497 is a 6-bit binary fractional rate multiplier with enable, common asynchronous clear, output strobe, and cascade inputs and outputs. The device is presented in Fig. 7.36. The rate input is
$$B = (B5, B4, B3, B2, B1, B0)_2$$
and the number of output pulses is
$$N_o = \frac{B}{2^6} N_i$$
The *Clear* control signal is active high and operates asynchronously to drive the counter flip-flops to the all-zero state. The rising edge of the *Clock* pulses causes the counter to toggle. The *Strobe* is an active-low enable signal for the pulse rate outputs Y and Z.

The *Enable input* and *Enable output* allow the modules to be cascaded. A 12-bit rate multiplier may be constructed by feeding the *Enable output* from the least significant module into the *Enable input* and *strobe* of the most significant module in the cascade. Both the *Enable input* and *Enable output* are active low.

The *Unity/cascade input* may be used to combine the outputs of cascaded units. The Z output from the least significant module is connected to the *Unity/cascade input* of the most significant one, effectively ORing the pulse

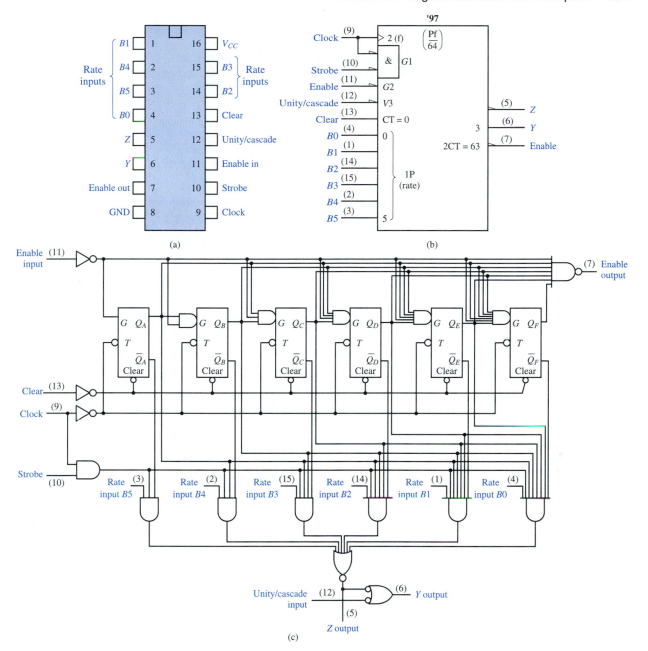

Figure 7.36   Six-bit binary rate multiplier, the SN7497. **(a)** Package pins.
(b) Logic symbol. **(c)** Logic diagram. *Source:* The TTL Data Book Volume 2,
Texas Instruments Inc., 1985.

trains from the two modules. Tie the *Unity/cascade input* high if a single module
is being used (making $Z = \bar{Y}$).

EXAMPLE 7.8

Examine the output equation for the SN7497 and contrast its operation with the design of Fig. 7.35.

If we establish the control conditions

$$Unity/cascade\ input = 1$$
$$Enable\ input = 0$$
$$Clear = 0$$
$$Strobe = 0$$

the output equation for the SN7497 has the following form:

$$Y = \overline{Clock} \cdot \quad (B5 \cdot \bar{Q}_A$$
$$+ B4 \cdot \bar{Q}_B \cdot Q_A$$
$$+ B3 \cdot \bar{Q}_C \cdot Q_B \cdot Q_A$$
$$+ B2 \cdot \bar{Q}_D \cdot Q_C \cdot Q_B \cdot Q_A$$
$$+ B1 \cdot \bar{Q}_E \cdot Q_D \cdot Q_C \cdot Q_B \cdot Q_A$$
$$+ B0 \cdot \bar{Q}_F \cdot Q_E \cdot Q_D \cdot Q_C \cdot Q_B \cdot Q_A)$$

This equation differs from our previous design in that it exchanges the roles of the flip-flop outputs Q and $\bar{Q}$. This change will move the positions of the pulses but leave the overall pulse counts unchanged. Also note that the *Clock* signal has been inverted so that the output pulses will be synchronized with $\overline{Clock}$ instead of *Clock*.

SN74167

The SN74167 of Fig. 7.37 is a decade fractional rate multiplier with enable, common asynchronous clear, preset to 9, output enable, and cascade inputs and outputs. It operates in a similar manner to the SN7497 just discussed. From the logic diagram, we can determine that the *Enable input*, *Enable output*, *Clear*, *Clock*, *Strobe*, and *Unity/cascade* input are identical in operation to the SN7497. The module differs in its counter operation. The decade counter has an active high *Set to 9* input that loads asynchronously the maximum count into the counter.

The rate equation for this device is

$$N_o = \frac{B}{10}\ N_i$$

where the rate constant $B = (B_3, B_2, B_1, B_0)_2$ is restricted to the values $0 \geq B \geq 9$.

EXAMPLE 7.9

Determine the logic equation for the Y output of the SN74167 using the same control conditions of Example 7.8.

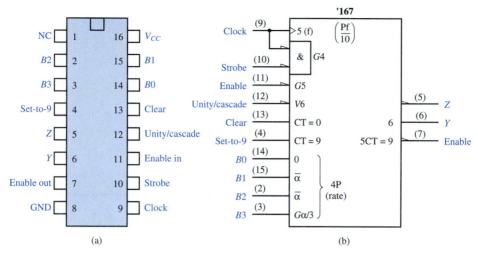

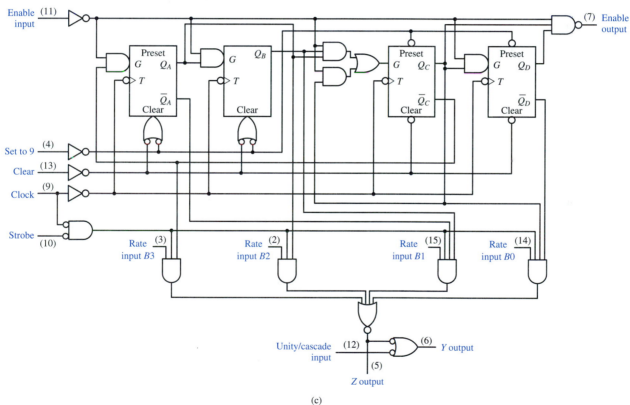

Figure 7.37   Decade rate multiplier, the SN74167. **(a)** Package pins. **(b)** Logic symbol. **(c)** Logic diagram.

From the logic diagram (with *Set to 9* tied low) we can trace the logic and write

$$
\begin{aligned}
Y = (\quad & B_3 \cdot \bar{Q}_C \\
+ \quad & B_2 \cdot Q_A \\
+ \quad & B_1 \cdot Q_B \cdot \bar{Q}_A \\
+ \quad & B_0 \cdot Q_D \cdot Q_C)
\end{aligned}
$$

This equation is much simpler than the one for the binary rate multipliers because we have the don't-care conditions for minterms 10, 11, 12, 13, 14, and 15. These are illegal states for the decade counter.

7.7.2 Cascading the Digital Fractional Rate Multipliers

The SN7497 and SN74167 are designed to be cascaded to achieve larger fractions. First, the modules may be used in parallel by using the enable control lines and logic gates on the module outputs.

EXAMPLE 7.10

Show the parallel connections for the SN74167 to produce a 0.297 fractional rate multiplier.

The fraction 0.297 can be implemented using three decade rate multiplier modules. The least significant module will be set to rate $B = (7)_{10}$. The second module in the cascade will have rate $B = (9)_{10}$. The first module will be connected for rate $B = (2)_{10}$. The three cascaded modules are shown in Fig. 7.38.

Finally, digital fractional rate multipliers may be used in a serial cascade in which the output of the first module drives the clock input of the second.

EXAMPLE 7.11

Design a rate multiplier to implement the rate equation

$$
N_o = \frac{63}{320} N_i
$$

We may accomplish this goal using one 7497 and one 74163 as illustrated in Fig. 7.39. Note that the desired rate equation may be expressed as

$$
N_o = \left(\frac{7}{10} \right) \left(\frac{18}{64} \right) N_i
$$

So $B = (0111)_2$ for the 74167 and $B = (010010)_2$ for the 7497.

◗ 7.8 Summary

In this chapter we examined the design and operation of a number of standard sequential logic modules, including shift registers and counters. Many of these modules are available as standard TTL functions [1], as well as being available in design libraries used to create VLSI circuits, programmable gate arrays, and

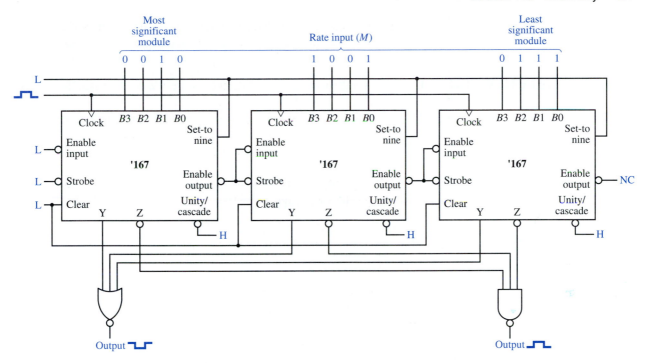

Figure 7.38   Cascaded decade rate multipliers.

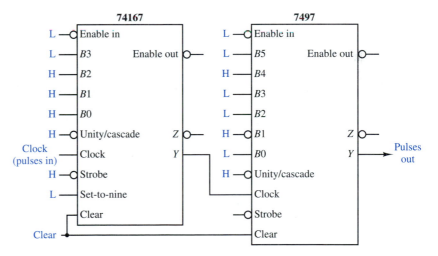

Figure 7.39   Serially cascaded rate multipliers.

printed circuit boards. A number of examples were presented to illustrate the use of these modules as building blocks to create larger circuits. It is often advantageous to utilize these modules in a design rather than creating custom circuits. In Chapter 8 we will present formal design methods for the design and analysis of synchronous sequential circuits. The reader is referred to [2], [3], and [4] for further examples of sequential logic modules and their applications.

REFERENCES

1. TEXAS INSTRUMENTS, *The TTL Data Book, Volume 2*. Dallas, Texas: Texas Instruments, Inc., 1988.

2. J. F. WAKERLY, *Digital Design Principles and Practices*. Englewood Cliffs, NJ: Prentice-Hall, 1990, pp. 349–369.

3. R. H. KATZ, *Contemporary Logic Design*. Menlo Park, CA: Benjamin/Cummings Publishing Co., 1994, pp. 282–321.

4. J. P. HAYES, *Introduction to Digital Logic Design*. Reading, MA: Addison-Wesley Publishing Co., 1993, pp. 405–447.

PROBLEMS

7.1 Use SN7400 series chips to design a shift register implementation for the MUX/DEMUX configuration of Fig. 4.29.

7.2 Develop a function table for the SN74198 8-bit bidirectional shift register presented in Fig. P7.2.

7.3 Use a 2-to-4 decoder, NAND gates, and edge-triggered D flip-flops to design a 4-bit shift register module that has the following function table:

S1	S0	Mode
0	0	Shift right (all 4 bits)
0	1	Shift left (all 4 bits)
1	0	Synchronous common clear
1	1	Synchronous parallel load

Draw a logic diagram for your module.

7.4 Use a 3-to-8 decoder, NAND gates, and edge-triggered D flip-flops to design a 4-bit shift register module that has the following function table:

S2	S1	S0	Mode
0	0	0	Shift right (all 4 bits)
0	0	1	Shift left (all 4 bits)
0	1	0	Synchronous common clear
0	1	1	Synchronous parallel load
1	0	0	Synchronous preset MSB to 1 and clear other bits
1	0	1	Synchronous data hold
1	1	0	Ring counter (Q output of LSB is fed back as serial input to the MSB)
1	1	1	Twisted-ring counter ($\bar{Q}$ output of LSB is fed back as serial input to the MSB)

Draw a logic diagram for your module.

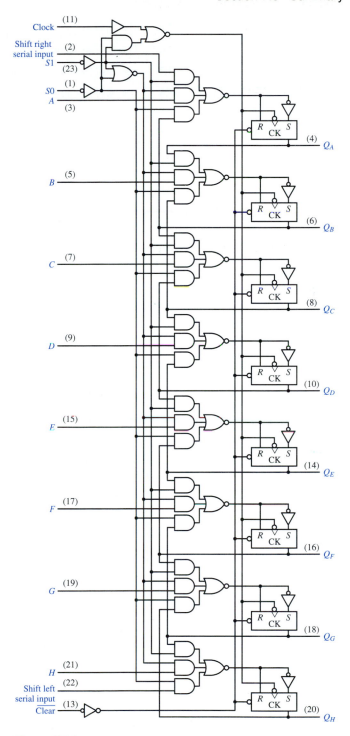

Figure P7.2   The SN74198 8-bit bidirectional shift register.

7.5 Use SN7400 series modules to design a synchronous modulo-15 counter.

7.6 Use SN7400 series modules to design an asynchronous modulo-15 counter.

7.7 Use SN7400 series modules to design an asynchronous modulo-65 counter.

7.8 Use SN7400 series modules to design a synchronous modulo-80 counter.

7.9 Use SN7400 series modules to design an eight-state ring counter. Provide an asynchronous initialize control signal.

7.10 Use SN7400 series modules to design a 14-state ring counter. Provide an asynchronous initialize control signal.

7.11 Use SN7400 series modules to design an eight-state twisted-ring counter. Provide an asynchronous initialize control signal.

7.12 Use SN7400 series modules to design a 14-state twisted-ring counter. Provide an asynchronous initialize control signal.

7.13 Use SN7400 series counter and decoder modules to design an eight-state ring-counter equivalent similar to Fig. 7.30. Provide an asynchronous initialize control signal.

7.14 Use SN7400 series counter and decoder modules to design a 14-state ring-counter equivalent similar to Fig. 7.30. Provide an asynchronous initialize control signal.

7.15 Design three equivalent timing signal generators using the counters of Problems 7.8, 7.10, and 7.12. The outputs of the three circuits should generate a pulse on the first and fifth clock pulses after the initialize signal. The sequence should repeat every eight clock pulses.

7.16 Design three equivalent timing signal generators using the counters of Problems 7.9, 7.11, and 7.13. The outputs of the nine circuits (three for each problem) should match the example of Fig. 7.34b, except that the timing waveforms will be repeated every 14 clock pulses instead of every 16 pulses as shown in Fig. 7.34.

7.17 Use SN7400 modules to implement a digital fractional rate multiplier with an output to input ratio of 5/10.

7.18 Use SN7400 modules to implement a digital fractional rate multiplier with an output to input ratio of 11/80.

7.19 Design a timing generator using the structure of Fig. P7.19a. The unit should generate four signals as shown in Fig. P7.19b to meet the following specification:

f_1 goes low on clock pulses 2, 9, 17, 38, and 60

f_2 goes high on clock pulses 2, 8, 15, 35, and 56

f_3 goes low on clock pulses 1, 8, 16, 37, and 63

f_4 goes high on clock pulses 3, 27, 39, 41, and 63

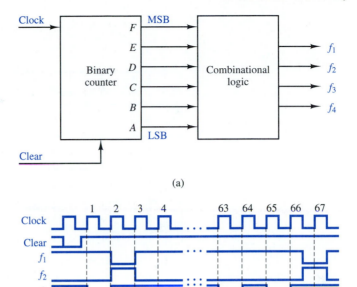

(a)

(b)

Figure P7.19 **(a)** Block diagram. **(b)** Timing diagram.

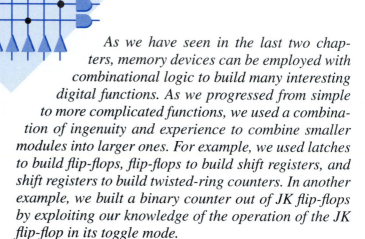

8

As we have seen in the last two chapters, memory devices can be employed with combinational logic to build many interesting digital functions. As we progressed from simple to more complicated functions, we used a combination of ingenuity and experience to combine smaller modules into larger ones. For example, we used latches to build flip-flops, flip-flops to build shift registers, and shift registers to build twisted-ring counters. In another example, we built a binary counter out of JK flip-flops by exploiting our knowledge of the operation of the JK flip-flop in its toggle mode.

Suppose that a digital designer is given an arbitrary state table and asked to find a schematic diagram for a hardware implementation. Ingenuity and knowledge of the JK flip-flop will not easily solve this problem. We call this the general synchronous sequential circuit synthesis problem. In this chapter we examine methods and tools to solve such problems.

Analysis and Synthesis of Sychronous Sequential Circuits

8.1 Synchronous Sequential Circuit Models

Before proceeding with the analysis and design of sequential circuits, it is appropriate to review the basic sequential circuit model and some related terminology. The operation of a synchronous sequential circuit, as modeled in Fig. 8.1, is controlled by a synchronizing pulse signal called a *clock*, which is applied to the memory portion of the circuit. A circuit that is controlled by a clock is termed a *synchronous sequential circuit*. One devoid of a clock signal is called an *asynchronous sequential circuit*. All sequential circuits can be placed in one of these two categories. In this chapter we consider only synchronous circuits; asynchronous circuits will be discussed in Chapter 10.

The memory in the block diagram of Fig. 8.1 is usually realized with edge-triggered and/or pulse-triggered flip-flops. In synchronous sequential circuit applications, the behavior of these two devices is almost identical; their outputs change only on a rising or falling clock signal transition. Therefore, the state of a synchronous sequential circuit may only change on a designated clock signal transition. For the examples of this chapter, all flip-flops will be assumed to be edge triggered.

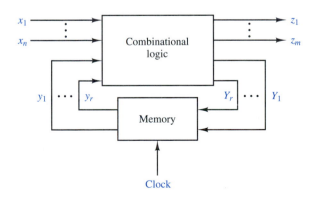

Figure 8.1   The sequential circuit model.

Recall from Chapter 6 that the n-tuple $(x_1, \ldots, x_n)$ in Fig. 8.1 is referred to as the circuit *input*, the m-tuple $(z_1, \ldots, z_m)$ is called the circuit *output*, and the r-tuples $(y_1, \ldots, y_r)$ and $(Y_1, \ldots, Y_r)$ represent the *present state* and *next state* of the circuit, respectively. The relationships that exist among these variables may be expressed mathematically as

$$z_i = g_i(x_1, \ldots, x_n, y_1, \ldots, y_r), \quad i = 1, \ldots, r \tag{8.1}$$
$$Y_i = h_i(x_1, \ldots, x_n, y_1, \ldots, y_r), \quad i = 1, \ldots, r \tag{8.2}$$

where the g_i and h_i are switching functions. Equations 8.1 and 8.2 may be written in vector notation as

$$\mathbf{z} = \mathbf{g}(\mathbf{x}, \mathbf{y}) \tag{8.3}$$
$$\mathbf{Y} = \mathbf{h}(\mathbf{x}, \mathbf{y}) \tag{8.4}$$

where

$$\mathbf{z} = \begin{bmatrix} z_1 \\ z_2 \\ \vdots \\ z_m \end{bmatrix}, \quad \mathbf{x} = \begin{bmatrix} x_1 \\ x_2 \\ \vdots \\ x_n \end{bmatrix}, \quad \mathbf{y} = \begin{bmatrix} y_1 \\ y_2 \\ \vdots \\ y_r \end{bmatrix}, \quad \mathbf{Y} = \begin{bmatrix} Y_1 \\ Y_2 \\ \vdots \\ Y_r \end{bmatrix} \tag{8.5}$$

These relationships may also be expressed in the form of state tables and state diagrams. These have two basic formats, depending on the relationship between the output signals z_j and the input signals x_i.

8.1.1 Mealy Model

In a *Mealy model* sequential circuit [1], the outputs are functions of both the inputs and the present state. The state diagram and state table of a Mealy model sequential circuit are shown in Figs. 8.2a and b, respectively. The Mealy model is called a *transition-assigned circuit* because the circuit output is associated with the state transitions, that is, the arcs in the state diagram. In other words, the circuit outputs are functions of the present state and inputs, as given by Eqs. 8.1 and 8.3. This relationship is illustrated by the following example.

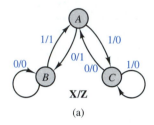

X/Z

(a)

Present state	Input x 0	1
A	$B/1$	$C/0$
B	$B/0$	$A/1$
C	$A/0$	$C/0$

Next state/output

(b)

Figure 8.2   Synchronous sequential circuit: Mealy model. **(a)** State diagram. **(b)** State table.

EXAMPLE 8.1

Let us determine the output response of the sequential circuit defined in Fig. 8.2 to the input sequence $x = 011010$.

Let us assume that the circuit is initially in state A. At time 0 an input of $x = 0$ is applied. From either the state diagram or the state table, we can read that the output is $z = 1$ and the next state will be B. Continuing for the remaining values in the input sequence, the circuit will behave as follows:

Time:	0	1	2	3	4	5	
Present state:	A	B	A	C	A	C	A
Input:	0	1	1	0	1	0	
Output:	1	1	0	0	0	0	
Next state:	B	A	C	A	C	A	

Hence, this input sequence applied to the machine in state A causes the output sequence

$$z = 110000$$

and leaves the circuit in final state A.

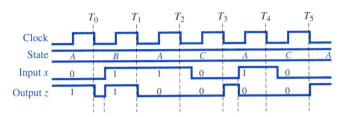

Figure 8.3   Mealy model timing diagram.

Figure 8.3 illustrates the actual circuit timing for the given input sequence. In this diagram it is assumed that the state changes on the high-to-low transition of the clock. Note that the output z can change any time either the input or the state changes, since z is a function of both. This gives rise to two unexpected output changes shown in the timing diagram. At time T_0, z drops to 0 when the state changes to B, and then goes back to 1 when input x changes to 1. A similar event occurs at time T_3. Hence, we must be careful to sample the output of a Mealy model circuit only when the circuit has stabilized after an input change.

8.1.2 Moore Model

A second arrangement for a state diagram is shown in Fig. 8.4. This format is called the *Moore model* for a sequential circuit [2], and it is distinguished from the Mealy model by identifying the outputs solely with the present state of the device. The output is then included inside the circles representing the states of the circuit.

The state table is also in a new format. The output may be removed from the next state entries in the state table since each next state will always have the same output entry; a new column of outputs is shown. It is important to remember that these outputs belong to the present state and not to the next one.

The output functional relationship given in Eqs. 8.1 and 8.3 can be modified, respectively, as follows for Moore-type circuits:

$$z_i = g_i(y_1, \ldots, y_r), \qquad i = 1, \ldots, m \tag{8.6}$$

$$\mathbf{z} = \mathbf{g}(\mathbf{y}) \tag{8.7}$$

This follows since the outputs are determined by the present state only.

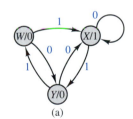

(a)

Present state	Input x 0	1	Outputs
W	Y	X	0
X	X	Y	1
Y	X	W	0

(b)

Figure 8.4   Synchronous sequential circuit - Moore model. **(a)** State diagram. **(b)** State table.

EXAMPLE 8.2

Consider the following input sequence to the Moore model of Fig. 8.4 with the starting state W:

Time:	0	1	2	3	4	5
Present state:	W	Y	W	X	X	Y	X
Input:	0	1	1	0	1	0
Output:	0	0	0	1	1	0
Next State:	Y	W	X	X	Y	X

The output is always identified by the present state from either the state diagram or the state table.

Figure 8.5 illustrates the actual circuit timing for the given input sequence. As in the previous example, all state changes occur on the high-to-low transition of the clock.

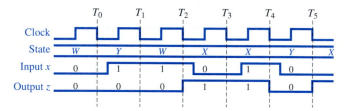

Figure 8.5 Moore model timing diagram.

In Fig. 8.5, note that all output changes in a Moore model circuit are synchronized to the clock, since output z is a function of the state only and can therefore change only when the state changes. Consequently, the output remains stable during any input changes, unlike the outputs of the Mealy model circuit illustrated previously in Fig. 8.3. Therefore, the outputs of a Moore model circuit typically exhibit better behavior that those of a Mealy model circuit; that is, input changes do not result in unwanted glitches in the outputs.

The primary advantage of using a Mealy versus a Moore model for a sequential circuit design is that, since the outputs of a Mealy model are functions of both the inputs and the state, the designer has more flexibility in designing output and state transition functions, and thus fewer states will be needed than in an equivalent Moore model circuit, where the outputs are functions of only the state variables.

In the sections that follow, examples of both Mealy and Moore model circuits will be presented.

8.2 Sequential Circuit Analysis

Before we dive into the synthesis problem, let us first reverse the process. That is, suppose we are given a schematic diagram of a synchronous sequential circuit and asked to describe its operation.

Analysis is the process of determining the output response of a given circuit or circuit model to a given input sequence. To do so, it is most convenient to first determine the model, for example, the state table or state diagram, of the given circuit. This process will first be illustrated by a series of examples and then summarized in the form of a step-by-step procedure.

8.2.1 Analysis of Sequential Circuit State Diagrams

Let us begin by examining the operation of a synchronous sequential circuit as described by a state diagram.

EXAMPLE 8.3

Consider the state diagram given in Fig. 8.6. Assume the diagram models a synchronous sequential circuit that has negative-edge-triggered flip-flops for memory elements.

Let us now construct a timing diagram that illustrates the circuit's behavior in response to the input sequence 001110110, assuming that the circuit starts in state 00. The desired timing diagram is shown in Fig. 8.7 and will now be explained.

First, a clock signal is needed to synchronize input signals and state changes. Since the memory elements are assumed to be negative-edge-triggered flip-flops, the state variables y_1 and y_2 change value only on a $1 \rightarrow 0$ transition of the clock signal. The values of the state variables following a clock transition are determined by the value of x and the values of the state variables y_1 and y_2 at the instant the clock transition occurs. The output z, however, is not synchronized with the clock. Output z is simply a combinational function of the input x and the state variables y_1 and y_2; therefore, it may change when any of these three signals change.

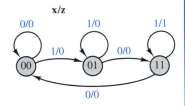

Figure 8.6   State diagram model of a synchronous sequential circuit.

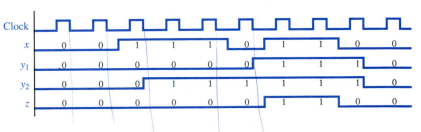

Figure 8.7   Timing diagram for a synchronous sequential circuit.

The previous example illustrates the following important point. A timing diagram can be constructed that represents the behavior of the circuit modeled by a state diagram (or state table) given the type of circuit, the type of memory element, an input sequence, and a starting state. The timing of the input signal transitions are not precisely known unless the input sequence is itself given in the form of a timing diagram.

8.2.2 Analysis of Sequential Circuit Logic Diagrams

Let us now consider the problem of analyzing a synchronous sequential circuit defined by a logic diagram. For such a sequential circuit we need to determine the state table or state diagram that defines its operation. From this state table or diagram we can then determine the response of the circuit to any given input sequence.

As an example, consider the sequential circuit shown in Fig. 8.8a. This sequential circuit is built of AND, OR, and NOT gates and a D flip-flop. For illustrative purposes the circuit is drawn in the form of the model presented in Fig. 8.1b. It is assumed that the circuit operates in a synchronous manner under the control of an external clock. In this case, since the memory element is a positive-edge-triggered D flip-flop, the memory changes state only on a $0 \rightarrow 1$ transition of a clock pulse.

Perhaps a more vivid understanding can be obtained if we first examine a timing diagram for the D flip-flop as shown in Fig. 8.8b. Note that the output signal Q is just the value of the flip-flop input data D at the instant the clock makes a $0 \rightarrow 1$ transition. The clock period, Δt, is selected to allow the circuit sufficient time for state changes and for new inputs to be applied before the next state transition is triggered.

Circuit Behavior Expressed as a Timing Diagram

Let us now examine the behavior of the circuit in Fig. 8.8a. The operation of the D flip-flop was described in Chapter 6, and the characteristics of the AND, OR, and NOT gates were demonstrated in Chapter 2. Using this information, a timing diagram for the example sequential circuit can be constructed for a given input sequence and a fixed starting state.

This sequential circuit has only one flip-flop and hence only two states, 0 and 1. The input, output, and state conditions for this network can be summarized as follows:

$$
\begin{array}{rl}
\text{Inputs:} & x = 0 \\
& x = 1 \\
\text{States:} & y = 0 \\
& y = 1 \\
\text{Outputs:} & z = 0 \\
& z = 1
\end{array}
$$

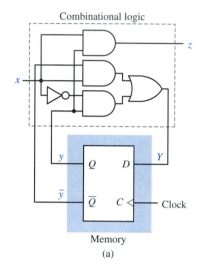

Combinational logic

Memory

(a)

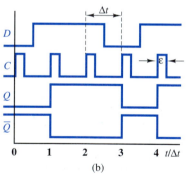

(b)

Figure 8.8 Introductory example. **(a)** Logic diagram. **(b)** Timing diagram.

The logic equations for the example, derived from the logic diagram of Fig. 8.8a, are the following:

$$z = xy$$
$$Y = x\bar{y} + \bar{x}y = x \oplus y \tag{8.8}$$

Using Eqs. (8.8), we can build the timing diagram shown in Fig. 8.9. The input sequence is

$$x = 01101000$$

and the starting state is $y = 0$. During the interval $t = 0$ to $t = 1$, the input is $x = 0$ and the present state is $y = 0$. Hence,

$$z = xy = 0 \cdot 0 = 0$$
$$Y = x \oplus y = 0 \oplus 0 = 0$$

Therefore, the clock pulse at $t = 1$ clocks the next state $Y = 0$ into the D flip-flop. During the period $t = 1$ to $t = 2$, the present state is $y = 0$ and the input changes to $x = 1$:

$$z = xy = 1 \cdot 0 = 0$$
$$Y = x \oplus y = 1 \oplus 0 = 1$$

As the clock pulse at $t = 2$ occurs, the state of the sequential device will change to 1, and so on. In a similar manner, the remainder of the timing diagram is determined.

From the timing diagram we observe that the output sequence is

$$z = 00100000$$

Note from the timing diagram that changes in Y occurred at $t = 3$ and at $t = 5$ that did not affect the state of the circuit. In each of these cases the value of Y changed again prior to the next clock transition. Only the value of Y at the clock transition determines the next state of y. Therefore, the momentary changes at $t = 3$ and $t = 5$ are ignored.

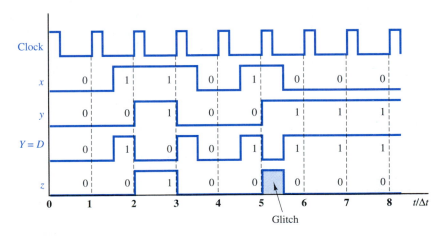

Figure 8.9   Timing diagram for the circuit of Fig. 8.4(a).

The timing diagram also shows a momentary change, or *glitch*, in the output at time $t = 5$. Since $z = xy$, the change in state variable y at time $t = 5$ results in $z = 1$ at that time, and then the subsequent change in input x causes z to return to its desired value of 0. Note that the width of this pulse on z depends on when input x changes.

Deriving the State Diagram and State Table

The operation of the sequential circuit of Fig. 8.8a may be completely defined by a state table that lists all possible operating conditions. Let us adopt the shorthand notation

$$y^k \quad \text{to represent} \quad y(k \, \Delta t) = y^k$$

where k is an integer and Δt is the period between clock pulses. The blank state table is shown in Fig. 8.10a. To fill in the upper left-hand corner, we must assume a present state $y^k = 0$ and the input $x^k = 0$. Following these signals through the circuit of Fig. 8.8a we find that the next state is $Y^k = y^{k+1} = 0$ and that the output is $z^k = 0$. Hence, the entry in the upper-left block is $y^{k+1}/z^k = 0/0$.

The initial conditions for the upper-right block are $y^k = 0$ and $x^k = 1$. Applying these signals in Fig. 8.8a yields $z^k = 0$ and $Y^k = y^{k+1} = 1$. The entry in this block is therefore $y^{k+1}/z^k = 1/0$. The two lower block entries are determined in a similar manner. The results of the analysis are shown in Fig. 8.10b.

We sometimes replace the present state vectors $\mathbf{y}$ by symbols to simplify notation; for example, in Fig. 8.10b, we may represent the states as follows:

$$\mathbf{y} = [y] = [0] \equiv A$$
$$\mathbf{y} = [y] = [1] \equiv B$$

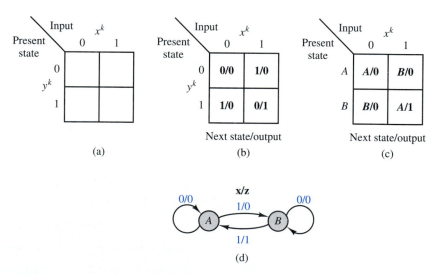

(a)

(b) Next state/output

(c) Next state/output

(d)

Figure 8.10 State table and diagram for the circuit of Fig. 8.4(a). **(a)** Blank table. **(b)** State transition table. **(c)** State table. **(d)** State diagram.

We call this mapping from a symbolic state to a binary value the *state assignment*. The state diagram and table drawn from the information contained in Fig. 8.10b are demonstrated in Figs. 8.10c and d.

Deriving the State Table from Karnaugh Maps

It is both interesting and informative to derive the state table shown in Fig. 8.10b directly from the circuit equations via K-maps. In Fig. 8.8a we have noted that

$$z = xy$$
$$Y = x \oplus y$$

Evaluated at time $t = k \, \Delta t$

$$z^k = x^k \cdot y^k$$
$$Y^k = x^k \oplus y^k = y^{k+1}$$

K-maps for these equations are shown in Figs. 8.11a and b. The state table is constructed by merely combining the two K-maps as shown in Fig. 8.11c. This table is identical to the one in Fig. 8.10b.

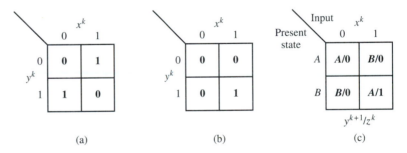

Figure 8.11 K-maps for the circuit of Fig. 8.4(a). **(a)** Map for $Y^k = y^{k+1}$. **(b)** Map for z. **(c)** State table.

This completes our introductory synchronous sequential circuit example. The following analysis procedure summarizes the processes illustrated in the preceding examples.

Synchronous Sequential Circuit Analysis Procedure

Step 1. If a state table or state diagram is given, proceed to steps 6 or 7, respectively. Otherwise, continue. Use combinational logic analysis techniques to determine the flip-flop input equations and the circuit output equations. Go to step 7 if only a timing diagram is needed.

Step 2. Construct K-maps for all the logic equations from step 1.

Step 3. Combine the K-maps for all flip-flop input equations into a single map.

Step 4. Using the characteristic equations of the flip-flops, construct a next-state map.

Step 5. Combine the next-state map and the output maps into a single map. This step results in a binary state table.

Step 6. Construct a binary state diagram from the binary state table if desired. Otherwise, go to step 7.

Step 7. Draw a timing diagram showing the clock, the given input sequence, and the starting state.

Step 8. On the timing diagram, derive the waveforms for the flip-flop input(s) and flip-flop state(s) for all the remaining circuit input values.

Step 9. On the timing diagram, derive the waveforms of the circuit output(s).

The following examples will illustrate this procedure. We begin by considering the problem of analyzing a clocked sequential circuit containing a T flip-flop.

EXAMPLE 8.4

Let us explore the behavior of the circuit in Fig. 8.12 by developing a timing diagram, state table, and state diagram. The timing diagram should show the circuit response to the input sequence $x = 01101000$, with the circuit beginning in state $y = 0$.

Timing Diagram

We begin by deriving excitation and output equations from the logic diagram of Fig. 8.12, using step 1 of the analysis procedure, from which we can generate a timing diagram using steps 7 to 9 of the procedure.

The operation of the T flip-flop and the characteristics of the AND, OR, and NOT gates have all been demonstrated earlier. This sequential circuit has

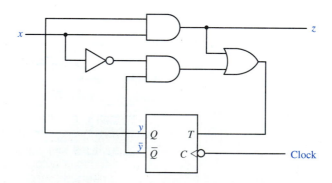

Figure 8.12   Synchronous sequential circuit with a T flip-flop.

only one flip-flop and hence only two states, 0 and 1. The input, output, and state conditions for this network are summarized as follows:

$$\text{Inputs:} \quad x = 0$$
$$x = 1$$
$$\text{States:} \quad y = 0$$
$$y = 1$$
$$\text{Outputs:} \quad z = 0$$
$$z = 1$$

The logic equations for the example are:

$$z = xy$$
$$T = xy + \bar{x}\bar{y} = x \odot y$$

Using these equations, we can construct the timing diagram shown in Fig. 8.13. The clocked T flip-flop characteristics described in Chapter 6 are also employed in the timing diagram's construction.

A specific timing diagram for the example sequential circuit is valid for only one given input sequence and a fixed starting state. The input sequence is

$$x = 01101000$$

and the starting state is $y = 0$. During the time $t/\Delta t = 0$ to $t/\Delta t = 1$, the input is $x = 0$ and the present state is $y = 0$. Hence, if we examine the logic equations during the clock pulse at the end of the period,

$$z = xy = 0 \cdot 0 = 0$$
$$T = x \odot y = 0 \odot 0 = 1$$

The variable T is the control for the T flip-flop. On the $1 \rightarrow 0$ transition of the clock pulse, the signal T will allow the clock pulse to trigger the flip-flop to the 1 state as shown for y in the interval $t/\Delta t = 1$ to $t/\Delta t = 2$. In a similar manner, the entire timing diagram is determined. Notice that all the input transitions are *not* synchronized with the clock pulse. The operation of the T flip-flop guarantees that the logic value on the input line x will be examined only at the falling edge of the clock pulse. Suppose an asynchronous input pulse occurs after time $t/\Delta t = 7$ (see dotted pulse in Fig. 8.13); although this asynchronous input pulse causes a change in the T input to the flip-flop, the pulse is ignored because it occurs while the clock is in logic state 0, so the flip-flop output is unchanged.

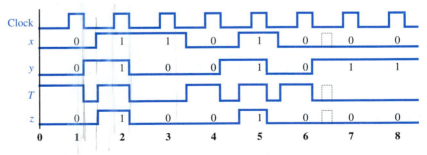

Figure 8.13   Timing diagram for the T flip-flop synchronous sequential circuit.

State Diagram and State Table Derivation

From the excitation and output equations generated in step 1 of the analysis, we can derive the state table and state diagram of the circuit using step 6 of the analysis procedure.

The operation of the sequential circuit of Fig. 8.12 is completely defined by its state table, which tabulates all possible operating conditions. The blank state table is shown in Fig. 8.14a. To fill in the upper-left corner of the state table, we assume that the present state is zero; that is, $y^k = 0$ and the input $x^k = 0$. Signals are examined only during the period ϵ while the clock pulse is high (1). Following these signals through the circuit of Fig. 8.12, we find that $z^k = 0$ and $T^k = 1$, and thus during the clock pulse the flip-flop will experience a state change, and hence the entry in the block under examination is $y^{k+1}/z^k = 1/0$. In other words, when the sequential circuit is in state $y^k = 0$ and the input is $x^k = 0$, the circuit changes state so that $y^{k+1} = 1$ and the output produced is $z^k = 0$.

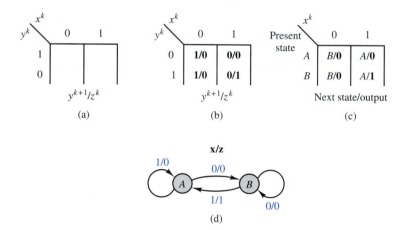

(a)   (b)   (c)

(d)

Figure 8.14 State table and diagram for the T flip-flop sequential circuit example. **(a)** Blank state table. **(b)** Transition table. **(c)** State table. **(d)** State diagram.

The initial conditions for the upper-right block are $y^k = 0$ and $x^k = 1$. These conditions yield $z^k = 0$ and $T^k = 0$, and therefore the flip-flop does not change state and hence the block entry is $y^{k+1}/z^k = 0/0$. The two lower-block entries are derived in a similar manner and are shown in Fig. 8.14b. The state table may also be taken from a judiciously chosen timing diagram. The reader is encouraged to try this procedure.

As shown in Example 8.3, sometimes the switching variable codes are replaced by symbols to simplify notation; if we code the sequential circuit's states as

$$0 \equiv A$$
$$1 \equiv B$$

the state table in Fig. 8.14c and the state diagram of Fig. 8.14d are obtained. At this point we may use the state diagram to determine the response of the circuit to an input sequence:

$$
\begin{array}{lccccccccc}
x & = & 0 & 1 & 1 & 0 & 1 & 0 & 0 & 0 \\
y & = & A & B & A & A & B & A & B & B & B \\
z & = & 0 & 1 & 0 & 0 & 1 & 0 & 0 & 0
\end{array}
$$

The starting state is A ($y = 0$) and the final state is B ($y = 1$). Note that this behavior is identical to the timing diagram of Fig. 8.14, which was to be expected.

State Table Derivation from K-maps

K-maps may also be used to determine the state table using steps 2 to 6 of the analysis procedure. The logic equations are

$$z^k = x^k y^k$$

$$T^k = x^k \odot y^k$$

where y^k is the present state and T^k determines the next state. K-maps for these equations are shown in Figs. 8.15a and b. The map for T^k defines the signal to the T input of the flip-flop when a clock pulse is present for various conditions of x and y. $T = 1$ causes the flip-flop to change state when a clock pulse occurs; for $T = 0$, there is no change in state.

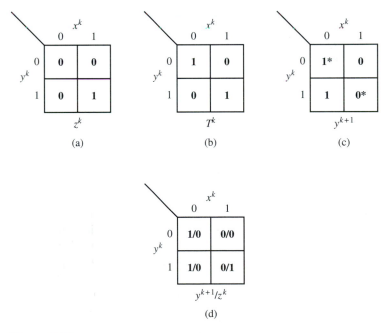

Figure 8.15 Derivation of the state table from K-maps. **(a)** Output K-map. **(b)** Excitation K-map. **(c)** Next state map. **(d)** Binary state table.

Using the map for T^k in Fig. 8.15b, we must now find the map for the next state y^{k+1}. This map is derived in Fig. 8.15c. The K-map variables are the input x^k and the present state y^k. The next-state entry is made by examining the corresponding entries in the map for T^k. The asterisks indicate the state changes caused by $T = 1$ minterms.

Finally, combining the next-state and output K-maps of Figs. 8.15a and c yields the state table in Fig. 8.15d, which is identical to the one shown in Fig. 8.14b. This completes the example.

EXAMPLE 8.5

Analyze the circuit shown in Fig. 8.16.

The circuit contains two clocked negative-edge-triggered JK flip-flops and hence has four states. An analysis similar to that presented previously yields the timing diagram and state table of Fig. 8.17. The input sequence and starting state are

$$x = 0011110$$
$$y_1^0 y_2^0 = 10$$

The equations that describe the circuit's operation are

$$J_1 = xy_2, \quad J_2 = x, \qquad z = xy_1y_2$$
$$K_1 = \bar{x}, \quad\;\; K_2 = \bar{x} + \bar{y}_1,$$

The K-maps for these equations are given in Fig. 8.18. The K-maps for J and K are combined into a single table shown in Fig. 8.19a. Using the J and K signals to determine the state changes yields the table of Fig. 8.19b. Finally,

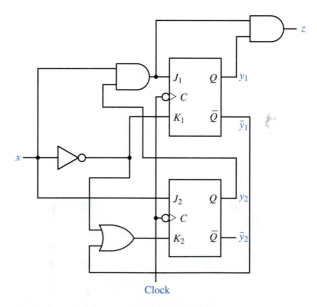

Clock

Figure 8.16   Synchronous sequential circuit with JK flip-flops.

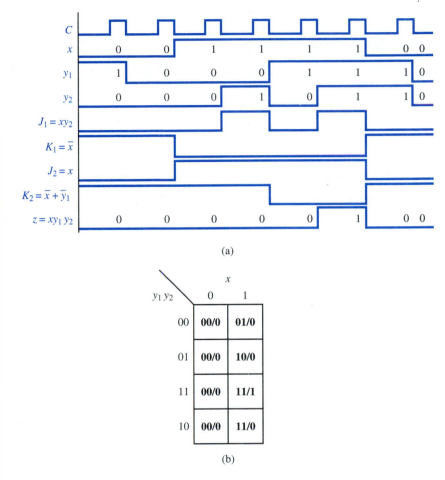

(a)

(b)

Figure 8.17 Timing diagram and state table for the example circuit. **(a)** Timing diagram. **(b)** State table.

combining the transition table with the table for the output z yields the binary state table shown in Fig. 8.19c.

8.2.3 Summary

In this section we have examined methods for analyzing various types of synchronous sequential circuits. The reader should now be able to take the logic diagram for any given sequential network, provided it is not extremely complicated, apply the analysis techniques of this chapter, and derive a state table and/or timing diagram description of the circuit. In the next section we shall reverse this procedure and find logic circuit diagrams to realize a specified state table or diagram.

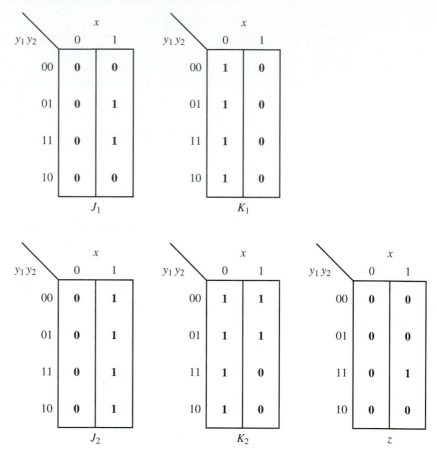

Figure 8.18 K-maps for logic equations that describe the example circuit.

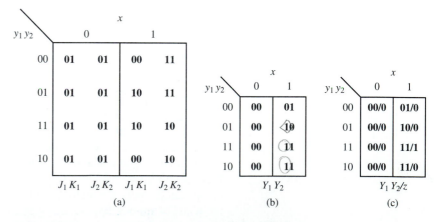

Figure 8.19 Combining the K-maps into the state table.

8.3 Synchronous Sequential Circuit Synthesis

In the previous section, the analysis of sequential circuits was introduced using several examples. In each case a logic diagram was given and the resulting analysis produced a state table, state diagram, and/or timing diagram. In this section the reverse procedure, the synthesis process, will be addressed [3–9]. For a given state table or diagram, well-defined tools will be used to generate an equivalent logic diagram for the sequential circuit in question. All sequential circuits in this chapter have clocked memory elements and are thus *synchronous* sequential circuits.

In our previous work, each time we analyzed a sequential circuit, we found that the resulting state table was completely determined, or specified. However, occasionally a circuit is connected in such a manner that the state table cannot be completely defined (for example, a circuit that causes a 1 input to both the *S* and *R* terminals of an SR flip-flop).

The synthesis of synchronous sequential circuits begins with the specification of the desired state table (or diagram). Circuits for which every next state/output pair is completely defined are termed *completely specified circuits*. Those for which several next states or outputs are arbitrary are termed *incompletely specified circuits*. An example of each type of circuit is shown

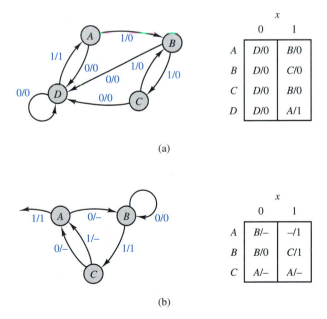

(a)

(b)

Figure 8.20   Types of sequential circuits. **(a)** Completely specified circuit. **(b)** Incompletely specified circuit.

in Fig. 8.20. The following sections deal with completely specified circuits. Incompletely specified circuits will be considered later in the chapter.

8.3.1 Synthesis Procedure

The procedure for designing synchronous sequential circuits will be introduced by a simple example.

EXAMPLE 8.6

Let us find a clocked D flip-flop realization for the sequential circuit defined in the state table of Fig. 8.21a.

First we must adopt some coding scheme for the symbolic states. This process is called *state assignment*. We arbitrarily choose the code in Fig. 8.21b. If we replace the symbolic states with their code equivalents, a binary state table is obtained or, in other words, the *transition table* shown in Fig. 8.21c. The transition table contains all the necessary information for generating the switching functions for the combinational logic portion of the circuit. Then we separate the transition table into an output K-map and D flip-flop input K-maps

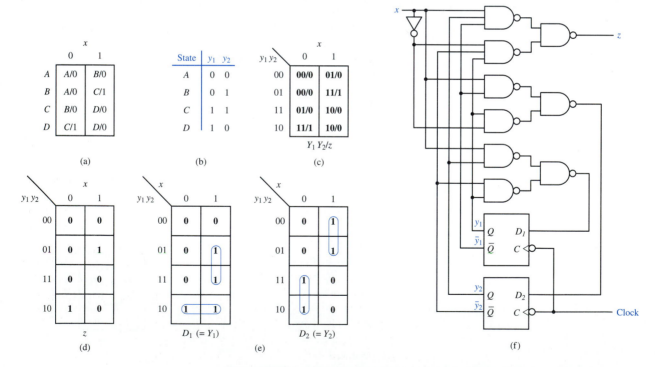

Figure 8.21 An introductory example. **(a)** State table. **(b)** State assignment. **(c)** Transition table. **(d)** Output K-map. **(e)** Excitation K-maps. **(f)** Logic diagram.

as shown in Figs. 8.21d and e. The flip-flop input maps are called *excitation maps*. From the excitation and output maps,

$$D_1 = y_1 \bar{y}_2 + x y_2$$
$$D_2 = \bar{x} y_1 + x \bar{y}_1 = x \oplus y_1$$
$$z = x \bar{y}_1 y_2 + \bar{x} y_1 \bar{y}_2$$

The logic diagram for the completed design is presented in Fig. 8.21f. The combinational logic is realized using two levels of NAND gates.

In the foregoing example, several questions remain unanswered. How do we choose the state assignment? What happens if the design requires another type of flip-flop? How do we know the given state table is the best one to use? Many state tables have extra states that may be eliminated.

Before we attempt to answer these questions, let us outline the complete synthesis procedure for synchronous sequential logic circuits.

Synchronous Sequential Circuit Synthesis Procedure

Step 1. From a word description of the problem, derive a state table.

Step 2. Use state reduction techniques to find the state table of a minimum-state equivalent circuit.

Step 3. Choose a state assignment and generate the state and output transition tables.

Step 4. Determine the memory device or flip-flop to be used and find the flip-flop excitation maps.

Step 5. From the excitation maps, produce the switching logic equations. Also, form output maps and determine the output logic equations.

Step 6. Draw the logic diagram of the sequential circuit using logic equations and the chosen memory devices.

The first step requires intuition on the part of the logic designer and must be learned through trial and error experience. Step 2 is used to minimize the number of memory elements required to build a circuit by eliminating unnecessary states from the state table. In step 3, we may either choose an arbitrary state assignment or else apply one of several algorithms that select state assignments to optimize the amount of combinational logic needed to realize a circuit. We shall see that the successful designer employs standard algorithms and rules of thumb in completing steps 2 and 3. We shall examine these algorithms and rules in Chapter 9, after we have gained some experience in the fundamentals of synchronous sequential circuit design.

Step 4 requires analysis of the characteristics of the selected flip-flop types, as presented in Chapter 6, to derive the flip-flop excitation maps. The skills required in step 5 are found in Chapter 3, and hence it is assumed that the reader is familiar with them. Step 6 is the obvious conclusion of the synthesis procedure and is included for completion.

Now that the problem has been defined, we shall first examine techniques for designing logic circuits to realize a given state table or state diagram. Then we will address the problem of creating state tables and diagrams from verbal problem descriptions. We will address the minimization methods used in steps 2 and 3 in Chapter 9.

8.3.2 Flip-flop Input Tables

In the introductory synthesis example of Fig. 8.21, an edge-triggered D flip-flop was employed for circuit realization. In particular, the characteristics of the D flip-flop were used to generate the excitation maps from the transition table. The transition table defines the necessary state transitions for each memory flip-flop. A *flip-flop input table* may be used to determine the required excitation inputs for each type of flip-flop memory element. Consider the input tables of Fig. 8.22, which represent the characteristics of the four primary flip-flop types discussed in Chapter 6. The notation in this table is as follows: t is the time at which the clock signal is activated; $Q(t)$ is the state of the flip-flop at the instant the clock signal is activated; $Q(t + \epsilon)$ is the next state of the flip-flop after the clock signal has been activated.

The D flip-flop is convenient to employ because its next state is simply its present input; hence the excitation maps are taken directly from the transition table. Any other flip-flop requires the application of the corresponding input

State transitions		Required inputs
$Q(t)$	$Q(t + \varepsilon)$	$D(t)$
0	0	0
0	1	1
1	0	0
1	1	1

(a)

State transitions		Required inputs	
$Q(t)$	$Q(t + \varepsilon)$	$S(t)$	$R(t)$
0	0	0	d
0	1	1	0
1	0	0	1
1	1	d	0

(b)

State transitions		Required inputs
$Q(t)$	$Q(t + \varepsilon)$	$T(t)$
0	0	0
0	1	1
1	0	1
1	1	0

(c)

State transitions		Required inputs	
$Q(t)$	$Q(t + \varepsilon)$	$J(t)$	$K(t)$
0	0	0	d
0	1	1	d
1	0	d	1
1	1	d	0

(d)

Figure 8.22   Flip-flop input tables. **(a)** D flip-flop. **(b)** Clocked SR flip-flop. **(c)** Clocked T flip-flop. **(d)** Clocked JK flip-flop.

table of Fig. 8.22 in the production of the excitation K-maps. The flip-flop input tables are derived from the flip-flop characteristic equations and excitation tables presented in Chapter 6.

EXAMPLE 8.7

Let us implement the sequential circuit of Fig. 8.21 using clocked JK flip-flops.

Assume the same state assignment. The transition table remains unchanged and is reproduced in Fig. 8.23a for convenience.

The flip-flop input table of Fig. 8.22d is used to obtain the excitation tables of Fig. 8.23b. One state transition is emphasized both in the transition table and in the corresponding entry of the excitation table; that is, the transition of y_2 shown in Fig. 8.23a from 1 to 0 requires $J_2 = d$ and $K_2 = 1$, as illustrated in Fig. 8.23b. Next the excitation tables are transformed into excitation K-maps and the required Boolean logic equations are minimized as follows:

$$J_1 = xy_2 \qquad K_1 = \bar{x}y_2$$
$$J_2 = x \oplus y_1 \qquad K_2 = x \odot y_1 = \bar{J}_2$$

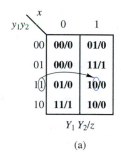

(a)

(b)

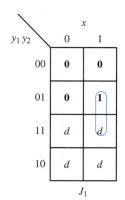 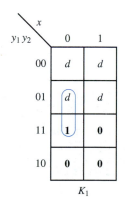 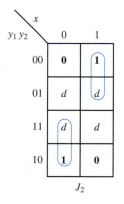 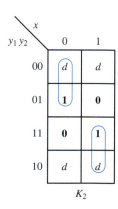

(c)

Figure 8.23 Generating the excitation maps. **(a)** Transition table. **(b)** Excitation tables. **(c)** Excitation maps.

The logic diagram is shown in Fig. 8.24. The output logic is unchanged from Fig. 8.21f.

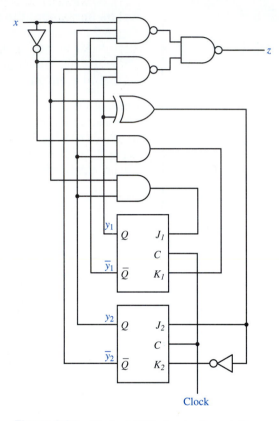

Figure 8.24 Clocked JK flip-flop implementation.

8.3.3 Application Equation Method for JK Flip-flops

In Chapter 6, we derived the next-state characteristic equation for a JK flip-flop:

$$Q^* = J\bar{Q} + \bar{K}Q$$

We may use this equation to our advantage in designing synchronous sequential circuits employing JK flip-flops. The technique is as follows:

1. Proceed in the synthesis process through the steps generating the binary state table, or transition table.

2. Instead of generating JK flip-flop excitation tables and K-maps, produce the excitation K-maps for a D flip-flop implementation.

3. For each next state variable Y_i, divide its K-map into two halves, one associated with y_i and one associated with $\bar{y}_i$.

4. Minimize the function Y_i on the K-map, but do not cross the boundaries dividing the map into halves. This generates a function in the form:
$$Y_i = (J_i)\bar{y}_i + (\bar{K}_i)y_i$$

5. We may now write the J_i and K_i expressions directly from the function in step 4.

EXAMPLE 8.8

Let us derive the excitation equations for the previous example using the application equation method.

The steps of the application equation method are performed as follows:

1. The transition table is given in Fig. 8.23a.

2. The excitation K-maps are derived from the transition table as shown in Fig. 8.25.

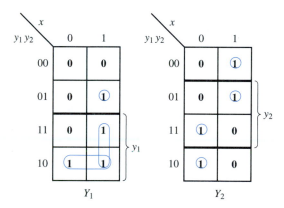

Figure 8.25   Excitation K-maps.

3. The Y_1 excitation map of Fig. 8.25 is divided by a thick line into two halves, corresponding to y_1 and $\bar{y}_1$. Likewise, the Y_2 excitation map is partitioned into halves corresponding to y_2 and $\bar{y}_2$.

4. Terms are circled on the excitation maps without crossing the boundaries that divide the maps. This produces the logic expressions:
$$Y_1 = (xy_2)\bar{y}_1 + (x + \bar{y}_2)y_1$$
$$Y_2 = (x\bar{y}_1 + \bar{x}y_1)\bar{y}_2 + (x\bar{y}_1 + \bar{x}y_1)y_2$$
$$= (x \oplus y_1)\bar{y}_2 + (x \oplus y_1)y_2$$

5. Since the expressions derived in step 4 are of the form
$$Y_i = (J_i)\bar{y}_i + (\bar{K}_i)y_i$$
we may write the J_i and K_i expressions directly from them:
$$J_1 = xy_2 \qquad K_1 = \overline{x + \bar{y}_2} = \bar{x}y_2$$
$$J_2 = x \oplus y_1 \qquad K_2 = \overline{x \oplus y_1} = x \odot y_1$$

8.3.4 Design Examples

The synthesis procedure for synchronous sequential circuits was presented earlier in this chapter as a six-step process. The reader should now be able to complete all the steps except steps 2 and 3, state reduction and state assignment. Let us postpone the development of the theory of these topics and, instead, dwell on some practical applications of the other four steps for the moment. This change of pace has two purposes: first, to allow the reader to practice her or his skills of state table/state diagram formulation and excitation map generation and, second, to provide a basis from which to present the state table reduction and state assignment problems.

The design procedure will be demonstrated by several examples. In each example it is assumed that the circuit is under the control of a periodic clock pulse and that transitions in the circuits occur only as initiated by this clock.

Sequence Recognizers

Sequence recognizers are synchronous sequential circuits that produce a designated response on their outputs when specific sequences of input values are detected. Each set of values in an input sequence is assumed to arrive prior to the active transition of the clock, with successive values in a sequence arriving during consecutive clock periods.

EXAMPLE **8.9**

states = # digits to
recognize

O/P (z) = 1 after
the sequence is being
pushed

Design a synchronous sequential circuit with one input x and one output z that recognizes the input sequence 01. 2 digits = # of states

This circuit can be used to recognize a 0 to 1 transition on the input x. In other words, the circuit should produce an output sequence $z = 01$ whenever the input sequence $x = 01$ occurs. For example, if the input sequence is

$$x = 010100000111101$$

then the output sequence will be

$$z = 010100000100001$$

The first step in the design procedure is the construction of a state diagram that represents the input/output behavior just described. The diagram is constructed as shown in Fig. 8.26. First it is assumed that the circuit is in some starting state A and that the first input is a 1. Since a 1 is not the first element in the input string to be recognized, the circuit remains in state A and yields an output $z = 0$, as shown in Fig. 8.26a. However, if the circuit is in the initial state A and the input is a 0, then, because this input is the first symbol in the string to be recognized, the circuit moves to a new state B and produces an output of 0, as shown in Fig. 8.26b. Now suppose that the circuit is in state B and that the input symbol is a 0. Because this is not the second symbol in the sequence 01, the circuit merely remains in state B and yields an output $z = 0$. Finally, if the circuit is in state B and the next input symbol is a 1, the circuit moves to state A and produces an output $z = 1$. Note that this final diagram, shown in Fig. 8.26d, satisfies the input/output sequence given previously and thus recognizes the input sequence $x = 01$. The state table that corresponds to the final state diagram is shown in Fig. 8.27a. We shall assume that this state table contains the minimum number of states possible for this circuit.

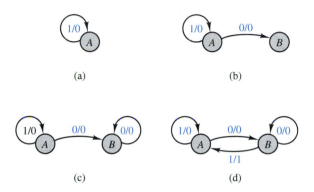

Figure 8.26   Sequence 01 recognizer state diagram.

The next step in the synthesis procedure is to determine the number of flip-flops required and the state assignment. The relationship between the number of states (N_S) and the number of flip-flops (N_{FF}) is given by the expression

$$2^{N_{FF}-1} < N_S \leq 2^{N_{FF}} \tag{8.9}$$

For example, a four-state circuit would require two flip-flops, a ten-state circuit would require four flip-flops, and so on. For the circuit described by the state table shown in Fig. 8.27a, only a single flip-flop is needed. The state assignment is arbitrarily chosen as $A = 0$ and $B = 1$; it could, however, just as easily have been selected in the opposite manner ($A = 1$, $B = 0$). We shall defer a more detailed explanation of state assignment until Chapter 9.

Once the state assignment has been chosen, the state table in Fig. 8.27a can be redrawn as the transition table of Fig. 8.27b. Here y^k denotes the present state of the circuit, which is the current output of the flip-flop. The symbol y^{k+1} denotes the next state of the circuit, that is, the output of the flip-flop after a transition has occurred. The K-map for the output is drawn separately merely for simplicity. Suppose that we want to realize the circuit with clocked set–reset flip-flops. The problem then becomes one of determining the proper signals on the set and reset input lines to effect the transitions shown in Fig. 8.27b. Using the clocked SR flip-flop input table of Fig. 8.22b, we may derive the excitation maps shown in Fig. 8.27c. For example, consider the transition in the upper-left corner of the transition table shown in Fig. 8.27b: $y^k = 0$, $x = 0$, and $y^{k+1} = 1$. To effect a state change from $y^k = 0$ to $y^{k+1} = 1$, the signals that must appear on the set and reset lines are $S = 1$ and $R = 0$. Hence, these signals appear in the corresponding positions in the excitation maps of Fig. 8.27c. Next consider the state transition in the upper-right corner of the transition table: $y^k = 0$, $x = 1$, and $y^{k+1} = 0$. Since no change in state must occur, the signal on the set line must be $S = 0$, while the signal on the reset line does not matter; that is, R is a don't-care. The reader should recall that an SR flip-flop will not change to the set state with $S = 0$ and $R = 0$ or $S = 0$ and $R = 1$. The remaining blocks in the excitation maps are determined in a similar manner.

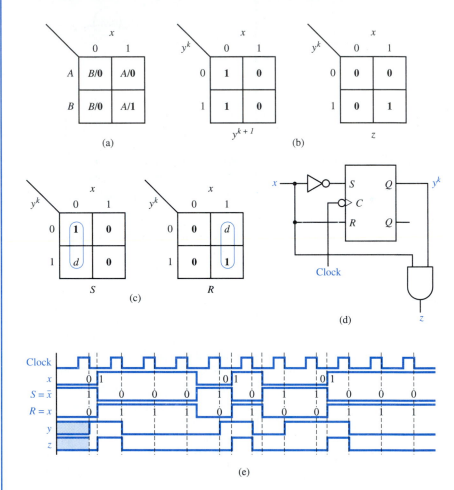

Figure 8.27   Synthesis of a sequence 01 recognizer. **(a)** State table. **(b)** Transition table and output map. **(c)** Excitation maps. **(d)** Logic diagram. **(e)** Timing diagram.

The excitation maps can now be used to derive the switching logic circuit equations:

$$S = \bar{x}$$
$$R = x$$
$$z = xy^k$$

The actual circuit obtained from these logic equations is shown in Fig. 8.27d. The reader may now check the circuit to see if it does indeed recognize the input sequence 01. A timing diagram with x shown as a level input signal that is not synchronized with the clock is drawn in Fig. 8.27e. Note that the circuit operates as follows:

1. A logic 0 on x causes the SR flip-flop to set on the next falling edge of the clock.
2. The flip-flop then remains at logic 1 waiting for the input to change from 0 to 1.
3. Then x goes high, and the output z also goes high.
4. Finally, the flip-flop resets on the next falling edge of the clock.

So the three 0 to 1 transitions on x have been detected as shown by the three pulses on z.

EXAMPLE 8.10

For completeness, let us realize the circuit of Example 8.9 with clocked T flip-flops and then with JK flip-flops.

If a clocked T flip-flop is used to implement the sequence recognizer, the excitation map for the flip-flop is as shown in Fig. 8.28a. This table is derived using the transition table in Fig. 8.27b. Recall that $T = 1$ if a state transition is to take place and $T = 0$ otherwise. See the input table for a clocked T flip-flop

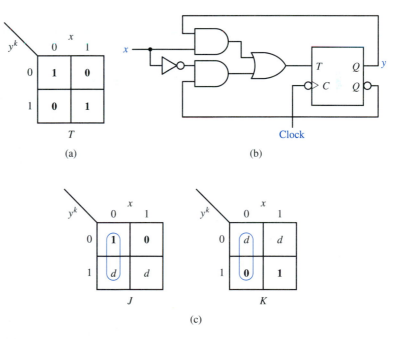

Figure 8.28   Clocked T and JK flip-flop realizations. (a) Clocked T flip-flop excitation map. (b) Clocked T flip-flop implementation. (c) Clocked JK excitation maps.

in Fig. 8.22c. From the excitation map in Fig. 8.28a, the logic equation for T is given by the expression

$$T = \bar{x}\bar{y} + xy = x \odot y$$

The output equation is identical to that obtained earlier. The implementation of the logic equation with a clocked T flip-flop is shown in Fig. 8.28b.

Fig. 8.28c shows the excitation maps for a realization using clocked JK flip-flops. The corresponding logic equations are:

$$J = \bar{x}, \quad K = x$$

Note that the logic equations for J and K are identical to those for S and R in the set–reset realization, and hence the clocked JK flip-flop realization is identical to that shown in Fig. 8.27d, with the SR flip-flop replaced by a JK flip-flop.

EXAMPLE 8.11

Let us design a synchronous sequential circuit with one input line and one output line that recognizes the input string $x = \underline{1111}$. The circuit is also required to recognize 4 digits = # states **overlapping sequences, as can be seen in the output string z that results from the following input string x:**

$$x = 1101111111010$$

$$z = 0000001111000$$

The state diagram and the corresponding reduced state table for the sequential circuit that will recognize the input string $x = 1111$ are shown in Figs. 8.29a and b. Note that if state A is assumed to be the initial state the circuit changes state every time an input $x = 1$ occurs, with the exception of the fourth and succeeding ones. Every time an $x = 0$ occurs, the circuit resets by returning to state A. The loop with $x = 1$ at state D satisfies the overlapping input sequence criterion by producing a 1 at the output when the fourth, fifth, sixth, and so on, logic 1 occurs at the input.

The state assignment for the example is arbitrarily chosen as follows:

$$A = 00$$
$$B = 01$$
$$C = 10$$
$$D = 11$$

The resulting transition table is shown in Fig. 8.29c. The output map is shown in Fig. 8.29d.

The excitation maps for a clocked SR flip-flop realization of the circuit are shown in Fig. 8.30. The logic equations obtained from Fig. 8.29d and Fig. 8.30 are

$$S_1 = y_2 x, \quad S_2 = \bar{y}_2 x, \qquad z = xy_1 y_2$$
$$R_1 = \bar{x}, \quad R_2 = \bar{x} + \bar{y}_1 y_2$$

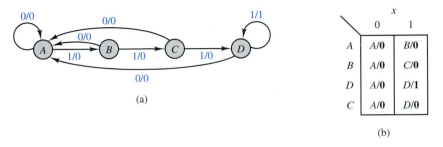

(a)

(b)

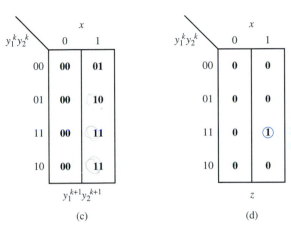

(c)

(d)

Figure 8.29   A sequence 1111 recognizer. **(a)** State diagram. **(b)** State table.
(c) Transition table. **(d)** Output map.

The excitation maps for a clocked T flip-flop realization of the circuit are given
in Fig. 8.31a, and the corresponding logic circuit equations are

$$T_1 = y_1\bar{x} + \bar{y}_1 y_2 x, \qquad z = x y_1 y_2$$
$$T_2 = y_2\bar{x} + \bar{y}_2 x + \bar{y}_1 y_2$$

Excitation maps for a clocked JK flip-flop realization of the circuit are given
in Fig. 8.31b. The logic equations obtained from these K-maps are given next,
and the hardware used to realize the equations is shown in Fig. 8.32:

$$J_1 = y_2 x, \quad J_2 = x, \qquad z = x y_1 y_2$$
$$K_1 = \bar{x}, \quad K_2 = \bar{y}_1 + \bar{x}$$

We can also derive the JK flip-flop excitation equations using the application equation method. The excitation K-maps are first derived from the
transition table as shown in Fig. 8.31c. From these, we derive the following
next-state equations.

$$Y_1 = (x y_2)\bar{y}_1 + (x)y_1$$
$$Y_2 = (x)\bar{y}_2 + (x y_1)y_2$$

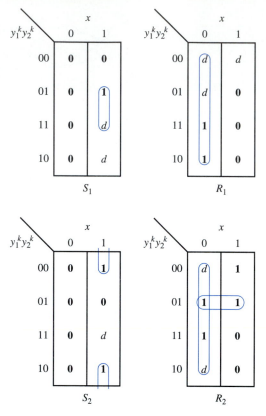

Figure 8.30 K-maps for a clocked SR realization.

Recalling that the excitation equations are of the form

$$Y_i = (J_i)\bar{y}_i + (\bar{K}_i)y_i$$

we can write the J and K excitation equations directly from the next-state equations, producing the same expressions derived earlier from the JK excitation maps.

EXAMPLE 8.12

Here we want to design a clocked sequential circuit that recognizes the input sequence consisting of exactly two zeros followed by a 10. In other words, the following output sequence should result from the given input sequence.

$$x = 001001000010010$$
$$z = 000100100001001$$

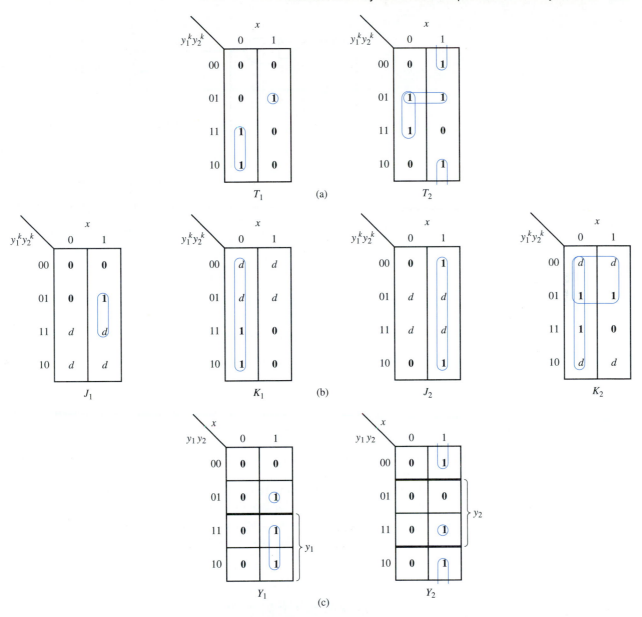

Figure 8.31 Clocked T and JK realizations. **(a)** Clocked T excitation maps.
(b) Clocked JK excitation maps. **(c)** Excitation K-maps.

One way to approach the design of a sequence recognizer is to establish a string of state transitions corresponding to the "correct" input sequence. Examine the partial state diagram of Fig. 8.33a. If the circuit begins in state

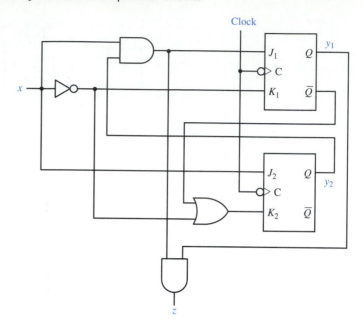

Figure 8.32 Clocked JK logic diagram.

A, an input sequence of 0010 will produce an output $z = 1$ coincident with the last $x = 0$ in the sequence. Note that we have added two extra states to be used for error conditions; that is, we will send the circuit to these states when the input sequence does not match the correct pattern. Figure 8.33b illustrates some obvious transitions to the error states. To complete the state diagram, we must have two arcs exiting each state, one for each input condition. Notice that the $x = 0$ arc exiting state E has not been defined. This arc should loop back to state C to allow for overlapping sequences, so it does *not* get routed to state G. The correct transition is recorded in Fig. 8.33c. Next we must complete the transitions exiting error states F and G. For state F, if an input $x = 0$ occurs, then a 10 sequence pattern exists, which can be the beginning of a valid input sequence , so we send the circuit to state B in the horizontal row of states in the state diagram. All other x inputs to the circuit in states F and G cause transitions within these error states, as shown in Fig. 8.33d. This completes the state diagram. We should now look for equivalent states in our design. Examining the state table for the circuit in Fig. 8.33e, we note that $A = F$ and $B = E$, since they have identical rows, and therefore we may eliminate rows E and F. Therefore, the reduced circuit is shown in Figs. 8.33f and g. More will be said about equivalent states and state table reduction in Chapter 9.

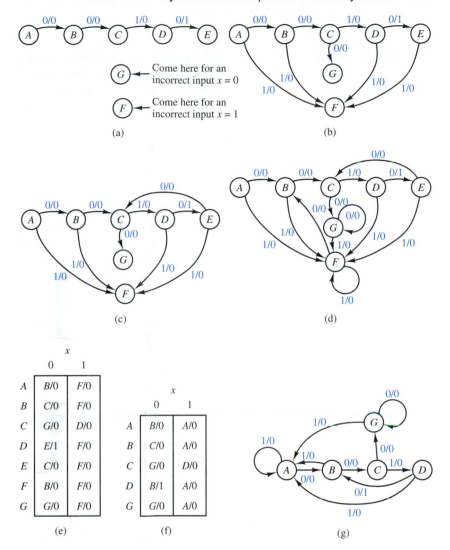

Figure 8.33 A sequence 0010 recognizer. **(a)** Partial state diagram. **(b)** State transitions to the error states. **(c)** Feedback for overlapping sequences. **(d)** Complete state diagram. **(e)** State table. **(f)** Reduced state table. **(g)** State diagram.

Realization of this circuit in hardware will require three flip-flops. To complete the solution, we need only follow the procedure as shown in the previous examples.

A number of problems may be approached in the same manner as for sequence recognizers. This is illustrated by the following example, in which we design an arithmetic circuit to operate on sequences of binary digits.

EXAMPLE 8.13

Let us design a serial binary adder that computes the sum of two n-bit binary numbers, $a_{n-1} \ldots a_1 a_0$ and $b_{n-1} \ldots b_1 b_0$, 1 bit at a time, beginning with the least significant bit.

The serial adder is to be used as illustrated in the block diagram of Fig. 8.34a. The addend and augend are stored in shift registers A and B, respectively. The sum replaces the addend in register A. Bits are presented to the serial adder from the shift registers. In clock cycle i, the adder inputs are addend bit a_i and augend bit b_i, and the output is the sum bit s_i, which is computed as the sum of the two inputs and the carry bit, c_{i-1}, produced while generating sum bit s_{i-1}. The circuit must remember the carry from the previous clock cycle. Therefore, the state of the adder in clock cycle i should reflect the value of c_{i-1}. Consequently, two states are needed for the circuit. State 0 represents the condition $c_{i-1} = 0$ and state 1 represents $c_{i-1} = 1$. At the end of each clock cycle, the sum bit s_i is shifted into register A to replace addend bit a_i, while b_i is returned to register B.

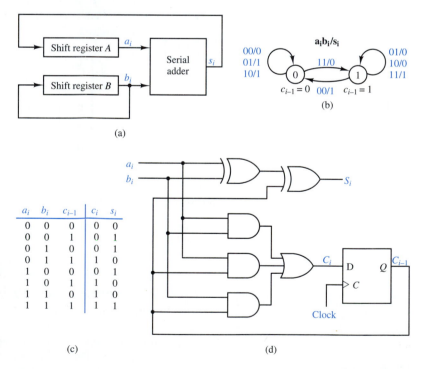

Figure 8.34   Serial binary adder design. **(a)** Block diagram. **(b)** State diagram. **(c)** State table. **(d)** Logic diagram.

The serial adder state diagram is given in Fig. 8.34b and the corresponding state table in Fig. 8.34c. Using a D flip-flop as the memory element, it can be shown that the excitation and output equations are simply the full-adder equations, Eqs. 4.19, derived in Chapter 4.

$$s_i = a_i \oplus b_i \oplus c_{i-1}$$
$$D = c_i = a_i b_i + a_i c_{i-1} + b_i c_{i-1}$$

where c_{i-1} represents the present state and c_i the next state of the controller. The completed logic diagram is given in Fig. 8.34d.

Counter Circuits

The design and operation of several different counter modules were presented in Chapter 7. However, we used ad hoc procedures in the design of those modules. In the examples that follow, we consider the design of counter circuits using the methods presented in this chapter. In these examples, Moore models are assumed, with the state and output reflecting the current value of the counter.

EXAMPLE 8.14

Design an up/down counter with four states (0, 1, 2, 3) using clocked JK flip-flops. A control signal x is to be used as follows: When $x = 0$ the circuit counts forward (up); when $x = 1$, backward (down).

A state diagram depicting this counter is illustrated in Fig. 8.35a. From this diagram the state table shown in Fig. 8.35b is derived. Notice that the output of the counter is just its present state. If we choose a state assignment

$$0 \rightarrow 00$$
$$1 \rightarrow 01$$
$$2 \rightarrow 10$$
$$3 \rightarrow 11$$

which is standard for counters, the transition table may be produced as illustrated in Fig. 8.35c. Using the input table for the clocked JK flip-flop (see Fig. 8.22), the excitation maps for the two flip-flops y_1 and y_2 are obtained in Fig. 8.35d. Using these K-maps, the following relations are found:

$$J_1 = K_1 = x \bar{y}_2 + \bar{x} y_2 = x \oplus y_2$$
$$J_2 = K_2 = 1$$

Hence, the logic diagram for the four-state up/down counter is drawn in Fig. 8.36. If the signal x is controlled by a toggle switch and the clock period is very slow (say 1 second), the action of this device may be observed by attaching light-emitting diodes (LEDs) to the flip-flop outputs.

Now let us tackle a more formidable counter design.

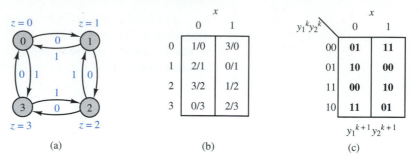

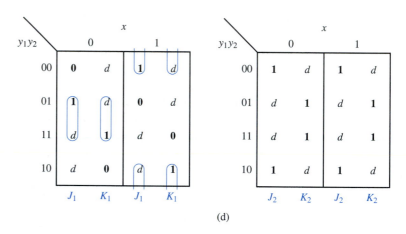

(d)

Figure 8.35 Up/down counter synthesis. **(a)** State diagram. **(b)** State table. **(c)** Transition table **(d)** Excitation maps.

EXAMPLE 8.15

Use clocked JK flip-flops to design a circuit that counts in the BCD code. The counter has one control signal, x. When $x = 1$, the counter counts; otherwise, it holds the current state. The output showing the value of the count is to be in the form of four lights. For example, if the count is 3, then the lights would read OFF, OFF, ON, ON.

Because of its simplicity, the state table can be constructed immediately. Ignoring the output for the moment, the state table for this example is shown in Fig. 8.37a.

To satisfy the output readout, the states will be assigned so that they are a direct indication of the count; that is, each is assigned its BCD representation, and hence the output can be obtained by merely monitoring the outputs of the

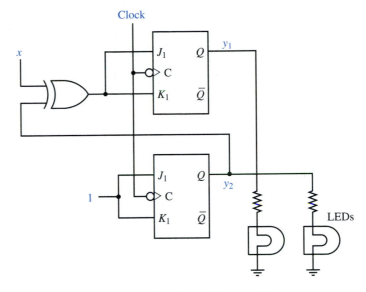

Figure 8.36   Implementation of an up/down counter.

flip-flops and using these signals to turn the lights on and off. Therefore, the state assignment is

$$
\begin{array}{ll}
0 \to 0000 & 5 \to 0101 \\
1 \to 0001 & 6 \to 0110 \\
2 \to 0010 & 7 \to 0111 \\
3 \to 0011 & 8 \to 1000 \\
4 \to 0100 & 9 \to 1001
\end{array}
$$

The transition table for this assignment is given in Fig. 8.37b. Next we derive the excitation maps for the four flip-flops using Fig. 8.22d. The resulting tables are presented in Fig. 8.37c. The d's in the tables represent don't-cares. These tables may be reorganized into K-map form as shown for input J_2 in Fig. 8.37d. All the resulting Boolean logic equations are listed next:

$$
\begin{array}{ll}
J_3 = y_2 y_1 y_0 x, & K_3 = y_0 x \\
J_2 = y_1 y_0 x, & K_2 = y_1 y_0 x \\
J_1 = \bar{y}_3 y_0 x, & K_1 = y_0 x \\
J_0 = x, & K_0 = x
\end{array}
$$

Note from the logic equations that the input x acts as a gating signal to disable or enable all flip-flop inputs simultaneously.

The actual implementation of the circuit using clocked JK flip-flops is shown in Fig. 8.37e.

x	0	1
0	0	1
1	1	2
2	2	3
3	3	4
4	4	5
5	5	6
6	6	7
7	7	8
8	8	9
9	9	0

(a)

$y_3^k y_2^k y_1^k y_0^k$ \ x	0	1
0000	0000	0001
0001	0001	0010
0010	0010	0011
0011	0011	0100
0100	0100	0101
0101	0101	0110
0110	0110	0111
0111	0111	1000
1000	1000	1001
1001	1001	0000
1010	$dddd$	$dddd$
1011	$dddd$	$dddd$
1100	$dddd$	$dddd$
1101	$dddd$	$dddd$
1110	$dddd$	$dddd$
1111	$dddd$	$dddd$

$y_3^{k+1} y_2^{k+1} y_1^{k+1} y_0^{k+1}$

(b)

Figure 8.37 Design of the BCD counter. **(a)** State table. **(b)** Transition table.

EXAMPLE 8.16

Let us use the application equation method to derive the excitation equations for flip-flop y_1 of the BCD counter in Example 8.15.

1. The transition table is given in Fig. 8.37b.
2. The excitation K-map for D flip-flop y_1 is given in Fig. 8.38.
3. The dark line across the K-map divides Y_1 into halves associated with y_1 and $\bar{y}_1$.
4. The next state equation is

$$Y_1 = (x \bar{y}_3 y_0) \bar{y}_1 + (\bar{x} + \bar{y}_0) y_1$$

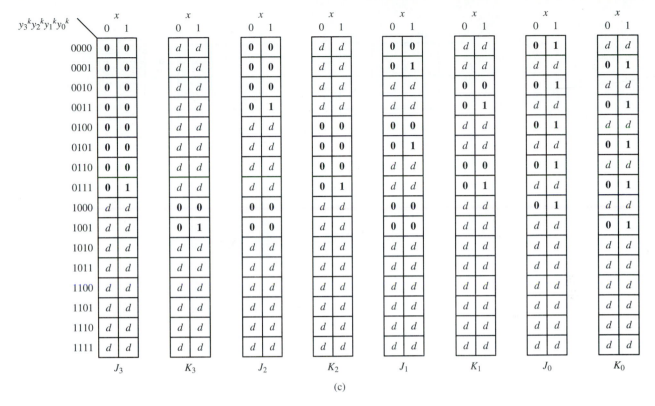

Figure 8.37   (Continued) design of the BCD counter. **(c)** Excitation tables for the BCD counter.

Notice that the product term groupings do not cross the dark line dividing the K-map.

5. The equations for J_1 and K_1 are

$$J_1 = x\bar{y}_3 y_0$$
$$\bar{K}_1 = \bar{x} + \bar{y}_0$$
$$K_1 = x y_0$$

Notice that these are the same equations obtained by the excitation table method in Example 8.15.

Finite-state Controllers

Many applications require control circuits that perform designated sequences of actions in response to externally applied signals or as a result of conditions produced within the circuit, such as a carry generated in an addition operation or a counter reaching a terminal value. Such control circuits are characterized

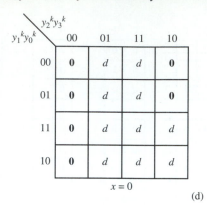

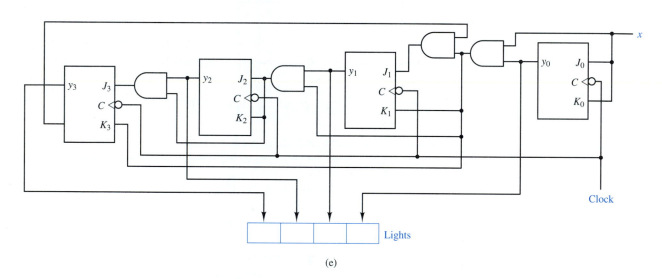

Figure 8.37 (Continued) design of the BCD counter. **(d)** K-map for J_2. **(e)** Realization of the BCD counter.

by having a finite number of states; hence they are referred to as *finite-state controllers*.

One of the most common applications of finite-state controllers is as control units for computers and other digital systems. Such systems comprise two parts: a data path and a control unit. The data path performs various operations on data elements, such as arithmetic operations and other transformations. Data paths typically comprise combinational logic modules, such as arithmetic logic units and multiplexers, and often include registers for data storage.

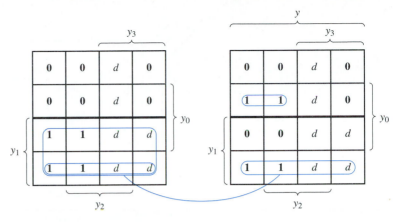

Figure 8.38 K-map for Y_1 (y_1^{k+1}).

The control unit supplies commands to the data path to enable selected operations. These commands must be sequenced properly to ensure that the proper operations are carried out in response to various inputs and conditions. We design a control unit for a digital system by identifying its inputs and outputs and then developing the control algorithm in the form of a state diagram.

Finite-state controllers are designed using the general synchronous sequential circuit synthesis procedure defined earlier. We begin by defining the inputs and outputs of the controller and then the algorithm to be implemented. The algorithm is often specified in state diagram format. Then the remaining steps of the synthesis procedure are performed. This is illustrated by the following examples.

EXAMPLE 8.17

We wish to design a finite-state controller for the robot of Fig. 8.39 so that it can find its way out of the maze shown in the figure.

The robot is to maneuver by turning whenever it comes in contact with an obstacle. On the nose of the robot is a sensor whose output $x = 1$ whenever it is in contact with an obstacle; $x = 0$ otherwise. The robot has two control lines: $z_1 = 1$, which turns the robot to the left, and $z_2 = 1$ which turns the robot to the right. When it encounters an obstacle, the robot should turn right until no obstacle is detected. The next time an obstacle is detected, the robot should turn left until the obstacle is cleared, and so on.

The robot controller requires four states as follows:

    State A = no obstacle detected, last turn was left
    State B = obstacle detected, turning right
    State C = no obstacle detected, last turn was right
    State D = obstacle detected, turning left

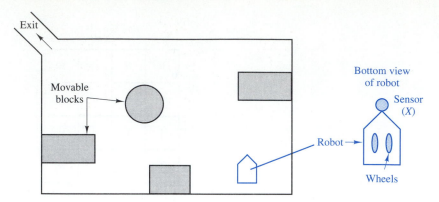

Figure 8.39 Robot and maze.

The control unit state diagram is given in Fig. 8.40a. Note that the controller stays in state A with no turns until an obstacle is encountered. Then it enters state B and turns right until it no longer detects the obstacle, at which time it enters state C and stops turning. The controller then remains in state C until another obstacle is detected, at which time it enters state D and turns left until the obstacle is no longer detected; it then returns to state A.

The state table is given in Fig 8.40b. Let us select the state assigment $A = 00$, $B = 01$, $C = 11$, and $D = 10$. The binary transition table is given in Fig. 8.40c. From the transition table, we can form the output tables for z_1 and z_2, shown in Fig. 8.40d, from which we can derive the following output equations.

$$z_1 = xy_1$$
$$z_2 = x\bar{y}_1$$

For the state variables, let us use JK flip-flops and the application equation method. The excitation tables for Y_1 and Y_2 are given in Fig. 8.40e. From these tables, we derive the excitation equations as follows.

$$Y_1 = (\bar{x}y_2)\bar{y}_1 + (x + y_2)y_1$$
$$J_1 = \bar{x}y_2$$
$$K_1 = \overline{x + y_2} = \bar{x}\bar{y}_2$$

$$Y_2 = (x\bar{y}_1)\bar{y}_2 + (\bar{x} + \bar{y}_1)y_2$$
$$J_2 = x\bar{y}_1$$
$$K_2 = \overline{\bar{x} + \bar{y}_1} = xy_1$$

The completed logic circuit diagram for the robot controller is given in Fig. 8.40f.

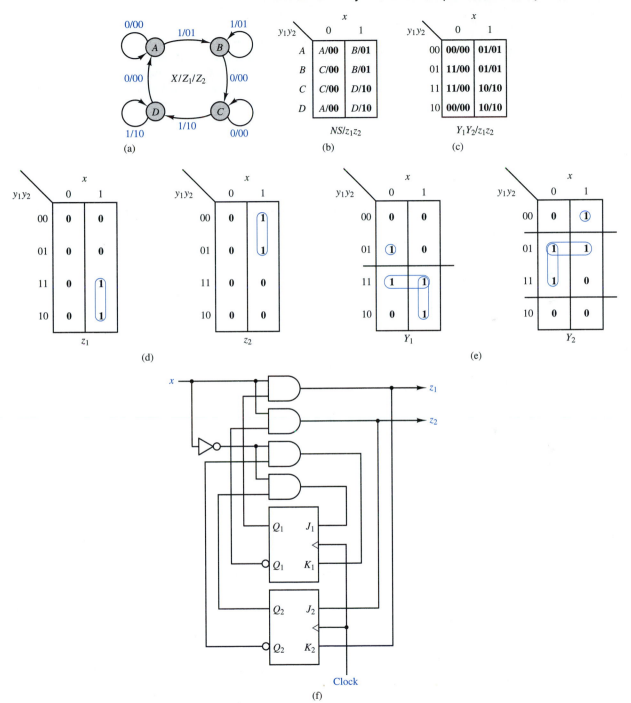

Figure 8.40 Robot controller design. **(a)** State diagram. **(b)** State table. **(c)** Transition table. **(d)** Output maps. **(e)** Excitation maps. **(f)** Logic circuit diagram.

EXAMPLE 8.18

Let us design a control unit for a simple coin-operated candy machine. Candy costs 20 cents, and the machine accepts nickels and dimes. Change should be returned if more than 20 cents is deposited. No more than 25 cents can be deposited on a single purchase; therefore, the maximum change is one nickel.

A block diagram of the candy machine is given in Fig. 8.41a. The control unit has two inputs, N and D, which are outputs of the coin detector. The coin detector generates a 1 on signal N if a nickel is deposited and a 1 on signal D output if a dime is deposited. The N and D lines automatically reset to 0 on the next clock pulse. We shall assume that it is physically impossible to insert two coins at the same time, and therefore we cannot have $N = D = 1$ in the same clock period.

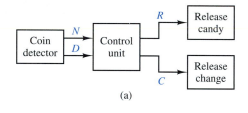

(a)

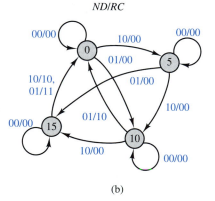

(b)

Figure 8.41 Coin-operated candy machine design. **(a)** Block diagram. **(b)** Control unit state diagram.

The control unit has two outputs, R and C. The candy is released by a 1 on signal R, and a nickel in change is released by a 1 on signal C.

The states of the control unit represent the total amount of money deposited for the current purchase. The set of states is thus {0, 5, 10, 15}. When a deposited coin increases the amount to 20 or 25 cents, the control unit will return to state 0 while releasing the candy, along with releasing change, if necessary.

The state diagram of Fig. 8.41b describes the operation of the candy machine control unit. For a given state, the R and C outputs depend on which coin is inserted; therefore, a Mealy model has been used. Note that the input combination $ND = 11$ is not specified since two coins cannot be deposited simultaneously.

The completion of a synchronous sequential logic circuit design from the state diagram of Fig. 8.41b is left as an exercise for the reader.

8.3.5 Algorithmic State Machine Diagrams

A variation of the state diagram that is useful when designing control units and other finite-state machines is the *algorithmic state machine* (ASM) diagram. An *algorithm* is a well-defined sequence of steps that produces a desired sequence of actions in response to a given sequence of inputs. The ASM diagram is a convenient tool for expressing algorithms to be realized by sequential logic circuits, much as a flow chart might be used to describe a software algorithm to be programmed on a computer. ASM diagrams are constructed of three elements:

> **State box:** Represents one state of the circuit, and is therefore equivalent to one node of a state diagram. The state name is listed in the box and, for Moore circuits, the outputs to be produced, that is, the actions to be performed while in that state. A state box always has a single entry point and a single exit point, as illustrated in Fig. 8.42a.
>
> **Decision box:** Represents a state transition decision based on a test of one circuit input. A decision box, as illustrated in Fig. 8.42b, lists the input to be tested and has a single entry point and two exit points, one for the input equal to 0 and one for the input equal to 1. A separate decision box is used for each input test.
>
> **Conditional output box:** Specifies outputs associated with state transitions for a given input in a Mealy circuit. A conditional output box is placed in the path between a decision box and a state box and has a single entry and exit point, as shown in Fig. 8.42c.

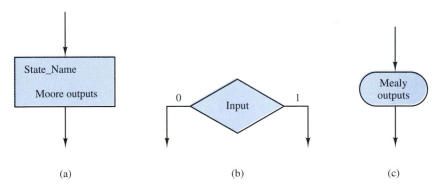

(a)   (b)   (c)

Figure 8.42   Elements of an ASM diagram. **(a)** State box. **(b)** Decision box. **(c)** Conditional output box.

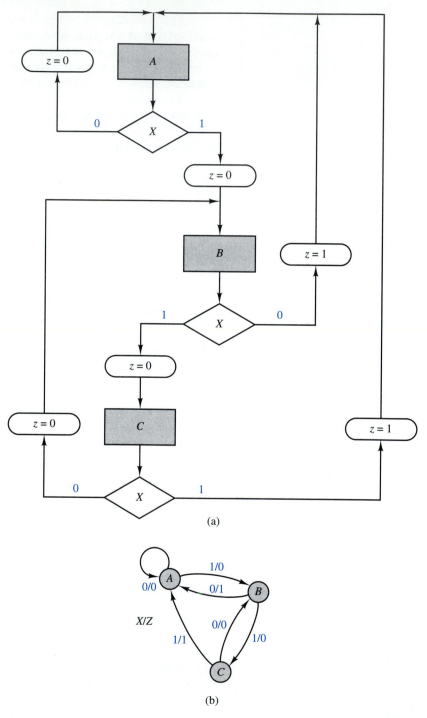

Figure 8.43   ASM Representation of a Mealy model sequential circuit. **(a)** ASM diagram. **(b)** Equivalent state diagram.

ASM diagrams can be used to develop both Mealy and Moore model circuits. The ASM diagram and corresponding state diagram for a Mealy circuit are presented in Figs. 8.43a and b, respectively. In the ASM diagram, note that output z is specified in conditional output boxes, one for each state and input combination. This corresponds to associating the output with the arcs of the state diagram.

The ASM diagram and corresponding state diagram for a Moore circuit are presented in Figs. 8.44a and b, respectively. Note that there are no conditional output boxes in the ASM diagram. The outputs of a Moore circuit are functions of only the state variables and are therefore specified within the state boxes in the ASM diagram and within the nodes of the state diagram.

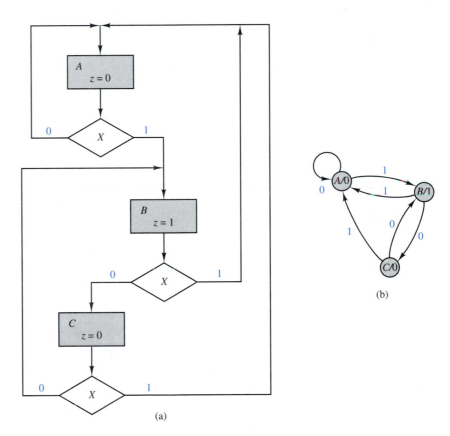

(a)

(b)

Figure 8.44 ASM representation of a Moore model sequential circuit. **(a)** ASM diagram. **(b)** Equivalent state diagram.

The use of ASM diagrams in sequential circuit design is demonstrated by the following two examples.

EXAMPLE 8.19

Let us design an ASM diagram for an 8-bit serial two's complementer that will implement Algorithm 1.4 presented in Chapter 1.

Algorithm 1.4 requires that we examine the bits of the number from right to left, copying the bits until the first 1 bit has been copied and then complementing the remaining bits. The ASM diagram of the serial two's complement algorithm is given in Fig. 8.45. Data bits are supplied to the circuit sequentially on input x, beginning with the least significant bit. The circuit output z is the corrected data bit. In state A, we are looking for the first 1 bit, and therefore $z = x$. In state B, the first 1 bit has been detected, and therefore $z = \bar{x}$. Note that a Mealy model has been used, since z is a function of x and the state. Therefore, all outputs are specified in conditional output boxes.

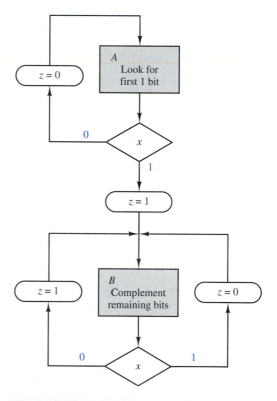

Figure 8.45   ASM representation of a serial two's complementer.

Now let us tackle a more formidable design problem involving a data path and a control unit.

EXAMPLE 8.20

We wish to design the control unit for a binary multiplier that will compute the 8-bit product of two 4-bit unsigned binary numbers using a series of add and shift operations. The multiplier begins when pulsed by a *Reset* signal and halts with the product on its outputs. A *Halt* signal indicates the end of the operation.

We develop the multiplication algorithm by first examining the "pencil and paper" algorithm, as described in Chapter 1. Consider the product of $(0111)_2$ and $(1010)_2$.

$$
\begin{array}{rcccccccl}
 & & & 0 & 1 & 1 & 1 & & \text{Multiplicand} \\
\times & & & 1 & 0 & 1 & 0 & & \text{Multiplier} \\
\hline
 & & & 0 & 0 & 0 & 0 & & \text{Partial product 1} \\
 & & 0 & 1 & 1 & 1 & & & \text{Partial product 2} \\
 & 0 & 0 & 0 & 0 & & & & \text{Partial product 3} \\
0 & 1 & 1 & 1 & & & & & \text{Partial product 4} \\
\hline
1 & 0 & 0 & 0 & 1 & 1 & 0 & & \text{Product}
\end{array}
$$

Multiplier bits are examined sequentially from right to left. If the multiplier bit is 1, the partial product is the multiplicand, and if the multiplier bit is 0, the partial product is simply 0000. Each new partial product is shifted one bit position to the left before adding it to the total. Alternatively, we can leave the position of the partial product fixed and shift the total to the right after each addition. We shall use the latter approach for our control unit.

The data path of the binary multiplier requires three registers and a binary adder, as illustrated in Fig. 8.46a. The registers serve the following functions.

> **A:** A 5-bit shift register that holds the four most significant bits of the product and the carry from the adder.
>
> **Q:** A 4-bit shift register. Q initially contains the multiplier. In each iteration, Q will be shifted one position to the right, with its leftmost bit replaced by 1 bit of the product, so that at the end of the operation Q will contain the lower 4 bits of the product.
>
> **M:** A 4-bit parallel register that holds the multiplicand.

In addition to these components, a 2-bit binary counter, *CNT*, is used to count the number of iterations. It will be initialized to 00 and incremented after each shift operation, returning to 00 after the fourth iteration. A logic gate will be used to indicate the 00 condition.

The product will be computed by adding the multiplicand to the current total in register A when the tested multiplier bit is 1. Instead of adding a partial product of 0000 to the total when the multiplier bit is 0, we shall simply omit the addition step.

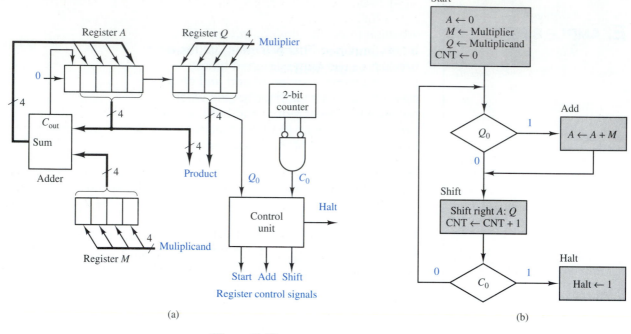

(a)

(b)

Figure 8.46 Binary multiplier. **(a)** Block diagram. **(b)** ASM diagram.

The controller has two inputs: Q_0 is the multiplier bit being tested and C_0 is 1 when the counter contains 00, indicating the end of the fourth add and shift cycle. The ASM diagram of the controller is given in Fig. 8.46b. A Moore model is used with the following four states:

> **Start:** Load the operands into the M and Q registers, and clear the A register and counter CNT.
>
> **Add:** Add the multiplicand (M) to the current partial product (A) by loading the sum and carry outputs of the binary adder into the A register.
>
> **Shift:** Shift the partial product and multiplier 1 bit to the right by enabling the shift control lines of the A and Q registers. Also, increment the counter by enabling its increment control line.
>
> **Halt:** Halt, leaving the final product in the A and Q registers.

One multiplier bit is tested in each iteration of the algorithm to determine whether to enter the *Add* state or to omit the *Add* state and go directly to the *Shift* state. The counter output is tested after the *Shift* state to determine whether to halt or perform another iteration.

The controller has four outputs, one corresponding to each state. The *Start* output activates the load control lines of the M and Q registers and the clear lines of the A register and counter. The *Add* output activates the load line of the A register. The *Shift* output activates the shift control lines of the A and Q

registers and the increment control line of the counter. The *Halt* output signals the end of the operation.

8.3.6 One-hot Finite-State Machine Design Method

In the design of sequential circuits described by ASM diagrams, a simplified design approach using the one-hot state assigment method is often used to reduce design time. A *one-hot state assigment* uses one state variable, and consequently one flip-flop, per state, as shown in Table 8.1. All the state variables except one are equal to 0 at any given time. The single state variable that is equal to 1 is called the *hot* state. Therefore, an n-state sequential circuit requires n state variables rather than $\lceil \log_2 n \rceil$. The resulting circuit contains more flip-flops, but can be designed more easily and often requires fewer combinational logic gates.

One-hot designs can be derived directly from ASM diagrams. Figure 8.47 illustrates logic circuit implementations of the various ASM constructs. D flip-flops are used for all memory elements, with one flip-flop per state box. Simple state sequencing is implemented by cascading the flip-flops, as illustrated in Fig. 8.47a. When in state A, flip-flop output $Q_A = 1$. Since $D_B = Q_A$, flip-flop output Q_B will be set to 1 on the next clock pulse, while Q_A resets to 0. In this manner, the hot state passes from one flip-flop to the next. For Moore circuits, the circuit outputs are simply the flip-flop outputs, as shown in Fig. 8.47a, since they are functions of only the state.

Control paths that merge on the ASM diagram are merged with an OR gate in the control circuit, as illustrated in Fig. 8.47b. In this circuit, flip-flop output Q_B will be set to 1 on the next clock pulse if either $Q_A = 1$ or $Q_C = 1$.

ASM decision boxes are implemented as illustrated in Fig. 8.47c. In this case, when flip-flop output $Q_A = 1$ and input $x = 0$, the AND gates set flip-flop inputs $D_B = 1$ and $D_C = 0$, causing flip-flop output Q_B to be set to 1 on the next clock pulse. If $x = 1$, then $D_B = 0$ and $D_C = 1$.

Conditional output boxes in an ASM diagram are realized by connecting the circuit outputs to the outputs of the AND gates that implement the decision boxes, as shown in Fig. 8.47c, since these signals are functions of both the state and the input.

TABLE 8.1 STATE ASSIGMENTS FOR A FOUR-STATE SEQUENTIAL CIRCUIT

State	Sequential Assignment $y_1 y_0$	One-hot Assignment $y_3 y_2 y_1 y_0$
A	00	0001
B	01	0010
C	10	0100
D	11	1000

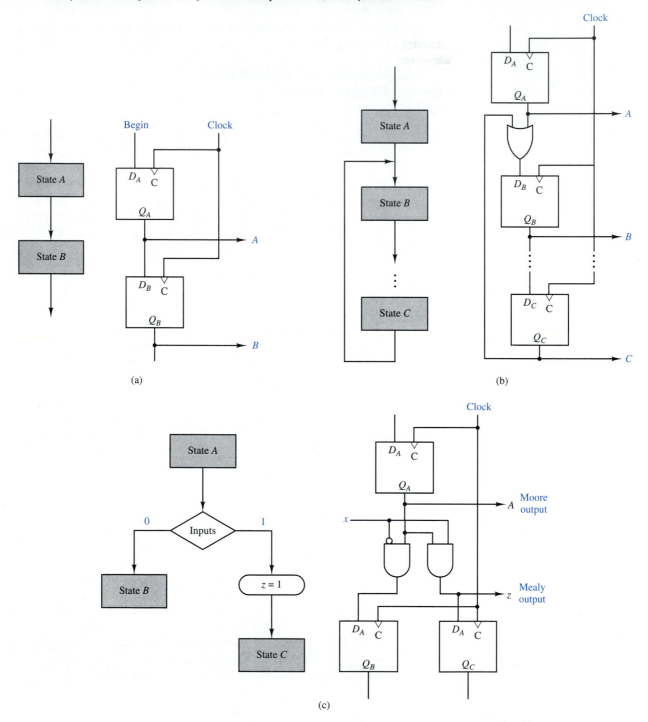

Figure 8.47 Controllers designed with the one-hot method. **(a)** Simple state sequencing. **(b)** Merging control paths. **(c)** Control decision.

The following example illustrates the one-hot design method for deriving Moore and Mealy model circuits from ASM diagrams.

EXAMPLE 8.21

Let us use the one-hot design method to implement the multiplier control unit ASM diagram of Fig. 8.46b and the serial two's complementer ASM diagram of Fig. 8.45.

Figure 8.48a shows the logic diagram of the multiplier control unit. Note that the circuit structure is derived directly from the ASM diagram. Since this is a Moore model, the outputs are simply driven by the four flip-flop outputs. The algorithm is initiated by providing a pulse on the *Begin* control line to set the first flip-flop to 1 in one clock cycle and then to 0 on the next clock cycle.

Figure 8.48b shows the serial two's complementer circuit. Again, the circuit structure is derived directly from the ASM diagram. In this case a Mealy model is used. Therefore, the output z is a function of the state variables and the input x. In this case, $z = 1$ if the circuit is in state 0 and $x = 1$ or, if the circuit is in state 1, $x = 0$.

8.4 Incompletely Specified Circuits

A sequential circuit is said to be *incompletely specified* if its state table contains don't-cares. These don't-cares arise normally in some circuits due to the fact that only a certain set of inputs can ever be applied. Hence, states and outputs that may occur because of forbidden inputs are never attained and we may assign them as don't-cares. The following example will illustrate this idea.

EXAMPLE 8.22

Let us design a detonator circuit as shown in Fig. 8.49a that exhibits the behavior of the state diagram in Fig. 8.49b.

When the device is active and $x = 0$, the device rests in an idle state A. The detonation sequence is initiated by setting $x = 1$. The device will move from state A to B, then C, and finally D, where it issues a pulse ($z = 1$) to detonate an explosive. The circuitry prior to the detonator circuit is designed so that once the first $x = 1$ occurs the device cannot be reset; that is, no $x = 0$ input will occur once $x = 1$ is received.

The partial state diagram and complete state table for the detonator are shown in Figs. 8.49b and c, respectively. Here again note that once the detonator sequence has begun it will continue without interruption until the detonate pulse is generated. The final state is a don't-care because the explosive has ignited. In the following analysis the detonator circuit will be realized using clocked T flip-flops. If we choose the state assignment ($y_2 y_1$) as

$$A = 00 \qquad C = 10$$
$$B = 01 \qquad D = 11$$

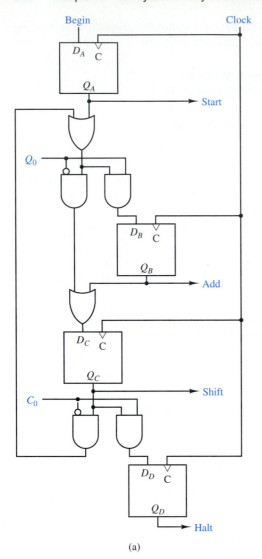

(a)

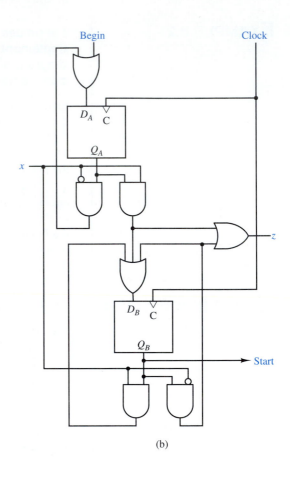

(b)

Figure 8.48 Controllers designed with the one-hot method. **(a)** Multiplier control unit. **(b)** Serial two's complementer control unit.

all the necessary tables for the circuit realization are shown in Fig. 8.50. The following equations follow directly from the tables:

$$T_1 = x$$
$$T_2 = y_1$$
$$z = y_1 y_2$$

The actual circuit for the detonator is shown in Fig. 8.51. Since our analysis is valid only during the clock pulse, we use the clock pulse to gate the output.

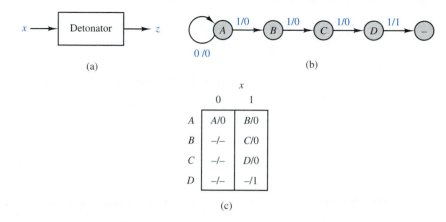

(a)   (b)

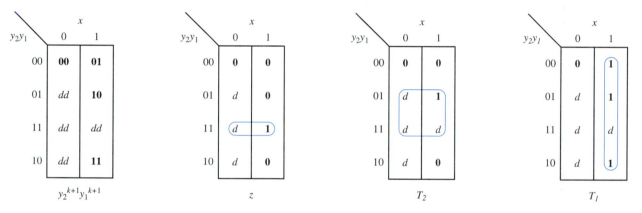

(c)

Figure 8.49 Detonator circuit. **(a)** Block diagram. **(b)** Partial state diagram. **(c)** State table.

Figure 8.50 Detonator transition, output, and excitation maps.

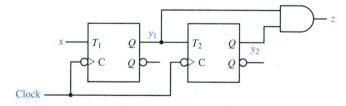

Figure 8.51 Detonator implementation.

It is important for the reader to realize that incompletely specified circuits have an advantage over completely specified circuits from a hardware realization standpoint. The advantage stems from the presence of don't-cares in the state table. In other words, these don't-cares may be able to be grouped with the ones in the excitation maps to produce a simpler circuit than would have been possible if all terms were completely specified. Figure 8.50 illustrates this case.

8.4.1 State Assignment and Circuit Realization

Once a reduced state table has been determined, the state assignment and circuit logic equations may be produced using exactly the same rules employed in the completely specified case. However, since certain entries in the state table are unspecified, there is usually a larger number of don't-cares in the generated K-maps, resulting in better logic minimization.

EXAMPLE 8.23

For the binary state table of Fig. 8.52a, let us complete the realization using D, clocked T, and clocked JK flip-flops.

From the binary state table, the K-maps for each realization are derived in Figs. 8.52b through e, and the corresponding logic equations are listed as follows:

$$D_2 = \bar{x}y_1 + y_2 y_1$$
$$D_1 = y_2 \bar{y}_1$$

$$T_2 = \bar{x}y_1 + y_2 \bar{y}_1$$
$$T_1 = y_2 + y_1$$

$$J_2 = \bar{x}y_1$$
$$K_2 = \bar{y}_1$$
$$J_1 = y_2$$
$$K_1 = 1$$

$$z = xy_2 + \bar{x}\bar{y}_1$$

Notice that the D and clocked T realization require eight inputs to the gates, and the clocked JK, two. In general, the clocked JK flip-flop gives better logic reduction because it has more control logic internal to the device itself.

8.5 Computer-aided Design of Sequential Circuits

The process of designing, verifying, constructing, and testing a sequential logic circuit is considerably more complex than for combinational logic circuits. This complexity increases significantly with the number of states in the circuit. Consequently, computer-aided design (CAD) methods are a virtual necessity in the development of any sequential circuit having more than a few states. In

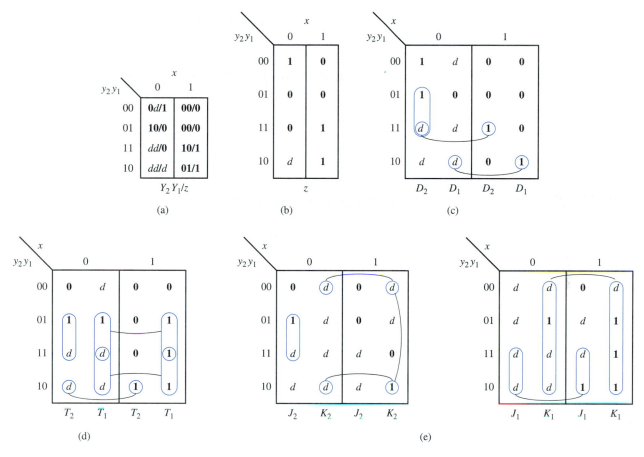

Figure 8.52 Logic realizations. **(a)** Binary state table. **(b)** K-map for z. **(c)** D flip-flops. **(d)** Clocked T flip-flops. **(e)** Clocked JK flip-flops.

this section we examine some CAD tools used in the synthesis and analysis of synchronous sequential circuits.

8.5.1 Design Capture and Synthesis

The design of a sequential circuit begins by expressing the desired behavior of the circuit in the form of a state diagram, ASM diagram, state table, or some other formal description. This description is then processed to synthesize a logic circuit that will realize the desired behavior. Many CAD tools are available that can process various sequential circuit representations. Some of these tools automatically perform one or more steps of the synthesis process. At different stages of the design process, logic simulation tools may be utilized to simulate the operation of the circuit to facilitate verification of the logic design and/or analysis of its timing behavior.

Many CAD systems support the development and capture of sequential circuit descriptions in several formats, which may include the following:

1. Schematic diagrams
2. Excitation and output logic equations
3. State tables
4. State or ASM diagrams
5. Finite-state machine descriptions in a hardware description language (HDL)

Where designs are captured in schematic diagram or logic equation form, the designer will already have performed the design synthesis process. In these cases, designs are entered primarily so that they can be evaluated using logic simulation. In some cases, however, schematics and logic equations can be analyzed by the CAD system to identify areas in which the design can be optimized.

State diagrams, ASM diagrams, state tables, and HDL descriptions express only the desired behavior of a finite-state machine, from which a circuit must be synthesized. Behavioral descriptions are often processed by automatic synthesis tools, which perform some or all of the steps in the design synthesis process, thus reducing design time. In addition, simulation of a behavioral model is often performed prior to synthesizing a circuit to verify that the model realizes the desired behavior.

Schematic Entry

Schematic capture for combinational logic circuits and modular digital designs was described in Chapters 2 and 4, respectively. The development of logic circuit diagrams for sequential circuits is similar, except that flip-flops and other sequential modules must be utilized, in addition to the basic logic gates, and are therefore included in one or more component libraries. In addition, clock signals to control state transitions must be defined, and asynchronous preset and clear signals to initialize flip-flop states may also be specified.

A number of device parameters must also be specified in sequential circuits that are not applicable to combinational circuits. Typical parameters include setup and hold times for latches, flip-flops, and other sequential module inputs; clock specifications; and propagation delays from both synchronous and asynchronous inputs to the outputs. These parameters are often specified for each component in a design library to reflect the actual characteristics of that component's technology. In addition to physical characteristics, some design systems allow default initial states to be assigned to memory elements for use during logic simulation.

Finite-state Machine Descriptions

State diagrams, state tables, and other finite-state machine descriptions all contain basically the same information, describing the desired circuit behavior in terms of state transitions and output changes in response to all possible input and state combinations. For example, Figs. 8.53a and b present a state diagram and the corresponding state table, respectively, of a finite state machine. State tables are often entered into a CAD system in truth table format, as shown in Fig. 8.53c.

Many CAD systems allow sequential circuit behavior to be expressed in a standard hardware description language, such as VHDL or Verilog; others may provide a vendor-specific HDL for this purpose. We earlier discussed the use of VHDL to describe combinational logic circuits in Chapter 2. Sequential behavior can also be readily expressed in VHDL. For example, Fig. 8.54 presents a VHDL description of the state diagram of Fig. 8.53a.

As described in Chapter 2, a VHDL description of a circuit module comprises an entity, which defines the module inputs and outputs, and an architecture, which defines the behavior and/or structural implementation of the module. The entity declaration in Fig. 8.54 defines circuit *seqckt* as having a clock input, *clk*, one signal input, *x*, and one output, *z*.

In a VHDL architecture description, sequential circuit behavior is usually described using one or more *process* structures. In the example of Fig. 8.54, process *clock* describes the memory element behavior and process *state_trans* defines the state transitions and outputs for each state and input combination. The latter contains the same information that would appear in a state diagram

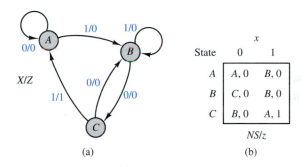

State	x	
	0	1
A	A, 0	B, 0
B	C, 0	B, 0
C	B, 0	A, 1

NS/z

(a) (b)

Current state	Inputs x	::	Next state	Outputs z
A	0	::	A	0
A	1	::	B	0
B	0	::	C	0
B	1	::	B	0
C	0	::	B	0
C	1	::	A	1

(c)

Figure 8.53 Sequential circuit description. **(a)** State diagram. **(b)** State table. **(c)** Truth table format.

```
ENTITY seqckt IS
  PORT(clk: in  bit;   -- clock signal
       x:   in  bit;   -- circuit input
       z:   out bit);  -- circuit output
END seqckt;


ARCHITECTURE mealy OF seqckt IS
   TYPE states IS (a,b,c);          -- three states
   SIGNAL state:      states := a; -- current state (initially a)
   SIGNAL next_state: states := a; -- next state (initial value a)
BEGIN
clock: PROCESS(clk)      -- react to transition on signal clk
        BEGIN
           IF clk'EVENT and clk = '1' THEN   -- rising edge of clk
             state <= next_state;            -- state change
           END IF;
        END PROCESS clock;
state_trans:  PROCESS(state,x) -- react to changes in state or input x
              BEGIN
                  next_state <= state;  -- update next_state
                  CASE state IS         -- state transitions and outputs
                    WHEN a => IF x = '0' THEN
                                   z <= '0';
                              ELSE
                                   next_state <= b;
                                   z <= '0';
                              END IF;
                    WHEN b => IF x = '0' THEN
                                   next_state <= c;
                                   z <= '0';
                              ELSE
                                   z <= '0';
                              END IF;
                    WHEN c => IF x = '0' THEN
                                   next_state <= b;
                                   z <= '0';
                              ELSE
                                   next_state <= a;
                                   z <= '1';
                              END IF;
                  END CASE;
              END PROCESS state_trans;
END mealy;
```

Figure 8.54 VHDL description of a sequential circuit.

or state table. Note that a special data type, *states*, is defined, having values (a, b, c). This allows the state and next state of the circuit to be specified symbolically until a state assignment is determined.

The *clock* PROCESS statement is executed on each transition of signal *clk*. Within the process, the IF statement allows the circuit *state* to change only when *clk* makes a transition and $clk = 1$. Therefore, state changes occur on the rising transition of *clk*.

The *state_trans* PROCESS reacts to changes in *state* or input x and therefore models the combinational logic portion of the sequential circuit. The CASE statement specifies a next state value and output for each state and input value and therefore describes a Mealy model.

The interested reader is referred to [10, 11] for additional information on using VHDL to model sequential circuits.

Computer-automated Logic Synthesis

Computer-automated synthesis tools are often used to perform some or all of the steps of the sequential circuit design process, beginning from a behavioral description of the circuit, in the form of a state diagram, state table, or HDL description, and ultimately generating a logic circuit diagram or net list.

In most cases, the designer has a number of options to direct the synthesis of a design. These options are specified before the synthesizer begins and may include the following.

1. *Select a state assigment method.* Some tools require the designer to provide a specific state assigment to be used during synthesis or else to designate one of several standard state assignment patterns. For example, Table 8.2 lists three of the state assignment options provided by Mentor Graphics *AutoLogic* synthesis tool [11]. Other assigment options may also be provided.

   Some of the more advanced logic synthesis tools include algorithms for deriving an optimal state assignment from a given state table. Several such algorithms will be described in Chapter 9.

2. *Select flip-flop types.* Some synthesis programs require specific flip-flop types to be designated. Others either select a default type or, in more

TABLE 8.2 STATE ASSIGNMENT OPTIONS FOR A FOUR-STATE MACHINE.

State	Sequential	Gray Code	One Hot
A	00	00	0001
B	01	01	0010
C	10	11	0100
D	11	10	1000

advanced systems, attempt to determine the optimal type for the given circuit. With computer automation, it is often feasible to synthesize a design a number of different ways, using different flip-flop options to determine which will require the smallest number of combinational logic gates.

3. *Specify combinational logic minimization algorithms for the excitation and output equations.* These equations are derived from flip-flop excitation and output tables. Most of the methods described in Chapter 3 may be applied to minimize these equations. Often multiple algorithms are made available to the designer, offering trade-offs in optimization versus design time.

Figure 8.55 shows a sequential circuit that was automatically synthesized from the VHDL description of Fig. 8.54 by Mentor Graphics *AutoLogic VHDL* synthesis tool [11]. This circuit was produced in two steps. In the first step, the VHDL description was converted to logic equations and a logic circuit generated without optimization. The synthesizer was told to use D flip-flops and the sequential state assigment of Table 8.2. The resulting circuit contained 17 primitive logic gates and six multiplexers, in addition to the two D flip-flops. This particular tool used only two-input logic gates and 2-to-1 multiplexers in implementing the combinational logic section. The second step optimized the design to that of Fig. 8.55, reducing the combinational logic portion to four gates and one multiplexer.

The reader is referred to [12] for additional information on automatic logic synthesis algorithms and methods.

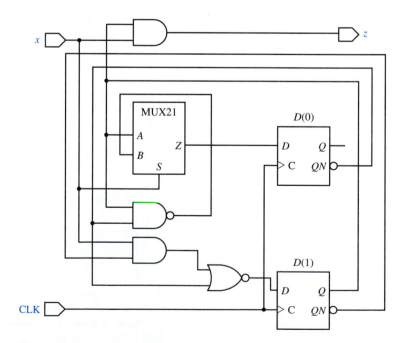

Figure 8.55 Logic circuit synthesized from a VHDL description.

8.5.2 Design Analysis and Verification

Analysis and verification of a sequential circuit design are most often done using logic simulation. Sequential circuit verification may include functional analysis, to ensure that the circuit realizes the behavior defined in the state table or other finite-state machine description, and also a timing analysis to determine performance characteristics.

Functional Analysis

Functional analysis of a sequential circuit design is used to verify that the logic function realized by the circuit matches the logical behavior described by the initial behavioral description, that is, to verify that the outputs are correct and that the proper state transition takes place for each state–input combination, as defined in the state table or other finite-state machine description.

It is often desirable to simulate the operation of a finite-state machine from its behavioral description prior to beginning the synthesis process to verify the correctness of the algorithm. The results of this behavioral simulation can then be compared to simulation results obtained from the synthesized logic circuit to ensure that the logic circuit does indeed realize the desired behavior.

Logic simulation of combinational logic circuits was described in Chapter 2. This process is similar for synchronous sequential circuits, although there are a number of additional considerations.

1. A clock signal must be defined in terms of its period and duty cycle, that is, the portion of the clock period during which the clock is high.

2. Signal waveforms to be applied to the circuit inputs must be defined. Note that the timing of each input change must be coordinated with the clock transition times so that all flip-flop excitation inputs will be stable prior to each clock transition. For example, if a clock with transitions every 100 ns is defined, beginning at time 0, then input changes must not be allowed to occur at any time which is a multiple of 100 ns.

   Some logic simulators allow sequences of input values to be specified in list form. Values are then automatically applied to the inputs prior to each clock transition.

3. The initial state of the circuit must be specified, that is, all memory element outputs set to specified initial values. Some simulators allow default states to be assigned as initial values. Others assign to each flip-flop a special unknown state value, usually X or U, to indicate that the flip-flop has not yet been set to a known value during circuit operation. The persistence of an X value on the output of a flip-flop indicates that the flip-flop has not been set to a specific 0 or 1 value, which may indicate a design error.

   For example, if a T flip-flop is initially set to an unknown state X, simply toggling the flip-flop will not be sufficient to determine the next state of the flip-flop, and thus the state of the flip-flop will remain X throughout simulation. This warns the designer that a reset signal or some other means must be provided to initialize the state of the flip-flop.

State transitions and output sequences are captured by the simulator and displayed in tabular form, as timing diagram waveforms, or both. Normally all flip-flop output values can be captured and examined, and therefore all state transitions can be verified. In an actual circuit, often only the external outputs are visible, with the state variables inaccessible from the pins on the circuit module. In these cases, circuit behavior must be deduced from the output sequences produced for each input test sequence.

In analyzing simulation results, the circuit state is checked for correctness after each clock transition. In a Mealy model circuit, output changes can be initiated by state or input changes and may therefore occur at any time within the clock period. In Moore model circuits, the outputs should change only when the state variables change and should therefore not be affected by transitions on the input signals.

Timing Analysis

Timing analysis involves estimation of propagation delays, which determine circuit performance, and checking for violation of timing constraints during operation of a circuit.

The performance of a synchronous sequential circuit is most often specified in terms of the maximum clock frequency at which the circuit may operate, which is the inverse of the minimum clock period, T_{min}. T_{min} is limited by the propagation delays through the flip-flops and combinational logic gates that comprise the circuit and is also limited by flip-flop setup time requirements.

Referring to the general synchronous sequential circuit model of Fig. 8.56, the various circuit propagation delays can be lumped into two parameters: the propagation delays through the flip-flops, t_{FF}, and those through the

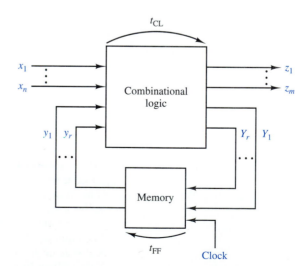

Figure 8.56 Propagation delays in a sequential circuit.

combinational logic, t_{CL}. Following an active transition of the clock, new values propagate through the flip-flops to the secondary variables, $y_1 \ldots y_r$, and then these values propagate through the combinational logic to the next state variables, $Y_1 \ldots Y_r$. Because of the setup time constraint, all flip-flop excitation inputs must be stable for a period of time of at least t_{su} prior to the next clock transition. Consequently, the minimum time between successive clock transitions is given by

$$T_{min} \geq t_{FF} + t_{CL} + t_{su} \tag{8.10}$$

and therefore T_{min} represents the minimum clock period.

Propagation delay t_{FF} is measured from the point of a clock transition to the time at which all the flip-flop outputs become stable and is therefore a function of the flip-flop t_{PHL} and t_{PLH} parameters described in Chapter 6. Since all flip-flops are synchronized to the same clock, t_{FF} is chosen as the maximum of the individual flip-flop t_{PHL} and t_{PLH} parameters to reflect the worst-case delay.

Propagation delay time t_{CL} is a function of the t_{PHL} and t_{PLH} parameters of the individual gates that make up the combinational logic block. The number of gates between each input and output of the combinational logic block may be different. Therefore, t_{CL} is computed as the worst-case path delay between the inputs and the next-state outputs.

The external outputs of a sequential circuit are typically not subject to constraints, as are the flip-flop excitation inputs. Therefore, the output timing is often not as critical. In a Mealy machine, the outputs are functions of the external inputs and the state variables. Therefore, an output change may be produced by either an input change, which would propagate to the output in time t_{CL}, or by a state variable change, in which case the change would propagate to the output after a delay of $t_{FF} + t_{CL}$.

In a Moore machine, the outputs are functions of only the state variables. Therefore, all output changes would occur after a delay of $t_{FF} + t_{CL}$ measured from the time of the clock transition.

Constraint checking is often done during logic simulation to ensure that no timing constraints are violated for the given clock and input sequences. As defined in Chapter 6, every flip-flop has a minimum setup time, t_{su}, and hold time, t_h, as illustrated in Fig. 8.57. For a clock transition at time t_k, changes

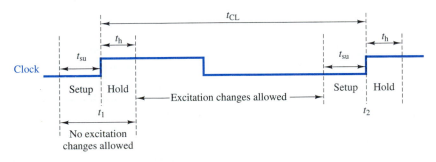

Figure 8.57 Sequential circuit timing constraints.

in the flip-flop excitation input values must not occur within the time period $[t_k - t_{su}, t_k + t_h]$, as labeled in Fig. 8.57.

Input changes must be timed to avoid setup and hold time constraint violations. Referring to Fig. 8.57, for clock transitions at times t_1 and t_2, changes in the flip-flop excitation inputs are only allowed within the time interval $[t_1 + t_h, t_2 - t_{su}]$. Since there is a time delay t_{CL} between an input change and a corresponding change in the next-state variables $Y_1 \ldots Y_r$, the time t_x of any input changes must satisfy the constraints:

$$t_1 + t_h < t_x + t_{CL} < t_2 - t_{su}$$

or

$$t_1 + t_h - t_{CL} < t_x < t_2 - t_{su} - t_{CL}$$

To perform constraint checking during logic simulation, t_{su} and t_h parameters must be specified for each flip-flop. During simulation, any flip-flop excitation input that changes within the time period spanning from t_{su} prior to the clock transition until t_h after the clock transition is flagged by the simulator as an error in the simulation output. In some cases, the simulator may set the state of a flip-flop to an indeterminate value, X, to warn the designer of a potential problem. This use of the indeterminate value indicates that a possible unknown state exists in the flip-flop due to violations of the setup and hold time constraints.

8.6 Summary

In this chapter we have presented procedures to analyze a synchronous sequential circuit, given its logic diagram, state table, or state diagram, and procedures to realize both completely and incompletely specified synchronous sequential logic circuits. Flip-flop input tables and the generation of excitation maps received attention, as did the development of state diagrams and state tables from verbal problem descriptions. Many design examples were completed to illustrate the synthesis techniques. The reader should now have a good grasp of the synchronous sequential circuit synthesis problem. In Chapter 9 we will examine methods for optimizing synchronous sequential circuits. For more detailed information on the synthesis problem, the reader is encouraged to pursue further reading from the selected references presented next.

REFERENCES

1. G. H. MEALY, "A Method for Synthesizing Sequential Circuits," *Bell Sys. Tech. J.*, Vol. 34, September 1955, pp. 1045–1079.

2. E. F. MOORE, "Gedanken—Experiments on Sequential Machines," *Automata Studies, Annals of Mathematical Studies*, No. 34. Princeton, NJ: Princeton University Press, 1956, pp. 129–153.

3. D. A. HUFFMAN, "The Synthesis of Sequential Switching Circuits," *J. Franklin Inst.*, Vol. 257, Nos. 3 and 4, March and April 1954, pp. 161–190, 275–303.

4. E. J. MCCLUSKEY, *Introduction to the Theory of Switching Circuits*. New York: McGraw-Hill Book Co., 1965.

5. ZVI KOHAVI, *Switching and Finite Automata Theory.* New York: McGraw-Hill Book Co., 1970.

6. TAYLOR L. BOOTH, *Digital Networks and Computer Systems.* New York: Wiley, 1971.

7. J. F. WAKERLY, *Digital Design Principles and Practices*, 2nd Ed., Chapter 2. Englewood Cliffs, NJ: Prentice Hall, 1994.

8. J. P. HAYES, *Introduction to Digital Logic Design*, Reading, MA: Addison-Wesley, 1993.

9. R. H. KATZ, *Contemporary Logic Design*, Menlo Park, CA: Benjamin/Cummings Publishing Co., 1994.

10. J. R. ARMSTRONG, *Chip-level Modeling with VHDL.* Englewood Cliffs, NJ: Prentice Hall, 1989.

11. *AUTOLOGIC VHDL REFERENCE MANUAL,* Mentor Graphics Corp., 8005 S.W. Boeckman Rd., Wilsonville, OR 97070, April 1992.

12. T. K. EDWARDS, *Automatic Logic Synthesis for Digital Systems*, New York: McGraw-Hill Book Co., 1992.

PROBLEMS

8.1 For the synchronous sequential circuit of Fig. P8.1, find:

(a) The state table using K-maps and $A \equiv 0$, $B \equiv 1$.

(b) The state diagram if the circuit input is in pulse form.

(c) The timing diagram for an input sequence $x = 00100110$ and the starting state $y^0 = 1$.

8.2 Given the synchronous sequential circuit of Fig. P8.2 with level inputs:

(a) Draw a timing diagram for $x = 000101011$ and $y^0 = 0$.

(b) Find the state diagram.

(c) Find the state table.

8.3 For the sequential circuit in Fig. P8.3, find:

(a) The state table $(A \equiv 0,\ B \equiv 1)$.

(b) The state diagram.

(c) A timing diagram if the starting state is $y^0 = 0$ and $x = 001011000$. This circuit is level synchronous.

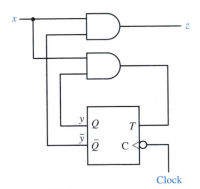

Figure P8.1

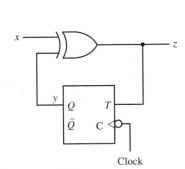

Figure P8.2

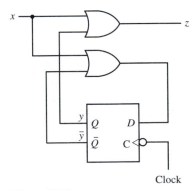

Figure P8.3

8.4   Draw the logic diagram for a synchronous sequential circuit using clocked T flip-flops and the switching functions

$$z = T_1 = x\bar{y}_2$$
$$T_2 = x \oplus y_1$$

Find a state diagram of the circuit using the assignment

	y_1	y_2
A :	0	0
B :	0	1
C :	1	1
D :	1	0

8.5   Draw the logic diagram for a clocked D flip-flop implementation of a sequential circuit employing the logic equations

$$Y_1 = \bar{x} \oplus y_1 = x \odot y_1$$
$$Y_2 = x + y_1 + y_2$$
$$z = xy_1\bar{y}_2$$

Find a binary state table for this circuit.

8.6   Analyze the synchronous sequential circuit of Fig. P8.6. Assume the inputs are binary levels and that the following state assignment is used:

	y_1	y_2
A :	0	0
B :	0	1
C :	1	1
D :	1	0

Use K-maps to find:

(a)   The state table.   **(b)**   The state diagram.

8.7   If the sequential circuit of Fig. P8.7 yields an output sequence

$$z = 11011111$$

when we apply the input sequence

$$x = 01101010$$

what is the starting state?

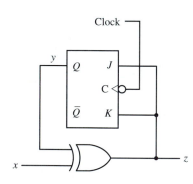

Figure P8.7

8.8   Find the state table for the sequential circuit in Fig. P8.8.

8.9   Consider a sequential circuit consisting of two cascaded circuits illustrated in Fig. P8.9. If the starting state is $y_1 = y_2 = 0$, what is the output sequence generated by the input sequence

$$x = 0110111010$$

8.10   Find the state diagram for the sequential circuit of Fig. P8.10 using the state assignment

	y_1	y_2
A :	0	0
B :	0	1
C :	1	1
D :	1	0

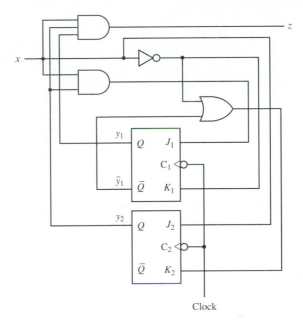

Figure P8.6

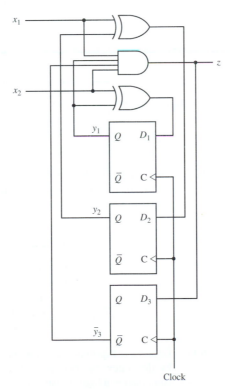

Clock

Figure P8.8

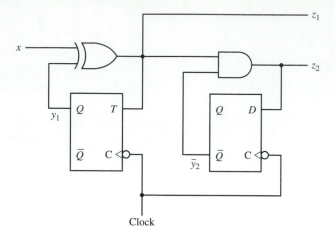

Figure P8.9

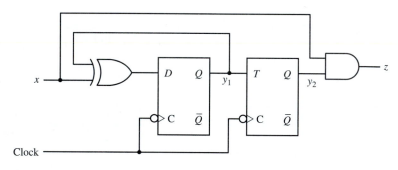

Figure P8.10

8.11 Find the D flip-flop implementation for the sequential circuit defined by the following state table. Use the state assigment listed. Draw the logic circuit diagram.

y_3	y_2	y_1		x 0	1
0	0	0	A	$D/0$	$C/0$
0	0	1	B	$E/0$	$A/1$
0	1	1	C	$F/1$	$B/0$
0	1	0	D	$A/1$	$F/1$
1	0	0	E	$C/0$	$E/0$
1	0	1	F	$B/0$	$D/1$

8.12 Obtain a D flip-flop realization for the synchronous sequential circuit specified by the following state table. Use the indicated state assignment. Write the combinational logic equations.

y_3	y_2	y_1		$x=0$	$x=1$
0	0	0	A	$B/0$	$E/0$
0	0	1	B	$A/1$	$C/1$
0	1	0	C	$B/0$	$C/1$
0	1	1	D	$C/0$	$E/0$
1	0	0	E	$D/1$	$A/0$

8.13   Determine four state diagrams for synchronous sequential circuits as specified by the following requirements. Each circuit has a single input line x and a single output line z.

(a) The first circuit must produce an output $z = 1$ when two consecutive logic 1 inputs x have occurred. The next input after the two logic ones resets the output to logic 0. For example,

$$x = 01100111110$$
$$z = 00100010100$$

(b) The second circuit must detect the input sequence 101 by producing $z = 1$ as the last 1 occurs. The output z is reset to 0 on the next clock pulse. Two 101 sequences may overlap. For example,

$$x = 010101101$$
$$z = 000101001$$

(c) Repeat Problem 8.13b but do not permit overlapping sequences. For example,

$$x = 010101101$$
$$z = 000100001$$

(d) The fourth circuit detects a 01 sequence. The sequence sets $z = 1$, which is reset only by a 00 input sequence. For all other cases, $z = 0$. For example,

$$x = 010100100$$
$$z = 011110110$$

8.14   Derive the minimum state diagram of a clocked sequential circuit that recognizes the input sequence 1010. Sequences may overlap. For example,

$$x = 00101001010101110$$
$$z = 00000100001010000$$

8.15   Find the state table of a synchronous sequential circuit that detects the input sequence 0101. The sequences may overlap as follows:

$$x = 010101001101011$$
$$z = 000101000000010$$

8.16   Obtain a minimum state diagram for a clocked sequential circuit that recognizes the input sequence 1001 including overlap. For example:

$$x = 0101001000110010010$$
$$z = 0000001000000010010$$

8.17   Derive the logic equations to implement the four-state sequential circuit defined by the following state table, using the indicated state assignment and:

(a) D flip-flops.   (c) Clocked SR flip-flops.

(b) Clocked JK flip-flops.

			x	
y_1	y_2		0	1
0	0	A	$B/0$	$C/0$
0	1	B	$D/0$	$A/1$
1	1	C	$A/1$	$D/0$
1	0	D	$D/1$	$B/1$

8.18   For the following circuit with the given state assignment, find a clocked JK flip-flop implementation. Write the logic equations and sketch the logic diagram.

			x	
y_1	y_2		0	1
0	0	A	$B/0$	$D/0$
0	1	B	$C/0$	$A/0$
1	0	C	$D/0$	$B/0$
1	1	D	$A/1$	$C/1$

8.19   Implement the circuit of Problem 8.18 using clocked T flip-flops.

8.20   Implement the circuit of Problem 8.18 using D flip-flops.

8.21   Given the following reduced state table and assignment, find the logic equations and logic diagram:
   (a) Using D flip-flops.   **(b)** Using clocked JK flip-flops.

			x	
y_1	y_2		0	1
0	0	A	$A/0$	$B/0$
0	1	B	$C/0$	$B/0$
1	1	C	$D/0$	$B/0$
1	0	D	$A/1$	$B/0$

8.22   Find the logic diagram of an implementation of the following sequential circuit, given the state assignment and:
   (a) D flip-flops.   **(c)** Clocked T flip-flops.
   (b) Clocked JK flip-flops.

			x	
y_1	y_2		0	1
0	0	A	$A/0$	$B/0$
0	1	B	$C/0$	$B/0$
1	1	C	$D/0$	$B/0$
1	0	D	$B/1$	$A/0$

8.23   Find a clocked JK flip-flop realization for the following reduced state table and assignment:

				x	
y_1	y_2	y_3		0	1
0	0	0	A	$B/0$	$D/0$
1	0	1	B	$A/0$	$C/1$
1	0	0	C	$D/1$	$C/0$
0	0	1	D	$B/1$	$E/1$
0	1	0	E	$C/0$	$A/0$
1	1	0	F	$E/0$	$F/1$

8.24   Design a 2-bit up/down, modulo-3 counter with the following function table using JK flip-flops.

s_1	s_0	Mode
0	0	Up
0	1	Down
1	0	Modulo 3
1	1	Modulo 3

8.25   Use D flip-flops to design a 3-bit counter/pseudorandom number generator. The circuit has one control input x. When $x = 0$, the circuit should operate as a binary up-counter. Otherwise, it should operate as a pseudorandom number generator according to the following function table.

Present State	Binary Up-Counter $x = 0$	Pseudo-Random No. Gen. $x = 1$
0	1	0
1	2	4
2	3	5
3	4	1
4	5	2
5	6	6
6	7	7
7	0	3
	Next State	

8.26   Design a serial subtractor that will perform the operation $A - B$, where $A = a_{n-1} \ldots a_1 a_0$ and $B = b_{n-1} \ldots b_1 b_0$. The operands are applied to the serial subtractor sequentially, beginning with bits a_0 and b_0. Use JK flip-flops.

8.27   Design a serial parity generation circuit. The circuit receives a sequence of bits and determines whether the sequence contains an even or odd number of ones. The circuit output p should be 0 for even parity, that is, if the sequence contains an even number of ones, and 1 for odd parity.

8.28   Design a logic circuit to implement the candy machine control unit designed in Example 8.18. Use JK flip-flops.

8.29   Design a logic circuit for the binary multiplier control unit whose ASM diagram was designed in Example 8.20 using a minimum number of JK flip-flops.

8.30   Modify the binary multiplier design of Example 8.20 so that it will perform a binary division operation, dividing an 8-bit dividend by a 4-bit divisor using a sequence of subtract and shift operations. The dividend should initially be loaded into the A and Q registers and the divisor placed in the M register. At the end of the algorithm, the quotient should be in the Q register and the remainder in the A register.

In Chapter 8 we examined methods for designing synchronous sequential circuits. Minimization was limited to applying combinational logic methods to reduce excitation and output equations. Significant savings can also be made in steps 2 and 3 of the synchonous sequential circuit synthesis procedure. First, in the design of state diagrams and/or state tables, it is often the case that more states than necessary are included. Since the number of states determines the number of memory elements, it is advantageous to reduce this number where possible. Second, the selection of an optimal state assignment has the effect of arranging the excitation K-maps to form larger groupings of minterms, thereby reducing the excitation and output equations. In this chapter we will discuss the identification and elimination of redundant states in both completely and incompletely specified sequential circuits. Then we will consider the optimal state assignment problem.

Simplification of Sequential Circuits

9.1 Redundant States

In a general sense we say that two states are *equivalent* if we cannot distinguish between them. In other words, we cannot determine in which of two equivalent states a sequential circuit starts by applying inputs and observing the outputs. If this condition exists for every input sequence, one of these states is redundant and can be removed without altering the circuit's behavior.

Redundant states normally arise in an early design phase when a word description of the sequential circuit's function is transformed into a state diagram or state table. The removal of redundant states is important for a number of reasons:

1. *Cost:* The number of memory elements is directly related to the number of states.
2. *Complexity:* The more states the circuit contains, the more complex the design and its associated implementation become.
3. *Aids failure analysis:* Diagnostic routines are often predicated on the assumption that no redundant states exist.

9.1.1 State Equivalence

Let us introduce the idea of state equivalence through a simple example. Consider the circuit shown in Figs. 9.1a and b. Suppose that the initial state is unknown. If an input $x = 0$ is applied to the circuit and the output is $z = 1$, all that is known concerning the initial state is that it is either A or B or C. Likewise, if the output is $z = 0$ when input $x = 0$ is applied, the initial state is either D or E. Note that a similar conclusion is obtained for the input $x = 1$. Therefore, we conclude that states A, B, and C are equivalent and that states D and E are equivalent for an input sequence of length 1, that is, *1-equivalent*. The behavior for input sequences of lengths 2 and 3 is shown in Figs. 9.1c and d. Note that states B and C and states D and E are 2-equivalent. States B and C are also 3-equivalent, and in fact it can be shown that these two states are K-equivalent for all K.

With these facts as basic background we now define precisely what is meant by equivalent states.

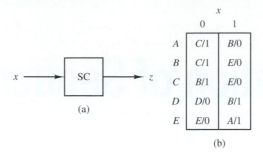

	x	
	0	1
A	C/1	B/0
B	C/1	E/0
C	B/1	E/0
D	D/0	B/1
E	E/0	A/1

(a)

(b)

Initial State	Input Sequences			
	00	01	11	10
A	11	10	01	00
B	11	10	00	01
C	11	10	00	01
D	00	01	11	10
E	00	01	11	10

(c)

Initial State	Input Sequences							
	000	001	010	011	100	101	110	111
A	111	110	100	101	011	010	000	001
B	111	110	100	101	000	001	011	010
C	111	110	100	101	000	001	011	010
D	000	001	011	010	111	110	100	101
E	000	001	011	010	111	110	101	100

(d)

Figure 9.1   Redundant states.
(a) Sequential circuit SC.
(b) State table. **(c)** Output
Sequences of length 2.
(d) Output sequences of length 3.

Definition

The states $S_1, S_2, \ldots, S_j$ of a sequential circuit are said to be *equivalent* if and only if, for every possible input sequence, the same output sequence will be produced by the circuit regardless of whether $S_1, S_2, \ldots, S_j$ is the initial state.

This definition can be stated in another manner for pairs of states. Let S_k and S_l be the next states of sequential circuit SC when input I_p is applied while the circuit is in states S_i and S_j, respectively. Then S_i and S_j are *equivalent* if and only if, for every possible input I_p,

1. The output produced by state S_i is equal to the output produced by state S_j.

2. The next states S_k and S_l are equivalent.

The second definition can be deduced from the first as follows. If S_i produces a different output for any input I_p than S_j produces for I_p, then S_i and S_j cannot be equivalent. Hence, the first condition is necessary. If S_k and S_l are not equivalent, there is an input sequence $I_1 I_2 \ldots I_k$ that produces a different output sequence for S_i as a starting state than for S_j as a starting state. Therefore, $I_p I_1 I_2 \ldots I_k$ will produce a different output sequence for S_i as a starting state than for S_j as a starting state. Hence, S_i and S_j cannot be equivalent unless the second condition is satisfied. Finally, the conditions are clearly sufficient for S_i and S_j to be equivalent; and therefore, the two definitions are synonymous. These two conditions form the basis for all state reduction techniques.

9.1.2 Equivalence and Compatibility Relations

Let x and y be elements of a set S. Suppose x and y are related by a property r, which is denoted $x \; r \; y$. A *relation* R on the set S is the set of all ordered pairs $(s_i, \; s_j)$ such that s_i and s_j are elements of S and such that $s_i \; r \; s_j$. R is *reflexive* if and only if $s_i \; r \; s_i$ for all s_i in S. R is *symmetric* if and only if $s_i \; r \; s_j$ implies that $s_j \; r \; s_i$. R is *transitive* if and only if $s_i \; r \; s_j$ and $s_j \; r \; s_k$ imply that $s_i \; r \; s_k$. An *equivalence relation* on S is a relation on S that is symmetric, reflexive, and transitive. The elements of S can be partitioned into disjoint subsets called *equivalence classes* by an equivalence relation.

It can be shown that state equivalence defines an equivalence relation on the set of states of a completely specified sequential circuit. Hence, the equivalence classes are used to define the states of the reduced state table.

A relation on S is said to be a *compatibility relation* if and only if the relation is reflexive and symmetric. Compatibility relations define subsets of S referred to as *compatibility classes*. These subsets are not, in general, disjoint. The subject of compatibility classes will be important when the reduction of incompletely specified state tables is discussed later in the chapter. The reader is referred to references [1–3] for more detailed discussions of equivalence and compatibility relations.

9.2 State Reduction in Completely Specified Circuits

We now present three techniques for determining equivalent states in completely specified sequential circuits:

1. Inspection
2. Partitioning
3. The implication table

In each case we use the technique to determine the equivalence classes of the circuit and then eliminate all but one state from each equivalence class to reduce the state table.

9.2.1 Inspection

The simplest and most obvious technique is that of recognizing equivalent states by inspection. In this approach, we need only recognize multiple rows in the state table that perform the same function and then remove the redundant states.

EXAMPLE 9.1

In this example we show three examples of equivalent rows. First, examine the sequential circuit defined by the state table shown in Fig. 9.2a. It can be reduced by inspection by noting that states B and D perform exactly the same function. Hence, state D can be removed from the table by simply removing row D and replacing state D in the remainder of the table by its equivalent state B. This procedure results in the state table shown in Fig. 9.2b.

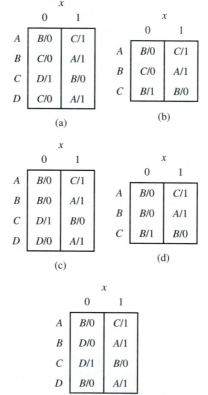

Figure 9.2 State equivalence by inspection. **(a)** Circuit 1. **(b)** Reduced circuit 1. **(c)** Circuit 2. **(d)** Reduced circuit 2. **(e)** Circuit 3.

Second, analyze the sequential circuit of Fig. 9.2c. If the circuit is in state B, under an input of logic 0 it stays in the same state (loops back to itself on a state diagram) with a 0 output, and under an input of logic 1 it transitions to state A with a 1 output. On the other hand, if the circuit is in state D, we could make the same statement: under an input of logic 0 it stays in the same state with a 0 output, and under an input of logic 1 it transitions to state A with a 1 output. Hence, states B and D are equivalent by inspection. The reduced state table is given in Fig. 9.2d.

Our third example is illustrated in Fig. 9.2e. This example closely resembles circuit 2; however, we have exchanged the next states for B and D in column $x = 0$. Now, analyzing the behavior of states B and D together, we note that if the pair of states are combined the behavior under input 0 requires the sequential circuit to remain in the same state (loops back to itself) with an output of logic 0, and under input $x = 1$, the sequential circuit transitions to state A with an output of logic 1. So the reduced circuit of Fig. 9.2d is also valid for circuit 3. This is another case of state reduction by inspection.

In summary, two states are equivalent by inspection when the next-state rows are identical or when the next-state rows are identical except for the "self-loop-back" entries.

9.2.2 Partitioning

The partitioning approach involves the successive determination of partitions P_K, $K = 1, 2, 3, \ldots, l$, in which each P_K is composed of a number of *blocks*, each of which consists of a group of one or more states. The states contained within a given block of P_K are K-equivalent. In other words, given a sequential circuit with states S_1, S_2, S_3, S_4, S_5, if $P_K = (S_1 S_3)(S_2 S_4)(S_5)$, then P_K contains three blocks and S_1 and S_3 are K-equivalent, as are S_2 and S_4. S_5 is not K-equivalent to any other state in the sequential circuit. For clarity, the sequential circuit described by Fig 9.1b will be used as an example in describing the partitioning procedure.

Partitioning Procedure

Step 1. The first partition P_1 is formed by placing two or more states in the same block of P_1 if and only if their *output* is identical for each input. For the example of Fig. 9.1b, $P_1 = (ABC)(DE)$, and hence the states within each block are 1-equivalent. This step guarantees that each block in P_1 satisfies condition 1 for equivalent states.

Step 2. Successive partitions P_K, $K = 2, 3, 4, \ldots, l$, are derived by placing two or more states in the same block of P_K if and only if for each input value their next states all lie in a *single* block of P_{K-1}. This iterative procedure is suggested by condition 2 for equivalent states.

Step 3. When $P_{K+1} = P_K$, that is, once the partition repeats, the states in each block of P_K that are K-equivalent are $(K + 1)$-equivalent, $(K + 2)$-equivalent, and so on, and P_K is said to be an *equivalence* partition. In our example, a quick check indicates that $P_4 = P_3$ and therefore states B and C are K-equivalent for any K; that is, they are equivalent. Condition 2 for equivalent states is now satisfied by P_K.

In performing this procedure for our example it is necessary to check the groups of states in each block of P_1. In the first block, the next states for A, B, and C with $x = 0$ all lie in the same block of P_1. However, for $x = 1$, the next state of A lies in a different block of P_1 than the next states of B and C. Therefore, the block (ABC) contained in P_1 is split into the blocks $(A)(BC)$ in P_2. See Fig. 9.3. The next states of states D and E lie in the same block of P_1 for both $x = 0$ and $x = 1$, and hence D and E will remain in the same block of P_2. Thus,

$$P_2 = (A)(BC)(DE)$$

and the states within each block are 2-equivalent. Hence, P_2 should correspond exactly to Fig. 9.1c.

Partition P_3 is obtained by examining each block of P_2. The next states of B and C lie in the same block of P_2 for each input, and hence the block (BC) remains intact in P_3. However, the next states for D and E with $x = 1$ lie in different blocks of P_2, and hence these two states must appear in different blocks of P_3. Therefore, $P_3 = (A)(BC)(D)(E)$. This agrees with Fig. 9.1d, and hence only states B and C are 3-equivalent.

This procedure of obtaining successive partitions is repeated until the condition stated in step 3 is obtained.

	Partition blocks				Action
Partition P_0	(ABCDE)				
Output for $x = 0$	11100				Separate (ABC) and (DE)
Output for $x = 1$	00011				Separate (ABC) and (DE)
Partition P_1	(ABC)		(DE)		
Next state for $x = 0$	CCB		DE		
Next state for $x = 1$	BEE		BA		Separate (A) and (BC)
Partition P_2	(A)	(BC)	(DE)		
Next state for $x = 0$	C	CB	DE		
Next state for $x = 1$	B	EE	BA		Separate (D) and (E)
Partition P_3	(A)	(BC)	(D)	(E)	
Next state for $x = 0$	C	CB	D	E	
Next state for $x = 1$	B	EE	B	A	
Partition $P_4 = P_3$	(A)	(BC)	(D)	(E)	

States B and C are equivalent.

Figure 9.3 State equivalence by partitioning.

EXAMPLE 9.2

Use the partitioning method to reduce the state table shown in Fig. 9.4a.

The partitions for the state table are

$$P_1 = (AD)(BE)(CF)(GH)$$
$$P_2 = (AD)(BE)(CF)(G)(H)$$
$$P_3 = P_2$$

The reduced state table using the following symbolic states is shown in Fig. 9.4b:

$$A' = (AD), \quad C' = (CF), \quad E' = (H),$$
$$B' = (BE), \quad D' = (G)$$

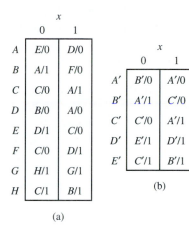

	x	
	0	1
A	E/0	D/0
B	A/1	F/0
C	C/0	A/1
D	B/0	A/0
E	D/1	C/0
F	C/0	D/1
G	H/1	G/1
H	C/1	B/1

(a)

	x	
	0	1
A'	B'/0	A'/0
B'	A'/1	C'/0
C'	C'/0	A'/1
D'	E'/1	D'/1
E'	C'/1	B'/1

(b)

Figure 9.4   Partitioning example. **(a)** State table. **(b)** Reduced state table.

EXAMPLE 9.3

Reduce the state table shown in Fig. 9.5a by applying the partitioning method.

The partitions are

$$P_1 = (ACG)(BDEH)(F)$$
$$P_2 = (A)(CG)(BH)(DE)(F), \qquad \text{from column } x = 0$$
$$\quad = (A)(C)(G)(BH)(DE)(F), \qquad \text{from column } x = 1$$
$$P_3 = P_2$$

Using the following symbolic states yields the reduced state table shown in Fig. 9.5b.

$$A' = (A), \quad C' = (C), \quad E' = (BH),$$
$$B' = (F), \quad D' = (G), \quad F' = (DE)$$

EXAMPLE 9.4

This example illustrates that the techniques described previously are applicable for sequential circuits with multiple inputs. The state table for a sequential circuit with two input lines is shown in Fig. 9.6a.

The partitions are

$$P_1 = (ADFG)(BCEH)$$
$$P_2 = (AFG)(D)(BCEH)$$
$$P_3 = (AF)(G)(D)(BCH)(E)$$
$$P_4 = P_3$$

	x	
	0	1
A	A/0	B/0
B	H/1	C/0
C	E/0	B/0
D	C/1	D/0
E	C/1	E/0
F	F/1	G/1
G	B/0	F/0
H	H/1	C/0

(a)

	x	
	0	1
A′	A′/0	E′/0
B′	B′/1	D′/1
C′	F′/0	E′/0
D′	E′/0	B′/0
E′	E′/1	C′/0
F′	C′/1	F′/0

(b)

Figure 9.5 Partitioning example. **(a)** State table. **(b)** Reduced state table.

	$x_1 x_2$			
	00	01	11	10
A	D/0	D/0	F/0	A/0
B	C/1	D/0	E/1	F/0
C	C/1	D/0	E/1	A/0
D	D/0	B/0	A/0	F/0
E	C/1	F/0	E/1	A/0
F	D/0	D/0	A/0	F/0
G	G/0	G/0	A/0	A/0
H	B/1	D/0	E/1	A/0

(a)

	$x_1 x_2$			
	00	01	11	10
A′	C′/0	C′/0	A′/0	A′/0
B′	B′/1	C′/0	D′/1	A′/0
C′	C′/0	B′/0	A′/0	A′/0
D′	B′/1	A′/0	D′/1	A′/0
E′	E′/0	E′/0	A′/0	A′/0

(b)

Figure 9.6 Multiple input example. **(a)** Original circuit. **(b)** Reduced circuit.

The reduced state table is shown in Fig. 9.6b, where the following state substitution has been used:

$$A' = (AF), \qquad C' = (D), \quad E' = (G)$$
$$B' = (BCH), \quad D' = (E),$$

9.2.3 Implication Table

The implication table is another tool that can be used to determine state equivalence. This technique is more general in that it can also be applied to incompletely specified sequential circuits; however, it can also be more time consuming than the partitioning approach.

Consider once again the example of Fig. 9.1b, repeated in Fig. 9.7a. This example will be used to explain the procedure.

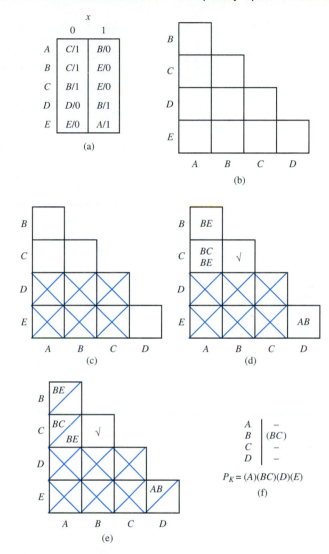

Figure 9.7   The implication table for a five-state circuit.
(a) State table. **(b)** Implication table. **(c)** Output partitioning.
(d) Implied pairs. **(e)** Completed table. **(f)** Equivalence
partition.

Implication Table Procedure

Step 1. Form a table using the structure shown in Fig. 9.7b, which is
derived by listing vertically all states in the table except the last and
horizontally all states except the first. The resulting table displays
all possible combinations of two states, and hence each cell in
the table corresponding to the intersection of a row and column
represents two states being tested for equivalence.

Step 2. Since only states with identical outputs can possibly be equivalent (condition 1 for equivalent states), a cross is placed in the cells corresponding to those pairs of states whose outputs are not equal for every input. This has been done in Fig. 9.7c for the example.

Step 3. Using condition 2 for equivalent states, the vacant cells in Fig. 9.7c must now be completed. Into these blocks are placed the pairs of next states whose equivalence is "implied" by the two states whose intersection defines the cell. As an illustration of this, consider the cell defined by states A and B. From the state table it can be seen that, for A and B to be equivalent states, B and E must be equivalent. Hence, the pair BE is listed in the cell defined by A and B as shown in Fig. 9.7d. Note that if the states of the implied pair, B and E, are not equivalent, then there exists an input string beginning with $x = 0$ that will produce different outputs depending on whether the initial state is A or B, meaning A and B are not equivalent.

   If the implied pairs for any cell contain only the states that define the cell or if the next states of the two states defining the cell are the same state for a given input, then a check mark ($\sqrt{}$) is placed in the cell indicating that the two states defining the cell are equivalent by *inspection* and independent of any implied pairs. This condition is illustrated in Fig. 9.7d by the cell defined by states B and C and is similar to the case of equivalence by inspection seen in the example of Fig. 9.2e.

Step 4. Once the table has been completely filled, successive passes are made through the entire table to determine if any cells should be crossed off other than those crossed out in step 2. A cell in the table is crossed out if it contains at least one implied pair that defines a cell in the table that has previously been crossed out. This operation has been performed for the example, and the resulting table is shown in Fig. 9.7e. For example, the cell defined by A and B was crossed out because it contained the pair BE which defines a cell that was already crossed out. This procedure is repeated until no additional cells can be crossed off.

Step 5. Finally, the table shown in Fig. 9.7f is obtained by listing as a column the states that define the horizontal row of the implication table. Then the implication table is examined column by column from left to right to see if any cells are not crossed out. The states that define any cell that has not been crossed out are equivalent and are listed as an equivalent pair in the table in Fig. 9.7f. Pairs are combined using transitivity.

$$(s_i, s_j)(s_j, s_k) \rightarrow (s_i, s_j, s_k) \tag{9.1}$$

In the example, all the cells in columns A, C, and D are crossed out and hence dashes are placed in these rows in the table of Fig. 9.7f. In column B of the implication table the cell defined by states B and C is not crossed out, and hence the pair (BC) is placed in row B of the table. The equivalence partition then consists of all the equivalent states found in the table, that is, (BC) together with the remaining states of the circuit that are not equivalent to any other state. Note that this equivalence partition is identical to that obtained earlier by partitioning.

EXAMPLE 9.5

Use an implication table to determine the equivalence partition for the sequential circuit of Fig. 9.4a.

The circuit is repeated as Fig. 9.8a. The analysis for this example is shown in Figs. 9.8b and c.

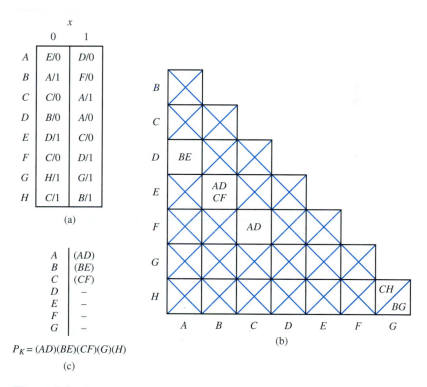

Figure 9.8   The implication table for an eight-state circuit. **(a)** State table. **(b)** Implication table. **(c)** Equivalence partition.

EXAMPLE 9.6

The equivalence partition for the sequential circuit described by the state table of Fig. 9.6a is determined in Fig. 9.9.

This example, although straightforward, does contain one salient feature. In row B of Fig. 9.9c is listed the set of equivalent states $(BC)(BH)$, while (CH) is listed in row C. Equation 9.1 may be used to combine these states into the larger equivalence class (BCH).

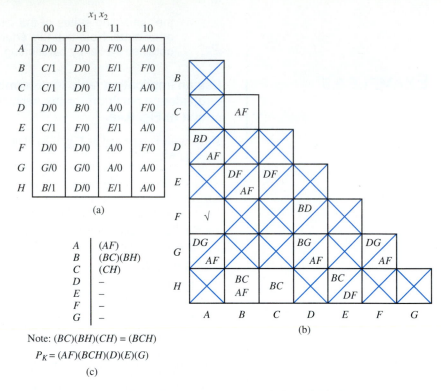

Figure 9.9 The implication table for a seven-state circuit. **(a)** State table. **(b)** Implication table. **(c)** Equivalence partition.

Examples 9.5 and 9.6, which illustrate the use of the implication table, can be compared with the previously used partitioning method. In general, the implication table approach is more routine, but it is also more tedious than the partitioning approach.

In this section we have examined three techniques for minimizing the number of states of synchronous sequential circuits. Any one may be used in the synthesis process.

9.3 State Reduction in Incompletely Specified Circuits

The minimization of state tables containing don't-cares requires special consideration. The following example will quickly illustrate this point.

EXAMPLE 9.7

Consider the problem of minimizing the following incompletely specified circuit:

$$x$$

	0	1
A	$B/—$	$E/0$
B	$B/1$	$E/—$
C	$F/0$	$C/0$
D	$B/1$	$A/1$
E	$D/0$	$C/—$
F	$D/—$	$C/1$

In this state table, four don't-cares appear. Because they are don't-cares, they can, of course, be assigned or specified in any way that we choose. Once these don't-cares are specified, the state table is no longer incompletely specified, and the state reduction techniques described previously can be applied to determine equivalent states and thus reduce the table. Suppose then that we assign the don't-cares in a manner that makes state A equivalent to B and E equivalent to F. Under this condition the table above will reduce to

$$x$$

	0	1
A'	$A'/1$	$D'/0$
B'	$D'/0$	$B'/0$
C'	$A'/1$	$A'/1$
D'	$C'/0$	$B'/1$

Note that this was a rather obvious simplification since we could see immediately from the original state table that states A and B would be equivalent as well as states E and F if the don't-cares were assigned in the proper manner. However, if the don't-cares in the original table are specified as zeros for present states A and E and specified as ones for states B and F, then states A, C, and E are equivalent, as are states B, D, and F. Hence, the state table reduces to

$$x$$

	0	1
A'	$B'/0$	$A'/0$
B'	$B'/1$	$A'/1$

Note that the latter simplification was not obvious and yet it yielded the simplest table.

The following ideas provide the basis for state table reduction in incompletely specified circuits.

9.3.1 State Compatibility

Because of the problems associated with assigning values to don't-care conditions, we must develop a different procedure to eliminate redundant states from the state tables of incompletely specified circuits. We begin by examining the sequences of inputs that can be applied to an incompletely specified circuit. Then we define state compatibility and methods for identifying compatible and incompatible states.

Applicable Input Sequences

An input sequence is said to be *applicable* to state S_i of an incompletely specified machine if and only if the following condition is satisfied: When the machine is in S_i and the input sequence is applied, all next states are specified except for possibly the last element of the sequence. For example, the input sequences 0111 and 1111 are applicable to state A of the machine defined in Fig. 8.49. But the sequence 11111 is not applicable to state A.

Compatible States

Two states S_i and S_j of an incompletely specified machine are said to be *compatible* $(S_i S_j)$ if and only if for each input sequence applicable to S_i and S_j the same output sequence will be produced when the outputs are specified, whether S_i or S_j is the starting state. States A and C in the state reduction example are compatible. Note that the following output sequences produced by input sequence 1111 for starting states A and C are the same when specified:

Input:		1		1		1		1	
State:	A		E		C		C		C
Output:		0		–		0		0	
State:	C		C		C		C		C
Output:		0		0		0		0	

State compatibility can be shown to define a compatibility relation on the states of an incompletely specified machine. Hence, a set of compatible states is called a *compatibility class*. A *maximal compatible* is a compatibility class that will not remain a compatibility class if any state not in the class is added. In the previous example, (AC), (AE), (CE), and (ACE) are compatibility classes. Of these four compatibility classes, only (ACE) is a maximal compatible.

States S_i and S_j of an incompletely specified machine are compatible if and only if the following two conditions are satisfied:

1. The outputs produced by S_i and S_j must be the same, when both are specified, for each possible input I_p.

2. The next states of S_i and S_j must be compatible, when both are specified, for each possible input I_p.

Incompatible States

Two states of an incompletely specified machine that fail to satisfy the preceding two conditions are said to be *incompatible*. A set of incompatible states forms an *incompatibility class*. A *maximal incompatible* is an incompatibility class to which no other incompatible state may be added without destroying the class.

EXAMPLE 9.8

Determine the compatibility classes and maximal compatibles for the state table of Fig. 9.10a.

The implication table is employed first to determine all pairs of compatible states as shown in Fig. 9.10b. This table is formed in the same manner as it was in the completely specified case. Note that the presence of don't-care output terms allows state B to be paired with state A in one instance and state C in another.

The reduction of the implication table is also performed as it was in the completely specified case. The determination of the compatibility classes is shown in Fig. 9.10c. Note that this procedure is reminiscent of that used to determine equivalent states in the completely specified case. In the row defined by state G, the pair (GH) is a compatibility class. This pair is taken from the last column of the implication table. Next we add the compatible pairs from column F of the implication table. Row F of the list in Fig. 9.10c now contains two compatible pairs, $(GH)(FG)$. As we add additional columns, moving from right to left in the implication table, the list of compatible pairs grows. For example, row E contains the pairs $(EG)(EH)(GH)(FG)$; but $(EG)(EH)(GH)$ can be combined into a larger compatibility class (EGH), so a second row for state E is included in Fig. 9.10c showing this step. We continue this process of adding compatible pairs and combining them into larger compatibility classes as we move from right to left in the implication table. The bottom row in Fig. 9.10c is the set of maximal compatibles.

Examination of the list of maximal compatibles illustrates the fundamental difference between compatibility in incompletely specified circuits and equivalence in completely specified circuits. In a completely specified circuit, if we found that state A was equivalent to state B and that state B was equivalent to state C, we were guaranteed without even checking that states A and C were equivalent because state equivalence is an equivalence relation. However, since the transitive property does not hold in general for incompletely specified circuits, there is no such guarantee. Consider the maximal compatible (BCG) in Fig. 9.10c. To be able to group all three states together we must have the compatible pairs (BC), (CG), and (BG); that is, (BC) and (CG) do not automatically imply (BG). A moment's reflection will show that this problem arises due to don't-cares in the state table.

EXAMPLE 9.9

Determine the incompatibility classes and maximal incompatibles for the sequential machine of Fig. 9.10a.

The implication table of Fig. 9.10b is employed to generate the incompatibility classes by extracting from it pairs of states that are *not* compatible, as shown in Fig. 9.10d. The set of maximal incompatibles is the list at the bottom of the table.

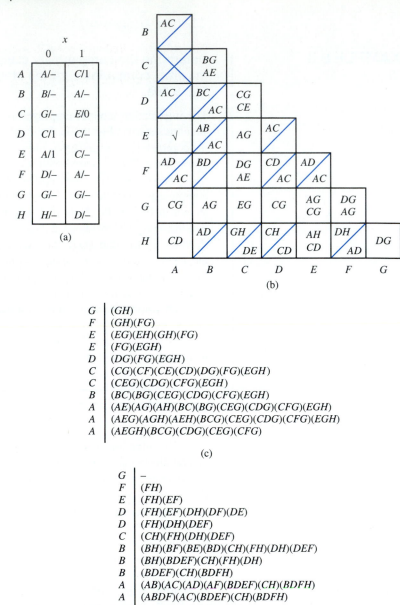

Figure 9.10   Generating maximal compatibles and incompatibles. **(a)** State table. **(b)** Implication table. **(c)** Compatibility classes. **(d)** Incompatibility classes.

The process of generating the maximal compatibles and incompatibles as demonstrated in Figs. 9.10c and d can be somewhat tedious, and hence we now introduce a graphical technique that aids in this process.

Merger Diagrams

The process of finding the maximal compatible sets of states from the compatible pairs derived from the implication table is aided measureably by a graphical technique called the *merger diagram*. First the states of the original machine can be conveniently represented as dots equally spaced around a circle; then a line is used to connect each related (compatible) pair of states. This completes the construction of the merger diagram. The same may be done to find maximal incompatible sets of states.

The maximal sets of states can be derived from the merger diagram by visually noting those sets in which every state is connected to every other state by a line segment. Thus the maximal sets form regular graphical patterns, as shown in Fig. 9.11. The rules for extracting maximal sets from a merger diagram are as follows:

> **Rule 1.** Make each maximal set as large as possible.
>
> **Rule 2.** Each state of the maximal set must be interconnected with every other state in the set by a line segment.
>
> **Rule 3.** Each related (compatible or incompatible) pair of states must appear in at least one maximal set.

The application of these rules is now demonstrated by an example.

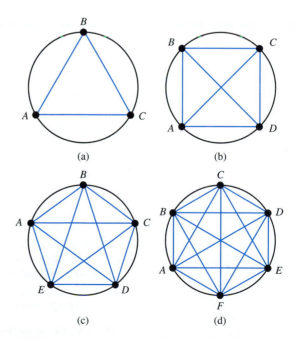

(a)

(b)

(c)

(d)

Figure 9.11   The merger diagram. **(a)** Three states.
(b) Four states. **(c)** Five states. **(d)** Six states.

EXAMPLE 9.10

The merger diagrams of Fig. 9.12 are constructed from the implication table of Fig. 9.10b. Consider the merger diagram for the maximal compatibles in Fig. 9.12a. The graphical pattern for the maximal compatible $(AEGH)$ has been emphasized. Note that any attempt to add another compatible state to this graphical grouping ends in failure. All remaining line segments (compatible pairs) may be covered using four triangles (BCG), (CDG), (CEG), and (CFG). Hence, we have found the set of maximal compatibles. The set of maximal incompatibles is extracted from Fig. 9.12b in a like manner.

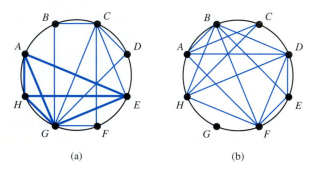

(a)   (b)

Figure 9.12 Example merger diagrams **(a)** Merger diagram for the maximal compatibles. **(b)** Merger diagram for the maximal incompatibles.

The reader is now familiar with the concept of incompletely specified sequential circuits, compatible states, incompatible states, and merger diagrams. With these tools we are now prepared to address the problem of state minimization for incompletely specified sequential circuits.

9.3.2 Minimization Procedure

The minimization of an incompletely specified state table for a sequential machine can be an involved process. In general, we must select a set of compatibility classes that meets the following three conditions:

1. *Completeness*: The union of all the sets in the chosen set of compatibility classes must contain all the states in the original machine.
2. *Consistency*: The chosen set of compatibility classes must be closed; that is, the implied next states of each compatibility class in the chosen set must be contained by some compatibility class within the set.
3. *Minimality*: The smallest number of compatibility classes that meet the preceding criteria should be chosen.

Once a set of compatibility classes has been found that meets these conditions, each class in the set corresponds to a state in the reduced state table. Unfortunately, the process of selecting the set of compatibility classes that meets the three conditions must be done by trial and error. Hence, it would be helpful to at least bound the number of states K required in the realization of the minimal-state circuit.

The upper bound U on the number of states in the minimal circuit is given by the expression

$$U = \text{minimum}\{\text{NSMC, NSOC}\}$$

where

$$\text{NSMC} = \text{number of sets of maximal compatibles}$$

$$\text{NSOC} = \text{number of states in the original circuit}$$

This equation simply states that we should need no more states in the minimal circuit than the number of states in the original circuit, and that if there exists some compatibility among states such that NSMC < NSOC, then we should require fewer states than NSOC.

The lower bound L on the number of states in the minimal circuit is given by the expression

$$L = \text{maximum}\{\text{NSMI}_1, \text{NSMI}_2, \ldots, \text{NSMI}_i, \ldots\}$$

where

$$\text{NSMI}_i = \text{number of states in the } i\text{th group of the set of}$$
$$\text{maximal incompatibles of the original circuit}$$

The reasonableness of this condition is illustrated by the fact that, if there exist two states in the original circuit that are incompatible, the minimal circuit will have to have at least two states in order to distinguish the incompatible ones.

At this point we may specify the algorithm for state reduction for incompletely specified sequential machines.

State Reduction Algorithm

Step 1. Find the maximal compatibles using the implication table and merger diagram.

Step 2. Find the maximal incompatibles using the implication table of step 1 and another merger diagram.

Step 3. Find the bounds on the number of required states, U and L.

Step 4. Find, by trial and error, a set of compatibility classes that satisfy completeness, consistency, and minimality.

Step 5. Produce the minimum state table. In general, it may still contain unspecified next states and outputs.

The trial and error selection of compatibility classes may begin by considering only the maximal compatibles. The set of maximal compatibles is always *complete* and *consistent*. However, the set may not be minimal. We may begin the search for a minimal set of compatibility classes by considering the maximal compatibles taken in groups of L, the lower bound.

EXAMPLE 9.11

Let us find a reduced state table for the incompletely specified machine of Fig. 9.10a.

First we construct a *closure table* by treating the maximal compatibles as states and finding their sets of next states, as shown in Fig. 9.13a. Each entry in the table is obtained from the original table by recording the next state of each state within a maximal compatible.

	x			x	
	0	1		0	1
(AEGH)	AGH	CDG	A'	$A'/1$	$C'/1$
(BCG)	BG	AEG	B'	$B'/-$	$A'/0$
(CDG)	CG	CEG	C'	$B', C', D', E'/1$	$D'/0$
(CFG)	DG	AEG	D'	$A'/1$	$D'/0$
(CEG)	AG	CEG	E'	$C'/-$	$A'/0$
	(a)			(b)	

Figure 9.13   State reduction. **(a)** Closure table. **(b)** Reduced state table.

Since NSMC = 5 and NSOC = 8, the upper bound on the number of states is

$$U = \min\{5,\ 8\} = 5$$

The lower bound is determined from the maximal incompatibles. The set of maximal incompatibles has been derived in Fig. 9.12b and is

$$(ABDF)(BDEF)(BDFH)(AC)(CH)$$

Therefore,

$$L = \max\{4,\ 4,\ 4,\ 2,\ 2\} = 4$$

The number of states in the reduced machine is bounded by

$$4 \leq K \leq 5$$

Since we want a minimal circuit, we begin with the lower bound to see if we can find four maximal compatibles that satisfy the conditions of completeness and consistency. By trial and error we find, using the closure table of Fig. 9.13a, that no set of four maximal compatibles will satisfy both completeness and consistency. Hence, all five maximal compatibles are required. By definition, the set of maximal compatibles is complete and consistent. Hence, the reduced machine will contain the five states

$$A' = (AEGH), \quad D' = (CEG)$$
$$B' = (BCG), \qquad E' = (CFG)$$
$$C' = (CDG)$$

The reduced state table that duplicates the performance of Fig. 9.10a is given by Fig. 9.13b.

The multiple next-state entry in Fig. 9.13b requires an explanation. Note that if the circuit is in state C' and $x = 0$ then the next state can be any of B', C', D', or E'. This multiple next-state entry exists because the closure table indicates that, for $x = 0$, $(CDG) \rightarrow CG$, and hence the next state could be (BCG), (CDG), (CEG), or (CFG).

For the previous example all maximal compatibles had to be used as states of the reduced machine. In some cases, only a subset of the maximal compatibles can be chosen for reducing the machine, as is illustrated in the next example.

EXAMPLE 9.12

We shall determine the reduced state table corresponding to the one given in Fig. 9.14a.

Steps 1 and 2 of the state reduction algorithm are performed in Figs. 9.14b, c, and d. From the implication table the compatible pairs are

$$(AB)(AC)(AD)(AE)(BD)(CD)(CE)$$

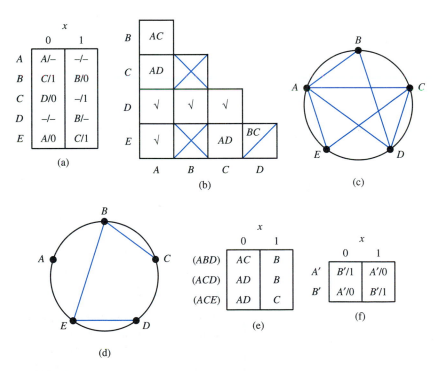

Figure 9.14   State reduction example. **(a)** State table. **(b)** Implication table. **(c)** Maximal compatibles. **(d)** Maximal incompatibles. **(e)** Closure table. **(f)** Reduced state table.

These compatible pairs are processed on the merger diagram of Fig. 9.14c to yield the maximal compatibles

$$(ABD)(ACD)(ACE)$$

In a similiar manner, the incompatible pairs are found from the implication table to be

$$(BC)(BE)(DE)$$

The merger diagram of Fig. 9.14d demonstrates that these pairs are the maximal incompatibles.

Step 3 of the state reduction algorithm calculates the bounds on the number of reduced states. The calculations follow:

$$\text{NSMC} = 3$$
$$\text{NSOC} = 5$$
$$\text{NSMI}_1 = 2$$
$$\text{NSMI}_2 = 2$$
$$\text{NSMI}_3 = 2$$

Hence,

$$U = \min\{3, 5\} = 3$$
$$L = \max\{2, 2, 2\} = 2$$

and

$$2 \le K \le 3$$

Step 4 of the algorithm is centered around the closure table of Fig. 9.14e. We begin our search for two compatibility classes that are complete and consistent by examining the maximal compatibles. Choosing the maximal compatibles (ABD) and (ACE) as trial states, we see that they satisfy completeness since the union of all the states contained in these two maximal compatibles contains all the states in the original circuit. They satisfy consistency, as shown in Fig. 9.14e, and also minimality, as indicated by the lower bound. Therefore, under the definitions,

$$A' = (ABD)$$
$$B' = (ACE)$$

the final minimal circuit for step 5 of the algorithm is shown in Fig. 9.14f.

EXAMPLE 9.13

We shall now derive the minimal circuit for the sequential machine shown in Fig. 9.15a.

The implication table for this state table is shown in Fig. 9.15b. The compatible pairs obtained from the table are

$$(AB)(AD)(BC)(BD)$$

Figure 9.15c is the corresponding merger diagram, and the maximal compatibles obtained from the diagram are

$$(ABD)(BC)(E)(F)$$

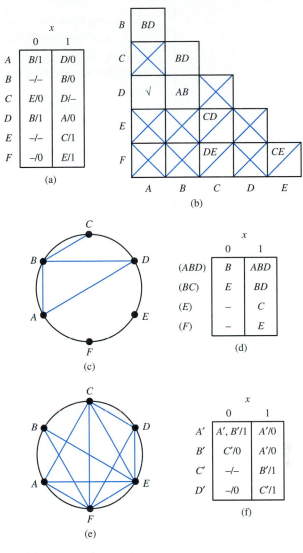

Figure 9.15 State reduction example. **(a)** State table.
(b) Implication table. **(c)** Maximal compatibles. **(d)** Closure
table. **(e)** Maximal incompatibles. **(f)** Reduced state table.

These maximal compatibles form the closure table shown in Fig. 9.15d. The
upper and lower bounds on the number of states in the minimal circuit are
obtained as follows:

$$\text{NSMC} = 4$$

$$\text{NSOC} = 6$$

$$U = \min\{4, 6\}$$

$$U = 4$$

The incompatible pairs are

$$(AC)(AE)(AF)(BE)(BF)(CD)(CE)(CF)(DE)(DF)(EF)$$

A merger diagram for the maximal incompatibles is given in Fig. 9.15e. From this figure, the maximal incompatibles are derived as

$$(CDEF)(ACEF)(BEF)$$

Now since $\text{NSMI}_1 = 4$, $\text{NSMI}_2 = 4$, and $\text{NSMI}_3 = 3$, then

$$L = \max\{4, 4, 3\}$$

$$L = 4$$

Now note that the bound conditions specify that

$$4 \leq K \leq 4$$

Hence, all the maximal compatibles may be chosen as states of the minimal circuit. Using the symbols

$$A' = (ABD)$$

$$B' = (BC)$$

$$C' = (E)$$

$$D' = (F)$$

the resulting minimal state table is shown in Fig. 9.15f.

Note that the resultant state table has considerable flexibility. When the circuit is in state A' and the input $x = 0$ is applied, the next state can be either A' or B'. This property will serve to simplify the hardware realization, as is shown next.

In the last three examples, step 4 of the state reduction algorithm was approached as a search through a very restricted set of compatibility classes, the set of maximal compatibles. While the consideration of only maximal compatibles is computationally desirable, a minimal reduced state table is not always obtained. If the compatibility classes are not required to be maximal, a better reduction is often obtained. An algorithm for making such a selection for step 4 that always leads to a minimal reduced table will be illustrated here by example.

EXAMPLE 9.14

Let us reduce the incompletely specified sequential circuit of Fig. 9.16a.

If we apply the state reduction algorithm, we find the following:

Step 1. Figures 9.16b and c. Maximal compatibles are
$$(ABC)(ACD)(ADE)$$

Step 2. Figure 9.16b and d. Maximal incompatibles are
$$(BD)(BE)(CE)$$

Step 3.
$$\text{NSMC} = 3$$
$$\text{NSOC} = 5$$
$$\text{NSMI}_1 = 2$$
$$\text{NSMI}_2 = 2$$

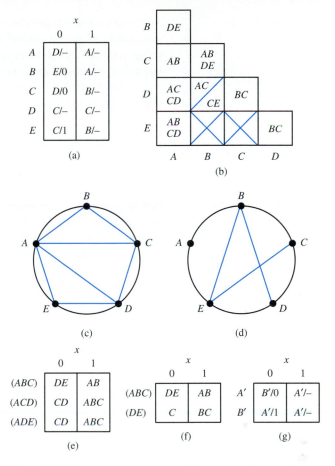

Figure 9.16 A counterexample. **(a)** State table. **(b)** Implication table. **(c)** Maximal compatibles. **(d)** Maximal incompatibles. **(e)** Closure table for maximal compatibles. **(f)** Closure table for maximal incompatibles. **(g)** Reduced state table.

$$\text{NSMI}_3 = 2$$
$$U = \min\{3, 5\} = 3$$
$$L = \max\{2, 2, 2\} = 2$$
$$2 \le K \le 3$$

Step 4. Consider the closure tables of Figs. 9.16e and f. No set of two maximal compatibles can be found that is complete and consistent. Hence, if we restrict ourselves to maximal compatibility classes, we must choose three states in the reduced machine. However, if we choose compatibility classes (ABC) and (DE), we find that this set is complete, consistent, and minimal.

Step 5. $A' = (ABC)$, $B' = (DE)$.

The minimal reduced state table is shown in Fig. 9.16g.

This completes our discussion of state reduction of incompletely specified sequential circuits. In general, a near-minimal reduced machine is produced by using maximal compatibles as states for the reduced machine. However, to guarantee a minimal machine, the algorithm developed in this chapter should be applied to find a minimal, complete, and consistent set of compatibility classes to act as states for the reduced machine.

9.4 Optimal State Assigment Methods

Up to this point we have always assumed some state assignment with no discussion of any alternatives. However, it is important for the reader to realize that two different assignments may yield vast differences in hardware. From a purely practical standpoint, many engineers might argue that what is needed is a quick, but not necessarily minimal, solution. However, if the system being designed is a basic module that will be manufactured in great quantities, a potential cost saving exists if the module can be built with fewer elements.

The following example will illustrate the need for some guidelines in choosing a good state assignment.

EXAMPLE 9.15

Consider the sequential circuit described by the minimum state table of Fig. 9.17. If the following state assignment is used

	y_1	y_2	y_3
A:	0	0	0
B:	0	0	1
C:	0	1	1
D:	0	1	0
E:	1	0	1
F:	1	1	0
G:	1	1	1

Present state	x 0	1
A	B/0	E/0
B	C/0	G/0
C	D/0	F/0
D	A/1	A/0
E	G/0	C/0
F	A/0	A/1
G	F/0	D/0

Next state/output

Figure 9.17   A seven-state machine.

then the logic equations that implement the circuit are

$$
\begin{aligned}
J_1 &= \bar{y}_2 x + y_3 x, & J_3 &= \bar{y}_2 \\
K_1 &= \bar{y}_3 + x, & K_3 &= y_2 \\
J_2 &= y_3, & z &= \bar{y}_3 y_2 \bar{y}_1 \bar{x} + \bar{y}_3 y_1 x \\
K_2 &= \bar{y}_3
\end{aligned}
$$

Consider also the following assignment:

	y_1	y_2	y_3
A:	0	0	0
B:	0	0	1
C:	0	1	0
D:	0	1	1
E:	1	0	0
F:	1	0	1
G:	1	1	0

Under this second assignment the logic equations that implement the circuit are

$$J_1 = x\bar{y}_3 + x\bar{y}_2, \qquad J_3 = y_2 + \bar{x}\bar{y}_1$$
$$K_1 = x + y_3, \qquad\qquad K_3 = 1$$
$$J_2 = y_1\bar{y}_3 + \bar{y}_1 y_3$$
$$K_2 = y_3 + \bar{x}y_1 + x\bar{y}_1 \qquad z = xy_1 y_3 + \bar{x}y_2 y_3$$

A quick gate count check shows that the first assignment requires three OR gates, four AND gates, and one NOT gate; the second assignment requires six OR gates, nine AND gates, and one NOT gate. Hence, the second assignment requires *twice* as many gates as the first assignment.

9.4.1 Unique State Assignments

The number of possible state assignments for a problem of any significance is quite large. For example, the number of possible state assignments for a five-state machine is over 100, and the number for possible assignments for a ten-state machine exceeds 10 million. It is unfortunate that no simple and efficient technique for choosing a state assignment exists [4–8]. In place of an optimal solution we shall offer in the following pages a few guidelines to aid the reader in choosing a reasonably good state assignment.

With this motivation, let us now examine several useful techniques for choosing a state assignment. As part of the synthesis procedure, a minimum state table was obtained in order to reduce the required number of memory elements needed to implement the synchronous sequential circuit. Once a minimum number of memory elements has been found, the proper choice of state assignment can drastically reduce the required number of logic gates needed to implement the excitation and output switching functions. Previously, we have seen that the total number of memory elements N_{FF} is related to the number of states N_S in the circuit by

$$2^{N_{FF}-1} < N_S \le 2^{N_{FF}}$$

Therefore, there will be

$$N_{SA} = \frac{2^{N_{FF}}!}{(2^{N_{FF}} - N_S)!}$$

ways of assigning the $2^{N_{FF}}$ combinations of binary state assignments to the N_S states. This expression is evaluated for several cases in Table 9.1.

It should be demonstrated that not all these assignments are unique with respect to the resulting excitation and output equations. This is done in the following example.

EXAMPLE 9.16

For the state table of Fig. 9.18a, let us compare the D flip-flop excitation equations resulting from an arbitrary assignment of state variables y_1 and y_2 to assigments derived by complementing y_1 and by swapping y_1 and y_2.

TABLE 9.1   NUMBER OF STATE ASSIGNMENTS.

N_S	N_{FF}	N_{SA}	N_{UA}
1	0	—	—
2	1	2	1
3	2	24	3
4	2	24	3
5	3	6,720	140
6	3	20,160	420
7	3	40,320	840
8	3	40,320	840
9	4	4.15×10^9	10,810,800
10	4	2.91×10^{10}	75,675,600

Present state

	x	
	0	1
A	$A/0$	$B/0$
B	$A/0$	$C/0$
C	$C/0$	$D/0$
D	$C/1$	$A/0$

(a)

Assignments

States	1 $y_1 y_2$	2 $y_1 y_2$	3 $y_1 y_2$
A	00	10	00
B	01	11	10
C	11	01	11
D	10	00	01

(b)

Figure 9.18 Equivalent state assigments for a sequential circuit. **(a)** State table. **(b)** State assignments.

For assignment 1 of Fig. 9.18b, the following excitation equations can be derived.

$$D_1 = y_1 \bar{x} + y_2 x$$
$$D_2 = y_1 \bar{x} + \bar{y}_1 x$$

We may derive another state assignment by complementing a given bit position to get a new state assignment. State assignment 2 of Fig. 9.18b is derived from assignment 1 by complementing the y_1 values. The resulting excitation equations are

$$D_1 = y_1 \bar{x} + \bar{y}_2 x$$
$$D_2 = \bar{y}_1 \bar{x} + y_1 x$$

These equations may be derived from the previous ones by simply complementing y_1 and D_1. The new logic equations are no better than the old ones, since both true and complemented variables are available from most flip-flop devices.

Now suppose we swap columns y_1 and y_2 of assignment 1 to get assignment 3 of Fig. 9.18b. The following excitation equations result:

$$D_1 = y_2\bar{x} + \bar{y}_2x$$
$$D_2 = y_2\bar{x} + y_1x$$

These can be derived from those of assignment 1 by simply swapping variables y_1 and y_2 in the equations. The cost of the logic needed to realize these equations is still essentially unchanged. Therefore, creating a new state assignment by simply complementing state variables or swapping state variables will not simplify the circuit.

For sequential circuits with only two states, there is really only one choice of state assignment. For three or four states the 24 possible assignments reduce to just 3 unique ones; see Table 9.2. Therefore, it is possible to synthesize the sequential circuit using all three assignments and to choose the best one. The number of possible unique state assignments N_{UA} for a sequential circuit with N_S states is given by

$$N_{UA} = \frac{(2^{N_{FF}} - 1)!}{(2^{N_{FF}} - N_S)!N_{FF}!}$$

Several cases for this expression are shown in Table 9.1. For more than four states, complete enumeration is impractical, so techniques for choosing a good assignment are necessary.

9.4.2 State Assignment Guidelines

Our approach to developing a set of state assignment guidelines is to find several rules that will yield a state assignment that reduces the complexity of the next-state equations for the implementation of a reduced state table. The state assignment problem for this case is to select a state coding that forces large groupings of the logic ones on the binary transition table, or transition K-map. The larger the groups of ones, the more the excitation and output equations can be simplified and the less complex the combinational circuitry becomes. Notice that next-state logic minimization suggests the use of D flip-flops, since excitation input D_i is equal to next state Y_i for each flip-flop.

TABLE 9.2   **UNIQUE STATE ASSIGNMENTS.**

	Assignments		
	1	**2**	**3**
States	y_1y_2	y_1y_2	y_1y_2
A	00	00	00
B	01	11	10
C	11	01	01
D	10	10	11

	x	
	0	1
A	C/0	D/0
B	C/0	A/0
C	B/0	D/0
D	A/1	B/1

Figure 9.19
A four-state
machine.

A Simple Example

To gain insight into finding a good assignment, let us examine an example four-state machine synthesized using all three of its unique state assignments, as listed in Table 9.2. Consider the state table of Fig. 9.19. First let us realize this reduced circuit using assignment 1 and D flip-flops. Substituting assignment 1 into Fig. 9.19 yields the transition table of Fig 9.20a, which may be rearranged into K-maps for z, D_2, and D_1, as displayed in Figs. 9.20b, c, and d. Hence, the logic equations for this assignment are as follows:

Assignment 1.
$$D_2 = \bar{y}_1\bar{y}_2 + \bar{x}\bar{y}_2 + xy_1y_2$$
$$D_1 = \bar{x}\bar{y}_2 + \bar{x}y_1 + x\bar{y}_1y_2$$
$$z = \bar{y}_1y_2$$

Figures 9.21 and 9.22 illustrate the same procedures for assignments 2 and 3. The resulting Boolean switching functions are as follows:

Assignment 2.
$$D_2 = x\bar{y}_1 + y_1\bar{y}_2$$
$$D_1 = \bar{x}\bar{y}_2 + \bar{x}y_1 + x\bar{y}_1y_2$$
$$z = \bar{y}_1y_2$$

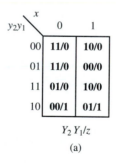

y_2y_1	x	
	0	1
00	11/0	10/0
01	11/0	00/0
11	01/0	10/0
10	00/1	01/1

$Y_2\,Y_1/z$

(a)

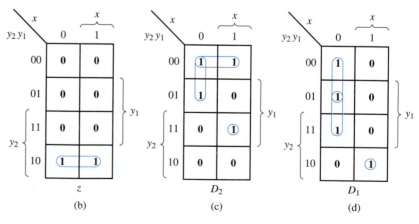

Figure 9.20   D flip-flop realization for assignment 1. **(a)** Transition table. **(b)** K-map for z. **(c)** K-map for D_2. **(d)** K-map for D_1.

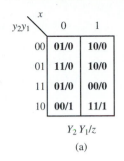

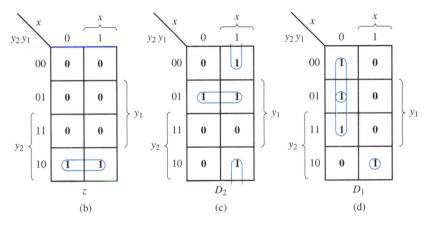

Figure 9.21   D flip-flop realization for assignment 2. **(a)** Transition table. **(b)** K-map for z. **(c)** K-map for D_2. **(d)** K-map for D_1.

Assignment 3.
$$D_2 = y_1\bar{y}_2 + x\bar{y}_2 + xy_1$$
$$D_1 = x\bar{y}_2 + \bar{x}\bar{y}_1$$
$$z = y_1 y_2$$

Now let us examine the results. If we specify a two-level sum of products logic implementation and count the number of inputs to gates, assignment 1 requires 20; assignment 2, 18; and assignment 3, 15. Assignment 3 gives the best results, but why? Aassignment 3 gives a better grouping of ones and zeros on the K-maps for D_1, D_2, and z.

State Assignment Rules

There are two ways to rearrange the ones on a K-map: vertically, by making the ones combine within a given column, and horizontally, by making the ones combine within a given row. If we assume that each row represents the next-state entries for a given present state and that the columns represent different input conditions, then optimal groupings of ones can be obtained by adopting the following general state assignment rules.

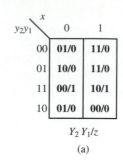

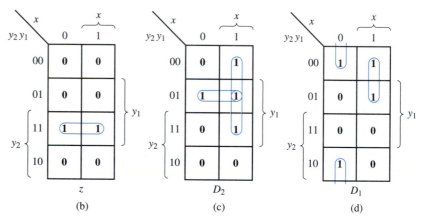

Figure 9.22 D flip-flop realization for assignment 3. **(a)** Transition table. **(b)** K-map for z. **(c)** K-map for D_2. **(d)** K-map for D_1.

Rule 1. States that have the same next states for a given input should be given logically adjacent assignments.

Rule 2. States that are the next states of a single present state, under logically adjacent inputs, should be given logically adjacent assignments.

Rule 1 forces ones to be grouped within a given column, while rule 2 forces ones to be grouped within a given row. Both of these rules may be applied by inspection of the reduced state table. This is illustrated by the following example.

EXAMPLE 9.17

Let us apply the preceding rules to the example of Fig. 9.19.

Rule 1: States A and B should be adjacent because they both go to state C under input 0; we denote this by A adj B. Also, A adj C is indicated.

Rule 2: Yields A adj B, A adj C, B adj D, and C adj D.

We may compare the adjacencies of states for the three assignments by plotting the states on *state assignment K-maps*, as shown in Fig. 9.23, with each cell representing the state variable combination assigned to one state of the circuit. Adjacent states are identified on these maps in the same manner as adjacent implicants or implicates on standard K-maps. From the K-maps of Fig. 9.23, it can be seen that assignment 3 fulfills all four adjacencies indicated by rules 1 and 2 and hence should produce the best results for this example.

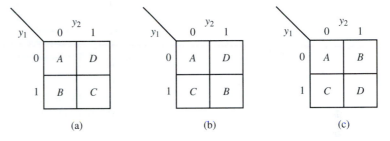

Figure 9.23   State adjacencies for four-state assignments. **(a)** Assignment 1. **(b)** Assignment 2. **(c)** Assignment 3.

In general, we are not always able to satisfy all the adjacencies suggested by rules 1 and 2. We do, however, try to satisfy as many as possible. In the event of conflicts, we resolve them in favor of rule 1 to achieve better groupings of ones within the columns.

Implication Graph

Another tool that aids the logic designer in selecting good state assignments is the implication graph. The *implication graph* for a sequential circuit is a flow graph whose nodes represent pairs of states. The nodes are connected by arcs, each of which represents state transitions between two pairs of states for a given input, as specified by the state table of the sequential circuit.

EXAMPLE 9.18

Let us derive an implication graph for the sequential circuit of Fig. 9.24a.

The implication graph for this circuit is shown in Fig. 9.24b.

An implication graph greatly resembles the implication table presented earlier and contains much of the same information; however, here it is displayed in a graphical form. The implication graph is constructed by first choosing a pair of states, say BD in the example, and finding its implied next-state pair under each input; the implied pairs are entered as new nodes on the graph. No entry is made on the graph if the pair of states has the same next state. For example, states B and D both go to state D under an input of 0 and to states A and B under an input of 1. Consequently, a state pair transition is indicated

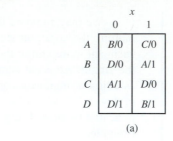

(a)

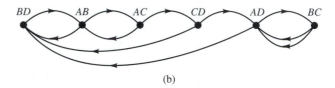

(b)

Figure 9.24 A four-state machine. **(a)** State table.
(b) Implication graph.

from BD to AB for the input $x = 1$, but no entry is made for $x = 0$. Now the procedure is repeated for each new implied pair until no new implied pairs can be generated.

An implication graph is said to be *complete* if it contains all possible pairs of states of a given sequential circuit. Normally, we deal with a partially complete implication graph. A *subgraph* is defined as part of a complete graph.

One particular type of subgraph is important for state assignment, the *closed* subgraph. A subgraph is *closed* if all outgoing arcs for each node within the subgraph terminate on nodes completely contained within the subgraph and if every state of the sequential circuit is represented by at least one node within the subgraph.

EXAMPLE 9.19

Two closed subgraphs for the sequential circuit of Fig. 9.25a are demonstrated in Fig. 9.25b. Notice that arcs may *enter* a closed subgraph from the exterior, but none may originate within the closed subgraph and exit.

The implication graph may be used in state assignment selection in the following manner. After we have applied rules 1 and 2 to a reduced state table, we have several suggested adjacencies. We may choose some of these to be implemented in a state assignment. Once we have made two states logically adjacent , it is possible to rearrange the state table so that the two states are physically adjacent. Considering these two adjacent states as present states of the sequential circuit, it is desirable to make their next-state pairs adjacent

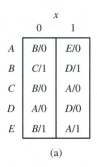

| | x | |
	0	1
A	B/0	E/0
B	C/1	D/1
C	B/0	A/0
D	A/0	D/0
E	B/1	A/1

(a)

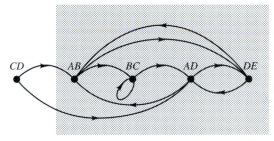

Closed subgraph

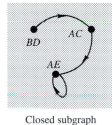

Closed subgraph

(b)

Figure 9.25   Closed subgraphs. **(a)** State table.
(b) Implication graph.

in order to provide larger groupings of ones on the transition table. The next example illustrates this point.

EXAMPLE 9.20

Let us use the implication graph of Fig. 9.24b to derive an optimal state assignment for the sequential circuit of Fig. 9.24a.

The application of rules 1 and 2 to the state table yields

> **Rule 1.** *B* adj *D*.
> **Rule 2.** *B* adj *C*, *D* adj *A*, *A* adj *D*, *D* adj *B*.

The adjacency *B* adj *D* is the most important one. If we make state *B* adjacent to state *D*, it is desirable to make *A* adj *B* as indicated by the implication graph. The adjacency was not suggested by either rule 1 or 2. In fact, the implication graph also suggests *A* adj *C* adj *D*. These adjacencies correspond to unique assignment 3 of Fig. 9.23c. The transition table for this assignment is produced in Fig. 9.26. The resulting excitation and output switching functions are

$$D_2 = \bar{x}y_2 + \bar{x}\bar{y}_1 + xy_1$$
$$D_1 = \bar{x}y_2 + x\bar{y}_2$$
$$z = xy_2 + \bar{x}y_1$$

These switching functions are optimal for this sequential circuit. The key to success in making the proper state assignment was the advent of A adj B by the implication graph. If we had ignored the graph entirely and made our assignment based entirely on rules 1 and 2, we would have arrived at assignment 2, and the realization would have been

$$D_2 = xy_1\bar{y}_2 + \bar{x}\bar{y}_1 + \bar{x}y_2 + \bar{y}_1 y_2$$
$$D_1 = \bar{y}_1\bar{y}_2 + x\bar{y}_1$$
$$z = xy_2 + \bar{y}_1 y_2 + \bar{x}y_1\bar{y}_2$$

which is not optimal.

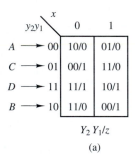

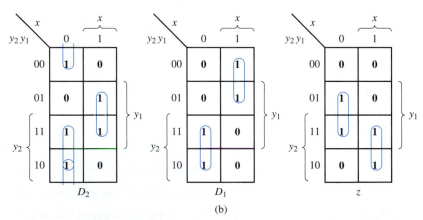

Figure 9.26 Example state assignment. **(a)** Transition table. **(b)** K-maps.

Example 9.20 illustrates the concept of establishing a *chain* of adjacency pairs. The chain is established by assigning adjacent pairs of states in accordance with the transition arcs of the implication graph. The ideal chains are those established by a closed subgraph. If a closed subgraph cannot be established, try to include a contiguous subgraph that contains a large number of transition arcs.

We shall now incorporate the implication graph into our state assignment guidelines by the following rule.

> **Rule 3.** Use the adjacencies suggested by rules 1 and 2 to construct a partially complete implication graph for the reduced state table. Then try to establish a chain of adjacency pairs on a closed or contiguous subgraph.

In applying rules 1, 2, and 3, let us emphasize that rules 1 and 3 are more important than rule 2.

The last state assignment guideline to be discussed is concerned with the mechanics of making the actual code choices. Generally, we try to minimize the total number of logic ones on the K-maps and to maximize the number of don't-cares. The following rule helps accomplish this goal:

> **Rule 4.** Search the next-state portion of the reduced state table for the "most transferred to" state. Assign it the all-logic-0 code by placing it on an assignment K-map in the block for minterm 0. Begin assigning other states according to the suggested adjacencies of rules 1, 2, and 3, saving the minterm blocks with the largest numbers of logic ones in their binary code for last. Satisfy as many of the suggested adjacencies as possible.

This completes the presentation of the state assignment guidelines. The procedure is now illustrated by a complete example.

EXAMPLE 9.21

Find a D flip-flop realization for the sequential circuit of Fig. 9.27a.

> **Rule 1.** A adj C, B adj D, A adj D.
>
> **Rule 2.** A adj D, B adj E, A adj B, C adj D.
>
> **Rule 3.** From rules 1 and 2 we plot the implication graph of Fig. 9.27b and identify two closed subgraphs, one containing A adj D, A adj E, B adj C, D adj E and the second containing only B adj D. Note that pair CE has been added to make the graph complete, that is, to show all pairs of states. For larger examples, generating a complete graph can make the graph too complex for hand evaluation. In such cases we would limit the graphs to only those nodes generated using rules 1 and 2.
>
> **Rule 4.** The state assignment K-map is given in Fig. 9.27c.

From this state assignment the following switching functions are generated as shown in Fig. 9.28:

$$D_3 = x\bar{y}_3$$
$$D_2 = x\bar{y}_3\bar{y}_1 + xy_2 + \bar{x}y_1$$
$$D_1 = \bar{x}\bar{y}_2\bar{y}_1$$
$$z = xy_2 + y_3y_2$$

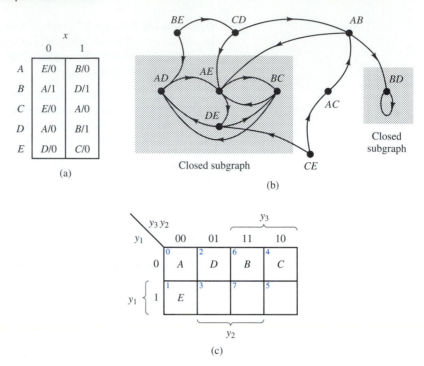

	x	
	0	1
A	$E/0$	$B/0$
B	$A/1$	$D/1$
C	$E/0$	$A/0$
D	$A/0$	$B/1$
E	$D/0$	$C/0$

(a)

(b)

(c)

Figure 9.27   State assignment procedure. **(a)** State table. **(b)** Closed subgraphs. **(c)** State assignment.

Output Logic

A word about the output equations is in order. In our state assignment procedure we have completely ignored any consideration of minimizing the output logic. If the number of Boolean next-state equations is much larger than the number of output equations, then apply the rules as stated to the next states and accept the results of the output equations. However, if the output equations are a significant part of the implementation logic, rules 1 and 2 are equally applicable for output logic minimization. In this text, however, we restrict ourselves to next-state analysis.

9.4.3 Partitioning

Recall that a *partition*, say P_i, on the set of states for a sequential machine is a collection of disjoint subsets, called *blocks* B_{ij}, that contain all the states of the machine. The process of making a state assignment for the sequential machine is equivalent to forcing a series of partitions with two blocks, called *two-block partitions*, on the set of states, one partition for each memory flip-flop.

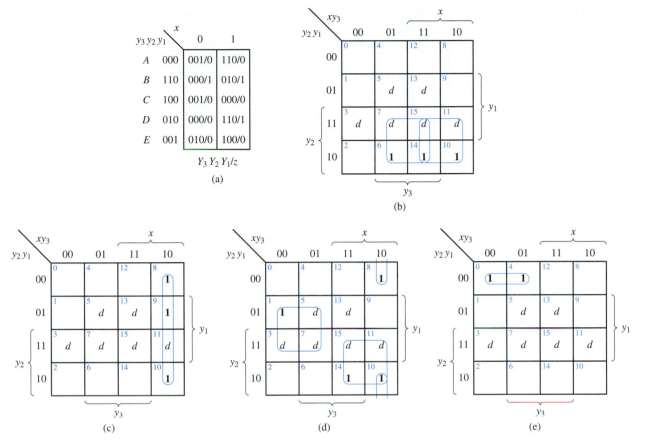

Figure 9.28   D flip-flop realization. **(a)** Transition table. **(b)** K-map for z. **(c)** K-map for D_3. **(d)** K-map for D_2. **(e)** K-map for D_1.

EXAMPLE 9.22

Find the two-block partitions forced on the sequential machine of Fig. 9.27a by the assignment of Fig. 9.27c.

The assigned code is

	y_3	y_2	y_1
A:	0	0	0
B:	1	1	0
C:	1	0	0
D:	0	1	0
E:	0	0	1

Each bit column of the assignment separates the states into two blocks, or subsets, those associated with logic 0 and those associated with logic 1.

$$
y_3 \rightarrow P_3 : \quad
\begin{array}{cc}
B_{31} & B_{32} \\
\hline
(ADE) & (BC)
\end{array}
$$

$$
y_2 \rightarrow P_2 : \quad
\begin{array}{cc}
B_{21} & B_{22} \\
\hline
(ACE) & (BD)
\end{array}
$$

$$
y_1 \rightarrow P_1 : \quad
\begin{array}{cc}
B_{11} & B_{12} \\
\hline
(ABCD) & (E)
\end{array}
$$

Closed Partitions

A partition on the set of states of a sequential machine is *closed* if and only if, for any block in the partition, all specified next states under each input fall into a single block of the partition.

EXAMPLE 9.23

Verify that P_3 is a closed partition for the sequential machine of Fig. 9.27a.

If we examine the next-state behavior of the blocks of partition P_3, we can observe

	Input		
Present Block	0	1	
B_{31}	B_{31}	B_{32}	Next
B_{32}	B_{31}	B_{31}	Block

The next states of the blocks of P_3 are also contained in blocks of P_3. Hence, partition P_3 is closed.

The presence of closed partitions on the states of a sequential machine can greatly reduce the dependence of next-state equations Y_i ($i = 1 \ldots r$) on the present-state variables y_i ($i = 1 \ldots r$). If a closed partition has two blocks, one of the state variables y_j can be used to code the blocks; that is, we can assign $y_j = 0$ for all the states in one of the blocks and $y_j = 1$ for all the states in the other block; this variable is called a *block bit*. The presence of the closed partition results in next-state variable Y_j being dependent only on the block bit y_j and the circuit inputs; that is,

$$
Y_j = h_j(x_1, x_2, \ldots, x_n, y_j)
$$

This is exemplified by deriving the next-state equation for Y_3 for the state assignment of Fig. 9.27c:

$$
Y_3 = x \bar{y}_3
$$

Closed partitions may be generated by using an implication graph. We begin by assuming that two states S_i and S_j are in the same partition block. By the definition of a closed partition, the implied next-state pairs of $S_i S_j$ must also lie together in some block of the closed partition. The implied pairs are then combined into disjoint blocks using the properties of equivalence relations.

EXAMPLE 9.24

Find a closed partition for the state table of Fig. 9.29a.

If states AB are chosen as a starting point, the partial implication subgraph of Fig. 9.29b is generated. The implied pairs are

$$(AB), (BC), (AC) \rightarrow (ABC)$$
$$(DE), (EF), (DF) \rightarrow (DEF)$$

Hence,

$$P_1 = (ABC)(DEF)$$

is a closed partition for the sequential machine.

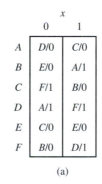

	0	1
A	D/0	C/0
B	E/0	A/1
C	F/1	B/0
D	A/1	F/1
E	C/0	E/0
F	B/0	D/1

(a)

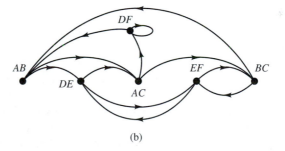

(b)

Figure 9.29 Closed partitions. **(a)** State table. **(b)** Partial implication graph.

The closed partition describes a property that exists in certain machines. If the closed partition has two blocks and the state assignment codes these blocks with a block bit, reduced next-state logic equations are obtained. Rule 3 of the state assignment procedure helps the logic designer find state assignments that correspond to closed partitions without requiring that the partitions themselves be generated.

Partition pairs

A second type of reduced dependency, called *cross dependency*, is exhibited by some sequential machines. These machines rely on pairs of partitions that are not necessarily closed. State transitions of sequential machines with cross dependency are described by block transitions between pairs of partitions, as is illustrated by the next example.

EXAMPLE 9.25

The sequential machine of Fig. 9.17 exhibits cross dependency under the minimal assignment

	y_3	y_2	y_1
A:	0	0	0
B:	0	0	1
C:	0	1	1
D:	0	1	0
E:	1	0	1
F:	1	1	0
G:	1	1	1

The two-block partitions for the assignment are

	B_{11}	B_{12}
P_1 :	$(ABCD)$	(EFG)

	B_{21}	B_{22}
P_2 :	(ABE)	$(CDFG)$

	B_{31}	B_{32}
P_3 :	(ADF)	$(BCEG)$

Close examination of the block behavior reveals the block transition table and diagram of Fig. 9.30.

The partitions P_2 and P_3 are not closed, but as a pair they exhibit reduced dependency, as shown by the following D flip-flop implementation:

$$D_1 = x\bar{y}_1 y_3 + \bar{x} y_1 y_3 + x\bar{y}_1 \bar{y}_2$$
$$\left.\begin{array}{l} D_2 = y_3 \\ D_3 = \bar{y}_2 \end{array}\right\} \text{cross dependency}$$
$$z = xy_1 \bar{y}_3 + \bar{x}\bar{y}_1 y_2 \bar{y}_3$$

The generation of partition pairs is beyond the scope of this text; the interested reader is referred to the references listed at the end of the chapter. Rule 3 of the state assignment procedure presented earlier helps the logic designer find cross-dependent assignments when they exist. Although the state assignment guidelines are not optimal, they can produce good state assignments even for machines with reduced dependency.

It is important for the reader to note that cross dependency, which is based on a pair of partitions, is a generalization of reduced dependency, which

Present block	Input	
	0	1
P_2: B_{21}	B_{32}	B_{32}
B_{22}	B_{31}	B_{31}
P_3: B_{31}	B_{21}	B_{21}
B_{32}	B_{22}	B_{22}

(a)

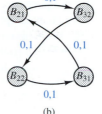

(b)

Figure 9.30 Cross dependency. **(a)** Block transition table. **(b)** Block transition diagram.

is based on a single closed partition. Reduced dependency can be considered to be a special case of cross dependency in which the pair of partitions is formed by using one closed partition twice.

9.4.4 Optimal State Assignments

Numerous authors have proposed procedures for obtaining "good" of "near-optimal" state assignments, and several claim that their procedures yield "optimal" assignments under some stated criteria of optimality. Several common optimality criteria are listed next:

1. Minimal gate and/or inputs-to-gates circuit

2. Minimal cost circuit

3. Circuit with reduced dependency

4. Criteria 1 to 3 for a specified flip-flop type

Several of the better methods for producing near-optimal assignments for D flip-flops are those developed by Dolotta and McClusky [9], Weiner and Smith [10], and Torng [11]. These methods search for reduced dependency in the specified state table for a sequential machine.

To this point we have examined only the case for D flip-flops. What happens if we want to use another type? In general, a *good* state assignment for D flip-flops will also be a *good* assignment for other flip-flop types. However, Curtis [12] has shown that an assignment that is optimal or near-optimal for one flip-flop type may be far from optimal for another. Curtis has extended the methods of Dolotta and McClusky and Weiner and Smith to provide near-optimal state assignments for specific flip-flop types or combinations of flip-flops of different types within one sequential machine realization.

To produce optimal assignments, the computational complexity of the proposed state assignment algorithms require the use of a general-purpose digital computer. Story et al. [13] and Haring [14] have developed such optimal algorithms. Story et al. find an optimal state assignment for clocked JK flip-flops.

For most applications an optimal or near-optimal solution for the state assignment problem is not required; a good assignment is adequate for most cases. However, in cases for which an optimal assignment is essential, the logic designer is referred to the open literature for state assignment algorithms that guarantee optimality.

This completes our presentation of the state assignment problem. We have tried to formulate some general guidelines to aid the designer in choosing a state assignment for a given sequential machine. Our guidelines do not guarantee a minimum logic realization. They do, however, generally give much better results than a completely arbitrary choice, as was made earlier in the text.

9.5 Summary

In this chapter we have presented synthesis procedures to realize both completely and incompletely specified synchronous sequential logic circuits. State reduction by inspection, partitioning, and the implication table was demonstrated. The concepts of state equivalence for completely specified circuits and state compatibility for incompletely specified circuits were contrasted. Flip-flop input tables and the generation of excitation maps received attention, as did the state assignment problem. Many design examples were completed to illustrate the synthesis techniques. The reader should now have a good grasp of the synchronous sequential circuit synthesis problem. For more detailed information on the synthesis problem, the reader is encouraged to pursue further reading from the selected references presented next. In addition, computer-aided methods are described in Downs and Schulz [15] and are implemented in a variety of CAD systems, such as Roth's *Logic Aid* [16].

REFERENCES

1. E. J. MCCLUSKEY, *Introduction to the Theory of Switching Circuits.* New York: McGraw-Hill Book Co., 1965.

2. ZVI KOHAVI, *Switching and Finite Automata Theory.* New York: McGraw-Hill Book Co., 1970.

3. TAYLOR L. BOOTH, *Digital Networks and Computer Systems.* New York: Wiley, 1971.

4. J. HARTMANIS, "On the State Assignment Problem for Sequential Machines I," *IRE Trans. Electronic Computers*, June 1961, pp. 157–165.

5. R. E. STEARNS AND J. HARTMANIS, "On the State Assignment Problem for Sequential Machines II," *IRE Trans. Electronic Computers*, December 1961, pp. 593–603.

6. M. C. PAULL AND S. H. UNGER, "Minimizing the Number of States in Incompletely Specified Sequential Switching Functions," *IRE Trans. Electronic Computers*, EC-8, No. 3, September 1959, pp. 356–357.

7. E. J. MCCLUSKEY AND S. H. UNGER, "A Note on the Number of Internal Variable Assignments for Sequential Switching Circuits," *IRE Trans. Electronic Computers*, EC-8, No. 4, December 1959, pp. 439–440.

8. R. M. KARP, "Some Techniques of State Assignment for Synchronous Sequential Machines," *IEEE Trans. Electronic Computers*, EC-13, No. 5, October 1964, pp. 507–518.

9.   T. A. DOLOTTA AND E. J. MCCLUSKEY, "The Coding of Internal States of Sequential Circuits," *IEEE Trans. Electronic Computers*, EC-13, No. 5, October 1964, pp. 549–562.

10.   P. WEINER AND E. J. SMITH, "Optimization of Reduced Dependences for Synchronous Sequential Machines," *IEEE Trans. Electronic Computers*, EC-16, No. 6, December 1967, pp. 835–847.

11.   H. C. TORNG, "An Algorithm for Finding Secondary Assignments of Synchronous Sequential Circuits," *IEEE Trans. Computers*, C-17, No. 5, May 1968, pp. 461–469.

12.   H. A. CURTIS, "Systematic Procedures for Realizing Synchronous Sequential Machines Using Flip-flop Memory: Part I," *IEEE Trans. Computers*, C-18, No. 12, December 1969, pp. 1121–1127.

13.   J. R. STORY, H. J. HARRISON, AND E. A. REINHARD, "Optimum State Assignment for Synchronous Sequential Circuits," *IEEE Trans. Computers*, C-21, No. 12, December 1972, pp. 1365–1373.

14.   D. R. HARING, *Sequential Circuit Synthesis: State Assignment Aspects*, M.I.T. Research Monograph No. 31. Cambridge, MA: The M.I.T. Press, 1966.

15.   T. DOWNS AND M. F. SCHULZ, *Logic Design with Pascal— Computer-aided Design Techniques*. New York: Van Nostrand Reinhold. 1988.

16.   C. H. ROTH JR., *User's Guide and Reference Manual for LogicAid*. St. Paul, MN: West Publishing Co., 1992.

PROBLEMS

9.1 Find a minimized state table for the following synchronous sequential circuit by

(a) Inspection.   (c) Implication table.

(b) Partitioning.

	I	J
A	B/0	A/1
B	C/0	A/0
C	C/0	B/0
D	E/0	D/1
E	C/0	D/0

9.2 Reduce the following state tables by inspection:

(a)

	I	J
A	B/1	C/0
B	A/1	C/0
C	D/1	A/0
D	C/1	A/1

(b)

	I	J
A	A/0	E/1
B	E/1	C/0
C	A/1	D/1
D	F/0	G/1
E	B/1	C/0
F	F/0	E/1
G	A/1	D/1

(c)

	I	J	K
A	A/0	B/1	E/1
B	B/0	A/1	F/1
C	A/1	D/0	E/0
D	F/0	C/1	A/0
E	A/0	D/1	E/1
F	B/0	D/1	F/1

9.3   Reduce the state tables of Problem 9.2 by partitioning.

9.4   Reduce the state tables of Problem 9.2 using implication tables.

9.5   Find a reduced state table for the following synchronous sequential circuit:

	I	J
A	B/0	C/0
B	D/0	E/0
C	F/0	G/0
D	A/1	B/1
E	C/0	D/0
F	F/0	G/0
G	B/0	F/0

9.6   Using an implication table, reduce the following sequential circuit to a minimum number of states:

	I	J
A	A/0	C/0
B	D/1	A/0
C	F/0	F/0
D	E/1	B/0
E	G/1	G/0
F	C/0	C/0
G	B/1	H/0
H	H/0	C/0

9.7   Reduce the number of states of the following sequential circuit:
(a) By partitioning.   (b) Using an implication table.

	I	J	K
A	D/1	C/0	E/1
B	D/0	E/0	C/1
C	A/0	E/0	B/1
D	A/1	B/0	E/1
E	A/1	C/0	B/1

9.8   Find a clocked D flip-flop realization for the following sequential circuit using each of the three unique assignments for four-state circuits:

	x	
	0	1
A	B/0	D/0
B	C/0	A/0
C	D/0	A/0
D	B/1	C/1

9.9 For the following state table, find circuit implementations with each of the three unique state assignments for four-state circuits and memory elements of:

(a) Clocked T flip-flops.   (c) Clocked SR flip-flops.

(b) Clocked JK flip-flops.

	x	
	0	1
A	C/0	D/0
B	C/0	A/0
C	B/0	D/0
D	A/1	B/1

9.10 Derive the logic equations to implement the four-state sequential circuit defined by the following state table, using the given state assignment and:

(a) D flip-flops.   (c) Clocked SR flip-flops.

(b) Clocked JK flip-flops.   (d) Clocked T flip-flops.

y_1	y_2		x	
			0	1
0	0	A	B/0	C/0
0	1	B	D/0	A/1
1	1	C	A/1	D/0
1	0	D	D/1	B/1

9.11 Find a state assignment for the following synchronous sequential circuit using the state assignment procedure presented in this chapter.

	x	
	0	1
A	B/0	E/0
B	D/0	A/1
C	D/1	A/0
D	B/1	C/1
E	A/0	A/0

9.12 Find a state assignment for the following sequential circuit. Choose the assignment for state A to be $y_3 = y_2 = y_1 = 0$.

	x	
	0	1
A	B/0	E/0
B	A/1	C/1
C	B/0	C/1
D	C/0	E/0
E	D/1	A/0

9.13 Find a state assignment for the following circuit:

	x	
	0	1
A	B/0	D/1
B	A/1	C/0
C	D/0	A/0
D	C/1	B/1

10

Many applications require the use of sequential circuits that are not synchronized in any way with a clock signal. These circuits are referred to as asynchronous sequential circuits. Asynchronous circuits require special attention since there is no clock signal to provide common timing information to the circuit elements. Hence, asynchronous circuits respond immediately to any change of input, rather than responding to the inputs present during a clock pulse. The absence of a clock signal also means that memory element transitions must be initiated by some other means. Therefore, precautions must be taken to avoid timing problems. The various facets and ramifications of asynchronous sequential circuit design will be discussed in this chapter.

Asynchronous Sequential Circuits

10.1 Types of Asynchronous Circuits

The first class of asynchronous circuits we will examine is *pulse-mode circuits*. These circuits have pulse inputs and unclocked memory elements. Flip-flops are commonly used for the memory in such circuits. Hence, the model shown in Fig. 10.1 will be adopted as the pulse-mode circuit model. Notice the close resemblance to the general sequential circuit model given in Chapter 6. However, restrictions are placed on pulse-mode circuits that make them significantly different from the circuits studied in Chapter 8. The following assumptions are made in the analysis and synthesis of pulse-mode asynchronous sequential circuits.

1. Pulses will not occur simultaneously on two or more input lines.
2. Memory element transitions are initiated only by input pulses.
3. Input variables are used only in the uncomplemented or the complemented forms, but not both.

The first assumption is a very practical one in that the probability of two pulses occurring at exactly the same time is small. This assumption is needed since a clock is not utilized to synchronize state changes. In a real-world situation, if we tried to apply two input pulses to a circuit at the same time,

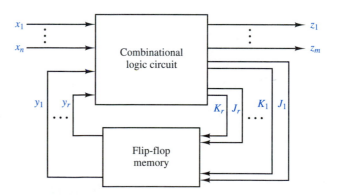

Figure 10.1 Pulse-mode circuit model.

say on input lines x_1 and x_2, one pulse would arrive before the other, and the performance of the circuit would be different depending on which pulse arrived first. Hence, the operation of the circuit would depend on parasitic resistance and capacitance values in the hardware. This is not acceptable for good design practice, and therefore we do not allow designs that permit coincident input pulses. In addition, input pulses should be spaced in time by at least the response time of the slowest memory element. This means that no memory element will be in the process of changing state when a new input pulse occurs. Hence, the behavior of the circuit will always be predictable.

Now consider the information provided by the input pulses to the circuit. It can be argued that since these pulses may occur asynchronously, or, in other words, at random unknown times, no information is provided to the device except when a pulse occurs. Hence, only the uncomplemented form of input pulses is used in the logic realizations of pulse-mode circuits.

The second class of asynchronous sequential circuits we will examine is *fundamental-mode circuits*. These circuits have level inputs and unclocked memory elements. Figure 10.2 shows the model of a fundamental-mode circuit. The memory elements are shown as delay lines in the model. However, in practice, the use of a physical delay line is often unnecessary, because sufficient delay is present in the other logic circuit elements. For this presentation, assume that all delays in the circuit can be lumped into the delay elements shown in the feedback paths. Also assume that each delay element has the same amount of delay Δt. These last two assumptions cannot always be justified in practice and will be removed at a later point in the chapter.

For fundamental-mode operation, inputs are restricted so that only one input variable is allowed to change value at a given instant of time. This restriction, which is similar to that required in pulse-mode circuits, exists since in practical situations two or more inputs are not likely to change value at precisely the same time. Hence, the second and succeeding changes could occur while the circuit is still responding to the first input change, in which case incorrect behavior of the circuit would be possible. A similar situation would exist if the time between

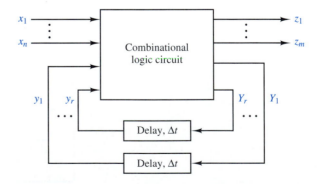

Figure 10.2 Fundamental-mode circuit model.

two input changes is too small. For predictable operation of fundamental-mode circuits, input changes should be spaced in time by at least Δt, the time needed for the circuit to settle into a stable state following an input change.

10.2 Analysis of Pulse-mode Asynchronous Circuits

In the analysis of pulse-mode asynchronous sequential circuits, it is important to recall that these circuits respond immediately to pulses on their inputs, rather than waiting for a clock signal, as in synchronous sequential circuits. The absence of a clock signal also means that memory element transitions must be initiated by some other means. Therefore, precautions must be taken to avoid timing problems by paying close attention to and understanding the significance of the three assumptions regarding pulse-mode operation presented in the previous section.

The first assumption, that pulses do not occur simultaneously on two or more input lines, means that a circuit with n input lines has only $n + 1$ input conditions, rather than 2^n, as is the case for synchronous circuits. Assumption 2 implies that a state transition can occur only if an input pulse occurs. Hence, the memory elements of the circuit respond only when an input pulse arrives. The third assumption guarantees that all devices trigger on the same edge of each pulse. It is important to keep these assumptions in mind while studying the examples that follow.

EXAMPLE 10.1

Let us examine the behavior of the pulsed asynchronous circuit shown in Fig. 10.3.

The analysis of this circuit proceeds in much the same fashion as the analysis of a synchronous circuit. The major differences are due to the absence of a clock signal and the assumptions listed previously.

The circuit has the following states and inputs:

$$\text{States:} \quad [y] = 0 \equiv A$$
$$[y] = 1 \equiv B$$

$$\text{Inputs:} \quad [x_1, x_2] = 00 \equiv I_0$$
$$[x_1, x_2] = 10 \equiv I_1$$
$$[x_1, x_2] = 01 \equiv I_2$$

Figure 10.4 shows a timing diagram for the circuit for a typical input sequence. Note that all state transitions correspond to the occurrence of an input pulse. On the leading edge of the input pulse, the S and R signals are activated. The flip-flop responds to its S and R inputs in τ seconds. The changing flip-flop output y then deactivates the S and R signals, and the circuit then waits for another input pulse on x_1 or x_2.

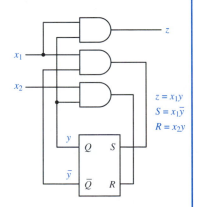

$z = x_1 y$
$S = x_1 \bar{y}$
$R = x_2 y$

Figure 10.3   A pulsed asynchronous sequential circuit.

The state table shown in Fig. 10.5a can be constructed from the timing diagram in Fig. 10.4. A symbolic state table is shown in Fig. 10.5b, with the three combinations of x_1x_2 designated as input conditions I_0, I_1, and I_2. Note that there is no column for the condition $x_1 = x_2 = 1$, since it has been assumed that simultaneous pulses cannot occur on multiple inputs.

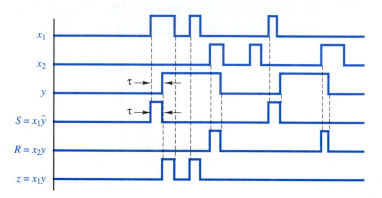

Figure 10.4   Timing diagram for example circuit.

A simplified state table is given in Fig. 10.5c. This table is obtained from the symbolic table using the following steps.

1. Eliminate the I_0 column, corresponding to input condition $x_1 = x_2 = 0$. Since no state change can occur when there is no pulse on either input, this column provides no significant information.

2. Interchange the I_2 and I_1 columns and replace the symbols I_1 with x_1 and I_2 with x_2, indicating pulses on x_1 and x_2, respectively.

The simplified state table completely describes the circuit behavior.

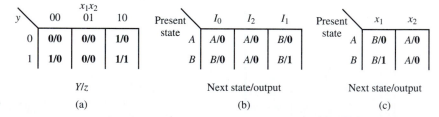

y	x_1x_2 00	01	10
0	0/0	0/0	1/0
1	1/0	0/0	1/1

Y/z

(a)

Present state	I_0	I_2	I_1
A	A/0	A/0	B/0
B	B/0	A/0	B/1

Next state/output

(b)

Present state	x_1	x_2
A	B/0	A/0
B	B/1	A/0

Next state/output

(c)

Figure 10.5   State tables for Example 10.1. **(a)** State table. **(b)** Symbolic state table. **(c)** Simplified state table.

A K-map development of the state table is given in Fig. 10.6. Since it is assumed that the input condition $x_1x_2 = 11$ will never occur, the corresponding K-map cells are left unspecified. The final step is accomplished by eliminating the 00 and 11 columns from the table and relabeling the 10 column as x_1 and the 01 column as x_2.

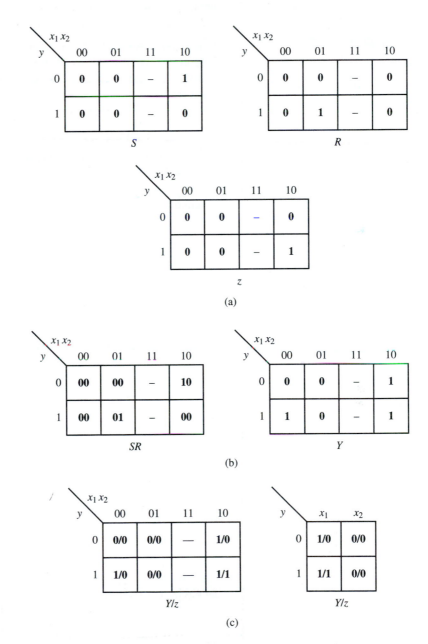

Figure 10.6   K-map development of state tables. **(a)** K-maps for the circuit. **(b)** Combined SR map and next-state (Y) map. **(c)** State tables.

Pulsed asynchronous circuits utilizing memory elements that are not edge triggered, that is, latches, are analyzed as shown in the preceding example. The analysis of a circuit that employs edge-triggered flip-flops will be considered next.

EXAMPLE 10.2

Consider the sequential circuit of Fig. 10.7. The analysis of this circuit will be completed using a timing diagram. The circuit is described by the logic equations

$$D_1 = \bar{y}_1, \quad D_2 = \bar{y}_1, \quad z = xy_1y_2$$
$$C_1 = xy_2, \quad C_2 = x$$

The timing diagram for the circuit has been constructed in Fig. 10.8. The input x is composed of asynchronous pulses, and the starting state of the circuit is $y_1 = y_2 = 0$. Notice that only three of the states of the circuit are shown on the diagram.

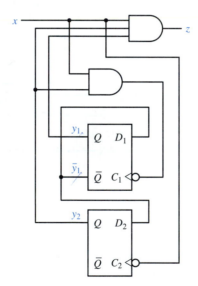

Figure 10.7   Pulsed sequential circuit with unclocked memory.

If the starting state had been $y_1 = 1$ and $y_2 = 0$, the sequential circuit would have been unable to change state because

$$D_1 = 0, \quad D_2 = 0,$$
$$C_1 = 0, \quad C_2 = x$$

The state variable y_2 would always stay at 0 and inhibit any state change in flip-flop output y_2.

A state table and diagram may be compiled for this circuit if we define the following:

Inputs: $I_0 \equiv$ no pulse on x
$I_1 \equiv$ pulse on x

States: $\overline{y_1 y_2}$
$A \equiv 00$
$B \equiv 01$
$C \equiv 10$
$D \equiv 11$

Outputs: $z = 0$
$z = 1$

The resulting state table and diagram are illustrated in Fig. 10.9. They are derived from the timing diagram in Fig. 10.8. Note that the state diagram has

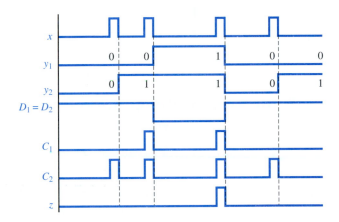

Figure 10.8   Timing diagram for Example 10.2.

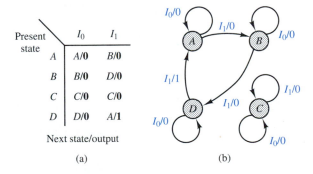

Present state	I_0	I_1
A	$A/0$	$B/0$
B	$B/0$	$D/0$
C	$C/0$	$C/0$
D	$D/0$	$A/1$

Next state/output

(a)

(b)

Figure 10.9   State table and diagram for Example 10.2.
(a) State table. **(b)** State diagram.

two separate parts and, as a result, if state C is the starting state, the sequential circuit is "hung" there. However, if state A, B, or D is the starting state, the circuit behaves as a typical sequential machine.

K-maps can be used for construction of the state table corresponding to the circuit of Fig. 10.7, using the D flip-flop characteristic equation, Eq. 6.12, and the following observation. The D flip-flop clock inputs will see a 1 to 0 transition only if an input pulse occurs. Hence, at most one such transition can occur for each input pulse.

The following equations are obtained by using Eq. 6.12 and the logic equations for the circuit in Fig. 10.7:

$$Y_1 = D_1 C_1 + y_1 \bar{C}_1$$
$$= \bar{y}_1 x y_2 + y_1(\bar{x} + \bar{y}_2)$$
$$= x \bar{y}_1 y_2 + \bar{x} y_1 + y_1 \bar{y}_2$$

$$Y_2 = D_2 C_2 + y_2 \bar{C}_2$$
$$= \bar{y}_1 x + y_2 \bar{x}$$

The K-map development of the state table is shown in Fig. 10.10.

10.3 Synthesis of Pulse-mode Circuits

The synthesis or design of pulse-mode circuits closely parallels the design of synchronous circuits discussed in Chapter 8. However, when designing pulse-mode circuits, remember that no clock pulse is present, inputs occur on only one line at a time, and only uncomplemented forms of input signals may be used.

The absence of a clock pulse implies that latch or flip-flop triggering must be accomplished by utilizing the pulses on the input signals, and therefore all circuit timing information must be obtained from the input pulses. Hence, the input pulses not only provide input information but also assume the functions performed by the clock pulse in synchronous circuits.

10.3.1 Design Procedure for Pulse-mode Circuits

The step-by-step design procedure outlined next is the same as that given for synchronous circuits. However, the details of some steps are different, as illustrated by the three examples that follow.

Step 1. Derive a state diagram and/or state table.

Step 2. Minimize the state table.

Step 3. Choose a state assignment and generate the transition/output table.

Step 4. Select the type of latch or flip-flop to be used and determine the excitation equations.

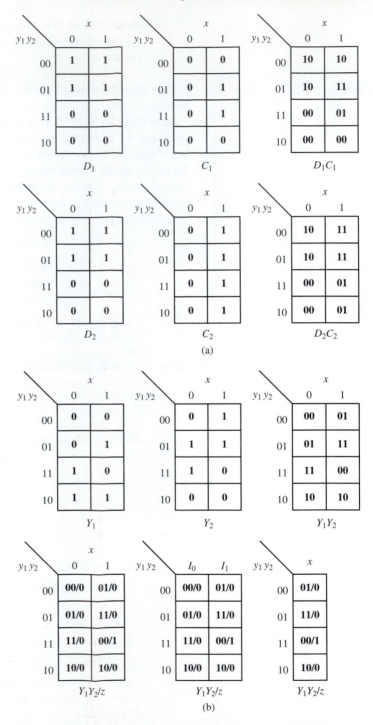

Figure 10.10 K-map state table development. **(a)** Flip-flop input maps. **(b)** Next-state maps.

Step 5. Determine the output equations.

Step 6. Choose the appropriate logic elements and draw the circuit diagram.

EXAMPLE 10.3

Let us design a pulse-mode circuit having two input lines, x_1 and x_2, and one output line, z, as shown in Fig. 10.11a. The circuit should produce an output pulse to coincide with the last input pulse in the sequence x_1—x_2—x_2. No other input sequence should produce an output pulse. Hence, this example is concerned with the design of a sequence detector for the sequence x_1—x_2—x_2.

Step 1. Define the following three states of the circuit:

A: indicates that the last input was x_1.
B: indicates that the sequence x_1–x_2 occurred.
C: indicates that the sequence x_1–x_2–x_2 occurred.

The corresponding state diagram is given in Fig. 10.11b. Note that the format of the state diagram is similar to that used for synchronous circuits. However, the transitions are labeled with the input variable and the output value rather than with both input and output values. Also, remember that the state transitions are triggered by the occurrence of the indicated input pulse and not by a clock pulse.

The state table corresponding to the state diagram of Fig. 10.11b is as follows:

Present state	x_1	x_2
A	$A/0$	$B/0$
B	$A/0$	$C/1$
C	$A/0$	$C/0$

Next state/output

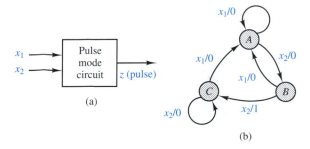

(a)

(b)

Figure 10.11 Pulse-mode example. **(a)** Pulse-mode circuit. **(b)** State diagram.

Step 2. The state table is minimum as given.

Step 3. A state assignment of $A = 00$, $B = 01$, $C = 10$ produces the following transition/output table.

$y_1 y_2$	x_1	x_2
00	00/0	01/0
01	00/0	10/1
10	00/0	10/0

$$Y_1 Y_2 / z$$

Step 4. Let us choose T flip-flops as the memory elements. The next state maps and corresponding flip-flop excitation maps are given in Fig. 10.12. These maps can be considered as reduced four-variable Karnaugh maps. Columns corresponding to $x_1 = x_2 = 0$

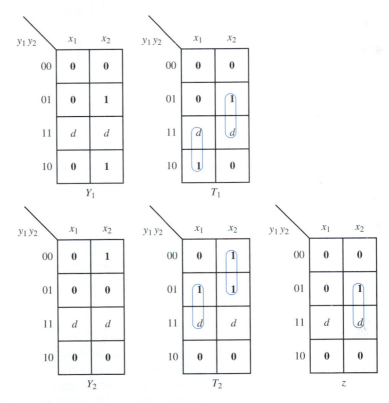

Figure 10.12 Next state, excitation, and output maps.

and $x_1 = x_2 = 1$ are omitted since they contain no pertinent information. The reader should verify that the omitted columns are not needed. Since the remaining columns are not adjacent on the complete map, groupings can be made only within a given column. Hence, the following excitation equations result:

$$T_1 = x_1 y_1 + x_2 y_2$$
$$T_2 = x_1 y_2 + x_2 \bar{y}_1$$

Step 5. The output map is given in Fig. 10.12, from which we derive the following equation:

$$z = x_2 y_2$$

Step 6. AND/OR logic can be used to realize the equations. Figure 10.13 shows the resulting circuit.

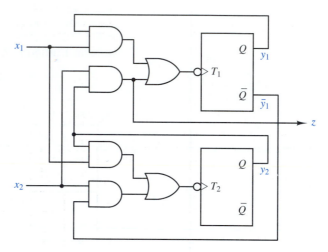

Figure 10.13   Logic diagram for the pulse-mode example.

In the previous example, the circuit realization took the form of a Mealy-type circuit since the output was a function of both an input and a state variable. A second example will now be presented that describes the realization of a Moore-type circuit. Recall that Mealy- and Moore-type circuits were defined in Chapter 8.

EXAMPLE 10.4

Let us design a pulse mode circuit with inputs x_1, x_2, x_3 and output z. The output must change from 0 to 1 if and only if the input sequence x_1–x_2–x_3 occurs while $z = 0$. The output must change from 1 to 0 only after an x_2 input occurs.

Step 1. Since the output must remain high between input pulses, a Moore-type circuit is required to realize the network in Fig. 10.14a. The state diagram and state table in Figs. 10.14b and c, respectively, satisfy the stated requirements.

Step 2. The table of Fig. 10.14c is reduced.

Step 3. Making the state assignment $A = 00$, $B = 01$, $C = 11$, $D = 10$ yields the transition/output table of Fig. 10.14d.

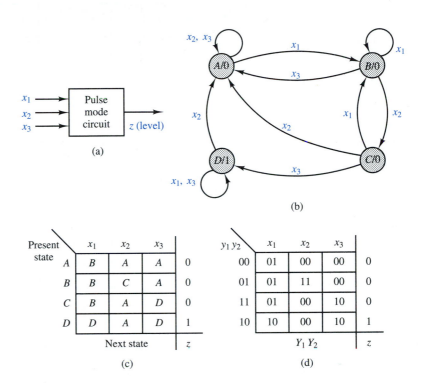

(a)

(b)

Present state	x_1	x_2	x_3	
A	B	A	A	0
B	B	C	A	0
C	B	A	D	0
D	D	A	D	1
		Next state		z

(c)

$y_1 y_2$	x_1	x_2	x_3	
00	01	00	00	0
01	01	11	00	0
11	01	00	10	0
10	10	00	10	1
		$Y_1 Y_2$		z

(d)

Figure 10.14   Pulse-mode example. **(a)** Pulse-mode circuit. **(b)** State diagram. **(c)** State table. **(d)** Transition/output table.

Step 4. Next-state maps and the corresponding excitation maps for SR latches are given in Fig. 10.15. Note that to use SR latches the duration of each input pulse must be sufficiently long to initiate a state change. Furthermore, remember that when using the reduced K-maps that groupings must be restricted to within a given column. The maps yield the following excitation equations:

$$S_1 = x_2 \bar{y}_1 y_2, \quad R_1 = x_1 y_2 + x_2 y_1$$
$$S_2 = x_1 \bar{y}_1, \quad R_2 = x_2 y_1 + x_3$$

Step 5. Since a Moore-type circuit is being realized, z will only be a function of state variables. A 1 output is produced only when the circuit is in state D. Hence,

$$z = y_1 \bar{y}_2$$

Step 6. Figure 10.16 shows the circuit diagram that results when AND/OR logic is used to realize the equations.

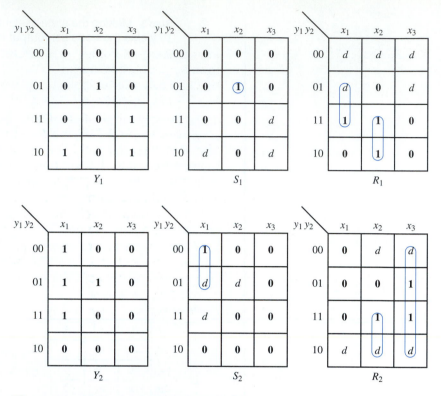

Figure 10.15   Next-state and SR excitation maps.

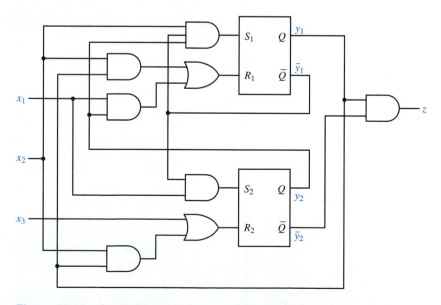

Figure 10.16   Circuit diagram for the pulse-mode example.

EXAMPLE 10.5

Let us design a pulse-mode circuit with inputs x_1, x_2, x_3 and output z. The circuit is to be used as a digital lock, as shown in Fig. 10.14a, with the combination $x_1{-}x_2{-}x_2{-}x_1{-}x_2$. Pulses on the inputs are produced by push buttons. Input x_3 is a reset signal to clear the lock. The output must change from 0 to 1 if and only if the input sequence $x_1{-}x_2{-}x_2{-}x_1{-}x_2$ occurs while $z = 0$. The output is to go high only during the last x_2 input. Once x_2 is released, the lock cannot be opened again unless a pulse on x_3 resets the logic. If any incorrect sequence is entered, the lock must wait for a reset pulse before the correct combination can be entered. In other words, after the lock has been opened, the sequence $x_3{-}x_1{-}x_2{-}x_2{-}x_1{-}x_2$ is required to open it again.

Step 1. The state diagram and state table of Figs. 10.17b and c, respectively, satisfy the stated requirements.

Step 2. The table of Fig. 10.17c is reduced.

Step 3. Using the state assignment rules of Chapter 9:

Rule 1: Try to satisfy the following adjacencies:

$$BC, \quad BE, \quad BF, \quad CE, \quad CF, \quad EF$$
$$AD, \quad AE, \quad AF, \quad DE, \quad DF, \quad EF$$

Rule 3: Establish an implication graph as shown in Fig. 10.17d. From the closed subgraph, circled on the graph, try to satisfy the following adjacencies:

$$CD, \quad DF, \quad EF, \quad CE, \quad BC$$

The state assignment in Fig. 10.17e represents a good choice for this circuit. Using this state assignment yields the transition table of Fig. 10.17f.

Step 4. From the transition table, excitation maps for SR latches are derived and given in Fig. 10.17g. Remember that, when using the reduced K-maps, groupings must be restricted to within a given column. The following excitation equations are derived from the maps.

$$S_1 = y_2 x_1 + x_2$$
$$R_1 = x_3$$

$$S_2 = \bar{y}_1 \bar{y}_2 x_1$$
$$R_2 = y_2 x_1 + y_3 x_2 + x_3$$

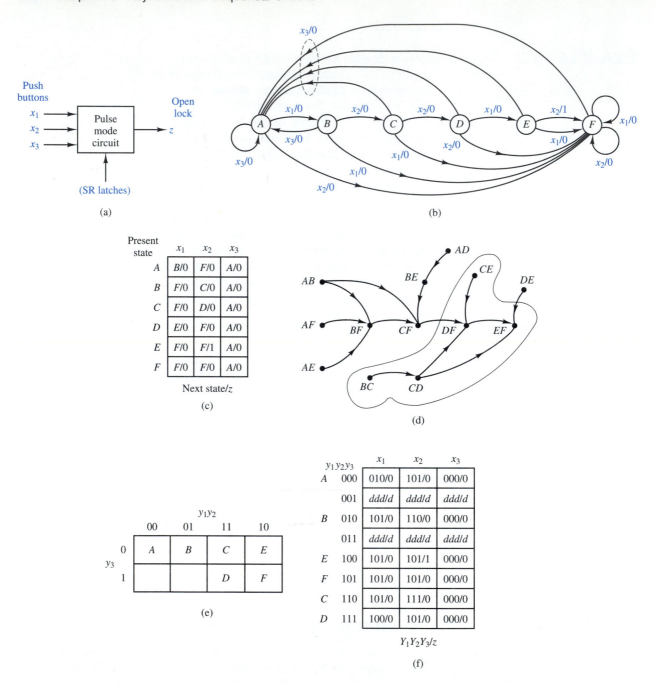

Figure 10.17 Digital combination lock example. **(a)** Digital combination lock. **(b)** State diagram. **(c)** State table. **(d)** Implication graph. **(e)** State assignment. **(f)** Transition/output table.

$y_1 y_2 y_3$	x_1	x_2	x_3
000	0*d*	10	0*d*
001	*dd*	*dd*	*dd*
010	10	10	0*d*
011	*dd*	*dd*	*dd*
100	*d*0	*d*0	01
101	*d*0	*d*0	01
110	*d*0	*d*0	01
111	*d*0	*d*0	01

$S_1 R_1$

$y_1 y_2 y_3$	x_1	x_2	x_3
000	10	0*d*	0*d*
001	*dd*	*dd*	*dd*
010	01	*d*0	01
011	*dd*	*dd*	*dd*
100	0*d*	0*d*	0*d*
101	0*d*	0*d*	0*d*
110	01	*d*0	01
111	01	01	01

$S_2 R_2$

$y_1 y_2 y_3$	x_1	x_2	x_3
000	0*d*	10	0*d*
001	*dd*	*dd*	*dd*
010	10	0*d*	0*d*
011	*dd*	*dd*	*dd*
100	10	10	0*d*
101	*d*0	*d*0	01
110	10	10	0*d*
111	01	*d*0	01

$S_3 R_3$

(g)

$y_1 y_2$

y_3	00	01	11	10
0	0	0	0	1
1	*d*	*d*	0	0

(h)

Figure 10.17   (Continued) Digital combination lock example. **(g)** Excitation K-maps. **(h)** Output K-map.

$$S_3 = (y_2 \bar{y}_3 + y_1 \bar{y}_3)x_1 + (\bar{y}_2 + y_1)x_2$$
$$R_3 = (y_2 y_3)x_1 + x_3$$

Step 5. The K-map for the output z is shown in Fig. 10.17h. The output equation is

$$z = y_1 \bar{y}_2 \bar{y}_3 x_2$$

Step 6. Construction of the detailed circuit diagram is left as an exercise for the reader.

This example completes our discussion of pulse-mode circuits. The remainder of the chapter will be concerned with fundamental-mode circuits.

10.4 Analysis of Fundamental-mode Circuits

Fundamental-mode circuit analysis requires careful attention because of the special behavioral characteristics of these types of circuits; that is, these circuits utilize unclocked memory and level inputs, whether synchronized by a clock signal or not. For example, consider the circuit defined by Fig. 10.18a. This network is composed of AND, OR, and NOT gates with one delay line memory

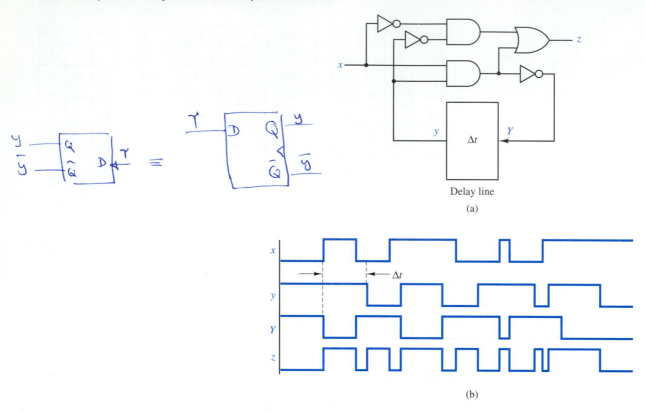

Figure 10.18 A level asynchronous sequential circuit. **(a)** Logic diagram. **(b)** Timing diagram.

element. The delay line memory element may be a physical component placed in the feedback path to introduce a delay of Δt between changes in output Y and feedback signal y. However, in many circuits, output Y is simply fed directly back to input y, in which case Δt represents the sum of the delays through the combinational logic gates, which determines the time between changes in input x or feedback signal y and corresponding changes in output Y.

This type of level asynchronous sequential circuit is perhaps the most difficult to analyze. A timing diagram for the circuit is shown in Fig. 10.18b. The logic equations for the network are

$$Y = \overline{xy} = \bar{x} + \bar{y}$$

$$z = xy + \bar{x}\bar{y} = x \odot y$$

Examining the equation for Y, we find that the complement of the input signal x serves as a control variable to mask out transitions in the delay line feedback loop. If $x = 0$ ($\bar{x} = 1$), then $Y = 1$; that is, the next state Y is independent of the present state y. When $x = 1$ ($\bar{x} = 0$), the next state Y is the complement of the present state y, that is, $Y = \bar{y}$, and the sequential circuit cycles back and forth between the 0 and 1 states.

This type of circuit is unique from all the other circuit types discussed previously in that no pulses are present to aid in the analysis. State transitions in synchronous sequential circuits are triggered by clock pulses and, in pulse-mode asynchronous circuits, by pulses on the circuit inputs. A state table and diagram are easily produced for these circuits by examining the circuit state and inputs at the exact instant of each active transition of the clock signal or input pulse. However, level asynchronous circuits are more difficult to describe. For convenience, we shall introduce a special notation for handling this unusual case.

The generic fundamental mode circuit model in Fig. 10.2 can be described by the following set of logic equations at time t:

$$z_i^t = g_i(x_1^t, \ldots, x_n^t, y_1^t, \ldots, y_r^t), \qquad i = 1, \ldots, m \qquad (10.1)$$

$$Y_j^t = h_j(x_1^t, \ldots, x_n^t, y_1^t, \ldots, y_r^t), \qquad j = 1, \ldots, r \qquad (10.2)$$

$$y_j^{t+\Delta t} = Y_j^t, \qquad j = 1, \ldots, r \qquad (10.3)$$

where

$$\mathbf{x} = (x_1, \ldots, x_n) = \text{input state}$$

$$\mathbf{y} = (y_1, \ldots, y_r) = \text{secondary state}$$

$$\mathbf{z} = (z_1, \ldots, z_m) = \text{output state}$$

$$\mathbf{Y} = (Y_1, \ldots, Y_r) = \text{excitation state}$$

$$(\mathbf{x}, \mathbf{y}) = \text{total state}$$

Alternatively, the equations may be written as

$$\mathbf{z}^t = \mathbf{g}(\mathbf{x}^t, \mathbf{y}^t) \qquad (10.4)$$

$$\mathbf{Y}^t = \mathbf{h}(\mathbf{x}^t, \mathbf{y}^t) \qquad (10.5)$$

$$\mathbf{y}^{t+\Delta t} = \mathbf{Y}^t \qquad (10.6)$$

10.4.1 Introduction

To introduce the analysis procedure for fundamental-mode circuits, consider the circuit shown in Fig. 10.19a. This circuit is described by the following set of equations:

$$z^t = g(x_1^t, x_2^t, y^t) = x_1^t x_2^t + \bar{x}_2^t y^t$$

$$Y^t = z^t$$

$$y^{t+\Delta t} = Y^t$$

where

$$(x_1, x_2) = \text{input state}$$

$$(y) = \text{secondary state}$$

$$(x_1, x_2, y) = \text{total state}$$

$$(z) = \text{output state}$$

$$(Y) = \text{excitation state}$$

Figure 10.19b illustrates the timing diagram of the circuit for a typical input sequence. The construction of timing diagrams was presented in Chapter 8, and the procedures discussed there remain valid here.

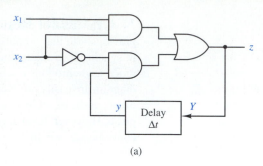

(a)

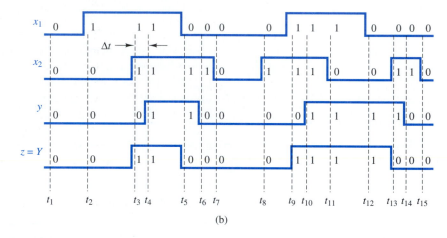

(b)

Figure 10.19 A fundamental-mode circuit. **(a)** Circuit diagram. **(b)** Timing diagram.

A situation of particular interest can be seen at time t_3 in Fig. 10.19b. Observe that Y changes from 0 to 1 in response to the 0 to 1 change in x_2. However, y does not follow with a 0 to 1 change until time t_4. This lag in the response of y is due to the delay element included in the feedback path. Since a delay of Δt has been assumed, $t_4 - t_3 = \Delta t$.

An *unstable state* is said to exist at time t_3, since $y \neq Y$. Other unstable states exist at times t_5, t_9, and t_{13}. When $y = Y$, a *stable state* exists.

It should be noted that unstable states exist for a period of time equal to Δt and are thus transient in nature. However, the transient behavior of fundamental-mode circuits is, in general, more critical for proper functioning of the device and therefore will be studied in more detail in a later section of the chapter.

In summary, a fundamental-mode circuit is in a *stable state* when the following relationship is satisfied:

$$\mathbf{y}^t = \mathbf{Y}^t \tag{10.7}$$

An *unstable state* is defined by the relationship

$$\mathbf{y}^t \neq \mathbf{Y}^t \tag{10.8}$$

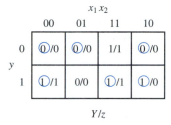

Figure 10.20 Excitation table.

10.4.2 Tabular Representations

It is often convenient to represent fundamental-mode circuits in tabular form. The first form to be considered is the *excitation table*. An excitation table presents both the excitation state and the output state as a function of the total state $(x_1, \ldots, x_n, y_1, \ldots, y_r)$. Hence, the excitation table is a tabular representation of Eqs. 10.1 and 10.2. The excitation table corresponding to Fig. 10.19a is given in Fig. 10.20. This table can be constructed by an appropriate combination of the K-maps for Y and z.

Note that each column of the table is associated with a unique input state, and each row of the table corresponds to a unique secondary state. Hence, each cell in the table represents a unique total state (x_1, x_2, y) of the circuit. Contained in each cell is the excitation state and output state specified for the corresponding total state by Eqs. 10.1 and 10.2, respectively. Stable states are indicated by encircling the corresponding excitation state.

Separation of the excitation and output functions into two separate tables is often desired. This has been done in Fig. 10.21 for the circuit shown in Fig. 10.19. Thus the excitation table can be represented in either the one- or two-table format. Both of these formats can be generalized by adding rows and columns as needed to accommodate additional states and inputs, as necessary.

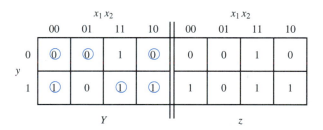

Figure 10.21 Excitation table (alternative form).

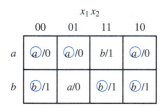

Figure 10.22 Flow table.

A *flow table* is another useful representation of a fundamental-mode circuit. Flow tables are similar to excitation tables; however, in a flow table, excitation states and secondary states are represented by letters or other nonbinary characters. Hence, a flow table specifies the circuit behavior, but does not specify the circuit realization. Figure 10.22 presents a flow table for the circuit in Fig. 10.19a.

Both flow tables and excitation tables can be used to determine the output response of a circuit to a given input sequence. The excitation table, however, provides both secondary and excitation state behavior as additional information.

The flow table in Fig. 10.23 illustrates the flow that corresponds to the time interval t_1 through t_7 in the timing diagram in Fig. 10.19b. Note the occurrence of unstable states in the flow sequence. Also, observe that an input change causes a horizontal move in the flow table. Vertical moves are produced by changes in secondary states that result from input changes. In other words,

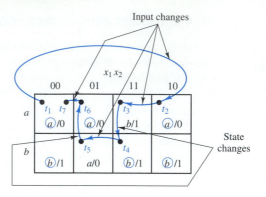

Figure 10.23 Flow table showing flow sequence.

an input change causes the circuit to move horizontally into a new column and then vertically within the column until it finds a stable state.

10.4.3 Analysis Procedure

The previous example suggests the following analysis procedure.

1. Determine the excitation and output equations from the circuit diagram.
2. Plot excitation and output K-maps for Y and z, and from these K-maps construct the excitation table.
3. Locate and circle all stable states in the excitation table.
4. Assign a unique nonbinary symbol to each row of the excitation table. Letters or the decimal equivalents of the secondary state codes are often used.
5. Construct the flow table by replacing each binary state in the excitation table with a symbol representing its state assignment.

This procedure will now be illustrated with the following example.

EXAMPLE 10.6

We wish to derive the flow table for the circuit given in Fig. 10.24a.

Step 1. The excitation and output equations for the network are

$$Y_1 = \bar{x}\bar{y}_2$$
$$Y_2 = x\bar{y}_1$$
$$z = \bar{x}y_1$$

Step 2. An excitation table is constructed from K-maps of Y_1, Y_2, and z as shown in Fig. 10.25a. The resulting table is given in Fig. 10.25b.

Step 3. Stable states can be located by the condition $y_1 y_2 = Y_1 Y_2$. These states are encircled as shown in Fig. 10.25b.

Step 4. Decimal equivalents of secondary state codes plus 1 are chosen to represent the corresponding rows in the excitation table, for example, $y_1 y_2 = (01) = 2$ in Fig. 10.25b.

Step 5. The resulting flow table is given in Fig. 10.25c. Note that the last two rows have been swapped to preserve numerical order.

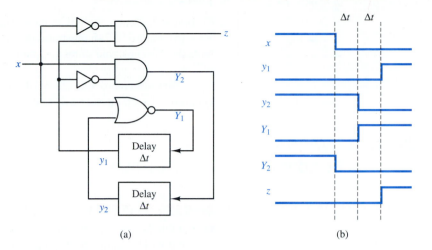

(a)   (b)

Figure 10.24   Fundamental-mode analysis example. **(a)** Circuit diagram.
(b) Timing diagram.

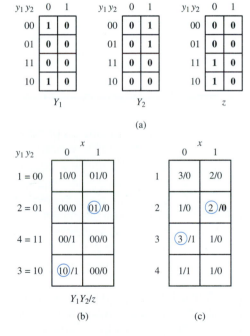

Figure 10.25   Excitation and
flow tables derived from K-maps.
(a) K-maps. **(b)** Excitation table.
(c) Flow table.

It is interesting to observe the state changes that occur in the circuit as it moves from stable state (2) when the input changes from 1 to 0. (*Note*: In the discussions that follow, parentheses will be used to denote stable states.) First, the circuit proceeds from stable state (2) to unstable state 1 in row 2. Next, the circuit moves to unstable state 3 in row 1. Finally, the device is transferred to stable state

(3) in row 3. Hence, the input change initiates a state sequence of $(2) \rightarrow 1 \rightarrow 3 \rightarrow (3)$. Figure 10.24b illustrates this sequence in the form of a timing diagram. Note that two unstable states are entered before the final stable state is reached.

This concludes our study of fundamental-mode circuit analysis. The synthesis of such circuits will be considered in the next section.

10.5 Synthesis of Fundamental-mode Circuits

The synthesis of fundamental-mode circuits may be accomplished by following a procedure similar to that previously described for pulse-mode circuits. However, a number of design considerations are unique to the fundamental-mode case and will be given special consideration later.

Fundamental-mode circuits cannot be conveniently represented by state diagrams or state tables since the total state is determined by both the input state and the secondary state. An alternative representation to the state diagram/state table, which is applicable for use with fundamental-mode devices, is the primitive flow table. A *primitive flow table* is a flow table that contains only one stable state per row.

A synthesis procedure for fundamental-mode circuits will now be defined. The procedure will be illustrated by two examples. A third example will be given later in the chapter.

10.5.1 Synthesis Procedure

Step 1. Construct a primitive flow table from a word description of the circuit to be realized.

Step 2. Determine a reduced flow table from the primitive flow table.

Step 3. Make a secondary state assignment.

Step 4. Construct the excitation table and the output table. Special rules will be given later for the output table construction.

Step 5. Determine the logic equations for each excitation state variable and each output state variable.

Step 6. Realize the logic equations with appropriate logic devices.

EXAMPLE 10.7

A two-input (x_1, x_2) and one-output (z) asynchronous sequential circuit is to be designed to meet the following specifications. Whenever $x_1 = 0$, $z = 0$. The first change in input x_2 that occurs while $x_1 = 1$ must cause the output to become $z = 1$. A $z = 1$ output must not change to $z = 0$ until $x_1 = 0$. A typical input/output response of the desired circuit is given in Fig. 10.26.

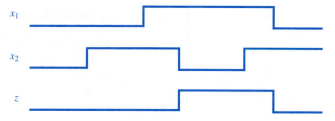

Figure 10.26   Typical input/output response.

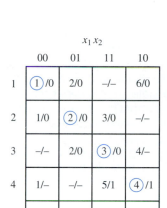

$x_1 x_2$

	00	01	11	10
1	①/0	2/0	–/–	6/0
2	1/0	②/0	3/0	–/–
3	–/–	2/0	③/0	4/–
4	1/–	–/–	5/1	④/1
5	–/–	2/–	⑤/1	4/1
6	1/0	–/–	5/–	⑥/0

Figure 10.27   Primitive flow table.

Step 1. A primitive flow table that satisfies the requirements of the circuit is given in Fig. 10.27. Several features of the table should be noted. First, there is a unique column for each input combination. In addition, each row contains one stable state with a specified output, two unstable states with unspecified outputs, and a column with an unspecified state and an unspecified output. The latter is always the column in which the values of both inputs differ from those of the column containing the stable state. Since fundamental-mode operation allows only one input change to occur at a given time, transitions corresponding to two or more input changes cannot occur. Hence, no next state is specified. Outputs of unstable states are specified as follows:

1. Assign an output of 0 to each unstable state that is a transient state between two stable states, each of which has an output of 0 associated with it.

2. Assign an output of 1 to each unstable state that is a transient state between two stable states, each of which has an output of 1 associated with it.

3. Assign a don't-care condition to each unstable state that is a transient state between two stable states, one of which has output 0 and the other output 1.

By assigning the outputs in this manner, momentary changes in the output will be avoided when the circuit passes through unstable states.

The need for each of the specified states will now be explained. Assume that the device is in state (1) and that x_2 changes from 0 to 1. No output change should occur under these conditions. Hence, state (2) is entered by way of unstable state 2. A change in x_1 from 0 to 1, while the device is in state (2), should not produce an output change either. Therefore, state (3) is entered through unstable state 3. If the circuit is in state (3) and x_2 changes from 1 to 0, an output change from 0 to 1 must take place. This change is produced by creating state (4) with output $z = 1$. Now assume that the device is in state (4) and that x_2 changes from 0 to 1. In this situation, no output change should occur, since $x_1 \neq 0$. Therefore, a stable state with $z = 1$ must exist in column 11. State (5) satisfies this requirement. State (6) is needed, since a stable state with $z = 0$ is necessary in column 10 when a 00 to 10 input

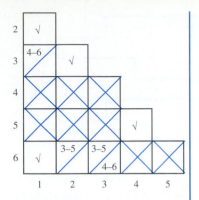

Figure 10.28 Implication table.

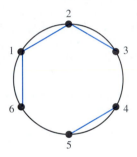

Figure 10.29 Merger diagram.

change occurs. The remaining transitions can be accommodated without defining additional states. For example, if the device is in state (6) and x_2 changes from 0 to 1, an output change from 0 to 1 should take place. This can be accomplished by a transition to state (5).

Step 2. Methods developed for the reduction of incompletely specified state tables may be applied to a primitive flow table to obtain a reduced flow table. The absence of present states in a primitive flow table poses no problem in the reduction procedure since each row is identified with a unique stable state. The concept of compatible states is thus replaced by the concept of compatible rows. Two rows are compatible (can be merged) if their states and outputs are compatible in each column of the primitive flow table. Compatibility of stable and unstable states is determined as follows. Stable state (i) and unstable state i are compatible. Stable state (i) and unstable state j are compatible if (i) is compatible with (j). Unstable state i is compatible with unstable state j if (i) is compatible with (j).

The implication table corresponding to the primitive flow table of Fig. 10.27 is given in Fig. 10.28. Compatible pairs of rows are seen to be (1, 2), (1, 6), (2, 3), and (4, 5). A merger diagram can be constructed as shown in Fig. 10.29 to illustrate the possible mergers.

Flow table reduction is completed by selecting a minimal closed cover. For the example, implication requirements are trivial. Hence, the problem simplifies to the selection of a minimal cover. An obvious minimal cover is {(1, 6), (2, 3), (4, 5)}, which leads to the reduced flow table of Fig. 10.30.

The equivalent flow table of Fig. 10.31 can be produced by relabeling the rows as a, b, and c.

	$x_1 x_2$			
	00	01	11	10
(1, 6)	①/0	2/0	5/–	⑥/0
(2, 3)	1/0	②/0	③/0	4/–
(4, 5)	1/–	2/–	⑤/1	④/1

Figure 10.30 Reduced flow table.

	$x_1 x_2$			
	00	01	11	10
a	ⓐ/0	b/0	c/–	ⓐ/0
b	a/0	ⓑ/0	ⓑ/0	c/–
c	a/–	b/–	ⓒ/1	ⓒ/1

Figure 10.31 Reduced flow table with states relabeled.

Step 3. Each row in the reduced flow table must be assigned a unique secondary state code. (The assignment must meet certain criteria to be discussed in a later section.) For now, an arbitrary choice will be assumed acceptable. In this example, two secondary state variables (y_1, y_2) are needed. The following assignment will be used:

Row	$y_1 y_2$
a	00
b	11
c	01

Step 4. The excitation table is constructed from the reduced flow table by replacing each letter by the corresponding secondary state code assigned in the previous step. Stable states are encircled. For this example, the excitation table is shown in Fig. 10.32a.

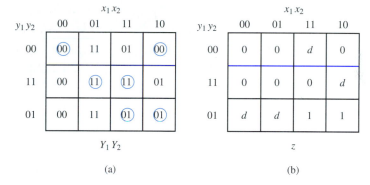

Figure 10.32   Excitation and output tables. **(a)** Excitation table. **(b)** Output table.

The output table of Fig. 10.32b is extracted from the reduced flow table.

Step 5. The logic equations for each excitation state variable and for each output state variable are obtained by transferring the information in the excitation and output tables to K-maps and then deriving the logic equations. Maps for the example are shown in Fig. 10.33, from which the following excitation and output equations are derived:

$$Y_1 = \bar{x}_1 x_2 + x_2 y_1$$
$$Y_2 = x_2 + x_1 y_2$$
$$z = \bar{y}_1 y_2$$

Step 6. Figure 10.34 shows a realization of the circuit with AND, OR, and NOT gates.

EXAMPLE 10.8

Let us design a two-input (x_1, x_2), two-output (z_1, z_2) fundamental-mode circuit that has the following specifications. When $x_1 x_2 = 00$, $z_1 z_2 = 00$. The output 10 will be produced

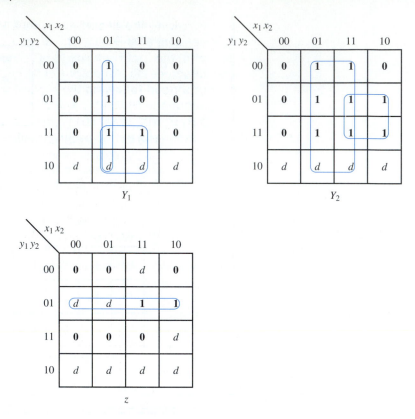

Figure 10.33   K-maps for the excitation and output tables.

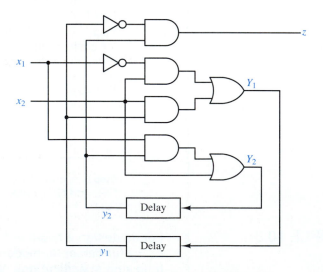

Figure 10.34   Realization of the synthesis example.

following the occurrence of the input sequence 00–01–11. The output will remain 10 until the input returns to 00, at which time it becomes 00. An output of 01 will be produced following the receipt of the input sequence 00–10–11. And once again, the output will remain 01 until a 00 input occurs, which returns the output to 00.

Step 1. When constructing the primitive flow table, it is helpful to note that at least one stable state must be defined in each column for each possible output that may be produced by the respective inputs. This observation leads to the partially complete primitive flow table of Fig. 10.35a. The flow table can be completed by establishing the necessary transitions between stable states. Such transitions can be accomplished by specifying the unstable states, as shown in the complete primitive flow table of Fig. 10.35b.

$x_1 x_2$

	00	01	11	10
1	①/00		–/–	
2		②/00		–/–
3		③/10		–/–
4		④/01		–/–
5	–/–		⑤/10	
6	–/–		⑥/01	
7		–/–		⑦/00
8		–/–		⑧/10
9		–/–		⑨/01

(a)

$x_1 x_2$

	00	01	11	10
1	①/00	2/00	–/dd	7/00
2	1/00	②/00	5/d0	–/dd
3	1/d0	③/10	5/10	–/dd
4	1/0d	④/01	6/01	–/dd
5	–/dd	3/10	⑤/10	8/10
6	–/dd	4/01	⑥/01	9/01
7	1/00	–/dd	6/0d	⑦/00
8	1/d0	–/dd	5/10	⑧/10
9	1/0d	–/dd	6/01	⑨/01

(b)

Figure 10.35 Primitive flow table development. **(a)** Partially complete primitive flow table. **(b)** Completed primitive flow table.

Step 2. Flow table reduction is begun by construction of an implication table as shown in Fig. 10.36. From the implication table, the compatible pairs of rows are found to be (1, 2), (1, 7), (2, 8), (3, 5),

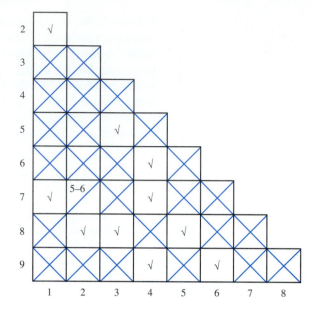

Figure 10.36   Implication table

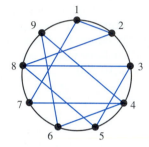

Figure 10.37   Merger diagram.

$x_1 x_2$

	00	01	11	10
a	(a)/00	(a)/00	b/d0	c/00
b	a/d0	(b)/10	(b)/10	(b)/10
c	(c)/00	a/00	d/0d	(c)/00
d	c/0d	(d)/01	(d)/01	(d)/01

Figure 10.38   Reduced flow table.

(3, 8), (4, 6), (4, 7), (4, 9), (5, 8), and (6, 9). The merger diagram, shown in Fig. 10.37, is helpful when selecting a cover.

Selection of a minimal closed cover yields the following set:

$$\{(1, 2), (1, 7), (3, 5, 8), (4, 6, 9)\}$$

The cover is used to produce the reduced flow table of Fig. 10.38, in which a is (1, 2), b is (3, 5, 8), c is (1, 7), and d is (4, 6, 9). Note that row 1 has been included in two states, a and c. Therefore, any unstable state in the primitive flow table whose next state is 1 may be arbitrarily replaced by a next state of either a or c in the reduced flow table.

Step 3. The following state assignment will be used:

Row	$y_1 y_2$
a	00
b	01
c	10
d	11

Step 4. The excitation and output tables are shown in Fig. 10.39.

Step 5. The following excitation and output equations can be obtained using the K-maps in Fig. 10.40.

$$Y_1 = y_1 y_2 + x_1 y_1 + \bar{x}_2 y_1 + x_1 \bar{x}_2 \bar{y}_2$$
$$Y_2 = x_1 x_2 + x_1 y_2 + x_2 y_2$$
$$z_1 = \bar{y}_1 y_2$$
$$z_2 = y_1 y_2$$

$x_1 x_2$

$y_1 y_2$	00	01	11	10
00	(00)	(00)	01	10
01	00	(01)	(01)	(01)
10	(10)	00	11	(10)
11	10	(11)	(11)	(11)

$Y_1 Y_2$

$x_1 x_2$

	00	01	11	10
00	00	00	$d0$	00
01	$d0$	10	10	10
10	00	00	$0d$	00
11	$0d$	01	01	01

$z_1 z_2$

Figure 10.39   Excitation and output tables.

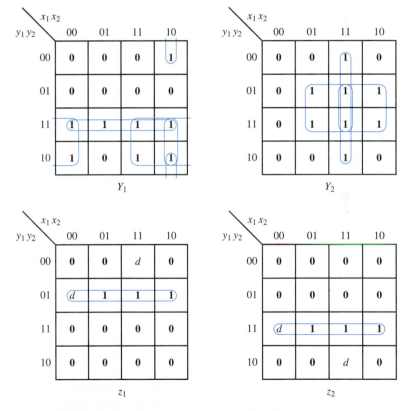

Figure 10.40   K-maps for the excitation and output tables.

Step 6. The circuit realization is shown in Fig. 10.41.

Sometimes we can implement a fundamental-mode circuit design without deriving a primitive flow table. This is illustrated by the following example.

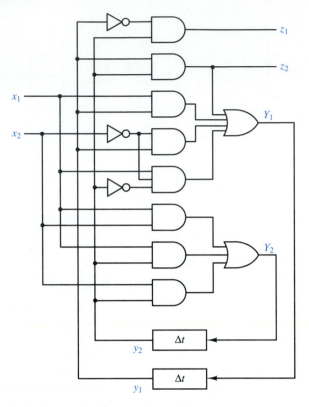

Figure 10.41 Realization of the design example.

EXAMPLE 10.9

We wish to implement a switch debounce filter, as illustrated in Fig. 10.42a. Mechanical switches are notorious noise generators in digital circuits because the contacts vibrate against each other as they *open* and *close*. Therefore, we want to design a fundamental-mode circuit that performs according to the timing diagram of Fig. 10.42b. As the push button releases from its contact on input x_1, a momentary oscillation is shown in the timing diagram. After a short time period (usually a few milliseconds for commercially available switches), the signal x_1 will stabilize to logic 1. Then as the contacts at x_2 close, they initially oscillate and finally pull down x_2 to logic 0. When the push button is released, the same sequence of events occurs in reverse.

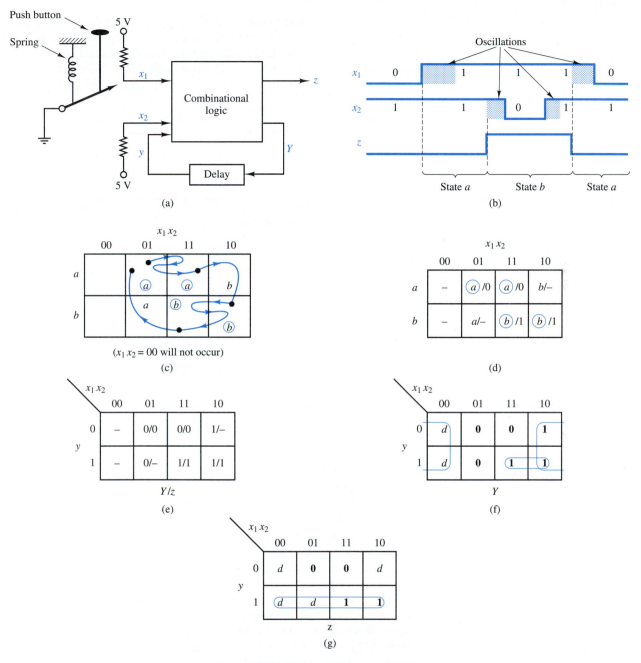

Figure 10.42   Switch debounce filter design. **(a)** Mechanical switch with debounce filter. **(b)** Desired timing behavior. **(c)** Desired flow sequence. **(d)** Complete reduced flow table. **(e)** Excitation table. **(f)** K-map for Y. **(g)** K-map for z.

In Fig. 10.42c, we have shown an example of a flow table (without the output z displayed) that illustrates the state behavior we are seeking. The oscillations in the inputs are "filtered" by allowing the circuit to bounce back and forth between stable states $\boxed{a}$ in the first row and $\boxed{b}$ in the second row. The oscillations are shown as a single cycle in the flow table, but in an actual switch might occur a dozen or more times! The complete flow table is shown in Fig. 10.42d.

The synthesis of this switch debounce filter proceeds as follows:

Step 1. Omitted in this case.

Step 2. The reduced flow table is given in Fig. 10.42d.

Step 3. Since only one state variable is needed, we make the assignment $a = 0$ and $b = 1$.

Step 4. The excitation table and K-maps for this circuit are shown in Figs. 10.42e, f, and g.

Step 5. The logic equations are

$$Y = \bar{x}_2 + x_1 y = \overline{x_2 \cdot \overline{(x_1 y)}}$$
$$z = y \quad \text{or} \quad z = Y$$

Note that the time delay element is usually implemented by connecting a wire from the output back to the input, so the output $z = y$ or $z = Y$ is essentially the same implementation.

Step 6. The logic diagram for our switch debounce filter is shown in Fig. 10.43a for a NAND gate realization. Notice that we can redraw the circuit as shown in Fig. 10.43b in the familiar cross-coupled NAND gate configuration for an SR latch!

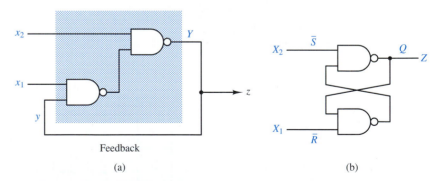

Feedback

(a)

(b)

Figure 10.43 Switch debounce filter logic circuit. **(a)** Logic diagram. **(b)** Equivalent logic diagram.

A fourth design example, which involves the selection of a secondary state assignment, will be presented later in the next section. Special requirements must be considered when making this assignment for a fundamental-mode circuit. These requirements will now be discussed.

10.6 Introduction to Races, Cycles, and Hazards

The characteristics of individual components from which a logic circuit is constructed influence the performance characteristics of the circuit. In particular, the relative response time of components has a significant effect on the behavior of fundamental-mode asynchronous circuits. These effects will now be considered.

Before proceeding, however, the sources of delays in fundamental-mode circuits will be briefly discussed. The fundamental-mode circuit model given in Fig. 10.2 shows feedback paths with delay elements. Additional delays are present in all physical circuits and result from the logic elements and the interconnection wires. Therefore, when circuits are realized without delay elements, delays inherent in the network are due only to the logic devices and wires.

The effects of delays on circuit performance will be divided into two categories. The first includes effects caused by delays in the feedback paths; the second considers the effects of delays in the logic and wires.

Inertial-type devices are often used as delay elements in feedback paths. An *inertial delay element* is an element that responds only to signals that persist for a time equal to or greater than the delay time of the device. To be specific, let ID represent an inertial delay with input Y, output y, and delay Δt, as shown in Fig. 10.44a. The output y assumes the value of input Y after a time of Δt if the duration of Y is greater than or equal to Δt. An input of duration less than Δt will not propagate to the output. The response of an inertial delay element to a typical input is shown in Fig. 10.44b.

Inertial delay elements serve to filter out unwanted transients that may occur in the feedback signals. These transients are produced as a result of the unequal response times of the logic elements and can cause incorrect behavior by the circuit if not eliminated.

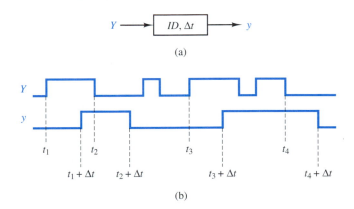

Figure 10.44 Inertial delay element. **(a)** Inertial delay element.
(b) Typical response sequence.

Inertial delay elements are more difficult to realize than are pure delay elements. However, the advantages provided by their use overcome the realization complexity. Therefore, for the remainder of the chapter, all delay elements will be considered to be inertial delays.

10.6.1 Races and Cycles

A *race condition* is said to exist in a fundamental-mode circuit when two or more secondary state variables must change value when the circuit is required to make a transition from one stable state to another stable state. In physical circuits, the amounts of delay in the different feedback paths are usually not the same. When unequal delays are possible, a race condition may cause unexpected or incorrect performance by the circuit. Such a condition will be illustrated later. Throughout the remainder of the discussion on fundamental-mode circuits, we will assume that the delay elements in one feedback path are not the same as those in another.

A race condition is said to be *noncritical* if the circuit always operates properly in the presence of the race. The circuit operates properly if it ends up in the correct stable state following any input change. However, in many cases a race may cause the circuit to enter and remain in an incorrect stable state. This latter case is referred to as a *critical* race condition. Critical races must always be avoided when designing a circuit. On the other hand, designers may often use noncritical races to their advantage.

The avoidance of critical race conditions can be accomplished by the proper assignment of secondary states. This assignment problem is nontrivial and will be considered in detail later. To more clearly understand the problems of race conditions, consider the following example.

EXAMPLE 10.10

Consider the flow table of Fig. 10.45 as a vehicle for analyzing critical and noncritical race conditions.

The state assignment $a = 00$, $b = 01$, $c = 10$, and $d = 11$ yields the excitation table in Fig. 10.46. Both critical and noncritical race conditions exist in this table. A circuit realization of the table is shown in Fig. 10.47.

In the following discussion, delay elements will be assumed to be inertial, and delays in both the logic gates and wires will be assumed to be negligible. The *total state* will refer to the value of the vector $x_1 x_2 y_1 y_2$, which is the combination of the input $x_1 x_2$ and the secondary state $y_1 y_2$.

An examination of the excitation table indicates that a race condition exists when a transition is made from total state 1011 to total state 0000. We will show that this race is noncritical through an analysis of the circuit for $\Delta_1 t > \Delta_2 t$ and for $\Delta_1 t < \Delta_2 t$. To simplify our discussion, let t_0 represent a time when the circuit is in state 1011, let t_1 represent the time when the input state changes from 10 to 00, let t_2 represent the time when the first delay element

$x_1 x_2$

	00	01	11	10
a	*a*/0	b/0	*a*/1	b/1
b	a/0	*b*/0	c/0	*b*/0
c	a/1	*c*/1	*c*/0	d/0
d	a/0	c/0	a/1	*d*/1

Figure 10.45 Flow table.

y_1y_2 \ x_1x_2	00	01	11	10	00	01	11	10
00	(00)	01	(00)	01	0	0	1	1
01	00	(01)	10	(01)	0	0	0	0
10	00	(10)	(10)	11	1	1	0	0
11	00	10	00	(11)	0	0	1	1
	Y_1Y_2				z			

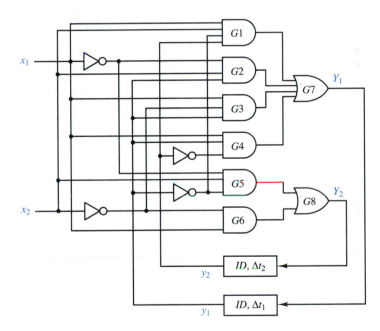

Figure 10.46 Excitation and output tables.

Figure 10.47 Circuit with races (for convenience, the output logic has been omitted).

responds, let t_3 represent the time when the second delay element responds, and let t_4 represent a time after t_3.

Consider now the following sequence of events. At time t_0, the circuit is in state 1011 and the gate outputs are $G1 = 0$, $G2 = 0$, $G3 = 1$, $G4 = 0$, $G5 = 0$, $G6 = 1$, $G7 = 1$, and $G8 = 1$. When the input changes from 10 to 00 at time t_1, all gate outputs become 0. Hence, $Y_1Y_2 = 00$. However, y_1y_2 remain 11 since they are delay element outputs. Therefore, the circuit is in an unstable state since $y_1 \neq Y_1$ and $y_2 \neq Y_2$.

The remaining analysis is influenced by the relative response times of the delay elements. Assume that $\Delta_1 t > \Delta_2 t$. At time $t_2 = t_1 + \Delta_2 t$, y_2 becomes 0 in response to an earlier change in Y_2. No further changes in Y_1 or Y_2 are produced by $y_2 = 0$. Hence, at $t_3 = t_1 + \Delta_1 t$, y_1 becomes 0 in response to $Y_1 = 0$. However, no change in $Y_1 Y_2$ is produced, and therefore the circuit has reached a stable state since $y_1 = Y_1$ and $y_2 = Y_2$. The following sequence of total states occurs as a result of the noncritical race when $\Delta_1 t > \Delta_2 t$:

$$1011\text{–}0011\text{–}0010\text{–}0000$$
$$t_0 \quad\ \ t_1 \quad\ \ t_2 \quad\ \ t_3$$

The reader is encouraged to verify that the following sequence is obtained when $\Delta_1 t < \Delta_2 t$:

$$1011\text{–}0011\text{–}0001\text{–}0000$$
$$t_0 \quad\ \ t_1 \quad\ \ t_2 \quad\ \ t_3$$

Timing diagrams of these state changes are given in Fig 10.48.

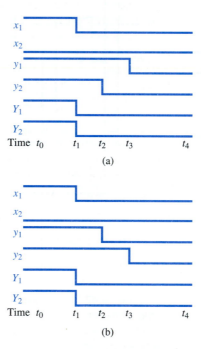

Figure 10.48 Timing for non-critical races. **(a)** $\Delta_1 t > \Delta_2 t$. **(b)** $\Delta_2 t > \Delta_1 t$.

It is important to note that the circuit response was a function of the relationship between $\Delta_1 t$ and $\Delta_2 t$. However, in each case the final stable state was the desired state. This is characteristic of noncritical races. The sequence of unstable states through which a circuit transitions is often unimportant as long as the correct final state is reached.

The occurrence of two or more consecutive unstable states is referred to as a *cycle*. We will delay our discussion of this topic until later.

In contrast to noncritical race conditions, a critical race condition may lead to erroneous circuit behavior. For example, consider the total state 1001, and let us analyze the circuit response as the input changes from 10 to 11. The gates in the circuit have the following outputs when in state 1001: $G1 = 0$, $G2 = 0$, $G3 = 0$, $G4 = 0$, $G5 = 0$, $G6 = 1$, $G7 = 0$, and $G8 = 1$. At time t_1, when the input changes to 11, gate $G1 = 1$ and $G6 = 0$, and hence $Y_1 = 1$ and $Y_2 = 0$. The remainder of the analysis is influenced by the relationship between $\Delta_1 t$ and $\Delta_2 t$. Assume now that $\Delta_1 t > \Delta_2 t$. At time $t_2 = t_1 + \Delta_2 t$, $y_2 = 0$ since $Y_2 = 0$. However, when y_2 becomes 0, it forces $Y_1 = 0$ before ID_1 responds to $Y_1 = 1$. Hence, $y_1 = 0 = Y_1$ and $y_2 = 0 = Y_2$, which implies that the device has stabilized in state 1100. This is an erroneous response, as indicated by the excitation table. The transition sequence is

$$1001-1101-1100-1100$$
$$t_0 \quad t_1 \quad t_2 \quad t_3$$

Let us now consider the case where $\Delta_1 t < \Delta_2 t$. Furthermore, assume that $2\Delta_1 t > \Delta_2 t$. At time $t_2 = t_1 + \Delta_1 t$, y_1 becomes 1 in response to $Y_1 = 1$. This change forces $G1$ to 0, which results in $Y_1 = 0$. At time $t_3 = t_1 + \Delta_2 t$, y_2 becomes 0 since $Y_2 = 0$. When y_2 becomes 0, $G4$ becomes 1, forcing $y_1 = 1$ again. By assuming that $2\Delta_1 t > \Delta_2 t$, then $t_3 - t_2 < \Delta_1 t$. Hence, the momentary change in Y_1 is not reflected in y_1. The device is now in the specified stable state 1110. The state sequence is then:

$$1001-1101-1111-1110-1110$$
$$t_0 \quad t_1 \quad t_2 \quad t_3 \quad t_4$$

A more detailed timing diagram is shown in Fig. 10.49. The reader is encouraged to examine the circuit for the other critical race conditions that exist.

The example illustrated that a critical race condition can result in erroneous circuit behavior. Clearly, such situations should be avoided. Hence, the problem of avoiding critical races will now be presented.

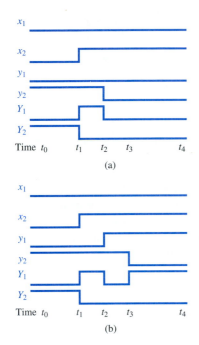

Figure 10.49 Critical race. **(a)** $\Delta_1 t > \Delta_2 t$. **(b)** $\Delta_1 t < \Delta_2 t$.

10.6.2 Avoidance of Race Conditions

Race conditions may be avoided through proper selection of the secondary state assignment. Simply stated, the secondary state must be assigned so that only one secondary variable at a time will be required to change for any state transition in the flow table. To accomplish this, it is often necessary to establish cycles between two stable states, as well as increase the number of state variables employed.

Now consider the problem of making a race-free assignment for the flow table in Fig. 10.45. An examination of the table indicates that transitions must be made from row a to row b, from row b to row c, from row c to row d, from row d to row a, and from row c to row a. This information is summarized in the *transition diagram* shown in Fig. 10.50a. Each node in the diagram corresponds to a row of the flow table. A line connects two nodes when transitions may occur between the corresponding rows. Lines are labeled with the input states that may exist when the transition occurs.

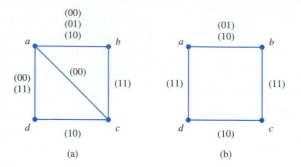

Figure 10.50 Transition diagrams for the example.
(a) Complete transition diagram. **(b)** Critical transition diagram.

As stated earlier, only critical race conditions must be avoided when designing a circuit. Figure 10.50b is a transition diagram that includes only transitions that may lead to a critical race. Only those transitions that take place in flow table columns containing two or more stable states are critical, since a critical race requires that there exists the possibility of reaching an incorrect stable state for a given input.

A critical race-free secondary state assignment will exist if the codes corresponding to connected nodes on the transition diagram differ in only 1 bit, which implies that only one secondary variable will be required to change in response to a given input change. The following assignment is clearly critical race-free for the transition diagram of Fig. 10.50b.

Row	y_1y_2
a	00
b	01
c	11
d	10

Figure 10.51 illustrates the excitation table and circuit realization for this assignment.

Numerous other critical race-free assignments exist for this example. A simple procedure for choosing such an assignment is to arbitrarily code one state, for example, $c = 10$, then code one of the connected states by changing 1 bit in the previous code, for example, $b = 00$, and then repeat this procedure until all states are coded, for example, $a = 01$ and $d = 11$. As a general rule, the state assignment problem is more complex than this and will be discussed in more detail in the following section.

10.6.3 Race-free State Assignments

We will now describe two methods for making race-free state assignments. The first method is based on the creation of cycles between stable states, while the

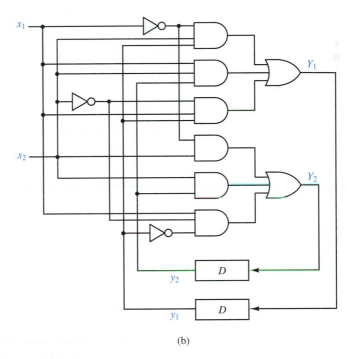

	$x_1 x_2$			
	00	01	11	10
00	⓪⓪	01	⓪⓪	01
01	00	⓪1	11	⓪1
11	00	⑪	⑪	10
10	00	11	00	⑩

$y_1 y_2$ (left label) $Y_1 Y_2$ (bottom label)

(a)

(b)

Figure 10.51   Critical race-free realization. **(a)** Excitation table. **(b)** Circuit realization.

	$x_1 x_2$			
	00	01	11	10
a	ⓐ/0	b/0	c/–	ⓐ/0
b	a/0	ⓑ/0	ⓑ/0	c/–
c	a/–	ⓒ/1	ⓒ/1	ⓒ/1

Figure 10.52   Reduced flow table.

second method requires the establishment of redundant rows in the flow table. The most economical assignments are usually obtained by the first method, but the second method is a more straightforward procedure.

Method 1.   Consider the reduced flow table of Fig. 10.52. The critical transition diagram in Fig. 10.53 indicates clearly that no assignment can be made to satisfy the needed adjacencies.

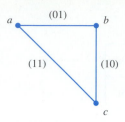

Figure 10.53   Critical transition digram

However, if the flow table is modified such that a cycle exists between any two stable states, then a race-free assignment can be made. To illustrate this approach, a cycle will be established between states a and c in column 11. The modified flow table is given in Fig. 10.54.

Note that the following sequence of states occurs during the transition from (a) in column 10 to (c) in column 11:

$$(a) \rightarrow d \rightarrow c \rightarrow (c)$$

Hence, the critical transition diagram becomes that shown in Fig. 10.55.

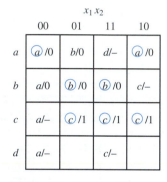

Figure 10.54   Modified flow table.

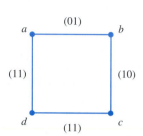

Figure 10.55   New critical transition diagram.

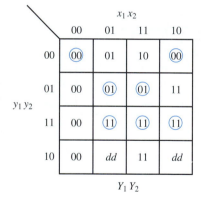

Figure 10.56   Excitation table.

Numerous race-free assignments exist for the modified flow table. An example is the following:

Row	$y_1 y_2$
a	00
b	01
c	11
d	10

The resulting excitation table is given in Fig. 10.56

Note the 00 excitation state assigned to state 0010. This assignment avoids the possibility of an unwanted stable state being established in row 10.

In the previous example, a cycle was created without the need to increase the number of state variables above the minimum required. This is not always possible, as will now be illustrated with the flow table in Fig. 10.57. The critical transition diagram in Fig. 10.58 indicates that not all required adjacencies can be met. In this case, cycles can be created to yield race-free state assignments only if three secondary state variables are used.

There are numerous ways in which to establish cycles in this problem that will avoid critical races. One way is to create a cycle between b and c in column 11, a cycle between b and d in column 01, and a cycle between c and d in

$x_1 x_2$

	00	01	11	10
a	Ⓐ /1	c/0	Ⓐ /0	b/0
b	a/1	Ⓑ /1	c/1	Ⓑ /0
c	d/0	Ⓒ /0	Ⓒ /1	d/1
d	Ⓓ /0	b/–	a/–	Ⓓ /1

Figure 10.57 Example flow table.

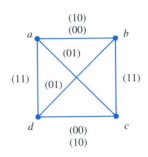

Figure 10.58 Critical transition diagram.

columns 00 and 10. These cycles are illustrated in the modified flow table in Fig. 10.59. The transition diagram for this modified flow table is given in Fig. 10.60.

An adjacency map is helpful when selecting the codes to meet the requirements given in the transition diagram. This technique has been used in Chapter 9. The map is similar in format to a K-map except that each cell represents a unique state code. Hence, adjacent cells represent adjacent codes. The three-variable map in Fig. 10.61 shows a state assignment that satisfies all adjacencies. Note that it was also necessary to employ another transition from d to b.

The corresponding state assignment is as follows:

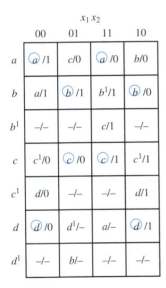

$x_1 x_2$

	00	01	11	10
a	Ⓐ /1	c/0	Ⓐ /0	b/0
b	a/1	Ⓑ /1	b^1/1	Ⓑ /0
b^1	–/–	–/–	c/1	–/–
c	c^1/0	Ⓒ /0	Ⓒ /1	c^1/1
c^1	d/0	–/–	–/–	d/1
d	Ⓓ /0	d^1/–	a/–	Ⓓ /1
d^1	–/–	b/–	–/–	–/–

Figure 10.59 Modified flow table with created cycles.

Row	$y_1 y_2 y_3$
a	000
b	001
b^1	011
c	010
c^1	110
d	100
d^1	101

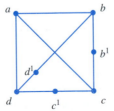

Figure 10.60 Transition diagram for the modified flow table.

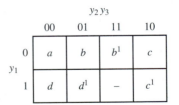

$y_2 y_3$

	00	01	11	10
y_1 0	a	b	b^1	c
1	d	d^1	–	c^1

Figure 10.61 State assignment satisfying required adjacencies.

An excitation table can then be produced and is shown in Fig. 10.62.

$y_1y_2y_3$ \ x_1x_2	00	01	11	10
000	(000)	010	(000)	001
001	000	(001)	011	(001)
011	*ddd*	*ddd*	010	*ddd*
010	110	(010)	(010)	110
110	100	*ddd*	*ddd*	100
100	(100)	101	000	(100)
101	*ddd*	001	*ddd*	*ddd*

$Y_1 Y_2 Y_3$

Figure 10.62 Excitation table derived with method 1.

Method 2. This method is based on the replication of rows in the reduced flow table. States are assigned to the expanded table in such a way that one row in each set of equivalent rows is adjacent to one row in each remaining set of equivalent rows. In addition, each row within a set of equivalent rows is adjacent to at least one other row of the same set. Hence, race-free transitions can be made between any two stable states by properly establishing row-to-row transitions.

For four-row flow tables, each row is duplicated in this approach. The state assignments for the expanded table are given in the following table:

y_2y_3 \ y_1	0	1
00	*a*	*a*
01	*b*	*d*
11	*b*	*d*
10	*c*	*c*

For this assignment, $a = 000$ is adjacent to $b = 001$ and $c = 010$, while $a = 100$ is adjacent to $d = 101$. The excitation table for the previous example is shown in Fig. 10.63.

	$y_1y_2y_3$ \ x_1x_2	00	01	11	10
a	000	(000)	010	(000)	001
a	100	(100)	000	(100)	000
b	001	000	(001)	011	(001)
b	011	001	(011)	010	(011)
c	010	110	(010)	(010)	110
c	110	111	(110)	(110)	111
d	101	(101)	001	100	(101)
d	111	(111)	101	101	(111)

$Y_1 Y_2 Y_3$

Figure 10.63 Excitation table derived with method 2.

In general, this second method is not as economical as the first since no don't-care conditions exist in the final excitation table. However, the second method requires no trial and error code selection since codes have been published for many different-sized tables. Figure 10.64 illustrates the assignment tables for six-row and eight-row tables.

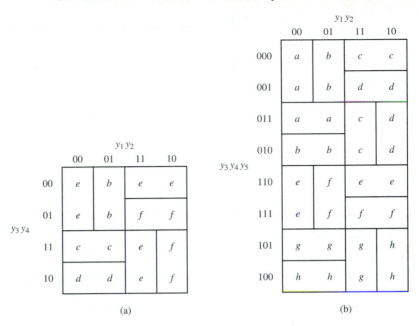

Figure 10.64 (a) Six-row tables:

$y_3 y_4$ \ $y_1 y_2$	00	01	11	10
00	e	b	e	e
01	e	b	f	f
11	c	c	e	f
10	d	d	e	f

(b) Eight-row tables:

$y_3 y_4 y_5$ \ $y_1 y_2$	00	01	11	10
000	a	b	c	c
001	a	b	d	d
011	a	a	c	d
010	b	b	c	d
110	e	f	e	e
111	e	f	f	f
101	g	g	g	h
100	h	h	g	h

Figure 10.64   Assignment tables for six- and eight-row tables. **(a)** Six-row tables. **(b)** Eight-row tables.

EXAMPLE 10.11

Figure 10.65 Primitive flow table for the example:

	$x_1 x_2$ 00	01	11	10
1	①/0	2/–	–/–	4/–
2	1/–	②/0	3/–	–/–
3	–/–	5/–	③/1	4/–
4	6/–	–/–	3/–	④/1
5	1/–	⑤/0	7/–	–/–
6	⑥/1	8/–	–/–	4/–
7	–/–	5/–	⑦/0	9/–
8	6/–	⑧/1	3/–	–/–
9	6/–	–/–	10/–	⑨/0
10	–/–	8/–	⑩/0	9/–
11	⑪/0	2/–	–/–	12/–
12	11/–	–/–	7/–	⑫/0

Figure 10.65   Primitive flow table for the example.

We wish to design a two-input (x_1, x_2), one-output (z) fundamental-mode circuit that will operate as follows. The output changes from 0 to 1 only on the first x_1 input change that follows an x_2 input change. A 1 to 0 output change occurs only when x_1 changes from 1 to 0 while $x_2 = 1$.

Step 1. The primitive flow table of Figure 10.65 satisfies the stated requirements. Note the presence of two states with output 0 in each column. This condition is a result of the requirement that a 0 to 1 output change should occur only on the first x_1 input change that follows an x_2 input change.

Step 2. The use of an implication table for the primitive flow table indicates that (1, 2), (3, 4), (4, 6), (4, 8), (5, 7), (6, 8), (9, 10), and (11, 12) are compatible rows. The corresponding merger diagram is shown in Fig. 10.66.

As the diagram indicates, rows 4, 6, and 8 can be merged into a single row. All other rows must be merged in pairs. The minimal reduced flow table that results from the merger diagram is shown in Fig. 10.67, where $a = (1, 2)$, $b = (3, 4)$, $c = (5, 7)$, $d = (4, 6, 8)$, $e = (9, 10)$, and $f = (11, 12)$. Note that the output assignment shown in the reduced flow table has been completed in order to avoid the occurrence of an output glitch, as described in items 2 and 3 of Step 1 of Example 10.7.

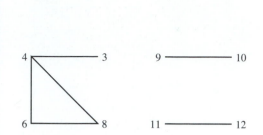

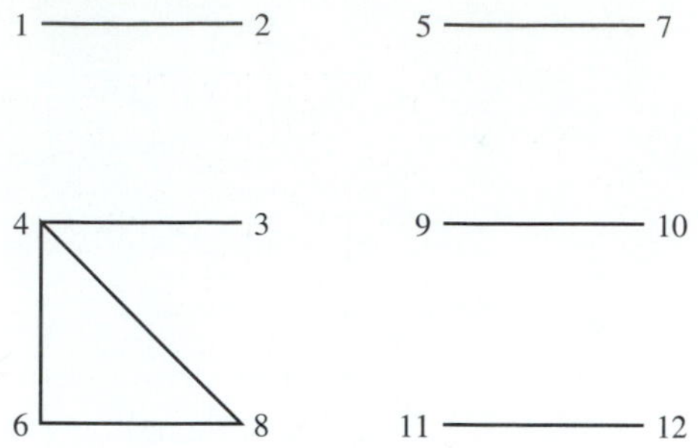

Figure 10.66 Merger diagram.

	x_1x_2 00	01	11	10
a	(*a*)/0	(*a*)/0	*b*/–	*b*/–
b	*d*/1	*c*/–	(*b*)/1	(*b*)/1
c	*a*/0	(*c*)/0	(*c*)/0	*e*/0
d	(*d*)/1	(*d*)/1	*b*/1	(*d*)/1
e	*d*/–	*d*/–	(*e*)/0	(*e*)/0
f	(*f*)/0	*a*/0	*c*/0	(*f*)/0

Figure 10.67 Minimal reduced flow table.

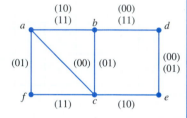

Figure 10.68 Critical transition diagram.

Step 3. The critical transition diagram is given in Fig. 10.68. A minimum of three secondary state variables is required since there are six rows in the reduced flow table. A three-variable assignment can be obtained through a judicious use of cycles.

Method 1 will be used to obtain a race-free assignment. Intermediate states c^1 and f^1, added as indicated in Fig. 10.69, permit this assignment to be made. The chosen assignment is illustrated by the map in Fig. 10.70.

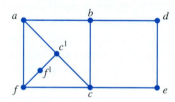

Figure 10.69 State assignment using method 1.

y_1 \ y_2y_3	00	01	11	10
0	*a*	*b*	*c*	c^1
1	*f*	*d*	*e*	f^1

Figure 10.70 Map of the chosen state assignment.

Step 4. Excitation and output tables are given in Fig. 10.71.

Step 5. The corresponding excitation and output equations are

$$Y_1 = \bar{x}_1\bar{x}_2\bar{y}_2y_3 + x_1\bar{x}_2y_2 + y_1y_2y_3 + x_1y_1\bar{y}_2\bar{y}_3 + \bar{x}_1y_1y_3 + \bar{x}_2y_1$$

$$Y_2 = \bar{x}_1x_2\bar{y}_1y_3 + x_1x_2y_1\bar{y}_3 + \bar{y}_1y_2y_3 + x_1y_2$$

$$Y_3 = \bar{y}_2y_3 + x_1\bar{x}_2\bar{y}_1 + y_1y_3 + x_2y_3$$

$$z = \bar{y}_2y_3$$

Step 6. A logic realization of these equations completes the design process.

$y_1y_2y_3$	x_1x_2 00	01	11	10	x_1x_2 00	01	11	10
a 000	(000)	(000)	001	001	0	0	–	–
b 001	101	011	(001)	(001)	1	–	1	1
c^1 010	000	–	011	–	0	–	0	–
c 011	010	(011)	(011)	111	0	0	0	0
f 100	(100)	000	110	(100)	0	0	0	0
d 101	(101)	(101)	001	(101)	1	1	1	1
f^1 110	–	–	010	–	–	–	0	–
e 111	101	101	(111)	(111)	–	–	0	0
		$Y_1Y_2Y_3$				z		

Figure 10.71   Excitation and output tables.

10.6.4 Hazards

The subject of hazards was initially discussed in Chapter 3 for combinational logic networks. Static and dynamic hazards can also be present in the combinational logic portion of sequential circuits and should be considered in sequential circuit design. The previous discussions remain valid here also, and therefore no further consideration will be given to this subject. It is important to note, however, that inertial delay elements can often be used to filter out transients caused by these hazards.

A third type of hazard is special to fundamental-mode circuits and will be briefly considered. In the discussion that follows, we will assume that all logic elements have some inherent delay associated with them. An *essential hazard* is a hazard caused by unequal delays along two or more paths that originate from the same input line. Such a hazard can cause the circuit to respond incorrectly to input changes. To illustrate this situation, consider the circuit shown in Fig. 10.72a. The excitation and output table for the circuit are given in Fig. 10.72b.

Assume that the circuit is in state $x = y_1 = y_2 = 0$. Hence, $Y_1 = Y_2 = 0$. Furthermore, assume that NOT gate $N1$ has a delay associated with it that is very large in comparison to the delays of the other elements in the circuit including the feedback delay. Now consider the response of the circuit to a 0 to 1 change in x at time t_1. A timing diagram of the response is shown in Fig. 10.72c. As this figure illustrates, the circuit becomes stable in state $x = 1$, $y_1 = 1$, and $y_2 = 0$. This is an incorrect response, as shown in the excitation table.

Critical events occur at times t_5, t_6, t_{10}, and t_{13}. The circuit is in the correct secondary state 01 at time t_5. However, since $N1$ has not yet responded to the input change, $A2$ becomes 1, which forces $Y_1 = 1$ at t_6. This subsequently causes $A3$ to go to 0. At t_{10}, $N1$ becomes 0, forcing $A2$ to 0, which causes

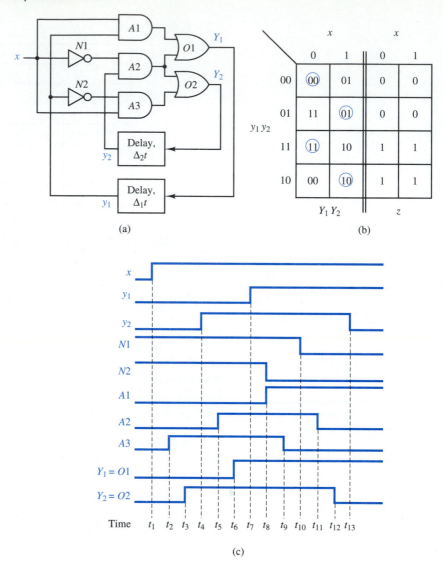

(a)

(b)

(c)

Figure 10.72   Circuit with essential hazard. **(a)** Circuit diagram. **(b)** Excitation and output tables. **(c)** Timing diagram.

$Y_2 = 0$. At t_{13}, y_2 responds to $Y_2 = 0$, and the circuit has reached a stable condition.

Hence, the delay in $N1$ has incorrectly forced $Y_1 = 1$ at t_6, which triggered the sequence of events leading to an incorrect stable state. The effect of such delays can be overcome by providing a sufficient amount of delay in the feedback paths.

10.6.5 Analysis

The analysis procedure given earlier in the chapter involved the determination of excitation tables, output tables, and flow tables from a circuit diagram. Given these tables, a thorough study is usually warranted to determine if any critical races or hazards exist in the circuit.

▶ 10.7 Summary

This chapter has been an introduction to the subject of asynchronous sequential circuits. Both pulse-mode and fundamental-mode circuits were considered. Attention was first given to the analysis and design of pulse-mode circuits. Analysis and design procedures were presented and were illustrated with several examples. The analysis and design of fundamental-mode circuits was considered next. Analysis and design procedures were again given and demonstrated by examples. Finally, a discussion of races and hazards was undertaken. Procedures for making race-free state assignments were presented and illustrated.

REFERENCES

1. S. H. CALDWELL, *Switching Circuits and Logical Design*. New York: Wiley, 1958.

2. D. A. HUFFMAN, "The Synthesis of Sequential Switching Circuits," *J. Franklin Institute*, Vol. 257, No. 3, Mar. 1954, pp. 161–190, and No. 4, Apr. 1954, pp. 275–303.

3. D. A. HUFFMAN, "A Study of Memory Requirements of Sequential Switching Circuits," *Tech. Report No. 293*, Research Laboratory of Electronics, Massachusetts Institute of Technology, Cambridge, MA, Mar. 14, 1955.

4. E. J. MCCLUSKEY, "Fundamental and Pulse Mode Sequential Circuits," *IFIP Congress Proc. 1962*. Amsterdam: North-Holland Publishing Company, 1963.

5. S. H. UNGER, *Asynchronous Sequential Switching Circuits*. New York: Wiley (Interscience Division), 1969.

PROBLEMS

10.1 Analyze the pulse-mode circuit shown in Fig. P10.1.
   (a) Determine a state table.
   (b) Construct a timing diagram for the circuit in response to the following input sequence. Include x_1, x_2, x_3, y_1, y_2, J_1, K_1, J_2, K_2, Y_1, Y_2, and z in your diagram.

10.2 Analyze the pulse-mode circuit shown in Fig. P10.2.
   (a) Determine a state table.
   (b) Determine the output response to the input sequence $x_1-x_2-x_1-x_1-x_1-x_1-x_2-x_2$ if the starting state is 00.
   (c) What form (level or pulse) will an output of $z = 1$ have? Why?

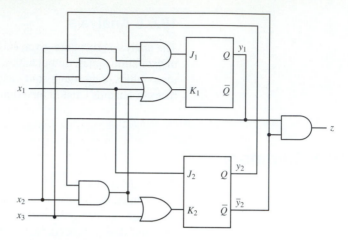

Figure P10.1

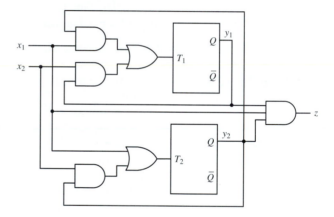

Figure P10.2

10.3 Determine a realization of the following pulse-mode state table. Use JK flip-flops with AND, OR, and NOT gates.

Present state	x_1	x_2	x_3
A	A/0	B/0	C/1
B	B/0	C/0	D/0
C	C/0	D/0	A/1
D	D/0	A/0	B/1

Next state/z

10.4 Design a pulse-mode circuit that meets the following specifications. Use AND, OR, and NOT gates with SR flip-flops to realize the circuit. The circuit will have two inputs x_1 and x_2 and one output z. An output pulse will be produced simultaneously with the last of a sequence of three input pulses if and only if the sequence contained at least two x_1 pulses.

10.5   A pulse-mode sequential circuit is needed that satisfies the following requirements. Two input lines x_1 and x_2 will be provided along with one output line z. An output transition from 0 to 1 will be produced only on the occurrence of the last x_2 pulse in the sequence $x_1 - x_2 - x_1 - x_2$. The output will be reset from 0 to 1 only by the first x_1 pulse that occurs following the 0 to 1 output transition. Allow overlapping sequences. Design the circuit using T flip-flops with AND, OR, and NOT gates.

10.6   Analyze the fundamental-mode circuit shown in Fig. P10.6.

    (a) Determine the excitation table and output table.

    (b) Construct a flow table.

    (c) Use the flow table to determine the output response to the input sequence $x_1 x_2$: 00–01–11–10–00–01–00–10. Assume initially that $x_1 = x_2 = y_1 = y_2 = Y_1 = Y_2 = 0$.

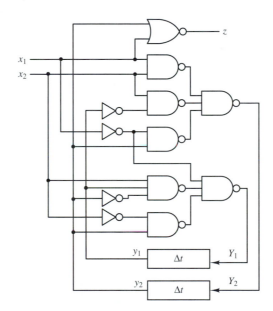

Figure P10.6

10.7   Consider the circuit in Fig. P10.7a. Analyze the circuit as follows:

    (a) Construct a timing diagram for the input sequence of Fig. P10.7b. Assume no delay in the logic gates. Also assume that initially $y_1 = Y_1 = 1$ and $y_2 = Y_2 = 0$. Include x_1, x_2, y_1, y_2, Y_1, Y_2, and z in the timing diagram.

    (b) Repeat part (a) assuming that each logic gate has a delay of $\frac{1}{2}\Delta t$.

10.8   Determine a primitive flow table for a fundamental-mode circuit that has the following requirements. One input x and one output z are needed. The output should follow the input on every other 0–1–0 transition, as indicated in Fig. P10.8.

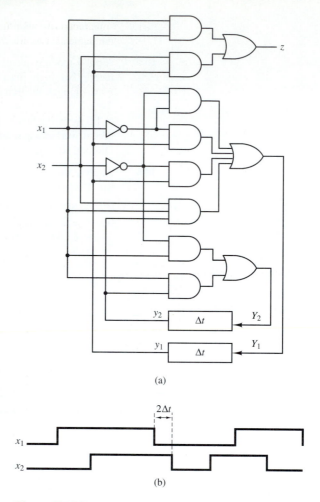

(a)

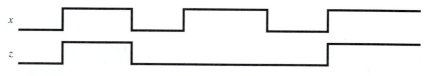

(b)

Figure P10.7 **(a)** Logic diagram. **(b)** Input sequence.

Figure P10.8

10.9 A fundamental-mode circuit must be designed to satisfy the following requirements. Two inputs (x_1, x_2) and one output (z) are required. The output $z = 0$ will always be produced when $x_1 = x_2$. When $x_1 = 0$ and x_2 changes from 0 to 1, an output $z = 1$ must occur. When $x_1 = 1$ and x_2 changes from 1 to 0, an output $z = 1$ must occur. Otherwise, no input change will cause an output change. Determine a primitive flow table for the circuit.

10.10   Construct a primitive flow table for a fundamental-mode circuit with the following specifications. The circuit must have two inputs (x_1, x_2) and two outputs (z_1, z_2). When $x_1 = x_2 = 0$, the outputs must be $z_1 = z_2 = 0$. If $x_2 = 1$ and x_2 changes from 0 to 1, an output $z_1 = 0$, $z_2 = 1$ will be produced. If $x_2 = 1$ and x_1 changes from 0 to 1, an output $z_1 = 1$, $z_2 = 0$ will be produced. Outputs are reset to $z_1 = z_2 = 0$ only when both x_1 and x_2 equal 0. No output change is produced by any other input change.

10.11   Reduce the following primitive flow table to a minimum row table:

$$x_1x_2$$

	00	01	11	10
1	①/0	2/–	–/–	3/–
2	4/–	②/1	5/–	–/–
3	1/–	–/–	5/–	③/0
4	④/–	2/–	–/–	6/–
5	–/–	2/–	⑤/–	6/–
6	1/–	–/–	5/–	⑥/1

10.12 Repeat Problem 10.11 for the following primitive flow table:

$$x_1x_2$$

	00	01	11	10
1	①/0	2/–	–/–	4/–
2	1/–	②/0	3/–	–/–
3	–/–	2/–	③/0	8/–
4	5/–	–/–	7/–	④/1
5	⑤/1	6/–	–/–	4/–
6	5/–	⑥/1	7/–	–/–
7	–/–	6/–	⑦/1	8/–
8	1/–	–/–	3/–	⑧/0

10.13 Determine a circuit realization for the following reduced flow table. Use the indicated state assignment. Assume AND, OR, and NOT gates are available for use in the realization.

$$x_1x_2$$

y_1y_2		00	01	11	10
00	a	ⓐ/0	ⓐ/1	b/–	c/–
01	b	a/–	ⓑ/0	ⓑ/0	d/–
11	c	a/–	a/–	ⓒ/1	ⓒ/1
10	d	a/–	b/–	c/–	ⓓ/0

10.14   Determine a minimum row flow table compatible with the following primitive flow table:

$$x_1 x_2$$

	00	01	11	10
1	①/1	6/–	–/–	5/–
2	②/0	4/–	–/–	3/–
3	2/–	–/–	9/–	③/0
4	2/–	④/0	7/–	–/–
5	1/–	–/–	7/–	⑤/1
6	1/–	⑥/1	7/–	–/–
7	–/–	4/–	⑦/0	10/–
8	⑧/0	4/–	–/–	10/–
9	–/–	6/–	⑨/1	3/–
10	1/–	–/–	9/–	⑩ /0

10.15   Repeat Problem 10.13 for the following flow table, but assume that only NAND gates are available for use in the circuit.

$$x_1 x_2$$

$y_1 y_2$	00	01	11	10
00 a	ⓐ/00	b/–	ⓐ/00	d/–
01 b	a/–	ⓑ/01	ⓑ/01	c/–
11 c	d/–	ⓒ/10	ⓒ/10	ⓒ/01
10 d	ⓓ/00	c/–	c/–	ⓓ/10

10.16 Repeat Problem 10.13 for the following reduced flow table.

x_1x_2

$y_1y_2y_3$	00	01	11	10
000 a	$\textcircled{a}$/1	c/–	b/–	$\textcircled{a}$/1
001 b	$\textcircled{b}$/0	d/–	$\textcircled{b}$/0	a/–
010 c	a/–	$\textcircled{c}$/0	e/–	$\textcircled{c}$/0
101 d	b/–	$\textcircled{d}$/1	f/–	$\textcircled{d}$/1
110 e	$\textcircled{e}$/1	f/–	$\textcircled{e}$/1	c/–
100 f	a/–	$\textcircled{f}$/0	$\textcircled{f}$/1	a/–

10.17 Given the following excitation table:

x_1x_2

y_1y_2	00	01	11	10
00	$\textcircled{00}$	$\textcircled{00}$	11	01
01	11	$\textcircled{01}$	10	$\textcircled{01}$
11	00	00	$\textcircled{10}$	$\textcircled{10}$
10	$\textcircled{11}$	10	$\textcircled{11}$	10

Y_1Y_2

(a) Find all race conditions in the table.

(b) Are the races critical or noncritical?

(c) Do any cycles exist in the table?

10.18 Analyze the circuit in Fig. P10.18 to determine if the circuit has a critical race. If so, draw a timing diagram to show the effect that the race can have on the circuit response.

10.19 Repeat Problem 10.18 for the circuit shown in Fig. P10.19.

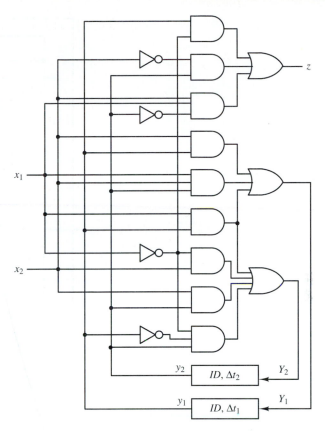

Figure P10.18

10.20   Determine a critical race-free state assignment for the following reduced flow table. Construct the corresponding excitation table.

$$x$$

	0	1
a	$\textcircled{a}$/0	d/–
b	$\textcircled{b}$/1	c/–
c	a/0	$\textcircled{c}$/0
d	b/0	$\textcircled{d}$/1

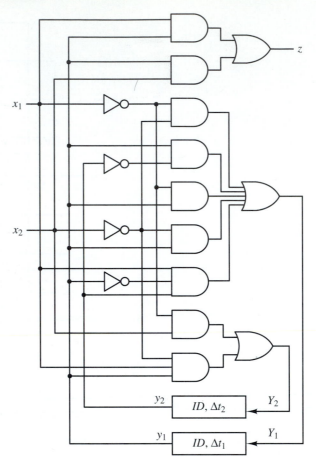

Figure P10.19

10.21 Repeat Problem 10.20 for the following reduced flow table:

$$x_1 x_2$$

	00	01	11	10
a	ⓐ/0	b/–	c/–	ⓐ/0
b	ⓑ/1	ⓑ/1	ⓑ/1	c/1
c	a/–	b/1	ⓒ/1	ⓒ/1

10.22   Given the following reduced flow table:

$$x_1 x_2$$

	00	01	11	10
a	$\textcircled{a}$/0	d/0	$\textcircled{a}$/1	c/0
b	$\textcircled{b}$/0	c/–	$\textcircled{b}$/0	d/–
c	b/0	$\textcircled{c}$/1	a/1	$\textcircled{c}$/0
d	a/0	$\textcircled{d}$/0	b/0	$\textcircled{d}$/1

(a) Use method 1 to find a critical race-free assignment for the table. Construct the corresponding excitation table.

(b) Repeat part (a) using method 2.

10.23   A fundamental-mode circuit is to be designed to function as an electronic lock. The lock has two switch inputs (x_1 and x_2). Design the circuit so that an open signal ($z = 1$) is produced only after the following conditions have been satisfied:

1. Begin with $x_1 = x_2 = 0$.

2. While $x_2 = 0$, x_1 is turned on, then off twice.

3. While x_1 remains off, x_2 is turned on to open the lock.

10.24   A fundamental-mode asynchronous sequential circuit is defined in Fig. P10.24 and the following equations.

$$Y_1 = \bar{x}_2 y_2 + x_1 y_1 + x_1 \bar{x}_2$$
$$Y_2 = \bar{x}_1 y_2 + \bar{x}_1 x_2 + x_2 y_1$$
$$z = x_1 \bar{x}_2 + x_2 \bar{y}_1 + \bar{x}_1 y_2$$

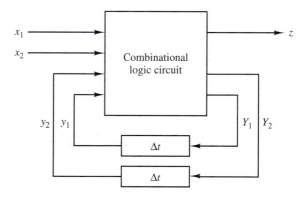

Figure P10.24

(a) Find a flow table.

(b) Using the flow table developed in part (a), find the output sequence for the input sequence $x_1x_2 = 00, 01, 11, 10, 11, 01, 00, 10$ if the delay lines are initially at zero (stable state $x_1 = x_2 = y_1 = y_2 = 0$).

10.25 Given the following reduced flow table, find a critical race-free secondary state assignment for this asynchronous sequential circuit. Find a two-level NOR realization using inertial delay elements.

$$x_1x_2$$

	00	01	11	10
a	$\textcircled{a}/0$	$b/-$	$\textcircled{a}/1$	$b/-$
b	$a/-$	$\textcircled{b}/0$	$c/-$	$\textcircled{b}/0$
c	$a/-$	$\textcircled{c}/1$	$\textcircled{c}/0$	$b/-$

10.26 Find a two-level NAND realization for the following primitive flow table:

$$x_1x_2$$

	00	01	11	10
a	$\textcircled{a}/0$	$b/-$	$-/-$	$c/-$
b	$a/-$	$\textcircled{b}/1$	$d/-$	$-/-$
c	$a/-$	$-/-$	$d/-$	$\textcircled{c}/1$
d	$-/-$	$b/-$	$\textcircled{d}/0$	$e/-$
e	$a/-$	$-/-$	$d/-$	$\textcircled{e}/0$

10.27 Find a two-level NOR implementation for a fundamental-mode asynchronous sequential circuit with two inputs (x_1, x_2) and one output (z) that satisfies the following conditions: First, z is always zero when $x_2 = 1$. The output z changes to logic 1 on the first $0 \rightarrow 1$ transition of x_1 when $x_2 = 0$ and remains at logic 1 until x_2 goes to logic 1 and forces z back to logic 0.

10.28 Find a two-level NAND realization of a fundamental-mode circuit that has two inputs (x_1, x_2) and one output (z) that satisfies the following conditions: First, $z = 0$ when $x_1 = 0$. The output z goes to logic 1 on the first $1 \rightarrow 0$ transition of x_2 when $x_1 = 1$. The output remains at logic 1 until x_1 returns to 0.

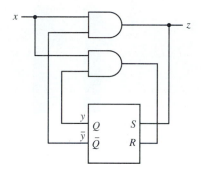

Figure P10.29

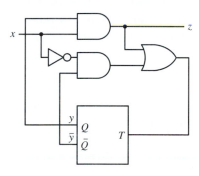

Figure P10.30

10.29 Consider the asynchronous sequential circuit presented in Fig. P10.29. If the circuit input is synchronous pulses, determine the following:
(a) The state table if $A \equiv 0$, $B \equiv 1$.
(b) The state diagram.
(c) The timing diagram for $x = 010011010$ and $y^0 = 0$.
Hint: You may use K-maps.

10.30 Analyze the asynchronous sequential circuit of Fig. P10.30. This circuit has synchronous pulses as its input x. Construct the following:
(a) A timing diagram for the input sequence $x = 01101000$ and $y^0 = 0$.
(b) A state table.
(c) A state diagram.
In your solution you may define the pulse widths of the input x to be equal to the time delay of the T flip-flop. Discuss what effect the following condition will have on the operation of this sequential circuit: Allow the input pulse to be somewhat longer than the flip-flop time delay. Show your conclusions on the timing diagram for part (a).

10.31 Analyze the asynchronous sequential circuit of Fig. P10.31 if the circuit input x is in the form of synchronous pulses. Find the following:
(a) The timing diagram if $x = 01010010100$ and $y_1^0 y_2^0 = 11$.
(b) The state table.
(c) The state diagram.
Hint: K-maps yield incorrect results because assumption 3 for pulse-type circuits is violated.

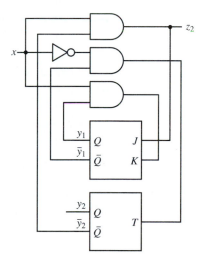

Figure P10.31

In Chapter 5 we examined programmable logic devices (PLDs), which are used to replace small scale integrated circuits in implementing combinational logic circuits. A number of programmable devices also support the implementation of sequential circuits, both synchronous and asynchronous. These devices contain either latches/flip-flops or logic gates that can be interconnected to create latches and flip-flops. In this chapter we examine two basic types of user-programmable circuits: programmable logic devices (PLDs), including field-programmable logic sequencers (FPLS) and programmable array logic devices (PALs) with registered or macrocell outputs, and programmable gate arrays, which include logic cell arrays (LCAs) and field-programmable gate arrays (FPGAs). After examining their basic structures, sequential circuit design with these devices will be discussed. Finally, computer-aided design (CAD) tools used to develop sequential circuits with programmable logic will be described.

Sequential Circuits with Programmable Logic Devices

11.1 Registered Programmable Logic Devices

As discussed in Chapter 8, the basic model of a sequential circuit is that of Fig. 11.1, comprising a combinational logic block and memory. The state of the circuit is stored in one or more memory elements, usually flip-flops or latches. The inputs to the combinational logic block are the external inputs to the circuit, $(x_1, \ldots x_n)$, and the circuit state variables, $(y_1, \ldots y_r)$, which are the outputs of the memory elements. The combinational logic block produces the external outputs of the circuit, $(z_1, \ldots z_m)$, and the next-state information, $(Y_1, \ldots Y_r)$, in the form of flip-flop excitation equations.

Several variations of the basic model of Fig. 11.1 are often used to illustrate various aspects of the sequential circuit structure. The most common is to partition the combinational logic block to distinguish the generation of outputs from next-state variables. This allows us to more easily distinguish a Mealy model from a Moore model, as defined in Chapter 8. Figure 11.2a shows a Mealy model, in which both the outputs and the next-state variables are functions of the inputs and the present state. Figure 11.2b shows a Moore model, in which the outputs are functions of the state variables only. For some

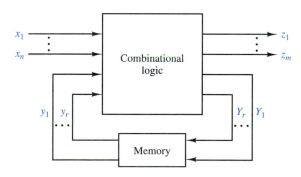

Figure 11.1 General model of a sequential logic circuit.

circuits, such as counters and shift registers, the Moore model outputs are simply the state variables, as shown in Fig. 11.2c.

In Figs. 11.2a and b, the outputs of the circuit are combinational; that is, they are outputs of combinational logic circuits and are thus asynchronous to the clock. Combinational outputs respond immediately whenever the inputs or the state variables change. In many cases it is desirable to synchronize output changes with a clock in the same manner as the state variable changes are synchronized to a clock. This is done by adding an output register to the circuit, as illustrated in Fig. 11.3, with the clock controlling both the state and the

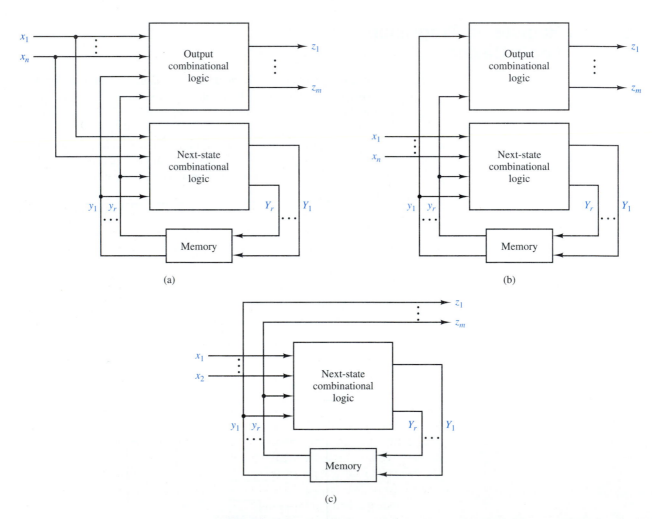

Figure 11.2 Sequential circuit models with separate combinational logic for outputs and next state. **(a)** Mealy model. **(b)** Moore model. **(c)** Moore model (outputs = state variables).

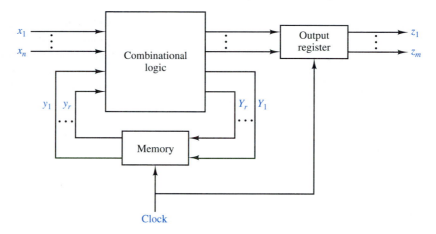

Figure 11.3 Sequential circuit model with synchronous outputs.

output flip-flops. The output register thus holds the outputs constant until the clock triggers a change in state.

Output registers are often used with nonsequential logic circuits as well to hold the outputs of a combinational logic circuit constant while inputs are changing. A clock then causes the outputs to all change simultaneously once the inputs are stable.

The PLDs described in Chapter 5 are ideal for implementing the combinational logic block(s) of a sequential circuit, with the restriction that all excitation and output equations be expressed in two-level SOP form. The sequential circuit is completed by adding memory elements. Many commercially available PLDs contain flip-flops or latches whose excitation inputs are driven by the outputs of a standard PLA or PAL. The outputs of the flip-flops/latches are often fed back to the inputs of the PLA/PAL circuit. Hence, these devices are ideally suited to implementing sequential circuits of the form of Fig. 11.1.

The general structure of a registered PLD is shown in Fig. 11.4. As with combinational PLDs, a registered PLD contains a programmable AND array whose outputs feed an OR array; the OR array is programmable in PLA-based devices and fixed in PAL-based devices. Each output of the OR array drives either an external output pin, in which case it is referred to as a *combinational output*, or an excitation input of a flip-flop. Flip-flop outputs may be connected to external pins, in which case the pins are referred to as *registered outputs*, or else the flip-flop outputs may be fed back to the AND array without being connected to external pins, in which case they are referred to as *buried registers*. Both combinational and registered outputs may likewise be fed back to the AND array. These different configurations are illustrated in Fig. 11.5.

Mealy models of the form of Fig. 11.2a can be implemented with registered PLDs as shown in Fig. 11.6a, by using combinational outputs for the output functions and flip-flops to store the state variables. Since the state variables need not be visible at the outputs, either buried registers or registered outputs

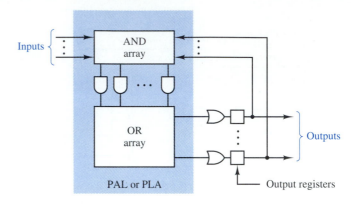

Figure 11.4 General structure of a registered PLD.

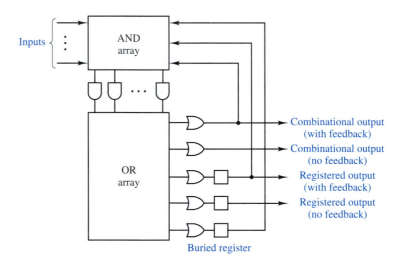

Figure 11.5 Registered PLD output options.

with feedback can be used. Moore models of the form of Fig. 11.2c require that the state flip-flops drive the external outputs, as shown in Fig. 11.6b, and thus registered outputs with feedback are needed. Moore models of the form of Fig. 11.2b are likewise implemented as in Fig. 11.6a, with the output equations generated in the AND/OR array as functions of the state variables only.

For Moore models of the form of Fig. 11.2c, combinational outputs are not required. However, all state variable flip-flops must drive external outputs. Typical examples include counters, shift registers, and accumulators.

To implement a sequential machine with synchronous outputs, as shown in Fig. 11.3, registered outputs are needed to latch the outputs, although these output values do not need to be fed back to the AND array.

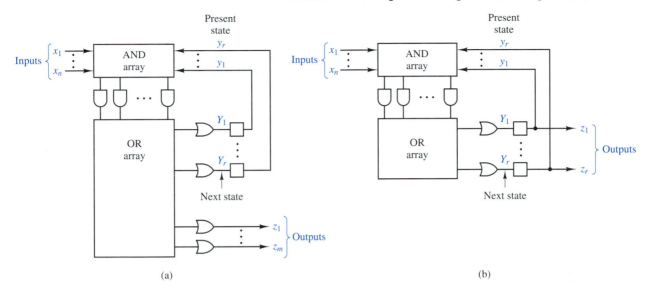

Figure 11.6   Sequential circuit models mapped onto registered PLDs.
(a) Mealy model. **(b)** Moore model ($z_i = y_i$).

Sequential PLDs often include a number of other useful programmable features. In some devices, the mode of operation of the flip-flops can be programmed, allowing the designer to configure each storage element as a D, T, JK, or SR flip-flop, as best fits the design. Another common option is programmable output polarity, allowing either true (Q) or complemented ($\bar{Q}$) flip-flop outputs to drive the external output pins.

Many PLD flip-flops have synchronous or asynchronous *clear* and/or *preset* inputs. Most clear/preset inputs are driven by single product terms generated in the AND array, although some devices connect an external control pin to these inputs to facilitate implementation of an external reset line.

Some PLDs support asynchronous sequential machine design by allowing individual flip-flop clock inputs to be driven by terms from the AND/OR array, rather than synchronizing all flip-flops to a single clock signal from an external pin on the device. In some cases, the user can select either synchronous or asynchronous operation for each flip-flop.

In the next sections we examine two primary classes of PLDs that are used in synchronous sequential machine applications: PLA-based devices, called field-programmable logic sequencers, and registered PAL devices.

11.1.1 Field-Programmable Logic Sequencers

The *field-programmable logic sequencer* (FPLS), introduced by Signetics in 1979 [1], is one of the oldest programmable logic elements developed to support sequential logic circuit implementation. A typical FPLS device is organized around a field-programmable logic array (FPLA). As described in Chapter 5, an FPLA contains a programmable AND array whose outputs feed a programmable OR array, as shown in Fig. 11.4. In an FPLS, the OR array outputs drive either flip-flop excitation inputs or combinational outputs. The outputs of the flip-flops are normally fed back to the AND array, allowing state variables to be realized.

Sequential circuits are realized in an FPLS by assigning state variables $(y_1, \ldots, y_r)$ to r flip-flops (buried registers or registered outputs with feedback), assigning the external outputs $(z_1, \ldots, z_m)$ to combinational output pins, and assigning the external inputs $(x_1, \ldots, x_n)$ to input pins. Most FPLS devices include some mixture of registered and combinational outputs, with the registered outputs realizing the state variables and the combinational outputs, the output variables. After assigning resources, the output equations and flip-flop excitation equations are derived in two-level SOP form, as described in Chapter 8, and then mapped onto the programmable AND and OR arrays.

Table 11.1 lists several FPLS devices available from Philips [1], which are typical of the devices available from various manufacturers. We will examine two of these in detail, the PLS105, which contains SR flip-flops, and the PLS155, which contains user-configurable flip-flops.

TABLE 11.1   SIGNETICS FPLS DEVICES [1]

Device	Organization	Registered Outputs	Buried Registers	FF Type
PLS105	$16 \times 48 \times 8$	8	6	SR
PLS155	$16 \times 45 \times 12$	4	0	D/JK/T
PLS157	$16 \times 45 \times 12$	6	0	D/JK/T
PLS167	$14 \times 48 \times 6$	6	6	SR
PLS168	$12 \times 48 \times 8$	8	6	SR
PLS179	$20 \times 45 \times 12$	8	6	D/JK/T

PLS105

The PLS105 FPLS device [1] was one of the first FPLS devices commercially available and is based on the PLS100 FPLA device. As shown in Fig. 11.7, the PLS105 contains 14 SR flip-flops. The outputs of eight of the flip-flops are connected to external output pins and are not fed back to the AND array, so they are not suitable for implementing state variables. These flip-flops would be used to create an output register. The outputs of the remaining six flip-flops, P_5 to P_0, are fed back to the AND array, but are not connected to external output pins. In this configuration, the latter six flip-flops are referred to as *buried registers*, since they are contained within the chip without their outputs being directly accessible. Thus, sequential machines with up to six state variables and eight outputs may be realized with a single PLS105.

All 14 of the flip-flops on the PLS105 are driven by a common clock input pin, CK, and a common preset input pin, PR/$\overline{\text{OE}}$. If the preset option is

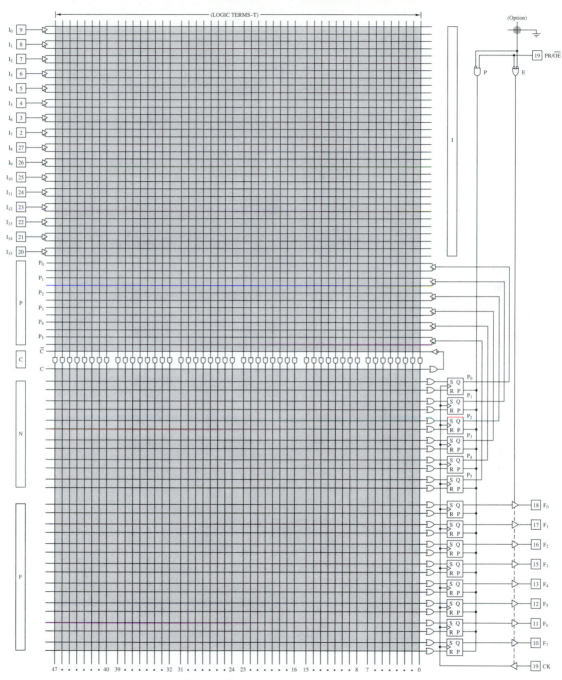

NOTES:
1. All AND gate inputs with a blown link float to a logic "1".
2. All OR gate inputs with a blown link float to a logic "0".
3. ● Programmable connection.

Figure 11.7 Philips PLS105 FPLS [1]. *Source*: Philips, "Programmable Logic Devices (PLD) Data Handbook," Philips Semiconductors, Sunnyvale, CA, 1994.

not needed, the $PR/\overline{OE}$ pin can be used to enable the tristate drivers connected to the output register.

The overall organization of the PLS105 is $16 \times 48 \times 8$, with 16 dedicated inputs I_{15} to I_0, 8 outputs F_7 to F_0, and 48 product terms generated in the AND array. The OR array of the PLA portion of the device has 29 outputs; 28 drive the S and R excitation inputs of the 14 flip-flops, and one complemented SOP expression, C, is produced and fed back to the AND array along with the six flip-flop outputs P_5 to P_0.

PLS155

The PLS155 [1], shown in Fig. 11.8, contains four registered outputs, F_3 to F_0, and eight combinational outputs, B_7 to B_0. All 12 of these signals are fed back as inputs to the AND array. Note that the combinational outputs are similar to those of a standard FPLA, such as the PLS100 described in Chapter 5. The data sheet for the PLS155 [1] lists its organization as $16 \times 45 \times 12$, indicating that there are 16 inputs, 45 product terms, and 12 outputs. Examination of Fig. 11.8 shows that there are only four dedicated inputs, I_3 to I_0. Tristate drivers on the eight combinational outputs can be disabled by product terms D_7 to D_0 to allow the corresponding pins to be used as inputs or enabled to drive the outputs.

The tristate drivers on the registered outputs can likewise be disabled to allow these pins to be used as inputs. In this case the inputs are not fed directly to the AND array. Instead, these pins force values onto the flip-flop excitation inputs, thus loading the flip-flops directly from the external pins. The flip-flop outputs are fed back as inputs to the AND array, allowing them to store the state variables of a sequential circuit. Hence, sequential circuits with up to four state variables can be implemented in a single PLS155 device.

The flip-flops of the PLS155 are flexible in that they can be programmed to operate as either JK or D flip-flops. Examine the circuit of flip-flop F_0, which is enlarged in Fig. 11.9. The storage element itself is a JK flip-flop. The *foldback buffer*, controlled by M_0, determines the actual mode of operation. If the buffer is disabled by $M_0 = 1$, it acts as an open circuit, making the J and K inputs to the flip-flop independent, as illustrated in Fig. 11.10a. If the buffer is enabled by $M_0 = 0$, as illustrated in Fig. 11.10b, the K input becomes equal to the complement of the J input. Note that the output of the foldback buffer is wire-ORed with the output of OR gate $G2$. Therefore, the output of $G2$ must be set to 0 to allow the foldback buffer output to determine the K input to the flip-flop. Recall from Chapter 6 that a JK flip-flop is made to operate as a D flip-flop by setting $J = D$ and $K = \bar{D}$. In this case, the D input is the output of OR gate $G1$.

If desired, M_0 can be fuse-programmed to 0 to configure the flip-flop permanently as a D flip-flop. Otherwise, the behavior of the flip-flop is determined by the output of AND gate F_C, allowing the flip-flop to be dynamically switched between JK and D modes of operation. If an SR flip-flop is desired, we simply use the JK flip-flop configuration with $J = S$ and $K = R$, with the combination $S = R = 1$ disallowed. Likewise, the equivalent of a T flip-flop

Figure 11.8 Philips PLS155 FPLS [1]. *Source*: Philips, "Programmable Logic Devices (PLD) Data Handbook," Philips Semiconductors, Sunnyvale, CA, 1994.

Notes:
1. All OR gate inputs with a blown link float to logic "0".
2. All other gates and control inputs with a blown link float to logic "1".
3. ⊕ denotes WIRE-OR
4. Programmable connection.

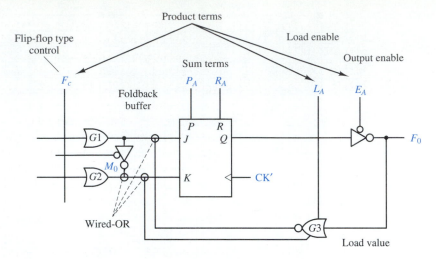

Figure 11.9   PLS155 programmable flip-flop.

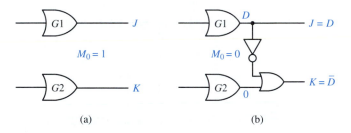

Figure 11.10   Equivalent circuits of the PLS155 flip-flop for JK
and D operation. **(a)** Foldback buffer disabled ($M_0 = 1$) (JK flip-
flop operation). **(b)** Foldback buffer enabled ($M_0 = 0$) (D flip-flop
operation).

can be created by setting $J = K = T$, programming both OR gates $G1$ and
$G2$ to supply T.

One additional feature of the four PLS155 flip-flops is that they can be
synchronously loaded from pins F_3 to F_0. This is done for flip-flop F_0 of Fig.
11.9 by setting the output of the *load* AND gate (L_A) to 1, which enables gate
$G3$ to apply the value on pin F_0 and its complement to the J and K inputs of
the flip-flop, respectively. The flip-flop is set or reset to the desired state on the
next clock pulse. Because of the wired-OR connections at the J and K inputs,
the outputs of gates $G1$ and $G2$ must be forced to 0 during a load operation.

11.1.2 Registered PALs

Registered PALs are similar to the FPLS devices just examined in that they
contain standard PAL configurations with one or more outputs driving flip-flop
excitation inputs. The notation used to designate registered PALs is the same as

for combinational PALs: PALxyz, where x is the total number of inputs, z is the total number of outputs, and y indicates the output architecture. Other suffixes are often appended to indicate the speed of the device, the power consumption, and the circuit technology (bipolar TTL, CMOS, UV-erasable, electrically erasable, and the like) [2]. Often a single PAL architecture is available in multiple technologies.

Many PAL devices are members of families that utilize a single basic PAL structure but have different output architectures. The most common output architectures are summarized in Table 11.2. For a simple registered PAL, the designation R indicates registered outputs. For example, a PAL16R6 has a total of 16 inputs and 6 registered outputs. This device will be examined in the next section.

TABLE 11.2   REGISTERED PAL OUTPUT ARCHITECTURES

Code	Meaning
R	Registered
RP	Registered with programmable polarity
RA	Registered asynchronous
X	XOR registered
A	Arithmetic registered
V	Versatile macrocell
S	Sequencer

Registered asynchronous outputs differ from standard registered outputs in that the flip-flop clock inputs are driven by product terms or SOP expressions generated in the AND/OR array, rather than by a single clock input pin. This allows asynchronous sequential circuits to be implemented as described in Chapter 10, since the individual flip-flops can be controlled independently as functions of the inputs and state variables.

XOR registered devices, such as the PAL16X4, and *arithmetic registered* devices, such as the PAL16A4, are similar in that exclusive-OR gates drive the excitation inputs of D flip-flops, facilitating the implementation of arithmetic functions, such as addition and subtraction. Typically, the two inputs to these XOR gates are SOP expressions generated in the AND/OR array of the PAL. The arithmetic registered architecture also includes special logic on the feedback lines to facilitate the implementation of carry and/or borrow signals between bits of various arithmetic circuits.

The output architecture designation V indicates *versatile* logic macrocells at the outputs, which contain a number of programmable options. A common example is the PAL22V10, which has 22 inputs and 10 outputs, with each output containing a programmable macrocell. The PAL22V10 will be examined in more detail later.

Table 11.3 lists several commonly used registered PALs and their configurations. The reader is referred to [2] for further details on these and other PAL devices.

TABLE 11.3   REGISTERED PALS [2]

Device	Dedicated Inputs	Dedicated Registered Outputs	I/O Pins	Products
PAL16R8	8	8	0	8
PAL16R6	8	6	2	8
PAL16R4	8	4	4	8
PAL16RP8	8	8	0	8
PAL16RA8	8	0–8	8–0	4
PAL16X4	8	4	4	8
PAL20R8	12	8	0	8
PAL20XRP8	10	8	2	8
PAL22V10	12	0–10	10–0	8–16
PAL32VX10	12	0–10	10–0	8–16
PAL23S8	9	4	4	8–12

PAL16R6

The PAL16R6 is one of the PAL16R8 family of 20-pin registered PAL devices. As shown in Fig. 11.11, the PAL16R6 contains eight dedicated input pins, I_8 to I_1, and eight output pins, of which two are combinational (I/O_8 and I/O_1) and six are registered (O_7 to O_2). Each registered output pin is driven by a D flip-flop whose outputs and their complements are fed back to the AND array. The combinational outputs are likewise fed back, making a total of 32 inputs to the AND array. Each D flip-flop excitation input is driven by one of the eight PAL SOP outputs. Hence, the PAL has a total of 32 inputs and 8 outputs. All six flip-flops are controlled by a single clock input pin CLK. All eight output pins are driven by tristate drivers that are controlled by the single $\overline{OE}$ control pin.

Other registered PALs in the PAL16R8 family include the 16R4 and 16R8, which use the same basic PAL circuit, but with different distributions of flip-flops and combinational outputs at the eight output pins. For example, the 16R4 has four combinational and four registered outputs, and the 16R8 has eight registered outputs and no combinational outputs.

Other devices in the PAL16R8 family, such as the PAL16A4, the PAL16X4, and the PAL16RP8, utilize the same basic PAL circuit, but have different output architectures. Additional registered PAL families are built around different PAL configurations. These are described more fully in [2].

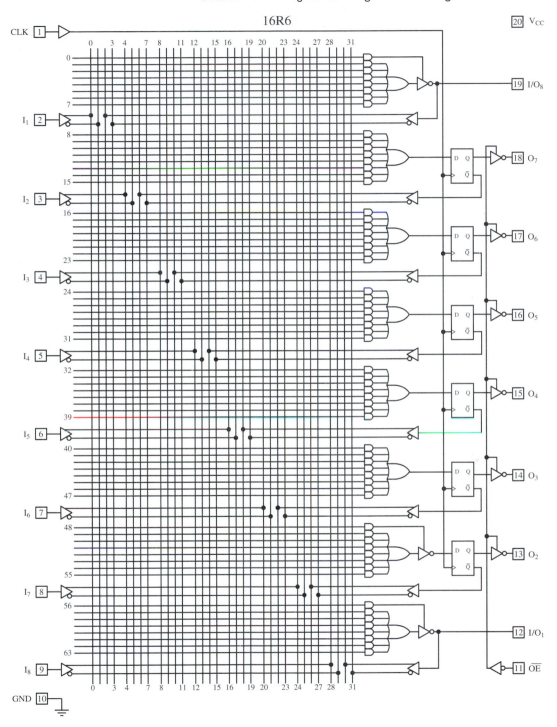

Figure 11.11   AMD PAL16R6 [2]. Copyright © Advanced Micro Devices, Inc., 1993. Reprinted with permission of copyright owner. All rights reserved.

11.1.3 PLDs with Programmable Logic Macrocells

To make registered PLDs more flexible, universal devices have been created that contain programmable logic macrocells instead of simple flip-flop configurations at the outputs. A *macrocell* is a logic circuit associated with an output pin that contains a flip-flop and a number of programmable options. This minimizes the number of device types needed for a given design, since the output cells of a single device can be configured in a variety of ways. Typical programmable options include the ability to either use or bypass the flip-flop, selection of the operational mode of the flip-flop (D, T, SR, or JK), selection of the true (Q) or complement ($\bar{Q}$) of the flip-flop as the output and/or as the feedback signal, the ability to make the flip-flop either a registered output or a buried register, and other options related to flip-flop clock, preset, and clear inputs.

A programmable macrocell can be configured to operate in a manner equivalent to most of the fixed registered-PAL output configurations. For this reason, a single device type can be used in a variety of applications. Consequently, fixed registered PALs are gradually being replaced by macrocell-based PALs.

Two of the more commonly used configurations are the PAL22V10 and the Altera EP910. These will be examined in this section.

PAL22V10

The PAL22V10 contains a 44×132 PAL that drives 10 output macrocells, as illustrated in Fig. 11.12. Each macrocell, as shown in Fig. 11.13, has four output options and two feedback options, which are programmed using fuses S_1 and S_0 according to Table 11.4.

The output of the macrocell is selected by a 4-to-1 multiplexer; output options include the PAL combinational output and its complement and the Q and $\bar{Q}$ flip-flop outputs. The output is programmed by fuse S_1 to be either combinational or registered and by fuse S_0 to be active high or low. Fuse S_1 also selects the feedback signal by controlling the feedback multiplexer. When S_1 selects a combinational output, the feedback signal comes directly from the I/O pin; otherwise, the feedback signal comes from the $\bar{Q}$ output of the flip-flop. Note that the feedback signal is supplied to the AND array in both complemented and uncomplemented forms.

TABLE 11.4 **PAL22V10 PROGRAMMABLE MACROCELL**

S_1	S_0	Output	Feedback
0	0	Combinational (active high)	I/O pin
0	1	Combinational (active low)	I/O pin
1	0	Registered (Q)	Flip-flop output $\bar{Q}$
1	1	Registered ($\bar{Q}$)	Flip-flop output $\bar{Q}$

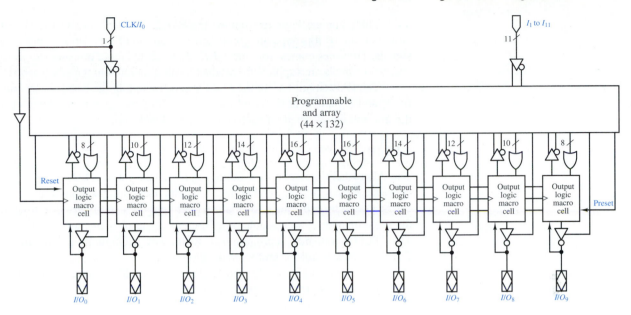

Figure 11.12 PAL22V10 PLD with programmable macrocells [2]. Copyright ⓒ Advanced Micro Devices, Inc., 1993. Reprinted with permission of copyright owner. All rights reserved.

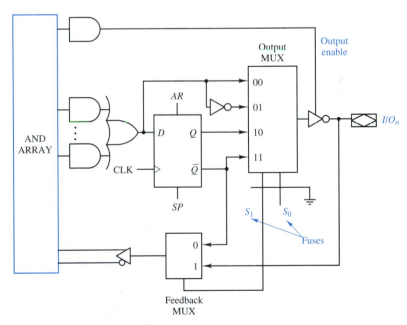

Figure 11.13 PAL22V10 programmable macrocell structure [2]. Copyright ⓒ Advanced Micro Devices, Inc., 1993. Reprinted with permission of copyright owner. All rights reserved.

The complete logic diagram of the PAL22V10 is shown in Fig. 11.14. Note that all 10 flip-flops are controlled by common *clock*, *preset*, and *reset* signals. The *clock* comes from the CLK/I_0 dedicated input pin, and the *preset* and *reset* signals are supplied by product terms generated in the AND array.

The PAL circuit has a total of 44 inputs, including the true (noninverted form) and complement (inverted form) of each of the 12 external inputs and the true and complement of each of the 10 feedback signals.

EP910

The Altera EP910 is one of a family of EPLD (erasable PLD) devices that contain a PAL with macrocell outputs [3]. The fuse configuration of an EPLD can be erased by exposing it to an ultraviolet light for a short period of time, in the same manner as an erasable programmable read-only memory (EPROM). The EPLD can then be reprogrammed with a new configuration. This makes EPLD devices useful for prototype development.

As shown in Fig. 11.15, the EP910 contains 24 macrocells. The PAL section of the EP910 has 72 inputs, which come from the true and complemented forms of 12 dedicated input pins and feedback lines from the 24 macrocells, and generates 72 product terms. Each of the 24 macrocells is driven by one PAL output, which is a sum of eight product terms. One additional product term controls the asynchronous reset input of the flip-flop in the macrocell, and another product term controls either the flip-flop clock input or the output enable control line of the tristate output driver.

The output macrocell structure, shown in Fig. 11.16, is similar to that of the PAL22V10 in that the output and feedback signals are selected by programmable multiplexers. However, the EP910 has several other programmable options. The operating mode of each flip-flop can be programmed (D, T, JK, or SR), as illustrated in Figs. 11.17a through d, or the flip-flop can be bypassed to create a combinational output, as in Fig. 11.17e. If a D or T flip-flop is used, the feedback multiplexer selects either the flip-flop output or the external I/O pin to supply the feedback signal. A two-position multiplexer selects the flip-flop clock input and output driver control signals. In one position, the external clock pin drives the flip-flop clock input, and a product term controls the output driver. In the other position, the multiplexer selects the product term to drive the flip-flop clock input and permanently enables the output driver. The external clock pin is normally used for synchronous sequential circuits, while the ability to use a product term to control the clock is needed for asynchronous operation.

Altera provides a family of EPLD devices whose features are similar to those of the EP910. These are summarized in Table 11.5.

▶ 11.2 Programmable Gate Arrays

A PLD is limited by its basic architecture to realizations of two-level SOP switching expressions for all outputs and excitation variables. In addition, the number and configurations of the registers is limited. In contrast, a *gate array*

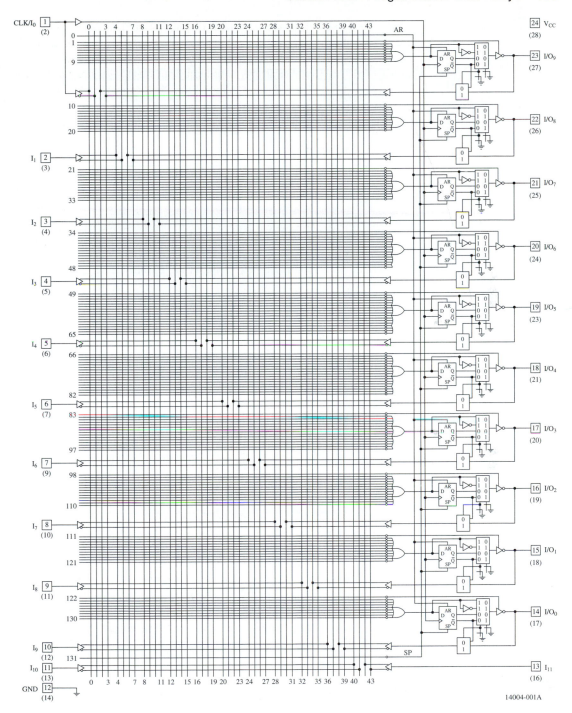

Figure 11.14 Complete PAL22V10 PLD logic diagram [2]. Copyright © Advanced Micro Devices, Inc., 1993. Reprinted with permission of copyright owner. All rights reserved.

Figure 11.15 Altera EP910 EPLD [3] *Source*: Altera, User-compatible Logic Databook, Altera Corp., Santa Clara, CA, 1988.

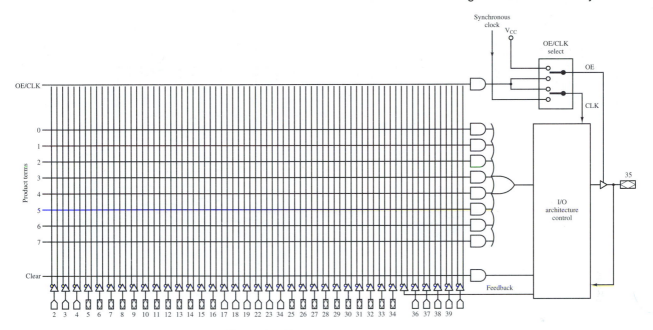

Figure 11.16   EP910 macrocell structure [3]. *Source*: Altera, User-configurable Logic Databook, Altera Corp., Santa Clara, CA, 1988.

TABLE 11.5   ALTERA EPLDS [3]

Device	Macrocells	Inputs
EP310, EP320	8	10
EP512	12	10
EP600, EP610	16	4
EP900, EP910	24	12
EP1800, EP1810	48	16

has no fixed interconnection architecture, but instead provides a pool of simple logic gates and other elements with no fixed connections between their inputs or outputs. Circuits are created by specifying desired interconnection patterns, with virtually no limits on these patterns. Gate arrays can be ordered from and configured by the manufacturer by providing the manufacturer with an interconnection pattern. In contrast, *field-programmable gate arrays* (FPGAs) are programmed by the user, using a special device programmer to create the interconnections between gates.

11.2.1 Logic Cell Arrays

The *logic cell array* (LCA) is a unique family of programmable devices introduced by Xilinx [4]. As illustrated in Fig. 11.18, each LCA contains a matrix

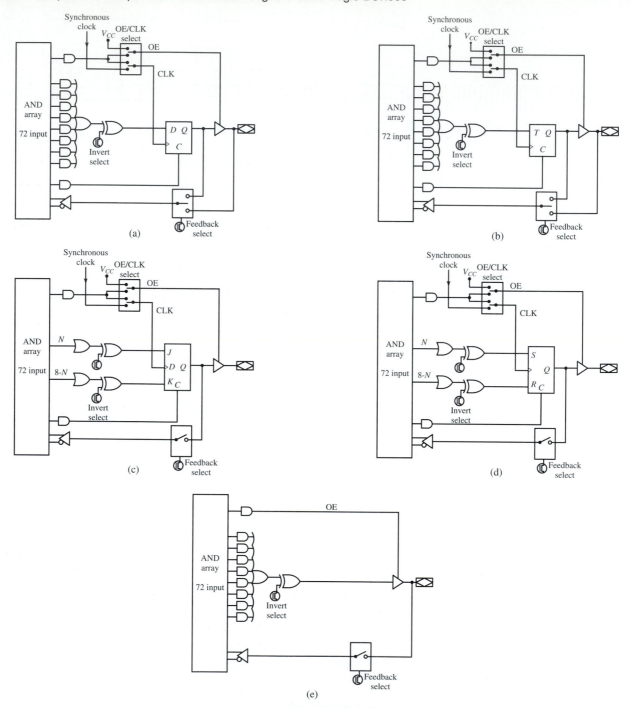

Figure 11.17 EP910 output architectures [3]. **(a)** D flip-flop. **(b)** T flip-flop. **(c)** JK flip-flop. **(d)** SR flip-flop. **(e)** Flip-flop bypassed. *Source*: Altera, User-configurable Logic Databook, Altera Corp., Santa Clara, CA, 1988.

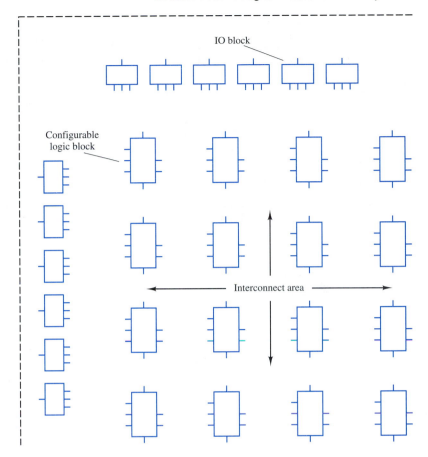

Figure 11.18 Xilinx logic cell array structure [4]. Figure courtesy of Xilinx, Inc.

of *configurable logic blocks* (CLBs), with each CLB containing a flip-flop and a small block of combinational logic. The matrix of CLBs is ringed by *user-configurable I/O blocks* (IOBs), which provide several different options at each I/O pin. The inputs and outputs of the CLBs and IOBs are interconnected with wire segments that lie in wiring channels between the rows and columns of blocks. Multiplexers at the block inputs and outputs connect the blocks to these wire segments, and matrices of switches at each row–column intersection connect the wire segments.

A circuit is created in an LCA by specifying the configuration of each CLB and IOB and by specifying the interconnections between these blocks. The configuration is programmed into the LCA by loading a pattern of ones and zeros into a volatile random-access memory (RAM) within the LCA each time the chip is powered up. If desired, changes can be made to the configuration while the LCA is operating, producing a dynamically changing design.

The IOB structure is shown in Fig. 11.19. Each I/O pin can be programmed to be a dedicated input or output or to be dynamically switched between input and output. The output driver control signal comes from a 3-to-1 multiplexer. If the OFF input of the multiplexer is selected, the output driver is disabled, and the pin operates as a dedicated input. If the ON input of the multiplexer is selected, the output driver is enabled, making the pin a dedicated output. If the TS (three-state control) input of the multiplexer is selected to control the driver, the driver is enabled when $TS = 0$ and is disabled when $TS = 1$. The TS signal is generated by logic within the LCA to make the pin switch dynamically between input and output operating modes.

When the I/O pin is used as an input, a 2-to-1 multiplexer selects either the buffered input signal or the output of a flip-flop to supply the signal to the LCA. This allows an input to be clocked into a flip-flop and held, creating a registered input.

The CLB, shown in Fig. 11.20, contains a combinational logic section and a storage element, along with a number of programmable multiplexers that are used to configure the output and flip-flop options. The combinational section has four inputs (A, B, C, and D) and two outputs (F and G) and can realize any function of four variables with a single output (with $F = G$) or any two functions (F and G) of three variables. These functions are realized by a lookup table stored in a high-speed 16-bit memory, similar to the manner in which logic functions are implemented with PROMs, as was described in Chapter 5.

The storage element can be programmed to operate as either a D flip-flop or a D latch, with the clock active high or low. The D input is driven by the F output of the combinational section. The clock, set, and reset inputs to the storage elements are selected by multiplexers. The clock can be synchronous,

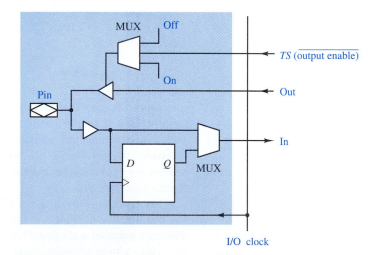

Figure 11.19 LCA I/O block structure [4]. Figure courtesy of Xilinx, Inc. © Xilinx, Inc., 1992. All rights reserved.

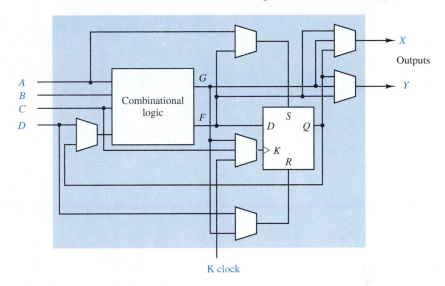

K clock

Figure 11.20   LCA configurable logic block (CLB) structure [4]. Figure courtesy of Xilinx, Inc. © Xilinx, Inc., 1992. All rights reserved.

with the clock signal distributed by the K pin that is common to all CLBs, or asynchronous, with the clock supplied by the combinational function block or the C input.

The two outputs of the CLB, X and Y, are selected by separate output multiplexers whose inputs are the F and G outputs of the combinational section and the flip-flop output Q. Thus, the CLB may have either combinational or registered outputs or both.

The inputs and outputs of the CLBs and IOBs are connected to metal segments (wires) that lie in the channels between the rows and columns of blocks. At each row/column intersection is a switch matrix that is programmed to connect the desired logic elements. Interconnections are made using three types of routing resources: general-purpose interconnects, long lines, and direct connections.

General-purpose interconnects lie in the channels between the rows and columns of CLBs and IOBs, as shown in Fig. 11.21. At each row/column intersection is a switch matrix that connects wire segments in the connected rows and columns. There are four horizontal wire segments between rows and five between columns, each segment running the length of the channel between switch matrixes.

Long lines extend across the entire CLB array, with two per vertical channel and one per row, as shown by the bold lines in Fig. 11.21. These are used to distribute clocks and other signals with minimum skew around the chip.

Separate *direct interconnects* exist between neighboring CLBs. The X output of each CLB can be directly connected to the C or D inputs of the CLB immediately above it or to the A or B inputs of the CLB immediately below

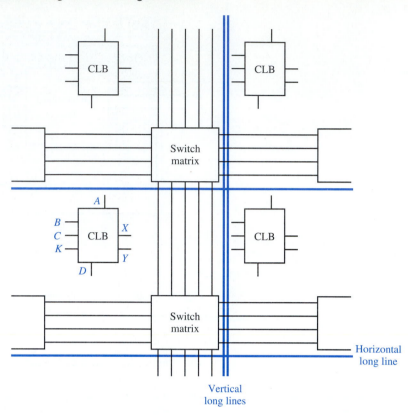

Figure 11.21   LCA general-purpose and long-line interconnects [4]. Figure courtesy of Xilinx, Inc. © Xilinx, Inc., 1992. All rights reserved.

it. The Y output of a CLB can be directly connected to the B input of the CLB immediately to its right. Thus, in laying out a design on an LCA, signal flow is usually from left to right horizontally and from the center toward the outside vertically.

The devices within a Xilinx LCA family share a common CLB and IOB architecture, but have different numbers of CLBs and IOBs, as summarized in Table 11.6. Several families are available, with additional functionality added to the CLBs and IOBs in the XC3000 and XC4000 series. The CLB and IOB configurations presented so far are those of the XC2000 series, which includes the XC2064, which has 58 IOBs and 64 CLBs arranged in an 8×8 matrix, and the XC2018, which has 74 IOBs and 100 CLBs arranged in a 10×10 matrix. The XC2064 is equivalent to approximately 1200 logic gates, while the XC2018 is equivalent to approximately 1800 gates.

The XC3000 series device capacities range from 2000 to 9000 equivalent logic gates. The CLB of the XC3000 extends the CLB design of the XC2000 series devices to a five-input combinational function block and two flip-flops, along with a control section to select a number of flip-flop and output options.

TABLE 11.6 XILINX LOGIC CELL ARRAY DEVICES [4]

Device	Equivalent Gates	CLBs	IOBs
XC2064	1,200	64	64
XC2018	1,800	100	64
XC3020	2,000	64	64
XC3030	3,000	100	80
XC3042	4,200	144	96
XC3064	6,400	224	120
XC3090	9,000	320	144
XC4002	2,000	64	64
XC4003	3,000	100	80
XC4004	4,000	144	96
XC4005	5,000	196	112
XC4006	6,000	256	128
XC4008	8,000	324	144
XC4010	10,000	400	160
XC4013	13,000	576	192
XC4016	16,000	676	208
XC4020	20,000	900	240

The newest family of devices, the XC4000 series, ranges from 8×8 to 30×30 matrices of CLBs and from 64 to 240 IOBs, providing the equivalent of 2000 to 20,000 logic gates. The architecture of the XC4000 family CLB is a considerable enhancement over that of the XC2000 and XC3000 families. As shown in Fig. 11.22, this CLB contains two independent storage elements and three function generators, with a total of 13 inputs and 4 outputs. Two of the outputs are combinational and two are registered. Two of the function generators have four inputs (F_1 to F_4 and G_1 to G_4), while the three inputs of the third function generator include the outputs of the other two function generators (F' and G') and one external input H_1. As in the XC2000 and XC3000 families, high-speed memory lookup is used to implement the function generators. When used together, the three function generators are capable of generating any two independent functions of four variables any single function of five variables, one function of four variables, and some functions of five variables, or some functions of up to nine variables. Thus, wider-input combinational functions can be realized in a single CLB than with previous LCA families.

Not shown in Fig. 11.22 is a special arithmetic carry circuit between the two function generators F and G. This allows a 2-bit adder to be created conveniently, with the carry between the modules handled by the special carry logic.

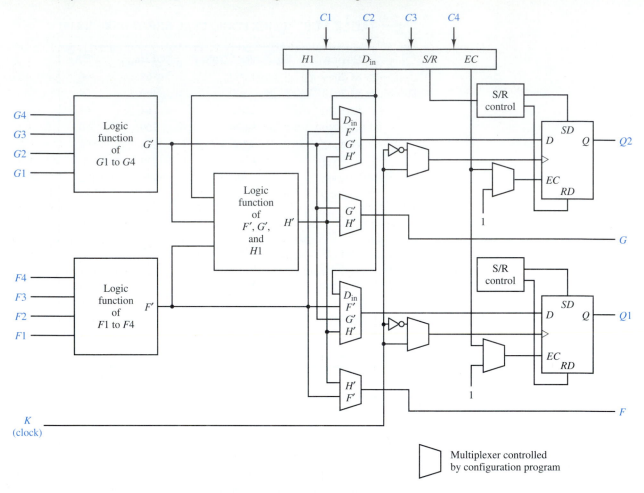

Figure 11.22   Xilinx XC4000 CLB architecture [4]. Figure courtesy of Xilinx, Inc. © Xilinx, Inc., 1992. All rights reserved.

The two storage elements of the XC4000 family CLB are edge-triggered D flip-flops with a common external clock input K. Each flip-flop is programmed independently to trigger on the rising or falling edge of the clock. To facilitate holding the state of a circuit, separate clock enable (EC) inputs are used on each flip-flop. Additionally, each flip-flop has a separate input that can be programmed as a set or a reset control line, with the two flip-flops configured independently. Note that the DIN, S/R, and EC inputs are connected to the external CLB inputs C_1 to C_4 using a multiplexer. This allows any of the four inputs to be connected in any order.

In addition to the improved CLB and IOB designs, the XC4000 also includes twice as many long line interconnections as the previous families, in addition to increased numbers of other routing resources.

is created by specifying a pattern of fuses to be blown to create the necessary interconnections between logic modules.

The devices within the ACT-1 family differ in numbers of available logic modules and I/O pins, as shown in Table 11.7. For example, the A1010 contains 295 logic modules and 57 I/O pins and is equivalent to approximately 1200 logic gates, while the A1020 contains 546 logic modules and 69 I/O pins and is equivalent to approximately 2000 gates.

TABLE 11.7   **ACTEL ACT-1 (A10XX) AND ACT-2 (A12XX) FAMILY DEVICES [5]**

Device	Equivalent Gates	Logic Modules	I/O
A1010	1200	295	57
A1020	2000	546	69
A1225	2500	451	82
A1240	4000	684	104
A1280	8000	1232	140

The ACT-2 family includes devices with considerably more logic gates and I/O pins, ranging from 2500 logic gates for the A1225 to 8000 gates for the A1280 (1232 logic modules and 104 I/O pins).

◗ 11.3 Sequential Circuit Design and PLD Device Selection

Sequential circuit design with programmable logic proceeds in the same manner as when using discrete gates and flip-flops.

1. Design a state diagram from the problem description and derive the state table.
2. Identify and remove redundant states.
3. Make a state variable assignment and derive a state transition table.
4. Select flip-flop types and derive excitation tables for each flip-flop.
5. Derive excitation equations from the excitation tables.
6. Derive output equations from the state table.
7. Map the equations onto logic gates and flip flops.

Steps 1 through 3 are independent of whether discrete gates or programmable logic devices are to be used for the implementation and are performed as discussed in Chapter 8. In step 4, the selection of flip-flop type may be dictated by the type of logic device to be used, or vice versa. In some FPLS devices and registered PLDs, the flip-flop type is fixed. In these cases we must work with the given types. In FPLS devices like the PLS155 and in some PAL devices with programmable output macrocells, each flip-flop type can be individually programmed, in which case we can proceed as if arbitrary discrete flip-flops were available and make a selection that best fits the problem.

The derivation of excitation and output equations may likewise be constrained by the device type. In FPLS devices and PLDs, we must utilize two-level sum of products formats to map the equations onto a programmable AND/OR array. In LCA devices, the optimal approach is to fit the excitation logic of each flip-flop into the same CLB that contains the flip-flop. In FPGA devices, there are fewer restrictions on the architecture of the flip-flop and its excitation logic, so the designer can concentrate on minimizing the number of cells utilized.

Once all equations are developed, realization of the design in the chosen device requires mapping of the logic equations onto the resources of the selected device. This is usually accomplished with the aid of special CAD tools that convert the equations to proper format and fit them into the target device, creating a fuse map that can be loaded into the device by a device programmer.

The selection of a programmable logic device to realize a given design is dictated by a number of key features of the design.

1. *Number of inputs.* The design will have one or more external "data" inputs, as well as a clock and possible set/reset control signals. Programmable device inputs include dedicated input lines that drive the AND/OR array, I/O lines that can be programmed to operate as inputs, and other dedicated inputs that drive flip-flop clock inputs, set/reset inputs, and so on.

2. *Number of storage elements.* The number of storage elements required for a design is a function of the number of state variables and the number of synchronous outputs that are required. State variables must be realized in flip-flops whose outputs are fed back to the AND/OR array. These flip-flops may be registered outputs or buried flip-flops. Synchronous outputs must be realized in registered outputs, although these do not need to be fed back to the AND/OR array. Where registered outputs are needed, either dedicated outputs or I/O lines configured to operate as outputs can be used.

3. *Flip-flop types.* The types of flip-flops available on a programmable device may be fixed, in which case the designer must decide whether the available types are suitable for the design. If not, another device must be selected. In many programmable devices, the operating mode of the flip-flops may be programmed. In these cases, the designer has maximum flexibility.

4. *Number of outputs.* A design may require combinational or registered outputs. In most cases, the outputs are separate from the state variables, although in some Moore machine designs, the state variables are also external outputs of the circuit. Programmable devices may have one or more dedicated outputs, either registered or combinational, and/or I/O lines that can be programmed to operate as outputs. Other output options may include programmable polarity.

5. *Combinational logic.* In PAL- and PLA-based devices, all excitation and output equations must be derived in two-level sum of products form that can be mapped onto AND/OR arrays. In registered PALs, the OR array is fixed, limiting the number of product terms that can be used in each excitation and output equation. In FPLS devices, the OR array is programmable, allowing an arbitrary number of product terms to be used in each equation, within the limits of the total number of product lines on the device. Sharing of product terms between expressions can be done to save product lines.

6. *Special features.* A variety of special features is available on many programmable devices that may be desirable or required for a given design. These include asynchronous clocking of flip-flops, logic terms to drive flip-flop set and reset inputs, and enable logic for tristate output drivers.

7. *Physical properties.* In many cases, designs are constrained by certain physical requirements, such as device package size, power consumption, operating speed, and chip cost and availability. In these cases, the designer may be forced to make trade-offs between device functionality and physical characteristics.

11.4 PLD Design Examples

The following examples illustrate the design and mapping of synchronous sequential circuit designs onto PLD devices.

EXAMPLE 11.1

Design a circuit with one input x and one output z that will produce an output of 1 whenever the last four inputs are 1, that is, a circuit that recognizes the input sequence $x = 1111$. Realize the circuit in a PAL16R6 device.

Using the design procedures described in Chapter 8, the state diagram and reduced state table are shown in Figs. 11.25a and b. The state assignment for the example is arbitrarily chosen as follows:

$$A = 00$$
$$B = 01$$
$$C = 10 \longrightarrow \text{mistake}, \quad C = 11$$
$$D = 11 \longrightarrow D = 10$$

The resulting transition table and output map are given in Figs. 11.25c and d. From these, we see that two flip-flops and one combinational output are required to realize the circuit.

Examination of the PAL16R6 circuit of Fig. 11.11 shows that there are six D flip-flops and two combinational outputs available. Let us use the flip-flops at outputs O_7 and O_6 for the state variables y_1 and y_2 and combinational output I/O_8 for the output z.

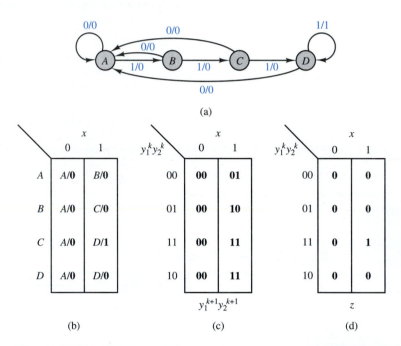

(a)

(b)

(c)

(d)

Figure 11.25 Sequential circuit that detects the input sequence $x = 1111$. **(a)** State diagram. **(b)** State table. **(c)** Transition table. **(d)** Output map.

The excitation equations for the D flip-flop excitation inputs D_1 and D_2 are derived from the transition table of Fig. 11.25c, and the output equation is derived from the output map of Fig. 11.25d.

$$D_1 = xy_1 + xy_2$$
$$D_2 = xy_1 + x\bar{y}_2$$
$$z = xy_1y_2$$
$$= \overline{\bar{x} + \bar{y}_1 + \bar{y}_2}$$

These equations are mapped onto the PAL16R6 as illustrated in Fig. 11.26. For illustration purposes, only the portion of the PAL16R6 used in the implementation is shown.

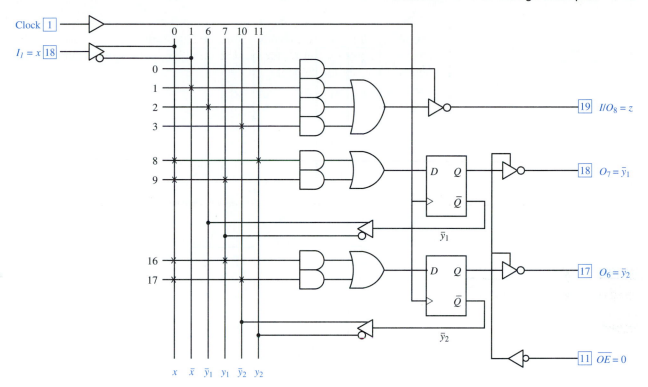

Figure 11.26   PAL16R6 realization of a sequence $x = 1111$ recognizer.

EXAMPLE 11.2

Repeat Example 11.1, but using the PLS155 FPLS device with the storage elements configured as JK flip-flops.

Observation of the PLS155 diagram in Fig. 11.8 shows that there are four registered and eight combinational outputs available. Let us map state variables y_1 and y_2 onto registered outputs F_3 and F_2, respectively, and map output z onto combinational output B_7.

We begin by deriving excitation maps for JK flip-flops from the transition table of Fig. 11.25c. These maps are shown in Fig. 11.27. From the excitation maps, the following excitation equations are derived.

$$J_1 = xy_2, \quad J_2 = x$$
$$K_1 = \bar{x}, \quad K_2 = \bar{x} + \bar{y}_1$$

These equations are mapped onto the PLS155 as illustrated in Fig. 11.28. Note that M_2 and M_3 must both be set to 1 to disable the foldback buffers of the flip-flops, configuring the flip-flops for JK operation.

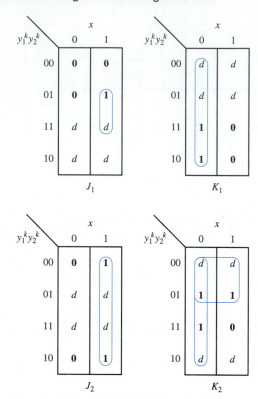

Figure 11.27 JK excitation maps for the sequence $x = 1111$ recognizer.

EXAMPLE 11.3

Design a 4-bit binary up/down counter with parallel load. The inputs include parallel data input lines A_3 to A_0, control signal $L/\bar{C}$, which is high to enable a parallel load of data and low to enable counting, control signal $U/\bar{D}$, which is 1 to signal up and 0 for down during counting, and a clock, CLK. The outputs are the 4-bit count Q_3 to Q_0 and a signal OVR, which indicates an overflow, that is, either a count from 1111 to 0000 or from 0000 to 1111 on the next clock pulse.

From this description, the counter requires six inputs, four registered outputs to realize the count, and one combinational output to realize the OVR output. Examining Table 11.3, we see that the counter would fit into any of the registered PLDs listed in the table, with the exception of the PAL16R8, which contains no combinational outputs. The other devices all have at least four registered outputs with feedback and at least six inputs. For this example, let us use the PAL16R4 device, which has eight dedicated inputs, four registered outputs, and four combinational outputs.

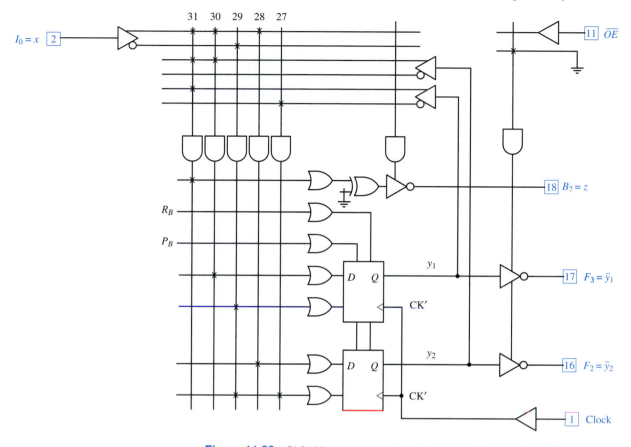

Figure 11.28   PLS155 realization of a sequence $x = 1111$ recognizer.

Since the PAL16R4 contains D flip-flops, we derive the following excitation equations, using the design procedures described in Chapter 8. The output drivers on the registered outputs of the PAL16R4 are inverting, as they are on the PAL16R6 shown in Fig. 11.11. Therefore, the values loaded into the flip-flops must be inverted.

$$D_0 = \bar{A}_0(L/\bar{C}) + \bar{Q}_0\overline{(L/\bar{C})}$$

$$D_1 = \bar{A}_1(L/\bar{C}) + \bar{Q}_1(\bar{Q}_0\overline{(U/\bar{D})} + Q_0(U/\bar{D})) \cdot \overline{(L/\bar{C})}$$

$$D_2 = \bar{A}_2(L/\bar{C}) + \bar{Q}_2(\bar{Q}_1\bar{Q}_0\overline{(U/\bar{D})} + Q_1Q_0(U/\bar{D})) \cdot \overline{(L/\bar{C})}$$

$$D_3 = \bar{A}_3(L/\bar{C}) + \bar{Q}_3(\bar{Q}_2\bar{Q}_1\bar{Q}_0\overline{(U/\bar{D})} + Q_2Q_1Q_0(U/\bar{D})) \cdot \overline{(L/\bar{C})}$$

Overflow occurs when counting up from $Q_3Q_2Q_1Q_0 = 1111$ or counting down from $Q_3Q_2Q_1Q_0 = 0000$. Therefore, the expression for the OVR output is

$$OVR = Q_3Q_2Q_1Q_0(U/\bar{D}) + \bar{Q}_3\bar{Q}_2\bar{Q}_1\bar{Q}_0\overline{(U/\bar{D})}$$

The excitation and output equations are mapped onto the PAL16R4 as shown in Fig. 11.29.

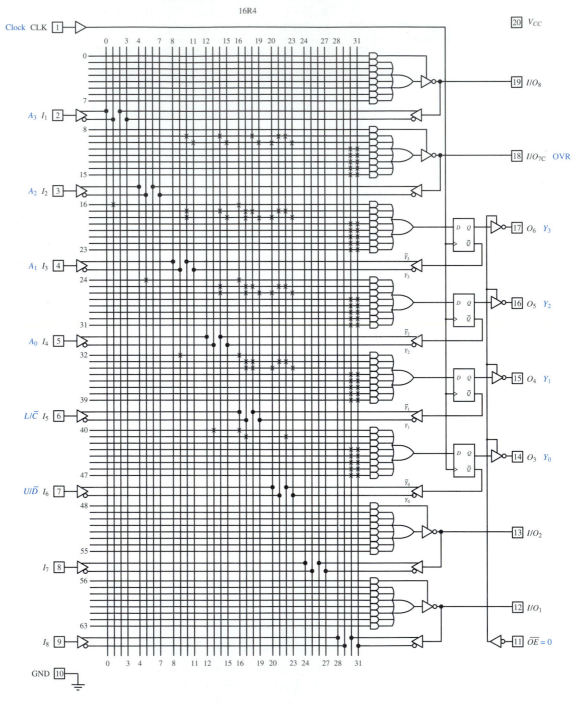

Figure 11.29 PAL16R4 realization of a 4-bit binary up/down counter with parallel load. Copyright © Advanced Micro Devices, Inc. Reprinted with permission of copyright owner. All rights reserved.

It is often desirable to use T flip-flops in binary counter designs. If this were the case in the previous example, we would select either an FPLS device, such as the PLS155 that has programmable flip-flop types, or else one of the PAL devices containing programmable output logic macrocells, such as the EP910 device, in which the flip-flop types can be programmed. The design would then be realized by deriving the T flip-flop excitation equations, configuring four registered outputs for T flip-flop operation, and then mapping the excitation equations onto the device.

11.5 Computer-aided Design of Sequential PLDs

In Chapter 5 we examined computer-aided design (CAD) tools for use in designing combinational PLDs. In this section we examine a number of features of these tools that support sequential circuit design.

Recall that most PLD CAD packages allow designs to be created and entered in several formats, including schematic diagrams, logic equations, truth tables, state diagrams, and state tables. As shown in Fig. 11.30, each design is translated, or *compiled*, into logic equation form and then the equations are minimized, using methods similar to those described in Chapter 3. The compiled design may then be simulated to verify its correctness and estimate timing and other parameters. When the design is correct, the logic equations are mapped onto a selected PLD device.

Most PLD design packages utilize a high-level language to express designs in logic equation, truth table, state table, or state machine format. Many of them also accept designs created with schematic capture programs. In these cases, the schematic is translated into logic equation form in the language used by that package. For example, Fig. 11.31 shows a schematic diagram for a 4-bit binary counter with an asynchronous clear input. This diagram was created with the Mentor Graphics *Design Architect* schematic editor and then translated by the Minc *PLDesigner* program into the PDL language. The resulting PDL listing is given in Fig. 11.32, and the reduced logic equations produced by the PDL compiler are given in Fig. 11.33.

The next section presents an overview of the sequential circuit support features of the PDL language. Other PLD design languages are similar to PDL. The reader is referred to [9, 10] for more details.

11.5.1 Sequential Circuit Design Representation with PDL

As discussed in Chapter 5, PDL (PLDesigner Design Language) is typical of the high-level languages used by PLD design tools. Designs can be entered in equation, truth table, state diagram, state table, and other behavioral forms. As illustrated by the example in Fig. 11.32, a PDL file includes a header section, which provides a verbal description of the design, an optional macro definition

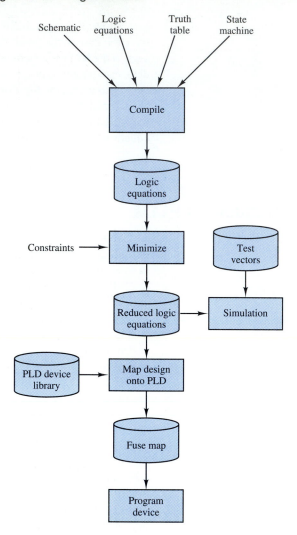

Figure 11.30   PLD design process.

section, which allows symbolic representations of functions and expressions, and a function definition section containing input and output signal declarations and the logic equations, truth tables, and/or state machine descriptions that describe the function to be realized.

Input and Output Signal Declarations

Every design has some number of external inputs and outputs and, in some cases, bidirectional input/output lines. In a PDL file these signals are defined, or *declared*, prior to listing the functional description of the design. In programmable logic devices, external inputs can either be dedicated input pins or

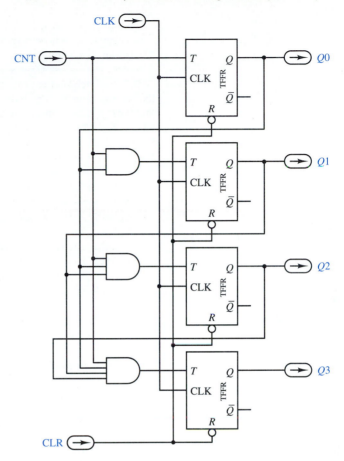

Figure 11.31   Four-bit counter schematic diagram.

I/O lines whose output drivers are disabled. Outputs can be combinational or registered, with or without a tristate driver. If registered, the register may be a flip-flop or latch that has a clock input and possibly asynchronous reset and/or present inputs. The following examples illustrate a number of input and output signal declaration formats.

```
INPUT x,y,[I3..I0];              ''dedicated inputs:
OUTPUT x,[c3..c0];               ''combinational outputs
OUTPUT x,y ENABLED_BY oe;        ''combinational outputs with tristate drivers
BIPUT x1,x2 ENABLED_BY oe;       ''bidirectional I/O line
OUTPUT b0,b1 CLOCKED_BY clk HIDDEN;           ''buried register
OUTPUT [q0..q3] CLOCKED_BY clk RESET_BY r PRESET_BY p; ''registered output
```

The ENABLED_BY keyword indicates a tristate driver associated with an output and defines the control signal for the driver. The CLOCKED_BY keyword

```
''============================================
'' Header Section
''============================================
TITLE    schematic.vpt ;
ENGINEER Joe E. Student;
COMPANY  State University ;
PROJECT  EE401 Homework Project ;
REVISION 1.0 ;
COMMENT  Four-bit up counter circuit ;
''============================================
'' Macro Definition Section
''============================================
''Macros for AND gates and T flip-flop

MACRO AND2(i0,i1) (i0 * i1) ;
MACRO AND3(i0,i1,i2) (i0 * i1 * i2) ;
MACRO AND4(i0,i1,i2,i3) (i0 * i1 * i2 * i3) ;
MACRO TFFR(tt,clk,r,q,qb)      { q.t =  tt ; }


''============================================
'' Function Definition Section
''============================================
FUNCTION schematic ;

'' Declare external input and output signals
   INPUT   CLK,CLR,CNT ;
   OUTPUT  Q3,Q2,Q1,Q0 CLOCKED_BY CLK RESET_BY /CLR ;

'' Instantiate three AND gates
   MACRO  N$14  AND4(CNT,Q0,Q1,Q2) ;
   MACRO  N$13  AND3(CNT,Q0,Q1) ;
   MACRO  N$11  AND2(CNT,Q0) ;

'' Instantiate four T flip-flops
   TFFR(N$14,CLK,CLR,Q3,_x_x_x_x) ;
   TFFR(N$13,CLK,CLR,Q2,_x_x_x_x) ;
   TFFR(N$11,CLK,CLR,Q1,_x_x_x_x) ;
   TFFR(CNT,CLK,CLR,Q0,_x_x_x_x) ;

END schematic ;
```

Figure 11.32   Four-bit counter PDL description generated from the schematic.

indicates the signal controlling one or more flip-flop clock inputs, and likewise the RESET_BY and PRESET_BY keywords define signals controlling flip-flop preset and reset control lines. Finally, the HIDDEN keyword indicates a register that does not drive an output pin, that is, a buried register. The keywords

```
Q3.CLK              = CLK ;  ''(1 term)
  .RESET            = /CLR ;  ''(1 term)
  .T                = Q2*Q1*Q0*CNT ;  ''(1 term)

Q2.CLK              = CLK ;  ''(1 term)
  .RESET            = /CLR ;  ''(1 term)
  .T                = Q1*Q0*CNT ;  ''(1 term)

Q1.CLK              = CLK ;  ''(1 term)
  .RESET            = /CLR ;  ''(1 term)
  .T                = Q0*CNT ;  ''(1 term)

Q0.CLK              = CLK ;  ''(1 term)
  .RESET            = /CLR ;  ''(1 term)
  .T                = CNT ;  ''(1 term)
```

Figure 11.33 PDL equations for the 4-bit counter generated by the PDL compiler.

RESET_BY, PRESET_BY, CLOCKED_BY, HIDDEN, and ENABLED_BY are used or omitted as needed to match the actual inputs and outputs of a particular logic device.

Logic Equations

Logic equations are expressed in PDL exactly as they would be written on paper. The available PDL logic operators were listed earlier in Table 5.5. For registered outputs, each flip-flop output is assigned a name in an OUTPUT declaration, and then all flip-flop excitation and control inputs are specified by appending suffixes to this name. For example, Figs. 11.34a and b show a JK flip-flop circuit and its PDL description. In this example, note that the J and K inputs of flip-flop $q0$ are designated as $q0.J$ and $q0.K$ respectively. Also note that separate expressions are not written for the flip-flop clock and preset inputs, since these signals are defined in the OUTPUT declaration of $q0$. Other flip-flop excitation input suffixes include {.D, .R, .S, .T}.

State Machine Description

Recall that a state diagram shows the states of a sequential machine, the transition between states caused by each input combination, and the outputs produced for each state–input combination. In Mealy machines, each output is a function of both state and input and is thus assigned to a state transition arc. In Moore machines, each output is a function of the state only and is thus assigned to the node representing the state.

Figures 11.35a and b present the state diagram and state table of a two-state Mealy machine. A PDL state machine description of this machine is listed

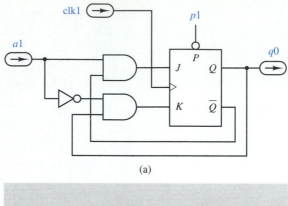

(a)

INPUT	a1;
OUTPUT	q0 CLOCKED_BY clk1 PRESET_BY p1;
q0.J	= a1 * /q0;
q0.K	= /a1 * q0;

(b)

Figure 11.34 JK flip-flop circuit. **(a)** Schematic diagram. **(b)** PDL description.

in Fig. 11.35c. As can be seen in the example, a PDL state machine description includes a CLOCKED_BY declaration, which defines the clock that triggers the state transitions, and an optional STATE_BITS declaration, which defines the names of the state variables.

Each state is assigned a symbolic name using a STATE declaration. The state declaration also defines the state transitions and outputs associated with the state. Two types of information must be defined for each state: state transitions and outputs. State transitions are specified by GOTO statements that indicate the next state for each state–input combination. Outputs are defined by logic equations.

Where there are multiple input combinations, a CASE GOTO construct can be used, as in the example illustrated in Figs. 11.36a and b, which show a state table and the PDL description of the state transitions and outputs for state A for each of the four combinations of the inputs $x_1 x_2$.

To define the outputs of a Moore machine, output expressions are defined immediately following the state name, as in the partial binary counter description of Fig. 11.37. If a specific state assignment is desired, it is specified with the STATE_BITS construct. The state variables are first defined, followed by the desired assignment for each state.

State Table Format

State machines can also be expressed in state table format, using the TRUTH_TABLE construct described earlier. In this case, each state variable is shown as

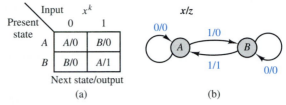

Input x^k

Present state	0	1
A	$A/0$	$B/0$
B	$B/0$	$A/1$

Next state/output

(a)

x/z

(b)

```
STATE_MACHINE example;
    CLOCKED_BY clk;                          "clock triggering state transitions
    STATE_BITS [y];                          "define the state variable
    STATE state_A [0]:                       "define actions if in state A
        IF (x) THEN
            BEGIN                            "action for x=1
                z = 0;                       "output is 0
                GOTO state_B;                "next state is B
            END;
        ELSE
            BEGIN                            "action for x=0
                z = 0;
                GOTO state_A;
            END;
    STATE state_B [1]:                       "define actions if in state B
        IF (x) THEN
            BEGIN                            "action for x=1
                z = 1;
                GOTO state_A;
            END;
        ELSE
            BEGIN                            "action for x=0
                z = 0;
                GOTO state_B;
            END;
END example;
```

(c)

Figure 11.35 Representing a state machine in PDL. **(a)** State table.
(b) State diagram. **(c)** PDL description.

both an input and an output in the truth table, with the output defining the next state of that variable. Figures 11.38a and b show PDL descriptions of the state table of Fig. 11.36a.

11.5.2 Processing a PDL Design File

After a PDL description of a design has been prepared, the PDL compiler is invoked to translate and reduce the design. This involves several steps. For a behavioral description, such as a state table or other state machine description,

$x_1 x_2$

$y_1 y_2$	00	01	11	10
00 = A	A, 0	A, 0	B, 0	C, 0
01 = B	C, 0	B, 0	D, 1	A, 1
11 = C	A, 1	C, 0	C, 1	D, 0
10 = D	A, 0	B, 1	D, 1	D, 1

(a)

```
STATE A: (/x1 * /x2):                    " action for x1=0, x2=0
              BEGIN
                  z = 0;
                  GOTO A;
              END;
         (/x1 * x2):                     " action for x1=0, x2=1
              BEGIN
                  z = 0;
                  GOTO A;
              END;
         (x1 * x2):                      " action for x1=1, x2=1
              BEGIN
                  z = 0;
                  GOTO B;
              END;
         (x1 * /x2):                     " action for x1=1, x2=0
              BEGIN
                  z = 0;
                  GOTO C;
              END;
      END;
```

(b)

Figure 11.36 Use of CASE construct to define state transitions. **(a)** State table. **(b)** Partial PDL description, showing actions for state A.

the compiler first synthesizes the machine by converting the state machine description to logic equations for all outputs and flip-flop excitation inputs. Once the design is in logic equation form, the equations are simplified to two-level SOP form, which can be mapped onto a PAL or PLA AND/OR array.

In the process of simplifying equations, the equations are minimized using one of four options that can be specified by the user. The first is to do no reduction at all, but to simply leave the equations in SOP format. The second option is to apply the *Espresso* algorithm, which reduces the equations quickly and with little memory usage, but without necessarily producing an optimum solution. The third option is to use the *Espresso* algorithm with

```
OUTPUTS c3,c2,c1,c0;
STATE_MACHINE count4;
    CLOCKED_BY clk;
    STATE_BITS [q3..q0];
    STATE cnt0 [0000b]:
        c3 = 0; c2 = 0; c1 = 0; c0 = 0; "Moore outputs
        if (clr) THEN
            GOTO cnt0;
        ELSE
            IF (cnt) THEN
                GOTO cnt1;
            ELSE
                GOTO cnt0;


    STATE cnt1 [0001b]:
        c3 = 0; c2 = 0; c1 = 0; c0 = 1; "Moore outputs
        if (clr) THEN
            GOTO cnt0;
        ELSE
            IF (cnt) THEN
                GOTO cnt2;
            ELSE
                GOTO cnt1;

    ....

END count4;
```

Figure 11.37   State machine description of a 4-bit counter with Moore outputs.

some of the *Quine–McCluskey* techniques applied to derive a better cover. The fourth option is to use the full *Quine–McCluskey* method, which produces an optimum solution, but at the expense of longer computation time and more memory usage.

For example, from the state tables of Fig. 11.38, the PDL compiler generated the logic equations given in Fig. 11.39.

After a design has been compiled, the next step is to verify its correctness using functional simulation. The PDL language allows test vectors and simulation controls to be specified within the design file, so compilation can be followed immediately by simulation with the *PLDsim* tool of the PLDsynthesis system. When PLDsynthesis is integrated into another design environment, such as the Mentor Graphics *Falcon Framework*, other simulators may also be used, such as the Mentor Graphics *QuickSim II* logic simulator. The reader is referred to [9] for further details on simulation within the PLDesigner and Falcon Framework environments.

```
FUNCTION statemach2;
MACRO StateA 0,0;
MACRO StateB 0,1;
MACRO StateC 1,1;
MACRO StateD 1,0;
INPUT x1, x2, clk;
OUTPUT z;
OUTPUT y1, y2 CLOCKED_BY clk;
TRUTH_TABLE
y1, y2,   x1,  x2   ::   y1, y2,   z;
StateA,   0,   0    ::   StateA,   0;
StateA,   0,   1    ::   StateA,   0;
StateA,   1,   0    ::   StateC,   0;
StateA,   1,   1    ::   StateB,   0;
StateB,   0,   0    ::   StateC,   0;
StateB,   0,   1    ::   StateB,   0;
StateB,   1,   0    ::   StateA,   1;
StateB,   1,   1    ::   StateD,   1;
StateC,   0,   0    ::   StateA,   1;
StateC,   0,   1    ::   StateC,   0;
StateC,   1,   0    ::   StateD,   0;
StateC,   1,   1    ::   StateC,   1;
StateD,   0,   0    ::   StateA,   0;
StateD,   0,   1    ::   StateB,   1;
StateD,   1,   0    ::   StateD,   1;
StateD,   1,   1    ::   StateD,   1;
END;
END statemach2;
          (a)
```

```
FUNCTION statemach;
INPUT x1,x2,clk;
OUTPUT z;
OUTPUT y1,y2 CLOCKED_BY clk;
TRUTH_TABLE
y1,   y2,   x1,   x2   ::   y1,   y2,   z;
0,    0,    0,    0    ::   0,    0,    0;
0,    0,    0,    1    ::   0,    0,    0;
0,    0,    1,    1    ::   0,    1,    0;
0,    0,    1,    0    ::   1,    1,    0;
0,    1,    0,    0    ::   1,    1,    0;
0,    1,    0,    1    ::   0,    1,    0;
0,    1,    1,    1    ::   1,    0,    1;
0,    1,    1,    0    ::   0,    0,    1;
1,    1,    0,    0    ::   0,    0,    1;
1,    1,    0,    1    ::   1,    1,    0;
1,    1,    1,    1    ::   1,    1,    1;
1,    1,    1,    0    ::   1,    0,    0;
1,    0,    0,    0    ::   0,    0,    0;
1,    0,    0,    1    ::   0,    1,    1;
1,    0,    1,    1    ::   1,    0,    1;
1,    0,    1,    0    ::   1,    0,    1;
END;
END statemach;
          (b)
```

Figure 11.38 PDL descriptions of a state table. **(a)** Symbolic state names used. **(b)** State variable values specified.

The next step in the process is mapping the reduced equations onto a selected device. The PLDesigner system includes a library of devices, from which those devices can be selected that best fit a design while meeting any user-specified criteria.

In PLDsynthesis, these user-specified criteria, or constraint values, include package type, logic family, manufacturer, temperature rating, maximum current, maximum frequency, maximum delay, and component price. Each constraint is assigned a weighting factor so that the selection of a device can be made by placing more importance on those constraint values considered most critical by the designer.

The output of the device fitting operation is a fuse map, which can then be downloaded to a device programmer to program the chip. In some cases,

```
Z.EQN      = X1*X2*Y2
           + Y1*/X1*/X2*Y2
           + /Y1*X1*Y2
           + Y1*X2*/Y2
           + Y1*X1*/Y2 ; "(5 terms)


Y1.CLK     = CLK ; "(1 term)
.D         = Y2*/Y1*/X2*/X1
           + Y1*X1
           + /Y2*/X2*X1
           + Y2*Y1*X2
           + Y2*X2*X1 ; "(5 terms)


Y2.CLK     = CLK ; "(1 term)
.D         = Y1*/X1*X2
           + Y1*Y2*X2
           + /Y1*/Y2*X1
           + /Y1*Y2*/X1 ; "(4 terms)
```

Figure 11.39 Reduced excitation and output equations for the state table of Fig. 11.38.

simulation information can be supplied to the device programmer to allow it to exercise the device and compare actual operations to simulated results.

11.6 Summary

In this chapter we have examined programmable logic devices, such as PLDs and FPGAs, that can be used in realizing synchronous and asynchronous sequential circuits. The mapping of both Mealy and Moore machines onto these devices was illustrated. Finally, CAD tools that can be used to develop PLD-based designs were examined, including a description of the Minc PLD synthesis system.

REFERENCES

1. PHILIPS, *Programmable Logic Devices (PLD) Data Handbook*. Sunnyvale, CA: Philips Semiconductors, 1994.

2. ADVANCED MICRO DEVICES, *PAL Device Data Book*. Sunnyvale, CA: Advanced Micro Devices, Inc., 1990.

3. ALTERA, *User-configurable Logic Databook*. Santa Clara, CA: Altera Corp., 1988.

4. XILINX, *The Programmable Gate Array Design Handbook*. San Jose, CA: Xilinx, Inc., 1987.

5. ACTEL, *ACT Family Field Programmable Gate Array Databook*. Sunnyvale, CA: Actel Corp., 1991.

6. PARAG K. LALA, *Digital System Design Using Programmable Logic Devices*. Englewood Cliffs, NJ: Prentice-Hall, 1990.

7. MARTIN BOLTON, *Digital Systems Design with Programmable Logic*. Reading, MA: Addison-Wesley, 1990.

8. MINC, INC., *PLDesigner Student Version Manual*. New York: McGraw-Hill Publishing Co., 1990.

9. *PLDSYNTHESIS USER'S MANUAL*, Wilsonville, OR: Mentor Graphics Corp.

10. *PDL LANGUAGE REFERENCE MANUAL*, Wilsonville, OR: Mentor Graphics Corp.

PROBLEMS

11.1 Design a PAL16R4 implementation of a synchronous sequential circuit that recognizes the input sequence 1010. Sequences may overlap. For example,

$$x = 00101001010101110$$

$$z = 00000100001010000$$

Derive the logic equations, then draw the PAL16R4 circuit diagram using the format of Fig. 11.26.

11.2 Design the four-state sequential circuit defined by the following state table, using the indicated state assignment. Identify the pin number to be assigned to each input, output, and state variable, and write the logic equations in a format suitable for implementation in:

(a) A PAL16R6.

(b) A PLS155, with the flip-flops configured for JK operation.

			x	
y_1	y_2		0	1
0	0	A	$B/0$	$C/0$
0	1	B	$D/0$	$A/1$
1	1	C	$A/1$	$D/0$
1	0	D	$D/1$	$B/1$

11.3 For the circuit described by the state table and state assignment given below, find a PLS155 implementation, configuring the flip-flops for JK operation.

(a) Write the logic equations and indicate the PLS155 pin number to be assigned to each input, output, and state variable.

(b) Sketch the logic diagram using the format of Fig. 11.28.

			x	
y_1	y_2		0	1
0	0	A	$B/0$	$D/0$
0	1	B	$C/0$	$A/0$
1	1	C	$D/0$	$B/0$
1	0	D	$A/1$	$C/1$

11.4 Repeat Problem 11.3, but implement the circuit with a 22V10, indicating the configuration of each macrocell used in the design.

11.5 Given the following reduced state table and assignment, find the synchronous sequential circuit logic equations and sketch the logic diagram using the following devices.

(a) PAL16R6.

(b) PLS155, with the flip-flops configured for JK operation.

(c) 22V10.

y_1	y_2		x 0	1
0	0	A	A/0	B/0
0	1	B	C/0	B/0
1	1	C	D/0	B/0
1	0	D	A/1	B/0

11.6 Design the Moore model sequential circuit described by the state table and state assignment given below, using the following devices (do not use combinational outputs). Derive the logic equations and then sketch the logic diagram.

(a) Use a PLS155 with the flip-flops configured for JK operation.

(b) Use a 22V10.

y_1	y_2		x 0	1	z
0	0	A	A	B	1
0	1	B	C	B	0
1	1	C	D	B	0
1	0	D	B	A	1

11.7 Find a PAL16R6 realization for the reduced state table below, using the one-hot state assignment shown.

y_1	y_2	y_3	y_4	y_5	y_6		x 0	1
1	0	0	0	0	0	A	B/0	D/0
0	1	0	0	0	0	B	A/0	C/1
0	0	1	0	0	0	C	D/1	C/0
0	0	0	1	0	0	D	B/1	E/1
0	0	0	0	1	0	E	C/0	A/0
0	0	0	0	0	1	F	E/0	F/1

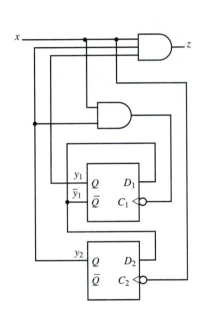

Figure P11.8

11.8 Implement the pulsed asynchronous sequential circuit given in Fig. P11.8, using an Altera EP910. Sketch the logic diagram in the format of Fig. 11.26, with the macrocells drawn as illustrated in Fig. 11.17. (*Hint*: three macrocells are needed.)

11.9 Design an 8-bit parallel load register using a PLS105. The register is to have 8 data inputs D_7–D_0, 8 outputs Q_7–Q_0, clock input *CLK*, and preset control input PRE. Sketch the logic diagram in the format of Fig. 11.28, or mark the inputs, outputs, and fuse connections on a copy of the PLS105 diagram.

11.10 Design a 4-bit bidirectional shift register and implement it in a PAL16R6. The shift register is to have serial inputs *Sin-Right* and *Sin-Left*, parallel inputs A, B, C, D, parallel outputs $Q_A Q_B Q_C Q_D$, a clock input *CLK*, and two function select inputs $S_1 S_0$. The shift register functions are defined in the following table:

S_1	S_0	Function
0	0	No operation
0	1	Load
1	0	Shift right
1	1	Shift left

(a) Derive the logic equations and indicate the pins to be assigned to each input, output, and state variable. Note that the PAL16R6 output drivers are inverting.

(b) Sketch the logic diagram in the format of Fig. 11.26, or else mark the inputs, outputs, and fuse connections on a copy of the PAL16R6 diagram.

11.11 Design a 4-bit up/down, modulo-12 counter using a PLS155 with the flip-flops configured for JK operation. The counter is to have parallel inputs $\{D, C, B, A\}$, outputs $\{Q_D, Q_C, Q_B, Q_A\}$, clock input CLK, and two function select inputs $S_1 S_0$. The counter functions are defined in the following table:

S_1	S_0	Mode
0	0	no operation
0	1	load
1	0	count up
1	1	count down

(a) Derive the logic equations and indicate the pins to be assigned to each input, output, and state variable.

(b) Mark the inputs, outputs, and fuse connections on a copy of the PLS155 diagram.

11.12 Design a serial subtractor that will perform the operation $A - B$, where $A = a_{n-1} \ldots a_1 a_0$ and $B = b_{n-1} \ldots b_1 b_0$. The operands are applied to the serial subtractor sequentially, beginning with bits a_0 and b_0. Use a PLS155 with the flip-flops configured for JK operation.

11.13 Design a serial parity detection circuit using a PLS105. The circuit receives a sequence of bits and determines whether the sequence contains an even or odd number of ones. The circuit output, p, should be 0 for even parity, that is, if the sequence contains an even number of 1's, and 1 for odd parity. Sketch the logic diagram, and indicate the configuration of all macrocells used in the design. Note that the state variable and output require separate flip-flops in the PLS105.

11.14 Design a logic circuit to implement the candy machine control unit designed in Example 8.18. Use a one-hot state assignment, and implement the circuit in a PAL16R6. Sketch the logic diagram or else mark the inputs, outputs, and fuse connections on a copy of the PAL16R6 diagram.

11.15 Design a logic circuit for the binary multiplier control unit whose ASM diagram was designed in Example 8.20, using a 22V10 and a one-hot state assignment.

11.16 Design a 1-bit binary counter using a single Xilinx XC2000 Family CLB. The counter is to have a clock input, *Clock*, an enable input, *Enable*, a synchronous reset input, *Reset*, and a single output, Q. Draw the CLB diagram, labeling the inputs and output and highlighting the paths through the multiplexers. Also write the truth table of the combinational logic block.

11.17 Repeat the sequential circuit design of Problem 11.2, but implement the circuit with two Xilinx XC2000 Family CLBs. Draw the logic diagrams of the CLBs, showing how the multiplexers are to be configured, and draw the interconnections between the CLBs, input x, and output z. Also list the truth table of each CLB combinational logic block.

11.18 Design the serial subtractor circuit described in Problem 11.12, using a single XC4000 CLB to realize the circuit. Show how each multiplexer in the CLB is configured, and give the truth tables or minterm lists of the combinational logic blocks used.

11.19 Realize each of the following switching functions with a single Actel ACT-1 family logic module.
(a) $f(a, b, c) = a\bar{b}\bar{c}$.
(b) $f(a, b, c, d) = \bar{a}b + ac + d$.
(c) A four-to-one multiplexer.
(d) $f(a, b, c) = ab + ac + bc$.

11.20 Implement the following memory devices with Actel ACT-1 family logic modules. Sketch the logic diagram for each.
(a) A gated D-latch with inputs D and C, and one output Q (use one module).
(b) A master-slave D flip-flop with inputs D and C, and one output Q, with output Q changing on the rising edge of C (use two modules).

11.21 Design the parity detection circuit described in Problem 11.13 using ACT-1 family logic modules. Use the master-slave D flip-flop design of Problem 11.20b for the memory element. Draw the logic diagram, showing all connections to the logic modules.

11.22 Write a PDL model of the synchronous sequential circuit represented by the following state table and assignment: (a) using state table format. (b) using state machine format.

			x	
y_1	y_2		0	1
0	0	A	A/0	B/0
0	1	B	C/0	B/0
1	1	C	D/0	B/0
1	0	D	B/1	A/0

11.23 Write a PDL state machine model for the sequence recognizer described in Problem 11.1.

11.24 Derive excitation and output equations for the synchronous sequential circuit described in Problem 11.4, then write a PDL model of the circuit in terms of these equations. Assume the circuit is to be implemented in a PAL16R4.

11.25 Design a PDL state machine model of the modulo-12 up/down counter described in Problem 11.11.

Testing is a critical part of the manufacturing process for a digital circuit device, circuit board, or system. Each part that leaves the factory must be thoroughly checked to verify that it will function as designed. The effort needed to develop a test procedure and the actual testing of a circuit can add significantly to its overall cost and delivery time. Consequently, both the development of a fault testing strategy, or test, and the application of the test to each circuit must be done as efficiently as possible, while providing a high likelihood of detecting any faulty circuit.

This chapter will introduce the types of faults that occur in digital logic circuits. Then methods will be described for deriving tests to detect and locate faults in both combinational and sequential logic circuits. To facilitate the testing process, design methods which improve the testability of logic circuits will be presented. Finally, the design of built-in test features that can be used in digital integrated circuits and in circuit boards will be described.

Logic Circuit Testing and Testable Design

12.1 Digital Logic Circuit Testing

The two primary objectives of testing are fault detection and fault location. A *fault* will be defined informally as any condition that causes a device to function improperly. *Fault detection testing* is the process of determining whether or not a fault is present in a given device. A set of inputs to a logic circuit that can be used to detect a fault in the circuit is a *fault detection test set* (FDTS). *Fault location testing* is the process of determining which fault is present in a faulty device. A *fault location test set* (FLTS) is a set of inputs that can be used to locate a fault. The *fault coverage* of a fault detection or fault location test is defined as the percentage of all the potential faults in a circuit that are detected or located by the test.

Figure 12.1 shows a typical digital circuit test setup. The *circuit under test* (CUT) is stimulated by applying the test vectors of a FDTS or FLTS to the CUT inputs. The operation of the CUT is evaluated by capturing its responses to the test vectors and comparing them to the expected values. In most automatic test equipment (ATE), as illustrated in Fig. 12.1a, test vectors are stored in a memory from which they are retrieved and applied to the CUT by a microprocessor. In some ATE systems and in circuits with built-in self-test (BIST), test patterns are generated automatically by special circuits, as illustrated in Fig. 12.1b.

Responses of the CUT to applied test vectors are evaluated by capturing and comparing them to expected values. This is done in most ATE systems by retrieving the expected values from a memory as each test vector is applied and comparing each to the corresponding circuit output. In most cases, lists of expected values are produced using logic simulation. In many ATE systems and where built-in test circuits are used, response data from an entire test sequence are compressed into a single value called a *signature*, which is then compared to the signature of a known-good circuit. This eliminates the expense of storing individual response vectors.

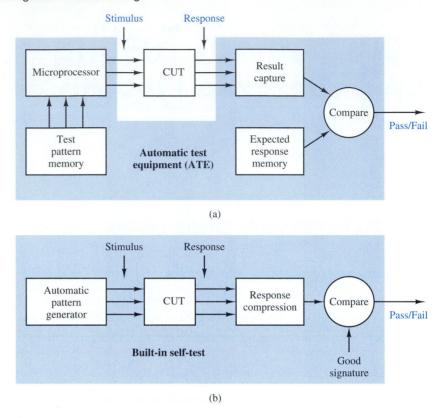

Figure 12.1   Digital logic circuit testing. **(a)** ATE test setup. **(b)** Built-in test setup.

12.2 Fault Models

We will now consider the concept of a fault in more detail. Logic networks may contain faults caused by broken or shorted interconnections, bad logic elements, improper power voltage, poor noise immunity, and so on. Faults may be categorized in several ways. A faulty condition that does not change with time is referred to as a *solid* or *permanent* fault. On the other hand, a fault that appears and disappears with time is called an *intermittent* fault. Other categories of faults specify the effect of a fault on the device. In this context, *logical faults* are faults that cause a given logic device to function as an entirely different logic device. *Nonlogical* faults include all faults other than logical faults. We will be concerned only with solid, logical faults.

To study the effect of faults on a logic circuit, a fault model must be established. A popular and useful model for representing faults in logic circuits is the *stuck-at fault model*. In this model, a fault in a circuit is represented as a wire in the circuit either stuck at logic 0 (s-a-0) or stuck at logic 1 (s-a-1). Figure 12.2 shows a circuit with a s-a-0 fault. The fault can be identified as wire (lead) ③ s-a-0. An abbreviated notation for the fault is 3/0. A faulty circuit can be considered as a logic circuit that realizes a function different from that realized

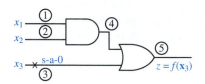

Figure 12.2   Stuck-at fault model for 3 s-a-0.

by the fault-free circuit. A standard functional notation will be adopted for the representation of faulty circuits. If $f(\mathbf{x}_n) = f(x_1, x_2, \ldots, x_n)$ represents a fault-free circuit, $f^{p/d}(\mathbf{x}_n)$ represents the same circuit with fault p/d, where p is a wire label, d can be 0 or 1 as appropriate for s-a-0 or s-a-1, and n is the number of input variables. The faulty circuit of Fig. 12.2 has the following representation:

$$f^{3/0}(\mathbf{x}_3) = x_1 x_2$$

Fault 2/1 would yield the function:

$$f^{2/1}(\mathbf{x}_3) = x_1 + x_3$$

A *single fault* exists when one and only one wire is stuck. When more than one wire is stuck, a *multiple fault* exists. Circuits with r wires have $2r$ possible single faults based on the stuck-at model. When multiple faults are considered, $3^r - 1$ faults can be enumerated. The latter number includes single faults as a special case of multiple faults.

The stuck-at model is justified by its simplicity and by its accurate representation of a large class of faults that occur in practical circuits. Open or shorted components such as transistors and diodes can be described as causing stuck-at faults in a circuit. Broken wires and wires shorted to ground or to high voltage can be represented as stuck-at faults.

Other potential faults in digital circuits are not as simple to model and detect. Examples include *bridging faults*, which are shorts between wires that allow a signal on one wire to affect the signal on another. Programmable logic suffers from a unique class of faults called *crosspoint faults*, which are the erroneous absence or presence of diodes and/or fuses at crosspoints in the logic array. Bridging and crosspoint faults both alter the logic function realized by the circuit in a manner different from stuck-at faults.

Many faults are *nonlogical* in that they do not alter the logic function realized by the circuit, but instead affect such circuit parameters as propagation delays and voltage/current levels. Nonlogical faults require special parametric tests and other test methods beyond the scope of this text.

In this chapter, we will focus our attention on single, stuck-at faults. However, the techniques presented are fundamental to testing for other fault types as well.

12.3 Combinational Logic Circuit Testing

We will now consider the problem of fault diagnosis for combinational logic networks. The following discussion serves to introduce the topics covered later.

Let $f(\mathbf{x}_n)$ represent the output of a logic network that is being tested for a possible fault. Clearly, the set of all 2^n possible inputs to the networks could be used as a FDTS. The use of all possible inputs for testing is referred to as *exhaustive testing* and is impractical for networks with a large number of input wires. However, the method is straightforward, as seen by the following example.

Consider the network shown in Fig. 12.2. Two copies of the network were tested by applying all eight possible input combinations to each copy and by observing the resulting network responses. Table 12.1 shows the results of the test. Copy 1 is seen to contain a fault, since some incorrect responses were obtained. Copy 1 has ③ s-a-0. On the other hand, copy 2 is judged to be fault-free.

TABLE 12.1 **EXHAUSTIVE TESTING**

| Tests | | | Responses | |
x_1	x_2	x_3	Copy 1	Copy 2
0	0	0	0	0
0	0	1	0	1
0	1	0	0	0
0	1	1	0	1
1	0	0	0	0
1	0	1	0	1
1	1	0	1	1
1	1	1	1	1

Most networks can be adequately tested without the use of the exhaustive approach, as will be seen on the following pages where the determination of efficient FDTSs for combinational logic networks will be discussed. An efficient FDTS is a set of input combinations that tests for any possible fault in a specified set of faults. The test set contains a minimum or near-minimum number of input combinations.

12.3.1 Test Generation

Test generation can be described as the process of determining a test for a given fault in a given network. When more than one such test exists, all tests that can be used to detect the fault are usually determined. This section contains a discussion of test generation for single stuck-at faults in combinational logic networks. Two methods for test generation are described: the exclusive-OR method and the path-sensitizing method. Also included are discussions of untestable faults and test generation for multiple output networks.

Let $f(\mathbf{x}_n)$ represent a fault-free logic network. A *test* T_i for fault p/d is any input $\mathbf{x}_n^j$ to the network for which the following relationship is satisfied:

$$f(\mathbf{x}_n^j) = \bar{f}^{p/d}(\mathbf{x}_n^j) \tag{12.1}$$

where the superscript j is the decimal value of the n binary inputs. For example, from Fig. 12.2, $\mathbf{x}_3^1 = (001)$ is a test for 3/0 since $f(\mathbf{x}_3^1) = 1 = \bar{0} = \bar{f}^{3/0}(\mathbf{x}_3^1)$. This definition is justified by observing that a test for a given fault must produce a different response when the fault is present than when the fault is absent. A given fault may have more than one test vector, and a given test vector may test for more than one fault.

The previous condition, which must be satisfied by an input in order to be a fault test, may be restated in terms of the exclusive-OR operation as follows:

$$f(\mathbf{x}_n^j) \oplus f^{p/d}(\mathbf{x}_n^j) = 1 \qquad (12.2)$$

This alternative description forms the basis of the first test generation procedure presented later.

A *fault table* is a table that displays a set of faults and a set of test inputs. Table 12.2 shows a fault table containing all single faults and all inputs for the network in Fig. 12.2. A 1 in row i, column j, (i, j), indicates that the input listed in row i is a test for the fault listed in column j. On the other hand, a 0 in (i, j) indicates that input i is not a test for fault j. For example, input 010 is a test for faults 1/1, 3/1, 4/1, and 5/1, but is not a test for 1/0, 2/0, 2/1, 3/0, 4/0, or 5/0.

TABLE 12.2   **FAULT TABLE**

Tests			Faults									
x_1	x_2	x_3	1/0	1/1	2/0	2/1	3/0	3/1	4/0	4/1	5/0	5/1
0	0	0	0	0	0	0	0	1	0	1	0	1
0	0	1	0	0	0	0	1	0	0	0	1	0
0	1	0	0	1	0	0	0	1	0	1	0	1
0	1	1	0	0	0	0	1	0	0	0	1	0
1	0	0	0	0	0	1	0	1	0	1	0	1
1	0	1	0	0	0	0	1	0	0	0	1	0
1	1	0	1	0	1	0	0	0	1	0	1	0
1	1	1	0	0	0	0	0	0	0	0	1	0

Exclusive-OR method

A straightforward method for generating all possible tests for a given fault in a network will now be described. Let $f(\mathbf{x}_n)$ represent a fault-free network, and let p/d be a fault for which tests are to be derived. The method starts with the construction of the truth tables of f and of $f^{p/d}$. Next, compute and record $f \oplus f^{p/d}$ for each row of the truth tables. These steps are illustrated in Table 12.3 for faults 1/0, 2/1, and 3/0 in the network of Fig. 12.2.

From the definition of a fault test, Eq. 12-2, it follows that tests for fault p/d are indicated by the ones in the column corresponding to $f \oplus f^{p/d}$. For example, fault 1/0 can be tested only by input 110, whereas fault 3/0 can be tested by either 001, 011, or 101.

Tests for fault p/d are minterms of the switching function $f \oplus f^{p/d}$. Hence, by expressing f and $f^{p/d}$ algebraically, an expression that gives all tests for p/d can be determined by application of Boolean algebra without the use of

TABLE 12.3 **EXCLUSIVE-OR METHOD**

Tests				Functions Realized by Faulty Circuits					
x_1	x_2	x_3	f	$f^{1/0}$	$f^{2/1}$	$f^{3/0}$	$f \oplus f^{1/0}$	$f \oplus f^{2/1}$	$f \oplus f^{3/0}$
0	0	0	0	0	0	0	0	0	0
0	0	1	1	1	1	0	0	0	1
0	1	0	0	0	0	0	0	0	0
0	1	1	1	1	1	0	0	0	1
1	0	0	0	0	1	0	0	1	0
1	0	1	1	1	1	0	0	0	1
1	1	0	1	0	1	1	1	0	0
1	1	1	1	1	1	1	0	0	0

truth tables. If $F^{p/d}$ represents all tests for fault p/d, then $F^{p/d} = f \oplus f^{p/d}$. For fault 1/0 in Fig. 12.2,

$$F^{1/0} = (x_1 x_2 + x_3) \oplus (x_3) = x_1 x_2 \bar{x}_3$$

The minterm $x_1 x_2 \bar{x}_3$ implies test 110. For 3/0,

$$F^{3/0} = (x_1 x_2 + x_3) \oplus (x_1 x_2)$$
$$= (\bar{x}_1 + \bar{x}_2) x_3$$
$$= \bar{x}_1 x_3 + \bar{x}_2 x_3$$

which has minterms $\bar{x}_1 \bar{x}_2 x_3$, $x_1 \bar{x}_2 x_3$, and $\bar{x}_1 x_2 x_3$, implying tests 001, 101, and 011.

The algebraic approach is especially beneficial when functions of a large number of variables are involved. For example, consider the network in Fig. 12.3. (Such a network might be used where only two-input gates are available.)

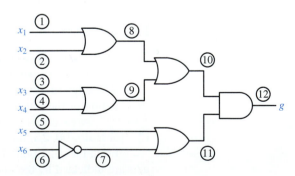

Figure 12.3   Network with fan-out.

The six-variable function that corresponds to this network is

$$g(\mathbf{x}_6) = (x_1 + x_2 + x_3 + x_4)(x_5 + \bar{x}_6)$$

Consider the generation of tests for 6/0. The truth table approach would require the formation of three tables of 64 entries each. Clearly, this requires more effort than the algebraic approach illustrated next for the same case:

$$G^{6/0} = g(\mathbf{x}_6) \oplus g^{6/0}(\mathbf{x}_6)$$
$$= [(x_1 + x_2 + x_3 + x_4)(x_5 + \bar{x}_6)] \oplus [x_1 + x_2 + x_3 + x_4]$$
$$= (x_1 + x_2 + x_3 + x_4)\bar{x}_5 x_6$$
$$= x_1\bar{x}_5 x_6 + x_2\bar{x}_5 x_6 + x_3\bar{x}_5 x_6 + x_4\bar{x}_5 x_6$$

Many tests for 6/0 are seen to exist.

Tests for internal faults such as 10/1 can also be determined by the preceding method as follows:

$$G^{10/1} = g(\mathbf{x}_6) \oplus g^{10/1}(\mathbf{x}_6)$$
$$= [(x_1 + x_2 + x_3 + x_4)(x_5 + \bar{x}_6)] \oplus [x_5 + \bar{x}_6]$$
$$= \bar{x}_1\bar{x}_2\bar{x}_3\bar{x}_4(x_5 + \bar{x}_6)$$
$$= \bar{x}_1\bar{x}_2\bar{x}_3\bar{x}_4 x_5 + \bar{x}_1\bar{x}_2\bar{x}_3\bar{x}_4\bar{x}_6$$

One test implied by $G^{10/1}$ is $x_1 = x_2 = x_3 = x_4 = x_6 = 0, x_5 = 1$.

While the Exclusive-OR method is straightforward, computation is often lengthy for the truth table approach and tedious for the algebraic approach. This is especially true when tests must be derived for all $2r$ single faults in a network. A test generation method that overcomes some of these computational difficulties is presented in the next section.

Path-sensitizing Method

The approach taken in the path-sensitizing method is to first select a path from the fault site to the network output. Inputs are then chosen so that the logic values of lines in the path are a function of the fault. A path has been *sensitized* from the fault site to the output when this condition has been established. Consider the OR gate in Fig. 12.4a for an example. Output z is dependent on the logic value at line ① when the logic value at line ② is 0. Let 1/0 be

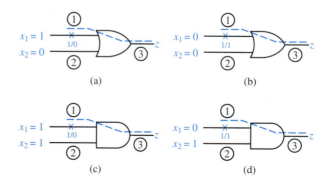

Figure 12.4   Path sensitizing for gates. **(a)** OR gate with 1/0. **(b)** OR gate with 1/1. **(c)** AND gate with 1/0. **(d)** AND gate with 1/1.

the fault for which a test is being derived. The input $x_1 = 1$, $x_2 = 0$ makes the output $z = 1$ when 1/0 is not present and $z = 0$ when the fault is present. Hence, $x_1 = 1$, $x_2 = 0$ sensitizes a path from the potential fault 1/0 to the output and is therefore a test for 1/0. The input $x_1 = x_2 = 0$ sensitizes a path for fault 1/1 as shown in Fig. 12.4b and is a test for 1/1. Paths can be sensitized in an AND gate as shown in Figs. 12.4c and d. In general, paths are sensitized through the basic logic gates as shown in Fig. 12.5.

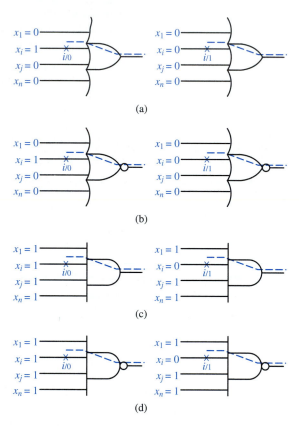

(a)

(b)

(c)

(d)

Figure 12.5 Path sensitizing in popular logic gates.
(a) OR gate. **(b)** NOR gate. **(c)** AND gate. **(d)** NAND gate.

Path sensitizing can be extended for use in networks of logic gates. This extension will now be described for the fan-out-free network shown in Fig. 12.6. First, a test will be determined for fault 1/0. Only one path from lead ①
to the network output exists and will be sensitized as shown in Fig. 12.6a. The input $x_1 = 1$ is required to establish the proper logic value at line ① to test for a stuck-at-0 fault, while the value $x_2 = 1$ is necessary for sensitizing the path through the AND gate. To extend the path through the OR gate to the output, input $x_3 = 0$ is needed. The test 110 has therefore been established for fault 1/0.

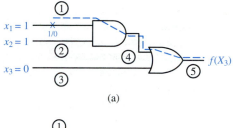

(a)

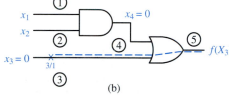

(b)

Figure 12.6 Path sensitizing for networks. **(a)** Path for 1/0. **(b)** Path for 3/1.

Now consider the test determination for fault 3/1. The input $x_3 = 0$ is required to initialize the path since a s-a-1 fault is being considered. A path is sensitized to the output by establishing logic value 0 at lead ④. This lead is labeled x_4 as shown in Fig. 12.6b. Setting $x_3 = x_4 = 0$ sensitizes the necessary path and is referred to as the *forward trace* step in the path-sensitizing method. To make $x_4 = 0$, x_1 and x_2 must be either 00, 01, or 10. Fixing x_1 and x_2 is referred to as the *backward trace* step in the method. The three tests 000, 010, or 100 have thus been found for 3/1.

The path-sensitizing method can be summarized as follows:

1. Select the fault for which tests are to be determined and select a path from the fault site to the network output.

2. Sensitize the path (forward trace).

3. Establish network inputs as required by step 2 (backward trace).

A useful application of path sensitizing besides test generation is the determination of the set of faults tested by a given input. Again consider the network in Fig. 12.6 with input 110. For clarity, the network has been redrawn in Fig. 12.7. Lines along the path from input x_1 to the network output are labeled $1 \rightarrow 0$, which has the following meaning: (logic value with *no* fault) $\rightarrow$ (logic value with fault). Hence, faults 1/0, 4/0, and 5/0 are all tested by input 110. The path from ② to ④ is also sensitized by $x_1 = 1$. Therefore, the input 110 tests for 2/0 also.

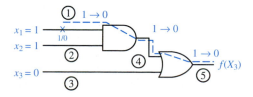

Figure 12.7 Propagation along a sensitized path.

The previous discussion can be summarized as follows. For a given sensitized path, each lead along the path is tested for an s-a-0 or s-a-1 fault. This property also leads to the following fact about fan-out-free networks. Fan-out-free networks can be tested for all possible single s-a-0 and s-a-1 faults by testing each input lead for s-a-0 and s-a-1 faults. Networks with fan-out do not exhibit this property.

The use of path sensitizing on networks with fan-out will now be considered. Care must be taken for this case. Three examples involving networks with fan-out will be presented to illustrate the potential problems. After identification of the problems, guidelines will be given for avoiding the problems.

A simple network with fan-out is shown in Fig. 12.8. Consider the derivation of a test for fault 2/0 in the network. Since line ② fans out, there are two paths from the fault site to the network output. Hence, there are two single paths and one double path that can be sensitized. These three cases are illustrated in

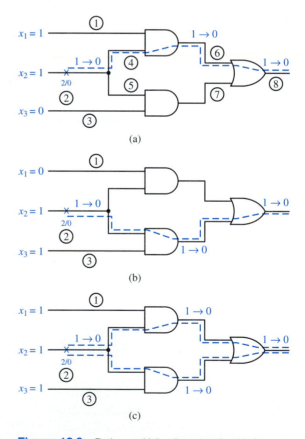

Figure 12.8 Path sensitizing in network with fan-out. **(a)** Single path produced by 110. **(b)** Single path produced by 011. **(b)** Double paths produced by 111.

Figs. 12.8a, b, and c, respectively. The notation $1 \rightarrow 0$ is again used to show that each case produces a test for 2/0. Hence, 110, 011, and 111 are all tests for 2/0.

Tests will now be derived for fault 2/0 in the fan-out network of Fig. 12.9. Note that this is a simple 2-to-1 multiplexer with x_2 being the selection control bit. Again, two single paths and one double path exist for the fault. Notice, however, that when the double path is sensitized the network output is 1 whether or not the fault 2/0 is present. Hence, the input 111 is not a test for the fault. But inputs 110 and 011 are both tests.

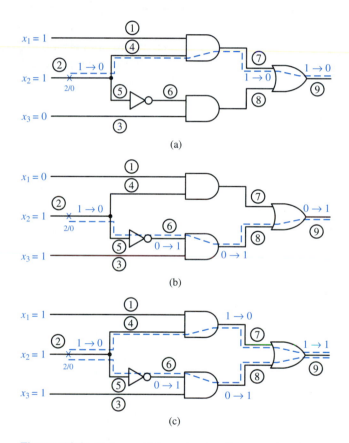

Figure 12.9 Path sensitizing-network with unequal parity. **(a)** Single path produced by 110. **(b)** Single path produced by 011. **(c)** Double path produced by 111 is not a test.

The last two examples illustrate that in one case a multiple path produced a test, but in another case a multiple path did not produce a test. Single paths produced tests for both examples. A generalization that might be considered after seeing these examples is that only single paths should be sensitized when deriving tests. However, the network shown in Fig. 12.10 provides a counterexample to such a generalization. This network is often used in place of an exclusive-OR gate, since it utilizes only simple two-input NAND gates with no additional inverters. The attempt to obtain a test for $\alpha/1$ by sensitizing a single path is shown in Fig. 12.10a. Contradictory requirements for network inputs are indicated because a 0 cannot be applied to α and still have a 0 on the lower input of the nonpath NAND gate as shown. Similar results are obtained when the other single path is sensitized. Figure 12.10b gives the successful derivation of a test when the double path is sensitized.

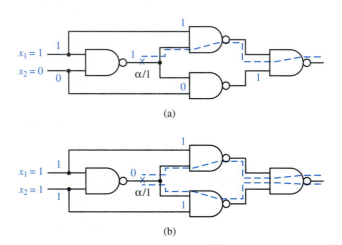

(a)

(b)

Figure 12.10 Counterexample to single path sensitizing. **(a)** Single path does not produce a test. **(b)** Double path produces a test.

The effect of fan-out on path sensitizing can be summarized by the following three cases:

Case 1. Both single and multiple paths produce tests.

Case 2. Only single paths produce tests.

Case 3. Only multiple paths produce tests.

The following guidelines are helpful for avoiding problems that can arise when using path sensitizing to derive tests for a fault in fan-out networks.

1. Attempt to derive tests using only single paths. Continue to step 2 only if no tests are found.

2. Attempt to derive tests using multiple paths. Check each potential test for validity. Stop when a test is found.

3. If there are m possible single paths, all possible multiple paths of 2, 3,..., m combinations must be examined before concluding that no test exists.

A procedure based on these guidelines does not guarantee that all tests for a given fault will be found.

12.3.2 Untestable faults

A fault p/d is said to be *testable* if and only if there exists at least one test for the fault. All faults considered in previous examples have been testable. However, not all faults are testable, as will be shown next. Such faults are referred to as *untestable* faults.

Consider fault 8/1 in the network given in Fig. 12.11a. It can be shown algebraically that $f_\alpha^{8/1} = f_\alpha$. Therefore, by the exclusive-OR method, $F_\alpha^{8/1} = 0$, which implies that no tests exist for fault 8/1. Hence, fault 8/1 is untestable.

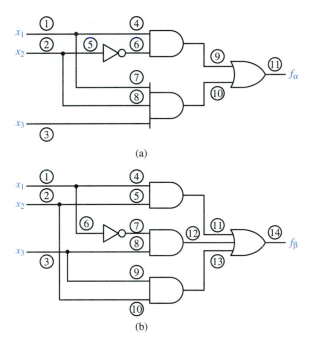

(a)

(b)

Figure 12.11   Networks with redundancy. **(a)** Literal redundancy. **(b)** Term redundancy.

A similar situation arises for fault 13/0 in the network of Fig. 12.11b. Function $f_\beta^{8/1} = f_\beta$, and therefore $F_\beta^{13/0} = 0$, and thus fault 13/0 is untestable. Note, however, that $F_\alpha^{8/0}$ and $F_\beta^{13/1}$ are nonzero, as shown next:

$$F_\alpha^{8/0} = (x_1\bar{x}_2 + x_1 x_2 x_3) \oplus (x_1\bar{x}_2)$$
$$= x_1 x_2 x_3$$
$$F_\beta^{13/1} = (x_1 x_2 + \bar{x}_1 x_3 + x_2 x_3) \oplus (1)$$
$$= x_1\bar{x}_2 + \bar{x}_1\bar{x}_3$$

Hence, 8/0 in f_α and 13/1 in f_β are testable.

The question of how to identify untestable faults thus arises. An answer to the question can be found in a study of redundancy in logic networks. A network contains *redundancy* if and only if there exists a line in the network that can be cut and replaced by an appropriate logical constant (0 or 1) without changing the function realized by the network. A network without redundancy is referred to as a *nonredundant* network. The networks in Fig. 12.11 both contain redundancy, as demonstrated next.

Line ⑧ of the network in Fig. 12.11a can be cut and replaced with a constant 1 input to the AND gate without modifying the logic function f_α. This can be easily justified with Boolean algebra. Hence, the literal x_2 is not needed in the expression and therefore indicates a redundancy in the network.

In Fig. 12.11b, line ⑬ can be cut and replaced by logic 0 without changing the function realized by the network. Therefore, the line is redundant.

Untestable single faults can occur only in networks with redundancy. The untestable faults correspond to redundant lines in the network and can be identified as follows. Let i be a redundant line in a network. If i can be cut and replaced by the logical constant value v (0 or 1, but not both), the fault i/v is untestable. However, fault $i/\bar{v}$ is testable. If i can by replaced by both v and $\bar{v}$, faults i/v and $i/\bar{v}$ are both untestable.

12.3.3 Multiple Output Networks

Most logic networks that occur in practice have more than one output terminal. In other words, more than one logic function is realized by the network. Figure 12.12 shows a network with two output terminals. When generating tests for a fault in this network, both output functions must be considered. Let $F^{p/d}$ represent the Boolean function that describes all possible tests for fault p/d. Then

$$F^{p/d} = F_1^{p/d} + F_2^{p/d}$$

where $F_1^{p/d}$ and $F_2^{p/d}$ represent all tests for fault p/d at terminals f_1 and f_2, respectively. For example, consider faults 1/0 and 3/1 in Fig. 12.12:

$$F^{1/0} = F_1^{1/0} + F_2^{1/0}$$
$$= [(x_1x_2 + x_2x_3) \oplus (x_2x_3)] + [(x_2x_3 + x_3x_4) \oplus (x_2x_3 + x_3x_4)]$$
$$= [x_1x_2\bar{x}_3] + [0]$$
$$= x_1x_2\bar{x}_3$$

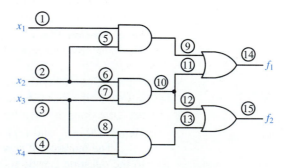

Figure 12.12   Multiple output network.

$F_2^{1/0} = 0$ since fault 1/0 cannot be observed at f_2.

$$
\begin{aligned}
F^{3/1} &= F_1^{3/1} + F_2^{3/1} \\
&= [(x_1 x_2 + x_2 x_3) \oplus (x_1 x_2 + x_2)] + [(x_2 x_3 + x_3 x_4) \oplus (x_2 + x_4)] \\
&= [\bar{x}_1 x_2 \bar{x}_3] + [x_2 \bar{x}_3 + \bar{x}_3 x_4] \\
&= x_2 \bar{x}_3 + \bar{x}_3 x_4
\end{aligned}
$$

In general, for a network with m output terminals, the tests for fault p/d are given by the following:

$$ F^{p/d} = F_1^{p/d} + F_2^{p/d} + \cdots + F_m^{p/d} $$

Many other algorithms exist for generating tests for faults in combinational logic circuits, most of which are designed to produce tests automatically from the circuit description. For example, the *D-algorithm* [20] is an automated path-sensitization method that utilizes special logic values to represent error conditions: D represents a signal whose correct value should be 1 but is erroneously 0, while $\bar{D}$ represents the opposite error condition. The D-algorithm automatically determines the inputs required to produce a D (or $\bar{D}$) at the site of a fault, and additional inputs required to propagate a D or $\bar{D}$ to a primary output. LASAR (Logic Automated Stimulus and Response) [20] likewise propagates error conditions by using "forcing" and "critical" values at each logic gate. PODEM [20] uses a branch and bound method to examine all input combinations by considering the values of one input signal at a time to determine if it can lead to a test.

12.3.4 Fault Detection Test Sets

Two methods for determining tests for a given single, testable s-a-0 or s-a-1 fault were presented in the previous section. The problem of selecting an FDTS for a given network will be considered in this section. An FDTS for a given network is said to be *complete* if there is at least one test in the set for every possible fault in the network. A *minimum* FDTS is a complete FDTS that contains the fewest number of tests of any complete FDTS. The network in Fig. 12.8 has the following minimum FDTS:

$$ \text{FDTS}_m = \{010, 011, 101, 110\} $$

We will derive this test set at the end of this section.

In the following paragraphs, methods for selecting minimum FDTSs will be considered. The selection of near-minimum FDTSs will also be described. The fault table of a network is assumed to be known before selection of a FDTS is begun. Any one of the methods presented in the previous section can be used to produce the fault table. However, the table need not contain all possible faults of a network when used in the selection process. Faults can be eliminated from the table when they are either equivalent to or dominate some other fault in the table.

Consider the AND gate of Fig. 12.13a. Its complete fault table is given in Fig. 12.13b. From this table it can be seen that faults 1/0, 2/0, and 3/0 have the exact same test set: {11}. Faults with the same test set are called *equivalent faults*. Since the test set for one of these faults will detect the others, all but one fault can be deleted from any set of equivalent faults in a test table.

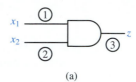

(a)

Tests		Faults					
x_1	x_2	1/0	1/1	2/0	2/1	3/0	3/1
0	0	0	0	0	0	0	1
0	1	0	1	0	0	0	1
1	0	0	0	0	1	0	1
1	1	1	0	1	0	1	0

(b)

Tests		Faults		
x_1	x_2	1/0	1/1	2/1
0	0	0	0	0
0	1	0	1	0
1	0	0	0	1
1	1	1	0	0

(c)

Figure 12.13 Fault table reduction. **(a)** AND gate. **(b)** Complete fault table. **(c)** Reduced fault table.

Next, note that the test set for fault 1/1, {01}, is a subset of the test set for fault 3/1, {01, 10, 00}. We say that a fault f_1 *dominates* another fault f_2 if the test set of f_2 is a proper subset of the test set of f_1. In this case, f_1 (the dominating fault) can be removed from the fault table since any test for f_2 will also be a test for f_1.

For the AND gate of Fig. 12.13a, the removal of faults using fault equivalence and fault dominance leaves the reduced fault table of Fig. 12.13c. Similar reductions can be made for the other logic gate types. Because of these reductions, only faults at network checkpoints must be considered. The *checkpoints of a network* are the wires of the network that satisfy either of the following descriptions:

1. All input wires that are not fan-out stems
2. All wires in the network that are fan-out branches

The term *fan-out stem* refers to the wire preceding the fanout point, and the term *fan-out branches* refers to the wires beyond the fan-out point. The checkpoints for the network in Fig. 12.8 are 1, 3, 4, and 5. Table 12.4 shows the corresponding fault table.

TABLE 12.4 FAULT TABLE WITH CHECKPOINT FAULTS ONLY FOR FIGURE 12.8

Tests			Faults							
x_1	x_2	x_3	1/0	1/1	3/0	3/1	4/0	4/1	5/0	5/1
0	0	0								
0	0	1								1
0	1	0		1			1			
0	1	1			1				1	
1	0	0						1		
1	0	1						1		1
1	1	0	1				1			
1	1	1								

A minimum fault detection test set can be selected from a fault table by choosing the fewest number of inputs that cover all faults. This process is equivalent to the prime implicant selection step of the Quine–McCluskey procedure, in which the fewest number of prime implicants is chosen that cover all minterms. The selection procedure described in Chapter 3 for the Quine–McCluskey procedure is directly applicable here and will not be repeated. Applying the procedure to Table 12.4 yields {010, 011, 101, 110} as a minimum test set.

The selection of a minimum test set can become lengthy for fault tables of moderate to large size. Hence, the use of procedures for selecting test sets that are not necessarily minimum is often more practical. As will be seen, such procedures often yield a minimum set. The near-minimum procedure described here is based on the computation of a weight for each input in the fault table. The *weight* of a given input is defined as the number of faults tested by the input. Inputs for the near-minimum test set are selected by the following procedure:

Step 1. Compute the weight of each input (row) in the fault table.

Step 2. Select the input with the largest weight. Make an arbitrary choice if more than one input has the largest weight.

Step 3. Reduce the fault table by deleting the input selected and all the faults covered by this input.

Step 4. Recompute the weight of each input in the reduced fault table.

Step 5. Terminate the procedure when all inputs in the reduced table have weight 0. Otherwise, repeat steps 2 through 5.

EXAMPLE 12.1

The procedure will now be illustrated by a different example circuit whose fault table is displayed in Table 12.5.

TABLE 12.5   FAULT TABLE WITH WEIGHTS

Tests	Faults									Weights
	1	2	3	4	5	6	7	8	9	
T_1					1		1			2
T_2							1	1		2
T_3				1	1					2
T_4	1				1	1				3
T_5	1		1			1			1	4
T_6		1	1					1	1	4

Step 1. The inputs are weighted as follows: T_1, 2; T_2, 2; T_3, 2; T_4, 3; T_5, 4; T_6, 4.
Step 2. Select T_5.
Step 3. The reduced fault table is given in Table 12.6a.

TABLE 12.6   FAULT TABLE REDUCTION PROCESS (a) T_5 REMOVED (b) T_1 REMOVED (c) T_6 REMOVED (d) T_3 REMOVED

Tests	Faults					Weights
	2	4	5	7	8	
T_1		1		1		2
T_2				1	1	2
T_3		1	1			2
T_4			1			1
T_6	1				1	2

(a)

Tests	Faults			Weights
	2	5	8	
T_2			1	1
T_3		1		1
T_4		1		1
T_6	1		1	2

(b)

Tests	Faults 5	Weights
T_2		0
T_3	1	1
T_4	1	1

(c)

Tests	Faults	Weights
T_2		0
T_4		0

(d)

Step 4. New weights are shown in the reduced Table 12.6a.

Step 5. Repeat steps 2 through 5.

Step 2. Select T_1.

Step 3. The reduced fault table is given in Table 12.6b.

Step 4. New weights are shown in the reduced Table 12.6b.

Step 5. Repeat steps 2 through 5.

Step 2. Select T_6.

Steps 3 and 4. See Table 12.6c.

Step 5. Repeat steps 2 through 5.

Step 2. Select T_3.

Steps 3 and 4. See Table 12.6d.

Step 5. Stop. Test set = $\{T_1,\ T_3,\ T_5,\ T_6\}$.

The choice of whether to find a minimum test set or to find a near-minimum test set will vary with the situation. When the most efficient test set is a necessity in order to minimize testing time, a minimum test set should be found. But when test selection time is more important than testing time, a near-minimum test set should be the objective.

12.3.5 Fault Location and Diagnosis

The problem of locating a given fault in a network can be described as the ability to distinguish the given fault from all other possible faults that may occur in the network. Two faults are *distinguishable* if and only if there exists at least one fault detection test for one of the faults that is not a test for the other fault. From Fig. 12.6, faults 1/1 and 2/1 are distinguishable. Among other distinguishable faults in Fig. 12.6 are 3/0 and 5/0. Two or more faults are *indistinguishable* or *equivalent* if and only if they have the exact same set of fault detection tests. In Fig. 12.6, {1/0, 2/0, 4/0} and {3/1, 4/1, 5/1} are seen to be two sets of indistinguishable faults.

Let $F^{i/d_i - j/d_j}$ be a Boolean function that represents all tests that distinguish between faults i/d_i and j/d_j in a network realizing $f(\mathbf{x}_n)$. Then

$$F^{i/d_i - j/d_j} = F^{i/d_i} \oplus F^{j/d_j} \tag{12.3}$$

where F^{i/d_i} and F^{j/d_j} describe all tests for i/d_i and j/d_j, respectively. If i/d_i and j/d_j are indistinguishable, $F^{i/d_i - j/d_j} = 0$.

For an illustration of Eq. 12.3, consider Fig. 12.6:

$$F^{1/1-2/1} = F^{1/1} \oplus F^{2/1}$$

$$= \bar{x}_1 x_2 \bar{x}_3 \oplus x_1 \bar{x}_2 \bar{x}_3$$

$$= \bar{x}_1 x_2 \bar{x}_3 + x_1 \bar{x}_2 \bar{x}_3$$

Therefore, tests 010 and 100 can distinguish between faults 1/1 and 2/1.

$$F^{1/0-2/0} = F^{1/0} \oplus F^{2/0}$$

$$= x_1 x_2 \bar{x}_3 \oplus x_1 x_2 \bar{x}_3$$

$$= 0$$

Hence, faults 1/0 and 2/0 are indistinguishable.

Faults that are distinguishable from all other faults can be precisely located by the use of a complete fault location test set (FLTS). However, a fault that is indistinguishable from other faults can be located only to within the set of equivalent faults. The precision to which an FLTS can locate a fault is called the *fault resolution* of the set.

A test set is a fault location test set if and only if the response of the network to the test input sequence uniquely identifies the fault with the desired resolution. A FDTS must produce a response that identifies the network as fault-free or that identifies the fault with the desired resolution. The set {001, 010, 011, 100, 110} is a FDTS for the network in Fig. 12.8.

The meanings of the responses that can be produced by a test set can be conveniently displayed in a *fault dictionary*. Table 12.7 shows a maximum resolution fault dictionary for the network in Fig. 12.8. Such a dictionary is constructed by determining the network responses to each input in the test set in the presence of each unique single fault condition.

TABLE 12.7   **FAULT DICTIONARY FOR FIGURE 12.8**

Test Sequence:	001	–	010	–	$x_1x_2x_3$ 011	–	100	–	110	Possible Conditions
Response	0		0		0		0		0	2/0,8/0
sequence,	0		0		0		0		1	3/0,5/0,7/0
z	0		0		1		0		0	1/0,4/0,6/0
	0		0		1		0		1	Fault-free
	0		0		1		1		1	4/1
	0		1		1		0		1	1/1, 3/1
	1		0		1		0		1	5/1
	1		0		1		1		1	2/1
	1		1		1		1		1	6/1,7/1,8/1

12.3.6 Random Testing

The test generation methods described so far are all *deterministic*, each test vector is explicitly selected to detect a specified set of faults. For very large circuits, the generation of complete deterministic tests sets is expensive and often impractical. Where built-in test methods are used, circuits that automatically generate deterministic test sets are especially difficult to construct.

In contrast, randomly generated test vectors are often capable of achieving high fault coverage (although usually less than 100%). Figure 12.14 shows the relationship between fault coverage and the number of test vectors applied during testing of a typical large circuit. The first few test vectors applied to a circuit usually detect a high percentage of the possible faults. Consequently, the fault coverage obtained by a small set of randomly generated test vectors may be

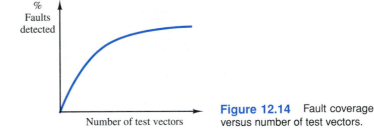

Figure 12.14 Fault coverage versus number of test vectors.

sufficiently high to produce an acceptable degree of confidence that the circuit is fault free. Random or pseudorandom test vectors are easily generated by algorithms implemented in software on a test microprocessor or using special on-chip test circuits.

In general, 2^{2^n} different functions can be realized by an n-input combinational logic circuit, all but one of them incorrect. For a given input vector, half of the possible functions produce an output of 0, and the other half produce an output of 1. Thus, a single test vector determines whether the circuit realizes one of the $(2^{2^n})/2 = 2^{2^n-1}$ faulty functions or is one of the $(2^{2^n})/2$ functions having the same output as the correct function. If a correct result is obtained, we may conclude that the circuit does not realize one of the 2^{2^n-1} faulty functions. A second vector rules out half of the remaining functions, and so on. In general, if correct responses are obtained for m test vectors, the probability that all faults in the circuit have been detected is approximately

$$P_D = \frac{\sum_{i=1}^{m} 2^{2^n-i}}{2^{2^n} - 1}$$

By applying a sufficiently large number of test vectors, m, P_D can be made very close to 1. However, this value is not exact. Many faults are resistant to testing by random patterns.

Consider the eight-input AND gate of Fig. 12.15a. The fault 9/1 is detected by any input vector except $x_1 \ldots x_8 = \{11111111\}$. Therefore, the probability that fault 9/1 is detected by a random pattern is $255/256$. In contrast, there is only one test for fault 1/1, which is $x_1 \ldots x_8 = \{01111111\}$. Therefore, the probability of fault 1/1 being detected by a random pattern is $1/256$.

In general, gates with a high fan-in are called *random pattern resistant*, because they are subject to faults with low probabilities of detection by random patterns. Other random pattern resistant faults include those on signal lines that are separated by many levels of logic from the primary inputs or the primary outputs. Careful design can often eliminate most of the random pattern resistant faults from a circuit.

When a circuit does contain random pattern resistant faults, deterministic tests are often used to detect them, with the rest of the circuit tested by a sequence of random patterns.

Testability analysis programs are available that evaluate the controllability and observability of faults in digital circuits. Examples include the Sandia

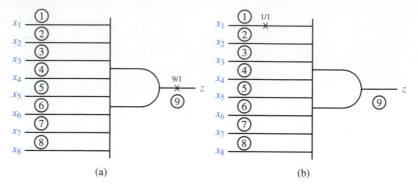

Figure 12.15   Testing with random patterns. **(a)** Fault 9/1 easily tested. **(b)** Fault 1/1 random pattern resistant.

Controllability Observability Analysis Program (SCOAP) [15]. The reader is referred to [16] for other examples.

12.4 Sequential Logic Circuit Testing

We will now turn out attention to the problem of fault diagnosis of sequential logic circuits. Synchronous sequential circuits that can be represented by the finite-state machine model given in Chapter 8 will be considered. A block diagram of the model is given in Fig. 8.1. The equations that describe the model are repeated here.

$$
\begin{aligned}
z_i &= g_i(x_1, \ldots, x_n, y_1, \ldots, y_r), & i &= 1, \ldots, m \\
Y_j &= h_j(x_1, \ldots, x_n, y_1, \ldots, y_r), & j &= 1, \ldots, r \\
y_j^{k+1} &= Y_j^k & j &= 1, \ldots, r
\end{aligned}
$$

In the discussions that follow, the circuit inputs $x_1, \ldots, x_n$ will be referred to as *primary inputs* to the combinational logic in the model. Circuit outputs $z_1, \ldots, z_m$ will be called *primary outputs*. The states $y_1, \ldots, y_r$ and next states $Y_1, \ldots, Y_r$ will be called *secondary inputs* and *secondary outputs*, respectively.

It will be assumed that in general only primary inputs can be independently controlled and that only primary outputs can be observed during testing. In other words, tests can only be applied at the $x_1, \ldots, x_n$ inputs, and test responses can only be observed at the $z_1, \ldots, z_m$ outputs. Hence, the states of the circuit cannot be observed directly.

It will also be assumed that the fault-free circuit is a realization of a reduced state table. In other words, the state table that corresponds to the fault-free circuit contains no equivalent states. Finally, it will be assumed that the fault-free circuit is strongly connected. A circuit is *strongly connected* if and only if there exists for each ordered pair of states (S_i, S_j) of the circuit an input sequence that will transfer the circuit from state S_i to state S_j.

Generally, a test sequence for a specified fault will consist of two disjoint subsequences called the *initialization sequence* (IS) and the *observation sequence* (OS). The purpose of the initialization sequence is to take the machine under test from an unknown starting state to a known state. Then the observation sequence makes the result of the state transition observable from the primary outputs.

An alternative to the use of an initialization sequence is the incorporation of special reset logic into the realization of the machine. However, the reset logic would be subject to failure and in many cases would not be practical for all possible states of a machine. Before presenting methods for developing initialization sequences, the following background material is necessary.

A *transfer sequence* (TS) for states S_i and S_j of a sequential machine is the shortest input sequence that will take the machine from state S_i to state S_j. The following example illustrates the derivation of transfer sequences.

EXAMPLE 12.2

Let us derive the minimum input sequence that will take the sequential circuit described by the state table in Fig. 12.16a from state A to state B.

To accomplish this, we assume the circuit is in state A and we form the tree shown in Fig. 12.16b. The tree, which is derived from the state table, indicates that an input of 0 or 1, when applied to the circuit in state A, will transfer the circuit to state A or state C, respectively. The complete tree is generated by following this procedure and terminating a branch whenever a state is duplicated.

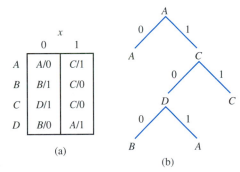

Figure 12.16   Deriving a transfer sequence. **(a)** State table. **(b)** Transfer tree.

Figure 12.16b shows that the shortest transfer sequence that will drive the circuit from state A to state B is $x = 100$.

A *homing sequence* (HS) is an input sequence that produces an output response that uniquely indicates the state of a machine after the homing sequence has been applied. A *preset homing sequence* is a homing sequence that does not employ the output response to determine subsequent inputs in the sequence. In other words, the symbols in the sequence are independent of the response to the sequence. The derivation of preset homing sequences will be illustrated by the following example.

EXAMPLE 12.3

Let us derive a homing sequence for the sequential circuit defined by the state table shown in Fig. 12.17a.

The homing sequence is derived using the homing tree shown in Fig. 12.17b. Each node of the tree represents a set of states referred to as an *ambiguity*, since it indicates a lack of knowledge about the actual state of the circuit. A branch is drawn from each node for each possible input to the circuit. The tree is constructed as follows. Assume the ambiguity $(ABCD)$, which indicates that the state of the circuit is unknown. Determine the ambiguity $(AB)(CD)$ for a 0 input. Note that the component (AB) corresponds to an output of 1, and the component (CD) corresponds to an output of 0. The complete homing tree is derived by generating the branches in this manner. A branch is terminated whenever all components of an ambiguity contain only a single state or when an ambiguity is repeated. The ambiguities containing only single state components are labeled with an (S), as shown in Fig. 12.17b. The input sequences that lead from the initial ambiguity $(ABCD)$ to an ambiguity containing only single state components are homing sequences.

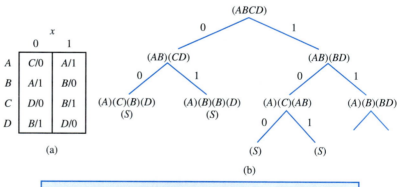

	x	
	0	1
A	$C/0$	$A/1$
B	$A/1$	$B/0$
C	$D/0$	$B/1$
D	$B/1$	$D/0$

(a)

(b)

Initial State	Input	Output	Final State
A	00	00	D
B	00	10	C
C	00	01	B
D	00	11	A

(c)

Figure 12.17 Preset homing sequence. **(a)** State table. **(b)** Homing tree. **(c)** Homing sequence 00.

An analysis of the homing sequence 00 is shown in Fig. 12.17c. Note that every output sequence can be identified with a unique final state.

All reduced sequential machines possess at least one homing sequence. By definition, a strongly connected machine has at least one transfer sequence for each ordered pair of states. Hence, a reduced, strongly connected machine M can be initialized to any desired state S_i by the following method:

1. Select a homing sequence (HS) for M.
2. Apply HS to M and observe the output response.
3. Determine the state of M after applying HS. Call this state S_j.
4. If $S_i \neq S_j$, apply a transfer sequence TS (S_i, S_j).

The generation of initialization sequences as described pertains to fault-free circuits. Hence, if an initialization sequence so generated is applied to a faulty circuit, the desired initialization may or may not occur. This suggests two questions. First, if the proper initialization does not occur, can the fault be detected by the method described here? Second, can initialization sequences be generated that are independent of the fault? Answers to these questions are beyond the scope of this text.

In practice, the design of initialization and observation sequences is often impractical for circuits having more than a small number of states. In such cases, special design for testability methods are used in the sequential circuit design to improve the ability to force the circuit into a desired state and to observe its outputs. As a result, the cost of developing a test for the circuit can be greatly reduced. We shall examine these methods in the next section.

12.5 Design for Testability

A number of design techniques have been developed to improve the testability of digital logic circuits, that is, to make it easier to derive and apply test procedures. Careful design can make logic signal lines in a circuit more controllable or observable. The *controllability* of a signal line is the ease with which it can be set to a desired logic value from the primary inputs of the circuit. The *observability* of a logic line is the ease with which the current logic value of that line can be propagated to an observable primary output.

In addition to improving controllability and observability through logic design methods, special circuits that participate in the application of test vectors and the capturing of results are often integrated into the circuit design. In many cases, these special built-in self-test (BIST) features are created with simple design modifications; in other cases, dedicated test circuits are added to the circuit.

This section will examine several techniques to improve sequential circuit testability, including the scan path design method to improve the controllability and observability of the state variables of sequential logic circuits and techniques for creating BIST circuits for use in integrated-circuit chips and printed-circuit boards.

12.5.1 Scan Path Design

A sequential circuit with n inputs and r memory elements, as shown in Fig. 12.18a, requires 2^{n+r} test vectors to perform an exhaustive test of the combinational logic block (CLB). However, the CLB state variable inputs $y_1 \ldots y_r$, that is, the memory element outputs, are not directly controllable from the primary inputs $x_1 \ldots x_n$. Likewise, the CLB next-state outputs $Y_1 \ldots Y_r$ are not directly observable from the primary outputs $z_1 \ldots z_m$. Therefore, significantly more than 2^{n+r} test vectors may be required to produce all the 2^{n+r} patterns at the CLB inputs and to verify that the proper CLB outputs were generated for each.

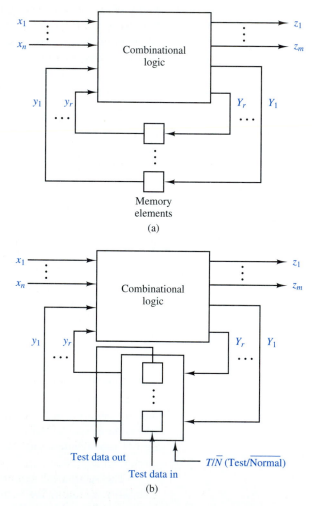

Figure 12.18 Incorporating scan design into a sequential circuit. **(a)** Generic sequential circuit model. **(b)** Flip-flops isolated from the combinational logic for testing.

Sequential circuit testability can be improved dramatically by isolating the memory elements during test operations and providing special inputs and outputs to control and observe their values.

Scan path design is a commonly used method to allow sequential circuit flip-flops to be configured for test and normal operation modes. As shown in Fig. 12.18b, a special control signal pin, $T/\bar{N}$, is added to the circuit to configure the flip-flops for either the test mode or normal mode of operation. To provide the two operating modes, a two-to-one multiplexer is added to each flip-flop excitation input, as illustrated in Fig. 12.19, with the multiplexer controlled by the $T/\bar{N}$ pin. In *normal mode* ($T/\bar{N} = 0$), the CLB next-state outputs $Y_1 \dots Y_r$ are connected to the excitation inputs of the flip-flops; that is, $D_i = Y_i$ for each flip-flop. Thus the circuit operates according to its state table. In *test mode* ($T/\bar{N} = 1$), each flip-flop input is connected to the output of the previous flip-flop; that is, $D_i = y_{i-1}$, configuring the flip-flops into a serial shift register, called the *scan path*. Note that the input to flip-flop y_1 is connected to the *Scan-in* pin, and the output of flip-flop y_r is connected to the *Scan-out* pin.

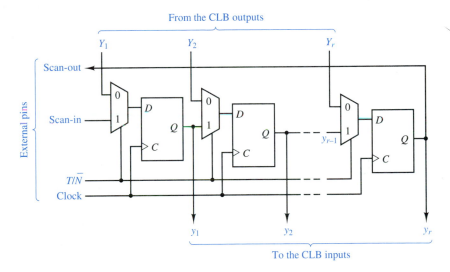

Figure 12.19   Scan path register design.

The test process for a synchronous sequential circuit implemented with the scan path design method is as follows:

Step 1. Verify the operation of the flip-flops by setting $T/\bar{N} = 1$ and shifting a designated pattern of ones and zeros through the scan path using the *Scan-in* line. Verify that the sequence on *Scan-out* is the same as the sequence applied to *Scan-in*.

Step 2. We can proceed in two ways: (a) verify the state table, or (b) test the CLB for stuck-at faults.

(a) To verify the state table of the circuit, the combinational logic block is tested as follows.

1. Set $T/\bar{N} = 1$ to select the test mode.
2. Shift a pattern $y_1 \ldots y_r$ into the flip-flops to force the circuit into a specific state.
3. If all state transitions in the state table have been verified, stop. Otherwise, apply an input pattern to $x_1 \ldots x_n$.
4. Observe the primary outputs $z_1 \ldots z_m$ and verify that $\mathbf{z} = f(\mathbf{x}, \mathbf{y})$.
5. Set $T/\bar{N} = 0$ to select the normal mode.
6. Clock the circuit to force a state transition, that is, to load $Y_1 \ldots Y_r$ into the flip-flops.
7. Set $T/\bar{N} = 1$ to select the test mode.
8. Shift out the new state, corresponding to the value of $Y_1 \ldots Y_r$ produced by the CLB, and verify that $\mathbf{y} = f(\mathbf{x}, \mathbf{y})$. While shifting out the current state, shift in the next pattern for $y_1 \ldots y_r$. Go to step 3.

(b) Apply the FDTS for the CLB.

EXAMPLE 12.4

Design a synchronous sequential circuit for the state table given in Fig. 12.20a using the scan path design method, and design a test sequence.

The binary state table for one specific state assignment for y_1 and y_2 is given in Fig. 12.20b. From this table, the following excitation and output equations are derived:

$$D_1 = Y_1 = \bar{x} y_1 + y_1 y_2$$
$$D_2 = Y_2 = x \bar{y}_1 + \bar{x} y_1 \bar{y}_2 + x y_2$$
$$z = x y_2 + y_1 y_2$$

The logic circuit is given in Fig. 12.20c. Note the multiplexers at the flip-flop inputs D_1 and D_2.

The circuit is tested as follows:

Step 1. Set $T/\bar{N} = 1$ to select the test mode and shift a sequence of ones and zeros through the scan path, say {010100110}, to verify that all flip-flops in the scan path can be changed between 0 and 1.

Step 2. Verify the state table of Fig. 12.20a. Figure 12.20d summarizes this test process, which verifies each of the state transitions and outputs of the state table. First the circuit is forced into state A by shifting 00 into the flip-flops, setting $y_1 y_2 = 00$, and setting $x = 0$. After verifying that $z = 0$, the circuit is returned to the normal mode by setting $T/\bar{N} = 0$, and the circuit is clocked to force a state transition. The new flip-flop outputs are then observed in the next test step by returning the circuit to the test mode and shifting out the contents of the flip-flops, verifying that state A was reached ($Y_1 Y_2 =$

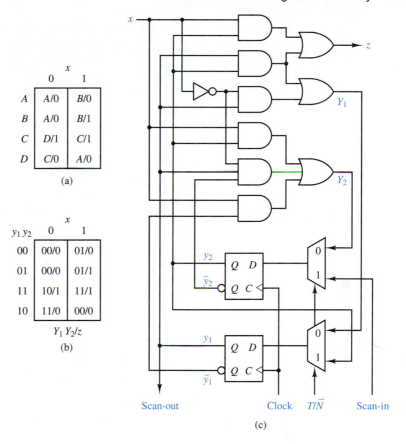

(a)

(b)

(c)

Test Clock Cycles	Test Inputs Shift in New State $y_1 y_2$	Apply Input x	Verify Output z	Test Outputs Shift out Previous Next State $Y_1 Y_2$
1–3	00	0	0	—
4–6	00	1	0	00
7–9	01	0	0	01
10–12	01	1	1	00
13–15	11	0	1	01
16–18	11	1	1	10
19–21	10	0	0	11
22–25	10	1	0	11
26–27	—	—	—	00

(d)

Figure 12.20   Scan path design of a synchronous sequential circuit. **(a)** State table. **(b)** Binary state table. **(c)** Logic diagram. **(d)** State transition test sequence.

00). While shifting out this result, the state for test 2 in the test table of Fig. 12.20d is shifted into the flip-flops. This process is repeated until all eight state transitions have been tested and verified.

In general, for a sequential circuit with n inputs and r state variables, the number of clock cycles needed to verify the state table is

$$N_{\text{clks}} = (2^n) \times (2^r) \times (r+1) + r$$
$$= (2^{n+r}) \times (r+1) + r \tag{12.4}$$

where $r + 1$ cycles are needed to shift in each state vector and clock the circuit for each of the 2^{n+r} state/input combinations, and r additional clock cycles are needed to shift out the final result. For the state table of the previous example,

$$N_{\text{clks}} = (2^{1+2}) \times (2+1) + 2$$
$$= 27 \text{ clock cycles}$$

12.6 Built-in Self-test

Built-in self-test (BIST) improves device testing by placing test pattern generation and/or response capture and evaluation circuitry within the circuit to be tested, as was depicted in Fig. 12.1b. This allows much of the testing to proceed automatically without the aid of a tester. Figure 12.21 illustrates the use of BIST circuits. Autonomous linear feedback shift register (ALFSR) elements are used to generate pseudorandom test patterns to apply to the combinational

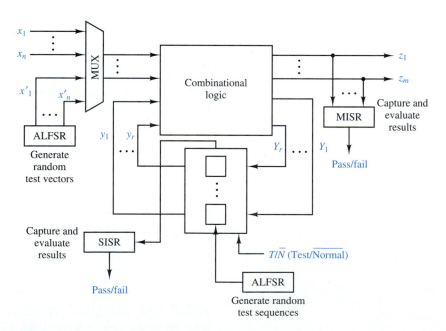

Figure 12.21 Sequential logic circuit with built-in self-test (BIST).

logic block and to the input of the scan path. Data from the primary outputs are captured and compressed by a multiple-input signature register (MISR), while serial data from the scan path are captured and compressed by a serial-input shift register (SISR). This section will describe the design and operation of each of these BIST elements.

12.6.1 Pseudorandom Test Vector Generation

The most common BIST circuit used to generate pseudorandom test vectors is the linear feedback shift register (LFSR). An LFSR is a series configuration of D flip-flops and exclusive-OR (XOR) gates whose design and operation are based on principles of polynomial arithmetic in cyclic coding theory.

When used for generating test vectors, an *autonomous LFSR* (ALFSR), that is, an LFSR with no external inputs, is often used. An n-stage ALFSR produces a periodic pseudorandom sequence of n-bit binary numbers according to a special *generating function* that is realized through feedback lines and XOR gates within the ALFSR. If the sequence contains all $2^n - 1$ nonzero values, resulting in a period of $2^n - 1$, the generating function is called a *primitive polynomial*. (The pattern 0000 is prevented from occurring because the LFSR would never leave this state.)

Figure 12.22a presents one general structure used for ALFSR designs. In this circuit, $a_{n-1} \ldots a_0$ are the outputs of the n flip-flops of the n-bit shift register, with a_n the input to the shift register, equal to the exclusive-OR of the feedback signals; that is,

$$a_n = \sum_{i=0}^{n-1} {}^{\oplus} a_i c_i$$
$$= a_0 c_0 \oplus a_1 c_1 \oplus \cdots \oplus a_{n-1} c_{n-1}$$

The coefficients $c_{n-1} \ldots c_0$ are selected to create the primitive polynomial $p(x)$, with $c_i = 1$ if flip-flop output a_i is fed back to the shift register input through the exclusive-OR gates, and $c_i = 0$ if a_i is not connected to the feedback circuit.

Figure 12.22b presents a 4-bit ALFSR based on the primitive polynomial

$$p(x) = x^4 + x + 1$$

At output a_0, the value a_1 is present after one clock period, a_2 after two clock periods, and so on. This sequence of outputs is often represented in polynomial form as

$$f(x) = a_4 x^4 + a_3 x^3 + a_2 x^2 + a_1 x + a_0$$

where x^k represents a time delay of k clock periods. Note that

$$a_4 = a_1 \oplus a_0$$

and

$$a_4 \oplus a_1 \oplus a_0 = 0$$

which corresponds to the primitive polynomial

$$p(x) = x^4 + x^1 + x^0$$
$$= x^4 + x + 1$$

If the register is initialized to a "seed" state of 1000, the sequence given in Fig. 12.22c results.

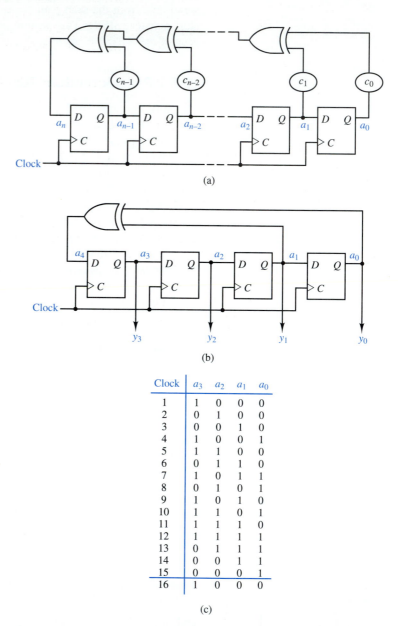

(a)

(b)

Clock	a_3	a_2	a_1	a_0
1	1	0	0	0
2	0	1	0	0
3	0	0	1	0
4	1	0	0	1
5	1	1	0	0
6	0	1	1	0
7	1	0	1	1
8	0	1	0	1
9	1	0	1	0
10	1	1	0	1
11	1	1	1	0
12	1	1	1	1
13	0	1	1	1
14	0	0	1	1
15	0	0	0	1
16	1	0	0	0

(c)

Figure 12.22 ALFSR structure 1 **(a)** General structure. **(b)** ALFSR with $p(x) = x^4 + x + 1$. **(c)** Generated number sequence.

Primitive polynomials for sequences of length $2^n - 1$ are published in a number of sources [13].

A second type of ALFSR structure, typically used when there are two or more feedback taps, is shown in Fig. 12.23a. As with the first structure, the c_i values indicate the presence or absence of feedback taps. The 4-bit ALFSR utilizing this structure is shown in Fig. 12.23b, producing the counting sequence shown in Fig. 12.23c. Its primitive polynomial is

$$p(x) = x^4 + x^3 + x^0$$

This polynomial is derived from that of Fig. 12.22b by replacing each element x^j of the primitive polynomial by x^{n-j}. In this configuration, one

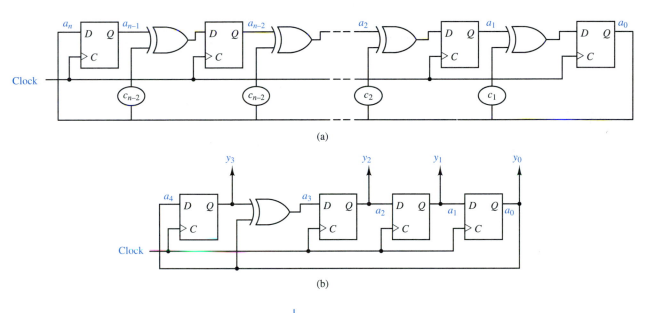

(a)

(b)

Clock	a_3	a_2	a_1	a_0
1	1	0	0	0
2	0	1	0	0
3	0	0	1	0
4	0	0	0	1
5	1	1	0	0
6	0	1	1	0
7	0	0	1	1
8	1	1	0	1
9	1	0	1	0
10	0	1	0	1
11	1	1	1	0
12	0	1	1	1
13	1	1	1	1
14	1	0	1	1
15	1	0	0	1
16	1	0	0	0

(c)

Figure 12.23 ALFSR structure 2. **(a)** General structure. **(b)** ALFSR with $p(x) = x^4 + x^3 + 1$. **(c)** Generated number sequence.

XOR gate is placed at the input to each flip-flop to which there is a feedback connection. As a result, at most one XOR gate delay occurs between clock cycles, whereas in the first structure all the XOR gates are contained in the feedback path, resulting in $k - 1$ gate delays for k feedback lines. Note that the first structure can be built with a standard shift register with XOR gates added externally, whereas the second structure requires XOR gates to be placed between the flip-flops.

12.6.2 Signature Analysis

The capture and analysis of the responses of a circuit to each individual test vector of a FDTS are often impractical, especially if the test circuits are built into the circuit module. In such cases, response data for an entire sequence of tests are usually compressed into a single data value called a *signature*. If the signature of a circuit obtained for a given test is incorrect, the circuit is known to be faulty. If the signature is correct, the circuit is most likely fault-free. However, since some information is lost during compression of the test results, it is possible for certain faults to go undetected; that is, the signatures of some faulty circuits may be the same as that of the fault-free circuit, making them undetectable with this test. This situation is referred to as *aliasing*, with the resulting signature referred to as an *alias* when equal to the signature of the good circuit. The percentage of undetectable faults due to aliasing is a function of the circuit design and the data compression algorithm used. In general, most signature analysis algorithms detect the great majority of likely faults, with a correct signature indicating a high probability that the circuit is fault-free.

A number of data compression methods are relatively simple to implement. Examples include counting the number of ones in a sequence of output values, which detects all odd numbers of errors and some even numbers of errors, counting the number of $0 \rightarrow 1$ and $1 \rightarrow 0$ transitions on the output lines, and computing parity over a sequence of outputs, which detects all single errors and all odd numbers of errors. These methods are easily implemented, although a number of output error patterns may go undetected due to aliasing.

Higher fault coverage can be achieved through the use of error-detection coding methods, often implemented with an LFSR. Let us assume that a test response sequence on an output line z can be represented by a polynomial $z(x)$:

$$z(x) = z_n x^n + z_{n-1} x^{n-1} + \cdots + z_1 x^1 + z_0$$

where x^k represents a time delay of k clock cycles, and z_k represents the data value at clock cycle k, as produced by the kth test vector. Recall from our earlier discussion that a k-bit LFSR represents a generator polynomial of degree k. Error detection is performed in cyclic coding theory by dividing the data sequence polynomial $z(x)$ by the generator polynomial of the LFSR, $p(x)$, producing a quotient $q(x)$ and remainder $r(x)$. Therefore,

$$z(x) = q(x)p(x) + r(x) \tag{12.5}$$

Polynomial division is performed serially by the LFSR as the response data sequence arrives. As the operation is performed, the $n - k$ bits of the quotient are shifted out of the LFSR, leaving the k-bit remainder $r(x)$ in the LFSR after the last step.

If a circuit fault results in one or more errors in the sequence of outputs, we can represent the output sequence by z^*, where

$$z^*(x) = z(x) \oplus e(x) \tag{12.6}$$

In Eq. 12.6, polynomial $e(x)$ represents an error sequence:

$$e(x) = e_n x^n + e_{n-1} x^{n-1} + \cdots + e_1 x^1 + e_0$$

where $e_k = 1$ if bit z_k is in error and $e_k = 0$ if bit z_k is correct. Note that $z_k \oplus e_k = \bar{z}_k$ if there is an error, and $z_k \oplus e_k = z_n$ if there is no error. The output sequence $z^*(x)$ can thus be represented by

$$z^*(x) = z(x) \oplus e(x) \tag{12.7}$$

$$= (e_n \oplus z_n)x^n + (e_{n-1} \oplus z_{n-1})x^{n-1} + \tag{12.8}$$

$$\cdots + (e_1 \oplus z_1)x^1 + (e_0 \oplus z_0)$$

The polynomial division performed on $z^*(x)$ by the LFSR produces

$$z^*(x) = q^*(x)p(x) + r^*(x) \tag{12.9}$$

where remainder $r^*(x)$ is the signature of the circuit. The circuit is assumed to be fault-free if $r^*(x) = r(x)$.

Note that, for an $(n - k)$-bit quotient, there are 2^{n-k} different quotients out of 2^n possible response sequences that have the same k-bit remainder $r(x)$. Only one of these test sequences and quotients corresponds to fault-free circuit operation. Therefore, the probability that an error is masked (missed), that is, the probability that $r^*(x) = r(x)$ for an incorrect sequence $z^*(x)$, is given by

$$P_M = \frac{2^{n-k} - 1}{2^n - 1} \tag{12.10}$$

For large values of n, Eq. 12.10 reduces to

$$P_M \approx \frac{2^{n-k}}{2^n} = 2^{-k} \tag{12.11}$$

which is a function only of the length of the LFSR. Therefore, assuming long response sequences, the probability of missing an error is reduced as the number of stages in the LFSR increases.

Figure 12.24a shows a LFSR with a single input; this configuration is called a *serial input signature register* (SISR). The generating function of a SISR is realized in the same manner as described previously for ALFSR elements. For the SISR in Fig. 12.24a, the generating function is

$$p(x) = x^4 + x + 1$$

since the feedback taps are at stages 1 and 0. The operation of the SISR is demonstrated in Fig. 12.24b for the input sequence $z(x) = 010001101110$. Figure 12.24c illustrates the response obtained when an erroneous input sequence occurs; in this case, 1 bit has been altered in the input sequence of Fig. 12.24c. Note that the error response, $r^*(x)$, differs from the expected response, $r(x)$.

When a logic circuit has m parallel outputs, $z_1 \ldots z_m$, m SISR elements can be used to compute individual signatures for each output. However, this is an expensive approach. A more efficient method is to use a *multiple-input signature register* (MISR), which effectively computes the signatures of parallel input sequences concurrently within a single LFSR circuit. A 4-bit MISR is shown in Fig. 12.25, which is based on the same generating function as the SISR of Fig. 12.24a.

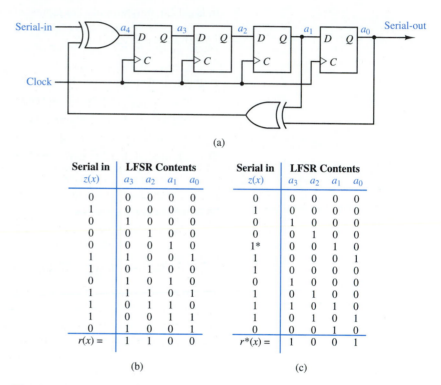

(a)

Serial in	LFSR Contents				Serial in	LFSR Contents			
$z(x)$	a_3	a_2	a_1	a_0	$z(x)$	a_3	a_2	a_1	a_0
0	0	0	0	0	0	0	0	0	0
1	0	0	0	0	1	0	0	0	0
0	1	0	0	0	0	1	0	0	0
0	0	1	0	0	0	0	1	0	0
0	0	0	1	0	1*	0	0	1	0
1	1	0	0	1	1	0	0	0	1
1	0	1	0	0	1	0	0	0	0
0	1	0	1	0	0	1	0	0	0
1	1	1	0	1	1	0	1	0	0
1	0	1	1	0	1	1	0	1	0
1	0	0	1	1	1	0	1	0	1
0	1	0	0	1	0	0	0	1	0
$r(x) =$	1	1	0	0	$r^*(x) =$	1	0	0	1

(b)   (c)

Figure 12.24 SISR operation. **(a)** SISR logic diagram. **(b)** Response to correct sequence. **(c)** Response to erroneous sequence.

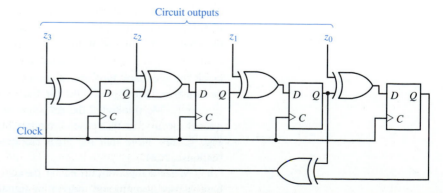

Figure 12.25 Multiple-input signature register (MISR).

In this case, the probability of missing an error in one of the m data sequences, where the response sequences contain n m-bit values, is given by

$$P_M = \frac{2^{nm-k} - 1}{2^{nm} - 1} \tag{12.12}$$

As is the case for the SISR, for long sequences, that is, for large nm,

$$P_M \approx \frac{2^{nm-k}}{2^{nm}} = 2^{-k} \tag{12.13}$$

Therefore, the probability of missing an error in a long sequence of data values is primarily a function of the number of stages in the MISR. Note that the number of parallel inputs to the MISR, m, may be less than the number of MISR stages, k. In this case, the inputs are combined with m of the k flip-flop inputs.

In general, an SISR or MISR of length $k \geq 2$ is capable of detecting all single-bit errors. If the LFSR generator polynomial $p(x)$ has an even number of terms [which occurs when $p(x)$ is divisible by $(x + 1)$], all odd numbers of errors can be detected. In addition, any *burst error*, that is, any group of consecutive errors, of length up to k can be detected. Therefore, the fault coverage is a function of the number of stages k in the LFSR, the number of parallel inputs m, and the length of the inputs sequence n, as well as the LFSR generating function $p(x)$ and the initial state of the LFSR. A more detailed description of signature analysis fault coverage properties is presented in [20].

12.6.3 Built-in Logic Block Observer

The addition of LFSR elements to a circuit to perform pattern generation and signature analysis adds to the complexity and expense of a circuit module. One approach that can minimize the total number of flip-flops in the circuit is to combine the pattern generation and signature analysis functions with the normal state register of the circuit. The resulting register structure is referred to as a *built-in logic block observer* (BILBO).

A 4-bit BILBO register is shown in Fig. 12.26. The BILBO has two control lines, B_1 and B_2, that select the mode of operation as summarized in Table 12.8. For $B_1 B_2 = 00$, the flip-flops are loaded with the parallel input lines, I_1 to I_4, thus operating as a normal parallel-load register. When $B_1 B_2 = 01$ and $B_1 B_2 = 11$, each flip-flop except for the first is loaded with the output of the flip-flop to its left; that is, $D_i = F_{i-1}$. When $B_1 B_2 = 01$, $D_1 = $ scan-in, and thus the BILBO is configured into a serial shift register to be used as a scan path. For $B_1 B_2 = 11$, D_1 is connected to the feedback signal, configuring the BILBO as an ALFSR. When $B_1 B_2 = 10$, each flip-flop input $D_i = I_i \oplus F_{i-1}$, and thus the LFSR functions as an MISR, assuming I_1 to I_4 are circuit outputs.

During normal circuit operation, the normal (parallel-load) mode is selected; the BILBO inputs are the next-state variables $Y_1 \ldots Y_4$ and the outputs are the current state $y_1 \ldots y_4$. During testing operations, the BILBO is set to the shift-register mode to scan values in and out. Test pattern generation and signature analysis are performed by setting the BILBO to the ALFSR mode to generate patterns and to the MISR mode to capture results and perform signature analysis.

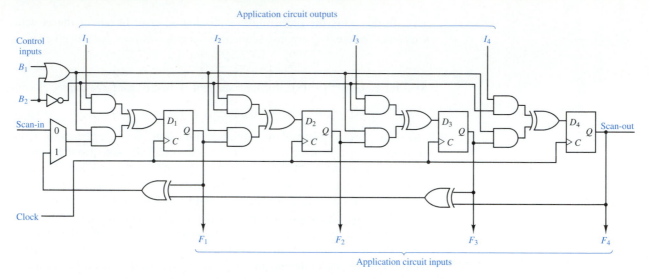

Figure 12.26 Built-in logic block observer (BILBO).

TABLE 12.8 **BILBO OPERATING MODES**

B_1	B_2	Input MUX	D_i	Function	Test Function
0	0	Scan-in	I_i	Parallel-load register	Normal (nontest) mode
0	1	Scan-in	F_{i-1}	Linear shift register	Scan path mode
1	0	Feedback	$I_i \oplus F_{i-1}$	MISR	Signature analysis
1	1	Feedback	F_{i-1}	ALFSR	Pattern generation

When using BILBOs, the circuit is typically partitioned into modules, as shown in Fig. 12.27, allowing selected BILBOs to operate as ALFSR elements and the others as MISR elements during testing. For the circuit of Fig. 12.27, the test procedure would be as follows.

Step 1. Use BILBO 1 as an ALFSR and BILBO 2 as an MISR to test CLB 1 as follows:

1. Place both BILBOs into scan-path mode and shift in initial values: the ALFSR seed value for BILBO 1 and all zeros for BILBO 2.

2. Place BILBO 1 into ALFSR mode and BILBO 2 into MISR mode.

3. Operate the circuit for the designated number of test cycles. BILBO 1 generates patterns for the inputs of CLB 1 and BILBO 2 performs signature analysis on the outputs of CLB 1.

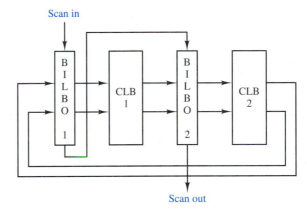

Figure 12.27   Circuit partitioning for testing with BILBOs.

4. Place both BILBOs into scan-path mode and shift out the final signature from BILBO 2 while shifting in the initial values for the next test.

Step 2. Use BILBO 2 as an ALFSR and BILBO 1 as an MISR to test CLB 2. Perform steps 2 to 4 of Step 1, swapping the roles of the two BILBOs.

After testing is complete, the BILBOs are returned to the parallel-load mode to allow them to operate as normal state variable flip-flops.

12.7 Board and System-level Boundary Scan

Digital logic circuit boards and systems present an even greater challenge to test engineers and digital designers than individual ICs and modules, although many of the testing and design for testability concepts discussed in this chapter can be extended to boards and systems. To address this problem, a number of manufacturers have formed the Joint Test Advisory Group (JTAG) and in 1988 developed the JTAG Testability Bus Specification, which in 1990 was adopted as IEEE Standard 1149.1 [18]. The goals of the 1149.1 testability bus include the following:

1. A standard interface between ATE systems and the devices on a printed circuit board (PCB), allowing test data to be transferred to the devices and diagnostic information to be received from them

2. A method for testing the interconnections between the chips on a PCB, which is a common source of faults on PCBs

3. A method for testing and locating individual faulty chips on a PCB

These goals are accomplished by extending scan path design methods to the entire circuit board. The testability bus consists primarily of four dedicated signal lines on a PCB, with a standard interconnection to ATE equipment and a special testability bus interface on each chip, including a built-in control circuit to interpret and execute test commands issued by the ATE system.

The basic configuration of a circuit module containing a testability bus interface is shown in Fig. 12.28. Two special features are included on each module: a *boundary scan register* (BSR) and a *test access port* (TAP). The BSR is an extension of the scan path design method, providing a shift register around the boundary of each chip, with a flip-flop placed between each circuit input/output line and the corresponding external pin, as illustrated in Fig. 12.29. These flip-flops can be configured into a serial shift register or made transparent for normal chip operation. Data are shifted into the BSR through the dedicated TDI (*test data in*) pin and shifted out through the TDO (*test data out*) pin.

The BSRs of the individual components on a circuit board are configured into a single serial shift register by connecting the TDO pin of one device to the TDI pin of the next, with one TDI pin and one TDO pin at the board connection to the ATE system. This is illustrated in Fig. 12.30. Using this shift register, the ATE system can supply test instructions and data to all chips on the board and receive test results and other diagnostic data from them. If desired, any individual chip can be temporarily eliminated from the shift register using a

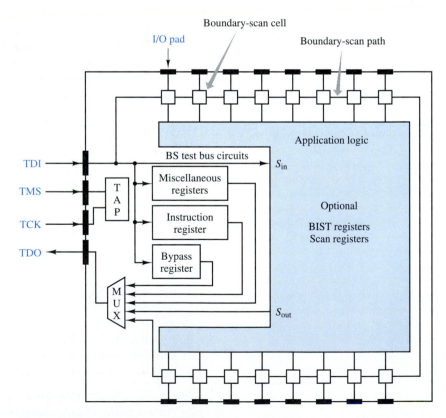

Figure 12.28 Circuit for use the with 1149.1 testability bus.

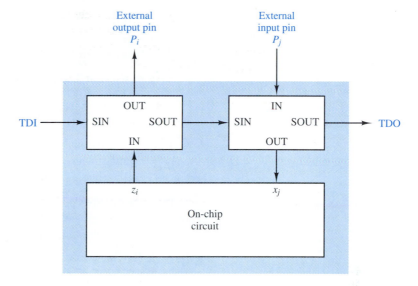

Figure 12.29   Boundary-scan cells between circuit I/O lines and external pins.

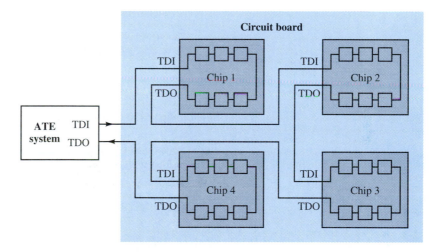

Figure 12.30   Circuit board configured as a single scan register.

1-bit *bypass register*, shown in Fig. 12.28, which routes incoming data from the TDI pin directly to the TDO pin on that chip, bypassing the on-chip BSR. In this manner, the ATE system can work with selected chips during testing.

The TAP has two inputs signals: TMS and TCK. TMS is used to broadcast commands from the ATE system to the chips, synchronized by a clock signal on the TCK pin. These commands cause the chips to interpret incoming bits on their TDI pins as either test instructions or test data. Instructions are routed to a special instruction register, shown in Fig. 12.28, while data are routed to the BSR or to an optional test data register.

Test operations are performed as follows.

1. A bit sequence is broadcast on TMS to force the devices to load their instruction registers with a sequence of bits sent by their TDI inputs.
2. A bit sequence is broadcast on TMS to force the devices to route a test data sequence from their TDI inputs to their BSRs.
3. Each TAP configures its chip according to the received test instruction.
4. The test instruction is executed, with results captured in the BSR.
5. The test results are shifted out to the ATE system using the TDO outputs.

Two general types of test operations can be performed: tests of interconnections between chips and internal tests of on-chip circuits. The primary test instructions include the following:

BYPASS: Bypass the BSR by routing TDI directly to TDO.
EXTEST: Drive data from the BSR onto the output pins.
SAMPLE: Capture data from the input pins into the BSR.
INTEST: Apply test vectors to the internal circuit from the BSR and capture the circuit response in the BSR.
RUNBIST: Initiate operation of on-chip BIST circuits.

The EXTEST, SAMPLE, and INTEST instructions all involve the use of the BSR. The configuration of a boundary scan cell is shown in Fig. 12.31. At each chip input pin, IN is the external input and OUT drives the on-chip circuit. At an output pin, IN is connected to the circuit output and OUT drives the external pin. The relationships between the boundary scan cells, the on-chip application circuitry, and the external I/O pins are illustrated in Figs. 12.28 and 12.29.

Referring to Fig. 12.31, during normal circuit operation, *Mode-Ctrl* = 0, connecting IN to OUT in each BSR cell, thereby bypassing the registers in the cells. During scan operations, *ShiftDR* = 1, causing SIN to be shifted to SOUT

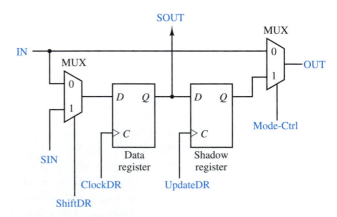

Figure 12.31   Boundary-scan cell.

by the scan flip-flop in each cell. SIN of the first cell is connected to the TDI input, and SOUT of the last cell is connected to the TDO output to complete the BSR.

When testing chip interconnections, data are driven onto each output pin by connecting OUT to the BSR cell shadow register. Data are captured from each input pin by clocking IN into the scan register. The captured data are then examined to ensure that the transmitted and received data are the same. In this manner, the interconnections between all signal pins on a board can be tested.

When testing an on-chip circuit, data are applied to the circuit inputs from the BSR cells by connecting the appropriate shadow register bits to OUT, and data from the circuit outputs are captured in the corresponding BSR cells by connecting IN to the scan register. Test vectors are shifted into the BSR prior to applying the test, and the captured data are shifted out of the BSR to examine the results. Thus, any individual chip on the board can be tested independently, provided that the chip incorporates the 1149.1 Testability Bus circuitry.

▶ 12.8 Summary

This chapter has introduced the subjects of fault diagnosis of logic circuits and design for testability. First, a general discussion of fault diagnosis was presented. Next, fault diagnosis for combinational and sequential logic networks was discussed. Methods for generating tests and for making a diagnosis were considered. Finally, design methods to facilitate digital logic circuit testing, both for individual circuits and entire circuit boards and systems, were presented. These methods facilitate testing with automatic test equipment or allow tests to be performed entirely within a chip.

REFERENCES

1. B. D. ARMSTRONG, "On Finding a Nearly Minimal Set of Fault Detection Tests for Combinational Logic Nets," *IEEE Trans. Computers*, Vol. EC-15, No.1, Feb. 1966, pp. 66–73.

2. A. AVIZIENIS, "Fault Tolerant Computing: An Overview," *Computer*, Vol. 5, No.1, Jan.–Feb. 1971, pp. 5–7.

3. D. C. BOSSEN AND S. J. HONG, "Cause-Effect Analysis for Multiple Fault Detection in Combinational Networks," *IEEE Trans. Computers*, Vol. C-20, No. 11, Nov. 1971, pp. 1252–1257.

4. W. G. BOURICIUS, E. P. HSIEH, G. R. PUTZOLU, J. P. ROTH, P. R. SCHNIEDER, AND C. J. TAN, "Algorithms for Detection of Faults in Logic Circuits," *IEEE Trans. Computers*, Vol. C-20, No. 11, Nov. 1971, pp. 1258–1264.

5. M. A. BREUER, "A Random and an Algorithmic Technique for Fault Detection Test Generation for Sequential Circuits," *IEEE Trans Computers*, Vol. C-20, No. 11, Nov. 1971, pp. 1364–1371.

6. H. Y. CHANG, E. G. MANNING, AND G. METZE, *Fault Diagnosis of Digital Systems*. New York: Wiley (Interscience Division), 1970.

7. A. D. FRIEDMAN AND P. R. MENON, *Fault Detection in Digital Circuits*. Englewood Cliffs, NJ: Prentice Hall, 1971.

8. F. C. HENNIE, *Finite-state Models for Logical Machines*. New York: Wiley, 1968.

9. W. H. KAUTZ, "Fault Testing and Diagnosis in Combinational Digital Circuits," *IEEE Trans. Computers*, Vol. C-17, No. 4, Apr. 1968, pp. 352–367.

10. Z. KOHAVI AND P. LAVALLEE, "Design of Sequential Machines with Fault Detection Capabilities," *IEEE Trans. Computers*, Vol. EC-16, No. 4, Aug. 1967, pp. 473–484.

11. E. F. MOORE, "Gedanken-Experiments on Sequential Machines," in *Automata Studies*, C. E. Shannon, ed. Princeton, NJ: Princeton University Press, 1956.

12. J. P. ROTH, W. G. BOURICIUS, AND P. R. SCHNEIDER, "Programmed Algorithms to Compute Tests to Detect and Distinguish between Failures in Logic Circuits," *IEEE Trans. Computers*, Vol. EC-16, No. 5, Oct. 1967, pp. 567–580.

13. W. W. PETERSON AND E. J. WELDON, JR., *Error-correcting Codes*, 2nd ed. Cambridge, MA: MIT Press, 1972.

14. B. KOENEMANN, J. MUCHA, AND G. ZWIEHOFF, "Built-in Logic Block Observation Techniques," *Digest of Papers, 1979 Test Conference*, IEEE Pub. 79CH1509-9C, Oct. 1979, pp. 37–41.

15. L. H. GOLDSTEIN, "Controllability/Observability Analysis of Digital Circuits," *IEEE Trans. Computers*, Vol. CAS-26, No. 9, Sept. 1979, pp. 685–693.

16. A. MICZO, *Digital Logic Testing and Simulation*. New York: Harper & Row, 1986.

17. M. ABRAMOVICI, M. BREUER, AND A. D. FRIEDMAN, *Digital Systems Testing and Testable Design*, New York: Computer Science Press, 1990.

18. *TEST ACCESS PORT AND BOUNDARY-SCAN ARCHITECTURE*, IEEE Standard 1149.1-1990, IEEE Standards Board, 345 East 47th St., New York, NY 10017, May 1990.

19. K. P. PARKER, *The Boundary-scan Handbook*. Norwell, MA: Kluwer Academic Pub., 1992.

20. J. E. SMITH, "Measures of Effectiveness of Fault Signature Analysis," *IEEE Trans. Computers*, Vol. C-29, No. 6, June 1980, pp. 510–514.

PROBLEMS

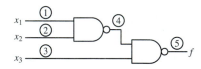

Figure P12.1

12.1 Determine the function realized by the network in Fig. P12.1 for each of the following faults:

(a) 1/0.   (c) 3/0.

(b) 1/1.   (d) 4/1.

12.2 Determine the function realized by the network in Fig. P12.2 for each of the following faults:

(a) 2/0.   (c) 9/0.

(b) 8/1.   (d) 5/0.

12.3 Use the exclusive-OR method to determine all tests for all faults listed in Problem 12.1.

12.4 Repeat Problem 12.3 using the path-sensitizing method.

12.5 Use the exclusive-OR method to determine all tests for all faults listed in Problem 12.2.

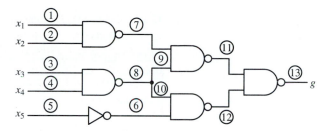

Figure P12.2

12.6 Repeat Problem 12.5 using the path-sensitizing method.

12.7 List all faults that can be detected by each of the following tests for the network in Fig. P12.2.

   (a) 10101.   **(c)** 11011.

   (b) 10100.   **(d)** 11010.

12.8 Construct a fault table containing all possible faults and all possible input combinations for the network in Fig. P12.1.

12.9 Construct a fault table containing only checkpoint faults for the network in Fig. P12.9.

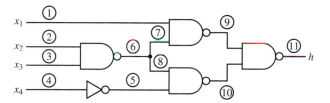

Figure P12.9

12.10 Find a minimum FDTS from the following fault table:

Tests			Faults							
x_1	x_2	x_3	a	b	c	d	e	f	g	h
0	0	0	1							1
0	0	1		1				1		
0	1	0	1		1				1	
0	1	1				1		1		
1	0	0	1							1
1	0	1		1			1		1	
1	1	0						1		1
1	1	1	1			1			1	1

12.11 Find a FDTS for the table in Problem 12.10 using the near-minimum selection procedure.

12.12 Repeat Problems 12.10 and 12.11 for the following fault table:

Tests	Faults								
	a	b	c	d	e	f	g	h	i
1	1		1						
2		1		1		1			
3			1		1				
4				1					1
5					1		1		
6		1							1
7							1	1	
8	1							1	

12.13 Determine all tests that can be used to distinguish each of the following pairs of faults in the network of Fig. P12.9.

(a) 1/0–4/1.

(b) 2/0–3/0.

(c) 7/0–8/0.

(d) 1/1–7/1.

12.14 Given the circuit in Fig. P12.14, determine an initialization sequence and an observation sequence for each of the following faults:

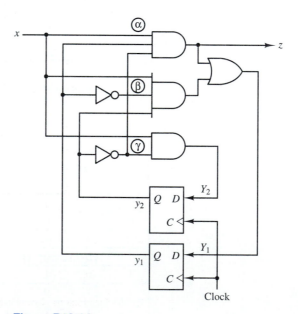

Figure P12.14

(a) $\alpha/1$.   (c) $\gamma/1$.

(b) $\beta/0$.

12.15   Repeat Problem 12.14 for the circuit given in Fig. P12.15 and the following faults:

(a) $\alpha/1$.   (c) $\gamma/0$.

(b) $\beta/0$.   (d) $\delta/1$.

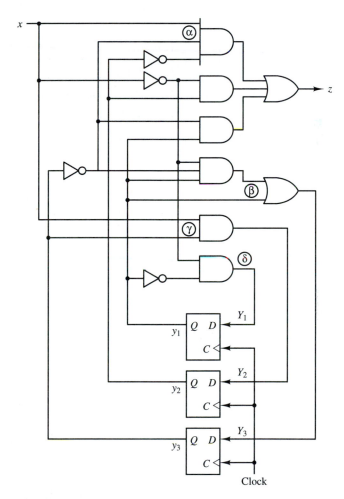

Figure P12.15

12.16   Reduce the following hypothetical test table by taking advantage of test coverage.

	Initial State	Observation Sequence, x				Output Sequence, z				Final State	Faults Tested
1	S_1	1				$\bar{D}$				S_2	a_0, c_1
2	S_2	0				$\bar{D}$				S_2	b_0, i_0
3	S_3	1				$\bar{D}$				S_3	g_0, f_0
4	S_4	0				D				S_1	h_1, b_1
5	S_2	1				$\bar{D}$				S_3	l_0, e_0
6	S_1	1	1			0	$\bar{D}$			S_3	j_0, g_1
7	S_3	1	0			0	$\bar{D}$			S_4	n_0, j_1
8	S_3	0	0			0	D			S_1	p_0, m_0
9	S_2	1	0			0	$\bar{D}$			S_4	f_1, h_0
10	S_4	0	1	1		1	0	$\bar{D}$		S_3	a_1, i_1
11	S_2	1	0	0		0	0	D		S_1	n_1, k_0
12	S_3	1	0	0		0	0	D		S_1	p_1, l_1
13	S_1	1	0	1		0	0	$\bar{D}$		S_3	d_0, k_1
14	S_2	1	0	0	1	0	0	1	$\bar{D}$	S_2	m_1, d_1
15	S_4	0	1	1	1	1	0	0	$\bar{D}$	S_3	e_1, c_0

12.17 Develop a test procedure for a circuit with the following reduced test table:

	Initial State	Observation Sequence, x				Output Sequence, z			Final State	Faults Tested
1	S_1	0	1	1	0	$\bar{D}$	$\bar{D}$		S_3	a_0, d_1, e_1, h_0
2	S_2	1	1	1	$\bar{D}$	1	D		S_1	b_1, e_0
3	S_3	0	1	0	0	1	$\bar{D}$		S_4	c_0, f_0
4	S_4	0	0	1	0	$\bar{D}$	D		S_1	a_1, c_1, f_1, g_0, h_1
5	S_1	1	0		0	$\bar{D}$			S_2	b_0, d_0, g_1

12.18 The circuit whose test table is given in Problem 12.17 is initialized to state S_1. An input sequence 011010 is applied to the circuit and the output response 001010 is observed. Is the circuit faulty? If yes, what fault is present?

12.19 The circuit shown in Fig. P12.19 is initialized to state $y_1 = 0$, $y_2 = 1$, and the input sequence $x = 010111$ is applied. Determine all single faults that would be detected by this sequence.

12.20 Find the state diagram and state table for Fig. 12.24a.

12.21 For the ALFSR shown in Fig. P12.21:

(a) Find the state diagram and state table.

(b) Determine the masking probability for the circuit.

(c) Determine the correct and error responses for the serial input sequences in Figs. 12.24b and c.

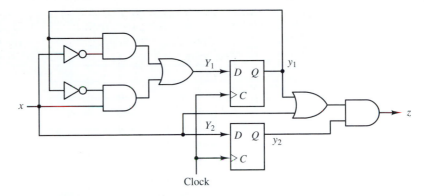

Figure P12.19

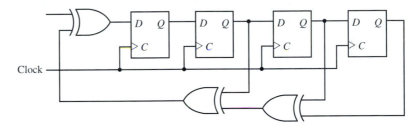

Figure P12.21

12.22 Design an 8-bit BILBO register with the following function table:

$B1$	$B2$	Function
0	0	AFLSR mode
0	1	Scan mode (shift register)
1	0	Normal mode (parallel load)
1	1	MISR mode

Let $p(x) = 1 + x + x^5 + x^6 + x^8$.

12.23 Design a 10-bit BILBO register with the following function table:

$B1$	$B2$	$B3$	Function
0	0	0	Scan mode (shift register)
0	1	0	Synchronous reset
1	0	0	MISR mode
1	0	1	ALFSR mode
1	1	0	Normal mode (parallel load)

Let $p(x) = 1 + x^3 + x^{10}$.

13

This text has presented methods for the various steps in the analysis and design of digital logic circuits. "Real" problems require that these methods be combined, with considerations of total cost, testability, and other practical issues. To illustrate, this chapter presents four comprehensive design case studies: an electronic slot machine game, a keyless automobile entry system, a single-lane traffic controller, and a grocery store cash register. All aspects of the design process will be examined in each case. First, the problem will be defined and system requirements determined. Then the functional modules needed to satisfy the requirements will be determined, with a logic circuit designed or a standard component selected to implement each module. Finally, the modules will be combined into a complete system. While standard TTL modules are used in these examples, the reader is encouraged also to consider programmable logic and other approaches.

Design Examples

13.1 Electronic Slot Machine

13.1.1 Problem Definition

A *slot machine* is a casino-style game in which a player deposits a coin and pulls a lever, causing a set of wheels to begin spinning. Each wheel has a number of digits or images painted around its circumference, which are displayed through a window. After the pull lever is released, the wheels freeze, each displaying one digit/image. If the displayed numbers/images match one of a set of specified patterns, a designated amount of money is won. The *payoff*, or the amount of money won, depends on the pattern matched and in some cases may also be a function of the amount of money deposited (or wagered).

There are a number of variations of this game, including hand-held electronic games that utilize no money. These operate by simply pulling a lever or pressing a button to initiate rolling and freezing of the number wheels. To minimize mechanical parts, an electronic display is often used to simulate rolling wheels by continuously changing the digits being displayed. Winning combinations are signaled by blinking lights and/or audible alarms. In some cases points are won and lost, allowing players to keep running scores while playing the game.

In this example, we will design an electronic slot machine game that is operated by depressing a push-button PLAY switch, causing numeric digits in the range [1 . . . 7] to be continuously displayed and changed on an electronic display panel in such a way as to give the appearance of rotating number wheels. The digits will freeze on the display after the PLAY button is released. If one of a specified set of numbers is displayed, a *payoff*, a designated number of points, will be awarded. In our machine, any combination of two or three identical digits will be designated as *winners*, with three identical digits returning a bigger payoff (more points) than two identical digits. The size of the payoff will also be a function of the value of the matching digit and a wager, which will be placed using two switches prior to pressing the PLAY button. Figure 13.1 shows the basic layout of the front panel of the game.

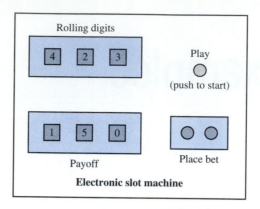

Figure 13.1   Electronic slot machine game.

13.1.2 System Requirements and Solution Plan

We begin the project by determining the requirements for the system and developing a plan to address these requirements. From the description of the game, several major subsystems are needed: two three-digit electronic displays for the rolling digits and the payoff, a PLAY button, two switches to place the wager, circuits to generate the numbers for the rolling digit display, and a circuit to identify winning patterns and compute the payoff. These subsystems are illustrated in the block diagram of Fig. 13.2 and are described briefly as follows.

1. **PLAY button.** A push-button switch will be used for the PLAY button of the slot machine. The button will be depressed to reset the game and start the random-number generators and released to stop them, at which time a decision will be made as to whether the player has won or lost.

2. **Rolling-digit display.** Three seven-segment LEDs (light-emitting diodes) will be used to display the digits produced by the number generators. These will be updated continuously while the PLAY button is being held down to simulate rolling number wheels. To add to this effect, the three digits will be changed at different frequencies and also frozen at different times following the release of the PLAY button to simulate wheels stopping one after the other.

3. **Number generators.** Three number generators form the basis of the game, each producing digits in the range $[1 \ldots 7]$. The number generators begin operating when the PLAY button is pressed and halt after the PLAY button is released. To make the number generators appear to be random, making it difficult for a player to predict their final values, they will be clocked at a fairly high rate, with each changed at a different rate. In addition, stopping each number generator at a different time following the release of the PLAY button will add to the difficulty of predicting the final digit values.

4. **Timing module.** The timing module will contain an oscillator circuit and various timing circuits to produce signals that control the number generators. One set of timing circuit outputs will initiate operation of the number generators when the PLAY button is pressed and halt them at

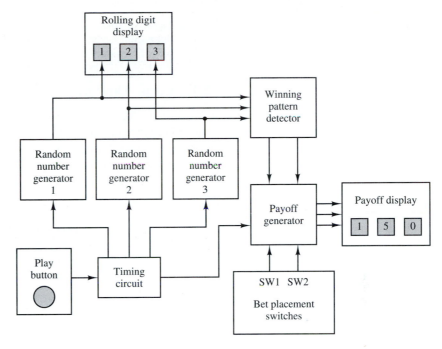

Figure 13.2   Electronic slot machine game block diagram.

different times after the PLAY button is released. A second set of outputs will make the number generators change at different rates.

5. **Wager placement inputs.** The number of points won will be multiplied by a scale factor in the range [1 ... 4] that will be selected by two switches that are set before pressing the PLAY button. This simulates placement of a wager on the outcome of the game. It can be assumed that some number of points is lost if a winning combination does not occur, with the loss being a function of the wager.

6. **Winning pattern detector.** This module will evaluate the outputs of the three number generators, after the number generators have all halted, to determine if the three final numbers produced by the number generators correspond to one of the winning combinations, that is, to determine whether two or three numbers match. The results will be sent to the payoff generator.

7. **Payoff generator.** The payoff generator will compute the payoff, the number of points won, based on whether a matching combination was detected and the value of the matching digit. The payoff will be proportional to the matching digit number. In addition, the payoff for three matching digits will be higher than for two matching digits. Finally, the payoff will be multiplied by a scale factor (1 to 4) corresponding to the amount wagered. A payoff of zero (000) will be displayed if no winning pattern is detected.

8. **Payoff display.** The number of points won will be displayed on a three-digit seven-segment LED display, driven by the outputs of the payoff generator.

13.1.3 Logic Design

To organize the logic circuit design process for the slot machine, each module identified in the requirements will be designed and tested independently. Then these modules will be combined to create the complete slot machine circuit. The following paragraphs present the designs of the individual modules.

PLAY Button

A mechanical push-button switch will be used for the PLAY button. The switch generates a logic 1 signal when depressed and logic 0 when released. A spring will return the switch to its original position when it is not being held down. To ensure reliable operation, that is, "clean" $0 \rightarrow 1$ and $1 \rightarrow 0$ transitions, a debounce circuit will be used.

A switch debounce circuit was developed in Chapter 10 (see Example 10.9) and is simply a pair of cross-coupled NAND gates (74LS00). The complete PLAY button circuit is illustrated in Fig. 13.3.

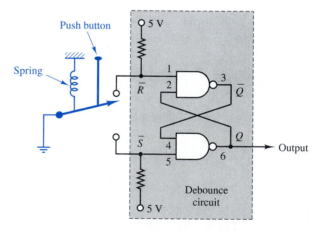

Figure 13.3   PLAY button and debounce circuit.

Number Generators

A truly random number generator would be ideal for this game, but it is not a trivial circuit. Instead, a simple synchronous binary counter circuit that counts continuously from 1 to 7 will be used for each of the three digits. The appearance of randomness will come from the operation of a timing circuit that will do three things:

1. The counters will be made to run sufficiently fast that it will be difficult for the player to predict the counter outputs when the PLAY button is released.

2. The three counters will be operated at different frequencies. The highest frequency will be 45 hertz (Hz) for one of the digits, with the other two being one-half and one-third of this frequency, or 22.5 and 15 Hz, respectively. The 15-Hz rate causes the digit to change 15 times per second, which will allow the digits to be seen while changing sufficiently fast to inhibit guessing the final value.

3. The three counters will be stopped at different times following the release of the PLAY button.

To produce the numbers 1 to 7, a binary counter will be used for each number generator that will be synchronously loaded with the value 1 after it has reached a count of 7. Although 3 bits would be sufficient, a 4-bit counter will be selected since 3-bit counters are not standard TTL modules. To allow different counting frequencies and stopping times to be used, separate clock and enable inputs are needed for each counter, in addition to parallel-load capability.

The SN74LS163A 4-bit synchronous binary counter meets the preceding requirements. Three SN74LS163A modules will be used for this design, as shown in Fig. 13.4

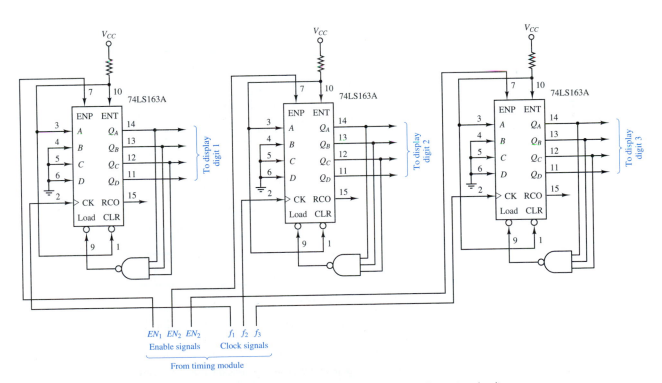

Figure 13.4   Number generation: 1-to-7 counter circuits.

Note that three independent count-enable signals $\{EN_1, EN_2, EN_3\}$ and three different clock signals $\{f_1, f_2, f_3\}$ are needed to control the three counters. The counter outputs will be sent to the rolling digit display and to the winning combination detector.

Timing Module

A block diagram of the timing module is shown in Fig. 13.5a. Three clock signals (f_1, f_2, f_3) and three enable signals (EN_1, EN_2, EN_3) are needed to control the counters in the number generator, as shown in Fig. 13.4. An oscillator circuit will be designed to produce a square wave of frequency $f_1 = 45$ Hz to use as the clock signal for the first counter. The frequency of this signal will then be divided by factors of 2 and 3 to produce two other signals at frequencies $f_2 = 22.5$ Hz and $f_3 = 15$ Hz, respectively. The desired operation of the three enable signals is illustrated by the timing diagram in Fig. 13.5b. All three enable signals will be set to 1 when the PLAY button is depressed. After the PLAY

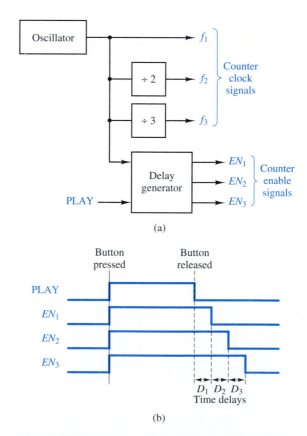

(a)

(b)

Figure 13.5 Timing module for the number generator.
(a) Timing generator. **(b)** Enable signal timing.

button is released, EN_1 will be set to 0 after a short delay D_1, EN_2 after a second delay D_2, and EN_3 after a third delay D_3.

The oscillator will be implemented with a 555 precision timer module configured to operate in *astable multivibrator* mode, as described in Chapter 6 and illustrated in Fig. 13.6. The oscillating frequency will be set to 45 Hz. The frequency of oscillation, f, was defined in Chapter 6 as

$$f = \frac{1.44}{(R_A + 2R_B)C} \tag{13.1}$$

Therefore, to obtain $f = 45$ Hz, the following component values are selected:

$$R_A = 15 k\Omega$$
$$R_B = 8.5 k\Omega$$
$$C = 1 \mu F$$

A divide-by-2 circuit and a divide-by-3 circuit will be used to generate the other two clock signals. Since the frequencies of pulse trains can be conveniently divided by binary counters, a 74LS92 modulo-12 binary counter will be used as shown in Fig. 13.6. The outputs of the 74LS92, Q_A, Q_B, Q_C, and Q_D, are simply pulse trains whose frequencies are 1/2, 1/3, 1/6, and 1/12 of the clock input, respectively. Therefore, output Q_A will provide $f_2 = f_1/2 = 22.5$ Hz, while Q_B will provide $f_3 = f_1/3 = 15$ Hz.

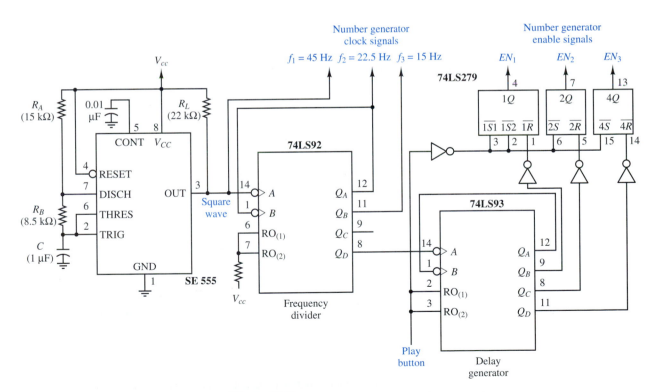

Figure 13.6   Timing module for the number generator.

The counter enable signals EN_1, EN_2, and EN_3 will be produced through three SR latches (SN74LS279). The latches will be set to 1 when the PLAY button is pressed and then reset to 0 at different times following the release of the PLAY button. To produce different reset times, a 74LS93 4-bit binary counter, shown in Fig. 13.6, will be cleared (with counting disabled) while the PLAY button is being pressed and will begin counting when the PLAY button is released. Three of the counter outputs will be used to reset the latches. $Q_B = 1$ (a count of 2) will turn off EN_1, $Q_C = 1$ (a count of 4) will turn off EN_2, and $Q_D = 1$ will turn off EN_3 (a count of 8). The 74LS93 counter will be clocked by output Q_D of the 74LS92 used for the number-generator clock signals. The frequency of the waveform on output Q_D of the 74LS92 is

$$f = 45\,\text{Hz}/12 = 3.75\,\text{Hz}$$

Recalling that clock period is the inverse of clock frequency, the delay times for the three enable signals will be

$$
\begin{array}{lll}
\text{Digit 1} & \frac{1}{f/2} = 2 \div 3.75\,\text{Hz} = 0.533\,\text{s} \\[4pt]
\text{Digit 2} & \frac{1}{f/4} = 4 \div 3.75\,\text{Hz} = 1.06\,\text{s} \\[4pt]
\text{Digit 3} & \frac{1}{f/8} = 8 \div 3.75\,\text{Hz} = 2.13\,\text{s}
\end{array}
$$

Rolling-digit Display

The output of each random number generator is a 4-bit binary number representing one of the binary-coded values [1 . . . 7]. Each digit will be displayed on a standard seven-segment LED display. Therefore, a BCD-to-7-segment code converter will be inserted between each number generator and display digit, as illustrated in Fig. 13.4.

A search of the *TTL Data Book* shows the functions 7446, 7447, 7448, and 7449 BCD-to-seven-segment converters. The 7446 and 7447 drive displays with active-low inputs (common-anode VLEDs) and the 7448 and 7449 drive displays with active-high inputs (common-cathode VLEDs). Let us select common-cathode VLEDs.

We shall select the 7448, resulting in the circuit of Fig. 13.7. It should be noted that current-limiting resistors may be needed between the 7448 outputs and the display inputs, depending on the input current requirements of the display.

Payoff Display

The *payoff display* is identical to the rolling-digit display. A three-digit BCD number generated by the *payoff generator* will be converted and displayed on three seven-segment LEDs using a copy of the circuit shown in Fig. 13.7.

Wager-placement Switches

The wager must be made prior to pressing the PLAY button. Transitions on the wager-placement switches do not initiate any actions. Therefore, simple nondebounced DIP switches can be used. A 2-bit register will latch the positions

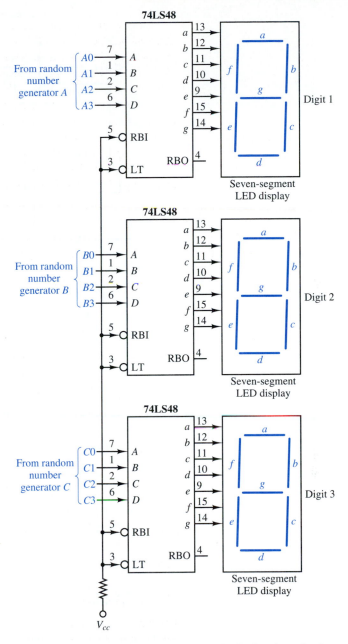

Figure 13.7   Three-digit seven-segment display interface circuit.

of these switches at the time the PLAY button is depressed to prevent the wager from being changed once the game has begun. The output of this register is supplied as an input to the *payoff generator*. The circuit is shown in Fig. 13.8.

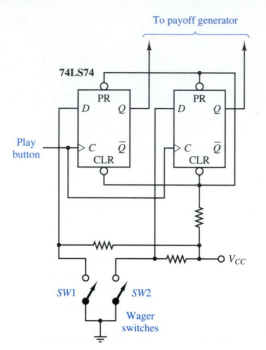

Figure 13.8   Wager-placement switches and register.

Winning Combination Detector

The *winning combination detector* determines if there are two or three matching digits from the number generators. This will be done by using 74LS85 four-bit comparators to detect matching values. Since there are three digits, $A = (A_3 A_2 A_1 A_0)$, $B = (B_3 B_2 B_1 B_0)$, and $C = (C_3 C_2 C_1 C_0)$, three comparators will be used, as shown in Fig. 13.9, to detect the conditions $A = B$, $A = C$, and $B = C$. Note that only the lowest 3 bits of each digit need to be checked, since the only valid digits are 1 to 7. A NOR gate will be used to signify that a match has been found by at least one of the comparators. Furthermore, if $A = B$ and $A = C$, it follows that $B = C$. Therefore, a single two-input AND gate will be used to detect the condition $A = B = C$. The complete circuit is given in Fig. 13.9.

The payoff computation circuit must know whether two or three digits match and the numeric value of the matching digit. A multiplexer can be used to select one of the input numbers, if it matches one or both of the others, to send to the payoff circuit. For this purpose, a 74LS157 quad 2-to-1 multiplexer is used, with the two 4-bit inputs connected to the signal lines for digits A and B, as shown in Fig. 13.9. If there is no pair of matching digits, as indicated by the output of the NOR gate, the multiplexer will be disabled by its control input, G, forcing its outputs to all zeros. If $B = C$, digit B will be selected by using the $B = C$ comparator output to control the multiplexer select line S. If there is a match and $B \neq C$, either $A = B$ or $A = C$, hence, digit A will be

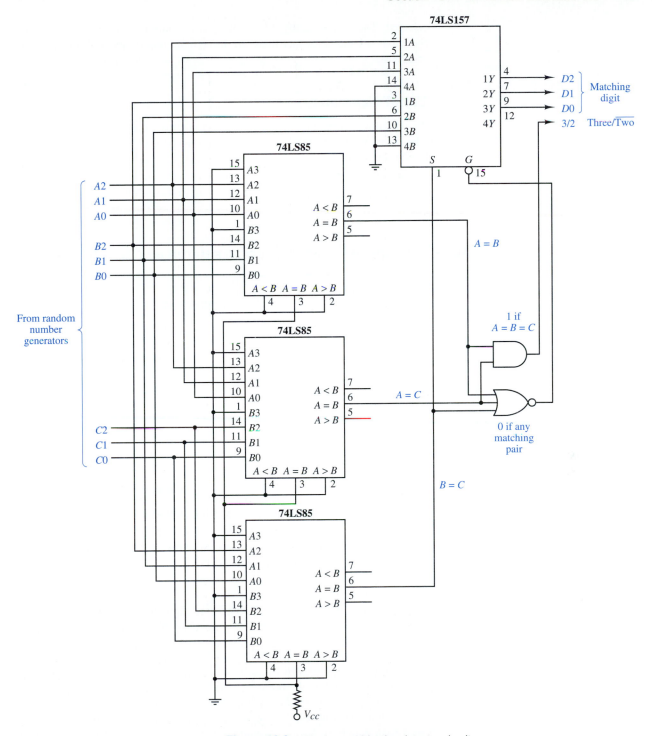

Figure 13.9   Winning combination detector circuit.

selected. The output of the AND gate is also routed to the payoff generator. Note that a 1 indicates that there are three matching digits, and a 0 indicates otherwise.

Payoff Generator

If a winning combination is detected, the number of points won is a function of whether two or three of the displayed digits match and the matching digit value. In addition, the number of points is multiplied by a factor of 1 to 4, depending on the wager that was placed on the wager switches. Table 13.1 displays the number of points to be awarded for each winning combination.

TABLE 13.1   **WINNINGS TABLE** (a) **DOUBLE MATCH** (b) **TRIPLE MATCH**

Digit	Wager				Digit	Wager			
	1	2	3	4		1	2	3	4
1	25	50	75	100	1	50	100	150	200
2	30	60	90	120	2	60	120	180	240
3	35	70	105	140	3	70	140	210	280
4	40	80	120	160	4	80	160	240	320
5	45	90	135	180	5	90	180	270	360
6	50	100	150	200	6	100	200	300	400
7	60	120	180	240	7	140	280	420	560

There are six inputs to the winnings computation circuit:

1. A 3-bit number (1 to 7) corresponding to the matching digit, or all zeros if there were no matching digits.

2. One bit indicating whether there were two or three matching digits, assuming there was at least one match.

3. A 2-bit number corresponding to the wager that was placed.

Since the number of points is a three-digit decimal number, the winnings computation circuit will have 12 output lines corresponding to three BCD digits.

To realize this circuit, a 64×12 PROM device could be used, that is, a PROM with 6 inputs and 12 outputs. However, 64×12 is not a standard commercially available configuration; therefore, we will use two PROMs, an 82LS129A (256×4) to drive the hundreds digit and an 82LS135 (256×8) to drive the tens and units digits. The complete payoff generator circuit is given in Fig. 13.10, which shows the assignment of signals to the 8-bit PROM address inputs and the PROM outputs. The PROM contents are listed in Table 13.2.

TABLE 13.2   **CONTENTS OF PAYOFF GENERATOR PROMS**

	Inputs		Prize		Inputs		Prize
$A(5)$	$A(4\text{-}3)$	$A(2\text{-}0)$	$O(11\text{-}8)O(7\text{-}4)O(3\text{-}0)$	$A(5)$	$A(4\text{-}3)$	$A(2\text{-}0)$	$O(11\text{-}8)O(7\text{-}4)O(3\text{-}0)$
—	—	000	000				
0	00	001	025	1	00	001	050
0	00	010	030	1	00	010	060
0	00	011	035	1	00	011	070
0	00	100	040	1	00	100	080
0	00	101	045	1	00	101	090
0	00	110	050	1	00	110	100
0	00	111	060	1	00	111	140
0	01	001	050	1	01	001	100
0	01	010	060	1	01	010	120
0	01	011	070	1	01	011	140
0	01	100	080	1	01	100	160
0	01	101	090	1	01	101	180
0	01	110	100	1	01	110	200
0	01	111	120	1	01	111	280
0	10	001	075	1	10	001	150
0	10	010	090	1	10	010	180
0	10	011	105	1	10	011	210
0	10	100	120	1	10	100	240
0	10	101	135	1	10	101	270
0	10	110	150	1	10	110	300
0	10	111	180	1	10	111	420
0	11	001	100	1	11	001	200
0	11	010	120	1	11	010	240
0	11	011	140	1	11	011	280
0	11	100	160	1	11	100	320
0	11	101	180	1	11	101	360
0	11	110	200	1	11	110	400
0	11	111	240	1	11	111	560

13.2 Keyless Auto Entry System

13.2.1 Problem Definition

Too many times, an automobile owner has walked up to his or her car and discovered that the keys have been locked inside the car. To solve this problem, a desirable feature would be a keyless entry system that would allow a car

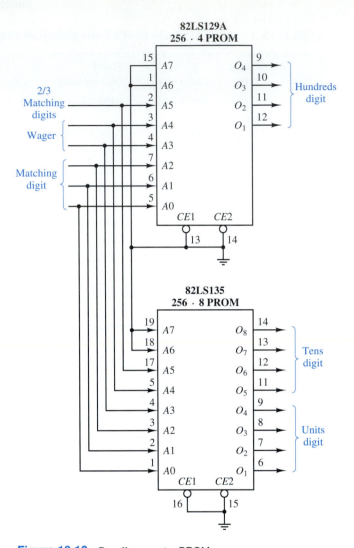

Figure 13.10 Payoff generator PROMs.

owner to enter a numeric combination code on a push-button keypad to unlock the car door.

For safety reasons, such a system would have to be designed to minimize the possibility of a thief discovering the code by trial and error, as can be done fairly easily with many combination locks. Several things could be done to make it more difficult to determine the correct code experimentally. One is to make the length of the code variable so that the thief would not know how many digits to enter. Table 13.3 shows the number of possible combinations there would be if four numeric keys (1, 2, 3, 4) were used, with codes of length 4, 5, 6, and 7 digits. The table also gives the approximate probabilities of making a correct guess on a single try.

TABLE 13.3 **KEYLESS ENTRY SYSTEM COMBINATIONS**

Code length	Number of combinations	Approximate probability of correct guess on the first try	Time to break code (1 code per minute)
4	256	4/1,000	4.25 hours
5	1,024	1/1,000	2.1 days
6	4,096	1/5,000	1.7 weeks
7	16,384	3/50,000	6.8 weeks

A further deterrent to thieves would be to automatically disable the system for several minutes if two or three incorrect attempts have been made to open the lock. Most thieves will not want to stand around and wait to make additional attempts, whereas this would be a minor inconvenience to the car owner as compared to calling a locksmith. Table 13.3 lists the estimated time that would be needed to try all codes, assuming one could be tried each minute with a 3-minute wait enforced after each three incorrect entries.

13.2.2 System Requirements

The keyless auto entry system will be operated by a five-button keypad near the outside door handle. To keep this project manageable, only four numeric buttons (1, 2, 3, 4) will be used. The entry code will be a user-defined sequence of four, five, six, or seven digits. A RESET button will also be provided, to be used in the event an error is made while entering the code. After pressing the RESET button, the correct entry code sequence must be reentered from the beginning.

To make it convenient for the car owner to set up a custom entry code that can be easily remembered, a setup panel will be provided inside the car on which the owner can set switches to program the digits of the combination and the length of the code.

The system will have a single output, UNLOCK, which will activate a mechanism to unlock the door. It is assumed that this electronic signal is overridden by the normal mechanical lock and key mechanism. A block diagram of the keyless auto entry system is shown in Fig. 13.11. It contains the following subsystems:

1. **Code entry keypad.** Four push-button switches will be used, representing the digits 1, 2, 3, and 4. A fifth push-button switch will activate the RESET function. Each switch will generate one logic-high pulse when pressed. To ensure clean pulses, each switch will be debounced. The signals produced by the four data switches will be sent to an encoder circuit, which will generate a single pulse each time one of the four numeric buttons is pressed, along with a 2-bit binary code to represent that button. The RESET button will generate a pulse to reset the system control unit. This button will be disabled for a designated "sleep" interval

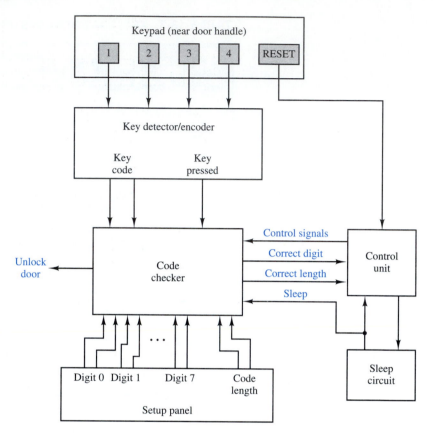

Figure 13.11 Keyless auto entry system block diagram.

any time three successive incorrect attempts have been made to open the lock.

2. **Setup panel.** A panel of 16 DIP switches, shown in Fig. 13.12a, will be provided to program the length of the code sequence and the digits comprising the code. Since valid code sequences can be 4, 5, 6, or 7 digits long, two DIP switches, $B7$ and $B8$, will be used to set the code sequence length as defined in Fig. 13.12b. Each digit of the code sequence must be one of the four numbers 1, 2, 3, or 4. Therefore, two DIP switches will be assigned to each digit of the code sequence and set as defined in Fig. 13.12c. Since the maximum code length is 7 digits, a total of 14 switches are needed to define any possible code sequence. Signals from the 16 DIP switches will be sent to the code checker module, which will determine if a correct code has been entered.

3. **Code checker.** The code checker determines if a sequence of digits entered by the keypad is the code sequence defined by the DIP switches on the setup panel. This module requires a counter to keep track of the number of digits entered and a circuit to compare each digit to the corresponding pair of switches on the setup panel. An UNLOCK signal

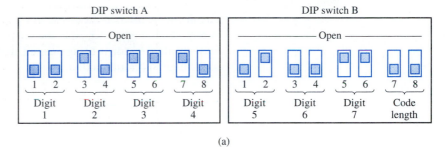

(a)

Code length	Switch $B7$	Switch $B8$
4	Closed	Closed
5	Closed	Open
6	Open	Closed
7	Open	Open

(b)

Digit	1st Switch	2nd Switch
1	Closed	Closed
2	Closed	Open
3	Open	Closed
4	Open	Open

(c)

Figure 13.12 Keyless entry system setup panel. **(a)** DIP switches. **(b)** Code length settings. **(c)** Digit codes.

will be generated by the control unit if a correct code sequence has been detected. An ERROR signal will be generated by the control unit if any entered digit is in error or if too many digits are entered. Both of these should be reset when the door is opened or when the lock is reset.

4. **Sleep circuit.** The function of the sleep circuit is to prevent the system from being reset for a period of 3 minutes following a third consecutive incorrect attempt to open the lock. This circuit will reset the system automatically after the 3 minutes has elapsed.

5. **Control unit.** The control unit will provide all timing and control signals for the other modules. In doing so, it will determine whether a code sequence is being entered, if a reset is needed following an error in entering a code sequence, or if the sleep circuit must be activated following three incorrect attempts to enter the correct code sequence.

13.2.3 Logic Design

The logic circuit design for the keyless auto entry system will be presented by describing each module identified in the requirements. Then the modules will be combined to create the complete circuit. The following paragraphs present the design of the individual modules.

Keypad Interface and Encoder

The keypad interface comprises five push-button switches, debounce circuitry, and an encoder circuit. A pair of cross-coupled NAND gates can be used for each switch as a debounce circuit, as shown in Fig. 13.3 for the previous example. To produce the 2-bit code for each button, a standard 4-to-1 priority encoder circuit can be used, as described in Chapter 4 (Fig. 4.19). The circuit diagram is repeated in Fig. 13.13. Note that there are three outputs: D indicates that at least one digit button is being pressed, and $d_1 d_0$ is the 2-bit code corresponding to the highest priority button.

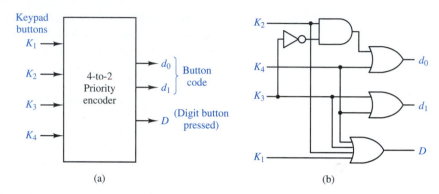

(a)   (b)

Figure 13.13   Four-to-one priority encoder for the code entry keypad. **(a)** Logic symbol. **(b)** Logic diagram.

For correct operation, the rest of the circuitry will expect the D signal to go high and then low again as each new button is pressed. If two buttons are pressed at the same time, only the higher numbered button will be detected.

Setup Panel

The 16 DIP switches on the setup panel will be set in advance and will be assumed to remain fixed throughout the operation of the system. Consequently, debounce circuitry is not needed. The DIP switches are configured as shown in Fig. 13.14. Each line is pulled up to a logic 1 value when the switch is OPEN and pulled down to logic 0 when CLOSED.

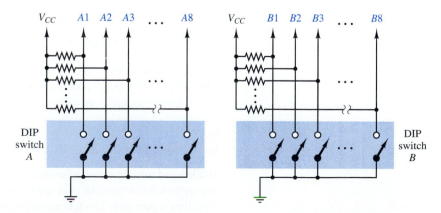

Figure 13.14   Setup panel DIP switches.

DIP switches $B7$ and $B8$ are routed directly to the circuit that checks the number of digits entered. The other 14 switches are routed to the circuit that compares them to the entered code.

Code Checker

The code checker performs two functions. First, it counts the number of digits entered at the keypad. Since the maximum entry code sequence length is seven digits, a 3-bit binary counter can be used for the digit counter. The digit counter will be incremented on the falling edge of each pulse on INCD and cleared whenever a RESET signal is generated on CLRD. In this example, we select a 74LS93 four-bit binary counter with asynchronous reset, connected as shown in Fig. 13.15.

The second 74LS93 shown in Fig. 13.15 counts the number of code entry attempts. This counter is incremented after each unsuccessful try on the falling edge of a pulse on INCT and cleared by a pulse on CLRT. At the counter outputs, a 1 is produced at output T of the AND gate when the count reaches 3, that is, when $Q_B Q_A = 11$. This signals the control unit that there have been three unsuccessful tries to enter the code.

The second function of the code checker is to compare the 2-bit code for the nth digit of a code sequence entered by the keypad to the setting of DIP switch pair n on the setup panel. One circuit is needed to select and route switch pair n to a comparator, to be compared to the code for the entered digit. Since there are seven pairs of switches, a dual 8-to-1 multiplexer can be used for this purpose. Two 74LS151 8-to-1 multiplexer modules will be used, as shown in Fig. 13.15. The switch pair is selected by the digit counter described previously. Pair 0 will be selected immediately after the counter is reset to 0, pair 1 after the first digit has been entered, and so on. Note that the 74LS93 is incremented on the falling edge of each pulse on INCD, while the comparison is performed while the pulse is high.

Two comparison circuits are needed, one to compare entered digits to the corresponding pairs of DIP switches and the second to compare the number of digits entered to the pair of switches that defines the code sequence length. In the first case, a 2-bit comparator could be used and, for the sequence length, a 3-bit comparator. Rather than design these circuits, 74LS85 four-bit comparator modules will be used for each, as shown in Fig. 13.15. For the first 74LS85, the upper inputs come from the keypad encoder and the lower inputs from the DIP switch multiplexer. For the second 74LS85, the upper inputs are from the digit counter, while the lower inputs are from DIP switches $B7$ and $B8$.

Sleep Circuit

The sleep circuit is to inhibit the operation of the system for a 3-minute period following three incorrect attempts to enter the combination. This will be done with a 555 timer module configured as shown in Fig. 13.16 for *monostable* (one-shot) operation. The 555 will be triggered by an active-low pulse from the control unit on signal $\overline{SLP}$ whenever a third consecutive incorrect code-entry

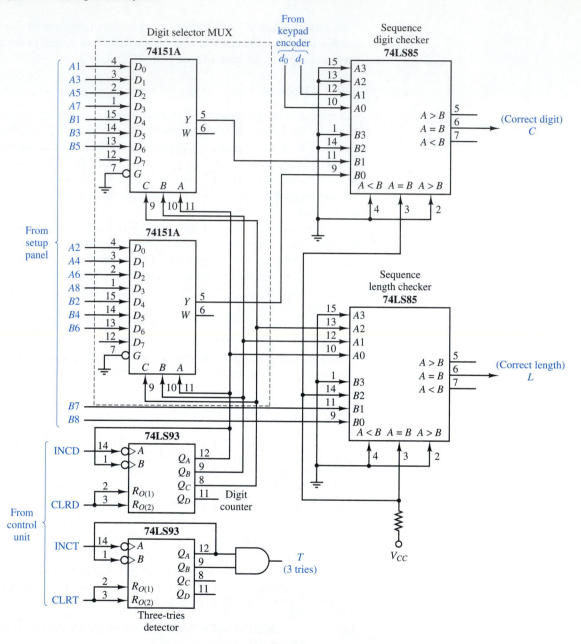

Figure 13.15   Code checker logic diagram.

sequence is detected, generating a SLEEP signal in the form of a pulse with a duration of 3 minutes that will prevent the control unit from being reset.

Recall from Chapter 6 that the 555 output pulse width is given by

$$t_W = 1.1(R_A)(C) \quad \text{s} \tag{13.2}$$

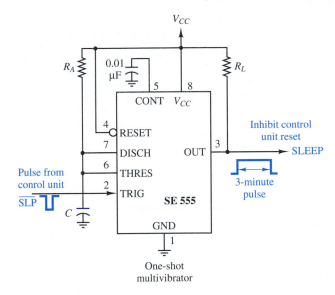

Figure 13.16   Sleep circuit "one-shot" logic diagram.

Therefore, the values $R_A = 3$ MΩ and $C = 60 \mu F$ produce a pulse of approximately 3 minutes in duration.

Control Unit

In response to entries from the keypad, the control unit is responsible for determining when to activate the UNLOCK mechanism, when to activate the SLEEP circuit, and when to reset the system.

As shown earlier, the keypad encoder produces a pulse on signal D whenever one of the four digit buttons is pressed, and the RESET button produces a pulse on signal R. Since these are the primary signals that initiate actions in the system, the control unit will be designed as a pulse mode asynchronous sequential circuit, as described in Chapter 10.

As pulses are generated on the D and R signals, three other conditions determine what the control unit should do. These conditions are represented by the C, L, and T signal lines as follows.

$C = 1$ if the current digit entered is correct, and 0 if the current digit is incorrect.

$L = 1$ if the number of digits entered is equal to the entry code sequence length, and 0 otherwise.

$T = 1$ if there have been three previous tries at entering the code sequence, and 0 otherwise.

As shown in Fig. 13.15, signal C is the output of the 74LS85 comparator that checks for correct digits, signal L is the output of the 74LS85 that compares the output of the digit counter to the selected code length, and T is produced by the counter of the "three-tries detector."

As discussed in Chapter 10, we begin the control unit design by developing a state diagram, which is shown in Fig. 13.17. From this state diagram we see that the control unit has three states:

> *INIT*: Initial state, waiting for the first digit to be entered.
>
> *ENTRY*: Digit entry state; the control unit remains in this state as long as correct digits are entered. This state is exited when a code-input error is detected, when the RESET button is pressed, or when an entire correct entry-code sequence has been entered.
>
> *ERROR*: Error state; the control unit enters this state if an error is made in the entry-code sequence, and if there have not been three previous errors. The control unit remains in this state until the RESET button is pressed, whereupon it returns to the *INIT* state.

The state table and binary state table for the control unit are given in Figs. 13.18a and b, respectively. Let us use JK flip-flops configured to operate as T flip-flops. The T flip-flop excitation table is given in Fig. 13.18c. From this table we can derive the T flip-flop excitation equations, and from the transition table we can derive the output equations for the pulse mode sequential circuit.

$$T_1 = (D\bar{C}\bar{L})\bar{y}_1 + (R\bar{T})y_1$$

$$T_2 = (DC\bar{L})\bar{y}_1\bar{y}_2 + (DCL)\bar{y}_1 + (D\bar{C}\bar{T} + D\bar{C}T + R\bar{T} + RT)y_2$$

$$= DC\bar{y}_1\bar{y}_2 + DCL\bar{y}_1 + D\bar{C}y_2 + Ry_2$$

$$UNLK = (DCL)\bar{y}_1$$

$$SLP = (D\bar{C}T)\bar{y}_1 + RT$$

$$INCD = (DC\bar{L})\bar{y}_1$$

$$INCT = R\bar{T}$$

$$CLRD = (DCL)\bar{y}_1 + R\bar{T}$$

$$CLRT = (DCL)\bar{y}_1$$

The logic diagram for the control unit is presented in Fig. 13.19.

13.3 One-lane Traffic Controller

In many places, two-way automobile traffic must be supported by a single-lane road, such as on narrow bridges in the country, roads under repair, and other narrow streets. As shown in Fig. 13.20, the single lane usually connects normal two-lane road segments. To control the two-way traffic in this single lane requires special traffic signals at each end of the single lane road that allow traffic to move in one direction for a period of time and then stop it to allow traffic to flow in the other direction, alternating back and forth. For each direction change, the traffic signal controller must halt traffic in one direction and wait until the lane is clear before allowing traffic to proceed in the opposite direction. To achieve optimum traffic flow, the period of time allotted to traffic

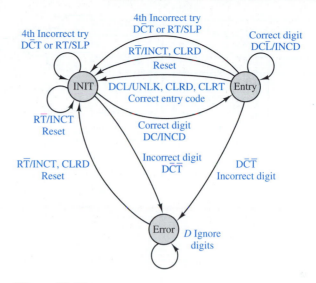

Figure 13.17   Control unit state diagram.

State:	$DC\bar{L}$	DCL	$DC\bar{T}$	$DC\bar{T}$	$R\bar{T}$	RT
INIT = 0	1/INCD	—	2	0/SLP	0/INCT, CLRD	0/SLP
ENTRY = 1	1/INCD	0/UNLK, CLRD, CLRT	2	0/SLP	0/INCT, CLRD	0/SLP
ERROR = 2	2	2	2	2	0/INCT, CLRD	—

Next state/outputs

(a)

$y_1 y_2$	$DC\bar{L}$	DCL	$DC\bar{T}$	$DC\bar{T}$	$R\bar{T}$	RT
INIT = 00	01	—	10	00	00	00
ENTRY = 01	01	00	10	00	00	00
11	—	—	—	—	—	—
ERROR = 10	10	10	10	10	00	—

$Y_1 Y_2$

(b)

$y_1 y_2$	$DC\bar{L}$	DCL	$DC\bar{T}$	$DC\bar{T}$	$R\bar{T}$	RT
INIT = 00	01	—	10	00	00	00
ENTRY = 01	00	01	11	01	01	01
11	—	—	—	—	—	—
ERROR = 10	00	00	00	00	10	—

$T_1 T_2$

(c)

Figure 13.18   Control unit state, transition, and excitation tables. **(a)** State table. **(b)** Binary state table. **(c)** T flip-flop excitation table.

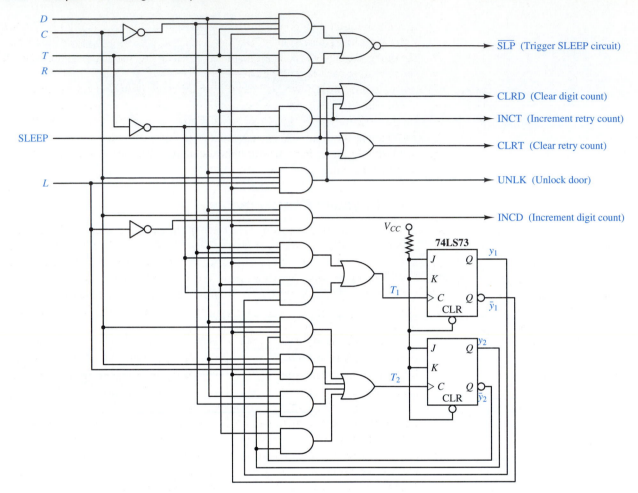

Figure 13.19 Control unit logic diagram.

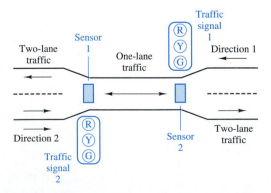

Figure 13.20 Two-way traffic on a one-lane road.

in each direction should be adjusted according to the traffic conditions, with the direction corresponding to heavier traffic allocated a longer period of time than the other. Traffic flow measurements can be made by using sensors embedded in the road at each end of the lane.

In this project we will design an adaptive traffic signal controller to coordinate traffic signals at the two ends of a one-lane road to support two-way traffic. A sensor will be positioned at each end of the road to detect cars entering and leaving the road. Time will be allocated to traffic flow in each direction according to traffic flow measurements obtained from the sensors during each 5-minute period.

13.3.1 System Requirements

The traffic controller will control the red, yellow, and green lamps of two traffic signals ($G1$, $Y1$, and $R1$ for signal 1 and $G2$, $Y2$, and $R2$ for signal 2), one at each end of the road. It is assumed that each of the six lights has a separate ON/OFF control line. Inputs to the traffic controller include signals from two sensors, $S1$ and $S2$, placed at each end of the road. Each sensor generates a pulse whenever crossed by a car. A manual RESET button will also be provided to initialize the controller.

The primary function of the controller is to determine when to switch the traffic lights from one color to the next. For cars moving in direction 1, $G1$ will be on for a time T_1, which will be recomputed every 5 minutes according to the traffic flow in each direction. After time T_1, the yellow light $Y1$ will be turned on for a single time unit T_Y (10 seconds will be used as the basic time unit for this example), after which red light $R1$ will be turned on until the controller is ready to activate $G1$ again. This timing pattern is illustrated in Fig. 13.21.

For cars moving in direction 2, light $G2$ will not be turned on until after the last car moving in direction 1 has left the road. The number of cars still on the road can be determined by comparing the number of cars entering the road, as signaled by one sensor, to the number of cars leaving the road, as signaled by the other sensor. When the difference between these counts is zero, it will

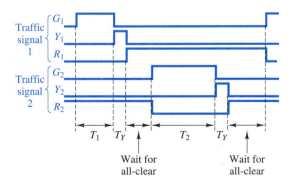

Figure 13.21   Traffic controller timing diagram.

be assumed that the road is clear. The duration of green light $G2$, T_2, will be computed as $T_2 = T_{tot} - T_1$, where T_{tot} is a total amount of green-light time. T_{tot} will be split between directions 1 and 2 according to the relative traffic flow in each direction.

Figure 13.22 presents a block diagram of the traffic light controller. The primary components of the controller include a time-base oscillator, a counter to determine whether cars remain on the road, a traffic counter to measure relative traffic flow in the two directions, a circuit to compute the green time allocations for the two directions, and a state machine control unit. The functions of these modules are described briefly as follows.

1. **Time-base oscillator.** The time-base oscillator will generate a clock signal that will be used to compute the times at which lights will be switched. The 10-second yellow light period will be assumed to be the shortest event in this system. All other switching times will be computed as multiples of 10 seconds. Thus, a clock signal with a period of 10 seconds will be used. The amount of green light time allocated to each direction will be recomputed every 5 minutes. Therefore, the oscillator will increment a counter that will be used to generate a pulse every 5 minutes.

2. **Cars-on-road counter.** To determine whether cars remain on the road prior to activating a green light, a counter will be used to compute the difference between the number of cars entering the road, N_E, and the number of cars leaving the road, N_L. The road is assumed to be all clear whenever $N_E - N_L = 0$. The number of cars entering the road is determined by counting pulses from one sensor, and the number of cars leaving is determined by counting pulses from the other sensor. Since the only condition of interest is whether $N_E - N_L = 0$, the actual counts are not needed. Therefore, an up/down counter will be used that will be incremented by pulses from sensor S_1 and decremented by pulses from sensor S_2. A counter output signal will indicate the condition $N_E - N_L = 0$.

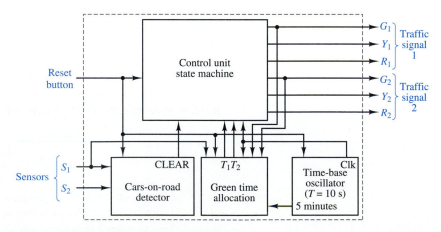

Figure 13.22   Traffic controller block diagram.

3. **Traffic counter.** To determine the relative amount of green light time allocated to each direction, a counter will be used to compute the difference between the numbers of cars traversing the road in each direction. As with the cars-on-road counter, the traffic counter will be incremented by cars moving in one direction and decremented by cars moving in the opposite direction. Pulses from S_1 will be used in both cases. The count will be sampled every 5 minutes, signaled by a pulse from the time-base oscillator, after which the counter will be reset to zero to begin the next 5-minute period.

4. **Green time allocation.** This module will recompute the green light durations T_1 and T_2 at the end of each 5-minute period based on the output of the traffic counter. Assuming D_1 to be the traffic count in direction 1 and D_2 to be the count in direction 2, T_1 will be increased if $D_1 - D_2 > 0$ and decreased if $D_1 - D_2 < 0$. T_2 will be computed as $T_{tot} - T_1$. Limit values will be used to ensure that neither T_1 nor T_2 drop below a minimum period of 40 seconds to prevent stalling traffic flow in either direction.

5. **State machine control unit.** The state machine control unit will coordinate the operation of the traffic light controller and generate the ON/OFF signals for the six lamps, cycling through them according to the timing diagram in Fig. 13.21, with switching times based on the outputs of the cars-on-road detector and the green time allocation module.

13.3.2 Logic Design

In this section, the designs of the individual modules described will be developed. Then these modules will be interconnected to complete the system design.

Time-base Generator

A clock signal with a period of 10 seconds will provide the time base for the controller. This clock signal will be generated by a 555 timer operating in astable multivibrator mode, as presented earlier in Fig. 13.6 for the slot machine example. From Eq. 13.2, a period of 10 seconds can be obtained by selecting the following resistor and capacitor values:

$$R_A = 200k\Omega$$
$$R_B = 200k\Omega$$
$$C = 24\,\mu F$$

The oscillator circuit output is signal CLK shown in Fig. 13.23.

A short pulse at the end of every 5-minute period is required to signal that it is time to sample the traffic counter and recompute the green time allocations. This pulse will be derived by a simple binary counter incremented by the clock generator. Since

$$5\ \text{min} = 5 \times 60\ \text{s}$$
$$= 30 \times 10\ \text{s}$$

a modulo-30 counter will be used. The 74LS390 is a dual, 4-bit decade asynchronous counter that can be used for this purpose, as shown in Fig. 13.23a. In this example, counter 1 is incremented once every 10 seconds, and counter 2 is incremented when counter 1 changes from $9 \rightarrow 0$. Referring to the K-map in

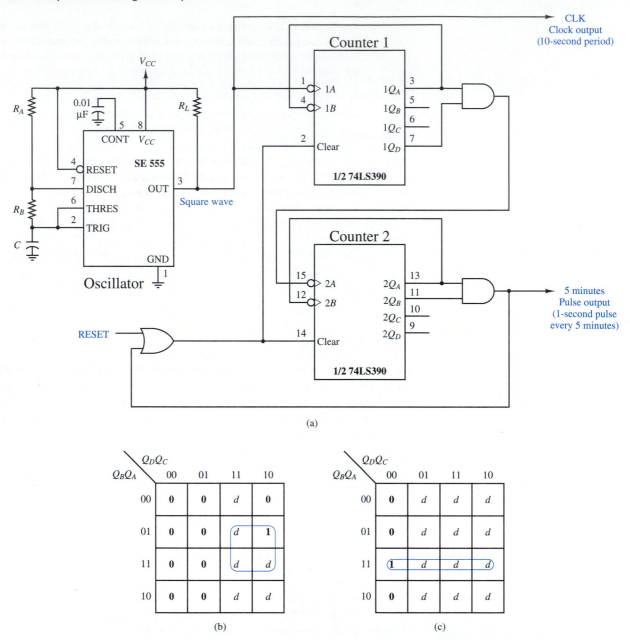

(a)

(b)   (c)

Figure 13.23 Time-base generator circuit design. **(a)** Logic diagram.
(b) Counter 1 = 9. **(c)** Counter 2 = 3.

Fig. 13.23b and realizing that counter 1 will never exceed 9, counter 2 should
be incremented for the condition

$$Q_A \cdot Q_D = 1$$

Likewise, counter 2 will never exceed a count of 3. Therefore, from the K-map in Fig. 13.23c, both counters should be reset for the counter 2 condition

$$Q_A \cdot Q_B = 1$$

In addition, both counters are also reset by the master RESET signal. The complete time-base generator circuit is shown in Fig. 13.23a.

Cars-on-Road Counter

As described previously, the road will be considered clear whenever the number of cars that leave the road, N_L, is equal to the number of cars that enter the road, N_E. To detect this condition, a binary up/down counter will be used as follows. Pulses from sensors S_1 and S_2 will be generated each time a car enters or leaves the road. For traffic in direction 1, pulses from S_1 indicate cars entering the road, while for direction 2 they indicate cars leaving the road, and vice versa for sensor S_2. Since only the difference between cars entering and leaving is significant, pulses from S_1 will be used to increment the counter, and pulses from S_2 will decrement the counter. Any time the count is zero, the counter will have been incremented and decremented an equal number of times; that is, $N_L - N_E = 0$, signaling that the road is clear.

The binary up/down counter used for this module must have a sufficient number of bits to count the largest number of cars that can enter the road without having left, that is, to compute the largest expected value of $N_L - N_E$. In this example it will be assumed that a 4-bit binary counter is sufficient, that is, that no more than 15 cars will ever be on the road at any one time. The 74LS193 is a 4-bit binary up/down counter with separate clock inputs for counting up and down. It will be configured as shown in Fig. 13.24, with the UP clock input controlled by pulses from sensor S_1 and the DOWN clock input controlled by S_2. A 4-input NOR gate detects a count of zero by producing an output of logic 1, indicating that $N_E = N_L$, thus indicating that all cars that entered the road have left.

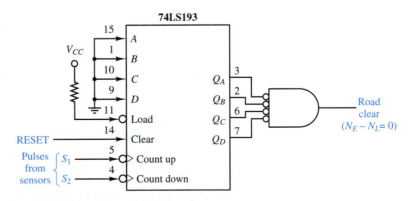

Figure 13.24   Cars-on-road counter logic diagram.

Traffic Counter

The operation of the traffic counter is similar to that of the cars-on-road counter in that it is to measure the difference between the number of cars traversing the road in each direction. An up/down counter can again be used, incremented by cars moving in one direction and decremented by cars moving in the opposite direction. In this case, only pulses from one sensor, S_1, will be used, with a signal from the control unit indicating the traffic direction. To minimize complexity, it will be assumed that the difference between the numbers of cars traversing the road in the two directions will be no more than 15, so a 4-bit counter will be sufficient.

Again the 74LS193 4-bit binary up/down counter will be used, as shown in Fig. 13.25. It will be incremented for each pulse on $S1$ while $G1$ is active, and decremented for each pulse on $S1$ while $G2$ is active. The counter will be reset every 5 minutes.

GREEN Time Allocation

The total amount of time allocated to green lights in one complete traffic cycle is

$$T_{\text{tot}} = T_1 + T_2$$

where T_1 is the amount of time allocated to green light $G1$ in direction 1 and T_2 the amount of time for light $G2$ in direction 2. If the traffic over a 5-minute period is greater in direction 1 than in direction 2, T_1 will be increased by one time unit and T_2 reduced by one time unit, keeping T_{tot} constant. To prevent traffic from being stalled in either direction, neither time will be reduced below a specified minimum value.

In this design, we shall assign $T_{\text{tot}} = 160$ s, which corresponds to 16 periods of clock signal CLK. This time will be split between T_1 and T_2. The circuit is shown in Fig. 13.25. The 74LS93 GREEN timer counter is incremented every 10 seconds while either light is green, that is, while $G1 = 1$ or $G2 = 1$. The clock signal is disabled when $G1 = G2 = 0$. $G1$ is assumed to be turned on at a count of 0. A 74LS85 comparator will detect the condition $t = T_1$, at which time $G1$ will be turned off and the counter will be stopped until $G2$ turns on. Then it will count to 15 ($Q_D Q_C Q_B Q_A = 1111$), at which time T_2 will be set to 1 to make the control unit turn off $G2$.

The allocation of time for T_1 will be determined by a second counter. This counter will be initialized to a value of 7 at reset time, setting $T_1 = T_2 = 80$ s. The counter will then be incremented or decremented after each 5-minute time period, according to the traffic counter, to adjust T_1. A minimum time of 40 seconds will be used for T_1 and T_2. Therefore, the counter will not be decremented if $T_1 = 3$ and will not be incremented if $T_1 = 12$. The conditions for inhibiting the decrementing and incrementing of the counter are derived from the K-maps of Fig. 13.26. Note that both maps contain don't-care conditions since the count will never be allowed to go below 3 or above 12. The logic expression used to inhibit the counter is the following:

$$\text{INHIBIT} = DN \cdot (\bar{Q}_D \bar{Q}_C) + \overline{DN} \cdot (Q_D Q_C)$$

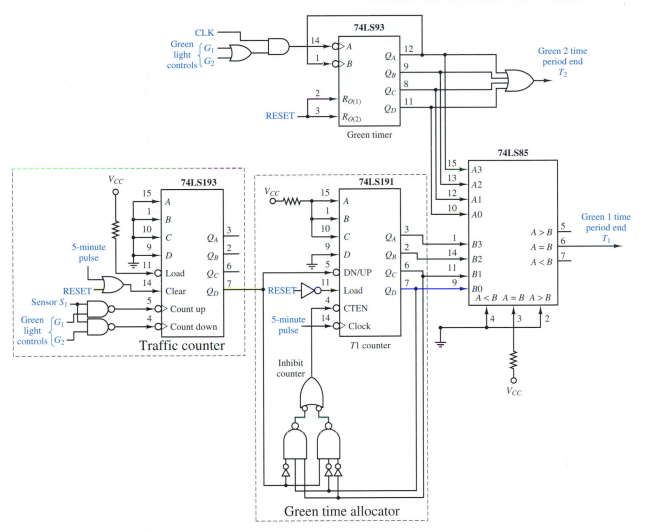

Figure 13.25 GREEN timer logic diagram.

where DN is the signal from the traffic counter controlling the $DN/\overline{UP}$ input of the T_1 counter. The INHIBIT signal is applied to the $\overline{CTEN}$ input of the T_1 counter, disabling the counter when INHIBIT = 1 and enabling the counter when INHIBIT = 0. The logic circuit is shown in Fig. 13.25.

Control Unit

The control unit requires six states, corresponding to the times during which the light is green and yellow in each direction and during which both lights are

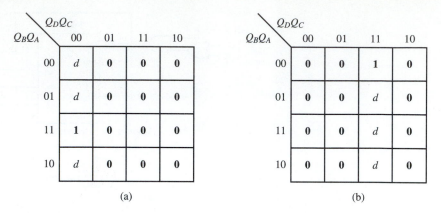

Figure 13.26 K-maps for logic to enforce green time limits. **(a)** Inhibit down count K-map. **(b)** Inhibit up count K-map.

red. The timing of these states was shown earlier in Fig. 13.21. The six states are defined as follows:

State	Light 1	Light 2
A	Green	Red
B	Yellow	Red
C	Red	Red
D	Red	Green
E	Red	Yellow
F	Red	Red

The desired state diagram is given in Fig. 13.27. Note that the control unit leaves states A and D after times T_1 and T_2, respectively, as defined previously. States B and E are each exited after a single clock period. States C and F are exited as soon as the number of cars exiting the road is equal to the number of cars that entered the road, that is, as soon as the output of the cars-on-road counter is zero, signaling the *all-clear* condition.

In this state machine, the state transitions occur in a fixed sequence, as in a simple modulo-6 counter; that is, the machine simply cycles through states A–B–C–D–E–F–A, and so on. The times of the state changes depend on the three inputs T_1, T_2, and *All clear*.

Several approaches can be used to design this state machine. One method would be to design a modulo-6 counter with a decoder to derive the six outputs. The counter would be incremented for each state change. Alternatively, a state machine design can be developed from a state table of six rows and eight columns, corresponding to the six states and three inputs. This implementation would require three flip-flops and assorted combinational logic.

For this example, let us use a one-hot state assignment, as defined in Chapter 8, and realize the state machine with a 6-bit shift register, as shown in Fig. 13.28. Each shift register output corresponds to one state of the machine.

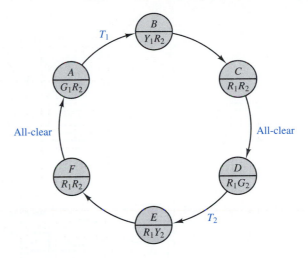

Figure 13.27 Traffic controller state diagram.

Outputs A and B control lights $G1$ and $Y1$, respectively, while outputs D and E control lights $G2$ and $Y2$. Light $R1$ is on whenever $G1$ and $Y1$ are both off, and likewise $R2$ is on whenever $G2$ and $Y2$ are both off. These output conditions are the following:

$$
\begin{array}{rclcrcl}
G_1 & = & Q_A & & G_2 & = & Q_D \\
Y_1 & = & Q_B & & Y_2 & = & Q_E \\
R_1 & = & \overline{(G_1 + Y_1)} & & R_2 & = & \overline{(G_2 + Y_2)}
\end{array}
$$

When the RESET button is pressed, bit 0 of the shift register will be initialized to 1 and the other bits to 0 to start the machine in state A. The shift enable input will then be activated and the register shifted one time for each condition indicated in the state diagram. These conditions are combined into the following shift-enable signal:

$$SHIFT\_EN = (A \cdot T_1) + B + (C \cdot CLR) + (D \cdot T_2) + E + (F \cdot CLR)$$

As shown in Fig. 13.28, the SHIFT_EN signal is ANDed with CLK to drive the two 74LS95 $CK1$ inputs, which provides the clock signal during shift operations. CLK also drives the 74LS95 $CK2$ inputs, which clocks the register during load operations.

13.4 Grocery Store Cash Register

Most retail establishments, including grocery stores, utilize electronic cash registers at their customer check-out stations. The basic functions of a cash register in a grocery store are to enter and display the prices of individual items being purchased and then compute and display the total bill. Many modern electronic point-of-sale terminals also compute discounts, keep track of inventories, compute change, and perform a variety of other functions. Magnetic

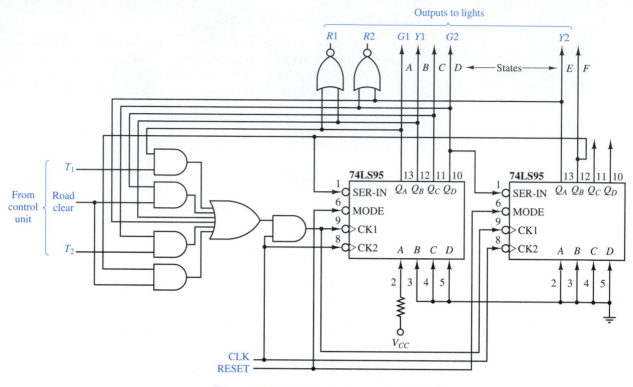

Figure 13.28 Traffic signal control unit logic diagram.

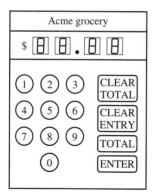

Figure 13.29 Grocery store cash register.

bar-code scanners and/or keyboards are used to enter prices, inventory numbers, discounts, and other information.

For this exercise, we shall design the control circuit for a minimum-function cash register that simply computes bills for lists of items. All item prices will be entered from a keyboard. The front would look something like the diagram in Fig. 13.29, with 14 buttons and a numeric display. The 14 buttons include the digits 0 to 9, and the following special functions:

ENTER: Pressed after each price has been keyed in.

TOTAL: Pressed after all prices have been entered to display the total bill.

CLEAR ENTRY: Pressed to clear the display if an error is made while keying in the price of an item.

CLEAR TOTAL: Pressed to clear the total out of the cash register prior to entering items for a new customer.

To keep the project manageable, we shall restrict all numbers to four decimal digits, with all prices and totals assumed to be in the range [\$00.01 ... \$99.99]. All numbers will be displayed as decimal values on seven-segment LED displays.

13.4.1 System Requirements

The main components of the cash register control circuit include a keypad and encoder for the 14 keys on the cash register, a four-digit display, an input register into which 4-bit BCD codes are shifted from the keypad encoder and sent to the display, and an accumulator, which computes the running total. All elements are controlled by signals from the keyboard. A block diagram of the cash register control circuit is shown in Fig. 13.30. The components are the following:

1. **Keypad.** The keypad comprises 14 push-button keys as described previously. Debounced push-button switches will be used. An encoder circuit will generate a BCD value corresponding to each numeric digit entered, along with a pulse to indicate that a DIGIT key has been pressed. Individual signals from the TOTAL, ENTER, CLEAR TOTAL, and CLEAR ENTRY buttons will be sent directly to the input and accumulator registers.

2. **Display.** Decimal digits will be displayed on four 7-segment LED elements. Since all numbers are to be in decimal, BCD-to-7 segment decoders will be used to drive the display. During price entry, digits will shift from right to left across the display as they are entered. For any number requiring less than four digits, leading zeros will not be displayed; that is, these digits will be blanked on the display to improve the readability of the displayed number.

3. **Input Register.** The input register will be loaded with numbers entered from the keypad and shifted from right to left until the ENTER key is pressed. The input register outputs will be sent to the display and to the accumulator, where the bill will be computed. If more than four digits are entered, only the last four will be kept. After the ENTER key has been pressed, the value will be kept in the input register so that another item of the same price may be added to the bill by simply pressing the ENTER

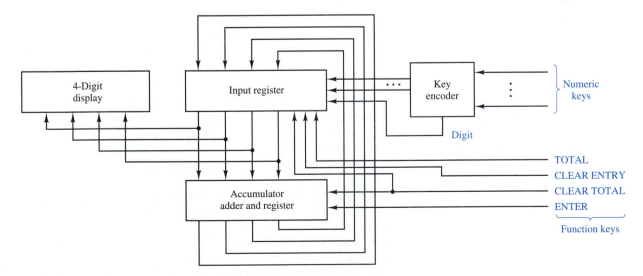

Figure 13.30   Cash register block diagram.

key again. When the TOTAL key is pressed, the input register will be loaded with the total bill from the accumulator. If an error is made while entering a price, the input register can be cleared by pressing the CLEAR ENTRY key. The input register is also cleared when the CLEAR TOTAL key is pressed to prepare for the next customer.

4. **Accumulator.** The accumulator maintains a running total of the current sale. To start a new customer transaction, the accumulator is cleared by pressing the CLEAR TOTAL key. Subsequently, each time the ENTER key is pressed, the price in the input register is added to the current total in the accumulator. Since all numbers are in decimal, a four-digit BCD adder will be used to compute the totals.

13.4.2 Logic Design

As with our previous examples, we will proceed with the cash register circuit design by first designing and testing separately each module described previously. Then these modules will be interconnected and tested until the entire system is operational. The following paragraphs present the designs of the individual modules.

Keypad

Each of the 14 buttons on the keypad will be a debounced, push-button switch as shown earlier in Fig. 13.3. The signals produced by the 10 numeric digit keys (0 to 9) will be encoded into a 4-bit BCD value and a signal DIGIT sent to the input register to indicate that a digit key has been pressed. The signals from the four special function keys will be sent directly to the input and accumulator registers to initiate the corresponding operations.

The BCD digit codes will be produced by a 10-to-4 priority encoder, constructed as illustrated in Fig. 13.31. The 10-to-4 encoder is constructed from two 74LS148 8-to-3 priority encoders. Buttons 0 to 7 drive the inputs of the first encoder, and buttons 8 and 9 drive the first two inputs of the second encoder. Since the 74LS148 inputs are active low, buttons 0 to 9 must produce a low signal when pressed. Consequently, the signals for each of buttons 0 to 9 will be taken from the upper NAND gate output (NAND gate output pin 3) of the debounce circuit of Fig. 13.3, which corresponds to the $\bar{Q}$ latch output. This output will be low when a button is pressed to set the debounce latch and return high when the button is released to reset the latch. Encoder outputs $A2$ to $A0$ provide the lowest 3 bits of the key number. The most significant bit is 0 for keys 0 to 7, and 1 for keys 8 and 9. When a digit key is pressed, the $\overline{GS}$ output of the affected encoder goes low. Therefore, the $\overline{GS}$ output of the first encoder can be used as the most significant bit of the BCD code, since it is 0 when one of keys 0 to 7 are pressed, and 1 otherwise. Note that the $A0$ outputs of the two encoders are ORed to produce the least significant bit of the BCD code as are the $A1$ and $A2$ outputs to produce the other two BCD code bits. The two $\overline{GS}$ outputs are likewise ORed to produce a pulse signal, DIGIT, that is sent to the input register to force it to capture the new digit.

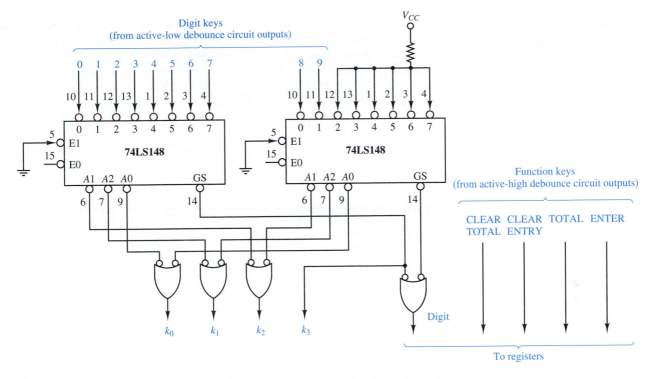

Figure 13.31   Cash register keypad encoder.

Input Register

The input register must store up to four digits for display, and these digits are also sent to the accumulator to compute price totals. To create the effect of digits shifting from right to left across the display during price entry, the register must be loaded serially with BCD digits from the keypad encoder when a pulse is received on the DIGIT line. When the TOTAL key is pressed, the register must be parallel loaded with the value from the accumulator to send the total price to the display. Finally, when either the CLEAR ENTRY or CLEAR TOTAL button is pressed, the input register should be cleared to all zeros.

The preceding functions require a 16-bit shift register supporting left-shift, parallel-load, and clear functions. The 74LS195A module is a 4-bit shift register with synchronous shift and parallel-load and asynchronous clear control inputs. We will use four of these modules for the input register, as shown in Fig. 13.32.

Each BCD digit is a 4-bit value. Rather than shifting a new digit into the input register 1 bit at a time, we will organize the register modules so that the entire digit can be shifted into the register in a single step. As shown in Fig. 13.32, the rightmost 74LS195A will contain the least significant bits of all four displayed digits, the next 74LS195A to the left will contain the next bit of each of the four digits, and so on. Thus, on a left shift the 4 bits corresponding to the leftmost digit on the display are shifted out of the register modules, while the bits for the new digit are shifted into them, one into each module.

The control signals for the input register are derived from the control signals generated by the keypad encoder. The register is to be cleared when either the CLEAR ENTRY or CLEAR TOTAL button is pressed. Hence, these signals are simply ORed to drive the input register asynchronous clear signal.

The register is to be parallel loaded with the current total from the accumulator when the TOTAL key is pressed and shifted left 1 bit when a DIGIT key is pressed. The 74LS195A is parallel loaded by setting the SHIFT/$\overline{\text{LOAD}}$ control input to 0 and pulsing the CLOCK input. A shift is performed by setting SHIFT/$\overline{\text{LOAD}}$ to 1 and pulsing the CLOCK input. Since the DIGIT signal will be 1 when a digit is entered, and therefore 0 when the TOTAL key is pressed, the DIGIT signal will be used to control the 74LS195A SHIFT/$\overline{\text{LOAD}}$ control input.

To supply the 74LS195A CLOCK input, the DIGIT and TOTAL signals should be ORed so that a pulse is generated whenever a digit key or the TOTAL key is pressed. Unfortunately, the DIGIT signal cannot be used directly, since it is activated in the keypad controller at the same time the 4-bit key code is being produced, as illustrated in Fig. 13.33. From the TTL data book, the minimum setup time for the 74LS195A serial input is 15 ns prior to the clock transition. In addition, the minimum setup time for the SHIFT/$\overline{\text{LOAD}}$ control input is 25 ns prior to the clock transition. To satisfy these requirements, it will be necessary to delay the pulse on the DIGIT signal. This delay will be produced by running the DIGIT signal through a string of inverters, as shown in

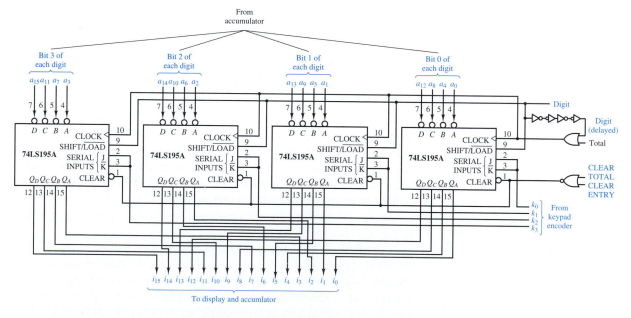

Figure 13.32   Input register.

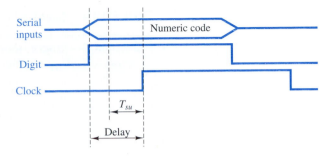

Figure 13.33 Input register shift timing.

Fig. 13.32, producing the CLOCK signal shown in the timing diagram of Fig. 13.33. Typical propagation delays of the 74LS04 inverter are $T_{PLH} = 9$ ns and $T_{PHL} = 10$ ns. Therefore, four inverters will delay the clock signal by a typical value of 38 to 40 ns after the DIGIT pulse goes high, satisfying the setup time requirements for both the CLOCK and SHIFT/$\overline{\text{LOAD}}$ control inputs. It will be assumed that the accumulator output is stable well in advance of the TOTAL key being pressed, allowing the TOTAL signal to be used for the load clock.

Accumulator

The accumulator comprises a 16-bit parallel-load register and a four-digit BCD adder. The accumulator is to be cleared when the CLEAR TOTAL button is pressed and loaded with the sum of its contents and the number in the input register when the ENTER key is pressed.

The accumulator register will be implemented with two 74LS273 octal D flip-flop modules, as shown in Fig. 13.35. The clock inputs will be controlled by the ENTER signal from the keypad, and the clear inputs will be controlled by the CLEAR TOTAL signal from the keypad.

Binary-coded decimal adders are not available as standard TTL modules. Therefore, we must create one from binary adders. Consider the addition of two BCD digits with a 4-bit binary adder. The sum of two decimal digits will be a number in the range $[0 \ldots 18]$. Table 13.4 lists the sum and carry outputs produced by a binary adder when its inputs are BCD digits, along with the corresponding sum and carry outputs desired from the BCD adder. Three unique cases can be identified in this table.

Case 1: $0 \leq \text{sum} \leq 9$. In this case the results produced by the binary adder are identical to those required from the BCD adder. Therefore, the results can be used with no adjustments.

Case 2: $10 \leq \text{sum} \leq 15$. In this case the binary adder produces sums in the range $(1010)_2 \ldots (1111)_2$, with no carry output. The corresponding decimal results can be obtained by adding $6_{10} = (0110)_2$ to the output of the binary adder. This operation produces a carry output and a sum in the range $[(0000)_2 \ldots (0101)_2]$, as desired.

TABLE 13.4   BINARY VERSUS BCD ADDITION

Decimal Sum	Binary Adder		BCD Adder		Binary-to-BCD Adjustment
	C_{out}	Sum	C_{out}	Sum	
0	0	0000	0	0000	+0000
1	0	0001	0	0001	+0000
2	0	0010	0	0010	+0000
3	0	0011	0	0011	+0000
4	0	0100	0	0100	+0000
5	0	0101	0	0101	+0000
6	0	0110	0	0110	+0000
7	0	0111	0	0111	+0000
8	0	1000	0	1000	+0000
9	0	1001	0	1001	+0000
10	0	1010	1	0000	+0110
11	0	1011	1	0001	+0110
12	0	1100	1	0010	+0110
13	0	1101	1	0011	+0110
14	0	1110	1	0100	+0110
15	0	1111	1	0101	+0110
16	1	0000	1	0110	+0110
17	1	0001	1	0111	+0110
18	1	0010	1	1000	+0110

Case 3: $16 \leq \text{sum} \leq 18$. In this case the binary and BCD adders both produce a carry-out, with the binary sum 6 less than the desired BCD result. The correct decimal results are again obtained by adding $6_{10} = (0110)_2$ to the output of the binary adder, as in case 2.

In cases 2 and 3, the decimal adder generates a carry-out for any sum greater than or equal to 10_{10}, whereas the binary adder generates a carry-out only if the sum is greater than or equal to 16_{10}. Consequently, adding 6 to the output of the binary adder for sums greater than 9_{10} will adjust the results to the desired value.

Figure 13.34a shows a two-stage circuit that adds two BCD digits by examining the output of the first binary adder and adjusting the result by adding 6 to it if the sum is in the range $[(1010)_2 \ldots (1111)_2]$ (case 2) or if the carry output is 1 (case 3). Using the K-map in Fig. 13.34b, which maps sum values greater than 9, the condition indicating the need to adjust the result is

$$Adjust = C_{out} + \Sigma_3 \Sigma_2 + \Sigma_3 \Sigma_1$$

Two 74LS83 four-bit adder modules are used, one to compute the sum and another to adjust the result. If $Adjust = 1$, then $(0110)_2$ is added to the output

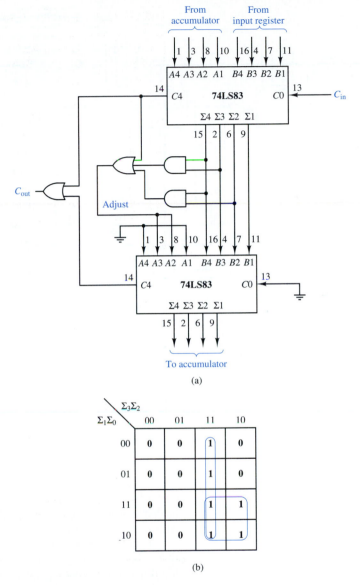

Figure 13.34   One-digit binary-coded decimal adder. **(a)** Logic diagram. **(b)** K-map of sum ≥ 10.

of the first adder; otherwise $(0000)_2$ is added. The complete 16-bit accumulator circuit is presented in Fig. 13.35.

Display

The four-digit cash register display is similar to the two three-digit displays designed earlier for the slot machine game. For the cash register display, each

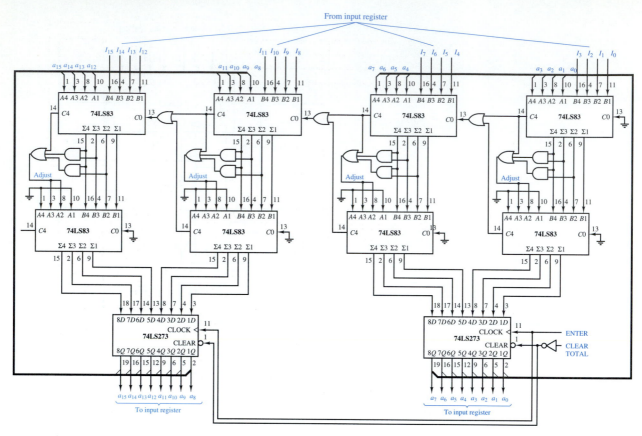

Figure 13.35   Binary-coded decimal accumulator.

of four BCD digits must be converted from BCD code to seven-segment code for display on a seven-segment LED element. As with the earlier designs, a 74LS48 code converter module can be used for this purpose.

For the cash register display, it is also required that any digits corresponding to leading zeros be blank on the display, that is, if a number begins with one or more zeros, these elements should be blank in the display. The 74LS48 includes a blanking control input, BI/RBO, that, when 0, forces all seven LED segments to be off.

For this application, whenever bits 15 to 12 of the input register are 0000, the BI/RBO input of the most significant 74LS48 will be forced to 0 to blank the most significant display element. The next digit, corresponding to bits 11 to 8 of the input register, will be blanked if and only if bits 11 to 8 are 0000 and the most significant digit is also blank. Likewise, the elements driven by bits 7 to 4 and bits 3 to 0 of the input register will be blanked if and only if all the upper digits are also zeros.

The final circuit for the display is given in Fig. 13.36.

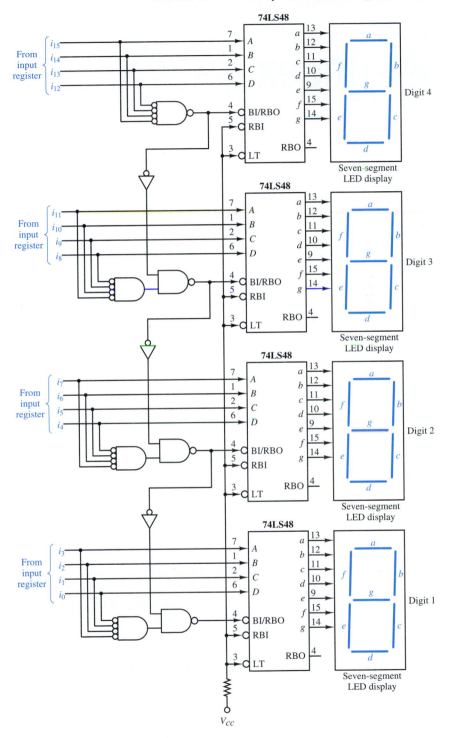

Figure 13.36   Cash register display with blanking control.

Index